The Tragedy
of Great
Power Politics

The Tragedy
of Great
Power Politics

John J. Mearsheimer

University of Chicago

W. W. NORTON & COMPANY · NEW YORK · LONDON

For information about permission to reproduce selections
from this book, write to Permissions, W. W. Norton & Company, Inc.,
500 Fifth Avenue, New York, NY 10110.

Manufacturing by the Maple-Vail Book Manufacturing Group
Book design by BTDnyc
Production manager: Leelo Märjamaa-Reintal

Library of Congress Cataloging-in-Publication Data

Mearsheimer, John J.
  The tragedy of Great Power politics / John J. Mearsheimer.
    p. cm.
  Includes bibliographical references and index.
  ISBN 0-393-02025-8
    1. World politics—19th century. 2. World politics—20th century.
  3. Great powers. 4. International relations. I. Title.

  D397 .M38   2001
  327.1'01—dc21
                                                2001030915

ISBN 0-393-32396-X pbk.

W. W. Norton & Company, Inc., 500 Fifth Avenue, New York, N.Y. 10110
www.wwnorton.com

W. W. Norton & Company Ltd., Castle House, 75/76 Wells Street, London W1T 3QT

1 2 3 4 5 6 7 8 9 0

CONTENTS

LIST OF MAPS

LIST OF TABLES

PREFACE

The twentieth century was a period of great international violence. In World War I (1914–18), roughly nine million people died on European battlefields. About fifty million people were killed during World War II (1939–45), well over half of them civilians. Soon after the end of World War II, the Cold War engulfed the globe. During this confrontation, the Soviet Union and its Warsaw Pact allies never directly fought the United States and its North Atlantic Treaty Organization allies, but many millions died in proxy wars in Korea, Vietnam, Afghanistan, Nicaragua, Angola, El Salvador, and elsewhere. Millions also died in the century's lesser, yet still fierce, wars, including the Russo-Japanese conflicts of 1904–5 and 1939, the Allied intervention in the Russian Civil War from 1918 to 1920, the Russo-Polish War of 1920–21, the various Arab-Israeli wars, and the Iran-Iraq War of 1980–88.

This cycle of violence will continue far into the new millennium. Hopes for peace will probably not be realized, because the great powers that shape the international system fear each other and compete for power as a result. Indeed, their ultimate aim is to gain a position of dominant power over others, because having dominant power is the best means to ensure one's own survival. Strength ensures safety, and the greatest strength is the greatest insurance of safety. States facing this incentive are fated to clash as each competes for advantage over the others. This is a tragic situation, but there is no escaping it unless the states that make up the system agree to form a world government. Such a vast transformation is hardly a realistic prospect, however, so conflict and war are bound to continue as large and enduring features of world politics.

One could challenge this gloomy view by noting that the twentieth century ended peacefully—with the end of the Cold War—and that relations among the great powers are quite peaceful as we begin the twenty-first century. This is certainly true, but predicting the future by simply extrapolating forward from the present does not make for sound analysis.

Consider what that approach would have told a European observer at the start of each of the previous two centuries. In 1800, Europe was in the midst of the French Revolutionary and Napoleonic Wars, which lasted twenty-three years (1792–1815) and involved all of that era's great powers. Extrapolating forward from that bloody year, one would have expected the nineteenth century to be filled with great-power conflict. In fact, it is among the least conflictual periods in European history. In 1900, on the other hand, there was no warfare in Europe that involved a great power, and little evidence portended that one was in the offing. Extrapolating forward from that tranquil year, one would have expected little conflict in Europe during the twentieth century. As we know, the opposite was the case.

General theories of international politics offer useful tools for anticipating what lies ahead. The most useful theories of this sort would describe how great powers normally behave toward each other and would explain their conduct. Useful theories would also account in good part for how the great powers have behaved in the past, including explaining why some historical periods were more conflictual than others. A theory that satisfies these requirements and helps us look backward to understand the past should also help us look forward and anticipate the future.

In this book I try to offer a theory with these attributes. My theory, which I label "offensive realism," is essentially realist in nature; it falls thus in the tradition of realist thinkers such as E. H. Carr, Hans Morgenthau, and Kenneth Waltz. Its elements are few and can be distilled in a handful of simple propositions. For example, I emphasize that great powers seek to maximize their share of world power. I also argue that multipolar systems which contain an especially powerful state—in other words, a potential hegemon—are especially prone to war.

These and other propositions in this book will be controversial. In their defense I try to show that the logic that underpins them is sound and compelling. I also test these propositions against the historical record. For evidence I look mainly at relations between the great powers since 1792. Finally, I use the theory to forecast the likely future shape of great-power relations.

This book was written to speak both to my fellow academics and to citizens who are interested in understanding the central forces that drive the behavior of the great powers. In pursuit of that goal, I have tried to make my arguments clear and easy to understand for those unsteeped in the jargon and debates of the scholarly world. I have tried to keep in mind the advice that the literary scholar Lionel Trilling once gave to the eminent sociologist C. Wright Mills: "You are to assume that you have been asked to give a lecture on some subject you know well, before an audience of teachers and students from all departments of a leading university, as well as an assortment of interested people from a nearby city. Assume that such an audience is before you and that they have a right to know; assume that you want to let them know. Now write."[1] I hope readers conclude that my efforts to follow this advice bore fruit.

ACKNOWLEDGMENTS

Although I am responsible for the arguments in this book, I received a great deal of help along the way from a small army of individuals and institutions.

Numerous colleagues were willing to spend their valuable time reading and commenting on the manuscript, and their fingerprints are all over this book. Almost every reader caused me either to abandon a wrongheaded argument, add a new argument, or qualify an existing argument. Indeed, I shudder to think how many foolish ideas and errors of fact would still be in this book were it not for the comments I received. Still, I did not accept all of their suggestions, and I bear full responsibility for any remaining problems.

I owe a profound debt of gratitude to Colin Elman, Michael Desch, Peter Liberman, Karl Mueller, Marc Trachtenberg, and especially Stephen Walt, all of whom not only read and commented on the entire manuscript once but also read and commented on some parts of it more than once. I am also grateful for comments provided by Robert Art, Deborah Avant, Richard Betts, Dale Copeland, Michael Creswell, Michael Doyle, David Edelstein, Benjamin Frankel, Hein Goemans, Jack Goldsmith, Joseph Grieco, Arman Grigorian, David Herrmann, Eric Labs, Karl Lautenschlager, Christopher Layne, Jack Levy, Michael Mandelbaum, Karen Mingst, Takayuki Nishi, Robert Pape, Barry Posen, Daryl Press, Cynthia Roberts, Robert Ross, Brian

Schmidt, Jack Snyder, Stephen Van Evera, and Alexander Wendt. My apologies to anyone I forgot.

Thanks are also owed to a host of research assistants who worked for me over the many years it took to write this book. They include Roshna Balasubramanian, David Edelstein, Daniel Ginsberg, Andrea Jett, Seth Jones, Keir Lieber, Daniel Marcinak, Justine Rosenthal, John Schussler, and Steven Weil. A special word of thanks is owed to Alexander Downes, who is largely responsible for producing the charts in this book, and who extensively researched a variety of subjects for me.

As the penultimate draft of the book was being completed, the Council on Foreign Relations in New York City selected me as its Whitney H. Shepardson Fellow for 1998–99. This wonderful fellowship is designed to help authors complete book projects in progress. Toward that end, the Council convened a study group that met three times in New York City to discuss different chapters from the book. Richard Betts did a superb job as chair of the group, which included Robert Jervis, Jack Levy, Gideon Rose, Jack Snyder, Richard Ullman, Kenneth Waltz, and Fareed Zakaria among its members. They were never short of criticism, but almost all of it was invaluable when I wrote the final draft. The Council also arranged for me to present chapters from the book to audiences in San Francisco and Washington, D.C. They, too, provided excellent comments.

After each session in New York with the Council study group, I took a taxicab to Columbia University, where I presented the same chapters to a workshop run by two graduate students, Arman Grigorian and Holger Schmidt. The Columbia students who attended each session offered many excellent comments, which helped me improve my arguments in a variety of ways.

The University of Chicago played a pivotal role in helping me write this book by providing a rich and exacting intellectual environment, as well as generous research support. A scholar could not ask for a better home. I have been especially fortunate at Chicago to have worked with a long list of talented graduate students who not only forced me to sharpen my arguments but taught me a lot about the theory and history of international politics. I also wish to thank the office staff in the Political Science

Department (Kathy Anderson, Heidi Parker, and Mimi Walsh) for providing me with logistical support over the years.

I would also like to acknowledge long-standing debts to four individuals who were my principal mentors when I began my career. William Schwartz introduced me to the study of international security when I was an undergraduate at West Point; Charles Powell nurtured me when I was a graduate student at the University of Southern California; and George Quester and Richard Rosecrance were my dissertation advisers at Cornell University. I would not have made it as a scholar, and thus would never have written this book, without their backing and without the support of the institutions where they taught and I studied. For all that help, I am forever grateful.

Roby Harrington, my editor at Norton, came up with the idea for this book and has worked with me on the project for longer than either he or I anticipated. His patience and wisdom are greatly appreciated. Traci Nagle did a splendid job of copy-editing the manuscript, while Avery Johnson and Rob Whiteside did a fine job overseeing the production of the book that is before you.

Finally, I thank my family for providing me with invaluable moral support. Writing a book is usually a protracted and painful process. I liken it to having to get up day after day to wrestle with a bear for hours on end. To finally whip the bear, it helps immensely to have strong support at home as well as in the arena of intellectual combat. I was fortunate to have both. Most important, I thank my wife, Pamela, to whom I owe so much. This book is dedicated to her.

The Tragedy
of Great
Power Politics

1

Introduction

Many in the West seem to believe that "perpetual peace" among the great powers is finally at hand. The end of the Cold War, so the argument goes, marked a sea change in how great powers interact with one another. We have entered a world in which there is little chance that the major powers will engage each other in security competition, much less war, which has become an obsolescent enterprise. In the words of one famous author, the end of the Cold War has brought us to the "the end of history."[1]

This perspective suggests that great powers no longer view each other as potential military rivals, but instead as members of a family of nations, members of what is sometimes called the "international community." The prospects for cooperation are abundant in this promising new world, a world which is likely to bring increased prosperity and peace to all the great powers. Even a few adherents of realism, a school of thought that has historically held pessimistic views about the prospects for peace among the great powers, appear to have bought into the reigning optimism, as reflected in an article from the mid-1990s titled "Realists as Optimists."[2]

Alas, the claim that security competition and war between the great powers have been purged from the international system is wrong. Indeed, there is much evidence that the promise of everlasting peace among the great powers was stillborn. Consider, for example, that even though the Soviet threat has disappeared, the United States still maintains about one hundred thousand troops in Europe and roughly the same number in Northeast Asia. It does so because it recognizes that dangerous rivalries would probably emerge among the major powers in these regions if U.S. troops were withdrawn. Moreover, almost every European state, including the United Kingdom and France, still harbors deep-seated, albeit muted, fears that a Germany unchecked by American power might behave aggressively; fear of Japan in Northeast Asia is probably even more profound, and it is certainly more frequently expressed. Finally, the possibility of a clash between China and the United States over Taiwan is hardly remote. This is not to say that such a war is likely, but the possibility reminds us that the threat of great-power war has not disappeared.

The sad fact is that international politics has always been a ruthless and dangerous business, and it is likely to remain that way. Although the intensity of their competition waxes and wanes, great powers fear each other and always compete with each other for power. The overriding goal of each state is to maximize its share of world power, which means gaining power at the expense of other states. But great powers do not merely strive to be the strongest of all the great powers, although that is a welcome outcome. Their ultimate aim is to be the hegemon—that is, the only great power in the system.

There are no status quo powers in the international system, save for the occasional hegemon that wants to maintain its dominating position over potential rivals. Great powers are rarely content with the current distribution of power; on the contrary, they face a constant incentive to change it in their favor. They almost always have revisionist intentions, and they will use force to alter the balance of power if they think it can be done at a reasonable price.[3] At times, the costs and risks of trying to shift the balance of power are too great, forcing great powers to wait for more favorable circumstances. But the desire for more power does not go away, unless a state achieves the ultimate goal of hegemony. Since no state is likely to achieve global hegemony, however, the world is condemned to perpetual great-power competition.

This unrelenting pursuit of power means that great powers are inclined to look for opportunities to alter the distribution of world power in their favor. They will seize these opportunities if they have the necessary capability. Simply put, great powers are primed for offense. But not only does a great power seek to gain power at the expense of other states, it also tries to thwart rivals bent on gaining power at its expense. Thus, a great power will defend the balance of power when looming change favors another state, and it will try to undermine the balance when the direction of change is in its own favor.

Why do great powers behave this way? My answer is that the structure of the international system forces states which seek only to be secure nonetheless to act aggressively toward each other. Three features of the international system combine to cause states to fear one another: 1) the absence of a central authority that sits above states and can protect them from each other, 2) the fact that states always have some offensive military capability, and 3) the fact that states can never be certain about other states' intentions. Given this fear—which can never be wholly eliminated—states recognize that the more powerful they are relative to their rivals, the better their chances of survival. Indeed, the best guarantee of survival is to be a hegemon, because no other state can seriously threaten such a mighty power.

This situation, which no one consciously designed or intended, is genuinely tragic. Great powers that have no reason to fight each other—that are merely concerned with their own survival—nevertheless have little choice but to pursue power and to seek to dominate the other states in the system. This dilemma is captured in brutally frank comments that Prussian statesman Otto von Bismarck made during the early 1860s, when it appeared that Poland, which was not an independent state at the time, might regain its sovereignty. "Restoring the Kingdom of Poland in any shape or form is tantamount to creating an ally for any enemy that chooses to attack us," he believed, and therefore he advocated that Prussia should "smash those Poles till, losing all hope, they lie down and die; I have every sympathy for their situation, but if we wish to survive we have no choice but to wipe them out."[4]

Although it is depressing to realize that great powers might think and act this way, it behooves us to see the world as it is, not as we would like it to be. For example, one of the key foreign policy issues facing the United States is the question of how China will behave if its rapid economic growth continues and effectively turns China into a giant Hong Kong. Many Americans believe that if China is democratic and enmeshed in the global capitalist system, it will not act aggressively; instead it will be content with the status quo in Northeast Asia. According to this logic, the United States should engage China in order to promote the latter's integration into the world economy, a policy that also seeks to encourage China's transition to democracy. If engagement succeeds, the United States can work with a wealthy and democratic China to promote peace around the globe.

Unfortunately, a policy of engagement is doomed to fail. If China becomes an economic powerhouse it will almost certainly translate its economic might into military might and make a run at dominating Northeast Asia. Whether China is democratic and deeply enmeshed in the global economy or autocratic and autarkic will have little effect on its behavior, because democracies care about security as much as non-democracies do, and hegemony is the best way for any state to guarantee its own survival. Of course, neither its neighbors nor the United States would stand idly by while China gained increasing increments of power. Instead, they would seek to contain China, probably by trying to form a balancing coalition. The result would be an intense security competition between China and its rivals, with the ever-present danger of great-power war hanging over them. In short, China and the United States are destined to be adversaries as China's power grows.

OFFENSIVE REALISM

This book offers a realist theory of international politics that challenges the prevailing optimism about relations among the great powers. That enterprise involves three particular tasks.

I begin by laying out the key components of the theory, which I call "offensive realism." I make a number of arguments about how great powers behave toward each other, emphasizing that they look for opportunities to gain power at each others' expense. Moreover, I identify the conditions that make conflict more or less likely. For example, I argue that multipolar systems are more war-prone than are bipolar systems, and that multipolar systems that contain especially powerful states—potential hegemons—are the most dangerous systems of all. But I do not just assert these various claims; I also attempt to provide compelling explanations for the behaviors and the outcomes that lie at the heart of the theory. In other words, I lay out the causal logic, or reasoning, which underpins each of my claims.

The theory focuses on the great powers because these states have the largest impact on what happens in international politics.[5] The fortunes of all states—great powers and smaller powers alike—are determined primarily by the decisions and actions of those with the greatest capability. For example, politics in almost every region of the world were deeply influenced by the competition between the Soviet Union and the United States between 1945 and 1990. The two world wars that preceded the Cold War had a similar effect on regional politics around the world. Each of these conflicts was a great-power rivalry, and each cast a long shadow over every part of the globe.

Great powers are determined largely on the basis of their relative military capability. To qualify as a great power, a state must have sufficient military assets to put up a serious fight in an all-out conventional war against the most powerful state in the world.[6] The candidate need not have the capability to defeat the leading state, but it must have some reasonable prospect of turning the conflict into a war of attrition that leaves the dominant state seriously weakened, even if that dominant state ultimately wins the war. In the nuclear age great powers must have a nuclear deterrent that can survive a nuclear strike against it, as well as formidable conventional forces. In the unlikely event that one state gained nuclear superiority over all of its rivals, it would be so powerful that it would be the only great power in the system. The balance of conventional forces would be largely irrelevant if a nuclear hegemon were to emerge.

My second task in this book is to show that the theory tells us a lot about the history of international politics. The ultimate test of any theory is how well it explains events in the real world, so I go to considerable lengths to test my arguments against the historical record. Specifically, the focus is on great-power relations from the start of the French Revolutionary and Napoleonic Wars in 1792 until the end of the twentieth century.[7] Much attention is paid to the European great powers because they dominated world politics for most of the past two hundred years. Indeed, until Japan and the United States achieved great-power status in 1895 and 1898, respectively, Europe was home to all of the world's great powers. Nevertheless, the book also includes substantial discussion of the politics of Northeast Asia, especially regarding imperial Japan between 1895 and 1945 and China in the 1990s. The United States also figures prominently in my efforts to test offensive realism against past events.

Some of the important historical puzzles that I attempt to shed light on include the following:

1) What accounts for the three longest and bloodiest wars in modern history—the French Revolutionary and Napoleonic Wars (1792–1815), World War I (1914–18), and World War II (1939–45)—conflicts that involved all of the major powers in the system?

2) What accounts for the long periods of relative peace in Europe between 1816 and 1852, 1871 and 1913, and especially 1945 and 1990, during the Cold War?

3) Why did the United Kingdom, which was by far the wealthiest state in the world during the mid-nineteenth century, not build a powerful military and try to dominate Europe? In other words, why did it behave differently from Napoleonic France, Wilhelmine Germany, Nazi Germany, and the Soviet Union, all of which translated their economic might into military might and strove for European hegemony?

4) Why was Bismarckian Germany (1862–90) especially aggressive between 1862 and 1870, fighting two wars with other great powers

and one war with a minor power, but hardly aggressive at all from 1871 until 1890, when it fought no wars and generally sought to maintain the European status quo?

5) Why did the United Kingdom, France, and Russia form a balancing coalition against Wilhelmine Germany before World War I, but fail to organize an effective alliance to contain Nazi Germany?

6) Why did Japan and the states of Western Europe join forces with the United States against the Soviet Union in the early years of the Cold War, even though the United States emerged from World War II with the most powerful economy in the world and a nuclear monopoly?

7) What explains the commitment of American troops to Europe and Northeast Asia during the twentieth century? For example, why did the United States wait until April 1917 to join World War I, rather than enter the war when it broke out in August 1914? For that matter, why did the United States not send troops to Europe before 1914 to prevent the outbreak of war? Similiarly, why did the United States not balance against Nazi Germany in the 1930s or send troops to Europe before September 1939 to prevent the outbreak of World War II?

8) Why did the United States and the Soviet Union continue building up their nuclear arsenals after each had acquired a secure second-strike capability against the other? A world in which both sides have an "assured destruction" capability is generally considered to be stable and its nuclear balance difficult to overturn, yet both superpowers spent billions of dollars and rubles trying to gain a first-strike advantage.

Third, I use the theory to make predictions about great-power politics in the twenty-first century. This effort may strike some readers as foolhardy, because the study of international relations, like the other social sciences, rests on a shakier theoretical foundation than that of the natural sciences. Moreover, political phenomena are highly complex; hence, precise political predictions are impossible without theoretical tools that are superior to those we now possess. As a result, all political forecasting is bound to include some error. Those who venture to predict, as I do here, should therefore proceed with humility, take care not to exhibit unwarranted confidence, and admit that hindsight is likely to reveal surprises and mistakes.

Despite these hazards, social scientists should nevertheless use their theories to make predictions about the future. Making predictions helps inform policy discourse, because it helps make sense of events unfolding in the world around us. And by clarifying points of disagreement, making explicit forecasts helps those with contradictory views to frame their own ideas more clearly. Furthermore, trying to anticipate new events is a good way to test social science theories, because theorists do not have the benefit of hindsight and therefore cannot adjust their claims to fit the evidence (because it is not yet available). In short, the world can be used as a laboratory to decide which theories best explain international politics. In that spirit, I employ offensive realism to peer into the future, mindful of both the benefits and the hazards of trying to predict events.

The Virtues and Limits of Theory

It should be apparent that this book is self-consciously theoretical. But outside the walls of academia, especially in the policy world, theory has a bad name. Social science theories are often portrayed as the idle speculations of head-in-the-clouds academics that have little relevance to what goes on in the "real world." For example, Paul Nitze, a prominent American foreign-policy maker during the Cold War, wrote, "Most of what has been written and taught under the heading of 'political science' by Americans since World War II has been . . . of limited value, if not counterproductive, as a guide to the actual conduct of policy."[8] In this view, theory should fall almost exclusively within the purview of academics, whereas policymakers should rely on common sense, intuition, and practical experience to carry out their duties.

This view is wrongheaded. In fact, none of us could understand the world we live in or make intelligent decisions without theories. Indeed, all students and practitioners of international politics rely on theories to comprehend their surroundings. Some are aware of it and some are not, some admit it and some do not; but there is no escaping the fact that we could not make sense of the complex world around us without simplifying theories. The Clinton administration's foreign policy rhetoric, for example, was heavily informed by the three main liberal theories of international relations: 1) the claim that prosperous and economically interdependent states are unlikely to fight each other, 2) the claim that democracies do not fight each other, and 3) the claim that international institutions enable states to avoid war and concentrate instead on building cooperative relationships.

Consider how Clinton and company justified expanding the membership of the North Atlantic Treaty Organization (NATO) in the mid-1990s. President Clinton maintained that one of the chief goals of expansion was "locking in democracy's gains in Central Europe," because "democracies resolve their differences peacefully." He also argued that the United States should foster an "open trading system," because "our security is tied to the stake other nations have in the prosperity of staying free and open and working with others, not working against them."[9] Strobe Talbott, Clinton's Oxford classmate and deputy secretary of state, made the same claims for NATO enlargement: "With the end of the cold war, it has become possible to construct a Europe that is increasingly united by a shared commitment to open societies and open markets." Moving the borders of NATO eastward, he maintained, would help "to solidify the national consensus for democratic and market reforms" that already existed in states like Hungary and Poland and thus enhance the prospects for peace in the region.[10]

In the same spirit, Secretary of State Madeleine Albright praised NATO's founders by saying that "[t]heir basic achievement was to begin the construction of the . . . network of rule-based institutions and arrangements that keep the peace." "But that achievement is not complete," she warned, and "our challenge today is to finish the post-war construction project . . . [and] expand the area of the world in which American interests and values will thrive."[11]

These examples demonstrate that general theories about how the world works play an important role in how policymakers identify the ends they seek and the means they choose to achieve them. Yet that is not to say we should embrace any theory that is widely held, no matter how popular it may be, because there are bad as well as good theories. For example, some theories deal with trivial issues, while others are opaque and almost impossible to comprehend. Furthermore, some theories have contradictions in their underlying logic, while others have little explanatory power because the world simply does not work the way they predict. The trick is to distinguish between sound theories and defective ones.[12] My aim is to persuade readers that offensive realism is a rich theory which sheds considerable light on the workings of the international system.

As with all theories, however, there are limits to offensive realism's explanatory power. A few cases contradict the main claims of the theory, cases that offensive realism should be able to explain but cannot. All theories face this problem, although the better the theory, the fewer the anomalies.

An example of a case that contradicts offensive realism involves Germany in 1905. At the time Germany was the most powerful state in Europe. Its main rivals on the continent were France and Russia, which some fifteen years earlier had formed an alliance to contain the Germans. The United Kingdom had a tiny army at the time because it was counting on France and Russia to keep Germany at bay. When Japan unexpectedly inflicted a devastating defeat on Russia between 1904 and 1905, which temporarily knocked Russia out of the European balance of power, France was left standing virtually alone against mighty Germany. Here was an excellent opportunity for Germany to crush France and take a giant step toward achieving hegemony in Europe. It surely made more sense for Germany to go to war in 1905 than in 1914. But Germany did not even seriously consider going to war in 1905, which contradicts what offensive realism would predict.

Theories encounter anomalies because they simplify reality by emphasizing certain factors while ignoring others. Offensive realism assumes that the international system strongly shapes the behavior of states. Structural factors such as anarchy and the distribution of power, I argue, are what matter most for explaining international politics. The theory pays little attention to individuals or domestic political considerations such as ideology. It tends to treat states like black boxes or billiard balls. For example, it does not matter for the theory whether Germany in 1905 was led by Bismarck, Kaiser Wilhelm, or Adolf Hitler, or whether Germany was democratic or autocratic. What matters for the theory is how much relative power Germany possessed at the time. These omitted factors, however, occasionally dominate a state's decision-making process; under these circumstances, offensive realism is not going to perform as well. In short, there is a price to pay for simplifying reality.

Furthermore, offensive realism does not answer every question that arises in world politics, because there will be cases in which the theory is consistent with several possible outcomes. When this occurs, other theories have to be brought in to provide more precise explanations. Social scientists say that a theory is "indeterminate" in such cases, a situation that is not unusual with broad-gauged theories like offensive realism.

An example of offensive realism's indeterminacy is that it cannot account for why the security competition between the superpowers during the Cold War was more intense between 1945 and 1963 than between 1963 and 1990.[13] The theory also has little to say about whether NATO should have adopted an offensive or a defensive military strategy to deter the Warsaw Pact in central Europe.[14] To answer these questions it is necessary to employ more fine-grained theories, such as deterrence theory. Nevertheless, those theories and the answers they spawn do not contradict offensive realism; they supplement it. In short, offensive realism is like a powerful flashlight in a dark room: even though it cannot illuminate every nook and cranny, most of the time it is an excellent tool for navigating through the darkness.

It should be apparent from this discussion that offensive realism is mainly a descriptive theory. It explains how great powers have behaved in the past and how they are likely to behave in the future. But it is also a prescriptive theory. States *should* behave according to the dictates of offensive realism, because it outlines the best way to survive in a dangerous world.

One might ask, if the theory describes how great powers act, why is it necessary to stipulate how they *should* act? The imposing constraints of the system should leave great powers with little choice but to act as the theory predicts. Although there is much truth in this description of great powers as prisoners trapped in an iron cage, the fact remains that they sometimes—although not often—act in contradiction to the theory. These are the anomalous cases discussed above. As we shall see, such foolish behavior invariably has negative consequences. In short, if they want to survive, great powers should always act like good offensive realists.

The Pursuit of Power

Enough said about theory. More needs to be said about the substance of my arguments, which means zeroing in on the core concept of "power." For all realists, calculations about power lie at the heart of how states think about the world around them. Power is the currency of great-power politics, and states compete for it among themselves. What money is to economics, power is to international relations.

This book is organized around six questions dealing with power. First, why do great powers want power? What is the underlying logic that explains why states compete for it? Second, how much power do states want? How much power is enough? These two questions are of paramount importance because they deal with the most basic issues concerning great-power behavior. My answer to these foundational questions, as emphasized above, is that the structure of the international system encourages states to pursue hegemony.

Third, what is power? How is that pivotal concept defined and measured? With good indicators of power, it is possible to determine the power levels of individual states, which then allows us to describe the architecture of the system. Specifically, we can identify which states qualify as great powers. From there, it is easy to determine whether the system is hegemonic (directed by a single great power), bipolar (controlled by two great powers), or multipolar (dominated by three or more great powers). Furthermore, we will know the relative strengths of the major powers. We are especially interested in knowing whether power is distributed more or less evenly among them, or if there are large power asymmetries.

In particular, does the system contain a potential hegemon—a power that is considerably stronger than any of its rival great powers?

Defining power clearly also gives us a window into understanding state behavior. If states compete for power, we learn more about the nature of that competition if we understand more fully what power is, and therefore what states are competing for. In short, knowing more about the true nature of power should help illuminate how great powers compete among themselves.

Fourth, what strategies do states pursue to gain power, or to maintain it when another great power threatens to upset the balance of power? Blackmail and war are the main strategies that states employ to acquire power, and balancing and buck-passing are the principal strategies that great powers use to maintain the distribution of power when facing a dangerous rival. With balancing, the threatened state accepts the burden of deterring its adversary and commits substantial resources to achieving that goal. With buck-passing, the endangered great power tries to get another state to shoulder the burden of deterring or defeating the threatening state.

The final two questions focus on the key strategies that states employ to maximize their share of world power. The fifth is, what are the causes of war? Specifically, what power-related factors make it more or less likely that security competition will intensify and turn into open conflict? Sixth, when do threatened great powers balance against a dangerous adversary and when do they attempt to pass the buck to another threatened state?

I will attempt to provide clear and convincing answers to these questions. It should be emphasized, however, that there is no consensus among realists on the answers to any of them. Realism is a rich tradition with a long history, and disputes over fundamental issues have long been commonplace among realists. In the pages that follow, I do not consider alternative realist theories in much detail. I will make clear how offensive realism differs from its main realist rivals, and I will challenge these alternative perspectives on particular points, mainly to elucidate my own arguments. But no attempt will be made to systematically examine any other realist theory. Instead, the focus will be on laying out my theory of offensive realism and using it to explain the past and predict the future.

...lso many nonrealist theories of international poli-
...iberal theories were mentioned earlier; there are
...ories, such as social constructivism and bureaucratic
...ust two. I will briefly analyze some of these theories
great-power politics after the Cold War (Chapter 10),
ma... they underpin many of the claims that international politics has u...rgone a fundamental change since 1990. Because of space
limitations, however, I make no attempt at a comprehensive assessment
of these nonrealist theories. Again, the emphasis in this study will be on
making the case for offensive realism.

Nevertheless, it makes good sense at this point to describe the theories
that dominate thinking about international relations in both the academic
and policy worlds, and to show how offensive realism compares with its
main realist and nonrealist competitors.

LIBERALISM VS. REALISM

Liberalism and realism are the two bodies of theory which hold places
of privilege on the theoretical menu of international relations. Most of
the great intellectual battles among international relations scholars take
place either across the divide between realism and liberalism, or within
those paradigms.[15] To illustrate this point, consider the three most influential realist works of the twentieth century:

1) E. H. Carr's *The Twenty Years' Crisis, 1919–1939*, which was published in the United Kingdom shortly after World War II started in
   Europe (1939) and is still widely read today.
2) Hans Morgenthau's *Politics among Nations*, which was first published in the United States in the early days of the Cold War
   (1948) and dominated the field of international relations for at
   least the next two decades.
3) Kenneth Waltz's *Theory of International Politics*, which has dominated the field since it first appeared during the latter part of the Cold
   War (1979).[16]

All three of these realist giants critique some aspect of liberalism in their writings. For example, both Carr and Waltz take issue with the liberal claim that economic interdependence enhances the prospects for peace.[17] More generally, Carr and Morgenthau frequently criticize liberals for holding utopian views of politics which, if followed, would lead states to disaster. At the same time, these realists also disagree about a number of important issues. Waltz, for example, challenges Morgenthau's claim that multipolar systems are more stable than bipolar systems.[18] Furthermore, whereas Morgenthau argues that states strive to gain power because they have an innate desire for power, Waltz maintains that the structure of the international system forces states to pursue power to enhance their prospects for survival. These examples are just a small sample of the differences among realist thinkers.[19]

Let us now look more closely at liberalism and realism, focusing first on the core beliefs shared by the theories in each paradigm, and second on the differences among specific liberal and realist theories.

Liberalism

The liberal tradition has its roots in the Enlightenment, that period in eighteenth-century Europe when intellectuals and political leaders had a powerful sense that reason could be employed to make the world a better place.[20] Accordingly, liberals tend to be hopeful about the prospects of making the world safer and more peaceful. Most liberals believe that it is possible to substantially reduce the scourge of war and to increase international prosperity. For this reason, liberal theories are sometimes labelled "utopian" or "idealist."

Liberalism's optimistic view of international politics is based on three core beliefs, which are common to almost all of the theories in the paradigm. First, liberals consider states to be the main actors in international politics. Second, they emphasize that the internal characteristics of states vary considerably, and that these differences have profound effects on state behavior.[21] Furthermore, liberal theorists often believe that some internal arrangements (e.g., democracy) are inherently preferable to others (e.g., dictatorship). For liberals, therefore, there are "good" and "bad" states in the international system. Good states pursue cooperative policies and hardly ever start wars on their own, whereas bad states cause conflicts with other states and are prone to use force to get their way.[22] Thus, the key to peace is to populate the world with good states.

Third, liberals believe that calculations about power matter little for explaining the behavior of good states. Other kinds of political and economic calculations matter more, although the form of those calculations varies from theory to theory, as will become apparent below. Bad states might be motivated by the desire to gain power at the expense of other states, but that is only because they are misguided. In an ideal world, where there are only good states, power would be largely irrelevant.

Among the various theories found under the big tent of liberalism, the three main ones mentioned earlier are particularly influential. The first argues that high levels of economic interdependence among states make them unlikely to fight each other.[23] The taproot of stability, according to this theory, is the creation and maintenance of a liberal economic order that allows for free economic exchange among states. Such an order makes states more prosperous, thereby bolstering peace, because prosperous states are more economically satisfied and satisfied states are more peaceful. Many wars are waged to gain or preserve wealth, but states have much less motive to initiate war if they are already wealthy. Furthermore, wealthy states with interdependent economies stand to become less prosperous if they fight each other, since they are biting the hand that feeds them. Once states establish extensive economic ties, in short, they avoid war and can concentrate instead on accumulating wealth.

The second, democratic peace theory, claims that democracies do not go to war against other democracies.[24] Thus, a world containing only democratic states would be a world without war. The argument here is not that democracies are less warlike than non-democracies, but rather that democracies do not fight among themselves. There are a variety of explanations for the democratic peace, but little agreement as to which one is correct. Liberal thinkers do agree, however, that democratic peace theory offers a direct challenge to realism and provides a powerful recipe for peace.

Finally, some liberals maintain that international institutions enhance the prospects for cooperation among states and thus significantly reduce the likelihood of war.[25] Institutions are not independent political entities that sit above states and force them to behave in acceptable ways. Instead, institutions are sets of rules that stipulate the ways in which states should cooperate and compete with each other. They prescribe acceptable forms of state behavior and proscribe unacceptable kinds of behavior. These rules are not imposed on states by some leviathan, but are negotiated by states, which agree to abide by the rules they created because it is in their interest to do so. Liberals claim that these institutions or rules can fundamentally change state behavior. Institutions, so the argument goes, can discourage states from calculating self-interest on the basis of how their every move affects their relative power position, and thus they push states away from war and promote peace.

Realism

In contrast to liberals, realists are pessimists when it comes to international politics. Realists agree that creating a peaceful world would be desirable, but they see no easy way to escape the harsh world of security competition and war. Creating a peaceful world is surely an attractive idea, but it is not a practical one. "Realism," as Carr notes, "tends to emphasize the irresistible strength of existing forces and the inevitable character of existing tendencies, and to insist that the highest wisdom lies in accepting, and adapting oneself to these forces and these tendencies."[26]

This gloomy view of international relations is based on three core beliefs. First, realists, like liberals, treat states as the principal actors in world politics. Realists focus mainly on great powers, however, because these states dominate and shape international politics and they also cause the deadliest wars. Second, realists believe that the behavior of great powers is influenced mainly by their external environment, not by their internal characteristics. The structure of the international system, which all states must deal with, largely shapes their foreign policies. Realists tend not to draw sharp distinctions between "good" and "bad" states, because all great powers act according to the same logic regardless of their culture, political system, or who runs the government.[27] It is therefore difficult to discriminate among states, save for differences in relative power. In essence, great powers are like billiard balls that vary only in size.[28]

Third, realists hold that calculations about power dominate states' thinking, and that states compete for power among themselves. That competition sometimes necessitates going to war, which is considered an acceptable instrument of statecraft. To quote Carl von Clausewitz, the nineteenth-century military strategist, war is a continuation of politics by other means.[29] Finally, a zero-sum quality characterizes that competition, sometimes making it intense and unforgiving. States may cooperate with each other on occasion, but at root they have conflicting interests.

Although there are many realist theories dealing with different aspects of power, two of them stand above the others: human nature realism, which is laid out in Morgenthau's *Politics among Nations,* and defensive realism, which is presented mainly in Waltz's *Theory of International Politics.* What sets these works apart from those of other realists and makes them both important and controversial is that they provide answers to the two foundational questions described above. Specifically, they explain why states pursue power—that is, they have a story to tell about the *causes* of security competition—and each offers an argument about how much power a state is likely to want.

Some other famous realist thinkers concentrate on making the case that great powers care deeply about power, but they do not attempt to explain why states compete for power or what level of power states deem satisfactory. In essence, they provide a general defense of the realist approach, but they do not offer their own theory of international politics. The works of Carr and American diplomat George Kennan fit this description. In his seminal realist tract, *The Twenty Years' Crisis,* Carr criticizes liberalism at length and argues that states are motivated principally by power considerations. Nevertheless, he says little about why states care about power or how much power they want.[30] Bluntly put, there is no theory in his book. The same basic pattern obtains in Kennan's well-known book *American Diplomacy, 1900–1950.*[31] Morgenthau and Waltz, on the other hand, offer their own theories of international relations, which is why they have dominated the discourse about world politics for the past fifty years.

Human nature realism, which is sometimes called "classical realism," dominated the study of international relations from the late 1940s, when Morgenthau's writings began attracting a large audience, until the early 1970s.[32] It is based on the simple assumption that states are led by human beings who have a "will to power" hardwired into them at birth.[33] That is, states have an insatiable appetite for power, or what Morgenthau calls "a limitless lust for power," which means that they constantly look for opportunities to take the offensive and dominate other states.[34] All states come with an *"animus dominandi,"* so there is no basis for discriminating among more aggressive and less aggressive states, and there certainly should be no room in the theory for status quo states.[35] Human nature realists recognize that international anarchy—the absence of a governing authority over the great powers—causes states to worry about the balance of power. But that structural constraint is treated as a second-order cause of state behavior. The principal driving force in international politics is the will to power inherent in every state in the system, and it pushes each of them to strive for supremacy.

Defensive realism, which is frequently referred to as "structural realism," came on the scene in the late 1970s with the appearance of Waltz's *Theory of International Politics.*[36] Unlike Morgenthau, Waltz does not assume that great powers are inherently aggressive because they are infused with a will to power; instead he starts by assuming that states merely aim to survive. Above all else, they seek security. Nevertheless, he maintains that the structure of the international system forces great powers to pay careful attention to the balance of power. In particular, anarchy forces security-seeking states to compete with each other for power, because power is the best means to survival. Whereas human nature is the deep cause of security competition in Morgenthau's theory, anarchy plays that role in Waltz's theory.[37]

Waltz does not emphasize, however, that the international system provides great powers with good reasons to act offensively to gain power. Instead, he appears to make the opposite case: that anarchy encourages states to behave defensively and to maintain rather than upset the balance of power. "The first concern of states," he writes, is "to maintain their position in the system."[38] There seems to be, as international relations theorist Randall Schweller notes, a "status quo bias" in Waltz's theory.[39]

Waltz recognizes that states have incentives to gain power at their rivals' expense and that it makes good strategic sense to act on that motive when the time is right. But he does not develop that line of argument in any detail. On the contrary, he emphasizes that when great powers behave aggressively, the potential victims usually balance against the aggressor and thwart its efforts to gain power.[40] For Waltz, in short, balancing checkmates offense.[41] Furthermore, he stresses that great powers must be careful not to acquire too much power, because "excessive strength" is likely to cause other states to join forces against them, thereby leaving them worse off than they would have been had they refrained from seeking additional increments of power.[42]

Waltz's views on the causes of war further reflect his theory's status quo bias. There are no profound or deep causes of war in his theory. In particular, he does not suggest that there might be important benefits to be gained from war. In fact, he says little about the causes of war, other than to argue that wars are largely the result of uncertainty and miscalculation. In other words, if states knew better, they would not start wars.

Robert Jervis, Jack Snyder, and Stephen Van Evera buttress the defensive realists' case by focusing attention on a structural concept known as the offense-defense balance.[43] They maintain that military power at any point in time can be categorized as favoring either offense or defense. If defense has a clear advantage over offense, and conquest is therefore difficult, great powers will have little incentive to use force to gain power and will concentrate instead on protecting what they have. When defense has the advantage, protecting what you have should be a relatively easy task. Alternatively, if offense is easier, states will be sorely tempted to try conquering each other, and there will be a lot of war in the system. Defensive realists argue, however, that the offense-defense balance is usually heavily tilted toward defense, thus making conquest extremely difficult.[44] In sum, efficient balancing coupled with the natural advantages of defense over

offense should discourage great powers from pursuing aggressive strategies and instead make them "defensive positionalists."[45]

My theory of offensive realism is also a structural theory of international politics. As with defensive realism, my theory sees great powers as concerned mainly with figuring out how to survive in a world where there is
no agency to protect them from each other; they quickly realize that
power is the key to their survival. Offensive realism parts company with
defensive realism over the question of how much power states want. For
defensive realists, the international structure provides states with little
incentive to seek additional increments of power; instead it pushes them
to maintain the existing balance of power. Preserving power, rather than
increasing it, is the main goal of states. Offensive realists, on the other
hand, believe that status quo powers are rarely found in world politics,
because the international system creates powerful incentives for states to
look for opportunities to gain power at the expense of rivals, and to take
advantage of those situations when the benefits outweigh the costs. A
state's ultimate goal is to be the hegemon in the system.[46]

It should be apparent that both offensive realism and human nature
realism portray great powers as relentlessly seeking power. The key difference between the two perspectives is that offensive realists reject
Morgenthau's claim that states are naturally endowed with Type A per-
sonalities. On the contrary, they believe that the international system
forces great powers to maximize their relative power because that is the
optimal way to maximize their security. In other words, survival mandates aggressive behavior. Great powers behave aggressively not because
they want to or because they possess some inner drive to dominate, but
because they have to seek more power if they want to maximize their
odds of survival. (Table 1.1 summarizes how the main realist theories
answer the foundational questions described above.)

No article or book makes the case for offensive realism in the sophisticated ways that Morgenthau does for human nature realism and Waltz
and others do for defensive realism. For sure, some realists have argued
that the system gives great powers good reasons to act aggressively.
Probably the best brief for offensive realism is a short, obscure book writ-

TABLE 1.1

The Major Realist Theories

	Human Nature Realism	Defensive Realism	Offensive Realism
What causes states to compete for power?	Lust for power inherent in states	Structure of the system	Structure of the system
How much power do states want?	All they can get. States maximize relative power, with hegemony as their ultimate goal.	Not much more than what they have. States concentrate on maintaining the balance of power.	All they can get. States maximize relative power, with hegemony as their ultimate goal.

ten during World War I by G. Lowes Dickinson, a British academic who was an early advocate of the League of Nations.[47] In *The European Anarchy,* he argues that the root cause of World War I "was not Germany nor any other power. The real culprit was the European anarchy," which created powerful incentives for states "to acquire supremacy over the others for motives at once of security and domination."[48] Nevertheless, neither Dickinson nor anyone else makes a comprehensive case for offensive realism.[49] My aim in writing this book is to fill that void.

POWER POLITICS IN LIBERAL AMERICA

Whatever merits realism may have as an explanation for real-world politics and as a guide for formulating foreign policy, it is not a popular school of thought in the West. Realism's central message—that it makes good sense for states to selfishly pursue power—does not have broad appeal. It is difficult to imagine a modern political leader openly asking the public to fight and die to improve the balance of power. No European or American leader did so during either world war or the Cold

War. Most people prefer to think of fights between their own state and rival states as clashes between good and evil, where they are on the side of the angels and their opponents are aligned with the devil. Thus, leaders tend to portray war as a moral crusade or an ideological contest, rather than as a struggle for power. Realism is a hard sell.

Americans appear to have an especially intense antipathy toward balance-of-power thinking. The rhetoric of twentieth-century presidents, for example, is filled with examples of realism bashing. Woodrow Wilson is probably the most well-known example of this tendency, because of his eloquent campaign against balance-of-power politics during and immediately after World War I.[50] Yet Wilson is hardly unique, and his successors have frequently echoed his views. In the final year of World War II, for example, Franklin Delano Roosevelt declared, "In the future world the misuse of power as implied in the term 'power politics' must not be the controlling factor in international relations."[51] More recently, Bill Clinton offered a strikingly similar view, proclaiming that "in a world where freedom, not tyranny, is on the march, the cynical calculus of pure power politics simply does not compute. It is ill-suited to a new era."[52] He sounded the same theme when defending NATO expansion in 1997, arguing that the charge that this policy might isolate Russia was based on the mistaken belief "that the great power territorial politics of the 20th century will dominate the 21st century." Instead, Clinton emphasized his belief that "enlightened self-interest, as well as shared values, will compel countries to define their greatness in more constructive ways . . . and will compel us to cooperate."[53]

Why Americans Dislike Realism

Americans tend to be hostile to realism because it clashes with their basic values. Realism stands opposed to Americans' views of both themselves and the wider world.[54] In particular, realism is at odds with the deep-seated sense of optimism and moralism that pervades much of American society. Liberalism, on the other hand, fits neatly with those values. Not surprisingly, foreign policy discourse in the United States often sounds as if it has been lifted right out of a Liberalism 101 lecture.

Americans are basically optimists.[55] They regard progress in politics, whether at the national or the international level, as both desirable and possible. As the French author Alexis de Tocqueville observed long ago, Americans believe that "man is endowed with an indefinite faculty of improvement."[56] Realism, by contrast, offers a pessimistic perspective on international politics. It depicts a world rife with security competition and war, and holds out little promise of an "escape from the evil of power, regardless of what one does."[57] Such pessimism is at odds with the powerful American belief that with time and effort, reasonable individuals can cooperate to solve important social problems.[58] Liberalism offers a more hopeful perspective on world politics, and Americans naturally find it more attractive than the gloomy specter drawn by realism.

Americans are also prone to believe that morality should play an important role in politics. As the prominent sociologist Seymour Martin Lipset writes, "Americans are utopian moralists who press hard to institutionalize virtue, to destroy evil people, and eliminate wicked institutions and practices."[59] This perspective clashes with the realist belief that war is an intrinsic element of life in the international system. Most Americans tend to think of war as a hideous enterprise that should ultimately be abolished from the face of the Earth. It might justifiably be used for lofty liberal goals like fighting tyranny or spreading democracy, but it is morally incorrect to fight wars merely to change or preserve the balance of power. This makes the Clausewitzian conception of warfare anathema to most Americans.[60]

The American proclivity for moralizing also conflicts with the fact that realists tend not to distinguish between good and bad states, but instead discriminate between states largely on the basis of their relative power capabilities. A purely realist interpretation of the Cold War, for example, allows for no meaningful difference in the motives behind American and Soviet behavior during that conflict. According to realist theory, both sides were driven by their concerns about the balance of power, and each did what it could to maximize its relative power. Most Americans would recoil at this interpretation of the Cold War, however, because they believe the United States was motivated by good intentions while the Soviet Union was not.

Liberal theorists do distinguish between good and bad states, of course, and they usually identify liberal democracies with market economies as the most worthy. Not surprisingly, Americans tend to like this perspective, because it identifies the United States as a benevolent force in world politics and portrays its real and potential rivals as misguided or malevolent troublemakers. Predictably, this line of thinking fueled the euphoria that attended the downfall of the Soviet Union and the end of the Cold War. When the "evil empire" collapsed, many Americans (and Europeans) concluded that democracy would spread across the globe and that world peace would soon break out. This optimism was based largely on the belief that democratic America is a virtuous state. If other states emulated the United States, therefore, the world would be populated by good states, and this development could only mean the end of international conflict.

Rhetoric vs. Practice

Because Americans dislike realpolitik, public discourse about foreign policy in the United States is usually couched in the language of liberalism. Hence the pronouncements of the policy elites are heavily flavored with optimism and moralism. American academics are especially good at promoting liberal thinking in the marketplace of ideas. Behind closed doors, however, the elites who make national security policy speak mostly the language of power, not that of principle, and the United States acts in the international system according to the dictates of realist logic.[61] In essence, a discernible gap separates public rhetoric from the actual conduct of American foreign policy.

Prominent realists have often criticized U.S. diplomacy on the grounds that it is too idealistic and have complained that American leaders pay insufficient attention to the balance of power. For example, Kennan wrote in 1951, "I see the most serious fault of our past policy formulation to lie in something that I might call the legalistic-moralistic approach to international problems. This approach runs like a red skein through our foreign policy of the last fifty years."[62] According to this line of argument, there is no real gap between America's liberal rhetoric and its foreign policy behavior, because the United States practices what it preaches. But this claim is wrong, as I will argue at length below. American foreign policy has usually been guided by realist logic, although the public pronouncements of its leaders might lead one to think otherwise.

It should be obvious to intelligent observers that the United States speaks one way and acts another. In fact, policymakers in other states have always remarked about this tendency in American foreign policy. As long ago as 1939, for example, Carr pointed out that states on the European continent regard the English-speaking peoples as "masters in the art of concealing their selfish national interests in the guise of the general good," adding that "this kind of hypocrisy is a special and characteristic peculiarity of the Anglo-Saxon mind."[63]

Still, the gap between rhetoric and reality usually goes unnoticed in the United States itself. Two factors account for this phenomenon. First, realist policies sometimes coincide with the dictates of liberalism, in which case there is no conflict between the pursuit of power and the pursuit of principle. Under these circumstances, realist policies can be justified with liberal rhetoric without having to discuss the underlying power realities. This coincidence makes for an easy sell. For example, the United States fought against fascism in World War II and communism in the Cold War for largely realist reasons. But both of those fights were also consistent with liberal principles, and thus policymakers had little trouble selling them to the public as ideological conflicts.

Second, when power considerations force the United States to act in ways that conflict with liberal principles, "spin doctors" appear and tell a story that accords with liberal ideals.[64] For example, in the late nineteenth century, American elites generally considered Germany to be a progressive constitutional state worthy of emulation. But the American view of Germany changed in the decade before World War I, as relations between the two states deteriorated. By the time the United States declared war on Germany in April 1917, Americans had come to see Germany as more autocratic and militaristic than its European rivals.

Similarly, during the late 1930s, many Americans saw the Soviet Union as an evil state, partly in response to Josef Stalin's murderous internal policies and his infamous alliance with Nazi Germany in August 1939. Nevertheless, when the United States joined forces with the Soviet Union in late 1941 to fight against the Third Reich, the U.S. government began a massive public relations campaign to clean up the image of America's new ally and make it compatible with liberal ideals. The Soviet Union was now portrayed as a proto-democracy, and Stalin became "Uncle Joe."

How is it possible to get away with this contradiction between rhetoric and policy? Most Americans readily accept these rationalizations because liberalism is so deeply rooted in their culture. As a result, they find it easy to believe that they are acting according to cherished principles, rather than cold and calculated power considerations.[65]

THE PLAN OF THE BOOK

The rest of the chapters in this book are concerned mainly with answering the six big questions about power which I identified earlier. Chapter 2, which is probably the most important chapter in the book, lays out my theory of why states compete for power and why they pursue hegemony.

In Chapters 3 and 4, I define power and explain how to measure it. I do this in order to lay the groundwork for testing my theory. It is impossible to determine whether states have behaved according to the dictates of offensive realism without knowing what power is and what different strategies states employ to maximize their share of world power. My starting point is to distinguish between potential power and actual military power, and then to argue that states care deeply about both kinds of power. Chapter 3 focuses on potential power, which involves mainly the size of a state's population and its wealth. Chapter 4 deals with actual military power. It is an especially long chapter because I make arguments about "the primacy of land power" and "the stopping power of water" that are novel and likely to be controversial.

In Chapter 5, I discuss the strategies that great powers employ to gain and maintain power. This chapter includes a substantial discussion of the utility of war for acquiring power. I also focus on balancing and buck-passing, which are the main strategies that states employ when faced with a rival that threatens to upset the balance of power.

In Chapters 6 and 7, I examine the historical record to see whether there is evidence to support the theory. Specifically, I compare the conduct of the great powers from 1792 to 1990 to see whether their behavior fits the predictions of offensive realism.

In Chapter 8, I lay out a simple theory that explains when great powers balance and when they choose to buck-pass, and then I examine that theory against the historical record. Chapter 9 focuses on the causes of war. Here, too, I lay out a simple theory and then test it against the empirical record.

Chapter 10 challenges the oft-made claim that international politics has been fundamentally transformed with the end of the Cold War, and that great powers no longer compete with each other for power. I briefly assess the theories underpinning that optimistic perspective, and then I look at how the great powers have behaved in Europe and Northeast Asia between 1991 and 2000. Finally, I make predictions about the likelihood of great-power conflict in these two important regions in the early twenty-first century.

2

Anarchy and the Struggle for Power

G reat powers, I argue, are always searching for opportunities to gain power over their rivals, with hegemony as their final goal. This perspective does not allow for status quo powers, except for the unusual state that achieves preponderance. Instead, the system is populated with great powers that have revisionist intentions at their core.[1] This chapter presents a theory that explains this competition for power. Specifically, I attempt to show that there is a compelling logic behind my claim that great powers seek to maximize their share of world power. I do not, however, test offensive realism against the historical record in this chapter. That important task is reserved for later chapters.

WHY STATES PURSUE POWER

M y explanation for why great powers vie with each other for power and strive for hegemony is derived from five assumptions about the international system. None of these assumptions alone mandates that states behave competitively. Taken together, however, they depict a world in which states have considerable reason to think and sometimes behave aggressively. In particular, the system encourages states to look for opportunities to maximize their power vis-à-vis other states.

How important is it that these assumptions be realistic? Some social scientists argue that the assumptions that underpin a theory need not conform to reality. Indeed, the economist Milton Friedman maintains that the best theories "will be found to have assumptions that are wildly inaccurate descriptive representations of reality, and, in general, the more significant the theory, the more unrealistic the assumptions."[2] According to this view, the explanatory power of a theory is all that matters. If unrealistic assumptions lead to a theory that tells us a lot about how the world works, it is of no importance whether the underlying assumptions are realistic or not.

I reject this view. Although I agree that explanatory power is the ultimate criterion for assessing theories, I also believe that a theory based on unrealistic or false assumptions will not explain much about how the world works.[3] Sound theories are based on sound assumptions. Accordingly, each of these five assumptions is a reasonably accurate representation of an important aspect of life in the international system.

Bedrock Assumptions

The first assumption is that the international system is anarchic, which does not mean that it is chaotic or riven by disorder. It is easy to draw that conclusion, since realism depicts a world characterized by security competition and war. By itself, however, the realist notion of anarchy has nothing to do with conflict; it is an ordering principle, which says that the system comprises independent states that have no central authority above them.[4] Sovereignty, in other words, inheres in states because there is no higher ruling body in the international system.[5] There is no "government over governments."[6]

The second assumption is that great powers inherently possess some offensive military capability, which gives them the wherewithal to hurt and possibly destroy each other. States are potentially dangerous to each other, although some states have more military might than others and are therefore more dangerous. A state's military power is usually identified with the particular weaponry at its disposal, although even if there were no weapons, the individuals in those states could still use their feet and hands to attack the population of another state. After all, for every neck, there are two hands to choke it.

The third assumption is that states can never be certain about other states' intentions. Specifically, no state can be sure that another state will not use its offensive military capability to attack the first state. This is not to say that states necessarily have hostile intentions. Indeed, all of the states in the system may be reliably benign, but it is impossible to be sure of that judgment because intentions are impossible to divine with 100 percent certainty.[7] There are many possible causes of aggression, and no state can be sure that another state is not motivated by one of them.[8] Furthermore, intentions can change quickly, so a state's intentions can be benign one day and hostile the next. Uncertainty about intentions is unavoidable, which means that states can never be sure that other states do not have offensive intentions to go along with their offensive capabilities.

The fourth assumption is that survival is the primary goal of great powers. Specifically, states seek to maintain their territorial integrity and the autonomy of their domestic political order. Survival dominates other motives because, once a state is conquered, it is unlikely to be in a position to pursue other aims. Soviet leader Josef Stalin put the point well during a war scare in 1927: "We can and must build socialism in the [Soviet Union]. But in order to do so we first of all have to exist."[9] States can and do pursue other goals, of course, but security is their most important objective.

The fifth assumption is that great powers are rational actors. They are aware of their external environment and they think strategically about how to survive in it. In particular, they consider the preferences of other states and how their own behavior is likely to affect the behavior of those other states, and how the behavior of those other states is likely to affect their own strategy for survival. Moreover, states pay attention to the long term as well as the immediate consequences of their actions.

As emphasized, none of these assumptions alone dictates that great powers as a general rule *should* behave aggressively toward each other. There is surely the possibility that some state might have hostile intentions, but the only assumption dealing with a specific motive that is common to all states says that their principal objective is to survive, which by itself is a rather harmless goal. Nevertheless, when the five assumptions are married together, they create powerful incentives for great powers to think and act offensively with regard to each other. In particular, three general patterns of behavior result: fear, self-help, and power maximization.

State Behavior

Great powers fear each other. They regard each other with suspicion, and they worry that war might be in the offing. They anticipate danger. There is little room for trust among states. For sure, the level of fear varies across time and space, but it cannot be reduced to a trivial level. From the perspective of any one great power, all other great powers are potential enemies. This point is illustrated by the reaction of the United Kingdom and France to German reunification at the end of the Cold War. Despite the fact that these three states had been close allies for almost forty-five years, both the United Kingdom and France immediately began worrying about the potential dangers of a united Germany.[10]

The basis of this fear is that in a world where great powers have the capability to attack each other and might have the motive to do so, any state bent on survival must be at least suspicious of other states and reluctant to trust them. Add to this the "911" problem—the absence of a central authority to which a threatened state can turn for help—and states have even greater incentive to fear each other. Moreover, there is no mechanism, other than the possible self-interest of third parties, for punishing an aggressor. Because it is sometimes difficult to deter potential aggressors, states have ample reason not to trust other states and to be prepared for war with them.

The possible consequences of falling victim to aggression further amplify the importance of fear as a motivating force in world politics. Great powers do not compete with each other as if international politics were merely an economic marketplace. Political competition among states is a much more dangerous business than mere economic intercourse; the former can lead to war, and war often means mass killing on the battlefield as well as mass murder of civilians. In extreme cases, war can even lead to the destruction of states. The horrible consequences of war sometimes cause states to view each other not just as competitors, but as potentially deadly enemies. Political antagonism, in short, tends to be intense, because the stakes are great.

States in the international system also aim to guarantee their own survival. Because other states are potential threats, and because there is no higher authority to come to their rescue when they dial 911, states cannot depend on others for their own security. Each state tends to see itself as vulnerable and alone, and therefore it aims to provide for its own survival. In international politics, God helps those who help themselves. This emphasis on self-help does not preclude states from forming alliances.[11] But alliances are only temporary marriages of convenience: today's alliance partner might be tomorrow's enemy, and today's enemy might be tomorrow's alliance partner. For example, the United States fought with China and the Soviet Union against Germany and Japan in World War II, but soon thereafter flip-flopped enemies and partners and allied with West Germany and Japan against China and the Soviet Union during the Cold War.

States operating in a self-help world almost always act according to their own self-interest and do not subordinate their interests to the interests of other states, or to the interests of the so-called international community. The reason is simple: it pays to be selfish in a self-help world. This is true in the short term as well as in the long term, because if a state loses in the short run, it might not be around for the long haul.

Apprehensive about the ultimate intentions of other states, and aware that they operate in a self-help system, states quickly understand that the best way to ensure their survival is to be the most powerful state in the system. The stronger a state is relative to its potential rivals, the less likely it is that any of those rivals will attack it and threaten its survival. Weaker states will be reluctant to pick fights with more powerful states because the weaker states are likely to suffer military defeat. Indeed, the bigger the gap in power between any two states, the less likely it is that the weaker will attack the stronger. Neither Canada nor Mexico, for example, would countenance attacking the United States, which is far more powerful than its neighbors. The ideal situation is to be the hegemon in the system. As Immanuel Kant said, "It is the desire of every state, or of its ruler, to arrive at a condition of perpetual peace by conquering the whole world, if that were possible."[12] Survival would then be almost guaranteed.[13]

Consequently, states pay close attention to how power is distributed among them, and they make a special effort to maximize their share of world power. Specifically, they look for opportunities to alter the balance of power by acquiring additional increments of power at the expense of potential rivals. States employ a variety of means—economic, diplomatic, and military—to shift the balance of power in their favor, even if doing so makes other states suspicious or even hostile. Because one state's gain in power is another state's loss, great powers tend to have a zero-sum mentality when dealing with each other. The trick, of course, is to be the winner in this competition and to dominate the other states in the system. Thus, the claim that states maximize relative power is tantamount to arguing that states are disposed to think offensively toward other states, even though their ultimate motive is simply to survive. In short, great powers have aggressive intentions.[14]

Even when a great power achieves a distinct military advantage over its rivals, it continues looking for chances to gain more power. The pursuit of power stops only when hegemony is achieved. The idea that a great power might feel secure without dominating the system, provided it has an "appropriate amount" of power, is not persuasive, for two reasons.[15] First, it is difficult to assess how much relative power one state must have over its rivals before it is secure. Is twice as much power an appropriate threshold? Or is three times as much power the magic number? The root of the problem is that power calculations alone do not determine which side wins a war. Clever strategies, for example, sometimes allow less powerful states to defeat more powerful foes.

Second, determining how much power is enough becomes even more complicated when great powers contemplate how power will be distributed among them ten or twenty years down the road. The capabilities of

individual states vary over time, sometimes markedly, and it is often difficult to predict the direction and scope of change in the balance of power.
Remember, few in the West anticipated the collapse of the Soviet Union
before it happened. In fact, during the first half of the Cold War, many in
the West feared that the Soviet economy would eventually generate
greater wealth than the American economy, which would cause a marked
power shift against the United States and its allies. What the future holds
for China and Russia and what the balance of power will look like in 2020
is difficult to foresee.

Given the difficulty of determining how much power is enough for
today and tomorrow, great powers recognize that the best way to ensure
their security is to achieve hegemony now, thus eliminating any possibility of a challenge by another great power. Only a misguided state would
pass up an opportunity to be the hegemon in the system because it
thought it already had sufficient power to survive.[16] But even if a great
power does not have the wherewithal to achieve hegemony (and that is
usually the case), it will still act offensively to amass as much power as it
can, because states are almost always better off with more rather than less
power. In short, states do not become status quo powers until they completely dominate the system.

All states are influenced by this logic, which means that not only do
they look for opportunities to take advantage of one another, they also
work to ensure that other states do not take advantage of them. After all,
rival states are driven by the same logic, and most states are likely to recognize their own motives at play in the actions of other states. In short,
states ultimately pay attention to defense as well as offense. They think
about conquest themselves, and they work to check aggressor states from
gaining power at their expense. This inexorably leads to a world of constant security competition, where states are willing to lie, cheat, and use
brute force if it helps them gain advantage over their rivals. Peace, if one
defines that concept as a state of tranquility or mutual concord, is not likely to break out in this world.

The "security dilemma," which is one of the most well-known concepts
in the international relations literature, reflects the basic logic of offensive

realism. The essence of the dilemma is that the measures a state takes to increase its own security usually decrease the security of other states. Thus, it is difficult for a state to increase its own chances of survival without threatening the survival of other states. John Herz first introduced the security dilemma in a 1950 article in the journal *World Politics*.[17] After discussing the anarchic nature of international politics, he writes, "Striving to attain security from . . . attack, [states] are driven to acquire more and more power in order to escape the impact of the power of others. This, in turn, renders the others more insecure and compels them to prepare for the worst. Since none can ever feel entirely secure in such a world of competing units, power competition ensues, and the vicious circle of security and power accumulation is on."[18] The implication of Herz's analysis is clear: the best way for a state to survive in anarchy is to take advantage of other states and gain power at their expense. The best defense is a good offense. Since this message is widely understood, ceaseless security competition ensues. Unfortunately, little can be done to ameliorate the security dilemma as long as states operate in anarchy.

It should be apparent from this discussion that saying that states are power maximizers is tantamount to saying that they care about relative power, not absolute power. There is an important distinction here, because states concerned about relative power behave differently than do states interested in absolute power.[19] States that maximize relative power are concerned primarily with the distribution of material capabilities. In particular, they try to gain as large a power advantage as possible over potential rivals, because power is the best means to survival in a dangerous world. Thus, states motivated by relative power concerns are likely to forgo large gains in their own power, if such gains give rival states even greater power, for smaller national gains that nevertheless provide them with a power advantage over their rivals.[20] States that maximize absolute power, on the other hand, care only about the size of their own gains, not those of other states. They are not motivated by balance-of-power logic but instead are concerned with amassing power without regard to how much power other states control. They would jump at the opportunity for large gains, even if a rival gained more in the deal. Power, according to this logic, is not a means to an end (survival), but an end in itself.[21]

Calculated Aggression

There is obviously little room for status quo powers in a world where states are inclined to look for opportunities to gain more power. Nevertheless, great powers cannot always act on their offensive intentions, because behavior is influenced not only by what states want, but also by their capacity to realize these desires. Every state might want to be king of the hill, but not every state has the wherewithal to compete for that lofty position, much less achieve it. Much depends on how military might is distributed among the great powers. A great power that has a marked power advantage over its rivals is likely to behave more aggressively, because it has the capability as well as the incentive to do so.

By contrast, great powers facing powerful opponents will be less inclined to consider offensive action and more concerned with defending the existing balance of power from threats by their more powerful opponents. Let there be an opportunity for those weaker states to revise the balance in their own favor, however, and they will take advantage of it. Stalin put the point well at the end of World War II: "Everyone imposes his own system as far as his army can reach. It cannot be otherwise."[22] States might also have the capability to gain advantage over a rival power but nevertheless decide that the perceived costs of offense are too high and do not justify the expected benefits.

In short, great powers are not mindless aggressors so bent on gaining power that they charge headlong into losing wars or pursue Pyrrhic victories. On the contrary, before great powers take offensive actions, they think carefully about the balance of power and about how other states will react to their moves. They weigh the costs and risks of offense against the likely benefits. If the benefits do not outweigh the risks, they sit tight and wait for a more propitious moment. Nor do states start arms races that are unlikely to improve their overall position. As discussed at greater length in Chapter 3, states sometimes limit defense spending either because spending more would bring no strategic advantage or because spending more would weaken the economy and undermine the state's power in the long run.[23] To paraphrase Clint Eastwood, a state has to know its limitations to survive in the international system.

Nevertheless, great powers miscalculate from time to time because they invariably make important decisions on the basis of imperfect information. States hardly ever have complete information about any situation they confront. There are two dimensions to this problem. Potential adversaries have incentives to misrepresent their own strength or weakness, and to conceal their true aims.[24] For example, a weaker state trying to deter a stronger state is likely to exaggerate its own power to discourage the potential aggressor from attacking. On the other hand, a state bent on aggression is likely to emphasize its peaceful goals while exaggerating its military weakness, so that the potential victim does not build up its own arms and thus leaves itself vulnerable to attack. Probably no national leader was better at practicing this kind of deception than Adolf Hitler.

But even if disinformation was not a problem, great powers are often unsure about how their own military forces, as well as the adversary's, will perform on the battlefield. For example, it is sometimes difficult to determine in advance how new weapons and untested combat units will perform in the face of enemy fire. Peacetime maneuvers and war games are helpful but imperfect indicators of what is likely to happen in actual combat. Fighting wars is a complicated business in which it is often difficult to predict outcomes. Remember that although the United States and its allies scored a stunning and remarkably easy victory against Iraq in early 1991, most experts at the time believed that Iraq's military would be a formidable foe and put up stubborn resistance before finally succumbing to American military might.[25]

Great powers are also sometimes unsure about the resolve of opposing states as well as allies. For example, Germany believed that if it went to war against France and Russia in the summer of 1914, the United Kingdom would probably stay out of the fight. Saddam Hussein expected the United States to stand aside when he invaded Kuwait in August 1990. Both aggressors guessed wrong, but each had good reason to think that its initial judgment was correct. In the 1930s, Adolf Hitler believed that his great-power rivals would be easy to exploit and isolate because each had little interest in fighting Germany and instead was determined to get someone else to assume that burden. He guessed right. In short, great powers constantly find themselves confronting situations in which they have to make important decisions with incomplete information. Not surprisingly, they sometimes make faulty judgments and end up doing themselves serious harm.

Some defensive realists go so far as to suggest that the constraints of the international system are so powerful that offense rarely succeeds, and that aggressive great powers invariably end up being punished.[26] As noted, they emphasize that 1) threatened states balance against aggressors and ultimately crush them, and 2) there is an offense-defense balance that is usually heavily tilted toward the defense, thus making conquest especially difficult. Great powers, therefore, should be content with the existing balance of power and not try to change it by force. After all, it makes little sense for a state to initiate a war that it is likely to lose; that would be self-defeating behavior. It is better to concentrate instead on preserving the balance of power.[27] Moreover, because aggressors seldom succeed, states should understand that security is abundant, and thus there is no good strategic reason for wanting more power in the first place. In a world where conquest seldom pays, states should have relatively benign intentions toward each other. If they do not, these defensive realists argue, the reason is probably poisonous domestic politics, not smart calculations about how to guarantee one's security in an anarchic world.

There is no question that systemic factors constrain aggression, especially balancing by threatened states. But defensive realists exaggerate those restraining forces.[28] Indeed, the historical record provides little support for their claim that offense rarely succeeds. One study estimates that there were 63 wars between 1815 and 1980, and the initiator won 39 times, which translates into about a 60 percent success rate.[29] Turning to specific cases, Otto von Bismarck unified Germany by winning military victories against Denmark in 1864, Austria in 1866, and France in 1870, and the United States as we know it today was created in good part by conquest in the nineteenth century. Conquest certainly paid big dividends in these cases. Nazi Germany won wars against Poland in 1939 and France in 1940, but lost to the Soviet Union between 1941 and 1945. Conquest ultimately did not pay for the Third Reich, but if Hitler had restrained himself after the fall of France and had not invaded the Soviet Union, conquest probably would have paid handsomely for the Nazis. In short, the historical record shows that offense sometimes succeeds and sometimes does not. The trick for a sophisticated power maximizer is to figure out when to raise and when to fold.[30]

HEGEMONY'S LIMITS

Great powers, as I have emphasized, strive to gain power over their rivals and hopefully become hegemons. Once a state achieves that exalted position, it becomes a status quo power. More needs to be said, however, about the meaning of hegemony.

A hegemon is a state that is so powerful that it dominates all the other states in the system.[31] No other state has the military wherewithal to put up a serious fight against it. In essence, a hegemon is the only great power in the system. A state that is substantially more powerful than the other great powers in the system is not a hegemon, because it faces, by definition, other great powers. The United Kingdom in the mid-nineteenth century, for example, is sometimes called a hegemon. But it was not a hegemon, because there were four other great powers in Europe at the time—Austria, France, Prussia, and Russia—and the United Kingdom did not dominate them in any meaningful way. In fact, during that period, the United Kingdom considered France to be a serious threat to the balance of power. Europe in the nineteenth century was multipolar, not unipolar.

Hegemony means domination of the system, which is usually interpreted to mean the entire world. It is possible, however, to apply the concept of a system more narrowly and use it to describe particular regions, such as Europe, Northeast Asia, and the Western Hemisphere. Thus, one can distinguish between *global hegemons*, which dominate the world, and *regional hegemons*, which dominate distinct geographical areas. The United States has been a regional hegemon in the Western Hemisphere for at least the past one hundred years. No other state in the Americas has sufficient military might to challenge it, which is why the United States is widely recognized as the only great power in its region.

My argument, which I develop at length in subsequent chapters, is that except for the unlikely event wherein one state achieves clear-cut nuclear superiority, it is virtually impossible for any state to achieve global hegemony. The principal impediment to world domination is the difficulty of projecting power across the world's oceans onto the territory of a rival great power. The United States, for example, is the most powerful state on the planet today. But it does not dominate Europe and Northeast Asia the way it does the Western Hemisphere, and it has no intention of trying to conquer and control those distant regions, mainly because of the stopping power of water. Indeed, there is reason to think that the American military commitment to Europe and Northeast Asia might wither away over the next decade. In short, there has never been a global hegemon, and there is not likely to be one anytime soon.

The best outcome a great power can hope for is to be a regional hegemon and possibly control another region that is nearby and accessible over land. The United States is the only regional hegemon in modern history, although other states have fought major wars in pursuit of regional hegemony: imperial Japan in Northeast Asia, and Napoleonic France, Wilhelmine Germany, and Nazi Germany in Europe. But none succeeded. The Soviet Union, which is located in Europe and Northeast Asia, threatened to dominate both of those regions during the Cold War. The Soviet Union might also have attempted to conquer the oil-rich Persian Gulf region, with which it shared a border. But even if Moscow had been able to dominate Europe, Northeast Asia, and the Persian Gulf, which it never came close to doing, it still would have been unable to conquer the Western Hemisphere and become a true global hegemon.

States that achieve regional hegemony seek to prevent great powers in other regions from duplicating their feat. Regional hegemons, in other words, do not want peers. Thus the United States, for example, played a key role in preventing imperial Japan, Wilhelmine Germany, Nazi Germany, and the Soviet Union from gaining regional supremacy. Regional hegemons attempt to check aspiring hegemons in other regions because they fear that a rival great power that dominates its own region will be an especially powerful foe that is essentially free to cause trouble in the fearful great power's backyard. Regional hegemons prefer that there be at least two great powers located together in other regions, because their proximity will force them to concentrate their attention on each other rather than on the distant hegemon.

Furthermore, if a potential hegemon emerges among them, the other great powers in that region might be able to contain it by themselves, allowing the distant hegemon to remain safely on the sidelines. Of course, if the local great powers were unable to do the job, the distant hegemon would take the appropriate measures to deal with the threatening state. The United States, as noted, has assumed that burden on four separate occasions in the twentieth century, which is why it is commonly referred to as an "offshore balancer."

In sum, the ideal situation for any great power is to be the only regional hegemon in the world. That state would be a status quo power, and it would go to considerable lengths to preserve the existing distribution of power. The United States is in that enviable position today; it dominates the Western Hemisphere and there is no hegemon in any other area of the world. But if a regional hegemon is confronted with a peer competitor, it would no longer be a status quo power. Indeed, it would go to considerable lengths to weaken and maybe even destroy its distant rival. Of course, both regional hegemons would be motivated by that logic, which would make for a fierce security competition between them.

POWER AND FEAR

That great powers fear each other is a central aspect of life in the international system. But as noted, the level of fear varies from case to case. For example, the Soviet Union worried much less about Germany in 1930 than it did in 1939. How much states fear each other matters greatly, because the amount of fear between them largely determines the severity of their security competition, as well as the probability that they will fight a war. The more profound the fear is, the more intense is the security competition, and the more likely is war. The logic is straightforward: a scared state will look especially hard for ways to enhance its security, and it will be disposed to pursue risky policies to achieve that end. Therefore, it is important to understand what causes states to fear each other more or less intensely.

Fear among great powers derives from the fact that they invariably have some offensive military capability that they can use against each other, and the fact that one can never be certain that other states do not intend to use that power against oneself. Moreover, because states operate in an anarchic system, there is no night watchman to whom they can turn for help if another great power attacks them. Although anarchy and uncertainty about other states' intentions create an irreducible level of fear among states that leads to power-maximizing behavior, they cannot account for why sometimes that level of fear is greater than at other times. The reason is that anarchy and the difficulty of discerning state intentions are constant facts of life, and constants cannot explain variation. The capability that states have to threaten each other, however, varies from case to case, and it is the key factor that drives fear levels up and down. Specifically, the more power a state possesses, the more fear it generates among its rivals. Germany, for example, was much more powerful at the end of the 1930s than it was at the decade's beginning, which is why the Soviets became increasingly fearful of Germany over the course of that decade.

This discussion of how power affects fear prompts the question, What is power? It is important to distinguish between potential and actual power. A state's potential power is based on the size of its population and the level of its wealth. These two assets are the main building blocks of military power. Wealthy rivals with large populations can usually build formidable military forces. A state's actual power is embedded mainly in its army and the air and naval forces that directly support it. Armies are the central ingredient of military power, because they are the principal instrument for conquering and controlling territory—the paramount political objective in a world of territorial states. In short, the key component of military might, even in the nuclear age, is land power.

Power considerations affect the intensity of fear among states in three main ways. First, rival states that possess nuclear forces that can survive a nuclear attack and retaliate against it are likely to fear each other less than if these same states had no nuclear weapons. During the Cold War, for example, the level of fear between the superpowers probably would have been substantially greater if nuclear weapons had not been invented. The logic here is simple: because nuclear weapons can inflict devastating destruction on a rival state in a short period of time, nuclear-armed rivals are going to be reluctant to fight with each other, which means that each side will have less reason to fear the other than would otherwise be the case. But as the Cold War demonstrates, this does not mean that war between nuclear powers is no longer thinkable; they still have reason to fear each other.

Second, when great powers are separated by large bodies of water, they usually do not have much offensive capability against each other, regardless of the relative size of their armies. Large bodies of water are formidable obstacles that cause significant power-projection problems for attacking armies. For example, the stopping power of water explains in good part why the United Kingdom and the United States (since becoming a great power in 1898) have never been invaded by another great power. It also explains why the United States has never tried to conquer territory in Europe or Northeast Asia, and why the United Kingdom has never attempted to dominate the European continent. Great powers located on the same landmass are in a much better position to attack and conquer each other. That is especially true of states that share a common border. Therefore, great powers separated by water are likely to fear each other less than great powers that can get at each other over land.

Third, the distribution of power among the states in the system also markedly affects the levels of fear.[32] The key issue is whether power is distributed more or less evenly among the great powers or whether there are sharp power asymmetries. The configuration of power that generates the most fear is a multipolar system that contains a potential hegemon—what I call "unbalanced multipolarity."

A potential hegemon is more than just the most powerful state in the system. It is a great power with so much actual military capability and so much potential power that it stands a good chance of dominating and controlling all of the other great powers in its region of the world. A potential hegemon need not have the wherewithal to fight all of its rivals at once, but it must have excellent prospects of defeating each opponent alone, and good prospects of defeating some of them in tandem. The key relationship, however, is the power gap between the potential hegemon and the second most powerful state in the system: there must be a marked gap between them. To qualify as a potential hegemon, a state must have—by some reasonably large margin—the most formidable army as well as the most latent power among all the states located in its region.

Bipolarity is the power configuration that produces the least amount of fear among the great powers, although not a negligible amount by any means. Fear tends to be less acute in bipolarity, because there is usually a rough balance of power between the two major states in the system. Multipolar systems without a potential hegemon, what I call "balanced multipolarity," are still likely to have power asymmetries among their members, although these asymmetries will not be as pronounced as the gaps created by the presence of an aspiring hegemon. Therefore, balanced multipolarity is likely to generate less fear than unbalanced multipolarity, but more fear than bipolarity.

This discussion of how the level of fear between great powers varies with changes in the distribution of power, not with assessments about each other's intentions, raises a related point. When a state surveys its environment to determine which states pose a threat to its survival, it focuses mainly on the offensive *capabilities* of potential rivals, not their intentions. As emphasized earlier, intentions are ultimately unknowable, so states worried about their survival must make worst-case assumptions about their rivals' intentions. Capabilities, however, not only can be measured but also determine whether or not a rival state is a serious threat. In short, great powers balance against capabilities, not intentions.[33]

Great powers obviously balance against states with formidable military forces, because that offensive military capability is the tangible threat to their survival. But great powers also pay careful attention to how much latent power rival states control, because rich and populous states usually can and do build powerful armies. Thus, great powers tend to fear states with large populations and rapidly expanding economies, even if these states have not yet translated their wealth into military might.

THE HIERARCHY OF STATE GOALS

S urvival is the number one goal of great powers, according to my theory. In practice, however, states pursue non-security goals as well. For example, great powers invariably seek greater economic prosperity to enhance the welfare of their citizenry. They sometimes seek to promote a particular ideology abroad, as happened during the Cold War when the the United States tried to spread democracy around the world and the Soviet Union tried to sell communism. National unification is another goal that sometimes motivates states, as it did with Prussia and Italy in the nineteenth century and Germany after the Cold War. Great powers also occasionally try to foster human rights around the globe. States might pursue any of these, as well as a number of other non-security goals.

Offensive realism certainly recognizes that great powers might pursue these non-security goals, but it has little to say about them, save for one important point: states can pursue them as long as the requisite behavior does not conflict with balance-of-power logic, which is often the case.[34] Indeed, the pursuit of these non-security goals sometimes complements the hunt for relative power. For example, Nazi Germany expanded into eastern Europe for both ideological and realist reasons, and the superpowers competed with each other during the Cold War for similar reasons. Furthermore, greater economic prosperity invariably means greater wealth, which has significant implications for security, because wealth is the foundation of military power. Wealthy states can afford powerful military forces, which enhance a state's prospects for survival. As the political economist Jacob Viner noted more than fifty years ago, "there is a long-run harmony" between wealth and power.[35] National unification is another goal that usually complements the pursuit of power. For example, the unified German state that emerged in 1871 was more powerful than the Prussian state it replaced.

Sometimes the pursuit of non-security goals has hardly any effect on the balance of power, one way or the other. Human rights interventions usually fit this description, because they tend to be small-scale operations that cost little and do not detract from a great power's prospects for survival. For better or for worse, states are rarely willing to expend blood and treasure to protect foreign populations from gross abuses, including genocide. For instance, despite claims that American foreign policy is infused with moralism, Somalia (1992–93) is the only instance during the past one hundred years in which U.S. soldiers were killed in action on a humanitarian mission. And in that case, the loss of a mere eighteen soldiers in an infamous firefight in October 1993 so traumatized American policymakers that they immediately pulled all U.S. troops out of Somalia and then refused to intervene in Rwanda in the spring of 1994, when ethnic Hutu went on a genocidal rampage against their Tutsi neighbors.[36] Stopping that genocide would have been relatively easy and it would have had virtually no effect on the position of the United States in the balance of power.[37] Yet nothing was done. In short, although realism does not prescribe human rights interventions, it does not necessarily proscribe them.

But sometimes the pursuit of non-security goals conflicts with balance-of-power logic, in which case states usually act according to the dictates of realism. For example, despite the U.S. commitment to spreading democracy across the globe, it helped overthrow democratically elected governments and embraced a number of authoritarian regimes during the Cold War, when American policymakers felt that these actions would help contain the Soviet Union.[38] In World War II, the liberal democracies put aside their antipathy for communism and formed an alliance with the Soviet Union against Nazi Germany. "I can't take communism," Franklin Roosevelt emphasized, but to defeat Hitler "I would hold hands with the Devil."[39] In the same way, Stalin repeatedly demonstrated that when his ideological preferences clashed with power considerations, the latter won out. To take the most blatant example of his realism, the Soviet Union formed a non-aggression pact with Nazi Germany in August 1939—the infamous Molotov-Ribbentrop Pact—in hopes that the agreement would at least temporarily satisfy Hitler's territorial ambitions in eastern Europe and turn the Wehrmacht toward France and the United Kingdom.[40] When great powers confront a serious threat, in short, they pay little attention to ideology as they search for alliance partners.[41]

Security also trumps wealth when those two goals conflict, because "defence," as Adam Smith wrote in *The Wealth of Nations,* "is of much more importance than opulence."[42] Smith provides a good illustration of how states behave when forced to choose between wealth and relative power. In 1651, England put into effect the famous Navigation Act, protectionist legislation designed to damage Holland's commerce and ultimately cripple the Dutch economy. The legislation mandated that all goods imported into England be carried either in English ships or ships owned by the country that originally produced the goods. Since the Dutch produced few goods themselves, this measure would badly damage their shipping, the central ingredient in their economic success. Of course, the Navigation Act would hurt England's economy as well, mainly because it would rob England of the benefits of free trade. "The act of navigation," Smith wrote, "is not favorable to foreign commerce, or to the growth of that opulence that can arise from it." Nevertheless, Smith considered the legislation "the wisest of all the commercial regulations of England" because it did more damage to the Dutch economy than to the English economy, and in the mid-seventeenth century Holland was "the only naval power which could endanger the security of England."[43]

CREATING WORLD ORDER

The claim is sometimes made that great powers can transcend realist logic by working together to build an international order that fosters peace and justice. World peace, it would appear, can only enhance a state's prosperity and security. America's political leaders paid considerable lip service to this line of argument over the course of the twentieth century. President Clinton, for example, told an audience at the United Nations in September 1993 that "at the birth of this organization 48 years ago . . . a generation of gifted leaders from many nations stepped forward to organize the world's efforts on behalf of security and prosperity. . . . Now history has granted to us a moment of even greater opportunity. . . . Let us resolve that we will dream larger. . . . Let us ensure that the world we pass to our children is healthier, safer and more abundant than the one we inhabit today."[44]

This rhetoric notwithstanding, great powers do not work together to promote world order for its own sake. Instead, each seeks to maximize its own share of world power, which is likely to clash with the goal of creating and sustaining stable international orders.[45] This is not to say that great powers never aim to prevent wars and keep the peace. On the contrary, they work hard to deter wars in which they would be the likely victim. In such cases, however, state behavior is driven largely by narrow calculations about relative power, not by a commitment to build a world order independent of a state's own interests. The United States, for example, devoted enormous resources to deterring the Soviet Union from starting a war in Europe during the Cold War, not because of some deep-seated commitment to promoting peace around the world, but because American leaders feared that a Soviet victory would lead to a dangerous shift in the balance of power.[46]

The particular international order that obtains at any time is mainly a by-product of the self-interested behavior of the system's great powers. The configuration of the system, in other words, is the unintended consequence of great-power security competition, not the result of states acting together to organize peace. The establishment of the Cold War order in Europe illustrates this point. Neither the Soviet Union nor the United States intended to establish it, nor did they work together to create it. In fact, each superpower worked hard in the early years of the Cold War to gain power at the expense of the other, while preventing the other from doing likewise.[47] The system that emerged in Europe in the aftermath of World War II was the unplanned consequence of intense security competition between the superpowers.

Although that intense superpower rivalry ended along with the Cold War in 1990, Russia and the United States have not worked together to create the present order in Europe. The United States, for example, has rejected out of hand various Russian proposals to make the Organization for Security and Cooperation in Europe the central organizing pillar of European security (replacing the U.S.-dominated NATO). Furthermore,

Russia was deeply opposed to NATO expansion, which it viewed as a serious threat to Russian security. Recognizing that Russia's weakness would preclude any retaliation, however, the United States ignored Russia's concerns and pushed NATO to accept the Czech Republic, Hungary, and Poland as new members. Russia has also opposed U.S. policy in the Balkans over the past decade, especially NATO's 1999 war against Yugoslavia. Again, the United States has paid little attention to Russia's concerns and has taken the steps it deems necessary to bring peace to that volatile region. Finally, it is worth noting that although Russia is dead set against allowing the United States to deploy ballistic missile defenses, it is highly likely that Washington will deploy such a system if it is judged to be technologically feasible.

For sure, great-power rivalry will sometimes produce a stable international order, as happened during the Cold War. Nevertheless, the great powers will continue looking for opportunities to increase their share of world power, and if a favorable situation arises, they will move to undermine that stable order. Consider how hard the United States worked during the late 1980s to weaken the Soviet Union and bring down the stable order that had emerged in Europe during the latter part of the Cold War.[48] Of course, the states that stand to lose power will work to deter aggression and preserve the existing order. But their motives will be selfish, revolving around balance-of-power logic, not some commitment to world peace.

Great powers cannot commit themselves to the pursuit of a peaceful world order for two reasons. First, states are unlikely to agree on a general formula for bolstering peace. Certainly, international relations scholars have never reached a consensus on what the blueprint should look like. In fact, it seems there are about as many theories on the causes of war and peace as there are scholars studying the subject. But more important, policymakers are unable to agree on how to create a stable world. For example, at the Paris Peace Conference after World War I, important differences over how to create stability in Europe divided Georges Clemenceau, David Lloyd George, and Woodrow Wilson.[49] In particular, Clemenceau was determined to impose harsher terms on Germany over the Rhineland than was either Lloyd George or Wilson, while Lloyd George stood out as the hard-liner on German reparations. The Treaty of Versailles, not surprisingly, did little to promote European stability.

Furthermore, consider American thinking on how to achieve stability in Europe in the early days of the Cold War.[50] The key elements for a stable and durable system were in place by the early 1950s. They included the division of Germany, the positioning of American ground forces in Western Europe to deter a Soviet attack, and ensuring that West Germany would not seek to develop nuclear weapons. Officials in the Truman administration, however, disagreed about whether a divided Germany would be a source of peace or war. For example, George Kennan and Paul Nitze, who held important positions in the State Department, believed that a divided Germany would be a source of instability, whereas Secretary of State Dean Acheson disagreed with them. In the 1950s, President Eisenhower sought to end the American commitment to defend Western Europe and to provide West Germany with its own nuclear deterrent. This policy, which was never fully adopted, nevertheless caused significant instability in Europe, as it led directly to the Berlin crises of 1958–59 and 1961.[51]

Second, great powers cannot put aside power considerations and work to promote international peace because they cannot be sure that their efforts will succeed. If their attempt fails, they are likely to pay a steep price for having neglected the balance of power, because if an aggressor appears at the door there will be no answer when they dial 911. That is a risk few states are willing to run. Therefore, prudence dictates that they behave according to realist logic. This line of reasoning accounts for why collective security schemes, which call for states to put aside narrow concerns about the balance of power and instead act in accordance with the broader interests of the international community, invariably die at birth.[52]

COOPERATION AMONG STATES

One might conclude from the preceding discussion that my theory does not allow for any cooperation among the great powers. But this conclusion would be wrong. States can cooperate, although cooperation is sometimes difficult to achieve and always difficult to sustain. Two factors inhibit cooperation: considerations about relative gains and concern about cheating.[53] Ultimately, great powers live in a fundamentally competitive world where they view each other as real, or at least potential, enemies, and they therefore look to gain power at each other's expense.

Any two states contemplating cooperation must consider how profits or gains will be distributed between them. They can think about the division in terms of either absolute or relative gains (recall the distinction made earlier between pursuing either absolute power or relative power; the concept here is the same). With absolute gains, each side is concerned with maximizing its own profits and cares little about how much the other side gains or loses in the deal. Each side cares about the other only to the extent that the other side's behavior affects its own prospects for achieving maximum profits. With relative gains, on the other hand, each side considers not only its own individual gain, but also how well it fares compared to the other side.

Because great powers care deeply about the balance of power, their thinking focuses on relative gains when they consider cooperating with other states. For sure, each state tries to maximize its absolute gains; still, it is more important for a state to make sure that it does no worse, and perhaps better, than the other state in any agreement. Cooperation is more difficult to achieve, however, when states are attuned to relative gains rather than absolute gains.[54] This is because states concerned about absolute gains have to make sure that if the pie is expanding, they are getting at least some portion of the increase, whereas states that worry about relative gains must pay careful attention to how the pie is divided, which complicates cooperative efforts.

Concerns about cheating also hinder cooperation. Great powers are often reluctant to enter into cooperative agreements for fear that the other side will cheat on the agreement and gain a significant advantage. This concern is especially acute in the military realm, causing a "special peril of defection," because the nature of military weaponry allows for rapid shifts in the balance of power.[55] Such a development could create a window of opportunity for the state that cheats to inflict a decisive defeat on its victim.

These barriers to cooperation notwithstanding, great powers do cooperate in a realist world. Balance-of-power logic often causes great powers to form alliances and cooperate against common enemies. The United Kingdom, France, and Russia, for example, were allies against Germany before and during World War I. States sometimes cooperate to gang up on a third state, as Germany and the Soviet Union did against Poland in 1939.[56] More recently, Serbia and Croatia agreed to conquer and divide Bosnia between them, although the United States and its European allies prevented them from executing their agreement.[57] Rivals as well as allies cooperate. After all, deals can be struck that roughly reflect the distribution of power and satisfy concerns about cheating. The various arms control agreements signed by the superpowers during the Cold War illustrate this point.

The bottom line, however, is that cooperation takes place in a world that is competitive at its core—one where states have powerful incentives to take advantage of other states. This point is graphically highlighted by the state of European politics in the forty years before World War I. The great powers cooperated frequently during this period, but that did not stop them from going to war on August 1, 1914.[58] The United States and the Soviet Union also cooperated considerably during World War II, but that cooperation did not prevent the outbreak of the Cold War shortly after Germany and Japan were defeated. Perhaps most amazingly, there was significant economic and military cooperation between Nazi Germany and the Soviet Union during the two years before the Wehrmacht attacked the Red Army.[59] No amount of cooperation can eliminate the dominating logic of security competition. Genuine peace, or a world in which states do not compete for power, is not likely as long as the state system remains anarchic.

CONCLUSION

In sum, my argument is that the structure of the international system, not the particular characteristics of individual great powers, causes them to think and act offensively and to seek hegemony.[60] I do not adopt Morgenthau's claim that states invariably behave aggressively because they have a will to power hardwired into them. Instead, I assume that the principal motive behind great-power behavior is survival. In anarchy, however, the desire to survive encourages states to behave aggressively. Nor does my theory classify states as more or less aggressive on the basis of their economic or political systems. Offensive realism makes only a handful of assumptions about great powers, and these assumptions apply equally to all great powers. Except for differences in how much power each state controls, the theory treats all states alike.

I have now laid out the logic explaining why states seek to gain as much power as possible over their rivals. I have said little, however, about the object of that pursuit: power itself. The next two chapters provide a detailed discussion of this important subject.

Wealth and Power

Power lies at the heart of international politics, yet there is considerable disagreement about what power is and how to measure it. In this chapter and the next, I define power and offer rough but reliable ways to measure it. Specifically, I argue that power is based on the particular material capabilities that a state possesses. The balance of power, therefore, is a function of tangible assets—such as armored divisions and nuclear weapons—that each great power controls.

States have two kinds of power: latent power and military power. These two forms of power are closely related but not synonymous, because they are derived from different kinds of assets. Latent power refers to the socio-economic ingredients that go into building military power; it is largely based on a state's wealth and the overall size of its population. Great powers need money, technology, and personnel to build military forces and to fight wars, and a state's latent power refers to the raw potential it can draw on when competing with rival states.

In international politics, however, a state's effective power is ultimately a function of its military forces and how they compare with the military forces of rival states. The United States and the Soviet Union were the most powerful states in the world during the Cold War because their military establishments dwarfed those of other states. Japan is not a great power today, even though it has a large and wealthy economy, because it has a small and relatively weak military, and it is heavily dependent on the United States for its security. Therefore, the balance of power is largely synonymous with the balance of military power. I define power largely in military terms because offensive realism emphasizes that force is the *ultima ratio* of international politics.[1]

Military power is based largely on the size and strength of a state's army and its supporting air and naval forces. Even in a nuclear world, armies are the core ingredient of military power. Independent naval forces and strategic air forces are not suited for conquering territory, nor are they much good by themselves at coercing other states into making territorial concessions. They certainly can contribute to a successful military campaign, but great-power wars are won mainly on the ground. The most powerful states, therefore, are those that possess the most formidable land forces.

This privileging of military power notwithstanding, states care greatly about latent power, because abundant wealth and a large population are prerequisites for building formidable military forces. During the Cold War, for example, American leaders worried about Soviet economic growth and were especially alarmed by Soviet scientific achievements (such as the Sputnik satellite launched in 1957), which they saw as signs that the Soviet Union's latent capabilities might one day exceed those of the United States. Today, the United States is increasingly worried about China, not because of its military, which is still relatively weak, but because China has more than 1.2 billion people and a rapidly modernizing economy. Should China become especially wealthy, it could readily become a military superpower and challenge the United States. These examples show that states pay careful attention to the balance of latent power as well as the balance of military power.

The next section discusses why it makes sense to define power in terms of material capabilities rather than outcomes, an approach favored by some scholars. I also explain why the balance of power is not an especially good predictor of military victory. The three sections that follow it focus on latent power. First, I discuss the fundamental importance of wealth for building powerful military forces, and then I describe the measures of wealth that I employ to capture latent power. Second, I use some historical cases to show that the rise and fall of great powers over the past two centuries has been due in good part to changes in the distribution of wealth among the major actors in the international system. Third, I explain why wealth and military power, although closely connected, are not synonymous, and I show that wealth cannot be used as a substitute measure for military might. Accordingly, I argue, we need separate indicators for latent power and military power.

THE MATERIAL BASIS OF POWER

At its most basic level, power can be defined in two different ways. Power, as I define it, represents nothing more than specific assets or material resources that are available to a state. Others, however, define power in terms of the outcomes of interactions between states. Power, they argue, is all about control or influence over other states; it is the ability of one state to force another to do something.[2] Robert Dahl, a prominent proponent of this view, maintains that "A has power over B to the extent that [A] can get B to do something that B would not otherwise do."[3] According to this logic, power exists only when a state exercises control or influence, and therefore it can be measured only after the outcome is determined. Simply put, the most powerful state is the one that prevails in a dispute.

It might seem that there is no meaningful difference between these two definitions. After all, when two great powers get into a conflict, should not the side with greater material capabilities prevail? Some students of international politics seem to believe that in war the state with greater resources should win almost all of the time, and that, therefore, the balance of power should do an excellent job of forecasting victory in war. There is a large body of quantitative studies, for example, that employs different measures of power to try to account for the outcome of interstate conflicts.[4] This belief also underpins Geoffrey Blainey's famous argument that war breaks out in good part because states cannot agree on the balance of power, but the subsequent fighting then establishes "an orderly ladder of power between victors and losers."[5] If the rival states had recognized the true balance beforehand, he argues, there would have been no war. Both sides would have foreseen the outcome and been motivated to negotiate a peaceful settlement based on existing power realities, rather than fight a bloody war to reach the same end.

But it is impossible to conflate these definitions of power, because the balance of power is not a highly reliable predictor of military success.[6] The reason is that non-material factors sometimes provide one combatant with a decisive advantage over the other. Those factors include, among others, strategy, intelligence, resolve, weather, and disease. Although material resources alone do not decide the outcome of wars, there is no question that the odds of success are substantially affected by the balance of resources, especially in protracted wars of attrition in which each side is trying to wear down the other by virtue of material superiority.[7] States certainly want to have more rather than less power over their rivals, because the more resources a state has at its disposal, the more likely it is to prevail in war. Of course, this is why states seek to maximize their share of world power. Nevertheless, increasing the likelihood of success does not mean that success is virtually certain. Indeed, there have been numerous wars where the victor was either less powerful or about as powerful as the loser, yet the victor prevailed because of non-material factors.

Consider strategy, which is how a state employs its forces against an opponent's forces, and which is probably the most important of the non-material factors. Clever strategies sometime allow states that are less powerful or no more powerful than their battlefield rivals to achieve victory.[8] The Germans, for example, employed a blitzkrieg strategy in the spring of 1940 to defeat the British and French armies, which were roughly of the same size and strength as the Wehrmacht.[9] The famous Schlieffen Plan, however, failed to produce a German victory against the same opponents in 1914, although a case can be made that the original version of the plan, which was more daring than the version that was finally executed, provided a blueprint for defeating France and the United Kingdom.[10] Strategy sometimes matters a lot.[11]

Russia's decisive defeat of Napoleon's army in 1812 highlights how these non-material factors can even help an outgunned defender win a war.[12] The French forces that spearheaded the invasion of Russia on June 23,

1812, outnumbered the Russian front-line armies by 449,000 to 211,000.[13] Counting reserve forces, Napoleon had a total of 674,000 troops at his disposal for the Russian campaign, while the entire Russian army numbered 409,000 regular soldiers at the start of the conflict. Moreover, the French forces were qualitatively superior to the Russian forces. Yet the Russians completely destroyed Napoleon's army during the next six months and won a decisive victory. By January 1, 1813, Napoleon had only 93,000 soldiers left to fight the Russians. A stunning 470,000 French soldiers had perished in Russia and another 100,000 were prisoners of war. The Russians, by contrast, lost a total of only 150,000 soldiers.

Weather, disease, and a smart Russian strategy defeated Napoleon. The Russians refused to engage the invasion force along their western border and instead withdrew toward Moscow, implementing a scorched-earth policy as they moved eastward.[14] The French army tried to catch the retreating Russian army and decisively defeat it in battle, but bad weather thwarted Napoleon's game plan. Torrential rain followed by blistering heat in the early weeks of the invasion slowed the attacking armies and allowed the Russians to escape. Disease and desertion soon became major problems for the French forces. Napoleon finally managed to engage the retreating Russian army in major battles at Smolensk (August 17) and Borodino (September 7). The French army won both battles, but they were Pyrrhic victories: French losses were high, the Russians refused to surrender, and the French army was drawn deeper into Russia. Napoleon occupied Moscow on September 14 but was forced to retreat in mid-October when the Russians still refused to quit the war. The subsequent retreat westward was a disaster for the French army, which disintegrated despite holding its own in battles with the pursuing Russian forces.[15] Weather again played an important role as winter set in on the retreating forces. Despite never winning a major battle in the 1812 campaign, the less powerful Russian army routed the more powerful French army.

It should be apparent that Blainey is wrong to argue that there would be no war if states could accurately measure the balance of power, because less powerful states can sometimes defeat more powerful states.[16] Therefore weaker states are sometimes going to initiate wars against stronger states.

The same logic also applies to states of roughly equal might. Furthermore, weaker states are sometimes going to stand up to stronger states that threaten to attack them, because there are often good reasons for defenders to think that they can fight, although outnumbered, and win.

In essence, then, it is not possible to equate the balance of tangible assets with outcomes, because non-material factors such as strategy sometimes profoundly affect outcomes. When defining power, therefore, one has to choose between material capabilities and outcomes as the basis for definition; the latter effectively incorporate the non-material as well as material ingredients of military success.

There are three reasons not to equate power with outcomes. First, when focusing on outcomes it becomes almost impossible to assess the balance of power before a conflict, since the balance can be determined only after we see which side wins. Second, this approach sometimes leads to implausible conclusions. For example, Russia might have decisively defeated Napoleon's armies in 1812, but Russia was not more powerful than France. Defining power in terms of outcomes, however, would effectively force one to argue that Russia was more powerful than France. Moreover, few would deny that the United States was a vastly more powerful state than North Vietnam, yet the weaker state was able to defeat the stronger in the Vietnam War (1965–72) because non-material factors trumped the balance of power. Third, one of the most interesting aspects of international relations is how power, which is a means, affects political outcomes, which are ends.[17] But there is little to say about the matter if power and outcomes are indistinguishable; there would be no difference between means and ends. We are then left with a circular argument.

POPULATION AND WEALTH: THE SINEWS OF MILITARY POWER

L atent power constitutes the societal resources that a state has available to build military forces.[18] Although there are always a variety of such resources, the size of a state's population and its wealth are the two most important components for generating military might. Population size matters a lot, because great powers require big armies, which can be raised only in countries with large populations.[19] States with small populations cannot be great powers. For example, neither Israel, with its population of 6 million, nor Sweden, with its population of 8.9 million, can achieve great-power status in a world in which Russia, the United States, and China have populations of 147 million, 281 million, and 1.24 billion, respectively.[20] Population size also has important economic consequences, because only large populations can produce great wealth, the other building block of military power.[21]

Wealth is important because a state cannot build a powerful military if it does not have the money and technology to equip, train, and continually modernize its fighting forces.[22] Furthermore, the costs of waging great-power wars are enormous. For example, the total direct cost of World War I (1914–18) for all the participants was about $200 billion.[23] The United States alone spent roughly $306 billion fighting the Axis powers between 1941 and 1945—roughly three times its gross national product (GNP) in 1940.[24] Accordingly, the great powers in the international system are invariably among the world's wealthiest states.

Although population size and wealth are essential ingredients of military power, I use wealth alone to measure potential power. This emphasis on wealth is not because it is more important than population, but because wealth incorporates both the demographic and the economic dimensions of power. As noted, a state must have a large population to produce great wealth. Therefore, it is reasonable to assume that the states with abundant wealth will also have large populations. In short, I am not ignoring population size, just assuming that it will be captured by the indicators I use to measure wealth.

It would be easier to use population size by itself to measure latent power, because a state's population is simpler to measure than its wealth. But it is not feasible to use population size to measure latent power, because population numbers often do not reflect wealth differences among states. Both China and India, for instance, had much larger populations than either the Soviet Union or the United States during the Cold

War, but neither China nor India achieved great-power status because they were nowhere near as wealthy as the superpowers. In essence, a large population does not ensure great wealth, but great wealth does require a large population. Therefore, only wealth can be used by itself as a measure of latent power.

The concept of wealth has various meanings and can be measured in different ways. For my purposes, however, it is essential to choose an indicator of wealth that reflects a state's latent power. Specifically, it must capture a state's mobilizable wealth and its level of technological development. "Mobilizable wealth" refers to the economic resources a state has at its disposal to build military forces. It is more important than overall wealth because what matters is not simply how wealthy a state might be, but how much of that wealth is available to spend on defense. It is also important to have industries that are producing the newest and most sophisticated technologies, because they invariably get incorporated into the most advanced weaponry. The development of steel in the mid-nineteenth century and jet aircraft in the mid-twentieth century, for example, profoundly changed the arsenals of the great powers. It behooved the great powers of the day to be on the cutting edge in those industries, as well as in other industries that contributed to building formidable military forces.

GNP, which represents a state's entire output over one year, is probably the most commonly used indicator of a state's wealth. In fact, I use it to measure wealth after 1960, as discussed below. But GNP is not always a good indicator of latent power, and employing it in the wrong circumstances can give a distorted picture of the balance of latent power. The essence of the problem is that GNP is primarily a measure of a state's overall wealth, and it does not always capture important differences in the mobilizable wealth and technological sophistication of different states.

Nevertheless, GNP does a reasonably good job of measuring these two dimensions of wealth when the relevant great powers are at similar levels of economic development. For example, two highly industrialized economies—such as the United Kingdom and Germany in 1890 or Japan and the United States in 1990—are likely to have similar leading-edge industries and roughly the same ratio of overall wealth to mobilizable wealth. The same logic applies when comparing two largely agrarian societies, such as Prussia and France in 1750.

But GNP is a poor indicator of latent power when the states being compared are at different levels of economic development. Consider what can happen when GNP is used to assess the potential power of a semi-industrialized state and a highly industrialized state. GNP, which represents the market value of all the goods and services that a state produces in a fixed period of time, is a function of both the size and the productivity of a state's labor force. The size of a state's labor force is directly related to its population size, while the productivity of its labor force is directly linked to the state's level of economic development. It is therefore possible for two states to have similar GNPs but substantially different population sizes and markedly different levels of industrialization. For example, one state might have a weak industrial base, but a relatively large population, a substantial portion of which is employed on farms, while the other state is highly industrialized, but has a considerably smaller population.[25]

The United Kingdom and Russia fit this profile for the hundred-year period between the fall of Napoleon in 1815 and the start of World War I in 1914. Their GNPs were similar over that period, although the United Kingdom far outdistanced Russia in terms of industrial output, as Table 3.1 makes clear. But Russia was able to hold its own in terms of GNP, because its huge peasant population grew at a robust pace over the nineteenth century.

Differences in industrial might like those between the United Kingdom and Russia, however, have important consequences for the balance of latent power. First, highly industrialized states invariably have considerably more surplus wealth to spend on defense than do semi-industrialized states, mainly because much of the physical product of the peasantry is consumed on the spot by the peasants themselves. Second, only states with the most advanced industries are capable of producing the large quantities of sophisticated weaponry that militaries need to survive in combat.[26]

Focusing on GNP alone, however, might lead one to think that the United Kingdom and Russia had the most powerful economies in Europe

TABLE 3.1

Indicators of British and Russian Wealth and Population, 1830–1913

	1830	1860	1880	1900	1913
GNP (billions of dollars)					
United Kingdom	8.2	16.1	23.6	36.3	44.1
Russia	10.6	14.4	23.3	32.0	52.4
Relative share of European wealth (percent)					
United Kingdom	53	68	59	37	28
Russia	15	4	3	10	11
Energy consumption (millions of metric tons of coal equivalent)					
United Kingdom	—	73.8	125.3	171.4	195.3
Russia	—	1.0	5.4	30.4	54.5
Iron/steel production (thousands of tons)					
United Kingdom	690	3,880	7,870	4,979	7,787
Russia	190	350	450	2,201	4,925
Relative share of world manufacturing output (percent)					
United Kingdom	9.5	19.9	22.9	18.5	13.6
Russia	5.6	7.0	7.6	8.8	8.2
Total industrial potential (United Kingdom in 1900 = 100)					
United Kingdom	17.5	45.0	73.3	100.0	127.2
Russia	10.3	15.8	24.5	47.5	76.6
Population (millions)					
United Kingdom	23.8	28.8	34.6	41.2	45.6
Russia	57.6	76.0	100.0	135.7	175.1

SOURCES: GNP figures, which are in 1960 U.S. dollars and prices, are from Paul Bairoch, "Europe's Gross National Product: 1800–1975," *Journal of European Economic History* 5, No. 2 (Fall 1976), p. 281. Relative shares of world manufacturing output are from Paul Bairoch, "International Industrialization Levels from 1750 to 1980," *Journal of European Economic History* 11, No. 2 (Fall 1982), p. 296. Figures for total industrial potential, which assign the United Kingdom in 1900 the baseline number of 100, are from ibid., p. 292. The energy consumption figures, the iron/steel production figures, and the population figures are from J. David Singer and Melvin Small, *National Material Capabilities Data, 1816–1985* (Ann Arbor, MI: Inter-University Consortium for Political and Social Research, February 1993). The figures for relative shares of European wealth are from Table 3.3.

between 1815 and 1914, and that they had the wherewithal to build for-midable military forces and dominate the region's politics. As a compari-son of Table 3.1 with Table 3.2 indicates, the United Kingdom and Russia led the other European great powers in terms of GNP during most of the period. In fact, this conclusion is wrong.[27] The United Kingdom certainly had more latent power than any other European state during the nine-teenth century, especially in the middle decades of that century, which are often called the *"Pax Brittanica."*[28] But as discussed below, the Russian economy was in an anemic state from at least the mid-nineteenth century through the 1920s. Russia had relatively little latent power during this period, which explains in good part why its military suffered crushing defeats in the Crimean War (1853–56), the Russo-Japanese War (1904–5), and World War I (1914–17).[29] In short, GNP fails to capture the poten-tially sharp difference in latent power between industrialized and semi-industrialized states.

The same problem arises when GNP is used to compare the latent power of contemporary China with Japan and the United States. Despite its rapid economic development over the past two decades, China is still a semi-industrialized state. Roughly 18 percent of its wealth remains tied up in agriculture.[30] Japan and the United States, on the other hand, are high-ly industrialized states; only 2 percent of their wealth is in agriculture. China, however, has almost five times as many people as the United States and about ten times as many people as Japan. Therefore, the bal-ance of latent power among those three states will be biased in China's favor if GNP is the chosen measure. This problem is likely to go away with time, because China's agricultural base will continue to shrink (it account-ed for 30 percent of wealth in 1980) as its economy modernizes. But for now, it must be factored into any analysis that uses GNP to measure China's latent power.

Thus, GNP is sometimes a sound measure of latent power, whereas at other times it is not. In those latter cases, one can either find an alterna-tive indicator that does a better job of capturing latent power, or use GNP but add the appropriate qualifiers.

In measuring the balance of latent power for the long historical period from 1792 to 2000, it is impossible to find one simple but reliable indica-

TABLE 3.2

Indicators of French and Prussian/German Wealth and Population, 1830–1913

	1830	1860	1880	1900	1913
GNP (billions of dollars)					
France	8.6	13.3	17.4	23.5	27.4
Germany	7.2	12.8	20.0	35.8	49.8
Relative share of European wealth (percent)					
France	21	14	13	11	12
Germany	5	10	20	34	40
Energy consumption (millions of metric tons of coal equivalent)					
France	—	13.2	29.1	48.0	62.8
Germany	—	15.0	47.1	113.0	187.8
Iron/steel production (thousands of tons)					
France	270	900	1,730	1,565	4,687
Germany	60	400	2,470	6,461	17,600
Relative share of world manufacturing output (percent)					
France	5.2	7.9	7.8	6.8	6.1
Germany	3.5	4.9	8.5	13.2	14.8
Total industrial potential (United Kingdom in 1900 = 100)					
France	9.5	17.9	25.1	36.8	57.3
Germany	6.5	11.1	27.4	71.2	137.7
Population (millions)					
France	32.4	37.4	37.5	38.9	39.7
Germany	12.9	18.0	45.1	56.0	67.0

NOTE: Figures labeled "Germany" are for Prussia in 1830 and 1860, and for Germany thereafter.

SOURCES: Same as those in Table 3.1.

tor of wealth. For one thing, there is little economic data available for the years between 1792 and 1815. The main place this causes problems is in Chapter 8, when the question arises of whether Napoleonic France had more latent power than its great-power rivals, especially the United Kingdom. I attempt to deal with the problem by describing what historians say about the relative wealth of the United Kingdom and France, and also by looking at population size, the other building block of military power. This information provides a rough but probably accurate picture of the balance of latent power during the Napoleonic years.

I measure latent power between 1816 and 1960 with a straightforward composite indicator that accords equal weight to a state's iron and steel production and its energy consumption. That indicator, which effectively represents a state's industrial might, does a good job of capturing both mobilizable wealth and level of technological development for that lengthy period.[31] From 1960 to the present, GNP is used to measure wealth. I switched indicators in 1960 for two reasons.[32] First, my composite indicator is not useful after 1970, because the role of steel in the major industrial economies began to decline sharply around that time.[33] Thus, a different measure of potential power is needed for the years after 1970; GNP was the obvious alternative. Second, the best available GNP figures for the Soviet Union and the United States, the two great powers in the system at the time, start in 1960 and run through the end of the Cold War.[34] So I employ GNP for the last thirty years of the Cold War (1960–90) and the first decade of the post–Cold War era (1991–2000), taking due note of the limits of GNP as an indicator of China's latent power today.[35]

THE ECONOMIC FOUNDATION OF MILITARY POWER

A brief look at the rise and decline of three European great powers during the last two centuries buttresses my claim that wealth underpins military power and that wealth by itself is a good indicator of latent power. The profound change that took place in the balance of power between France and Germany (Prussia before 1870) during the nineteenth century, as well as Russia's changing position in the balance of power between 1800 and 2000, shows the crucial role of wealth in determining power.

Napoleonic France was the most powerful state in Europe between 1793 and 1815; in fact, it came close to conquering the entire continent. Prussia was probably the weakest of the great powers at that time. It was decisively defeated by Napoleon's armies in 1806 and was effectively knocked out of the European balance of power until 1813, when it took advantage of France's devastating defeat in Russia to join the balancing coalition that finally finished off Napoleon at Waterloo in June of 1815. By 1900, however, the tables had turned almost completely, and Wilhelmine Germany was emerging as Europe's next potential hegemon, while France needed alliance partners to help check its German neighbor. France and its allies subsequently went to war in 1914 and 1939 to prevent Germany from dominating Europe.

Changes in the relative wealth of France and Germany during the hundred years after Waterloo largely account for the shift in military power between them. As is clear from Table 3.2, France was considerably wealthier than Prussia from 1816 until the late 1860s, when Otto von Bismarck transformed Prussia into Germany. In fact, Germany first gained an edge over France in steel production in 1870, the year that the Franco-Prussian War broke out.[36] From that point until the start of World War I, the wealth gap between France and Germany steadily widened in the latter's favor. By 1913, Germany was roughly three times as wealthy as France.

This marked change in the relative wealth of France and Germany was due in part to the fact that Germany industrialized more rapidly than France in the late nineteenth and early twentieth centuries. The main cause, however, was a significant shift in the size of their respective populations, which illustrates how changes in wealth also capture changes in population. The data in Table 3.2 show that France had about a 2.5:1 advantage in population over Prussia in 1830, but that by 1913 Germany had gained roughly a 1.7:1 population advantage over France. This demographic flip-flop was the result of two factors. The French birthrate in the nineteenth century was especially low, while the German birthrate was among the highest in Europe. Furthermore, the unified German state that Bismarck built around Prussia had a substantially larger population than Prussia itself. For example, Prussia had 19.3 million people in 1865, whereas Germany had 34.6 million people in 1870.[37]

Russia offers another case of a state whose position in the balance of power has been markedly affected by the fortunes of its economy. Russia was probably Napoleonic France's most formidable military rival. Indeed, the Russian army played the key role in driving Napoleon from power between 1812 and 1815. There was even fear in the wake of France's collapse that Russia might try to dominate Europe.[38] But Russia did not make a run at hegemony after 1815. Instead, its position in the European balance of power declined over the next hundred years. As noted, Russia fought three wars against other great powers during that period and suffered humiliating defeats in each: the Crimean War, the Russo-Japanese War, and World War I.

A comparison of Russia's performance in the Napoleonic Wars, World War I, and World War II shows how weak Russia had become by 1914. Each conflict was dominated by a potential hegemon that invaded Russia. Napoleonic France and Nazi Germany were able to concentrate the bulk of their armies against Russia, although each had to maintain some forces in other theaters as well.[39] Nevertheless, Russia decisively defeated both of those aggressors. During World War I, however, Germany deployed approximately two-thirds of its fighting forces on the western front against the French and British armies, while the remaining one-third fought against the Russian army on the eastern front.[40] Although the German army was fighting the Russian army with its best hand tied behind its back, it still managed to defeat Russia and knock it out of the war, a feat that neither Napoleon nor Hitler could accomplish with both hands free.

Russia's decline reached its nadir in the years immediately after World War I, when Poland invaded the newly created Soviet Union and scored major victories.[41] The Red Army briefly turned the tide before the Poles regained the initiative and won a limited victory. Starting in the early 1930s, however, the Soviets began to build a formidable military machine, which beat the Japanese army in a brief war in 1939, and then defeated the vaunted German Wehrmacht in World War II. The Soviet Union was so powerful after 1945 that only the United States could prevent it from dominating all of Europe. The Soviet Union remained a formidable military power for more than forty years after Hitler's defeat, until it broke apart into fifteen separate states in 1991.

The ups and downs in Russian military power over the past two centuries can be explained in good part by changes in Russia's position in the hierarchy of wealth. Although we do not have much data on the wealth of the great powers between 1800 and 1815, it seems clear that the United Kingdom and France had the most powerful economies in Europe.[42] Nevertheless, it does not appear that Russia was decidedly less wealthy than either the United Kingdom or France in those years.[43] But even if that were the case, the Russian economy was still able to support the Russian military in its fight against Napoleon, although Russia received subsidies from the United Kingdom at various points in the conflict. In short, there is no evidence that the French army had an important advantage over the Russian army because France was wealthier than Russia.[44]

Russia's position in the balance of wealth declined sharply over the seventy-five years following Napoleon's defeat (see Table 3.3), mainly because Russia industrialized much more slowly than did the United Kingdom, France, and Germany. Russia's lack of industrial might had important military consequences. For example, in the two decades before World War I, Russia could not afford to build large railroad networks in its western regions, which made it difficult for Russia to mobilize and move its armies rapidly to the Russo-German border. Germany, on the other hand, had a well-developed railroad system, so it could move its forces quickly to that same border. To rectify that asymmetry, France, which was allied with Russia against Germany, subsidized the building of Russian railroads.[45] In essence, by the eve of World War I, Russia was a semi-industrialized state about to go to war against a highly industrialized Germany.[46]

Not surprisingly, Russia's war economy could not support its army's needs. Rifle production was so woeful that in 1915, "only part of the army

TABLE 3.3

Relative Share of European Wealth, 1816–1940

	1816	1820	1830	1840	1850	1860	1870	1880	1890	1900	1910	1913	1920	1930	1940
United Kingdom	43%	48%	53%	64%	70%	68%	64%	59%	50%	37%	30%	28%	44%	27%	24%
Prussia/Germany	8%	7%	5%	5%	4%	10%	16%	20%	25%	34%	39%	40%	38%	33%	36%
France	21%	18%	21%	16%	12%	14%	13%	13%	13%	11%	12%	12%	13%	22%	9%
Russia/Soviet Union	19%	18%	15%	9%	7%	4%	2%	3%	5%	10%	10%	11%	2%	14%	28%
Austria-Hungary	9%	9%	7%	6%	7%	4%	5%	4%	6%	7%	8%	8%	—	—	—
Italy	—	—	—	—	—	—	0%	1%	1%	1%	2%	2%	3%	5%	4%

NOTE: "Wealth" here is a straightforward composite indicator that assigns equal weight to iron/steel production and energy consumption. Specifically, I determined the total amount of iron/steel that all the great powers produced for a given year, and then I calculated the percentage of that total accounted for by each great power. I performed a similar calculation for energy consumption. Then I averaged together each state's percentages for iron/steel and energy. However, percentages for 1830–50 are based on iron/steel production alone because energy consumption data is unavailable. Note that the calculations of European wealth used here and throughout this book are based solely on figures for the relevant great powers and do not include minor powers such as Belgium and Denmark. Finally, note that Germany was Prussia before 1870.

SOURCES: All data are from Singer and Small, *National Material Capabilities Data.*

was armed, with others waiting for casualties to get arms."[47] Artillery was so lacking by as late as 1917 that Germany had 6,819 heavy pieces, while Russia had only 1,430. Jonathan Adelman estimates that at best only 30 percent of the Russian army's equipment needs were met during the war. Another way to look at Russia's problem is to consider the following comparisons for the period from 1914 through 1917:

1) Germany produced 47,300 airplanes; Russia produced 3,500.
2) Germany produced 280,000 machine guns; Russia produced 28,000.
3) Germany produced 64,000 artillery pieces; Russia produced 11,700.
4) Germany produced 8,547,000 rifles; Russia produced 3,300,000.

Thus, it is hardly surprising that less than half the German army was able to defeat the entire Russian army in World War I.

Stalin ruthlessly but effectively modernized the Soviet economy in the 1930s, so that by the start of World War II Germany enjoyed only a modest advantage in wealth over the Soviet Union (see Table 3.3).[48] Thus, the Soviet war economy was able to compete effectively with the German war economy in World War II. Indeed, the Soviets outproduced the Germans in virtually every category of military weaponry for the years from 1941 through 1945:

1) The Soviet Union produced 102,600 airplanes; Germany produced 76,200.
2) The Soviet Union produced 1,437,900 machine guns; Germany produced 1,048,500.
3) The Soviet Union produced 11,820,500 rifles; Germany produced 7,845,700.
4) The Soviet Union produced 92,600 tanks; Germany produced 41,500.
5) The Soviet Union produced 350,300 mortars; Germany 68,900.[49]

No wonder the Red Army defeated the Wehrmacht on the eastern front.[50]

Although the Soviet economy suffered enormous damage in World War II (see Table 3.4), the Soviet Union emerged from that conflict with the most powerful economy in Europe.[51] Not surprisingly, it had the military might in the late 1940s to dominate the region. But the United States, which was far wealthier than the Soviet Union (see Table 3.5), was determined to prevent the Soviets from becoming a European hegemon. In the first three decades after World War II, the Soviet economy grew rapidly as it recovered from that war, and the wealth gap with its bipolar rival narrowed considerably. It appeared that General Secretary Nikita Khrushchev's boast in 1956 that the Soviet Union would "bury" the United States might prove true.[52]

TABLE 3.4

Relative Share of European Wealth, 1941–44

	1941	1942	1943	1944
United States	54%	58%	61%	63%
Germany	22%	23%	23%	19%
Soviet Union	12%	7%	7%	9%
United Kingdom	9%	9%	9%	9%
Italy	3%	3%	—	—

NOTE: "Wealth" is measured with the same composite indicator used in Table 3.3, save for the fact that I use energy production here instead of energy consumption. Although the United States is not a European power, it is included in this table because it was deeply involved in the fighting in Europe during World War II.

SOURCES: Energy and steel figures for the United States are from B. R. Mitchell, *International Historical Statistics: The Americas, 1750–1988,* 2d ed. (New York: Stockton Press, 1993), pp. 356, 397. The figures for the United Kingdom and Italy are from B. R. Mitchell, *International Historical Statistics: Europe, 1750–1988,* 3d ed. (New York: Stockton Press, 1992), pp. 457–58, 547. The figures for the Soviet Union are from Mark Harrison, *Soviet Planning in Peace and War, 1938–1945* (Cambridge: Cambridge University Press, 1985), p. 253. The German figures require explanation, because the numbers one uses depend on what territory is considered part of Germany. There are roughly three choices: 1) "older Germany," which covers the pre-1938 borders; 2) "greater Germany," which includes Austria, the Sudetenland, and territories conquered in the war, such as Alsace-Lorraine and the Polish regions of Olsa and Dombrowa, all of which were incorporated into the Third Reich; and 3) "greater Germany plus the occupied states" that Germany exploited for gain. On these distinctions, see United States Strategic Bombing Survey (USSBS), *The Effects of Strategic Bombing on the German War Economy*, European War Report 3 (Washington, DC: USSBS, October 31, 1945), p. 249. Also see Patricia Harvey, "The Economic Structure of Hitler's Europe," in Arnold Toynbee and Veronica M. Toynbee, eds., *Hitler's Europe* (Oxford: Oxford University Press, 1954), pp. 165–282. For German steel production between 1941 and 1945, I used the relevant figures for the third category above, which are from USSBS, *Effects of Strategic Bombing*, p. 252. However, reliable energy production figures for Germany for the World War II years are difficult to find. See ibid., p. 116. Using Soviet sources, Jonathan Adelman estimates the total amounts of electricity and steel produced by Germany and the Soviet Union during World War II. Adelman, *Prelude to the Cold War: The Tsarist, Soviet, and U.S. Armies in the Two World Wars* (Boulder, CO: Lynne Rienner, 1988), p. 219. Since Adelman's figure for German steel production (133.7 million tons) is close to my total (127 million), I assume his electricity figure is reliable. To apportion energy on a yearly basis, I simply applied the steel ratio for each year. For example, if 27 percent of German steel produced during the war was produced in 1943, I assume that 27 percent of all electricity was produced in that year, as well.

TABLE 3.5

Relative Share of Superpower Wealth, 1945–90

	1945	1950	1955	1960	1965	1970	1975	1980	1985	1990
United States	84%	78%	72%	67%	67%	65%	63%	65%	66%	68%
Soviet Union	16%	22%	28%	33%	33%	35%	37%	35%	34%	32%

NOTE: Figures for 1945, 1950, and 1955 are based on the same composite indicator used in Table 3.3.

SOURCES: All data for 1945–55 are from Singer and Small, *National Material Capabilities Data*. Figures for 1960–90 are based on gross national product (GNP) data from the U.S. Arms Control and Disarmament Agency's *World Military Expenditures and Arms Transfer Database*. It should be noted that there is still uncertainty and disagreement among experts about the actual size of the Soviet Union's GNP during the period 1945–91. In my opinion, however, this is the best available data.

However, the Soviet economy began to falter in the early 1980s because it was not keeping pace with the American economy in developing computers and other information technologies.[53] This problem did not manifest itself in an abrupt drop in GNP relative to the United States, although Soviet leaders expected that over the long term. They also recognized that this incipient technological backwardness would eventually hurt the Soviet military as well. Marshal Nikolai Ogarkov was dismissed as the chief of the Soviet general staff in the summer of 1984 for saying publicly that Soviet industry was falling badly behind American industry, which meant that Soviet weaponry would soon be inferior to American weaponry.[54] Soviet leaders recognized the gravity of the situation and tried to fix the problem. But their economic and political reforms went awry, touching off a crisis of nationalism, which not only allowed the United States to win the Cold War but shortly thereafter led to the dissolution of the Soviet Union.

This discussion of the importance of wealth for building military power might suggest that the distribution of latent power among states should roughly reflect the distribution of military power, and therefore it should be feasible to equate the two kinds of power. My argument that great powers aim to maximize their share of world power might reinforce that notion, since it seems to imply that states will translate their wealth into military power at roughly the same rate. But that is not the case, and thus economic might is not always a sound indicator of military might.

THE GAP BETWEEN LATENT POWER
AND MILITARY POWER

The alliance patterns that formed during the Cold War illustrate the problems that arise when wealth is equated with military power. The United States was much wealthier than the Soviet Union from the start to the finish of that conflict, but that was especially true between 1945 and 1955, when the North Atlantic Treaty Organization and the Warsaw Pact were formed (see Table 3.5). Yet the United Kingdom, France, West Germany, and Italy in Europe, and Japan in Asia, opted to join an American-led coalition aimed at containing the Soviet Union. If wealth were an accurate measure of power, those less powerful states should have joined forces with the Soviet Union to check the United States, not the other way around. After all, if wealth is the metric for assessing power, the United States was clearly the mightier superpower.[55]

Power realities do not always reflect the hierarchy of wealth, for three reasons. First, states convert varying portions of their wealth into military might. Second, the efficiency of that transformation varies from case to case, occasionally with important consequences for the balance of power. And third, great powers buy different kinds of military forces, and those choices also have implications for the military balance.

Diminishing Returns

Wealthy states sometimes do not build additional military forces—even though they could in principle afford them—because they recognize that doing so would not give them a strategic advantage over their rivals. Spending more makes little sense when a state's defense effort is subject to diminishing returns (that is, if its capabilities are already on the "flat of the curve") or if opponents can easily match the effort and maintain the balance of power. If launching an arms race is unlikely to leave the initiator in a better strategic position, in short, it will sit tight and wait for more favorable circumstances.

The United Kingdom in the nineteenth century is an example of a state that hit the flat of the curve in terms of the military payoff from additional defense spending. Between 1820 and 1890, the United Kingdom was far and away the wealthiest state in Europe. It never controlled less than 45 percent of great-power wealth during those seven decades, and in the middle two decades of the century (1840–60), it possessed close to 70 percent (see Table 3.3). France, which was the United Kingdom's closest competitor during those twenty years, never controlled more than 16 percent of European industrial might. No other European great power has ever enjoyed such an overwhelming economic advantage over its rivals. If wealth alone was a sound indicator of power, the United Kingdom would probably have been Europe's first hegemonic power, or at least a potential hegemon that the other great powers would have had to balance against.

But it is apparent from the historical record that this was not the case.[56] Despite its abundant wealth, the United Kingdom did not build a military force that posed a serious threat to France, Germany, or Russia. Indeed, the United Kingdom spent a much smaller percentage of its wealth on defense between 1815 and 1914 than any of its great-power rivals.[57] The United Kingdom was just another state in the European balance of power. Consequently, the other great powers never formed a balancing coalition to contain it, as happened with Napoleonic France, Wilhelmine Germany, Nazi Germany, and the Soviet Union.[58]

The United Kingdom did not raise a large army and attempt to conquer Europe because it would have faced huge problems trying to project power across the English Channel and onto the European continent. Large bodies of water, as discussed in the next chapter, tend to rob armies of offensive capability. At the same time, the stopping power of water made it especially difficult for any continental power to cross the channel and invade the United Kingdom. Thus, the United Kingdom wisely concluded that it made no strategic sense to build a large army that was of little utility for offense and unnecessary for defending the homeland.

The United States provides another example from the nineteenth century of a rich state maintaining a relatively small military establishment. The United States was wealthy enough by 1850 to qualify as a great power, but it is generally agreed that it did not achieve that exalted status until 1898, when it began building a muscular military that could compete with those of the European great powers.[59] This matter is discussed at greater length in Chapter 7. Suffice it to say here that the tiny American army notwithstanding, the United States was a highly expansionist state during the nineteenth century, pushing the European great powers back across the Atlantic Ocean and expanding its borders westward to the Pacific Ocean. The United States was bent on establishing hegemony in the Western Hemisphere, a goal it clearly had achieved by the start of the twentieth century.

The American military remained much smaller than its European counterparts during the latter half of the nineteenth century because it could dominate the hemisphere on the cheap. Local rivals such as the various Native American tribes and Mexico were outgunned by even a small U.S. army, and the European great powers were unable to confront the United States in a serious way. The Europeans not only had to devote significant resources to defending their homelands from attack by each other, but projecting power across the Atlantic Ocean onto the North American continent was a difficult task.

Another reason that states sometimes keep a lid on their military budgets is that they conclude that aggressive defense spending is likely to be bad for the economy, which will ultimately undermine state power, since economic might is the foundation of military might. During the 1930s, for example, British policymakers kept a tight rein on defense spending despite facing multiple threats around the globe, because they feared that massive increases would wreck the British economy, which they referred to as the "fourth arm of defence."[60] Similarly, the administration of President Dwight Eisenhower (1953–61) was dominated by fiscal conservatives who tended to see high levels of defense spending as a threat to the American economy. This was one of the reasons why U.S. defense spending was curtailed in the 1950s and why greater emphasis was placed on nuclear weapons. A nuclear-based strategy, it was believed, would provide the basis for a stable and fiscally viable defense policy for the long haul.[61]

Allies also affect the level of resources that a great power devotes to its defense. For sure, any two great powers involved in an intense security competition or fighting a war with each other are going to spend heavily on their military. But if one of those rivals has wealthy allies and the other does not, the state with rich friends will probably have to spend less on defense than its rival. During the Cold War, for example, the Soviet Union committed a larger percentage of its wealth to defense than did the United States.[62] This asymmetry was due in part to the fact that the United States had wealthy allies such as the United Kingdom, France, Italy, and especially West Germany and Japan. The Soviet Union, on the other hand, had impoverished allies such as Czechoslovakia, Hungary, and Poland.[63]

Finally, there are those cases in which a wealthy state cannot build powerful military forces because it is occupied by a great power that wants it to remain militarily weak. Austria and Prussia, for example, were each defeated and knocked from the ranks of the great powers by France during the Napoleonic Wars, and France was occupied by Nazi Germany from mid-1940 until the late summer of 1944, when it was finally liberated by British and American troops. The United States maintained troops in West Germany and Japan during the Cold War, and although it was surely a benevolent occupier, it did not allow either of its allies to build the requisite military might to become a great power. The United States preferred to keep Japan at bay, even though Japan was about as wealthy as the Soviet Union by the mid-1980s, if not sooner. Indeed, the available evidence indicates that Japan had a larger GNP than the Soviet Union's by 1987.[64] This case shows that although all great powers are wealthy states, not all wealthy states are great powers.

Different Levels of Efficiency

It is also unwise to liken the distribution of economic might with the distribution of military might because states convert their wealth into military power with varying degrees of efficiency. Indeed, there is sometimes a large efficiency gap between rival great powers that has a marked effect on the balance of power. The fight to the death between Nazi Germany and the Soviet Union in World War II illustrates this point.

Germany controlled some 36 percent of European wealth by 1940, while the Soviet Union possessed about 28 percent (see Table 3.3). In the spring of 1940, Germany conquered Belgium, Denmark, France, the Netherlands, and Norway and immediately began exploiting their economies, adding to its wealth advantage over the Soviet Union.[65] The Wehrmacht then invaded the Soviet Union in June 1941, and within six months Germany controlled almost all Soviet territory west of Moscow, which was prime real estate. By late 1941, the Soviet Union had lost territory that held 41 percent of its railway lines, 42 percent of its electricity-generating capacity, 71 percent of its iron ore, 63 percent of its coal, and 58 percent of its capacity to make crude steel.[66] In the spring of 1942, the Nazi war machine further extended its reach by driving deep into the oil-rich Caucasus region. The Soviet Union lost roughly 40 percent of its national income between 1940 and 1942.[67] Germany appears to have held more than a 3:1 advantage in economic might over the Soviet Union by 1942 (see Table 3.4).

Despite Germany's profound advantage in latent power, the Soviet war economy amazingly outproduced the German war economy over the course of the war and helped shift the balance of power in the Red Army's favor. As described earlier, the Soviet Union produced 2.2 times as many tanks as Germany and 1.3 times as many airplanes between 1941 and 1945. What is most astonishing is that the Soviets even outproduced the Germans in the early years of the war, when German control of Soviet territory was at its peak and the Allied bombing campaign was having barely any effect on the German war economy. The Soviet Union, for example, produced 24,446 tanks in 1942; Germany produced 9,200. The ratio of artillery pieces for 1942 was 127,000 to 12,000 in the Soviets' favor.[68] This asymmetry in weapons production eventually led to a significant Soviet advantage in the balance of ground forces. When Germany invaded the Soviet Union in June 1941, the Soviets had a slight advantage in number of divisions—211:199—the key indicator of military strength. By January 1945, however, there were 473 Soviet divisions and only 276 German divisions, and the average Red Army division was far better equipped with weapons and vehicles than the average Wehrmacht division.[69]

How did the Soviet Union manage to produce so much more weaponry than a far wealthier Nazi Germany? One possible answer is that the Soviet Union spent a larger percentage of its available wealth on the military than did the Third Reich. But in fact Germany devoted a slightly larger percentage of its national income to defense than did the Soviet Union. The German advantage in defense spending over the Soviets in 1942, for example, was 63 to 61 percent; in 1943 it was 70 to 61 percent.[70] The Allies' strategic bombing campaign might well have hurt German war production in the last months of the war, but as noted above, the Soviet Union was turning out greater numbers of weapons than Germany long before the bombing campaign began to have any significant effect on German output. The Soviet effort was also helped by the U.S. Lend-Lease program, although that aid accounts for only a small percentage of Soviet output.[71] The main reason that the Soviet Union produced so many more weapons than Germany is that the Soviets did a much better job of rationalizing their economy to meet the demands of total war. In particular, the

Soviet (and American) economy was far better organized than the German economy for mass producing weaponry.[72]

Different Kinds of Military Forces

The final reason why wealth is not a reliable indicator of military might is that states can buy different kinds of military power, and how they build their armed forces has consequences for the balance of power. This matter is discussed at length in the next chapter. The key issue here is whether a state has a large army with significant power-projection capability. But not all states spend the same percentage of their defense dollars on their army, and not all armies have the same power-projection capabilities.

During the period from 1870 to 1914, for example, when great powers spent their defense dollars on either their army or their navy, the United Kingdom earmarked a significantly larger share of its military budget to its navy than did either France or Germany.[73] These different patterns of defense spending made good strategic sense, since the United Kingdom was an insular state that needed a large and powerful navy to protect its seaborne commerce and to transport its army across the large bodies of water that separated it from the European continent as well as the vast British empire. France and Germany, on the other hand, were continental powers with much smaller empires, so they were less dependent on their navies than was the United Kingdom. They were also more dependent on their armies than the United Kingdom, however, because they had to worry constantly about an invasion by a neighboring state. The United Kingdom was much less concerned about being attacked, because it was separated from the other European great powers by the English Channel, a formidable barrier to invasion. Consequently, the United Kingdom had a much smaller army than did either France or Germany.

Furthermore, the small British army had little power-projection capability against the other European great powers, because the same geographical obstacle that made it difficult for rivals to invade the United Kingdom made it difficult for the United Kingdom to invade the continent. Kaiser Wilhelm summed up the U.K. military weakness when he said to a British visitor in 1911, "Excuse my saying so, but the few divisions you could put into the field could make no appreciable difference."[74] In short, the United Kingdom was not as powerful as either France or Germany during the forty-four years before World War I, even though it was wealthier than France for that entire period, and wealthier than Germany for roughly three-quarters of that time (see Table 3.3).

It should be apparent that there are sometimes important differences in how wealth and power are distributed among the great powers, but that those incongruities are not caused by states passing up opportunities to maximize their share of world power. For sound strategic reasons, states build different kinds of military establishments, and they expend different amounts of their wealth on their fighting forces. Moreover, states distill military power from wealth at varying levels of efficiency. All of these considerations affect the balance of power.

Thus, although wealth is the foundation of military might, it is impossible to simply equate wealth with military might. It is necessary to come up with separate indicators of military power; the next chapter takes on this task.

4

The Primacy
of Land Power

Power in international politics is largely a product of the military forces that a state possesses. Great powers, however, can acquire different kinds of fighting forces, and how much of each kind they buy has important implications for the balance of power. This chapter analyzes the four types of military power among which states choose—independent sea power, strategic airpower, land power, and nuclear weapons—to determine how to weigh them against each other and come up with a useful measure of power.

I make two main points in the discussion below. First, land power is the dominant form of military power in the modern world. A state's power is largely embedded in its army and the air and naval forces that support those ground forces. Simply put, the most powerful states possess the most formidable armies. Therefore, measuring the balance of land power by itself should provide a rough but sound indicator of the relative might of rival great powers.

Second, large bodies of water profoundly limit the power-projection capabilities of land forces. When opposing armies must cross a large expanse of water such as the Atlantic Ocean or the English Channel to attack each other, neither army is likely to have much offensive capability against its rival, regardless of the size and quality of the opposing armies.

The stopping power of water is of great significance not just because it is a central aspect of land power, but also because it has important consequences for the concept of hegemony. Specifically, the presence of oceans on much of the earth's surface makes it impossible for any state to achieve global hegemony. Not even the world's most powerful state can conquer distant regions that can be reached only by ship. Thus, great powers can aspire to dominate only the region in which they are located, and possibly an adjacent region that can be reached over land.

For more than a century strategists have debated which form of military power dominates the outcome of war. U.S. admiral Alfred Thayer Mahan famously proclaimed the supreme importance of independent sea power in *The Influence of Sea Power upon History, 1660–1783* and his other writings.[1] General Giulio Douhet of Italy later made the case for the primacy of strategic airpower in his 1921 classic, *The Command of the Air.*[2] Their works are still widely read at staff colleges around the world. I argue that both are wrong: land power is the decisive military instrument. Wars are won by big battalions, not by armadas in the air or on the sea. The strongest power is the state with the strongest army.

One might argue that nuclear weapons greatly diminish the importance of land power, either by rendering great-power war obsolete or by making the nuclear balance the essential component of military power in a competitive world. There is no question that great-power war is less likely in a nuclear world, but great powers still compete for security even under the nuclear shadow, sometimes intensely, and war between them remains a real possibility. The United States and the Soviet Union, for example, waged an unremitting security competition for forty-five years, despite the presence of nuclear weapons on both sides. Moreover, save for the unlikely scenario in which one great power achieves nuclear superiority, the nuclear balance matters little for determining relative power. Even in a nuclear world, armies and the air and naval forces that support them are the core ingredient of military power.

The alliance patterns that formed during the Cold War are evidence that land power is the principal component of military might. In a world dominated by two great powers, we would expect other key states to join forces with the weaker great power to contain the stronger one. Throughout the

Cold War, not only was the United States much wealthier than the Soviet Union, but it also enjoyed a significant advantage in naval forces, strategic bombers, and nuclear warheads. Nevertheless, France, West Germany, Italy, Japan, the United Kingdom, and eventually China considered the Soviet Union, not the United States, to be the most powerful state in the system. Indeed, those states allied with the United States against the Soviet Union because they feared the Soviet army, not the American army.[3] Moreover, there is little concern about a Russian threat today—even though Russia has thousands of nuclear weapons—because the Russian army is weak and in no position to launch a major ground offensive. Should it recover and become a formidable fighting force again, the United States and its European allies would start worrying about a new Russian threat.

This chapter comprises eight sections. I compare the different kinds of conventional military power in the first four sections, aiming to show that land power dominates independent sea power and strategic airpower. In the first section, I describe these different kinds of military power more fully and explain why land power is the main instrument for winning wars. In the next two sections, I discuss the various missions that navies and air forces perform and then consider the evidence on how independent naval and air forces have affected the outcomes of great-power wars. The role of land power in modern military history is examined in the fourth section.

The fifth section analyzes how large bodies of water sharply curtail the power-projection capabilities of armies and thus shift the balance of land power in important ways. The impact of nuclear weapons on military power is discussed in the sixth section. I then describe how to measure land power in the seventh section, which is followed by a short conclusion that describes some implications for international stability that follow from my analysis of power.

CONQUEST VS. COERCION

Land power is centered around armies, but it also includes the air and naval forces that support them. For example, navies transport armies across large bodies of water, and sometimes they attempt to project ground forces onto hostile beaches. Air forces also transport armies, but more important, they aid armies by delivering firepower from the skies. These air and naval missions, however, are directly assisting the army, not acting independently of it. Thus, these missions fit under the rubric of land power.

Armies are of paramount importance in warfare because they are the main military instrument for conquering and controlling land, which is the supreme political objective in a world of territorial states. Naval and air forces are simply not suited for conquering territory.[4] The famous British naval strategist Julian Corbett put the point well regarding the relationship between armies and navies: "Since men live upon the land and not upon the sea, great issues between nations at war have always been decided—except in the rarest cases—either by what your army can do against your enemy's territory and national life, or else by the fear of what the fleet makes it possible for your army to do."[5] Corbett's logic applies to airpower as well as sea power.

Navies and air forces, however, need not act simply as force multipliers for the army. Each can also independently project power against rival states, as many navalists and airpower enthusiasts like to emphasize. Navies, for example, can ignore what is happening on the battlefield and blockade an opponent, while air forces can fly over the battlefield and bomb the enemy's homeland. Both blockades and strategic bombing seek to produce victory by coercing the adversary into surrendering before its army is defeated on the battlefield. Specifically, the aim is to cause the opponent to surrender either by wrecking its economy and thus undermining its ability to prosecute the war, or by inflicting massive punishment on its civilian population.

The claims of Douhet and Mahan notwithstanding, neither independent naval power nor strategic airpower has much utility for winning major wars. Neither of those coercive instruments can win a great-power war operating alone. Only land power has the potential to win a major war by itself. The main reason, as discussed below, is that it is difficult to coerce a great power. In particular, it is hard to destroy an enemy's economy solely by blockading or bombing it. Furthermore, the leaders as well as the people in modern states are rarely willing to surrender even after absorbing tremendous amounts of punishment. Although blockading navies and strategic bombers cannot produce victory by themselves, they sometimes can help armies gain victory by damaging the economy that underpins the adversary's military machine. But even in this more limited capacity, air and naval forces usually do not play more than an auxiliary role.

Land power dominates the other kinds of military power for another reason: only armies can expeditiously defeat an opponent. Blockading navies and strategic bombing, as discussed below, cannot produce quick and decisive victories in wars between great powers. They are useful mainly for fighting lengthy wars of attrition. But states rarely go to war unless they think that rapid success is likely. In fact, the prospect of a protracted conflict is usually an excellent deterrent to war.[6] Consequently, a great power's army is its main instrument for initiating aggression. A state's offensive potential, in other words, is embedded largely in its army.

Let us now look more closely at the different missions that navies and air forces perform in wartime, paying special attention to how blockades and strategic bombing campaigns have affected the outcomes of past great-power conflicts.

THE LIMITS OF INDEPENDENT NAVAL POWER

A navy bent on projecting power against a rival state must first gain *command of the sea*, which is the bedrock mission for naval forces.[7] Command of the sea means controlling the lines of communication that crisscross the ocean's surface, so that a state's commercial and military ships can freely move across them. For a navy to command an ocean, it need not control all of the sea all of the time, but it must be able to control the strategically important parts whenever it wants to use them, and deny the enemy the ability to do likewise.[8] Gaining command of the sea can be achieved by destroying rival navies in battle, by blockading them in their ports, or by denying them access to critical sea lanes.

A navy that commands the oceans may have the freedom to move about those moats, but it still must find a way to project power against its rival's homeland; command of the sea by itself does not provide that capability. Navies can perform three power-projection missions where they are directly supporting the army, not acting independently.

Amphibious assault takes place when a navy moves an army across a large body of water and lands it on territory controlled by a rival great power.[9] The attacking forces meet armed resistance either when they arrive at their landing zones or shortly thereafter. Their aim is to engage and defeat the defender's main armies, and to conquer some portion, if not all, of its territory. The Allied invasion of Normandy on June 6, 1944, is an example of an amphibious assault.

Amphibious landings, in contrast, occur when the seaborne forces meet hardly any resistance when they land in enemy territory and are able to establish a beachhead and move well inland before engaging enemy forces.[10] The insertion of British troops into French-controlled Portugal during the Napoleonic Wars, discussed below, is an example of an amphibious landing; the landing of German army units in Norway in the spring of 1940 is another.

Troop transport by a navy involves moving ground forces across an ocean and landing them on territory controlled by friendly forces, from where they go into combat against the enemy army. The navy effectively serves as a ferry service. The American navy performed this mission in World War I, when it moved troops from the United States to France, and again in World War II, when it moved troops from the United States to the United Kingdom. These different kinds of amphibious operations are considered below, when I discuss how water limits the striking power of armies. Suffice it to say here that invasion from the sea against territory defended by a rival great power is usually a daunting task. Troop transport is a much easier mission.[11]

There are also two ways that navies can be used independently to project power against another state. In *naval bombardment,* enemy cities or selected military targets, usually along a rival's coast, are hit with sustained firepower from guns or missiles on ships and submarines, or by aircraft flying from carriers. The aim is to coerce the adversary either by punishing its cities or by shifting the military balance against it. This is not a serious strategy; naval bombardment is pinprick warfare, and it has little effect on the target state.

Although navies often bombarded enemy ports in the age of sail (1500–1850), they could not deliver enough firepower to those targets to be more than a nuisance.[12] Moreover, naval gunfire did not have the range to hit targets located off the coast. Horatio Nelson, the famous British admiral, summed up the futility of naval bombardment with sailing navies when he said, "A ship's a fool to fight a fort."[13] The industrialization of navies after 1850 significantly increased the amount of firepower navies could deliver, as well as their delivery range. But industrialization had an even more profound effect on the ability of land-based forces to find and sink navies, as discussed below. Thus, twentieth-century surface navies tended to stay far away from enemy coastlines in wartime.[14] More important, however, if a great power were to try to coerce an adversary with a conventional bombing campaign, it would surely use its air force for that purpose, not its navy.

The two great naval theorists of modern times, Corbett and Mahan, believed that a *blockade* is the navy's ace strategy for winning great-power wars. Blockade, which Mahan called "the most striking and awful mark of sea power," works by strangling a rival state's economy.[15] The aim is to cut off an opponent's overseas trade—to deny it imports that move across water and to prevent it from exporting its own goods and materials to the outside world.

Once seaborne trade is severed, there are two ways a blockade might coerce a rival great power into surrendering. First, it can inflict severe punishment on the enemy's civilian population, mainly by cutting off food imports and making life miserable, if not deadly, for the average citizen. If enough people are made to suffer and die, popular support for the war will evaporate, a result that will either cause the population to revolt or force the government to stop the war for fear of revolt. Second, a blockade can so weaken an enemy's economy that it can no longer continue the fight. Probably the best way to achieve this end is to cut off a critical import, such as oil. Blockading navies usually do not discriminate between these two approaches but instead try to cut off as much of an opponent's overseas trade as possible, hoping that one approach succeeds. Regardless, blockades do not produce quick and decisive victories, because it takes a long time for a navy to wreck an adversary's economy.

States usually implement blockades with naval forces that prevent oceangoing commerce from reaching the target state. The United Kingdom, for example, has historically relied on its surface navy to blockade rivals such as Napoleonic France and Wilhelmine Germany. Submarines can also be used to cut an enemy state's overseas trade, as Germany attempted to do against the United Kingdom in both world wars, and the United States did against Japan in World War II. The Americans also used surface ships, land-based aircraft, and mines to blockade Japan. But navies are not always necessary to carry out a blockade. A state that dominates a continent and controls its major ports can stop trade between the states located on that continent and states located elsewhere, thus blockading the outside states. Napoleon's Continental System (1806–13), which was aimed at the United Kingdom, fits this model.

The History of Blockades

There are eight cases in the modern era in which a great power attempted to coerce another great power with a wartime blockade: 1) France blockaded the United Kingdom during the Napoleonic Wars, and 2) the United Kingdom did likewise to France; 3) France blockaded Prussia in 1870; 4) Germany blockaded the United Kingdom and 5) the United Kingdom and the United States blockaded Germany and Austria-Hungary in World War I; 6) Germany blockaded the United Kingdom and 7) the United Kingdom and the United States blockaded Germany and Italy in World War II; and 8) the United States blockaded Japan in World War II. The Union's blockade of the Confederacy during the American Civil War (1861–65) is a possible ninth case, although neither side was technically a great power; I will consider it here nonetheless.[16]

In evaluating these cases, two questions should be kept in mind. First, is there evidence that blockades alone can coerce an enemy into surrendering? And second, can blockades contribute importantly to victory by ground armies? Is the influence of blockades on the final outcome of wars likely to be decisive, roughly equal to that of land power, or marginal?

The British economy was certainly hurt by Napoleon's Continental System, but the United Kingdom stayed in the war and eventually came out on the winning side.[17] The British blockade of Napoleonic France did not come close to wrecking the French economy, which was not particularly vulnerable to blockade.[18] No serious scholar argues that the British blockade played a key role in Napoleon's downfall. France's blockade of Prussia in 1870 had hardly any effect on the Prussian economy, much less on the Prussian army, which won a decisive victory over the French army.[19] Germany's submarine campaign against British shipping in World War I threatened to knock the United Kingdom out of the war in 1917, but that blockade ultimately failed and the British army played the key role in defeating Wilhelmine Germany in 1918.[20] In that same conflict, the British and American navies imposed a blockade of their own on Germany and Austria-Hungary that badly damaged those countries' economies and caused great suffering among their civilian populations.[21] Nevertheless, Germany surrendered only after the kaiser's armies, which were not seriously affected by the blockade, were shattered in combat on the western front in the summer of 1918. Austria-Hungary, too, had to be defeated on the battlefield.

In World War II, Hitler launched another U-boat campaign against the United Kingdom, but again it failed to wreck the British economy and knock the United Kingdom out of the war.[22] The Anglo-American blockade of Nazi Germany in that same conflict had no significant effect on the German economy, which was not particularly vulnerable to blockade.[23] Nor did the Allied blockade cause Italy's economy much harm, and it certainly had little to do with Italy's decision to quit the war in mid-1943. Regarding the American Civil War, the Confederacy's economy was hurt by the Union blockade, but it did not collapse, and General Robert E. Lee surrendered only after the Confederate armies had been soundly defeated in battle. Moreover, Lee's armies were not beaten in battle because they suffered from material shortages stemming from the blockade.[24]

The American blockade of Japan during World War II is the only case in which a blockade wrecked a rival's economy, causing serious damage to its military forces. Moreover, it is the only case among the nine of success-ful coercion, since Japan surrendered before its Home Army of two mil-lion men was defeated in battle.[25] There is no question that the blockade played a central role in bringing Japan to its knees, but it was done in tan-dem with land power, which played an equally important role in produc-ing victory. Japan's decision to surrender unconditionally in August 1945 merits close scrutiny, because it is a controversial case, and because it has significant implications for analyzing the efficacy of strategic airpower as well as blockades.[26]

A good way to think about what caused Japan to surrender is to distin-guish between what transpired before August 1945 and what happened in the first two weeks of that critical month. By late July 1945, Japan was a defeated nation, and its leaders recognized that fact. The only important issue at stake was whether Japan could avoid unconditional surrender, which the United States demanded. Defeat was inevitable because the bal-ance of land power had shifted decisively against Japan over the previous three years. Japan's army, along with its supporting air and naval forces, was on the verge of collapse because of the devastating American block-ade, and because it had been worn down in protracted fighting on two fronts. The Asian mainland was Japan's western front, and its armies had been bogged down there in a costly war with China since 1937. Japan's eastern front was its island empire in the western Pacific, where the United States was its principal foe. American ground forces, with exten-sive air and naval support for sure, had defeated most of the Japanese forces holding those islands and were gearing up to invade Japan itself in the fall of 1945.

By the end of July 1945, the American air force had been firebombing Japan's major cities for almost five months, and it had inflicted massive destruction on Japan's civilian population. Nevertheless, this punishment campaign neither caused the Japanese people to put pressure on their government to end the war nor caused Japan's leaders to think seriously about throwing in the towel. Instead, Japan was on the ropes because its army had been decimated by blockade and years of debilitating ground combat. Still, Japan refused to surrender unconditionally.

Why did Japan continue to hold out? It was not because its leaders thought that their badly weakened army could thwart an American invasion of Japan. In fact, it was widely recognized that the United States had the military might to conquer the home islands. Japanese policymakers refused to accept unconditional surrender because they thought that it was possible to negotiate an end to the war that left Japan's sovereignty intact. The key to success was to make the United States think that it would have to pay a large blood price to conquer Japan. The threat of costly victory, they reasoned, would cause the United States to be more flexible on the diplomatic front. Furthermore, Japanese leaders hoped that the Soviet Union, which had stayed out of the Pacific war so far, would mediate the peace talks and help produce an agreement short of unconditional surrender.

Two events in early August 1945 finally pushed Japan's leaders over the line and got them to accept unconditional surrender. The atomic bombings of Hiroshima (August 6) and Nagasaki (August 9) and the specter of more nuclear attacks caused some key individuals, including Emperor Hirohito, to push for quitting the war immediately. The final straw was the Soviet decision to join the war against Japan on August 8, 1945, and the Soviet attack on the Kwantung Army in Manchuria the following day. Not only did that development eliminate any possibility of using the Soviet Union to negotiate a peace agreement, but Japan was now at war with both the Soviet Union and the United States. Moreover, the rapid collapse of the Kwantung Army at the hands of the Red Army suggested that the Home Army was likely to fall rather quickly and easily to the American invasion force. In short, Japan's strategy for gaining a conditional surrender was in tatters by August 9, 1945, and this fact was widely recognized by the Japanese military, especially the army, which had been the principal roadblock to quitting the war.

The evidence from these cases of blockade suggests two conclusions about their utility for winning wars. First, blockades alone cannot coerce an enemy into surrendering. The futility of such a strategy is shown by the fact that no belligerent has ever tried it. Moreover, the record shows that even blockades used together with land power rarely have produced coercive results, revealing the general inability of blockades to coerce. In the nine cases surveyed above, the blockading state won five times and lost four times. In four of the five victories, however, there was no coercion; the victor had to conquer the other state's army. In the single case of successful coercion, the U.S. navy's blockade of Japan was only partially responsible for the outcome. Land power mattered at least as much as the blockade.

Second, blockades rarely do much to weaken enemy armies, hence they rarely contribute in important ways to the success of a ground campaign. The best that can be said for blockade is that it sometimes helps land power win protracted wars by damaging an adversary's economy. Indeed, the blockade of Japan is the only case in which a blockade mattered as much as land power for winning a great-power war.

Why Blockades Fail

Numerous factors account for the limited impact of blockades in great-power wars. They sometimes fail because the blockading navy is checked at sea and cannot cut the victim's sea lines of communication. The British and American navies thwarted Germany's blockades in both world wars by making it difficult for German submarines to get close enough to Allied shipping to launch their torpedoes. Furthermore, blockades sometimes become porous over the course of a long war, because of leakage or because neutral states serve as entrepôts. The Continental System, for example, eroded over time because Napoleon could not completely shut down British trade with the European continent.

Even when a blockade cuts off virtually all of the target state's seaborne commerce, its impact is usually limited for two reasons. First, great powers have ways of beating blockades, for example by recycling, stockpiling, and substitution. The United Kingdom was heavily dependent on imported food before both world wars, and the German blockades in those conflicts aimed to starve the British into submission. The United Kingdom dealt with this threat to its survival, however, by sharply increasing its production of foodstuffs.[27] When Germany had its rubber supply cut off in World War II, it developed a synthetic substitute.[28] Furthermore, great powers can conquer and exploit neighboring states, especially since the coming of railroads. Nazi Germany, for example, thoroughly exploited the European continent in World War II, greatly reducing the impact of the Allied blockade.

Modern bureaucratic states are especially adept at adjusting and rationalizing their economies to counter wartime blockades. Mancur Olson demonstrates this point in *The Economics of the Wartime Shortage*, which compares the blockades against the United Kingdom in the Napoleonic Wars, World War I, and World War II.[29] He notes that "Britain endured the greatest loss of food supplies in World War II, the next greatest loss in World War I, and the smallest loss in the Napoleonic wars." At the same time, the United Kingdom was more dependent on food imports during the twentieth century than it was during the Napoleonic period. Therefore, one would expect "the amount of suffering for want of food" to be greatest in World War II and least in Napoleon's day.

But Olson finds the opposite to be true: suffering due to lack of food in the Napoleonic period "was probably much greater than in either of the world wars." His explanation for this counterintuitive finding is that the administrative abilities of the British state increased markedly over time, so that its capacity to reorganize its economy in wartime and ameliorate the effects of blockade was "least remarkable in the Napoleonic period, more remarkable in World War I, and most remarkable in World War II."

Second, the populations of modern states can absorb great amounts of pain without rising up against their governments.[30] There is not a single case in the historical record in which either a blockade or a strategic bombing campaign designed to punish an enemy's population caused significant public protests against the target government. If anything, it appears that "punishment generates more public anger against the attacker than against the target government."[31] Consider Japan in World War II. Not only was its economy devastated by the American blockade, but Japan was subjected to a strategic bombing campaign that destroyed vast tracts of urban landscape and killed hundreds of thousands of civilians.

Yet the Japanese people stoically withstood the withering punishment the United States dished out, and they put little pressure on their government to surrender.[32]

Finally, governing elites are rarely moved to quit a war because their populations are being brutalized. In fact, one could argue that the more punishment that a population suffers, the more difficult it is for the leaders to quit the war. The basis of this claim, which seems counterintuitive, is that bloody defeat greatly increases the likelihood that after the war is over the people will seek revenge against the leaders who led them down the road to destruction. Thus, those leaders have a powerful incentive to ignore the pain being inflicted on their population and fight to the finish in the hope that they can pull out a victory and save their own skin.[33]

THE LIMITS OF STRATEGIC AIRPOWER

There are important parallels in how states employ their air forces and their navies in war. Whereas navies must gain command of the sea before they can project power against rival states, air forces must gain command of the air, or achieve what is commonly called *air superiority,* before they can bomb enemy forces on the ground or attack an opponent's homeland. If an air force does not control the skies, its strike forces are likely to suffer substantial losses, making it difficult, if not impossible for them to project power against the enemy.

American bombers, for example, conducted large-scale raids against the German cities of Regensburg and Schweinfurt in August and October 1943 without commanding the skies over that part of Germany. The attacking bombers suffered prohibitive losses as a result, forcing the United States to halt the attacks until long-range fighter escorts became available in early 1944.[34] During the first days of the Yom Kippur War in October 1973, the Israeli Air Force (IAF) attempted to provide much-needed support to the beleaguered Israeli ground forces along the Suez Canal and on the Golan Heights. But withering fire from Egyptian and Syrian surface-to-air missiles and air-defense guns forced the IAF to curtail that mission.[35]

Once an air force controls the skies, it can pursue three power-projection missions in support of army units fighting on the ground. In a *close air support* role, an air force flies above the battlefield and provides direct tactical support to friendly ground forces operating below. The air force's principal goal is to destroy enemy troops from the air, in effect serving as "flying artillery." This mission requires close coordination between air and ground forces. *Interdiction* involves air force strikes at the enemy army's rear area, mainly to destroy or delay the movement of enemy supplies and troops to the front line. The target list might include supply depots, reserve units, long-range artillery, and the lines of communication that crisscross the enemy's rear area and run up to its front lines. Air forces also provide *airlift*, moving troops and supplies either to or within a combat theater. These missions, of course, simply augment an army's power.

But an air force can also independently project power against an adversary with *strategic bombing*, in which the air force strikes directly at the enemy's homeland, paying little attention to events on the battlefield.[36] This mission lends itself to the claim that air forces alone can win wars. Not surprisingly, airpower enthusiasts tend to embrace strategic bombing, which works much like its naval equivalent, the blockade.[37] The aim of both strategic bombing and blockading is to coerce the enemy into surrendering either by massively punishing its civilian population or by destroying its economy, which would ultimately cripple its fighting forces. Proponents of economic targeting sometimes favor striking against the enemy's entire industrial base and wrecking it *in toto*. Others advocate strikes limited to one or more "critical components" such as oil, ball bearings, machine tools, steel, or transportation networks—the Achilles' heel of the enemy's economy.[38] Strategic bombing campaigns, like blockades, are not expected to produce quick and easy victories.

Over the past decade, some advocates of airpower have argued that strategic bombing can secure victory by decapitating the enemy's political leadership.[39] Specifically, bombers might be used either to kill a rival state's political leaders or to isolate them from their people by attacking the leadership's means of communication as well as the security forces that allow it to control the population. More benign elements in the adversary's camp, it is hoped, would then stage a coup and negotiate peace. Advocates of decapitation also claim that it might be feasible to isolate a political leader from his military forces, making it impossible for him to command and control them.

Two further points about independent airpower are in order before looking at the historical record. Strategic bombing, which I take to mean non-nuclear attacks on the enemy's homeland, has not been an important kind of military power since 1945, and that situation is unlikely to change in the foreseeable future. With the development of nuclear weapons at the end of World War II, great powers moved away from threatening each other's homelands with conventionally armed bombers and instead relied on nuclear weapons to accomplish that mission. During the Cold War, for example, neither the United States nor the Soviet Union planned to launch a strategic bombing campaign against the other in the event of a superpower war. Both states, however, had extensive plans for using their nuclear arsenals to strike each other's territory.

But old-fashioned strategic bombing has not disappeared altogether. The great powers continued employing it against minor powers, as the Soviet Union did against Afghanistan in the 1980s and the United States did against Iraq and Yugoslavia in the 1990s.[40] Having the capability to bomb small, weak states, however, should not count for much when assessing the balance of military might among the great powers. What should count the most are the military instruments that the great powers intend to use against *each other*, and that no longer includes strategic bombing. Thus, my analysis of independent airpower is relevant primarily to the period between 1915 and 1945, not to the recent past, the present, or the future.

The historical record includes fourteen cases of strategic bombing: five involve great powers attacking other great powers, and nine are instances of great powers striking minor powers. The campaigns between rival great powers provide the most important evidence for determining how to assess the balance of military might among the great powers. Nevertheless, I also consider the cases involving minor powers, because some might think that they—especially the U.S. air campaigns against Iraq and Yugoslavia—provide evidence that great powers can use their air forces to coerce another great power. That is not so, however, as will become apparent.

The History of Strategic Bombing

The five cases in which a great power attempted to coerce a rival great power with strategic bombing are in World War I, when 1) Germany bombed British cities; and in World War II, when 2) Germany struck again at British cities, 3) the United Kingdom and the United States bombed Germany, 4) the United Kingdom and the United States attacked Italy, and 5) the United States bombed Japan.

The nine instances in which a great power attempted to coerce a minor power with strategic airpower include 1) Italy against Ethiopia in 1936; 2) Japan versus China from 1937 to 1945; 3) the Soviet Union against Finland in World War II; the United States versus 4) North Korea in the early 1950s, 5) North Vietnam in the mid-1960s, and 6) North Vietnam again in 1972; 7) the Soviet Union against Afghanistan in the 1980s; and the United States and its allies versus 8) Iraq in 1991 and 9) Yugoslavia in 1999.

These fourteen cases should be evaluated in terms of the same two questions that informed the earlier analysis of blockades: First, is there evidence that strategic bombing alone can coerce an enemy into surrendering? Second, can strategic airpower contribute importantly to victory by ground armies? Is the influence of strategic bombing on the final outcome of wars likely to be decisive, roughly equal to that of land power, or marginal?

Bombing Great Powers

The German air offensives against British cities in World Wars I and II not only failed to coerce the United Kingdom to surrender, but Germany also lost both wars.[41] Furthermore, there is no evidence that either of those bombing campaigns seriously damaged the United Kingdom's military capability. Thus, if there is a case to be made for the decisive influence of strategic bombing, it depends largely on the Allied bombing of the so-called Axis powers—Germany, Italy, and Japan—in World War II.

A good reason to be skeptical about claims that bombing was of central importance to the outcomes of these three conflicts is that, in each case, serious bombing of the target state did not begin until well after it was clear that each was going down to defeat. Germany, for example, went to war with the United Kingdom in September 1939 and with the United States in December 1941. Germany surrendered in May 1945, although it was clear by the end of 1942, if not sooner, that Germany was going to lose the war. The Wehrmacht's last major offensive against the Red Army was at Kursk in the summer of 1943, and it failed badly. After much debate, the Allies finally decided at the Casablanca Conference in January 1943 to launch a serious strategic bombing campaign against Germany. But the air offensive was slow getting started, and the bombers did not begin pounding the Third Reich until the spring of 1944, when the Allies finally gained air superiority over Germany. Even historian Richard Overy, who believes that airpower played a central role in winning the war against Germany, acknowledges that it was only "during the last year of the war [that] the bombing campaign came of age."[42]

Italy went to war with the United Kingdom in June 1940 and the United States in December 1941. But unlike Germany, Italy quit the war in September 1943, before it had been conquered. The Allied bombing campaign against Italy began in earnest in July 1943, roughly two months before Italy surrendered. By that point, however, Italy was on the brink of catastrophic defeat. Its army was decimated and it no longer was capable of defending the Italian homeland from invasion.[43] In fact, the Wehrmacht was providing most of Italy's defense when the Allies invaded Sicily from the sea in July 1943.

Japan's war with the United States started in December 1941 and ended in August 1945. The serious pounding of Japan from the air began in March 1945, about five months before Japan surrendered. At that point, however, Japan had clearly lost the war and was facing the prospect of surrendering unconditionally. The United States had destroyed Japan's empire in the Pacific and effectively eliminated what remained of the Japanese navy at the Battle of Leyte Gulf in October 1944. Moreover, the American naval blockade had wrecked the Japanese economy by March 1945, an act that had profoundly negative consequences for Japan's army, a large portion of which was bogged down in an unwinnable war with China.

The fact is that these strategic bombing campaigns were feasible only late in the war when the Axis powers were badly battered and headed for defeat. Otherwise, the target states would not have been vulnerable to a sustained aerial assault. The United States, for example, was unable to conduct a major bombing campaign against Japan until it had destroyed most of Japan's navy and air force and had fought its way close to the home islands. Only then were American bombers near enough to make unhindered attacks on Japan. Nor could the United States effectively employ its strategic bombers against Germany until it had gained air superiority over the Third Reich. That difficult task took time and was feasible only because Germany was diverting huge resources to fight the Red Army.

The best case that can be made for the three Allied strategic bombing campaigns is that they helped finish off opponents who were already well on their way to defeat—which hardly supports the claim that independent airpower was a decisive weapon in World War II. In particular, one might argue that those strategic air campaigns helped end the war sooner rather than later, and that they also helped the Allies secure better terms than otherwise would have been possible. Except for the Italian case, however, the evidence seems to show that strategic bombing had little effect on how these conflicts ended. Let us consider these cases in more detail.

The Allies attempted to coerce Germany into surrendering by inflicting pain on its civilian population and by destroying its economy. The Allied punishment campaign against German cities, which included the infamous "firebombings" of Hamburg and Dresden, destroyed more than 40 percent of the urban area in Germany's seventy largest cities and killed roughly 305,000 civilians.[44] The German people, however, fatalistically absorbed the punishment, and Hitler felt no compunction to surrender.[45] There is no doubt that Allied air strikes, along with the advancing ground forces, wrecked Germany's industrial base by early 1945.[46] But the war was almost over at that point, and more important, the destruction of German industry was still not enough to coerce Hitler into stopping the war. In the end, the American, British, and Soviet armies had to conquer Germany.[47]

The strategic bombing campaign against Italy was modest in the extreme compared to the pummeling that was inflicted on Germany and Japan.[48] Some economic targets were struck, but no attempt was made to demolish Italy's industrial base. The Allies also sought to inflict pain on Italy's population, but in the period from October 1942 until August 1943 they killed about 3,700 Italians, a tiny number compared to the 305,000 Germans (between March 1942 and April 1945) and 900,000 Japanese (between March and August 1945) killed from the air. Despite its limited lethality, the bombing campaign began to rattle Italy's ruling elites in the summer of 1943 (when it was intensified) and increased the pressure on them to surrender as soon as possible. Nevertheless, the main reason that Italy was desperate to quit the war at that point—and eventually did so on September 8, 1943—was that the Italian army was in tatters and it stood hardly any chance of stopping an Allied invasion.[49] Italy was doomed to defeat well before the bombing campaign began to have an effect. Thus, the best that can be said for the Allied air offensive against Italy is that it probably forced Italy out of the war a month or two earlier than otherwise would have been the case.

When the American bombing campaign against Japan began in late 1944, the initial goal was to use high-explosive bombs to help destroy Japan's economy, which was being wrecked by the U.S. navy's blockade.[50] It quickly became apparent, however, that this airpower strategy would not seriously damage Japan's industrial base. Therefore, in March 1945, the United States decided to try instead to punish Japan's civilian population by firebombing its cities.[51] This deadly aerial campaign, which lasted until the war ended five months later, destroyed more than 40 percent of Japan's 64 largest cities, killed approximately 785,000 civilians, and forced about 8.5 million people to evacuate their homes.[52] Although Japan surrendered in August 1945 before the United States invaded and conquered the Japanese homeland—making this a case of succesful coercion—the firebombing campaign played only a minor role in convincing Japan to quit the war. As discussed earlier, blockade and land power were mainly responsible for the outcome, although the atomic bombings and the Soviet declaration of war against Japan (both in early August) helped push Japan over the edge.

Thus coercion failed in three of the five cases in which a great power was the target state: Germany's air offensives against the United Kingdom in World Wars I and II, and the Allied bombing campaign against Nazi Germany. Moreover, strategic bombing did not play a key role in the Allies' victory over the Wehrmacht. Although Italy and Japan were coerced into surrendering in World War II, both successes were largely due to factors other than independent airpower. Let us now consider what happened in the past when the great powers unleashed their bombers against minor powers.

Bombing Small Powers

Despite the significant power asymmetry in the nine instances in which a great power's strategic bombers struck at a minor power, coercion did not happen in five of the cases. Italy bombed Ethiopian towns and villages in 1936, sometimes using poison gas.[53] Nevertheless, Ethiopia refused to surrender, forcing the Italian army to conquer the entire country. Japan bombed Chinese cities between 1937 and 1945, killing large numbers of Chinese civilians.[54] But China did not surrender and ultimately the United States decisively defeated Japan. The United States conducted the famous "Rolling Thunder" bombing campaign against North Vietnam from 1965 to 1968. Its aim was to force the North Vietnamese to stop fueling the war in South Vietnam and accept the existence of an independent South Vietnam.[55] The effort failed and the war went on.

The Soviet Union waged a bombing campaign against Afghanistan's population centers between 1979 and 1989 in order to coerce the Afghan rebels to stop their war against the Soviet-backed government in Kabul.[56] The Soviets, not the rebels, eventually quit the war. Finally, in early 1991, the United States launched a strategic air offensive against Iraq to coerce

Saddam Hussein into abandoning Kuwait, which his army had conquered in August 1990.[57] The bombing campaign failed to coerce Saddam, however, and the United States and its allies eventually had to employ ground forces to accomplish their mission. This bombing campaign is noteworthy because the United States employed a decapitation strategy: it tried to kill Saddam from the air, and it also attempted to isolate him from his population and from his military forces in Kuwait. This strategy failed on all counts.[58]

Coercion did succeed in four of the cases involving small powers, but strategic bombing appears to have played a peripheral role in achieving that end in all but one of those cases. When the Soviet Union invaded Finland on November 30, 1939, Soviet leader Josef Stalin launched a modest bombing campaign against Finnish cities, killing roughly 650 civilians.[59] By all accounts, the bombing campaign had little to do with Finland's decision to stop the war in March 1940 before it was defeated and conquered by the Red Army. Finland quit fighting because it recognized that its army was badly outnumbered and stood hardly any chance of winning the war.

During the Korean War, the United States attempted to coerce North Korea into quitting the war by punishing it from the air.[60] This effort actually involved three distinct campaigns. From late July 1950 until late October 1950, American bombers concentrated on bombing North Korea's five major industrial centers. Between May and September 1952, the main targets were a handful of hydroelectric plants in North Korea, as well as Pyongyang, the North Korean capital. American bombers struck North Korean dams between May and June 1953, aiming to destroy North Korea's rice crop and starve it into surrendering.

Since the armistice terminating the war was not signed until July 27, 1953, the first two punishment campaigns clearly did not end the war. Indeed, it is apparent from the available evidence that neither of those campaigns affected North Korean behavior in any meaningful way. Although the campaign to destroy North Korea's rice crop immediately preceded the signing of the armistice, bombing the dams did not devastate North Korea's rice crop and cause mass starvation. North Korea was finally coerced into signing the armistice by President Dwight Eisenhower's nuclear threats, and by the realization that neither side had the necessary combination of capability and will to alter the stalemate on the ground. In short, conventional aerial punishment did not cause this successful coercion.

In addition to the failed "Rolling Thunder" campaign against North Vietnam (1965–68), the United States launched the "Linebacker" bombing campaigns in 1972.[61] North Vietnam eventually signed a cease-fire agreement in early 1973 that allowed the United States to withdraw from the war and delayed further North Vietnamese ground offensives against South Vietnam. Although technically this was a case of successful coercion, in fact, the agreement merely postponed North Vietnam's final victory over South Vietnam until 1975. Nevertheless, strategic bombing played a small role in causing North Vietnam to accept a cease-fire with the United States.

Contrary to the popular perception at the time, American bombers inflicted relatively little punishment on North Vietnam's civilian population. About thirteen thousand North Vietnamese died from the 1972 air campaign, a level of suffering that was hardly likely to cause a determined foe like North Vietnam to cave in to American demands.[62] The main reason North Vietnam agreed to a cease-fire in January 1973 was that the U.S. air force had thwarted a North Vietnamese ground offensive in the spring of 1972, thereby creating a powerful incentive for North Vietnam to facilitate a rapid withdrawal of all American forces from Vietnam before going on the offensive again. Signing the cease-fire did just that, and two years later North Vietnam won a complete military victory over South Vietnam, which fought its final battles without the help of American airpower.

The recent war conducted by the North Atlantic Treaty Organization (NATO) against Yugoslavia appears at first glance to be the one case in which strategic airpower alone coerced an adversary into submission.[63] The United States and its allies began bombing Yugoslavia on March 24, 1999. Their aim was to get Slobodan Milosevic, Yugoslavia's president, to stop repressing the Albanian population in the province of Kosovo and allow NATO troops into that province. The air campaign lasted seventy days. Milosevic caved in to NATO's demands on June 8, 1999. NATO did not launch a ground attack into Kosovo, although the rebel Kosovo Liberation Army skirmished with Yugoslav ground forces throughout the campaign.

Not much evidence is available about why Milosevic capitulated, but it seems clear that bombing did not come close to bringing Yugoslavia to its knees, and that bombing alone is not responsible for the outcome.[64] The bombing campaign was initially a small-scale effort, because NATO leaders believed that Milosevic would concede defeat after a few days of light punishment from the air. Although NATO intensified the air war when that approach failed, it did not have the political will to inflict significant pain on Yugoslavia. Consequently, NATO's bombers went to great lengths not to kill Yugoslav civilians while striking against a limited number of economic and political targets in Yugoslavia. The bombing campaign killed about five hundred civilians.[65] Not surprisingly, there is hardly any evidence that Milosevic threw in the towel because of pressure from his people to end their suffering.

It appears that a variety of factors account for Milosevic's decision to cave into NATO's demands. The threat of further punishment from the air was probably a key factor, but two other factors appear to have been at least as important. NATO was beginning preparations for a massive ground invasion of Yugoslavia, and in late May the U.S. administration of President Bill Clinton sent a clear message to Milosevic via the Russians that NATO would soon send ground troops into Kosovo if he did not surrender. Furthermore, Russia, which was Yugoslavia's key ally and was bitterly opposed to the war, essentially sided with NATO in early June and put significant pressure on Milosevic to end the conflict immediately. NATO also softened its demands a bit to make a settlement more attractive to the Yugoslav leader. In sum, the punishment campaign alone did not produce victory against Yugoslavia, although it seems to have been an important factor.

The evidence from these fourteen cases supports the following conclusions about the utility of strategic bombing. First, strategic bombing alone cannot coerce an enemy into surrendering. Save for the case of Yugoslavia, no great power (or alliance of great powers) has ever tried to win a war by relying solely on its air force, and even in that case NATO eventually threatened a ground invasion to coerce Milosevic. Strategic bombing was employed in tandem with land power from the start in the other thirteen cases. This record shows the futility of relying on strategic bombing alone. Furthermore, there is little evidence that past bombing campaigns so markedly affected the war's outcome as to indicate that strategic bombing by itself can compel the surrender of another great power. Even when strategic bombing is used along with land power, the record shows that strategic bombing plausibly played a major role in shaping the outcome only once. Strategic bombing is generally unable to coerce on its own.

Consider that in nine out of the fourteen cases, the great power employing strategic airpower won the war. In three of those nine cases, however, the victor did not coerce its adversary but had to defeat it on the ground: Italy against Ethiopia, the Allies against Nazi Germany, and the United States against Iraq. In the remaining six cases, the great power employing strategic airpower successfully coerced its adversary. Strategic bombing, however, played a subordinate role in determining the outcome of five of those six cases: the United States against Japan, the Soviet Union against Finland, the Allies against Italy, and the United States against Korea and Vietnam (1972). Land power was the key to victory in each case, although blockade was also an essential ingredient of success in the U.S.-Japan case.

The war over Kosovo is the only instance in which strategic bombing appears to have played a key role in causing successful coercion. But that case is not cause for optimism about the utility of independent airpower. Not only was Yugoslavia an especially weak minor power fighting alone against the mighty United States and its European allies, but other factors besides the bombing campaign moved Milosevic to acquiesce to NATO's demands.

The second lesson to be drawn from the historical record is that strategic bombing rarely does much to weaken enemy armies, and hence it rarely contributes importantly to the success of a ground campaign. During World War II, independent airpower did sometimes help great powers win lengthy wars of attrition against rival great powers, but it played only an ancillary role in those victories. In the nuclear era, great powers have employed that coercive instrument only against minor powers, not against each other. But even against weaker states, strategic bombing has been about as effective as it was against other great powers. In short, it is hard to bomb an adversary into submission.

Why Strategic Bombing Campaigns Fail

Strategic bombing is unlikely to work for the same reasons that blockades usually fail to coerce an opponent: civilian populations can absorb tremendous pain and deprivation without rising up against their government. Political scientist Robert Pape succinctly summarizes the historical evidence regarding aerial punishment and popular revolt: "Over more than seventy-five years, the record of air power is replete with efforts to alter the behavior of states by attacking or threatening to attack large numbers of civilians. The incontrovertible conclusion from these campaigns is that air attack does not cause citizens to turn against their government. . . . In fact, in the more than thirty major strategic air campaigns that have thus far been waged, air power has never driven the masses into the streets to demand anything."[66] Furthermore, modern industrial economies are not fragile structures that can be easily destroyed, even by massive bombing attacks. To paraphrase Adam Smith, there is a lot of room for ruin in a great power's economy. This targeting strategy makes even less sense against minor powers, because they invariably have small industrial bases.

But what about decapitation? As noted, that strategy failed against Iraq in 1991. It was also tried on three other occasions, none of which are included in the previous discussion because they were such small-scale attacks. Nevertheless, the strategy failed all three times to produce the desired results. On April 14, 1986, the United States bombed the tent of Muammar Qaddafi. The Libyan leader's young daughter was killed, but he escaped harm. It is widely believed that the terrorist bombing of Pan Am flight 103 over Scotland two years later was retribution for that failed assassination attempt. On April 21, 1996, the Russians targeted and killed Dzhokhar Dudayev, the leader of rebel forces in the province of Chechnya.

The aim was to coerce the Chechens into settling their secessionist war with Russia on terms that were favorable to the Kremlin. In fact, the rebels vowed to avenge Dudayev's death, and a few months later (August 1996) the Russian troops were forced out of Chechnya. Finally, the United States launched a brief four-day attack against Iraq in December 1998. "Operation Desert Fox," as the effort was code-named, was another attempt to decapitate Saddam; it failed.[67]

Decapitation is a fanciful strategy.[68] The case of Dudayev notwithstanding, it especially difficult in wartime to locate and kill a rival political leader. But even if decapitation happens, it is unlikely that the successor's politics will be substantially different from those of the dead predecessor. This strategy is based on the deep-seated American belief that hostile states are essentially comprised of benign citizens controlled by evil leaders. Remove the evil leader, the thinking goes, and the forces of good will triumph and the war will quickly end. This is not a promising strategy. Killing a particular leader does not guarantee that one of his closest lieutenants will not replace him. For example, had the Allies managed to kill Adolf Hitler, they probably would have gotten Martin Bormann or Hermann Goering as his replacement, neither of whom would have been much, if any, improvement over Hitler. Furthermore, evil leaders like Hitler often enjoy widespread popular support: not only do they sometimes represent the views of their body politic, but nationalism tends to foster close ties between political leaders and their populations, especially in wartime, when all concerned face a powerful external threat.[69]

The variant of the strategy that calls for isolating the political leadership from the broader population is also illusory. Leaders have multiple channels for communicating with their people, and it is virtually impossible for an air force to knock all of them out at once and keep them shut down for a long period of time. For example, bombers might be well-suited for damaging an adversary's telecommunications, but they are ill-suited for knocking out newspapers. They are also ill-suited for destroying the secret police and other instruments of suppression. Finally, causing coups that produce friendly leaders in enemy states during wartime is an extremely difficult task.

Isolating a political leader from his military forces is equally impractical. The key to success in this variant of the strategy is to sever the lines of communication between the battlefield and the political leadership. There are two reasons why this strategy is doomed to fail, however. Leaders have multiple channels for communicating with their military, as well as with their population, and bombers are not likely to shut them all down simultaneously, much less keep them all silent for a long time. Moreover, political leaders worried about this problem can delegate authority in advance to the appropriate military commanders, in the event that the lines of communication are cut. During the Cold War, for example, both superpowers planned for that contingency because of their fear of nuclear decapitation.

It seems clear from the historical record that blockades and strategic bombing occasionally affect the outcome of great-power wars but rarely play a decisive role in shaping the final result. Armies and the air and naval forces that support them are mainly responsible for determining which side wins a great-power war. Land power is the most formidable kind of conventional military power available to states.[70] In fact, it is a rare event when a war between great powers is not settled largely by rival armies fighting it out on the battlefield. Although some of the relevant history has been discussed in the preceding sections and chapters, a brief overview of the great-power wars since 1792 shows that wars are won on the ground.

THE DOMINATING INFLUENCE OF ARMIES

There have been ten wars between great powers over the past two centuries, three of which were central wars involving all of the great powers: the French Revolutionary and Napoleonic Wars (1792–1815), World War I (1914–18), and World War II (1939–45); the latter actually involved distinct conflicts in Asia and Europe.

In the wake of the French Revolution, France fought a series of wars over twenty-three years against different coalitions of European great powers, including Austria, Prussia, Russia, and the United Kingdom. The out-come of almost every campaign was determined by battles between rival armies, not battles at sea. Consider, for example, the impact of the famous naval Battle of Trafalgar on the course of the war. The British navy deci-sively defeated the French fleet in that engagement on October 21, 1805, one day after Napoleon had won a major victory against Austria in the Battle of Ulm. Britain's victory at sea, however, had little effect on Napoleon's fortunes. Indeed, over the course of the next two years, Napoleon's armies achieved their greatest triumphs, defeating the Austrians and the Russians at Austerlitz (1805), the Prussians at Jena and Auerstadt (1806), and the Russians at Friedland (1807).[71]

Furthermore, the United Kingdom blockaded the European continent and Napoleon blockaded the United Kingdom. But neither blockade markedly influenced the war's outcome. In fact, the United Kingdom was eventually forced to send an army to the continent to fight against Napoleon's army in Spain. That British army and, even more important, the Russian army that decimated the French army in the depths of Russia in 1812 were largely responsible for putting Napoleon out of business.

The balance of land power was also the principal determinant of victory in World War I. In particular, the outcome was decided by long and costly battles on the eastern front between German and Russian armies, and on the western front between German and Allied (British, French, and American) forces. The Germans scored a stunning victory in the east in October 1917, when the Russian army collapsed and Russia quit the war. The Germans almost duplicated that feat on the western front in the spring of 1918, but the British, French, and American armies held fast; shortly thereafter the German army fell apart, and with that the war ended on November 11, 1918. Strategic bombing played hardly any role in the final outcome. The Anglo-American blockade of Germany surely contributed to the victory, but it was a secondary factor. "The Great War," as it was later called, was settled main-ly by the millions of soldiers on both sides who fought and often died in bloody battles at places like Verdun, Tannenberg, Passchendaele, and the Somme.

The outcome of World War II in Europe was determined largely by bat-tles fought between rival armies and their supporting air and naval forces.

Nazi land power was almost exclusively responsible for the tidal wave of early German victories: against Poland in September 1939, France and the United Kingdom between May and June 1940, and the Soviet Union between June and December 1941. The tide turned against the Third Reich in early 1942, and by May 1945, Hitler was dead and his successors had surrendered unconditionally. The Germans were beaten decisively on the battlefield, mainly on the eastern front by the Red Army, which lost a staggering eight million soldiers in the process but managed to cause at least three out of every four German wartime casualties.[72] British and American armies also helped wear down the Wehrmacht, but they played a considerably smaller role than the Soviet army, mainly because they did not land on French soil until June 1944, less than a year before the war ended.

The Allies' strategic bombing campaign failed to cripple the German economy until early 1945, when the war's outcome had already been settled on the ground. Nevertheless, airpower alone did not wreck Germany's industrial base; the Allied armies closing in on the Third Reich also played a major role in that effort. The British and American navies imposed a blockade on the Third Reich, but it, too, had a minor impact on the war's outcome. In short, the only way to defeat a formidable continental power like Nazi Germany is to smash its army in bloody land battles and conquer it. Blockades and strategic bombing might help the cause somewhat, but they are likely to matter primarily on the margins.

Americans tend to think that the Asian half of World War II began when Pearl Harbor was attacked on December 7, 1941. But Japan had been on the warpath in Asia since 1931 and had conquered Manchuria, much of northern China, and parts of Indochina before the United States entered the war. Immediately after Pearl Harbor, the Japanese military conquered most of Southeast Asia, and virtually all of the islands in the western half of the Pacific Ocean. Japan's army was its principal instrument of conquest, although its navy often transported the army into combat. Japan conducted a strategic bombing campaign against China, but it was a clear-cut failure (as discussed earlier in this chapter). Also, starting in 1938, Japan tried to cut off China's access to the outside world with a blockade, which reduced the flow of arms and goods into China to a trickle by 1942. Nevertheless, China's armies continued to hold their own on the battlefield, refusing to surrender to their Japanese foes.[73] In short, land power was the key to Japan's military successes in World War II.

The tide turned against Japan in June 1942, when the American navy scored a stunning victory over the Japanese navy at the Battle of Midway. Over the next three years, Japan was worn down in a protracted two-front war, finally surrendering unconditionally in August 1945. As noted earlier, land power played a critical role in defeating Japan. The U.S. navy's blockade of the Japanese homeland, however, was also a deciding factor in that conflict. The firebombing of Japan, including Hiroshima and Nagasaki, certainly caused tremendous suffering in the targeted cities, but it played only a minor role in causing Japan's defeat. This is the only great-power war in modern history in which land power alone was not principally responsible for determining the outcome, and in which one of the coercive instruments—airpower or sea power—played more than an auxiliary role.

Seven other great power vs. great power wars have been fought over the past two hundred years: the Crimean War (1853–56), the War of Italian Unification (1859), the Austro-Prussian War (1866), the Franco-Prussian War (1870–71), the Russo-Japanese War (1904–5), the Russian Civil War (1918–21), and the Soviet-Japanese War (1939). None of these cases involved strategic bombing, and only the Russo-Japanese War had a significant naval dimension, although neither side blockaded the other. The rival navies mainly fought for command of the sea, which was important because whichever side dominated the water had an advantage in moving land forces about the theater of operations.[74] All seven conflicts were settled between rival armies on the battlefield.

Finally, the outcome of a major conventional conflict during the Cold War would have been determined in large part by events on the central front, where NATO and Warsaw Pact armies would have clashed head-on. For sure, the tactical air forces supporting those armies would have influenced developments on the ground. Still, the war would have been decided largely by how well the rival armies performed against each other. Neither side would have mounted a strategic bombing campaign against the other, mainly because the advent of nuclear weapons rendered that mission moot. Furthermore, there was no serious possibility of the NATO allies using independent naval power to their advantage, mainly because the Soviet Union was not vulnerable to blockade as Japan was in World War II.[75] Soviet submarines probably would have tried to cut the sea lines of communication between the United States and Europe, but they surely would have failed, just as the Germans had in both world wars. As was the case with Napoleonic France, Wilhelmine Germany, and Nazi Germany, a hegemonic war with the Soviet Union would have been settled on the ground by clashing armies.

THE STOPPING POWER OF WATER

There is one especially important aspect of land power that merits further elaboration: how large bodies of water sharply limit an army's power-projection capability. Water is usually not a serious obstacle for a navy that is transporting ground forces across an ocean and landing them in a friendly state. But water is a forbidding barrier when a navy attempts to deliver an army onto territory controlled and well-defended by a rival great power. Navies are therefore at a significant disadvantage when attempting amphibious operations against powerful land-based forces, which are likely to throw the seaborne invaders back into the sea. Generally speaking, land assaults across a common border are a much easier undertaking. Armies that have to traverse a large body of water to attack a well-armed opponent invariably have little offensive capability.

Why Water Stymies Armies

The basic problem that navies face when conducting seaborne invasions is that there are significant limits on the number of troops and the amount of firepower that a navy can bring to bear in an amphibious operation.[76] Thus, it is difficult for navies to insert onto enemy shores assault forces that are powerful enough to overwhelm the defending troops. The specific nature of this problem varies from the age of sail to the industrial age.[77]

Before the 1850s, when ships were powered by sail, navies were considerably more mobile than armies. Not only did armies have to negotiate obstacles such as mountains, forests, swamps, and deserts, they also did not have access to good roads, much less railroads or motorized vehicles. Land-based armies therefore moved slowly, which meant that they had considerable difficulty defending a coastline against a seaborne invasion. Navies that commanded the sea, on the other hand, could move swiftly about the ocean's surface and land troops on a rival's coast well before a land-based army could get to the beachhead to challenge the landing. Since amphibious landings were relatively easy to pull off in the age of sail, great powers hardly ever launched amphibious assaults against each other's territory; instead they landed where the opponent had no large forces. In fact, no amphibious assaults were carried out in Europe from the founding of the state system in 1648 until steam ships began replacing sailing ships in the mid-nineteenth century.

Despite the relative ease of landing troops in enemy territory, navies were not capable of putting large forces ashore and supporting them for long periods. Sailing navies had limited carrying capacity, and thus they were rarely capable of providing the logistical support that the invading forces needed to survive in hostile territory.[78] Nor could navies quickly bring in reinforcements with the necessary supplies. Furthermore, the enemy army, which was fighting on its own territory, would eventually reach the amphibious force and was likely to defeat it in battle. Consequently, great powers in the age of sail launched remarkably few amphibious landings in Europe against either the homeland of rival great powers or territory controlled by them. In fact, there were none during the two centuries prior to the start of the Napoleonic Wars in 1792, despite the fact that Europe's great powers were constantly at war with each other during that long period.[79] The only two amphibious landings in Europe during the age of sail were the Anglo-Russian operation in Holland (1799) and the British invasion of Portugal (1808). The seaborne forces were defeated in both cases, as discussed below.

The industrialization of war in the nineteenth century made large-scale amphibious invasions more feasible, but they remained an especially formidable task against a well-armed opponent.[80] From the invader's perspective, the most favorable development was that new, steam-driven navies had greater carrying capacity than sailing navies, and they were not beholden to the prevailing wind patterns. Consequently, steam-driven navies could land greater numbers of troops on enemy beaches and sustain them there for longer periods of time than could their predecessors. "Steam navigation," Lord Palmerston warned in 1845, had "rendered that which was before unpassable by a military force [the English Channel] nothing more than a river passable by a steam bridge."[81]

But Palmerston greatly exaggerated the threat of invasion to the United Kingdom, as there were other technological developments that worked against the seaborne forces. In particular, the development of airplanes, submarines, and naval mines increased the difficulty of reaching enemy shores, while the development of airplanes and railroads (and later, paved roads, trucks, and tanks) made it especially difficult for amphibious forces to prevail after they put ashore.

Railroads, which began spreading across Europe and the United States in the mid-nineteenth century, played an important role in the German wars of unification against Austria (1866) and France (1870–71), and in the American Civil War (1861–65).[82] Amphibious forces hardly benefit from railroads as they move across large bodies of water. Also, seaborne forces cannot bring railroads with them, and it is difficult to capture and make use of enemy railroads—at least in the short term. Railroads, however, markedly increase a land-based army's ability to defeat an amphibious operation, because they allow the defender to rapidly concentrate large forces at or near the landing sites. Armies on rails also arrive on the battlefield in excellent physical shape, because they avoid the wear and tear that comes with marching on foot. Furthermore, railroads are an excellent tool for sustaining an army locked in combat with an amphibious force. For these same reasons, the development in the early 1900s of paved roads and motorized as well as mechanized vehicles further advantaged the land-based army against the seaborne invader.

Although airplanes were first used in combat in the 1910s, it was not until the 1920s and 1930s that navies began developing aircraft carriers that could be used to support amphibious operations.[83] Nevertheless, the territorial state under assault benefits far more from airpower than do the amphibious forces, because many more aircraft can be based on land than on a handful of aircraft carriers.[84] A territorial state is essentially a huge aircraft carrier that can accommodate endless numbers of airplanes, whereas an actual carrier can accommodate only a small number of air-planes. Therefore, other things being equal, the territorial state should be able to control the air and use that advantage to pound the amphibious forces on the beaches, or even before they reach the beaches. Of course, the seaborne force can ameliorate this problem if it can rely on land-based aircraft of its own. For example, the assault forces at Normandy in June 1944 relied heavily on aircraft stationed in England.

Land-based air forces also have the capability to sink a rival navy. It is actually dangerous to place naval forces near the coast of a great power that has a formidable air force. Between March and December 1942, for example, Allied convoys sailing between British and Icelandic ports and the Soviet port of Murmansk passed close to Norway, where substantial German air forces were located. Those land-based aircraft wreaked havoc on the convoys until late 1942, when German airpower in the region was substantially reduced.[85] Thus, even if a navy commands the sea, it cannot go near a territorial state unless it also commands the air, which is difficult to achieve with aircraft carriers alone, because land-based air forces usual-ly outnumber sea-based air forces by a large margin.

Submarines were also employed for the first time in World War I, mainly by Germany against Allied shipping in the waters around the United Kingdom and in the Atlantic.[86] Although the German submarine campaign ultimately failed, it demonstrated that a large submarine force could destroy unescorted merchant ships with relative ease. German sub-marines also seriously threatened the United Kingdom's formidable sur-face navy, which spent the war playing a cat-and-mouse game in the North Sea with the German navy. In fact, the commanders of the British fleet lived in constant fear of German submarines, even when they were in home port. But they were especially fearful of venturing into the North Sea and being drawn near the German coast, where submarines might be lying in wait. "The submarine danger," as naval historian Paul Halpern notes, "had indeed contributed the most toward making the North Sea for capital ships somewhat similiar to the no-man's-land between the opposing trench systems on land. They would be risked there, but only for specific purposes."[87] The submarine threat to surface ships has important implications for navies bent on launching amphibious assaults against a rival's coast. In particular, an opponent with a formidable submarine force could sink the assaulting forces before they reached the beaches or sink much of the striking navy after the assaulting forces had landed, thereby stranding the seaborne troops on the beaches.

Finally, naval mines, fixed explosives that sit under the water and explode when struck by passing ships, increase the difficulty of invading a territorial state from the sea.[88] Navies used mines effectively for the first time in the American Civil War, but they were first employed on a massive scale during World War I. The combatants laid down roughly 240,000 mines between 1914 and 1918, and they shaped the course of the war in important ways.[89] Surface ships simply cannot pass unharmed through heavily mined waters; the minefields must be cleared first, and this is a difficult, sometimes impossible, task in wartime. A territorial state can therefore use mines effectively to defend its coast against invasion. Iraq, for example, mined the waters off the Kuwaiti coast before the United States and its allies began to amass forces to invade in the Persian Gulf War. When the ground war started on February 24, 1991, the U.S. marines did not storm the Kuwaiti beaches but remained on their ships in the gulf.[90]

Although amphibious operations against a land mass controlled by a great power are especially difficult to pull off, they are feasible under special circumstances. In particular, they are likely to work against a great power that is on the verge of catastrophic defeat, mainly because the victim is not going to possess the wherewithal to defend itself. Furthermore, they are likely to succeed against great powers that are defending huge expanses of territory. In such cases, the defender's troops are likely to be widely dispersed, leaving their territory vulnerable to attack somewhere on the periphery. In fact, uncontested amphibious landings are possible if a defending great power's forces are stretched thinly enough. It is especially helpful if the defender is fighting a two-front war, because then some sizable portion of its force will be pinned down on a front far away from the seaborne assault.[91] In all cases, the invading force should have clear-cut air superiority over the landing sites, so that its air force can provide close air support and prevent enemy reinforcements from reaching the beachheads.[92]

But if none of these circumstances applies and the defending great power can employ a substantial portion of its military might against the amphibious forces, the land-based forces are almost certain to inflict a devastating defeat on the seaborne invaders. Therefore, when surveying the historical record, we should expect to find cases of amphibious operations directed against a great power only when the special circumstances described above apply. Assaults from the sea against powerful land forces should be rare indeed.

The History of Amphibious Operations

A brief survey of the history of seaborne invasions provides ample evidence of the stopping power of water. There is no case in which a great power launched an amphibious assault against territory that was well-defended by another great power. Before World War I, some British naval planners argued for invading Germany from the sea at the outset of a general European war.[93] That idea, however, was considered suicidal by military planners and civilian policymakers alike. Corbett surely reflected mainstream thinking on the matter when he wrote in 1911, "Defeat the enemy's fleet as we may, he will be but little the worse. We shall have opened the way for invasion, but any of the great continental powers can laugh at our attempts to invade single-handed."[94] German chancellor Otto von Bismarck apparently did just that when asked how he would respond if the British army landed on the German coastline. He reportedly replied that he would "call out the local police and have it arrested!"[95] The United Kingdom did not seriously contemplate invading Germany either before or after World War I broke out but instead convoyed its army to France, where it took its place on the western front alongside the French army. The United Kingdom followed a similiar strategy after Germany invaded Poland on September 1, 1939.

During the Cold War, the United States and its allies never seriously considered launching an amphibious attack against the Soviet Union.[96] Moreover, American policymakers recognized during the Cold War that if the Soviet army had overrun Western Europe, it would have been almost impossible for the U.S. and British armies to launch a second Normandy invasion to get back on the European continent.[97] In all likelihood, the Soviet Union would not have faced a two-front war, and thus it would have been able to concentrate almost all of its best divisions in France. Moreover, the Soviets would have had a formidable air force to use against the invading forces.

Virtually all of the cases in modern history of amphibious assaults launched against territory controlled by a great power occurred under the special circumstances specified above. During the French Revolutionary and Napoleonic Wars (1792–1815), for example, the British navy conducted two amphibious landings and one amphibious assault into territory controlled by France. Both landings ultimately failed, although the assault was a success.

Great Britain and Russia landed amphibious troops in French-dominated Holland on August 27, 1799.[98] Their aim was to force France, which was already locked in combat with Austrian and Russian armies in the center of Europe, to fight a two-front war. However, shortly after the Anglo-Russian forces landed in Holland to open up the second front, France won key victories on the other front. Austria then quit the war, leaving France free to concentrate its military might against the invasion forces, which were poorly equipped and supplied from the start (this was the age of sail). To avoid disaster, the British and Russian armies did an about-face and tried to exit Holland by sea. But they failed to get off the continent and were forced to surrender to the French army on October 18, 1799, less than two months after the initial landing.

The second amphibious landing took place along the Portuguese coast in August 1808, at a time when Napoleon's military machine was deeply involved in neighboring Spain.[99] Portugal was then under the control of a small and weak French army, which made it possible for the United Kingdom to land troops on a strip of coastline controlled by friendly Portuguese fighters. The British invasion force pushed the French army out of Portugal and then moved into Spain to engage the main French armies on the Iberian Peninsula. Badly mauled by Napoleon's forces, the British army had to evacuate Spain by sea in January 1809, six months after landing in Portugal.[100] In both cases, the initial landings were possible because the main body of French troops was engaged elsewhere and the British navy was able to find safe landing sites in otherwise hostile territory. Once the amphibious forces were confronted with powerful French forces, however, they quickly headed for the beaches.

The British military launched a successful amphibious assault against French forces at Aboukir, Egypt, on March 8, 1801. The defenders were actually the remnants of the army that Napoleon had brought to Egypt in the summer of 1798.[101] The British navy had soon thereafter severed that army's lines of communication with Europe, dooming it to eventual destruction. Recognizing the bleak strategic situation facing him, Napoleon snuck back to France in August 1798. Thus, by the time Britain invaded Egypt in 1801, the French forces there had been withering on the vine for almost three years and were in poor shape to fight a war. Moreover, they were led by an especially incompetent commander. Thus, Britain's assault forces faced a less-than-formidable adversary in Egypt. In fact, the French army made little effort to defend the beaches at Aboukir and performed poorly in subsequent battles with British troops. French forces in Egypt surrendered on September 2, 1801.

The Crimean War (1853–56) is one of two cases in modern history in which a great power invaded the homeland of another great power from the sea (the Allied invasion of Sicily in July 1943 is the other case). In September 1854, roughly 53,000 British and French troops landed on the Crimean Peninsula, a remote piece of Russian territory that jutted into the Black Sea.[102] Their aim was to challenge Russian control of the Black Sea by capturing the Russian naval base at Sevastopol, which was defended by about 45,000 Russian troops.[103] The operation was an amphibious landing, not an amphibious assault. The Anglo-French forces put ashore approximately fifty miles north of Sevastopol, where they met no Russian resistance until after they had established a beachhead and moved well inland. Despite considerable British and French ineptitude, Sevastopol fell in September 1855. Russia lost the war soon thereafter; a peace treaty was signed in Paris in early 1856.

A number of exceptional circumstances account for the Crimean case. First, the United Kingdom and France threatened Russia in two widely separated theaters: the Baltic Sea and the Black Sea. But because the Baltic Sea was close to Russia's most important cities, and the Black Sea was far away from them, Russia kept most of its army near the Baltic Sea. Even after British and French troops landed in the Crimea, Russian forces in the Baltic region remained put. Second, the possibility of an Austrian attack against Poland pinned down additional Russian troops that might have otherwise been sent to the Crimea. Third, the communications and transportation network in mid-nineteenth-century Russia was primitive, and therefore it was difficult for Russia to supply its forces around Sevastopol. Field Marshal Helmuth von Moltke, the architect of Prussia's victories against Austria (1866) and France (1870–71), opined, "If Russia had had a railway to Sevastopol in 1856, the war would certainly have had a different outcome."[104] Finally, the United Kingdom and France had limited aims in the Crimea: they did not seriously threaten to enlarge their foothold there, and they certainly did not threaten to move north and inflict a decisive defeat on Russia. Only a British and French seaborne assault across the Baltic Sea might have led to a major Russian defeat. However, Russia kept sufficient forces in the Baltic region to deter such an attack.

During World War I, no seaborne invasions were carried out against territory controlled by Germany or any other great power. The disastrous Gallipoli campaign was the only major amphibious operation of the war.[105] British and French forces attempted to capture the Gallipoli Peninsula, which was part of Turkey and was of critical importance for gaining access to the Black Sea. Turkey was not a great power, but it was allied with Germany, although German troops did not fight with the Turks. Nevertheless, the Turks contained the attacking Allied forces in their beachheads and eventually forced them to withdraw by sea from Gallipoli.

Numerous amphibious operations took place in World War II against territory controlled by a great power. In the European theater, British and American forces launched five major seaborne assaults.[106] Allied forces invaded Sicily in July 1943, when Italy was still in the war (although barely), and the Italian mainland in September 1943, just after Italy quit the war.[107] Both invasions were successful. After conquering southern Italy, the Allies mounted a large-scale invasion at Anzio in January 1944.[108] The aim was to turn the German army's flank by landing a large seaborne force about fifty-five miles behind German lines. Although the landings went smoothly, the Anzio operation was a failure. The Wehrmacht pinned down the assaulting forces in their landing zones, where they remained until the German army began retreating northward toward Rome. The final two invasions were against German forces occupying France: Normandy in June 1944 and southern France in August 1944. Both were successful and contributed to the downfall of Nazi Germany.[109]

Leaving Anzio aside for the moment, the other four seaborne assaults were successful in part because the Allies enjoyed overwhelming air superiority in each case, which meant that the landing forces but not the defending forces were directly supported by flying artillery. Allied airpower was also used to thwart the movement of German reinforcements to the landing areas, which provided time for the Allies to build up their forces before they had to engage the Wehrmacht's main units. Furthermore, Germany, which was occupying and defending Italy and France when these invasions occurred, was fighting a two-front war and the majority of its forces were pinned down on the eastern front.[110] The German armies in Italy and France also had to cover vast stretches of coastline, so they had to spread their forces out, leaving them vulnerable to Allied amphibious assaults, which were concentrated at particular points along those coasts. Imagine the Normandy invasion against a Wehrmacht that controlled the skies above France and was not at war with the Soviet Union: the Allies would not have dared invade.

The successful landing at Anzio was due to these same factors: decisive air superiority and limited German resistance at the landing sites. The Allies, however, did not move quickly to exploit this initial advantage and score a stunning success. Not only were they slow to move inland from their beacheads, but Allied airpower failed to prevent the Wehrmacht from moving powerful forces to the landing areas, where they were able to contain the invasion force. Moreover, no effort was made to bring in reinforcements to strengthen the initial landing force, mainly because the Anzio operation did not matter much for the outcome of the Italian campaign.

Amphibious operations in the Pacific theater during World War II fall into two categories. In the six months immediately after Pearl Harbor, Japan conducted roughly fifty amphibious landings and assaults in the western Pacific against territory defended mainly by British but also by American troops.[111] The targets included Malaysia, British Borneo, Hong Kong, the Philippines, Timor, Java, Sumatra, and New Guinea, to name just a few. Almost all of these amphibious operations were successful, leaving Japan with a vast island empire by mid-1942. Japan's amphibious successes were due to the special circumstances described above: air superiority over the landing sites, and weak and isolated Allied forces that were incapable of defending the lengthy coastlines assigned to them.[112]

The U.S. military conducted fifty-two amphibious invasions against Japanese-held islands in the Pacific during World War II.[113] Those campaigns were essential for destroying the island empire Japan had built earlier in the war with its own amphibious operations. Some of the American invasions were small in scale, and many were unopposed landings. Others, such as that at Okinawa, turned deadly when the invading forces moved inland and encountered strong Japanese resistance. Some, such as Tarawa, Saipan, and Iwo Jima, involved major seaborne assaults against heavily defended beaches. Virtually all of these seaborne invasions were successful, although the price of victory was sometimes high.

This impressive record was due in part to American air superiority. As the U.S. Strategic Bombing Survey notes, "Our series of landing operations were always successful because air domination was always established in the objective area before a landing was attempted."[114] Control of the air not only meant that the invading American forces had close air support, while the Japanese had none, but it also allowed the United States to concentrate its forces against particular islands on the perimeter of Japan's Pacific empire and cut the flow of supplies and reinforcements to those outposts.[115] "Thus, the perimeter defense points became isolated, nonreinforceable garrisons—each subject to individual destruction in detail."[116] Furthermore, Japan was fighting a two-front war and only a small portion of its army was located on those Pacific islands; most of its army was located on the Asian mainland and in Japan itself.

Finally, it is worth noting that the United States was making plans to invade Japan when World War II ended in August 1945. There is little doubt that American seaborne forces would have assaulted Japan's main islands if it had not surrendered, and that the invasion would have been successful.

Amphibious operations against Japan were feasible in late 1945 because Japan was a fatally crippled great power, and the assault forces essentially would have delivered the coup de grâce. From the Battle of Midway in June 1942 through the capture of Okinawa in June 1945, the U.S. military had devastated Japanese forces in the Pacific.[117] By the summer of 1945, Japan's Pacific empire was in ruins and the remnants of its once-formidable navy were largely useless against the American military machine. The Japanese economy, which had been only about one-eighth the size of the American economy at the start of World War II, was in shambles by the spring of 1945.[118] Furthermore, by the summer of 1945, Japan's air force, like its navy, was wrecked, which meant that American planes dominated the skies over Japan. All Japan had left to defend its homeland was its army. But even here fortune smiled on the United States, because more than half of Japan's ground units were stuck on the Asian mainland, where they would not be able to affect the American invasion.[119] In short, Japan was a great power in name only by the summer of 1945, and thus it was feasible for American policymakers to countenance an invasion. Even so, they were deeply committed to avoiding an amphibious assault against Japan itself, because they feared high numbers of casualties.[120]

Continental vs. Insular Great Powers

The historical record illustrates in another way the difficulty of assaulting a great power's territory from the sea compared to invading it over land. Specifically, one can distinguish between *insular* and *continental* states. An insular state is the only great power on a large body of land that is surrounded on all sides by water. There can be other great powers on the planet, but they must be separated from the insular state by major bodies of water. The United Kingdom and Japan are obvious examples of insular states, since each occupies a large island by itself. The United States is also an insular power, because it is the only great power in the Western Hemisphere. A continental state, on the other hand, is a great power located on a large body of land that is also occupied by one or more other great powers. France, Germany, and Russia are obvious examples of continental states.

Insular great powers can be attacked only over water, whereas continental powers can be attacked over land and over water, provided they are not landlocked.[121] Given the stopping power of water, one would expect insular states to be much less vulnerable to invasion than continental states, and continental states to have been invaded across land far more often than across water. To test this argument, let us briefly consider the history of two insular great powers, the United Kingdom and the United States, and two continental great powers, France and Russia, focusing on how many times each has been invaded by another state, and whether those invasions were by land or sea.

Until 1945, the United Kingdom had been a great power for more than four centuries, during which time it was involved in countless wars. Over that long period, however, it was never invaded by another great power, much less a minor power.[122] For sure, adversaries sometimes threatened to send invasion forces across the English Channel, yet none ever launched the assault boats. Spain, for example, planned to invade England in 1588. But the defeat of the the Spanish Armada that same year in waters off England's coast eliminated the naval forces that were supposed to have escorted the Spanish army across the English Channel.[123] Although both

Napoleon and Hitler considered invading the United Kingdom, neither made an attempt.[124]

Like the United Kingdom, the United States has not been invaded since it became a great power in 1898.[125] Britain launched a handful of large-scale raids against American territory during the War of 1812, and Mexico raided Texas in the War of 1846–48. Those conflicts, however, took place long before the United States achieved great-power status, and even then, neither the United Kingdom nor Mexico seriously threatened to conquer the United States.[126] More important, there has been no serious threat to invade the United States since it became a great power at the end of the nineteenth century. In fact, the United States is probably the most secure great power in history, mainly because it has always been separated from the world's other great powers by two giant moats—the Atlantic and Pacific Oceans.

The story looks substantially different when the focus shifts to France and Russia. France has been invaded seven times by rival armies since 1792, and it was conquered three of those times. During the French Revolutionary and Napoleonic Wars (1792–1815), rival armies attacked France on four separate occasions (1792, 1793, 1813, and 1815), finally inflicting a decisive defeat on Napoleon with the last invasion. France was invaded and defeated by Prussia in 1870–71 and was paid another visit by the German army in 1914, although France narrowly escaped defeat in World War I. Germany struck once again in 1940, and this time it conquered France. All seven of these invasions came across land; France has never been invaded from the sea.[127]

Russia, the other continental state, has been invaded five times over the past two centuries. Napoleon drove to Moscow in 1812, and France and the United Kingdom assaulted the Crimean Peninsula in 1854. Russia was invaded and decisively defeated by the German army in World War I. Shortly thereafter, in 1921, Poland, which was not a great power, invaded the newly established Soviet Union. The Germans invaded again in the summer of 1941, beginning one of the most murderous military campaigns in recorded history. All of these invasions came across land, save for the Anglo-French attack in the Crimea.[128]

In sum, neither of our insular great powers (the United Kingdom and the United States) has ever been invaded, whereas our continental great powers (France and Russia) have been invaded a total of twelve times since 1792. These continental states were assaulted across land eleven times, but only once from the sea. The apparent lesson is that large bodies of water make it extremely difficult for armies to invade territory defended by a well-armed great power.

The discussion so far has focused on conventional military forces, emphasizing that land power is more important than either independent naval power or strategic airpower for winning great-power wars. Little has been said, however, about how nuclear weapons affect military power.

NUCLEAR WEAPONS AND THE BALANCE OF POWER

Nuclear weapons are revolutionary in a purely military sense, simply because they can cause unprecedented levels of destruction in short periods of time.[129] During much of the Cold War, for example, the United States and the Soviet Union had the capability to destroy each other as functioning societies in a matter of days, if not hours. Nevertheless, there is little agreement about how nuclear weapons affect great-power politics and, in particular, the balance of power. Some argue that nuclear weapons effectively eliminate great-power security competition, because nuclear-armed states would not dare attack each other for fear of annihilation. The preceding discussion of conventional military power, according to this perspective, is largely irrelevant in the nuclear age. But others make the opposite argument: because nuclear weapons are horribly destructive, no rational leader would ever use them, even in self-defense. Thus, nuclear weapons do not dampen security competition in any significant way, and the balance of conventional military power still matters greatly.

I argue that in the unlikely event that a single great power achieves nuclear superiority, it becomes a hegemon, which effectively means that it has no great-power rivals with which to compete for security. Conventional forces matter little for the balance of power in such a world. But in the more likely situation in which there are two or more great powers with survivable nuclear retaliatory forces, security competition between them will continue and land power will remain the key component of military power. There is no question, however, that the presence of nuclear weapons makes states more cautious about using military force of any kind against each other.

Nuclear Superiority

In its boldest and most well-known form, nuclear superiority exists when a great power has the capability to destroy an adversary's society without fear of major retaliation against its own society. In other words, nuclear superiority means that a state can turn a rival great power into "a smoking, radiating ruin" and yet remain largely unscathed itself.[130] That state could also use its nuclear arsenal to destroy its adversary's conventional forces, again without fear of nuclear retaliation. The best way for a state to achieve nuclear superiority is by arming itself with nuclear weapons while making sure no other state has them. A state with a nuclear monopoly, by definition, does not have to worry about retaliation in kind if it unleashes its nuclear weapons.

In a world of two or more nuclear-armed states, one state might gain superiority if it develops the capability to neutralize its rivals' nuclear weapons. To achieve this superiority, a state could either acquire a "splendid first strike" capability against its opponents' nuclear arsenals or develop the capability to defend itself from attack by their nuclear weapons.[131] Nuclear superiority does not obtain, however, simply because one state has significantly more nuclear weapons than another state. Such an asymmetry is largely meaningless as long as enough of the smaller nuclear arsenal can survive a first strike to inflict massive punishment on the state with the bigger arsenal.

Any state that achieves nuclear superiority over its rivals effectively becomes the only great power in the system, because the power advantage bestowed on that state would be tremendous. The nuclear hegemon could threaten to use its potent arsenal to inflict vast destruction on rival states, effectively eliminating them as functioning political entities. The potential victims would not be able to retaliate in kind—which is what makes this threat credible. The nuclear hegemon could also use its deadly weapons for military purposes, like striking large concentrations of enemy ground forces, air bases, naval ships, or key targets in the adversary's command-and-control system. Again, the target state would not have a commensurate capability, thereby giving the nuclear hegemon a decisive advantage, regardless of the balance of conventional forces.

Every great power would like to achieve nuclear superiority, but it is not likely to happen often, and when it does occur, it probably is not going to last for a long time.[132] Non-nuclear rivals are sure to go to great lengths to acquire nuclear arsenals of their own, and once they do, it would be difficult, although not impossible, for a great power to reestablish superiority by insulating itself from nuclear attack.[133] The United States, for example, had a monopoly on nuclear weapons from 1945 until 1949, but it did not have nuclear superiority in any meaningful sense during that brief period.[134] Not only was America's nuclear arsenal small during those years, but the Pentagon had not yet developed effective means for delivering it to the appropriate targets in the Soviet Union.

After the Soviet Union exploded a nuclear device in 1949, the United States tried, but failed, to gain nuclear superiority over its rival. Nor were the Soviets able to gain a decisive nuclear advantage over the Americans at any time during the Cold War. Thus, each side was forced to live with the fact that no matter how it employed its own nuclear forces, the other side was still likely to have a survivable nuclear retaliatory force that could inflict unacceptable damage on an attacker. This "Texas standoff" came to be called "mutual assured destruction" (MAD), because both sides probably would have been destroyed if either initiated a nuclear war. However desirable it might be for any state to transcend MAD and establish nuclear superiority, it is unlikely to happen in the foreseeable future.[135]

Military Power in a MAD World

A MAD world is highly stable at the nuclear level, because there is no incentive for any great power to start a nuclear war that it could not win; indeed, such a war would probably lead to its destruction as a functioning society. Still, the question remains: what effect does this balance of terror have on the prospects for a conventional war between nuclear-armed great powers? One school of thought maintains that it is so unlikely that nuclear weapons would be used in a MAD world that great powers are free to fight conventional wars almost as if nuclear weapons did not exist. Former secretary of defense Robert McNamara, for example, argues that "nuclear weapons serve no useful military purpose whatsoever. They are totally useless—except only to deter one's opponent from using them."[136] Nuclear weapons, according to this logic, have little effect on state behavior at the conventional level, and thus great powers are free to engage in security competition, much the way they did before nuclear weapons were invented.[137]

The problem with this perspective is that it is based on the assumption that great powers can be highly confident that a large-scale conventional war will not turn into a nuclear war. In fact, we do not know a great deal about the dynamics of escalation from the conventional to the nuclear level, because (thankfully) there is not much history to draw on. Nevertheless, an excellent body of scholarship holds that there is some reasonable chance that a conventional war among nuclear powers might escalate to the nuclear level.[138] Therefore, great powers operating in a MAD world are likely to be considerably more cautious when contemplating a conventional war with one another than they would be in the absence of nuclear weapons.

A second school of thought argues that great powers in a MAD world have little reason to worry about the conventional balance because nuclear-armed great powers are simply not going to attack each other with conventional forces because of fear of nuclear escalation.[139] Great powers are remarkably secure in a MAD world, so the argument goes, and thus there is no good reason for them to compete for security. Nuclear weapons have made great-power war virtually unthinkable and have thus rendered obsolete Carl von Clausewitz's dictum that war is an extension of politics by other means. In effect, the balance of terror has trivialized the balance of land power.

The problem with this perspective is that it goes to the other extreme on the escalation issue. In particular, it is based on the assumption that it is likely, if not automatic, that a conventional war would escalate to the nuclear level. Furthermore, it assumes that all the great powers think that conventional and nuclear war are part of a seamless web, and thus there is no meaningful distinction between the two kinds of conflict. But as the first school of thought emphasizes, the indisputable horror associated with nuclear weapons gives policymakers powerful incentives to ensure that conventional wars do not escalate to the nuclear level. Consequently, it is possible that a nuclear-armed great power might conclude that it could fight a conventional war against a nuclear-armed rival without the war turning nuclear, especially if the attacking power kept its goals limited and did not threaten to decisively defeat its opponent.[140] Once this possibility is recognized, great powers have no choice but to compete for security at the conventional level, much the way they did before the advent of nuclear weapons.

It is clear from the Cold War that great powers operating in a MAD world still engage in intense security competition, and that they care greatly about conventional forces, especially the balance of land power. The United States and the Soviet Union competed with each other for allies and bases all over the globe from the start of their rivalry after World War II until its finish some forty-five years later. It was a long and harsh struggle. Apparently, neither nine American presidents nor six Soviet leaderships bought the argument that they were so secure in a MAD world that they did not have to pay much attention to what happened outside their borders. Furthermore, despite their massive nuclear arsenals, both sides invested tremendous resources in their conventional forces, and both sides were deeply concerned about the balance of ground and air forces in Europe, as well as in other places around the globe.[141]

There is other evidence that casts doubt on the claim that states with an assured destruction capability are remarkably secure and do not have to worry much about fighting conventional wars. Most important, Egypt and Syria knew that Israel had nuclear weapons in 1973, but nevertheless they launched massive land offensives against Israel.[142] Actually, the Syrian offensive on the Golan Heights, located on Israel's doorstep, briefly opened the door for the Syrian army to drive into the heart of Israel. Fighting also broke out between China and the Soviet Union along the Ussuri River in the spring of 1969 and threatened to escalate into a full-blown war.[143] Both China and the Soviet Union had nuclear arsenals at the time. China attacked American forces in Korea in the fall of 1950, despite the fact that China had no nuclear weapons of its own and the United States had a nuclear arsenal, albeit a small one.

Relations between India and Pakistan over the past decade cast further doubt on the claim that nuclear weapons largely eliminate security competition between states and make them feel as though they have abundant security. Although both India and Pakistan have had nuclear weapons since the late 1980s, security competition between them has not disappeared. Indeed, they were embroiled in a serious crisis in 1990, and they fought a major border skirmish (involving more than a thousand battle deaths) in 1999.[144]

Finally, consider how Russia and the United States, who still maintain huge nuclear arsenals, think about conventional forces today. Russia's deep-seated opposition to NATO expansion shows that it fears the idea of NATO's conventional forces moving closer to its border. Russia obviously does not accept the argument that its powerful nuclear retaliatory force provides it with absolute security. The United States also seems to think that it has to worry about the conventional balance in Europe. After all, NATO expansion was predicated on the belief that Russia might someday try to conquer territory in central Europe. Moreover, the United States continues to insist that Russia observe the limits outlined in the Treaty on Conventional Armed Forces in Europe, signed on November 19, 1990, before the Soviet Union collapsed.

Thus, the balance of land power remains the central ingredient of military power in the nuclear age, although nuclear weapons undoubtedly make great-power war less likely. Now that the case for land power's primacy has been detailed, it is time to describe how to measure it.

MEASURING MILITARY POWER

Assessing the balance of land power involves a three-step process. First, the relative size and quality of the opposing armies must be estimated. It is important to consider the strength of those forces in peacetime as well as after mobilization, because states often maintain small standing armies that expand quickly in size when the ready reserves are called to active duty.

There is no simple way to measure the power of rival armies, mainly because their strength depends on a variety of factors, all of which tend to vary across armies: 1) the number of soldiers, 2) the quality of the soldiers, 3) the number of weapons, 4) the quality of the weaponry, and 5) how those soldiers and weapons are organized for war. Any good indicator of land power should account for all these inputs. Comparing the number of basic fighting units in opposing armies, be they brigades or divisions, is sometimes a sensible way of measuring ground balances, although it is essential to take into account significant quantitative and qualitative differences between those units.

During the Cold War, for example, it was difficult to assess the NATO–Warsaw Pact conventional balance, because there were substantial differences in the size and composition of the various armies on the central front.[145] To deal with this problem, the U.S. Defense Department devised the "armored division equivalent," or ADE, score as a basic measure of ground force capability. This ADE score was based mainly on an assessment of the quantity and quality of weaponry in each army.[146] Political scientist Barry Posen subsequently made an important refinement to this measure, which was a useful indicator of relative army strength in Europe.[147]

Although a number of studies have attempted to measure force balances in particular historical cases, no study available has systematically and carefully compared force levels in different armies over long periods of time. Consequently, there is no good database that can be tapped to measure military power over the past two centuries. Developing such a database would require an enormous effort and lies beyond the scope of this book. Therefore, when I assess the power of opposing armies in subsequent chapters, I cobble together the available data on the size and quality of the relevant armies and come up with rather rough indicators of military might. I start by counting the number of soldiers in each army, which is reasonably easy to do, and then attempt to account for the other four factors that affect army strength, which is a more difficult task.

The second step in assessing the balance of land power is to factor any air forces that support armies into the analysis.[148] We must assess the inventory of aircraft on each side, focusing on available numbers and quality. Pilot efficiency must also be taken into account as well as the strength of each side's 1) ground-based air defense systems, 2) reconnaissance capabilities, and 3) battle-management systems.

Third, we must consider the power-projection capability inherent in armies, paying special attention to whether large bodies of water limit an army's offensive capability. If there is such a body of water, and if an ally lies across it, one must assess the ability of navies to protect the movement of troops and supplies to and from that ally. But if a great power can cross the water only by directly assaulting territory on the other side of the water that is well-defended by a rival great power, the assessment of naval power is probably unnecessary, because such amphibious assaults are rarely possible. Thus the naval forces that might support that army are rarely useful, and hence judgments about their capabilities are rarely relevant to strategy. In those special circumstances where amphibious operations are feasible against a rival great power's territory, however, it is essential to assess the ability of the relevant navy to project seaborne forces ashore.

CONCLUSION

Armies, along with their supporting air and naval forces, are the paramount form of military power in the modern world. Large bodies of water, however, severely limit the power-projection capabilities of armies, and nuclear weapons markedly reduce the likelihood that great-power armies will clash. Nevertheless, even in a nuclear world, land power remains king.

This conclusion has two implications for stability among the great powers. The most dangerous states in the international system are continental powers with large armies. In fact, such states have initiated most of the past wars of conquest between great powers, and they have almost always attacked other continental powers, not insular powers, which are protected by the water surrounding them. This pattern is clearly reflected in European history over the past two centuries. During the years of almost constant warfare between 1792 and 1815, France was the main aggressor as it conquered or tried to conquer other continental powers such as Austria, Prussia, and Russia. Prussia attacked Austria in 1866, and although France declared war on Prussia in 1870, that decision was provoked by Prussia, which invaded and conquered France. Germany began World War I with the Schlieffen Plan, which aimed to knock France out of the war so that the Germans could then turn eastward and defeat Russia. Germany began World War II with separate land offensives against Poland (1939), France (1940), and the Soviet Union (1941). None of these aggressors attempted to invade either the United Kingdom or the United States. During the Cold War, the principal scenario that concerned NATO planners was a Soviet invasion of Western Europe.

In contrast, insular powers are unlikely to initiate wars of conquest against other great powers, because they would have to traverse a large body of water to reach their target. The same moats that protect insular powers also impede their ability to project power. Neither the United Kingdom nor the United States, for example, has ever seriously threatenened to conquer another great power. British policymakers did not contemplate starting a war against either Wilhelmine or Nazi Germany, and during the Cold War, American policymakers never seriously countenanced a war of conquest against the Soviet Union. Although the United Kingdom (and France) declared war against Russia in March 1854 and then invaded the Crimean Peninsula, the United Kingdom had no intention of conquering Russia. Instead, it entered an ongoing war between Turkey and Russia for the purpose of checking Russian expansion in the region around the Black Sea.

The Japanese attack against the United States at Pearl Harbor in December 1941 might appear to be another exception to this rule, since Japan is an insular state, and it struck first against another great power. However, Japan did not invade any part of the United States, and Japanese leaders certainly gave no thought to conquering it. Japan merely sought to establish an empire in the western Pacific by capturing the various islands located between it and Hawaii. Japan also initiated wars against Russia in 1904 and 1939, but in neither case did Japan invade Russia or even think about conquering it. Instead, those fights were essentially for control of Korea, Manchuria, and Outer Mongolia.

Finally, given that oceans limit the ability of armies to project power, and that nuclear weapons decrease the likelihood of great-power army clashes, the most peaceful world would probably be one where all the great powers were insular states with survivable nuclear arsenals.[149]

This concludes the discussion of power. Understanding what power is, however, should provide important insights into how states behave, especially how they go about maximizing their share of world power, which is the subject of the next chapter.

5

Strategies for Survival

I t is time to consider how great powers go about maximizing their share of world power. The first task is to lay out the specific goals that states pursue in their competition for power. My analysis of state objectives builds on previous chapters' discussion of power. Specifically, I argue that great powers strive for hegemony in their region of the world. Because of the difficulty of projecting power over large bodies of water, no state is likely to dominate the entire globe. Great powers also aim to be wealthy—in fact, much wealthier than their rivals, because military power has an economic foundation. Furthermore, great powers aspire to have the mightiest land forces in their region of the world, because armies and their supporting air and naval forces are the core ingredient of military power. Finally, great powers seek nuclear superiority, although that is an especially difficult goal to achieve.

The second task is to analyze the various strategies that states use to shift the balance of power in their favor or to prevent other states from shifting it against them. *War* is the main strategy states employ to acquire relative power. *Blackmail* is a more attractive alternative, because it relies on the threat of force, not the actual use of force, to produce results. Thus, it is relatively cost-free. Blackmail is usually difficult to achieve, however, because great powers are likely to fight before they submit to threats from other great powers. Another strategy for gaining power is *bait and bleed*, whereby a state tries to weaken its rivals by provoking a long and costly war between them. But this scheme is also difficult to make work. A more promising variant of the strategy is *bloodletting*, in which a state takes measures to ensure that any war in which an adversary is involved is protracted and deadly.

Balancing and *buck-passing* are the principal strategies that great powers use to prevent aggressors from upsetting the balance of power.[1] With balancing, threatened states seriously commit themselves to containing their dangerous opponent. In other words, they are willing to shoulder the burden of deterring, or fighting if need be, the aggressor. With buck-passing, they try to get another great power to check the aggressor while they remain on the sidelines. Threatened states usually prefer buck-passing to balancing, mainly because the buck-passer avoids the costs of fighting the aggressor in the event of war.

The strategies of *appeasement* and *bandwagoning* are not particulary useful for dealing with aggressors. Both call for conceding power to a rival state, which is a prescription for serious trouble in an anarchic system. With bandwagoning, the threatened state abandons hope of preventing the aggressor from gaining power at its expense and instead joins forces with its dangerous foe to get at least some small portion of the spoils of war. Appeasement is a more ambitious strategy. The appeaser aims to modify the behavior of the aggressor by conceding it power, in the hope that this gesture will make the aggressor feel more secure, thus dampening or eliminating its motive for aggression. Although appeasement and bandwagoning are ineffective and dangerous strategies, because they allow the balance of power to shift against the threatened state, I will discuss some special circumstances where it may make sense for a state to concede power to another state.

It is commonplace in the international relations literature to argue that balancing and bandwagoning are the key alternative strategies available to threatened great powers, and that great powers invariably opt to balance against dangerous adversaries.[2] I disagree. Bandwagoning, as emphasized, is not a productive option in a realist world, for although the bandwagoning state may achieve more absolute power, the dangerous aggressor gains more. The actual choice in a realist world is between balancing and buck-passing, and threatened states prefer buck-passing to balancing whenever possible.[3]

Finally, I relate my theory to the well-known realist argument that *imitation* of the successful practices of rival great powers is an important consequence of security competition. While I acknowledge the basic point as correct, I argue that imitation tends to be defined too narrowly, focusing on copycatting defensive but not offensive behavior. Moreover, great powers also care about *innovation,* which often means finding clever ways to gain power at the expense of rival states. Although a variety of state strategies are considered in this chapter, the primary focus is on three: war is the main strategy for gaining additional increments of power, whereas balancing and buck-passing are the main strategies for preserving the balance of power. An explanation of how threatened states choose between balancing and buck-passing is laid out in Chapter 8, and an explanation for when states are likely to choose war is put forth in Chapter 9.

OPERATIONAL STATE GOALS

Although I have emphasized that great powers seek to maximize their share of world power, more needs to be said about what that behavior entails. This section will therefore examine the different goals that states pursue and the strategies they employ in their hunt for more relative power.

Regional Hegemony

Great powers concentrate on achieving four basic objectives. First, they seek regional hegemony. Although a state would maximize its security if it dominated the entire world, global hegemony is not feasible, except in the unlikely event that that a state achieves nuclear superiority over its rivals (see below). The key limiting factor, as discussed in the preceding chapter, is the difficulty of projecting power across large bodies of water, which makes it impossible for any great power to conquer and dominate regions separated from it by oceans. Regional hegemons certainly pack a powerful military punch, but launching amphibious assaults across oceans against territory controlled and defended by another great power would be a suicidal undertaking. Not surprisingly, the United States, which is the only regional hegemon in modern history, has never seriously considered conquering either Europe or Northeast Asia. A great power could still conquer a neighboring region that it could reach by land, but it would still fall far short of achieving global hegemony.

Not only do great powers aim to dominate their own region, they also strive to prevent rivals in other areas from gaining hegemony. Regional hegemons fear that a peer competitor might jeopardize their hegemony by upsetting the balance of power in their backyard. Thus, regional hegemons prefer that there be two or more great powers in the other key regions of the world, because those neighbors are likely to spend most of their time competing with each other, leaving them few opportunities to threaten a distant hegemon.

How regional hegemons prevent other great powers from dominating far-off regions depends on the balance of power in those areas. If power is distributed rather evenly among the major states, so that there is no potential hegemon among them, the distant hegemon can safely stay out of any conflicts in those regions, because no state is powerful enough to conquer all of the others. But even if a potential hegemon comes on the scene in another region, the distant hegemon's first preference would be to stand aside and allow the local great powers to check the threat. This is quintessential buck-passing at play, and as discussed below, states prefer to buck-pass than to balance when faced with a dangerous opponent. If the local great powers cannot contain the threat, however, the distant hegemon would move in and balance against it. Although its main goal would be containment, the distant hegemon would also look for opportunities to undermine the threat and reestablish a rough balance of power in the region, so that it could return home. In essence, regional hegemons act as offshore balancers in other areas of the world, although they prefer to be the balancer of last resort.

One might wonder why a state that stood astride its own region would care whether there was another regional hegemon, especially if the two competitors were separated by an ocean. After all, it would be almost impossible for either regional hegemon to strike across the water at the other. For example, even if Nazi Germany had won World War II in Europe, Adolf Hitler could not have launched an amphibious assault across the Atlantic Ocean against the United States. Nor could China, if it someday becomes an Asian hegemon, strike across the Pacific Ocean to conquer the American homeland.

Nevertheless, rival hegemons separated by an ocean can still threaten one another by helping to upset the balance of power in each other's backyard. Specifically, a regional hegemon might someday face a local challenge from an upstart state, which would surely have strong incentives to ally with the distant hegemon to protect itself from attack by the neighboring hegemon. At the same time, the distant hegemon might have reasons of its own for collaborating with the upstart state. Remember that there are many possible reasons why states might attempt to take advantage of each other. In such cases, water's stopping power would have little effect on the distant hegemon's power-projection capability, because it would not have to launch an amphibious attack across the sea, but could instead transport troops and supplies across the water to the friendly territory of its ally in the rival hegemon's backyard. Ferrying troops is far easier to accomplish than invading a rival great power from the sea, although the distant hegemon would still need to be able to move freely across the ocean.

To illustrate this logic, consider the following hypothetical example. If Germany had won World War II in Europe and Mexico's economy and population had grown rapidly during the 1950s, Mexico probably would have sought an alliance with Germany, and might have even invited Germany to station troops in Mexico. The best way for the United States to have precluded a scenario of this kind would have been to ensure that its power advantage over Mexico remained large, and that Germany, or any other rival great power, was bogged down in a regional security competition, thus poorly positioning it to meddle in the Western Hemisphere. Of course, if Germany had been a hegemon in Europe, it would have had the same incentives to do whatever was possible to end the United States's dominance of the Western Hemisphere, which is why Germany would have been likely to join forces with Mexico against the United States in the first place.

Real-world evidence shows the importance of gaining hegemony in one's own region while making sure that rivals in distant regions are bogged down in security competition. France, for example, put troops in Mexico during the American Civil War (1861–65) against the wishes of the United States. But the U.S. military was in no position to challenge the French deployment, because it was involved in a major war with the Confederacy. Soon after winning the war, the United States forced France to remove its troops from Mexico. Shortly thereafter, in early 1866, Austria threatened to send its own troops to Mexico. That threat never materialized, however, because Austria became involved in a serious crisis with Prussia that led to a major war between them in the summer of 1866.[4]

Although every great power would like to be a regional hegemon, few are likely to reach that pinnacle. As mentioned already, the United States is the only great power that has dominated its region in modern history. There are two reasons why regional hegemons tend to be a rare species. Few states have the necessary endowments to make a run at hegemony. To qualify as a potential hegemon, a state must be considerably wealthier than its local rivals and must possess the mightiest army in the region. During the past two centuries, only a handful of states have met those criteria: Napoleonic France, Wilhelmine Germany, Nazi Germany, the Soviet Union during the Cold War, and the United States. Furthermore, even if a state has the wherewithal to be a potential hegemon, the other great powers in the system will seek to prevent it from actually becoming a regional hegemon. None of the European great powers mentioned above, for example, was able to defeat all of its rivals and gain regional hegemony.

Maximum Wealth

Second, great powers aim to maximize the amount of the world's wealth that they control. States care about relative wealth, because economic might is the foundation of military might. In practical terms, this means that great powers place a high premium on having a powerful and dynamic economy, not only because it enhances the general welfare, but also because it is a reliable way to gain a military advantage over rivals. "National self-preservation and economic growth," Max Weber maintained, are "two sides of the same coin."[5] The ideal situation for any state is to experience sharp economic growth while its rivals' economies grow slowly or hardly at all.

Parenthetically, great powers are likely to view especially wealthy states, or states moving in that direction, as serious threats, regardless of whether or not they have a formidable military capability. After all, wealth can rather easily be translated into military might. A case in point is Wilhelmine Germany in the late nineteenth and early twentieth centuries. The mere fact that Germany had a large population and a dynamic economy was reason enough to scare Europe's other great powers, although German behavior sometimes fueled those fears.[6] Similiar fears exist today regarding China, which has a huge population and an economy that is undergoing rapid modernization. Conversely, great powers are likely to worry less about states that are moving down the pecking order of wealthy states. The United States, for example, fears Russia less than it did the former Soviet Union, in part because Russia does not control nearly as much of the world's wealth as the Soviet Union did in its heyday; Russia cannot build as powerful an army as did its Soviet predecessor. If China's economy hits the skids and does not recover, fears about China will subside considerably.

Great powers also seek to prevent rival great powers from dominating the wealth-generating areas of the world. In the modern era, those areas are usually populated by the leading industrial states, although they might be occupied by less-developed states that possess critically important raw materials. Great powers sometimes attempt to dominate those regions themselves, but at the very least, they try to ensure that none falls under the control of a rival great power. Areas that contain little intrinsic wealth are of less concern to great powers.[7]

During the Cold War, for example, American strategists focused their attention on three regions outside of the Western Hemisphere: Europe, Northeast Asia, and the Persian Gulf.[8] The United States was determined that the Soviet Union not dominate any of those areas. Defending Western Europe was America's number one strategic priority because it is a wealthy region that was directly threatened by the Soviet army. Soviet control of the European continent would have sharply shifted the balance of power against the United States. Northeast Asia was strategically important because Japan is among the world's wealthiest states, and it faced a Soviet threat, albeit a less serious threat than the one confronting Western Europe. The United States cared about the Persian Gulf mainly because of oil, which fuels the economies of Asia and Europe. Consequently, the American military was designed largely to fight in these three areas of the world. The United States paid less attention to Africa, the rest of the Middle East, Southeast Asia, and the South Asian subcontinent, because there was little potential power in those regions.

Preeminent Land Power

Third, great powers aim to dominate the balance of land power, because that is the best way to maximize their share of military might. In practice, this means that states build powerful armies as well as air and naval forces to support those ground forces. But great powers do not spend all of their defense funds on land power. As discussed below, they devote considerable resources to acquiring nuclear weapons; sometimes they also buy independent sea power and strategic airpower. But because land power is the dominant form of military power, states aspire to have the most formidable army in their region of the world.

Nuclear Superiority

Fourth, great powers seek nuclear superiority over their rivals. In an ideal world, a state would have the world's only nuclear arsenal, which would give it the capability to devastate its rivals without fear of retaliation. That huge military advantage would make that nuclear-armed state a global hegemon, in which case my previous discussion of regional hegemony would be irrelevant. Also, the balance of land power would be of minor importance in a world dominated by a nuclear hegemon. It is difficult, however, to achieve and maintain nuclear superiority, because rival states will go to great lengths to develop a nuclear retaliatory force of their own. As emphasized in Chapter 4, great powers are likely to find themselves operating in a world of nuclear powers with the assured capacity to destroy their enemies—a world of mutual assured destruction, or MAD.

Some scholars, especially defensive realists, argue that it makes no sense for nuclear-armed states in a MAD world to pursue nuclear superiority.[9] In particular, they should not build counterforce weapons—i.e., those that could strike the other side's nuclear arsenal—and they should not build defensive systems that could shoot down the adversary's incoming nuclear warheads, because the essence of a MAD world is that no state can be assured that it has destroyed *all* of its rival's nuclear weapons, and thus would remain vulnerable to nuclear devastation. It makes more sense, so the argument goes, for each state to *be* vulnerable to the other side's nuclear weapons. Two reasons underpin the assertion that nuclear-armed states should not pursue nuclear superiority. MAD is a powerful force for stability, so it makes no sense to undermine it. Furthermore, it is almost impossible to gain meaningful military advantage by building counterforce weapons and defenses. No matter how sophisticated those systems might be, it is almost impossible to fight and win a nuclear war, because nuclear weapons are so destructive that both sides will be annihilated in the conflict. Thus, it makes little sense to think in terms of gaining military advantage at the nuclear level.

Great powers, however, are unlikely to be content with living in a MAD world, and they are likely to search for ways to gain superiority over their nuclear-armed opponents. Although there is no question that MAD makes war among the great powers less likely, a state is likely to be more secure if it has nuclear superiority. Specifically, a great power operating under MAD still has great-power rivals that it must worry about, and it still is vulnerable to nuclear attack, which although unlikely, is still possible. A great power that gains nuclear superiority, on the other hand, is a hegemon and thus has no major rivals to fear. Most important, it would not face the threat of a nuclear attack. Therefore, states have a powerful incentive to be nuclear hegemons. This logic does not deny that meaningful nuclear superiority is an especially difficult goal to achieve. Nevertheless, states will pursue nuclear advantage because of the great benefits it promises. In particular, states will build lots of counterforce capability and push hard to develop effective defenses in the hope that they might gain nuclear superiority.

In sum, great powers pursue four main goals: 1) to be the only regional hegemon on the globe, 2) to control as large a percentage of the world's wealth as possible, 3) to dominate the balance of land power in their region, and 4) to have nuclear superiority. Let us now move from goals to strategies, starting with the strategies that states employ to increase their relative power.

STRATEGIES FOR GAINING POWER

War

War is the most controversial strategy that great powers can employ to increase their share of world power. Not only does it involve death and destruction, sometimes on a vast scale, but it became fashionable in the twentieth century to argue that conquest does not pay and that war is therefore a futile enterprise. The most famous work making this point is probably Norman Angell's *The Great Illusion*, which was published a few years before the start of World War I.[10] This basic theme is also central to the writings of many contemporary students of international politics. Nevertheless, the argument is wrong: conquest can still improve a state's power position.

The claim that war is a losing proposition takes four basic forms. Some suggest that aggressors almost always lose. I dealt with this claim in Chapter 2, where I noted that in the past, states that initiated war won roughly 60 percent of the time. Others maintain that nuclear weapons make it virtually impossible for great powers to fight each other, because of the danger of mutual annihilation. I dealt with this issue in Chapter 4, arguing that nuclear weapons make great-power war less likely, but they do not render it obsolete. Certainly none of the great powers in the nuclear age has behaved as if war with another major power has been ruled out.

The other two perspectives assume that wars are winnable, but that successful conquest leads to Pyrrhic victories. The two focus, respectively, on the costs and on the benefits of war. These concepts are actually linked, since states contemplating aggression invariably weigh its expected costs and benefits.

The costs argument, which attracted a lot of attention in the 1980s, is that conquest does not pay because it leads to the creation of empires, and the price of maintaining an empire eventually becomes so great that economic growth at home is sharply slowed. In effect, high levels of defense spending undermine a state's relative economic position over time, ultimately eroding its position in the balance of power. Ergo, great powers would be better off creating wealth rather than conquering foreign territory.[11]

According to the benefits argument, military victory does not pay because conquerors cannot exploit modern industrial economies for gain, especially those that are built around information technologies.[12] The root of the conqueror's problem is that nationalism makes it hard to subdue and manipulate the people in defeated states. The victor may try repression, but it is likely to backfire in the face of massive popular resistance. Moreover, repression is not feasible in the information age, because knowledge-based economies depend on openness to function smoothly. Thus, if the conqueror cracks down, it will effectively kill the goose that lays the golden eggs. If it does not crack down, however, subversive ideas will proliferate inside the defeated state, making rebellion likely.[13]

There is no question that great powers sometimes confront circumstances in which the likely costs of conquest are high and the expected benefits are small. In those cases, it makes no sense to start a war. But the general claim that conquest almost always bankrupts the aggressor and provides no tangible benefits does not stand up to close scrutiny.

There are many examples of states expanding via the sword and yet not damaging their economies in the process. The United States during the first half of the nineteenth century and Prussia between 1862 and 1870 are obvious cases in point; aggression paid handsome economic dividends for both states. Moreover, little scholarly evidence supports the claim that high levels of defense spending necessarily hurt a great power's economy.[14] The United States, for example, has spent enormous sums of money on defense since 1940, and its economy is the envy of the world today. The United Kingdom had a huge empire and its economy eventually lost its competitive edge, but few economists blame its economic decline on high levels of defense spending. In fact, the United Kingdom historically spent considerably less money on defense than did its great-power rivals.[15] Probably the case that best supports the claim that large military budgets ruin a state's economy is the demise of the Soviet Union in the late 1980s. But scholars have reached no consensus on what caused the Soviet economy to collapse, and there is good reason to think that it was due to profound structural problems in the economy, not military spending.[16]

Regarding the benefits argument, conquerors can exploit a vanquished state's economy for gain, even in the information age. Wealth can be extracted from an occupied state by levying taxes, confiscating industrial output, or even confiscating industrial plants. Peter Liberman shows in his seminal work on this subject that contrary to the views of Angell and others, modernization not only makes industrial societies wealthy and therefore lucrative targets, but it also makes coercion and repression easier—not harder—for the conqueror.[17] He notes, for example, that although information technologies have a "subversive potential," they also have an "Orwellian" dimension, which facilitates repression in important ways. "Coercive and repressive conquerors," he argues, "can make defeated modern societies pay a large share of their economic surplus in tribute."[18]

During World War II, for example, Germany was able, "through financial transfers alone . . . to mobilize an annual average of 30 percent of French national incomes, 42–44 percent of Dutch, Belgian, and Norwegian prewar national income, and at least 25 percent of Czech prewar national income."[19] Germany also extracted significant economic resources from the Soviet Union during World War II. The Soviets then returned the favor in the early years of the Cold War by exploiting the East German economy for gain.[20] Nevertheless, occupation is not cost-free for the conqueror, and there will be cases where the costs of exploiting another state's economy outweigh the benefits. Still, conquest sometimes pays handsome dividends.

It is also possible for conquerors to gain power by confiscating natural resources such as oil and foodstuffs. For example, any great power that conquers Saudi Arabia would surely reap significant economic benefits from controlling Saudi oil. This is why the United States created its Rapid Deployment Force in the late 1970s; it feared that the Soviet Union might invade Iran and capture the oil-rich area of Khuzestan, which would enhance Soviet power.[21] Moreover, once in Iran, the Soviets would be well positioned to threaten Saudi Arabia and other oil-rich states. During both world wars, Germany was bent on gaining access to the grain and other foodstuffs produced in the Soviet Union so that it could feed its own people cheaply and easily.[22] The Germans also coveted Soviet oil and other resources.

But even if one rejects the notion that conquest pays economic dividends, there are three other ways that a victorious aggressor can shift the balance of power in its favor. The conqueror might employ some portion of the vanquished state's population in its army or as forced labor in its homeland. Napoleon's military machine, for example, made use of manpower raised in defeated states.[23] In fact, when France attacked Russia in the summer of 1812, roughly half of the main invasion force—which totalled 674,000 soldiers—was not French.[24] Nazi Germany also employed soldiers from conquered states in its army. For example, "of the thirty-eight SS divisions in existence in 1945, none was composed entirely of native Germans, and nineteen consisted largely of foreign personnel."[25] Moreover, the Third Reich used forced labor to its advantage. Indeed, it appears that there were probably as many as 7.6 million foreign civilian workers and prisoners of war employed in Germany by August 1944, which was one-fourth of the total German work force.[26]

Furthermore, conquest sometimes pays because the victor gains strategically important territory. In particular, states can gain a buffer zone that helps protect them from attack by another state, or that can be used to launch an attack on a rival state. For example, France gave serious consideration to annexing the Rhineland before and after Germany was defeated in World War I.[27] Israel's strategic position was certainly enhanced in June 1967 with the acquisition of the Sinai Peninsula, the Golan Heights, and the West Bank in the Six-Day War. The Soviet Union went to war against Finland in the winter of 1939–40 to gain territory that would help the Red Army thwart a Nazi invasion.[28] The Wehrmacht, on the other hand, conquered part of Poland in September 1939 and used it as a launching pad for its June 1941 invasion of the Soviet Union.

Finally, war can shift the balance of power in the victor's favor by eliminating the vanquished state from the ranks of the great powers. Conquering states can achieve this goal in different ways. They might destroy a defeated rival by killing most of its people, thereby eliminating it altogether from the international system. States rarely pursue this drastic option, but evidence of this kind of behavior exists to make states think about it. The Romans, for example, annihilated Carthage, and there is reason to think that Hitler planned to eliminate Poland and the Soviet Union from the map of Europe.[29] Spain destroyed both the Aztec and the Inca empires in Central and South America, and during the Cold War, both superpowers worried that the other would use its nuclear weapons to launch a "splendid first strike" that would obliterate them. Israelis often worry that if the Arab states ever inflicted a decisive defeat on Israel, they would impose a Carthaginian peace.[30]

Alternatively, conquering states might annex the defeated state. Austria, Prussia, and Russia, for example, partitioned Poland four times in the past three centuries.[31] The victor might also consider disarming and neutralizing the beaten state. The Allies employed this strategy against Germany after World War I, and in the early years of the Cold War, Stalin flirted with the idea of creating a unified but militarily weak Germany.[32] The famous "Morgenthau Plan" proposed that post-Hitler Germany be de-industrialized and turned into two largely agrarian states, so that it no longer could build powerful military forces.[33] Finally, conquering states might divide a defeated great power into two or more smaller states, which is what Germany did to the Soviet Union in the spring of 1918 with the Treaty of

Brest-Litovsk, and is also what the United Kingdom, the United States, and the Soviet Union effectively did to Germany after World War II.

Blackmail

A state can gain power at a rival's expense without going to war by threatening to use military force against its opponent. Coercive threats and intimidation, not the actual use of force, produce the desired outcome.[34] If this blackmail works, it is clearly preferable to war, because blackmail achieves its goals without bloody costs. However, blackmail is unlikely to produce marked shifts in the balance of power, mainly because threats alone are usually not enough to compel a great power to make significant concessions to a rival great power. Great powers, by definition, have formidable military strength relative to each other, and therefore they are not likely to give in to threats without a fight. Blackmail is more likely to work against minor powers that have no great-power ally.

Nevertheless, there are cases of successful blackmail against great powers. For example, in the decade before World War I, Germany attempted to intimidate its European rivals on four occasions and succeeded once.[35] Germany initiated diplomatic confrontations with France and the United Kingdom over Morocco in 1905 and again in 1911. Although Germany was clearly more powerful than either the United Kingdom or France, and probably more powerful than both of them combined, Germany suffered diplomatic defeats both times. In the other two cases, Germany tried to blackmail Russia into making concessions in the Balkans. In 1909, Austria annexed Bosnia without any prompting from Germany. When Russia protested, Germany used the threat of war to force Russia to accept Austria's action. Blackmail worked in this case, because the Russian army had not recovered from its shattering defeat in the Russo-Japanese War (1904–5) and thus was in no position to confront the mighty German army in a war. The Germans tried to intimidate the Russians again in the summer of 1914, but by then the Russian army had recovered from its defeat a decade earlier. The Russians stood their ground, and the result was World War I.

Among three other well-known cases of blackmail, only one had a significant effect on the balance of power. The first case was a dispute in 1898 between the United Kingdom and France over control of Fashoda, a strategically important fort at the headwaters of Africa's Nile River.[36] The United Kingdom warned France not to attempt to conquer any part of the Nile because it would threaten British control of Egypt and the Suez Canal. When the United Kingdom learned that France had sent an expeditionary force to Fashoda, it told France to remove it or face war. France backed down, because it knew the United Kingdom would win the ensuing war, and because France did not want to pick a fight with the United Kingdom when it was more worried about the emerging German threat on its eastern border. The second case is the famous Munich crisis of 1938, when Hitler threatened war to compel the United Kingdom and France to allow Germany to swallow up the Sudetenland, which was at the time part of Czechoslovakia. The third case is when the United States forced the Soviet Union to remove its ballistic missiles from Cuba in the fall of 1962. Of these cases, only Munich had a telling effect on the balance of power.

Bait and Bleed

Bait and bleed is a third strategy that states might employ to increase their relative power. This strategy involves causing two rivals to engage in a protracted war, so that they bleed each other white, while the baiter remains on the sideline, its military strength intact. There was concern in the United States during the Cold War, for example, that a third party might surreptitiously provoke a nuclear war between the superpowers.[37] Also, one of the superpowers might have considered provoking its rival to start a losing war in the Third World. For example, the United States could have encouraged the Soviet Union to get entrapped in conflicts like the one in Afghanistan. But that was not American policy. In fact, there are few examples in modern history of states pursuing a bait-and-bleed strategy.

The best case of bait and bleed I can find is Russia's efforts in the wake of the French Revolution (1789) to entice Austria and Prussia into starting a war with France, so that Russia would be free to expand its power in central Europe. Russia's leader, Catherine the Great, told her secretary in November 1791, "I am racking my brains in order to push the courts of Vienna and Berlin into French affairs. . . . There are reasons I cannot talk about; I want to get them involved in that business to have my hands free. I have much unfinished business, and it's necessary for them to be kept busy and out of my way."[38] Although Austria and Prussia did go to war against France in 1792, Russia's prompting had little influence on their decision. Indeed, they had compelling reasons of their own for picking a fight with France.

Another case that closely resembles a bait-and-bleed strategy involves Israel.[39] In 1954, Pinhas Lavon, Israel's defense minister, directed saboteurs to blow up important American and British targets in the Egyptian cities of Alexandria and Cairo. The aim was to fuel tensions between the United Kingdom and Egypt, which it was hoped would convince the United Kingdom to abandon its plan to withdraw its troops from bases near the Suez Canal. The strike force was caught and the operation turned into a fiasco.

The fundamental problem with a bait-and-bleed strategy, as the Lavon affair demonstrates, is that it is difficult to trick rival states into starting a war that they would otherwise not fight. There are hardly any good ways of causing trouble between other states without getting exposed, or at least raising suspicions in the target states. Moreover, the states being baited are likely to recognize the danger of engaging each other in a protracted war while the baiter sits untouched on the sidelines, gaining relative power on the cheap. States are likely to avoid such a trap. Finally there is always the danger for the baiter that one of the states being baited might win a quick and decisive victory and end up gaining power rather than losing it.

Bloodletting

Bloodletting is a more promising variant of this strategy. Here, the aim is to make sure that any war between one's rivals turns into a long and costly conflict that saps their strength. There is no baiting in this version; the rivals have gone to war independently, and the bloodletter is mainly concerned with causing its rivals to bleed each other white, while it stays out of the fighting. As a senator, Harry Truman had this strategy in mind in June 1941 when he reacted to the Nazi invasion of the Soviet Union by saying, "If we see that Germany is winning we ought to help Russia, and if Russia is winning we ought to help Germany, and that way let them kill as many as possible."[40]

Vladimir Lenin, too, had this strategy in mind when he took the Soviet Union out of World War I while the fighting between Germany and the Allies (the United Kingdom, France, and the United States) continued in the west. "In concluding a separate peace now," he said on January 20, 1918, "we rid ourselves . . . of both imperialistic groups fighting each other. We can take advantage of their strife, which makes it difficult for them to reach an agreement at our expense, and use that period when our hands are free to develop and strengthen the Socialist Revolution." As John Wheeler-Bennett notes, "Few documents illustrate more succinctly Lenin's . . . understanding of the value of *Realpolitik* in statesmanship."[41] The United States also pursued this strategy against the Soviet Union in Afghanistan during the 1980s.[42]

STRATEGIES FOR CHECKING AGGRESSORS

Great powers not only seek to gain power over their rivals, they also aim to prevent those foes from gaining power at their expense. Keeping potential aggressors at bay is sometimes a rather simple task. Since great powers maximize their share of world power, they invest heavily in defense and typically build formidable fighting forces. That impressive military capability is usually sufficient to deter rival states from challenging the balance of power. But occasionally, highly aggressive great powers that are more difficult to contain come on the scene. Especially powerful states, like potential hegemons, invariably fall into this category. To deal with these aggressors, threatened great powers can choose between two strategies: balancing and buck-passing. They invariably prefer buck-passing, although sometimes they have no choice but to balance against the threat.

Balancing

With balancing, a great power assumes direct responsibility for preventing an aggressor from upsetting the balance of power.[43] The initial goal is to deter the aggressor, but if that fails, the balancing state will fight the ensuing war. Threatened states can take three measures to make balancing work. First, they can send clear signals to the aggressor through diplomatic channels (and through the actions described below) that they are firmly committed to maintaining the balance of power, even if it means going to war. The emphasis in the balancer's message is on confrontation, not conciliation. In effect, the balancer draws a line in the sand and warns the aggressor not to cross it. The United States pursued this type of policy with the Soviet Union throughout the Cold War; France and Russia did the same with Germany before World War I.[44]

Second, threatened states can work to create a defensive alliance to help them contain their dangerous opponent. This diplomatic maneuver, which is often called "external balancing," is limited in a bipolar world, because there are no potential great-power alliance partners, although it is still possible to ally with minor powers.[45] During the Cold War, for example, both the United States and the Soviet Union had no choice but to ally with minor powers, because they were the only great powers in the system. Threatened states place a high premium on finding alliance partners, because the costs of checking an aggressor are shared in an alliance—an especially important consideration if war breaks out. Furthermore, recruiting allies increases the amount of firepower confronting the aggressor, which in turn increases the likelihood that deterrence will work.

These benefits notwithstanding, external balancing has a downside: it is often slow and inefficient. The difficulties of making an alliance work smoothly are reflected in the comment of the French general who said at the end of World War I, "Since I have seen alliances at work, I have lost something of my admiration for Napoleon [who almost always fought without allies against alliances]."[46] Putting together balancing coalitions quickly and making them function smoothly is often difficult, because it takes time to coordinate the efforts of prospective allies or member states, even when there is wide agreement on what needs to be done. Threatened states usually disagree over how the burdens should be distributed among alliance members. After all, states are self-interested actors with powerful incentives to minimize the costs they pay to contain an aggressor. This problem is compounded by the fact that alliance members have an impulse to buck-pass among themselves, as discussed below. Finally, there is likely to be friction among coalition members over which state leads the alliance, especially when it comes to formulating strategy.

Third, threatened states can balance against an aggressor by mobilizing additional resources of their own. For example, defense spending might be increased or conscription might be implemented. This action, which is commonly referred to as "internal balancing," is self-help in the purest sense of the term. But there are usually significant limits on how many additional resources a threatened state can muster against an aggressor, because great powers normally already devote a large percentage of their resources to defense. Because they seek to maximize their share of world power, states are effectively engaged in internal balancing all the time. Nevertheless, when faced with a particularly aggressive adversary, great powers will eliminate any slack in the system and search for clever ways to boost defense spending.

There is, however, one exceptional circumstance in which a great power will increase defense spending to help deter an aggressor. Offshore balancers like the United Kingdom and the United States tend to maintain relatively small military forces when they are not needed to contain a potential hegemon in a strategically important area. Usually, they can afford to have a small army because their distant rivals tend to focus their attention on each other, and because the stopping power of water provides them with abundant security. Therefore, when it is necessary for an offshore balancer to check a potential hegemon, it is likely to sharply expand the size and strength of its fighting forces, as the United States did in 1917, when it entered World War I, and in 1940, the year before it entered World War II.

Buck-Passing

Buck-passing is a threatened great power's main alternative to balancing.[47] A buck-passer attempts to get another state to bear the burden of deterring or possibly fighting an aggressor, while it remains on the sidelines. The buck-passer fully recognizes the need to prevent the aggressor from increasing its share of world power but looks for some other state that is threatened by the aggressor to perform that onerous task.

Threatened states can take four measures to facilitate buck-passing. First, they can seek good diplomatic relations with the aggressor, or at least not do anything to provoke it, in the hope that it will concentrate its attention on the intended "buck-catcher." During the late 1930s, for example, both France and the Soviet Union tried to pass the buck to each other in the face of a deadly threat from Nazi Germany. Each tried to have good relations with Hitler, so that he would aim his gunsight at the other.

Second, buck-passers usually maintain cool relations with the intended buck-catcher, not just because this diplomatic distancing might help foster good relations with the aggressor, but also because the buck-passer does not want to get dragged into a war on the side of the buck-catcher.[48] The aim of the buck-passer, after all, is to avoid having to fight the aggressor. Not surprisingly, then, a hostile undertone characterized relations between France and the Soviet Union in the years before World War II.

Third, great powers can mobilize additional resources of their own to make buck-passing work. It might seem that the buck-passer should be able to take a somewhat relaxed approach to defense spending, since the strategy's objective is to get someone else to contain the aggressor. But save for the exceptional case of the offshore balancer discussed earlier, that conclusion would be wrong. Leaving aside the fact that states maximize relative power, buck-passers have two other good reasons to look for opportunities to increase defense spending. By building up its own defenses, a buck-passer makes itself an imposing target, thus giving the aggressor incentive to focus its attention on the intended buck-catcher. The logic here is simple: the more powerful a threatened state is, the less likely it is that an aggressor will attack it. Of course, the buck-catcher must still have the wherewithal to contain the aggressor without the buck-passer's help.

Buck-passers also build formidable military forces for prophylactic reasons. In a world where two or more states are attempting to buck-pass, no state can be certain that it will not catch the buck and have to stand alone against the aggressor. It is better to be prepared for that eventuality. During the 1930s, for example, neither France nor the Soviet Union could be sure it would not catch the buck and have to stand alone against Nazi Germany. But even if a state successfully passes the buck, there is always the possibility that the aggressor might quickly and decisively defeat the buck-catcher and then attack the buck-passer. Thus, a state might improve its defenses as an insurance policy in case buck-passing fails.

Fourth, it sometimes makes sense for a buck-passer to allow or even facilitate the growth in power of the intended buck-catcher. That burden-bearer would then have a better chance of containing the aggressor state, which would increase the buck-passer's prospects of remaining on the sidelines. Between 1864 and 1870, for example, the United Kingdom and Russia stood by and allowed Otto von Bismarck's Prussia to conquer territory in the heart of Europe and create a unified German Reich that was considerably more powerful than its Prussian predecessor. The United Kingdom reasoned that a united Germany would not only deter French and Russian expansion into the heart of Europe, but it would also divert their attention away from Africa and Asia, where they might threaten the British empire. The Russians, on the other hand, hoped that a united Germany would keep Austria and France in check, and that it would also stifle Polish national aspirations.

The Allure of Buck-Passing

Buck-passing and putting together a balancing coalition obviously represent contrasting ways of dealing with an aggressor. Nevertheless, there is a strong tendency to buck-pass or "free-ride" inside balancing coalitions, although the danger that buck-passing will wreck the alliance is a powerful countervailing force. During the early years of World War I, for example, British policymakers tried to minimize the amount of fighting their troops did on the western front and instead get their alliance partners, France and Russia, to assume the costly burden of wearing down the German army.[49] The United Kingdom hoped then to use its still-fresh troops to win the final battles against Germany and to dictate the terms of peace. The United Kingdom would "win the peace," because it would emerge from the war in a substantially more powerful position than either the defeated Germans or the battle-worn French and Russians. The United Kingdom's allies quickly figured out what was going on, however, and forced the British army to participate fully in the awful task of bleeding the German army white. As always, states worry about relative power.[50]

Britain's attempt to free-ride on its allies, along with the history described in Chapters 7 and 8, gives evidence of the powerful impulse to buck-pass among threatened states. Indeed, great powers seem clearly to prefer buck-passing to balancing. One reason for this preference is that buck-passing usually provides defense "on the cheap." After all, the state that catches the buck pays the substantial costs of fighting the aggressor if deterrence fails and war breaks out. Of course, buck-passers sometimes spend considerable sums of money on their own military to facilitate buck-passing and to protect against the possibility that buck-passing might fail.

Buck-passing can also have an offensive dimension to it, which can make it even more attractive. Specifically, if the aggressor and the buck-catcher become involved in a long and costly war, the balance of power is likely to shift in the buck-passer's favor; it would then be in a good position to dominate the postwar world. The United States, for example, entered World War II in December 1941 but did not land its army in France until June 1944, less than a year before the war ended. Thus, the burden of wearing down the formidable Wehrmacht fell largely on the shoulders of the Soviet Union, which paid a staggering price to reach Berlin.[51] Although the United States would have preferred to invade France before 1944 and was thus an inadvertent buck-passer, there is no question that the United States benefited greatly from delaying the Normandy invasion until late in the war, when both the German and the Soviet armies were battered and worn.[52] Not surprisingly, Josef Stalin believed that the United Kingdom and the United States were purposely allowing Germany and the Soviet Union to bleed each other white so that those offshore balancers could dominate postwar Europe.[53]

Passing the buck is also an attractive option when a state faces more than one dangerous rival but does not have the military might to confront them all at once. Buck-passing might help reduce the number of threats. For example, the United Kingdom faced three menacing adversaries in the 1930s—Germany, Italy, and Japan—but it did not have the military power to check all three of them at once. The United Kingdom attempted to alleviate the problem by passing the burden of dealing with Germany to France, so it could concentrate instead on Italy and Japan.

Buck-passing is not a foolproof strategy, however. Its chief drawback is that the buck-catcher might fail to check the aggressor, leaving the buck-passer in a precarious strategic position. For example, France could not handle Nazi Germany alone, and therefore the United Kingdom had to form a balancing coalition with France against Hitler in March 1939. By then, however, Hitler controlled all of Czechoslovakia and it was too late to contain the Third Reich; war broke out five months later in September 1939. During that same period, the Soviet Union successfully passed the buck to France and the United Kingdom and then sat back expecting to watch Germany engage those two buck-catchers in a long, bloody war. But the Wehrmacht overran France in six weeks during the spring of 1940, leaving Hitler free to attack the Soviet Union without having to worry much about his western flank. By buck-passing rather than engaging Germany at the same time that France and the United Kingdom did, the Soviets wound up fighting a much harder war.

Furthermore, in cases where the buck-passer allows the military might of the buck-catcher to increase, there is the danger that the buck-catcher might eventually become so powerful that it threatens to upset the balance of power, as happened with Germany after it was unified in 1870. Bismarck actually worked to uphold the balance for the next twenty years. Indeed, a united Germany served to keep Russia and France in check on the European continent, as the United Kingdom hoped it would. But the situation changed markedly after 1890, as Germany grew increasingly powerful and eventually attempted to dominate Europe by force. Buck-passing in this case was, at best, a mixed success for the United Kingdom and Russia: effective in the short run, but disastrous in the long run.

Although these potential problems are surely cause for concern, they ultimately do little to diminish buck-passing's appeal. Great powers do not buck-pass thinking that it will lead to failure. On the contrary, they expect the strategy to succeed. Otherwise, they would eschew buck-passing and form a balancing coalition with the other threatened states in the system. But it is difficult to predict the future in international politics. Who would have guessed in 1870 that Germany would become the most powerful state in Europe by the early twentieth century and precipitate two world wars? Nor is balancing a foolproof alternative to buck-passing. Indeed, balancing is often inefficient, and states that balance together sometimes suffer catastrophic defeats, as happened to the United Kingdom and France in the spring of 1940.

It should be apparent that buck-passing sometimes leads to the same outcome as a bait-and-bleed strategy. Specifically, when buck-passing leads to war, the buck-passer, like the baiter, improves its relative power position by remaining on the sidelines while its main rivals wear themselves down. Furthermore, both strategies can fail in the same way if one of the combatants wins a quick and decisive victory. Nevertheless, there is an important difference between the two strategies: buck-passing is principally a deterrence strategy, with war-fighting as the default option, whereas bait and bleed purposely aims to provoke a war.

STRATEGIES TO AVOID

Some argue that balancing and buck-passing are not the only strategies that threatened states might employ against a dangerous opponent. Appeasement and bandwagoning, so the argument goes, are also viable alternatives. But that is wrong. Both of those strategies call for conceding power to an aggressor, which violates balance-of-power logic and increases the danger to the state that employs them. Great powers that care about their survival should neither appease nor bandwagon with their adversaries.

Bandwagoning happens when a state joins forces with a more powerful opponent, conceding that its formidable new partner will gain a disproportionate share of the spoils they conquer together.[54] The distribution of power, in other words, will shift further against the bandwagoner and in the stronger state's favor. Bandwagoning is a strategy for the weak. Its underlying assumption is that if a state is badly outgunned by a rival, it makes no sense to resist its demands, because that adversary will take what it wants by force anyway and inflict considerable punishment in the process. The bandwagoner must just hope that the troublemaker is merciful. Thucydides' famous dictum that "the strong do what they can and the weak suffer what they must" captures the essence of bandwagoning.[55]

This strategy, which violates the basic canon of offensive realism—that states maximize relative power—is rarely employed by great powers, because they have, by definition, the wherewithal to put up a decent fight against other great powers, and because they certainly have the incentive to stand up and fight. Bandwagoning is employed mainly by minor powers that stand alone against hostile great powers.[56] They have no choice but to give in to the enemy, because they are weak and isolated. Good examples of bandwagoning are the decisions by Bulgaria and Romania to ally with Nazi Germany in the early stages of World War II and then shift their allegiance to the Soviet Union near the end of the war.[57]

With appeasement, a threatened state makes concessions to an aggressor that shift the balance of power in the recipient's favor. The appeaser usually agrees to surrender all or part of the territory of a third state to its powerful foe. The purpose of this allowance is behavior modification: to push the aggressor in a more pacific direction and possibly turn it into a status quo power.[58] The strategy rests on the assumption that the adversary's aggressive behavior is largely the result of an acute sense of strategic vulnerability. Therefore, any steps taken to reduce that insecurity will dampen, and possibly eliminate, the underlying motive for war. Appeasement accomplishes this end, so the argument goes, by allowing the appeaser to demonstrate its good intentions and by shifting the military balance in the appeased state's favor, thus making it less vulnerable and more secure, and ultimately less aggressive.

Unlike the bandwagoner, who makes no effort to contain the aggressor, the appeaser remains committed to checking the threat. But like bandwagoning, appeasement contradicts the dictates of offensive realism and therefore it is a fanciful and dangerous strategy. It is unlikely to transform a dangerous foe into a kinder, gentler opponent, much less a peace-loving state. Indeed, appeasement is likely to whet, not shrink, an aggressor state's appetite for conquest. There is little doubt that if a state concedes a substantial amount of power to an acutely insecure rival, that foe would presumably feel better about its prospects for survival. That reduced level of fear would, in turn, lessen that rival's incentive to shift the balance of power in its favor. But that good news is only part of the story. In fact, two other considerations trump that peace-promoting logic. International anarchy, as emphasized, causes states to look for opportunities to gain additional increments of power at each other's expense. Because great powers are programmed for offense, an appeased state is likely to interpret any power concession by another state as a sign of weakness—as evidence that the appeaser is unwilling to defend the balance of power. The appeased state is then likely to continue pushing for more concessions. It would be foolish for a state not to gain as much power as possible, because a state's prospects for survival increase as it accumulates additional increments of power. Furthermore, the appeased state's capability to gain even more power would be enhanced—probably substantially—by the additional power it was granted by the appeaser. In short, appeasement is likely to make a dangerous rival more, not less, dangerous.

CONCEDING POWER FOR REALIST REASONS

There are, however, special circumstances in which a great power might concede some power to another state yet not act contrary to balance-of-power logic. As noted earlier, it sometimes makes good sense for a buck-passer to allow the buck-catcher to gain power if it enhances the buck-catcher's prospects of containing the aggressor by itself. Furthermore, if a great power confronts two or more aggressors at the same time, but has neither the resources to check all of them nor an ally to which it can pass the buck, the besieged state probably should prioritize between its threats and allow the balance with the lesser threat to shift adversely, so as to free up resources to deal with the primary threat. With any luck, the secondary threat will eventually become a rival of the primary threat, thus making it possible to forge an alliance with the former against the latter.

This logic explains in part the United Kingdom's rapprochement with the United States in the early twentieth century.[59] At that time, the United States was clearly the dominant power in the Western Hemisphere, although the United Kingdom still had significant interests in the region, which sometimes led to serious disputes with the Americans. However, it decided to abandon the region and establish good relations with the United States, in part because the United Kingdom, all the way across the Atlantic Ocean, was in no position to confront the United States in its own backyard. But the United Kingdom also faced growing threats in other regions of the globe, especially the rise of Germany in Europe, which was potentially a far greater threat to the United Kingdom than was the United States, an ocean away. This changing threat environment motivated the United Kingdom to make concessions to the Americans so that it could concentrate its resources against Germany. Eventually, Germany threatened the United States as well, causing the Americans and the British to fight together as allies against Germany in both world wars.

Finally, conceding power to a dangerous adversary might make sense as a short-term strategy for buying time to mobilize the resources needed to contain the threat. The state making the allowance must not only be dealing from a short-term position of weakness but must also have superior long-term mobilization capability. Few instances of this kind of behavior can be found in the historical record. The only case I know of is the Munich agreement of September 1938, in which the United Kingdom allowed the Sudetenland (which was an integral part of Czechoslovakia) to be absorbed by Nazi Germany, in part because British policymakers believed that the balance of power favored the Third Reich but that it would shift in favor of the United Kingdom and France over time. In fact, the balance shifted against the Allies after Munich: they probably would have been better off going to war against Germany in 1938 over Czechoslovakia rather than over Poland in 1939.[60]

CONCLUSION

There is one final matter regarding how states act to gain and maintain power that merits attention. Kenneth Waltz has made famous the argument that security competition drives great powers to imitate the successful practices of their opponents.[61] States are socialized, he argues, to "conform to common international practices." Indeed, they have no choice but to do so if they hope to survive in the rough-and-tumble of world politics. "The close juxtaposition of states promotes their sameness through the disadvantages that arise from a failure to conform to successful practices."[62] Waltz links this concept of imitation with balancing behavior: states, he maintains, learn that they must check opponents who threaten to disrupt the balance of power. The result of this tendency toward sameness is clearly maintenance of the status quo. After all, balancing is the critical conforming behavior, and it works to preserve, not upset, the balance of power. This is straightforward defensive realism.

For sure, there is a powerful tendency for states to imitate the successful practices of other states in the system. It also makes sense to identify balancing as a strategy that states would want to imitate, although it is not clear why states need to be socialized to balance against aggressors. The structure of the system alone should compel states to balance against dangerous rivals or rely on other states to contain them.

But Waltz overlooks two closely related aspects of state behavior that make international politics more offense-oriented and more dangerous than he allows. States not only emulate successful balancing behavior, they also imitate successful aggression. For example, one reason that the United States sought to reverse Saddam Hussein's conquest of Kuwait in 1990–91 was fear that other states might conclude that aggression pays and thus initiate more wars of conquest.[63]

Furthermore, great powers not only imitate each other's successful practices, they also prize innovation.[64] States look for new ways to gain advantage over opponents, by developing new weapons, innovative military doctrines, or clever strategies. Important benefits often accrue to states that behave in an unexpected way, which is why states worry so much about strategic surprise.[65] The case of Nazi Germany highlights this point. Hitler surely emulated the successful practices of rival European states, but he also pursued novel strategies that sometimes surprised his adversaries. Security competition, in other words, pushes states to deviate from accepted practice as well as to conform with it.[66]

In summary, I have explained how states maximize their share of world power, focusing on the specific goals they pursue as well as the strategies they employ to achieve those goals. Now, I turn to the historical record to determine whether there is evidence that great powers constantly seek to gain advantage over rivals.

6

Great Powers in Action

My theory offered in Chapter 2 attempts to explain why great powers tend to have aggressive intentions and why they aim to maximize their share of world power. I tried there to provide a sound logical foundation for my claims that status quo powers are rarely seen in the international system, and that especially powerful states usually pursue regional hegemony. Whether my theory is ultimately persuasive, however, depends on how well it explains the actual behavior of the great powers. Is there substantial evidence that great powers think and act as offensive realism predicts?

To answer yes to this question and show that offensive realism provides the best account of great-power behavior, I must demonstrate that 1) the history of great-power politics involves primarily the clashing of revisionist states, and 2) the only status quo powers that appear in the story are regional hegemons—i.e., states that have achieved the pinnacle of power. In other words, the evidence must show that great powers look for opportunities to gain power and take advantage of them when they arise. It must also show that great powers do not practice self-denial when they have the wherewithal to shift the balance of power in their favor, and that the appetite for power does not decline once states have a lot of it. Instead, powerful states should seek regional hegemony whenever the possibility arises. Finally, there should be little evidence of policymakers saying that they are satisfied with their share of world power when they have the capability to gain more. Indeed, we should almost always find leaders thinking that it is imperative to gain more power to enhance their state's prospects for survival.

Demonstrating that the international system is populated by revisionist powers is not a simple matter, because the universe of potential cases is vast.[1] After all, great powers have been competing among themselves for centuries, and there is lots of state behavior that is fair game for testing my argument. To make the inquiry manageable, this study takes four different perspectives on the historical record. Although I am naturally anxious to find evidence that supports offensive realism, I make a serious effort to argue against myself by looking for evidence that might refute the theory. Specifically, I try to pay equal attention to instances of expansion and of non-expansion and to show that the cases of non-expansion were largely the result of successful deterrence. I also attempt to employ consistent standards when measuring the constraints on expansion in the cases examined.

First, I examine the foreign policy behavior of the five dominant great powers of the past 150 years: Japan from the time of the Meiji Restoration in 1868 until the country's defeat in World War II; Germany from the coming to power of Otto von Bismarck in 1862 until Adolf Hitler's final defeat in 1945; the Soviet Union from its inception in 1917 until its collapse in 1991; Great Britain/the United Kingdom from 1792 until 1945; and the United States from 1800 to 1990.[2] I choose to examine wide swaths of each state's history rather than more discrete time periods because doing so helps show that particular acts of aggression were not instances of aberrant behavior caused by domestic politics, but, as offensive realism would predict, part of a broader pattern of aggressive behavior.

Japan, Germany, and the Soviet Union are straightforward cases that provide strong support for my theory. They were almost always looking for opportunities to expand through conquest, and when they saw an opening, they usually jumped at it. Gaining power did not temper their offensive proclivities; it whetted them. In fact, all three great powers sought regional hegemony. Germany and Japan fought major wars in pursuit of that goal; only the United States and its allies deterred the Soviet Union from trying to conquer Europe. Furthermore, there is considerable evidence that policymakers in these states talked and thought like offensive realists. It is certainly hard to find evidence of key leaders expressing satisfaction with the existing balance of power, especially when their state had the capability to alter it. In sum, security considerations appear to have been the main driving force behind the aggressive policies of Germany, Japan, and the Soviet Union.

The United Kingdom and the United States, however, might appear to have behaved in ways that contradict offensive realism. For example, the United Kingdom was by far the wealthiest state in Europe during much of the nineteenth century, but it made no attempt to translate its considerable wealth into military might and gain regional hegemony. Thus, it seems that the United Kingdom was not interested in gaining relative power, despite the fact that it had the wherewithal to do so. During the first half of the twentieth century, it looks like the United States passed up a number of opportunities to project power into Northeast Asia and Europe, yet instead it pursued an isolationist foreign policy—hardly evidence of aggressive behavior.

Nonetheless, I will argue that the United Kingdom and the United States did behave in accordance with offensive realism. The United States aggressively pursued hegemony in the Western Hemisphere during the nineteenth century, mainly to maximize its prospects of surviving in a hostile world. It succeeded, and it stands as the only great power in modern history to have achieved regional hegemony. The United States did not attempt to conquer territory in either Europe or Northeast Asia during the twentieth century, because of the great difficulty of projecting power across the Atlantic and Pacific Oceans. Nevertheless, it acted as an offshore balancer in those strategically important areas. The stopping power of water also explains why the United Kingdom never attempted to dominate Europe in the nineteenth century. Because they require detailed discussion, the American and British cases are dealt with in the next chapter.

Second, I examine the foreign policy behavior of Italy from its creation as a unified state in 1861 until its defeat in World War II. Some might concede that the mightiest great powers look for opportunities to gain power, yet still think that the other great powers, especially the weaker ones, behave like status quo powers. Italy is a good test case for this line of argument, because it was clearly "the least of the great powers" for virtually the entire time it ranked as a player in European politics.[3] Despite Italy's lack of military might, its leaders were constantly probing for opportunities to gain power, and when one presented itself, they rarely hesitated to seize it. Furthermore, Italian policymakers were motivated to be aggressive in large part by balance-of-power considerations.

Third, one might concede that "the number of cases in which a strong dynamic state has stopped expanding because of satiation or has set modest limits to its power aims has been few indeed" but nevertheless maintain that those great powers were foolish to behave aggressively, because offense usually led to catastrophe.[4] Those states ultimately would have been more secure if they had concentrated on maintaining the balance of power, not attempting to alter it by force. This self-defeating behavior, so the argument goes, cannot be explained by strategic logic but must instead be the result of misguided policies pushed by selfish interest groups on the home front. Defensive realists often adopt this line of argument. Their favorite examples of self-defeating behavior are Japan before World War II, Germany before World War I, and Germany before World War II: each state suffered a crushing military defeat in the ensuing war. I challenge this general line of argument, paying careful attention to the German and Japanese cases, where the evidence shows that they were not engaged in self-defeating behavior fueled by malign domestic politics.

Finally, I examine the nuclear arms race between the United States and the Soviet Union during the Cold War. Defensive realists suggest that once nuclear-armed rivals develop the capability to destroy each other as functioning societies, they should be content with the world they have created and not attempt to change it. In other words, they should become status quo powers at the nuclear level. According to offensive realism, however, those rival nuclear powers will not simply accept mutual assured destruction (MAD) but instead will strive to gain nuclear superiority over the other side. I will attempt to show that the nuclear weapons policies of both superpowers were largely consistent with the predictions of offensive realism.

With the exception of the American and British cases, which are discussed in the next chapter, my four different cuts at the historical record are dealt with here in the order in which they were described above. Therefore, let us begin with an assessment of Japanese foreign policy between the Meiji Restoration and Hiroshima.

JAPAN (1868–1945)

Before 1853, Japan had little contact with the outside world, especially the United States and the European great powers. More than two centuries of self-imposed isolation had left Japan with a feudal political system and an economy that was not in the same league as those of the leading industrial states of the day. The great powers used "gunboat diplomacy" to "open up" Japan in the 1850s by forcing it to accept a series of unequal commercial treaties. At the same time, the great powers were striving to gain control over territory on the Asian continent. Japan was powerless to affect these developments; it was at the mercy of the great powers.

Japan reacted to its adverse strategic position by imitating the great powers both at home and abroad. Japanese leaders decided to reform their political system and compete with the West economically and militarily. As Japan's foreign minister put it in 1887, "What we must do is to transform our empire and our people, make the empire like the countries of Europe and our people like the peoples of Europe. To put it differently, we have to establish a new, European-style empire on the edge of Asia."[5]

The Meiji Restoration in 1868 was the first major step on the road to rejuvenation.[6] Although the main emphasis in the early years of modernization was on domestic policy, Japan almost immediately began acting like a great power on the world stage.[7] Korea was Japan's initial target of conquest, but by the mid-1890s it was apparent that Japan was bent on controlling large portions of the Asian continent; by the end of World War I, it was clear that Japan sought hegemony in Asia. Japan's offensive inclinations remained firmly intact until 1945, when it was decisively defeated in World War II. During the nearly eight decades between the Meiji Restoration and the Japanese surrender in Tokyo Bay, Japan took advantage of almost every favorable shift in the balance of power to act aggressively and increase its share of world power.[8]

There is wide agreement among students of Japanese foreign policy that Japan was constantly searching for opportunities to expand and gain more power between 1868 and 1945, and that security concerns were the main driving force behind its behavior. For example, Nobutaka Ike writes, "It would appear in retrospect that a recurring theme of the epoch was war, either its actual prosecution or preparation for it. . . . The evidence leads one to the conjecture that war represented an integral part of Japan's modernization process."[9] Even Jack Snyder, a prominent defensive realist, recognizes that "from the Meiji restoration in 1868 until 1945, all Japanese governments were expansionist."[10]

Regarding Japan's motive, Mark Peattie captures the prevailing wisdom when he notes that, "security—or rather insecurity—in relation to the advance of Western power in Asia seems, by the evidence, to have been the dominant concern in the acquisition of the component territories of the Japanese empire."[11] Even E. H. Norman, an incisive critic of the authoritarian cast of the Meiji Restoration, concludes that all lessons of history "warned the Meiji statesmen that there was to be no half-way house between the status of a subject nation and that of a growing, victorious empire."[12] General Ishiwara Kanji forcefully made that same point at the Tokyo war-crimes trials in May 1946, when he challenged an American prosecutor with these words:

Haven't you heard of Perry [Commodore Matthew Perry of the U.S. navy, who negotiated the first U.S.-Japan trade treaty]? Don't you know anything about your country's history? . . . Tokugawa Japan believed in isolation; it didn't want to have anything to do with other countries and had its doors locked tightly. Then along came Perry from your country in his black ships to open those doors; he aimed his big guns at Japan and warned, "If you don't deal with us, look out for these; open your doors, and negotiate with other countries too." And then when Japan did open its doors and tried dealing with other countries, it learned that all those countries were a fearfully aggressive lot. And so for its own defense it took your country as its teacher and set about learning how to be aggressive. You might say we became your disciples. Why don't you subpoena Perry from the other world and try him as a war criminal?[13]

Targets and Rivals

Japan was principally concerned with controlling three areas on the Asian mainland: Korea, Manchuria, and China. Korea was the primary target because it is located a short distance from Japan (see Map 6.1). Most Japanese policymakers surely agreed with the German officer who described Korea as "a dagger thrust at the heart of Japan."[14] Manchuria was number two on Japan's target list, because it, too, is located just across the Sea of Japan. China was a more distant threat than either Korea or Manchuria, but it was still an important concern, because it had the potential to dominate all of Asia if it ever got its act together and modernized its economic and political systems. At the very least, Japan wanted to keep China weak and divided.

Japan was also interested at different times in acquiring territory in Outer Mongolia and Russia. Moreover, Japan sought to conquer large portions of Southeast Asia and, indeed, accomplished that goal in the early years of World War II. Furthermore, Japan had its sights on a number of islands that lie off the Asian continent. They included Formosa (now Taiwan), the Pescadores, Hainan, and the Ryukyus. The story of Japan's efforts to achieve hegemony in Asia, however, unfolded largely on the Asian continent and involved Korea, Manchuria, and China. Finally, Japan conquered a large number of islands in the western Pacific Ocean when it went to war against Germany in 1914 and the United States in 1941.

Neither China nor Korea was capable of checking Japan's imperial ambitions, although China helped the great powers stymie Japan's drive

Targets of Japanese Expansion in Asia, 1868–1945

RUSSIA

SAKHALIN

OUTER MONGOLIA • Nomonhan

MANCHURIA

Kurile Islands

Jehol

Chungkuefung

LIAODONG PENINSULA

Vladivostok

Sea of Japan

Port Arthur

Hopei

Dairen

KOREA

JAPAN

Tsingtao

Seoul

CHINA

Yellow Sea

Tokyo

Pacific Ocean

Shanghai

East China Sea

Bonin Islands

Iwo Jima

Hong Kong (Br.)

Ryukyu Islands

Okinawa

FORMOSA (Taiwan)

Pescadores Islands

Hainan

Mariana Islands

South China Sea

PHILIPPINES (U.S.)

Guam (U.S.)

FRENCH INDOCHINA

Caroline Islands

Marshall Islands

Saigon

British Borneo

Dutch East Indies

MAP 6.1

for regional hegemony between 1937 and 1945. Unlike Japan, which modernized after its initial contacts with the West, both China and Korea remained economically backward until well after 1945. Consequently, Japan gained a significant military advantage over China and Korea in the late nineteenth century and was eventually able to annex Korea and to conquer large portions of China. Japan might have dominated the Asian continent by the early twentieth century had it not been contained by the great powers.

Russia, the United Kingdom, and the United States played key roles in checking Japan between 1895 and 1945. Russia is part of Asia as well as of Europe, and thus it qualifies as both an Asian and a European great power. Indeed, Russia was Japan's principal great-power rival in Northeast Asia, and it was the only great power that fought against Japan's armies on the continent. Of course, Russia had imperial ambitions of its own in Northeast Asia, and it challenged Japan for control of Korea and Manchuria. Nevertheless, there were times, as during the Russo-Japanese War (1904–5), when the Russian military was so weak that it could not stand up to Japan. The United Kingdom and the United States also played important roles in containing Japan, although they relied mainly on economic and naval power, not their armies. France and Germany, for the most part, were minor players in the Far East.

Japan's Record of Expansion

In the first few decades after the Meiji Restoration, Japanese foreign policy focused on Korea, which remained isolated from the outside world, although it was still loosely viewed as a tributary state of China.[15] Japan was determined to open up Korea diplomatically and economically, much the way the Western powers had opened up Japan at mid-century. But the Koreans resisted Japan's overtures, prompting a fierce debate in Japan between 1868 and 1873 over whether to use force to accomplish that end. The decision was ultimately made to forego war and concentrate instead on domestic reform. A Japanese surveying team, however, clashed with Korean coastal forces in 1875. War was narrowly averted when Korea accepted the Treaty of Kang-wah (February 1876), which opened three Korean ports to Japanese commerce and declared Korea an independent state.

Nevertheless, China still considered Korea its vassal state, which inevitably led to an intense rivalry between China and Japan over Korea. Indeed, fighting broke out in late 1884 between Chinese and Japanese troops stationed in Seoul. But war was averted because both sides feared that the European great powers would take advantage of them if they fought with each other. Nevertheless, Sino-Japanese competition over Korea continued, and in the summer of 1894 another crisis broke out. This time, Japan decided to go to war against China and settle the issue on the battlefield. Japan quickly defeated China and imposed a harsh peace treaty on the losers.[16] With the Treaty of Shimonoseki, signed on April 17, 1895, China ceded the Liaodong Peninsula, Formosa, and the Pescadores to Japan. The Liaodong Peninsula was part of Manchuria and included the important city of Port Arthur. Furthermore, China was forced to recognize Korea's independence, which effectively meant that Korea would become a ward of Japan, not China. Japan also received important commercial rights in China and exacted a large indemnity from China, leaving little doubt that Japan was bent on becoming a major player in Asian politics.

The great powers, especially Russia, were alarmed by Japan's growing power and its sudden expansion on the Asian continent. Russia, France, and Germany decided to rectify the situation; a few days after the peace treaty was signed, they forced Japan to return the Liaodong Peninsula to China. The Russians were determined to prevent Japan from controlling any part of Manchuria, because they intended to control it themselves. Russia also made it clear that it would contest Japan for control of Korea. Japan was allowed to keep Formosa and the Pescadores. With this "Triple Intervention," Russia replaced China as Japan's rival for control of Korea and Manchuria.[17]

By the early twentieth century, Russia was the dominant force in Manchuria, having moved large numbers of troops there during the Boxer Rebellion (1900). Neither Japan nor Russia was able to gain the upper hand in Korea, mainly because Korean policymakers skillfully played the two great powers off against each other so as to avoid being devoured by either side. Japan found this strategic landscape unacceptable and offered the Russians a simple deal: Russia could dominate Manchuria if Japan could control Korea. But Russia said no, and Japan moved to rectify the problem by going to war against Russia in early February 1904.[18]

Japan won a resounding victory at sea and on land, which was reflected in the peace treaty that was signed at Portsmouth, New Hampshire, on September 5, 1905. Russia's influence in Korea was ended, ensuring that Japan would now dominate the Korean Peninsula. Moreover, Russia transferred the Liaodong Peninsula to Japan, including control of the South Manchuria Railway. Russia also surrendered the southern half of Sakhalin Island to Japan; Russia had controlled it since 1875. Japan had reversed the outcome of the Triple Intervention and gained a large foothold on the Asian continent.

Japan moved quickly to consolidate its gains, annexing Korea in August 1910.[19] Japan had to proceed more cautiously in Manchuria, however, because Russia still maintained a large army in Northeast Asia and a serious interest in Manchuria. Moreover, the United States was alarmed by Japan's growing might and sought to contain it by keeping Russia strong and using it as a balancing force against Japan. Faced with this new strategic environment, Japan agreed with Russia in July 1907 to divide Manchuria into separate spheres of influence. Japan also recognized Russia's special interests in Outer Mongolia, while Russia recognized Japan's domination of Korea.

Japan continued its offensive ways when World War I broke out on August 1, 1914. Japan entered the war on the Allies' side within the month and quickly conquered the Pacific islands controlled by Germany (the Marshalls, the Carolines, and the Marianas), as well as the German-controlled city of Tsingtao on China's Shandong Peninsula. China, which was then in the midst of major political turmoil and in a precarious strategic position, asked Japan to return control of those cities to China. Japan not only refused the request, but in January 1915, it presented China with the infamous "Twenty-one Demands," which called for China to make major economic and political concessions to Japan that would have eventually turned China into a Japanese vassal state like Korea.[20] The United States forced Japan to abandon its most radical demands, and China grudgingly agreed to Japan's more limited demands in May 1915. It was apparent from these events that Japan was bent on dominating China sooner rather than later.

Japan's foreign policy ambitions were on display again in the summer of 1918 when its troops invaded northern Manchuria and Russia itself in the wake of the Bolshevik Revolution (October 1917).[21] Russia was in the midst of a bloody civil war, and Japan intervened in tandem with the United Kingdom, France, and the United States. The Western powers, who were still fighting against the kaiser's armies on the western front, hoped with this intervention to get Russia back into the war against Germany. In practice, that meant helping the anti-Bolshevik forces win the civil war. Although Japan contributed seventy thousand troops to the intervention force, more than any other great power, it showed little interest in fighting the Bolsheviks and instead concentrated on establishing control over the areas it occupied: the northern part of Sakhalin Island, northern Manchuria, and eastern Siberia. Japan's intervention in Russia was difficult from the start, because of harsh weather, an unfriendly population, and the vast size of the territory it occupied. After the Bolsheviks triumphed in the civil war, Japan began withdrawing its troops from Russia, pulling out of Siberia in 1922 and northern Sakhalin in 1925.

By the end of World War I, the United States felt that Japan was getting too big for its britches, and it set out to rectify the situation. At the Washington Conference in the winter of 1921–22, the United States forced Japan to accept three treaties that effectively reversed Japan's gains in China during World War I and put limits on the sizes of the American, British, and Japanese navies.[22] These treaties included much rhetoric about the need for cooperation in future crises and the importance of maintaining the political status quo in Asia. But Japan was dissatisfied with the Washington treaties from the start, mainly because it was determined to expand its empire in Asia, whereas the treaties were designed to contain it. Still, Japan's leaders signed the treaties because they felt that Japan was in no position to challenge the Western powers, who had just emerged victorious from World War I. In fact, Japan did little to upset the status quo throughout the 1920s, which was a relatively peaceful decade in Asia as well as in Europe.[23]

Japan was back to its aggressive ways in the early 1930s, however, and its foreign policy became increasingly aggressive over the course of the decade.[24] Japan's Kwantung Army initiated a crisis with China on September 18, 1931.[25] The "Mukden incident," as it came to be known, was a pretext for going to war to conquer all of Manchuria. The Kwantung Army won the war quickly, and in March 1932, Japan helped establish the "independent" state of Manchukuo, which was a de facto Japanese colony.

With both Korea and Manchuria firmly under its control by early 1932, Japan set its sights on dominating China itself. Indeed, Japan had begun probing and pushing into China even before the formal establishment of Manchukuo.[26] In January 1932, fighting broke out in Shanghai between China's Nineteenth Route Army and Japanese naval units. Japan was forced to send ground troops into Shanghai, and the ensuing battles lasted for almost six weeks before the United Kingdom arranged a truce in May 1932. In early 1933, Japanese troops moved into Jehol and Hopei, two provinces in northern China. When a truce there was finally worked out in late May 1933, Japan remained in control of Jehol, and the Chinese were forced to accept a demilitarized zone across the northern part of Hopei.

In case anyone still had doubts about Japan's intentions, its foreign ministry issued an important statement on April 18, 1934, proclaiming that East Asia was in Japan's sphere of influence and warning the other great powers not to help China in its struggle with Japan. In effect, Japan fashioned its own version of the Monroe Doctrine for East Asia.[27] Japan finally launched a full-scale assault against China in the late summer of 1937.[28] By the time Hitler invaded Poland on September 1, 1939, Japan controlled large portions of northern China as well as a number of enclaves along China's coast.

Japan was also involved in a series of border conflicts with the Soviet Union in the late 1930s, including a pair of major battles at Chungkuefung (1938) and Nomonhan (1939).[29] Leaders of the Kwantung

Army were bent on expanding beyond Manchuria into Outer Mongolia and the Soviet Union itself. The Red Army decisively defeated the Kwantung Army in both fights, and Japan quickly lost its appetite for further northward expansion.

Two critical events in Europe during the early years of World War II—the fall of France in the spring of 1940 and the German invasion of the Soviet Union a year later—opened up new opportunities for Japanese aggression in Southeast Asia and the western Pacific.[30] Japan took advantage of them but ended up in a war with the United States that lasted from December 1941 until August 1945, in which Japan was decisively defeated and eliminated from the ranks of the great powers.

GERMANY (1862–1945)

In the years from 1862 to 1870 and from 1900 to 1945, Germany was bent on upsetting the European balance of power and increasing its share of military might. It initiated numerous crises and wars during those fifty-five years and made two attempts in the twentieth century to dominate Europe. Between 1870 and 1900, Germany was concerned mainly with preserving, not changing, the balance of power. But Germany had not become a satiated power, as it made clear in the first half of the twentieth century. The cause of its benign late-nineteenth-century behavior was that Germany did not have sufficient power at the time to challenge its rivals.

Germany's aggressive foreign policy behavior was driven mainly by strategic calculations. Security was always a burning issue for Germany because of geography: it is located in the center of Europe with few natural defensive barriers on either its eastern or its western flank, which makes it vulnerable to invasion. Consequently, German leaders were always on the lookout for opportunities to gain power and enhance the prospects for their country's survival. This is not to deny that other factors influenced German foreign policy. Consider, for example, German behavior under its two most famous leaders, Otto von Bismarck and Adolf Hitler. Although Bismarck is usually considered an artful practitioner of realpolitik, he was motivated by nationalism as well as security concerns when he started and won wars in 1864, 1866, and 1870–71.[31] Specifically, he not only sought to expand Prussia's borders and make it more secure, but also was determined to create a unified German state.

There is no doubt that Hitler's aggression was motivated in good part by a deep-seated racist ideology. Nevertheless, straightforward power calculations were central to Hitler's thinking about international politics.[32] Since 1945, scholars have debated how much continuity links the Nazis and their predecessors. In the foreign policy realm, however, there is widespread agreement that Hitler did not represent a sharp break with the past but instead thought and behaved like German leaders before him. David Calleo puts the point well: "In foreign policy, the similarities between imperial and Nazi Germany are manifest. Hitler shared the same geopolitical analysis: the same certainty about conflict among nations, the same craving and rationale for hegemony over Europe. The First World War, he could claim, only sharpened the validity of that geopolitical analysis."[33] Even without Hitler and his murderous ideology, Germany surely would have been an aggressive state by the late 1930s.[34]

Targets and Rivals

France and Russia were Germany's two principal rivals between 1862 and 1945, although during brief periods Russo-German relations were friendly. Franco-German relations, on the other hand, were almost always bad over that entire period. The United Kingdom and Germany got on reasonably well before 1900, but relations soured in the early twentieth century and the United Kingdom, like France and Russia, ended up fighting against Germany in both world wars. Austria-Hungary was Germany's bitter enemy in the early years of Bismarck's reign, but they became allies in 1879 and stayed linked until Austria-Hungary disintegrated in 1918. Relations between Italy and Germany were generally good from 1862 until 1945, although Italy did fight against Germany in World War I. The United States fought against Germany in both world wars, but otherwise there was no significant rivalry between them during those eight decades.

The list of particular targets of German aggression for the period between 1862 and 1945 is long, because Germany had ambitious plans for expansion after 1900. Wilhelmine Germany, for example, not only sought to dominate Europe, but also wanted to become a world power. This ambitious scheme, known as *Weltpolitik,* included the acquisition of a large colonial empire in Africa.[35] Nevertheless, Germany's most important goal during the first half of the twentieth century was expanding on the European continent at the expense of France and Russia, which it attempted to do in both world wars. Germany had more limited goals from 1862 to 1900, as discussed below, because it was not powerful enough to overrun Europe.

Germany's Record of Expansion

Bismarck took over the reins of government in Prussia in September 1862. There was no unified German state at the time. Instead, an assortment of German-speaking political entities, scattered about the center of Europe, were loosely tied together in the German Confederation. Its two most powerful members were Austria and Prussia. Over the course of the next nine years, Bismarck destroyed the confederation and established a unified German state that was considerably more powerful than the Prussia it replaced.[36] He accomplished that task by provoking and winning three wars. Prussia joined with Austria in 1864 to defeat Denmark and then joined with Italy in 1866 to defeat Austria. Finally, Prussia defeated France in 1870, in the process making the French provinces of Alsace and Lorraine part of the new German Reich. There is little doubt that Prussia acted as offensive realism would predict from 1862 until 1870.

Bismarck became chancellor of the new Germany on January 18, 1871, and remained in office for nineteen years, until Kaiser Wilhelm fired him on March 20, 1890.[37] Although Germany was the most powerful state on the European continent during those two decades, it fought no wars and its diplomacy was concerned mainly with maintaining, not altering, the balance of power. Even after Bismarck left office, German foreign policy remained on essentially the same course for another decade. Not until the early twentieth century did Germany's diplomacy turn provocative and its leaders begin to think seriously about using force to expand Germany's borders.

What accounts for this thirty-year hiatus of rather peaceful behavior by Germany? Why did Bismarck, who was so inclined toward offense during his first nine years in office, become defense-oriented in his last nineteen years? It was not because Bismarck had a sudden epiphany and became "a peace-loving diplomatic genius."[38] In fact, it was because he and his successors correctly understood that the German army had conquered about as much territory as it could without provoking a great-power war, which Germany was likely to lose. This point becomes clear when one considers the geography of Europe at the time, the likely reaction of the other European great powers to German aggression, and Germany's position in the balance of power.

There were few minor powers on Germany's eastern and western borders. Indeed there were none on its eastern border, which abutted Russia and Austria-Hungary (see Map 6.2). This meant that it was difficult for Germany to conquer new territory without invading the homeland of another great power—i.e., France or Russia. Furthermore, it was apparent to German leaders throughout these three decades that if Germany invaded either France or Russia, Germany would probably end up fighting against both—and maybe even the United Kingdom—in a two-front war.

Consider what happened in the two major Franco-German crises of this period. During the "War in Sight Crisis" of 1875, both the United Kingdom and Russia made it clear that they would not stand by and watch Germany crush France, as they had done in 1870.[39] During the "Boulanger Crisis" of 1887, Bismarck had good reason to think that Russia would aid France if a Franco-German war broke out.[40] When that crisis ended, Bismarck negotiated the famous Reinsurance Treaty (June 13, 1887) between Germany and Russia. His aim was to keep the wire open to the Russian tsar and forestall a military alliance between France and Russia. But as George Kennan points out, Bismarck probably realized, "like many other people—that in the event of a Franco-German war it would be impossible, treaty or no treaty, to prevent the Russians from

Europe in 1914

MAP 6.2

coming in against the Germans in a short space of time."[41] Virtually all doubt about the issue was erased between 1890 and 1894, when France and Russia formed an alliance against Germany.

Although Germany was the most powerful state in Europe between 1870 and 1900, it was not a potential hegemon, and thus it did not have sufficient power to be confident that it could defeat France and Russia at the same time, much less the United Kingdom, France, and Russia all at once. In fact, Germany probably would have found France alone to be a formidable opponent before 1900. Potential hegemons, as discussed in Chapter 2, possess the most powerful army and the most wealth of any state in their region.

Germany did have the number one army in Europe, but it was not substantially more powerful than the French army during the late nineteenth century. The German army was the larger of the two fighting forces in the first few years after the Franco-Prussian War (1870–71), and at the close of the nineteenth century (see Table 6.1). Although France had more soldiers in its army than Germany did in the 1880s and early 1890s, this numerical advantage was largely meaningless, because it was due to to the fact that France—unlike Germany—had a much larger pool of poorly trained reserves who would contribute little to the outcome of any war between the two countries. In general, the German army had a clear qualitative advantage over its French counterpart, although the gap was not as marked as it had been during the Franco-Prussian War.[42]

Regarding wealth, Germany had a sizable advantage over France and Russia from 1870 to 1900 (see Table 3.3). But the United Kingdom was much wealthier than Germany during that same period. For example, Germany controlled 20 percent of European wealth in 1880, while France controlled 13 percent and Russia 3 percent. The United Kingdom, however, possessed 59 percent of the total, which gave it nearly a 3:1 advantage over Germany. In 1890, Germany's share had grown to 25 percent, while the figures for France and Russia were 13 percent and 5 percent, respectively. But the United Kingdom still controlled 50 percent of European wealth, which gave it a 2:1 advantage over Germany.

In sum, German aggression during the last three decades of the nineteenth century probably would have led to a great-power war that it was not well-positioned to win. The Second Reich would have ended up fight-

TABLE 6.1

Manpower in European Armies, 1875–95

	1875		1880		1885		1890		1895	
	Standing army	War potential	Standing army	War potential	Standing army	War potential	Standing army	War potential	Standing army	War potential
Austria-Hungary	278,470	838,700	239,615	771,556	284,495	1,071,034	336,717	1,818,413	354,252	1,872,178
United Kingdom	192,478	539,776	194,512	571,769	188,657	577,334	210,218	618,967	222,151	669,553
France	430,703	1,000,000	502,697	2,000,000	523,833	2,500,000	573,277	2,500,000	598,024	2,500,000
Germany	419,738	1,304,541	419,014	1,304,541	445,392	1,535,400	492,246	2,234,631	584,734	3,000,000
Russia	765,872	1,213,259	884,319	2,427,853	757,238	1,917,904	814,000	2,220,798	868,672	2,532,496
Italy	214,667	460,619	214,667	460,619	250,000	1,243,556	262,247	1,221,478	252,829	1,356,999

NOTE: "War potential" (referred to in *The Statesman's Year-Book* as an army's "war footing") represents the total number of men who would be in the army immediately after mobilization; it thus encompasses a country's active army plus all its reserves, however poorly trained they may be. These numbers should be taken with a grain of salt because they are only estimates, and they include many reservists who were only partially trained, and sometimes not trained at all. *The Statesman's Year-Book* does not list a war footing for the United Kingdom; I obtained it by adding the various reserves, militias, and volunteer forces it does list to the active British army at home and in the empire.

SOURCES: All figures are from *The Statesman's Year-Book* (London: Macmillan, various years), except for France's 1875 and 1880 war potential, and Italy's 1885 standing army, which are the author's estimates. Years and page numbers are as follows (years refer to editions of *The Statesman's Year-Book*). Austria-Hungary: 1876, p. 17; 1881, p. 17; 1886, p. 19; 1891, p. 350; 1896, p. 356; United Kingdom: 1876, pp. 226–27; 1881, pp. 224–25; 1886, pp. 242–43; 1891, pp. 55–56; 1896, pp. 55–56; France: 1876, p. 70; 1881, p. 70; 1886, p. 76; 1891, p. 479; 1895, p. 487; Germany: 1876, p. 102; 1881, p. 108; 1891, pp. 538–39; 1896, pp. 547–48; Russia: 1876, p. 371; 1882, p. 380; 1887, p. 430; 1891, pp. 870, 872; 1896, pp. 886, 888; Italy: 1876, p. 311; 1881, p. 311; 1886, p. 337; 1891, p. 693; 1896, p. 702.

ing two or three great powers at the same time, and it did not have enough relative power to win that kind of war. Germany was powerful enough to set alarm bells ringing in the United Kingdom, France, and Russia when there was even a hint that it might go on the offensive, but it was not yet powerful enough to fight all three of its great-power rivals at once. So Germany was forced to accept the status quo from 1870 to 1900.

By 1903, however, Germany was a potential hegemon.[43] It controlled a larger percentage of European industrial might than did any other state, including the United Kingdom, and the German army was the most powerful in the world. It now had the capability to consider going on the offensive to gain more power. It is not surprising that at about this time Germany began to think seriously about altering the European balance of power and becoming a world power.

Germany's first serious move to challenge the status quo was its decision at the turn of the century to build a formidable navy that would challenge the United Kingdom's command of the world's oceans and allow it to pursue *Weltpolitik*.[44] The result was a naval arms race between the United Kingdom and Germany that lasted until World War I. Germany initiated a major crisis with France over Morocco in March 1905. Its aim was to isolate France from the United Kingdom and Russia and prevent them from forming a balancing coalition against Germany. In fact, the crisis backfired on Germany and those three states formed the Triple Entente. Although Germany's leaders did not start the so-called Bosnian crisis in October 1908, they intervened on Austria-Hungary's behalf and forced the crisis to the brink of war before Russia backed down and accepted a humiliating defeat in March 1909. Germany initiated a second crisis over Morocco in July 1911, and again the aim was to isolate and humiliate France. It too did not work: Germany was forced to back down and the Triple Entente tightened. Most important, Germany's leaders were principally responsible for starting World War I in the summer of 1914. Their aim was to defeat Germany's great-power rivals decisively and redraw the map of Europe to ensure German hegemony for the foreseeable future.[45]

The Treaty of Versailles (1919) defanged Germany throughout the Weimar period (1919–33).[46] Germany was not allowed to have an air force, and the size of its army could not exceed one hundred thousand men. Both conscription and the famous German General Staff were outlawed. The German army was so weak in the 1920s that German leaders seriously feared an invasion by the Polish army, which had attacked the Soviet Union in 1920 and defeated the Red Army.[47] Although Germany was in no position to acquire territory by force, virtually all of its leaders during the Weimar period were committed to upsetting the status quo and at least gaining back the territory in Belgium and Poland that had been taken from Germany at the end of World War I.[48] They were also intent on restoring German military might.[49] This revisionist bent among Weimar's ruling elites explains in part why there was so little resistance to Hitler's military and foreign policies after he came to power in 1933.

Germany's leading statesman during Weimar was Gustav Stresemann, who was foreign minister from 1924 until his death in 1929. His views on foreign policy appeared to be rather tame, at least compared to those of many of his political rivals, who complained that he was not aggressive enough in pushing Germany's revisionist agenda. He signed both the Locarno Pact (December 1, 1925) and the Kellogg-Briand Pact (August 27, 1928), which were attempts to foster international cooperation and eliminate war as a tool of statecraft. He also brought Germany into the League of Nations (September 8, 1926) and rarely spoke about using force to upset the balance of power. Nevertheless, there is a broad consensus among scholars that Stresemann was no idealist but was instead "a convinced adherent of the doctrine that *Machtpolitik* was the sole determining factor in international relations and that only a nation's power potential could determine its standing in the world."[50] Moreover, he was deeply committed to expanding Germany's borders. He signed nonaggression treaties and used accommodating language with the United Kingdom and France, because he thought that clever diplomacy was the only way that a militarily feeble Germany could get back some of its lost territory. If Germany had possessed a formidable army during his tenure at the foreign ministry, he almost certainly would have used it—or threatened to use it—to gain territory for Germany.

Little needs to be said about Nazi Germany (1933–45), since it is universally recognized as one of the most aggressive states in world history.[51]

When Hitler came to power in January 1933, Germany was still a military weakling. He immediately set out to rectify that situation and build a powerful Wehrmacht that could be employed for aggressive purposes.[52] By 1938, Hitler felt it was time to begin expanding Germany's borders. Austria and the Czechoslovakian Sudetenland were acquired in 1938 without firing a shot, as was the rest of Czechoslovakia and the Lithuanian city of Memel in March 1939. Later that year, the Wehrmacht invaded Poland, then Denmark and Norway in April 1940, Belgium, Holland, Luxembourg, and France in May 1940, Yugoslavia and Greece in April 1941, and the Soviet Union in June 1941.

THE SOVIET UNION (1917–91)

Russia had a rich history of expansionist behavior before the Bolsheviks came to power in October 1917. Indeed, "the Russian Empire as it appeared in 1917 was the product of nearly four centuries of continuous expansion."[53] There is considerable evidence that Vladimir Lenin, Josef Stalin, and their successors wanted to follow in the tsars' footsteps and further expand Soviet borders. But opportunities for expansion were limited in the Soviet Union's seventy-five-year history. Between 1917 and 1933, the country was essentially too weak to take the offensive against rival major powers. After 1933, it had its hands full just trying to contain dangerous threats on its flanks: imperial Japan in Northeast Asia and Nazi Germany in Europe. During the Cold War, the United States and its allies were determined to check Soviet expansion all across the globe. Nevertheless, the Soviets had some chances to expand, and they almost always took advantage of them.

There was a deep-seated and long-standing fear among Russia's rulers that their country was vulnerable to invasion, and that the best way to deal with that problem was to expand Russia's borders. Not surprisingly, Russian thinking about foreign policy before and after the Bolshevik Revolution was motivated largely by realist logic. Describing the "discourse of Russia's statesmen" between 1600 and 1914, William Fuller writes, "They generally employed the cold-blooded language of strategy and analysis. They weighed the international impact of what they proposed to do; they pondered the strengths and weaknesses of their prospective enemies; and they justified their policies in terms of the benefits they anticipated for Russian power and security. One is struck by the omnipresence of this style of reasoning."[54]

When the Bolsheviks came to power in 1917, they apparently believed that international politics would immediately undergo a fundamental transformation and that balance-of-power logic would be relegated to the boneyard of history. Specifically, they thought that with some help from the Soviet Union, communist revolutions would spread across Europe and the rest of the world, creating like-minded states that would live in peace before finally withering away altogether. Thus, Leon Trotsky's famous quip in November 1917, when he was appointed commissar for foreign affairs: "I shall issue some revolutionary proclamations to the peoples and then close up shop." Similarly, Lenin said in October 1917, "What, are we going to have foreign affairs?"[55]

World revolution never happened, however, and Lenin quickly became "a political realist second to none."[56] In fact, Richard Debo argues that Lenin abandoned the idea of spreading communism so fast that he doubts Lenin ever took the idea seriously.[57] Stalin, who ran Soviet foreign policy for almost thirty years after Lenin died, was also driven in large part by the cold logic of realism, as exemplified by his willingness to cooperate with Nazi Germany between 1939 and 1941.[58] Ideology mattered little for Stalin's successors, not simply because they too were deeply affected by the imperatives of life in an anarchic system, but also because "Stalin had undercut deep faith in Marxist-Leninist ideological universalism and killed its genuine advocates; he had reduced the party ideologues to propagandist pawns in his global schemes."[59]

In short, Soviet foreign policy behavior over time was driven mainly by calculations about relative power, not by communist ideology. "In the international sphere," as Barrington Moore notes, "the Communist rulers of Russia have depended to a great extent on techniques that owe more to Bismarck, Machiavelli, and even Aristotle than they do to Karl Marx or

Lenin. This pattern of world politics has been widely recognized as a system of inherently unstable equilibrium, described in the concept of the balance of power."[60]

This is not to say that communist ideology did not matter at all in the conduct of Soviet foreign policy.[61] Soviet leaders paid some attention to promoting world revolution in the 1920s, and they also paid attention to ideology in their dealings with the Third World during the Cold War. Moreover, there was often no conflict between the dictates of Marxist ideology and realism. The Soviet Union, for example, clashed with the United States from 1945 until 1990 for ideological as well as balance-of-power reasons. Also, virtually every time the Soviet Union behaved aggressively for security-related reasons, the action could be justified as promoting the spread of communism. But whenever there was a conflict between the two approaches, realism invariably won out. States do whatever is necessary to survive and the Soviet Union was no exception in this regard.

Targets and Rivals

The Soviet Union was concerned mainly with controlling territory and dominating other states in Europe and Northeast Asia, the two regions in which it is located. Until 1945, its principal rivals in those areas were local great powers. After 1945, its main adversary in both Europe and Northeast Asia was the United States, with which it competed all across the globe.

Germany was the Soviet Union's main European rival between 1917 and 1945, although they were allies from 1922 to 1933 and from 1939 to 1941. The United Kingdom and France had frosty and sometimes hostile relations with Moscow from the time of the Bolshevik Revolution until the early years of World War II, when the United Kingdom and the Soviet Union finally came together to fight the Nazis. During the Cold War, the Soviet Union and its Eastern European allies were arrayed against the United States and its Western European allies; indeed, the Soviet Union's chief foreign policy goal over the course of its history was to control Eastern Europe. Soviet leaders surely would have liked to dominate Western

Europe as well and become Europe's first hegemon, but that was not feasible, even after the Red Army destroyed the Wehrmacht in World War II, because the North Atlantic Treaty Organization stood squarely in its way.

In Northeast Asia, Japan was the Soviet Union's archenemy from 1917 until 1945. Like tsarist Russia, the Soviet Union sought to control Korea, Manchuria, the Kurile Islands, and the southern half of Sakhalin Island, all of which were dominated by Japan during this period. When World War II ended in 1945, the United States became Moscow's main enemy in Northeast Asia; China became an important Soviet ally after Mao Zedong's victory over the Nationalists in 1949. However, China and the Soviet Union had a serious falling out in the late 1950s, which led China to ally with the United States and Japan against the Soviet Union in the early 1970s. The Soviet Union gained control of the Kuriles and all of Sakhalin Island in 1945, and Manchuria came under the firm control of China after 1949, leaving Korea as the region's main battleground during the Cold War.

Soviet leaders were also interested in expanding into the Persian Gulf region, especially into oil-rich Iran, which shared a border with the Soviet Union. Finally, during the Cold War, Soviet policymakers were determined to win allies and gain influence in virtually every area of the Third World, including Africa, Latin America, the Middle East, Southeast Asia, and the South Asian subcontinent. Moscow was not bent on conquering and controlling territory in those less-developed regions, however. Instead, it sought client states that would be useful in its global competition with the United States.

The Soviet Union's Record of Expansion

The Soviet Union was engaged in a desperate fight for survival during the first three years of its existence (1917–20).[62] Immediately after the Bolshevik Revolution, Lenin pulled the Soviet Union out of World War I, but in the process he was forced to make huge territorial concessions to Germany in the Treaty of Brest-Litovsk (March 15, 1918).[63] Shortly thereafter, the Western allies, who were still fighting against Germany on the western front, inserted ground forces into the Soviet Union.[64] Their aim was to force the Soviet Union to rejoin the war against Germany. That did not happen, however, in large part because the German army was defeated on the battlefield in the late summer and early fall of 1918, and World War I ended on November 11, 1918.

Germany's defeat was good news for the Soviet leaders, because it spelled the death of the Brest-Litovsk treaty, which had robbed the Soviet Union of so much of its territory. Moscow's troubles were far from over, however. A bloody civil war between the Bolsheviks and various rival groups had broken out in the first months of 1918. To make matters worse, the Western allies supported the anti-Bolshevik forces, also known as the "Whites," in their fight with the Bolshevik "Reds" and kept their intervention forces in the Soviet Union until the summer of 1920. Although the Bolsheviks sometimes appeared to be on the verge of losing the civil war, the balance of power shifted decisively against the Whites in early 1920, and it was then only a matter of time before they were defeated. But before that could happen, the newly created state of Poland took advantage of Soviet weakness and invaded the Ukraine in April 1920. Poland hoped to break apart the Soviet Union and make Belorussia and Ukraine independent states. The hope was that those new states would then join a Polish-dominated federation of independent eastern European states.

The Polish army scored major victories in the early fighting, capturing Kiev in May 1920. But later that summer the Red Army turned the tide of battle, so much so that by the end of July, Soviet forces reached the Soviet-Polish border. Amazingly, the Soviets now had an opportunity to invade and conquer Poland, and maybe with help from Germany (the other great power unhappy about Poland's existence), redraw the map of eastern Europe. Lenin quickly seized the opportunity and sent the Red Army toward Warsaw.[65] But the Polish army, with help from France, routed the invading Soviet forces and pushed them out of Poland. Both sides were exhausted from the fighting by then, so they signed an armistice in October 1920 and a formal peace treaty in March 1921. By that point the civil war was effectively over and the Western allies had withdrawn their troops from Soviet territory.[66]

Soviet leaders were in no position to pursue an expansionist foreign policy during the 1920s or early 1930s, mainly because they had to concentrate on consolidating their rule at home and rebuilding their economy, which had been devestated by all the years of war.[67] For example, the Soviet Union controlled a mere 2 percent of European industrial might by 1920 (see Table 3.3). But Moscow did pay some attention to foreign affairs. In particular, it maintained close relations with Germany from April 1922, when the Treaty of Rapallo was signed, until Hitler came to power in early 1933.[68] Although both states were deeply interested in altering the territorial status quo, neither possessed a serious offensive military capability. Soviet leaders also made an effort in the 1920s to spread communism around the globe. But they were always careful not to provoke the other great powers into moving against the Soviet Union and threatening its survival. Virtually all of these efforts to foment revolution, whether in Asia or Europe, came up short.

Probably the most important Soviet initiative of the 1920s was Stalin's decision to modernize the Soviet economy through forced industrialization and the ruthless collectivization of agriculture. He was motivated in large part by security concerns. In particular, he believed that if the Soviet economy continued to lag behind those of the world's other industrialized states, the Soviet Union would be destroyed in a future great-power war. Speaking in 1931, Stalin said, "We have lagged behind the advanced countries by fifty to a hundred years. We must cover that distance in ten years. Either we'll do it or they will crush us."[69] A series of five-year plans, initiated in October 1928, transformed the Soviet Union from a destitute great power in the 1920s into Europe's most powerful state by the end of World War II.

The 1930s was a decade of great peril for the Soviet Union; it faced deadly threats from Nazi Germany in Europe and imperial Japan in Northeast Asia. Although the Red Army ended up in a life-and-death struggle with the Wehrmacht during World War II, not with the Japanese army, Japan was probably the more dangerous threat to the Soviet Union throughout the 1930s.[70] Indeed, Soviet and Japanese troops engaged in a series of border clashes in the late 1930s, culminating in a brief war at

Nomonhan in the summer of 1939. Moscow was in no position to take the offensive in Asia during the 1930s, but instead concentrated on containing Japanese expansion. Toward that end, the Soviets maintained a powerful military presence in the region and provided considerable assistance to China after the start of the Sino-Japanese War in the summer of 1937. Their aim was to keep Japan bogged down in a war of attrition with China.

The Soviet Union's main strategy for dealing with Nazi Germany contained an important offensive dimension.[71] Stalin apparently understood soon after Hitler came to power that the Third Reich was likely to start a great-power war in Europe and that there was not much chance of reconstituting the Triple Entente (the United Kingdom, France, Russia) to deter Nazi Germany or fight against it if war broke out. So Stalin pursued a buck-passing strategy. Specifically, he went to considerable lengths to develop friendly relations with Hitler, so that the Nazi leader would strike first against the United Kingdom and France, not the Soviet Union. Stalin hoped that the ensuing war would be long and costly for both sides, like World War I on the western front, and thus would allow the Soviet Union to gain power and territory at the expense of the United Kingdom, France, and especially Germany.

Stalin finally succeeded in passing the buck to the United Kingdom and France in the summer of 1939 with the signing of the Molotov-Ribbentrop Pact, in which Hitler and Stalin agreed to gang up on Poland and divide it between them, and Hitler agreed to allow the Soviet Union a free hand in the Baltic states (Estonia, Latvia, and Lithuania) and Finland. This agreement meant that the Wehrmacht would fight against the United Kingdom and France, not the Soviet Union. The Soviets moved quickly to implement the pact. After conquering the eastern half of Poland in September 1939, Stalin forced the Baltic countries in October to allow Soviet forces to be stationed on their territory. Less than a year later, in June 1940, the Soviet Union annexed those three tiny states. Stalin demanded territorial concessions from Finland in the fall of 1939, but the Finns refused to make a deal. So Stalin sent the Red Army into Finland in November 1939 and took the territory he wanted by force.[72] He was also able to convince Hitler in June 1940 to allow the Soviet Union to absorb

Bessarabia and Northern Bukovina, which were part of Romania. In short, the Soviet Union made substantial territorial gains in eastern Europe between the summers of 1939 and 1940.

Nevertheless, Stalin's buck-passing strategy came up short in the spring of 1940 when the Wehrmacht overran France in six weeks and pushed the British army off the continent at Dunkirk. Nazi Germany was now more powerful than ever and it was free to invade the Soviet Union without having to worry much about its western flank. Recalling how Stalin and his lieutenants reacted to news of the debacle on the western front, Nikita Khrushchev wrote, "Stalin's nerves cracked when he learned about the fall of France. . . . The most pressing and deadly threat in all history faced the Soviet Union. We felt as though we were facing the threat all by ourselves."[73] The German onslaught came a year later, on June 22, 1941.

The Soviet Union suffered enormous losses in the early years of World War II but eventually turned the tide against the Third Reich and began launching major offensives westward, toward Berlin, in early 1943. The Red Army, however, was not simply concerned with defeating the Wehrmacht and recapturing lost Soviet territory. Stalin was also determined to conquer territory in Eastern Europe that the Soviets would dominate after Germany was defeated.[74] The Red Army had to conquer Poland and the Baltic states to defeat the German army, but the Soviets also launched major military operations to capture Bulgaria, Hungary, and Romania, even though those offensives were not essential for defeating Germany and probably delayed the final victory.

The Soviet Union's appetite for power and influence in Northeast Asia was also evident during World War II. In fact, Stalin managed to win back more territory than Russia had controlled in the Far East before its defeat by Japan in 1905. The Soviets had managed to keep out of the Pacific war until the final days of that conflict, when the Red Army attacked Japan's Kwantung Army in Manchuria on August 9, 1945. This Soviet offensive was in large part a response to long-standing pressure from the United States to join the war against Japan after Germany was defeated. Stalin, however, demanded a price for Soviet participation, and Winston Churchill and Franklin Roosevelt responded by striking a secret deal with him at Yalta in February 1945.[75] For joining the fight against Japan, the Soviets were promised the Kurile Islands and the southern half of Sakhalin Island. In Manchuria, they were given a lease on Port Arthur as a naval base and recognition of the Soviet Union's "preeminent interests" over the commercial port of Dairen and the region's two most important railroads.

No firm decision was reached on Korea's future during World War II, although the Red Army occupied the northern part of that country during the closing days of the conflict.[76] In December 1945, the United States and the Soviet Union effectively agreed to jointly administer Korea as a trusteeship. But that plan fell apart quickly, and in February 1946, Stalin began building a client state in North Korea. The United States did the same in South Korea.

With Germany and Japan in ruins, the Soviet Union emerged from World War II as a potential hegemon in Europe and Northeast Asia. If it were possible, the Soviets surely would have moved to dominate both of those regions. Indeed, if ever a state had good reason to want to rule over Europe it was the Soviet Union in 1945. It had been invaded twice by Germany over a thirty-year period, and each time Germany made its victim pay an enormous blood price. No responsible Soviet leader would have passed up an opportunity to be Europe's hegemon in the wake of World War II.

Hegemony was not feasible, however, for two reasons. First, given the enormous amount of damage the Third Reich inflicted on Soviet society, Stalin had to concentrate on rebuilding and recovering after 1945, not fighting another war. Thus, he cut the size of the Soviet military from 12.5 million troops at the end of World War II to 2.87 million by 1948.[77] Second, the United States was an enormously wealthy country that had no intention of allowing the Soviet Union to dominate either Europe or Northeast Asia.[78]

In light of these constraints, Stalin sought to expand Soviet influence as far as possible without provoking a shooting war with the United States and its allies.[79] Actually, the available evidence indicates that he hoped to avoid an intense security competition with the United States, although he was not successful in that endeavor. In short, Stalin was a cautious expansionist during the early part of the Cold War. His four main targets were Iran, Turkey, Eastern Europe, and South Korea.

The Soviets occupied northern Iran during World War II, while the British and the Americans occupied southern Iran.[80] All three great powers agreed at the time to evacuate Iran within six months after the war against Japan ended. The United States pulled its troops out on January 1, 1946, and British troops were on schedule to come out by March 2, 1946. Moscow, however, made no move to leave Iran. Furthermore, it was supporting separatist movements among both the Azeri and the Kurdish populations in northern Iran, as well as Iran's communist Tudeh Party. Both the United Kingdom and the United States put pressure on Stalin to remove his troops from Iran, which he did in the spring of 1946.

Regarding Turkey, which was neutral during World War II until March 1945, Stalin demanded in June 1945 that the Turkish provinces of Ardahan and Kars, which had been part of Russia from 1878 to 1918, be given back to the Soviet Union.[81] He also asked for military bases on Turkish territory so that the Soviets could help control the Dardanelles, the Turkish straits linking the Black Sea with the Mediterranean Sea. In support of these demands, Stalin massed Soviet troops on the Turkish border at one point. But these wants were never realized because the United States was determined to prevent Soviet expansion in the eastern Mediterranean.

The principal realm of Soviet expansion in the early Cold War was Eastern Europe, and almost all of it was due to the fact that the Red Army conquered most of the area in the final stages of World War II. Estonia, Latvia, and Lithuania were formally incorporated into the Soviet Union after the war, as was the eastern one-third of Poland, part of East Prussia, Bessarabia, northern Bukovina, Czechoslovakia's eastern province of Subcarpathian Ruthenia, and three slices of territory on Finland's eastern border (see Map 6.3). Bulgaria, Hungary, Poland, and Romania were turned into satellite states immediately after the war. Czechoslovakia suffered the same fate in February 1948, and a year later the Soviets created another satellite state in East Germany.

Soviet Expansion in Eastern Europe during the Early Cold War

Annexed by Soviet Union

Soviet Satellites

Neutral countries

NORWAY

FINLAND

SWEDEN

Baltic Sea

ESTONIA

DENMARK

LATVIA

LITHUANIA

SOVIET UNION

EAST PRUSSIA

EAST GERMANY

POLAND

EASTERN POLAND

WEST GERMANY

CZECHOSLOVAKIA

NORTHERN BUKOVINA

SWITZ.

AUSTRIA

HUNGARY

SUBCARPATHIAN RUTHENIA

BESSARABIA

ITALY

ROMANIA

Black Sea

Adriatic Sea

YUGOSLAVIA

BULGARIA

ALBANIA

GREECE

TURKEY

Mediterranean Sea

MAP 6.3

Finland and Yugoslavia were the only states in Eastern Europe to escape complete Soviet domination. Their good fortune was due mainly to two factors. First, both states had clearly demonstrated in World War II that it would be difficult and costly for the Soviet army to conquer and occupy them for an extended period of time. The Soviet Union, which was attempting to recover from the massive damage it had suffered at the hands of the Nazis, already had its hands full occupying the other states in Eastern Europe. Thus, it was inclined to avoid costly operations in Finland and Yugoslavia. Second, both states were willing to maintain a neutral position in the East-West conflict, which meant that they were not a military threat to the Soviet Union. If either Finland or Yugoslavia had shown an inclination to ally with NATO, the Soviet army probably would have invaded it.[82]

The Soviet Union also attempted to gain power and influence in Northeast Asia during the early Cold War, although that region clearly received less attention than did Europe.[83] Despite some distrust between Stalin and Mao, the Soviets provided aid to the Chinese Communists in their fight against the Nationalist forces under Chiang Kai-shek. The Chinese Communists won the civil war in 1949 and allied with the Soviet Union against the United States. One year later, the Soviets supported North Korea's invasion of South Korea, which led to a three-year war that left Korea divided along roughly the same line that had divided it before the war.[84]

By the early 1950s, the United States and its allies around the globe had a formidable containment policy firmly in place, and there was little opportunity for further Soviet expansion in Europe, Northeast Asia, or the Persian Gulf. In fact, Stalin's decision to back North Korea's invasion of South Korea in late June 1950 was the last case of Soviet-sponsored aggression in any of those critically important areas for the remainder of the Cold War. Soviet efforts at expansion between 1950 and 1990 were confined to the Third World, where it met with occasional success, but always with firm resistance from the United States.[85]

After decades of competition with the United States for control over Europe, the Soviet Union suddenly reversed course in 1989 and abandoned its empire in Eastern Europe. That bold move effectively brought the Cold War to an end. The Soviet Union itself then broke apart into fifteen remnant states in late 1991. With few exceptions, the first wave of scholars to study these events argued that the Cold War ended because key Soviet leaders, especially Mikhail Gorbachev, underwent a fundamental transformation in their thinking about international politics during the 1980s.[86] Rather than seeking to maximize the Soviet Union's share of world power, Moscow's new thinkers were motivated by the pursuit of economic prosperity and liberal norms of restraint in the use of force. Soviet policymakers, in short, stopped thinking and acting like realists and instead adopted a new perspective emphasizing the virtues of cooperation among states.

As more evidence becomes available, however, it is becoming increasingly apparent that the first-wave explanation of Soviet behavior at the end of the Cold War is incomplete, if not wrong. The Soviet Union and its empire disappeared in large part because its smokestack economy could no longer keep up with the technological progress of the world's major economic powers.[87] Unless something drastic was done to reverse this economic decline, the Soviet Union's years as a superpower were numbered.

To fix the problem, Soviet leaders sought to gain access to Western technology by greatly reducing East-West security competition in Europe, liberalizing their political system at home, and cutting their losses in the Third World. But that approach backfired because political liberalization unleashed the long-dormant forces of nationalism, causing the Soviet Union itself to fall apart.[88] In sum, the conventional wisdom from the initial wave of scholarship on the end of the Cold War had it backwards: far from abandoning realist principles, the behavior and thinking of Soviet leaders reinforce the pattern of history that states seek to maximize their power in order to remain secure from international rivals.[89]

ITALY (1861–1943)

There is much agreement among students of Italian foreign policy that although Italy was the weakest of the great powers between 1861 and 1943, it constantly sought opportunities to expand and gain more power.[90]

Richard Bosworth, for example, writes that "pre-1914 Italy was a power on the make, looking for a bargain package deal which would offer the least of the great powers a place in the sun."[91] The foreign policy of post–World War I Italy, which was dominated by Benito Mussolini, shared the same basic goal. Fascist Italy (1922–43) merely faced a different set of opportunities than its predecessor, liberal Italy (1861–1922). Writing in 1938, four years before Italy collapsed in World War II, Maxwell Macartney and Paul Cremona wrote, "In the past Italian foreign policy has certainly not been dominated by abstract ideals. Nowhere have the implications of Machiavelli's *mot* on the political inutility of innocence been more thoroughly grasped than in his native country."[92]

Targets and Rivals

One gets a good sense of the breadth of Italy's appetite for territorial conquest by considering its main targets over the course of the eight decades that it was a great power. It focused its aggressive intentions on five different areas: North Africa, which included Egypt, Libya, and Tunisia; the Horn of Africa, which included Eritrea, Ethiopia, and Somaliland; the southern Balkans, which included Albania, Corfu, the Dodecanese Islands, and even parts of southwestern Turkey; southern Austria-Hungary, which included Dalmatia, Istria, the Trentino (the southern part of Tyrol), and Venetia; and southeastern France, which included Corsica, Nice, and Savoy (see Map 6.4).

Italy's main rivals for control of these areas were Austria-Hungary (at least until that multiethnic state broke apart in 1918) in the Balkans, and France in Africa. Of course, Italy also had its sights on territory that was part of Austria-Hungary and France, which had long "regarded the Italian peninsula as a free field for diplomatic and military maneuver."[93] The Ottoman Empire, which was falling apart between 1861 and its final demise in 1923, was also an important factor in Italy's calculations: that empire controlled large swaths of territory in the Balkans and North Africa.

Although Italy's hostile aims were ever-present, its army was ill-equipped for expansion. In fact, it was a remarkably inefficient fighting force.[94] Not only was it incapable of holding its own in a fight against the

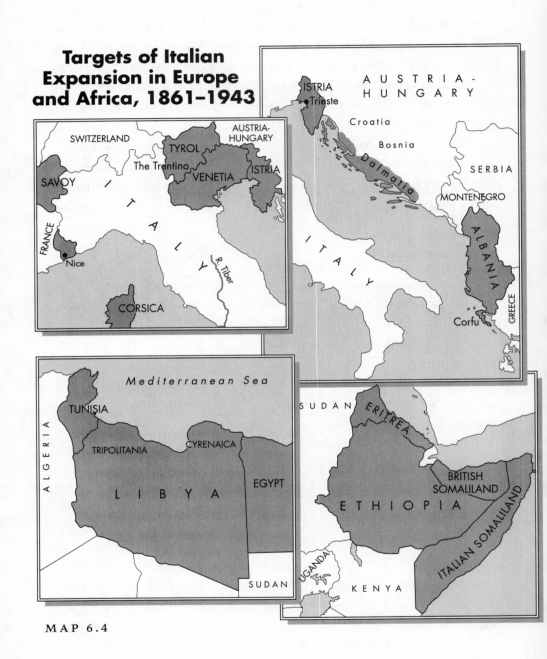

Targets of Italian Expansion in Europe and Africa, 1861–1943

MAP 6.4

other European great powers, it also could be counted on to perform poorly against the fighting forces of smaller European powers as well as native armies in Africa. Bismarck put the point well when he said that "Italy had a large appetite and rotten teeth."[95] Consequently, Italian leaders tended to avoid direct military engagements with other great powers unless their adversary was about to lose a war or had substantial numbers of its troops bogged down on another front.

Because of Italy's lack of military prowess, its leaders relied heavily on diplomacy to gain power. They paid careful attention to choosing alliance partners and were adept at playing other great powers off against each other for Italy's benefit. In particular, they operated on the assumption that although they were playing a weak hand, Italy possessed sufficient military might to tip the balance between other major powers, who would recognize that fact and make concessions to Italy to win its allegiance. Brian Sullivan labels this approach "the strategy of the decisive weight."[96] World War I probably provides the best example of that strategy in action. When the conflict broke out on August 1, 1914, Italy remained on the sidelines, where it dickered with each of the warring sides to get the best possible deal before entering the conflict.[97] Both sides made Italy generous offers, because each believed that the Italian army might tip the balance one way or the other. Although Italy had been formally allied with Austria-Hungary and Germany before World War I, it joined the war in May 1915 on the Allies' side, because the United Kingdom and France were willing to concede more territory to Italy than were its former allies.

Liberal and Fascist Italy's Record of Expansion

Italy's first efforts at territorial expansion were in Europe. In 1866, Italy joined forces with Prussia to fight against Austria. The Prussians crushed the Austrians in battle, but the Italians were defeated by the Austrians. In the peace settlement, however, Italy was awarded Venetia, a large area on its northern frontier that had been part of Austria. Italy then sat out the Franco-Prussian War (1870–71), although it conquered Rome in September 1870 when it was obvious that France, which had previously protected

Rome's independence, would lose its war with Prussia. Italy, as Denis Mack Smith notes, "thus casually gained Rome, like Venice, as just another by-product of Prussian victory."[98] During the "Great Eastern Crisis," which broke out in 1875 when the Ottoman Empire's control over southeastern Europe seemed to slip precipitously, Italy began scheming to take territory from Austria-Hungary. But the schemes failed and Italy came away empty-handed from the Congress of Berlin (1878), which ended the crisis.

Italy shifted its focus away from Europe and toward Africa in the early 1880s. Even before unification in 1861, Italian elites had shown significant interest in conquering territory along the North African coast. Tunisia was the number one target. But France beat Italy to the punch and captured Tunisia in 1881, which soured Italian relations with France for the next twenty years and caused Italy to form the Triple Alliance with Austria-Hungary and Germany in 1882. That same year, Italy attempted to join the British occupation of Egypt, but Bismarck nixed that scheme. Italy then turned its attention to the Horn of Africa, an area to which the other great powers paid little attention. An Italian expeditionary force was sent to the region in 1885, and within a decade, Italy had its first two colonies: Eritrea and Italian Somaliland. It failed to conquer Ethiopia, however. In fact, the Ethiopian army inflicted a major defeat on the Italian army at Adowa in 1895.

By 1900, Italy was again looking to expand in North Africa and Europe. Opportunities to expand presented themselves in both regions as the Ottoman Empire began losing its grip on Libya and the Balkans. Relations between Triple Alliance partners Austria-Hungary and Italy went sour at this point, in large part because they became rivals in the Balkans. This burgeoning rivalry opened the door for Italy to think seriously about taking Istria and the Trentino away from Austria-Hungary.

Italy went to war with the Ottoman Empire over Libya in 1911; when the war ended a year later, Italy had won control over its third African colony. During that conflict, Italy also conquered the Dodecanese Islands, whose inhabitants were mostly Greek. But World War I provided Italy with its greatest opportunity to expand its power and enhance its security.

As noted, Italian policymakers bargained hard with both sides before joining forces with the United Kingdom, France, and Russia. Italy's basic aims were to secure a "defensible land frontier" with Austria-Hungary and "domination of the Adriatic," the large body of water that separates Italy from the Balkans.[99] In the famous Treaty of London, the Allies promised Italy that after the war was won, it could have 1) Istria, 2) the Trentino, 3) a large chunk of the Dalmatian coast, 4) permanent control over the Dodecanese Islands, 5) the Turkish province of Adalia, 6) control of the Albanian city of Valona and the area immediately surrounding it, and 7) a sphere of influence in central Albania.[100] The Italians, as A.J.P. Taylor notes, "were certainly not modest in their claims."[101]

Italy suffered more than a million casualties in World War I, but it came out on the winning side. After the war, Italy not only expected to get what it was promised in 1915, it also saw new opportunities for expansion with the collapse of Austria-Hungary, the Ottoman Empire, and Russia. Thus, as Sullivan notes, "Italians began planning for control over the oil, grain, and mines of Romania, the Ukraine, and the Caucasus, and for protectorates over Croatia and the eastern Red Sea coast."[102] For a variety of reasons, however, Italy's grand ambitions were never realized. In the final postwar settlement, it gained only Istria and the Trentino, which were nevertheless strategically important areas.[103] Italy also continued to occupy the Dodecanese Islands, over which it was given formal control in 1923 by the Treaty of Lausanne.

Thus, in the six decades between unification and Mussolini's coming to power in October 1922, liberal Italy had acquired Rome, Venetia, Istria, the Trentino, and the Dodecanese Islands in Europe, and Eritrea, Libya, and Italian Somaliland in Africa. Fascist Italy quickly set about building on its predecessor's record of successful conquests. In August 1923, Mussolini's army invaded the Greek island of Corfu at the mouth of the Adriatic Sea, but the United Kingdom forced Italy to abandon its conquest. He also set his sights on Albania, which Italy had occupied during World War I but had given up in 1920 when the local population rebelled against the foreign rulers. Mussolini supported an Albanian chieftan in the mid-1920s, who then signed an agreement with Italy that effectively made Albania an

Italian protectorate. But that was not enough for the fascist leader, who formally annexed Albania in April 1939.

Ethiopia was another key target for Mussolini. Italy began making plans to occupy it in the mid-1920s, and "from at least 1929 onwards surreptitiously occupied places inside Ethiopia."[104] In October 1935, Italy launched a full-scale war against Ethiopia, and one year later it gained formal control over that African state. Finally, Italy sent troops to fight in the Spanish Civil War (1936–39) on the side of General Francisco Franco's reactionary junta. Italy's main aim was to acquire the Balearic Islands in the western Mediterranean, which would allow Italy to threaten France's lines of communication with North Africa, and the United Kingdom's lines of communication between Gibraltar and Malta.[105]

Mussolini saw World War II as an excellent chance to conquer foreign territory and gain power for Italy. Specifically, Nazi Germany's stunning military successes in the early years of the war "gave Italy unprecedented leverage and freedom of action."[106] Mussolini's first major step was to declare war against France on June 10, 1940, one month after Germany invaded France, and at a point when it was clear that France was doomed to defeat. Italy entered the war at this opportune moment to acquire French territory and colonies. Nice, Savoy, Corsica, Tunisia, and Djibouti were the main targets, although Italy was also interested in acquiring other French-controlled areas such as Algeria, as well as parts of the British empire, such as Aden and Malta. Mussolini also demanded that the French navy and air force be turned over to Italy. Germany met hardly any of Italy's demands, however, because Hitler did not want to give France any incentive to resist the Nazi occupation.

Despite this setback, Mussolini continued looking for opportunities to conquer territory. In the early summer of 1940, he offered to join forces with Nazi Germany if it invaded the United Kingdom. In August 1940, Italy captured British Somaliland. At the same time, Mussolini was contemplating invasions of Greece, Yugoslavia, and Egypt, which was defended by a small British army. In September 1940, Italy invaded Egypt with the hope of reaching the Suez Canal. The following month, Italy invaded Greece. Both operations turned into military disasters for the Italian army, although the Wehrmacht came to its rescue in both.[107] These military debacles notwithstanding, Italy declared war against the Soviet Union in the summer of 1941, when it appeared that the Red Army would be the Nazi war machine's next victim. Italy sent about two hundred thousand troops to the eastern front. Again, Mussolini hoped to get some of the spoils of victory for Italy, but his hopes were never realized, and Italy surrendered to the Allies in September 1943.

In sum, Mussolini, like Italy's liberal leaders before him, was a relentless expansionist.

SELF-DEFEATING BEHAVIOR?

The preceding four cases—Japan, Germany, the Soviet Union, and Italy—support the claim that great powers seek to increase their share of world power. Moreover, these cases also show that great powers are often willing to use force to achieve that goal. Satiated great powers are rare in international politics. This description of how great powers have acted over time is, in fact, not that controversial, even among defensive realists. Jack Snyder, for example, writes that "the idea that security can be achieved through expansion is a pervasive theme in the grand strategy of great powers in the industrial era."[108] Furthermore, in *Myths of Empire*, he offers detailed case studies of great-power behavior in the past that provide abundant evidence of the offensive proclivities of such states.

One might recognize that history is replete with examples of great powers acting aggressively but still argue that this behavior cannot be explained by the logic of offensive realism. The basis of this claim, which is common among defensive realists, is that expansion is misguided. Indeed, they regard it as a prescription for national suicide. Conquest does not pay, so the argument runs, because states that try to expand ultimately meet defeat. States would be wiser to maintain the status quo by pursuing policies of "retrenchment, selective appeasement, shoring up vital rather than peripheral areas, or simply benign neglect."[109] That states do otherwise is evidence of irrational or nonstrategic behavior, behavior that cannot be prompted by the imperatives of the international system. Rather, this behavior is primarily the result of malign domestic political forces.[110]

There are two problems with this line of argument. As I have already discussed, the historical record does not support the claim that conquest hardly ever pays and that aggressors invariably end up worse off than they were before the war. Exapansion sometimes pays big dividends; at other times it does not. Furthermore, the claim that great powers behave aggressively because of pernicious domestic politics is hard to sustain, because all kinds of states with very different kinds of political systems have adopted offensive military policies. It is not even the case that there is at least one type of political system or culture—including democracy— that routinely eschews aggression and works instead to defend the status quo. Nor does the record indicate that there are especially dangerous periods—for example, the nuclear age—during which great powers sharply curtail their offensive tendencies. To argue that expansion is inherently misguided implies that all great powers over the past 350 years have failed to comprehend how the international system works. This is an implausible argument on its face.

There is a more sophisticated fallback position, however, that may be discerned in the writings of the defensive realists.[111] Although they usually argue that conquest rarely pays, they also admit on other occasions that aggression succeeds a good part of the time. Building on that more variegated perspective, they divide the universe of aggressors into "expanders" and "overexpanders." Expanders are basically the smart aggressors who win wars. They recognize that only limited expansion makes good strategic sense. Attempts to dominate an entire region are likely to be self-defeating, because balancing coalitions invariably form against states with large appetites, and such states end up suffering devastating defeats. Expanders might occasionally start a losing war, but once they see the writing on the wall, they quickly retreat in the face of defeat. In essence, they are "good learners."[112] For defensive realists, Bismarck is the archetypical smart aggressor, because he won a series of wars without committing the fatal error of trying to become a European hegemon. The former Soviet Union is also held up as an example of an intelligent aggressor, mainly because it had the good sense not to try to conquer all of Europe.

Overexpanders, on the other hand, are the irrational aggressors who start losing wars yet do not have the good sense to quit when it becomes apparent that they are doomed to lose. In particular, they are the great powers who recklessly pursue regional hegemony, which invariably leads to their own catastrophic defeat. Defensive realists contend that these states should know better, because it is clear from history that the pursuit of hegemony almost always fails. This self-defeating behavior, so the argument goes, must be the result of warped domestic politics. Defensive realists usually point to three prominent overexpanders: Wilhelmine Germany from 1890 to 1914, Nazi Germany from 1933 to 1941, and imperial Japan from 1937 to 1941. Each of these aggressors started a war that led to a devastating loss. It is not an exaggeration say that the claim that offensive military policies lead to self-defeating behavior rests primarily on these three cases.

The main problem with this "moderation is good" perspective is that it mistakenly equates irrational expansion with military defeat. The fact that a great power loses a war does not necessarily mean that the decision to initiate it was the result of an ill-informed or irrational decision-making process. States should not start wars that they are certain to lose, of course, but it is hard to predict with a high degree of certainty how wars will turn out. After a war is over, pundits and scholars often assume that the outcome was obvious from the start; hindsight is 20-20. In practice, however, forecasting is difficult, and states sometimes guess wrong and get punished as a result. Thus, it is possible for a rational state to initiate a war that it ultimately loses.

The best way to determine whether an aggressor such as Japan or Germany was engaged in self-defeating behavior is to focus on the decision-making process that led it to initiate war, not the outcome of the conflict. A careful analysis of the Japanese and German cases reveals that, in each instance, the decision for war was a reasonable response to the particular circumstances each state faced. As the discussion below makes clear, these were not irrational decisions fueled by malign political forces on the home front.

There are also problems with the related argument that pursuing regional hegemony is akin to tilting at windmills. To be sure, the United States is the only state that has attempted to conquer its region and succeeded. Napoleonic France, Wilhelmine Germany, Nazi Germany, and imperial Japan all tried but failed. One out of five is not an impressive success rate. Still, the American case demonstrates that it is possible to achieve regional hegemony. There are also examples of success from the distant past: the Roman Empire in Europe (133 B.C.–235 A.D.), the Mughal Dynasty on the South Asian subcontinent (1556–1707), and the Ch'ing Dynasty in Asia (1683–1839), to name a few. Furthermore, even though Napoleon, Kaiser Wilhelm, and Hitler all lost their bids to dominate Europe, each won major battlefield victories, conquered huge tracts of territory, and came close to achieving their goals. Only Japan stood little chance of winning hegemony on the battlefield. But as we shall see, Japanese policymakers knew that they would probably lose, and went to war only because the United States left them with no reasonable alternative.

Critics of offensive policies claim that balancing coalitions form to defeat aspiring hegemons, but history shows that such coalitions are difficult to put together in a timely and efficient manner. Threatened states prefer to buck-pass to each other rather than form an alliance against their dangerous foe. For example, the balancing coalitions that finished off Napoleonic France and Nazi Germany came together only after these aggressors had conquered much of Europe. Moreover, in both cases, the defensive alliances did not form until after the drive for hegemony had been blunted by a significant military defeat in Russia, which effectively fought both Napoleon and Hitler without allies.[113] The difficulty of constructing effective defensive alliances sometimes provides powerful states with opportunities for aggression.

Finally, the claim that great powers should have learned from the historical record that attempts at regional hegemony are doomed is not persuasive. Not only does the American case contradict the basic point, but it is hard to apply the argument to the first states that made a run at regional hegemony. After all, they had few precedents, and the evidence from the earliest cases was mixed. Wilhelmine Germany, for example, could look at both Napoleonic France, which failed, and the United States, which succeeded. It is hard to argue that German policymakers should have read history to say that they were sure to lose if they attempted to conquer Europe. One might concede that point but argue that Hitler certainly should have known better, because he could see that Wilhelmine Germany as well as Napoleonic France had failed to conquer Europe. But, as discussed below, what Hitler learned from those cases was not that aggression did not pay, but rather that he should not repeat his predecessor's mistakes when the Third Reich made its run at hegemony. Learning, in other words, does not always lead to choosing a peaceful outcome.

Thus, the pursuit of regional hegemony is not a quixotic ambition, although there is no denying that it is difficult to achieve. Since the security benefits of hegemony are enormous, powerful states will invariably be tempted to emulate the United States and try to dominate their region of the world.

Wilhelmine Germany (1890–1914)

The indictment against the Kaiserreich for engaging in self-defeating behavior has two counts. First, its aggressive actions caused the United Kingdom, France, and Russia to form an alliance—the Triple Entente—against Germany. Thus, it is guilty of self-encirclement. Second, Germany then started a war with that balancing coalition in 1914 that it was almost sure to lose. Not only did Germany have to fight a two-front war as a result of its self-encirclement, but it had no good military strategy for quickly and decisively defeating its rivals.

These charges do not bear up under close inspection. There is no doubt that Germany made certain moves that helped cause the Triple Entente. Like all great powers, Germany had good strategic reasons for wanting to expand its borders, and it sometimes provoked its rivals, especially after 1900. Nevertheless, a close look at how the Entente was formed reveals that the main driving force behind its creation was Germany's growing economic and military might, not its aggressive behavior.

Consider what motivated France and Russia to come together between 1890 and 1894, and then what motivated the United Kingdom to join them between 1905 and 1907. As noted, both France and Russia worried about Germany's growing power during the 1870s and 1880s. Bismarck himself feared that they might form an alliance against Germany. After Russia threatened to come to France's aid during the "War in Sight Crisis" (1875), Bismarck built an alliance structure that was designed to isolate France from the other European great powers. Although he successfully kept France and Russia from allying against Germany during his tenure in office, Russia probably would not have stood by and watched Germany defeat France, as it had in 1870–71. Indeed, it was apparent by the late 1880s that France and Russia were likely to form an alliance against Germany in the near future, whether Bismarck remained in power or not. Soon after Bismarck left office in March 1890, France and Russia began negotiating an alliance, which was put in place four years later. But Germany did not behave offensively in the years before or immediately after Bismarck left office. His successors precipitated no significant crises between 1890 and 1900.[114] So it is hard to argue in this instance that aggressive German behavior caused self-encirclement.[115]

One might argue that Bismarck's successors caused Russia to join with France not by behaving aggressively but by foolishly failing to renew the Reinsurance Treaty between Germany and Russia. Bismarck negotiated this arrangement in 1887 in a desperate move to keep Russia and France apart. There is widespread agreement among scholars, however, that the treaty was a dead letter by 1890 and that there was no substitute diplomatic strategy available. Indeed, W. N. Medlicott maintains that, the Reinsurance Treaty notwithstanding, Bismarck's "Russian policy was in ruins" by 1887.[116] Even if Bismarck had remained in power past 1890, it is unlikely that he could have forestalled the Franco-Russian alliance with clever diplomacy. "Neither Bismarck nor an even greater political genius at the head of German foreign policy," Imanuel Geiss argues, "could probably have prevented . . . an alliance between Russia and France."[117] France and Russia came together because they were scared of Germany's growing power, not because Germany behaved aggressively or foolishly.

Germany did behave aggressively in the early twentieth century, when the United Kingdom joined with France and Russia to form the Triple Entente. But even here, the United Kingdom was motivated more by Germany's growing power than by its aggressive behavior.[118] Germany's decision in 1898 to build a fleet that could challenge the British navy surely soured relations between the United Kingdom and Germany, but it did not drive the United Kingdom to make an alliance with France and Russia. After all, the best way for the United Kingdom to have dealt with this naval arms race was to have won it hands down, not to have committed itself to fight a land war against Germany, which would have mandated spending precious defense dollars on the army rather than the navy. The Moroccan crisis of 1905, which was the first instance of overtly aggressive German behavior, certainly played an important role in the establishment of the Triple Entente between 1905 and 1907. But the main factor behind the United Kingdom's decision to form that three-cornered alliance was Russia's devastating defeat in the Russo-Japanese War (1904–5), which had little to do with German behavior.[119] Russia was effectively knocked out of the European balance of power with that defeat, which meant a sudden and dramatic improvement in Germany's power position on the continent.[120] British leaders recognized that France alone was not likely to fare well in a war with Germany, so they allied with France and Russia to rectify the balance and contain Germany. In sum, changes in the architecture of the European system, not German behavior, were the main cause of the Triple Entente.

The German decision to push for war in 1914 was not a case of wacky strategic ideas pushing a state to start a war it was sure to lose. It was, as noted, a calculated risk motivated in large part by Germany's desire to break its encirclement by the Triple Entente, prevent the growth of Russian power, and become Europe's hegemon. The precipitating event was a crisis in the Balkans between Austria-Hungary and Serbia, in which Germany sided with the former and Russia with the latter.

German leaders clearly understood that they would have to fight a two-front war and that the Schlieffen Plan did not guarantee victory. Nevertheless, they thought that the risk was worth taking, especially since

Germany was so much more powerful than either France or Russia at the time, and there was good reason to think that the United Kingdom might remain on the sidelines.[121] They almost proved right. The Schlieffen Plan narrowly missed producing a quick and decisive victory in 1914.[122] As political scientist Scott Sagan notes, it was for good reason that the French referred to their last-second victory near Paris in September 1914 as "the Miracle of the Marne."[123] Moreover, Germany almost won the subsequent war of attrition between 1915 and 1918. The Kaiser's armies knocked Russia out of the war in the fall of 1917, and they had the British and especially the French armies on the ropes in the spring of 1918. Had it not been for American intervention at the last moment, Germany might have won World War I.[124]

This discussion of German behavior before World War I points to an anomaly for offensive realism. Germany had an excellent opportunity to gain hegemony in Europe in the summer of 1905. Not only was it a potential hegemon, but Russia was reeling from its defeat in the Far East and was in no position to defend itself against a German attack. Also, the United Kingdom was not yet allied with France and Russia. So France stood virtually alone against the mighty Germans, who "had an opportunity without parallel to change the European balance in their favor."[125] Yet Germany did not seriously consider going to war in 1905 but instead waited until 1914, when Russia had recovered from its defeat and the United Kingdom had joined forces with France and Russia.[126] According to offensive realism, Germany should have gone to war in 1905, because it almost surely would have won the conflict.

Nazi Germany (1933–41)

The charge against Hitler is that he should have learned from World War I that if Germany behaved aggressively, a balancing coalition would form and crush it once again in a bloody two-front war. The fact that Hitler ignored this obvious lesson and rushed headlong into the abyss, so the argument goes, must have been the result of a deeply irrational decision-making process.

This indictment does not hold up on close inspection. Although there is no question that Hitler deserves a special place in the pantheon of mass murderers, his evilness should not obscure his skill as an adroit strategist who had a long run of successes before he made the fatal mistake of invading the Soviet Union in the summer of 1941. Hitler did indeed learn from World War I. He concluded that Germany had to avoid fighting on two fronts at the same time, and that it needed a way to win quick and decisive military victories. He actually realized those goals in the early years of World War II, which is why the Third Reich was able to wreak so much death and destruction across Europe. This case illustrates my earlier point about learning: defeated states usually do not conclude that war is a futile enterprise, but instead strive to make sure they do not repeat mistakes in the next war.

Hitler's diplomacy was carefully calculated to keep his adversaries from forming a balancing coalition against Germany, so that the Wehrmacht could defeat them one at a time.[127] The key to success was preventing the Soviet Union from joining forces with the United Kingdom and France, thus recreating the Triple Entente. He succeeded. In fact, the Soviet Union helped the Wehrmacht carve up Poland in September 1939, even though the United Kingdom and France had declared war against Germany for having invaded Poland. During the following summer (1940), the Soviet Union stood on the sidelines while the German army overran France and pushed the British army off the continent at Dunkirk. When Hitler invaded the Soviet Union in 1941, France was out of the war, the United States was not yet in, and the United Kingdom was not a serious threat to Germany. So the Wehrmacht was effectively able to fight a one-front war against the Red Army in 1941.[128]

Much of Hitler's success was due to the machinations of his rivals, but there is little doubt that Hitler acted skillfully. He not only played his adversaries off against one another, but he went to considerable lengths to convince them that Nazi Germany had benign intentions. As Norman Rich notes, "To conceal or obscure whatever his real intentions may have been, Hitler dedicated no small part of his diplomatic and propagandistic skill. In his public speeches and diplomatic conversations he monotonously intoned his desire for peace, he signed friendship treaties and nonaggression pacts, he was lavish with assurances of good will."[129] Hitler surely understood that the blustery rhetoric of Kaiser Wilhelm and other German leaders before World War I had been a mistake.

Hitler also recognized the need to fashion a military instrument that could win quick victories and avoid the bloody battles of World War I. To that end he supported the building of panzer divisions and played an important role in designing the blitzkrieg strategy that helped Germany win one of the most stunning military victories of all time in France (1940).[130] Hitler's Wehrmacht also won stunning victories against minor powers: Poland, Norway, Yugoslavia, and Greece. As Sebastian Haffner notes, "From 1930 until 1941 Hitler succeeded in practically everything he undertook, in domestic and foreign politics and eventually also in the military field, to the amazement of the world."[131] If Hitler had died in July 1940 after France capitulated, he probably would be considered "one of the greatest of German statesmen."[132]

Fortunately, Hitler made a critical mistake that led to the destruction of the Third Reich. He unleashed the Wehrmacht against the Soviet Union in June 1941, and this time the German blitzkrieg failed to produce a quick and decisive victory. Instead, a savage war of attrition set in on the eastern front, which the Wehrmacht eventually lost to the Red Army. Compounding matters, the United States came into the war in December 1941 and, along with the United Kingdom, eventually opened up a second front in the west. Given the disastrous consequences of attacking the Soviet Union, one might think that there was abundant evidence beforehand that the Soviet Union would win the war, that Hitler was warned repeatedly that launching Operation Barbarossa was tantamount to committing national suicide, and that he did it anyway because he was not a rational calculator.

The evidence, however, does not support this interpretation. There was little resistance among the German elite to Hitler's decision to invade the Soviet Union; in fact, there was considerable enthusiasm for the gambit.[133] For sure, some German generals were dissatisfied with important aspects of the final plan, and a few planners and policymakers thought that the

Red Army might not succumb to the German blitzkrieg. Nevertheless, there was a powerful consensus within the German elite that the Wehrmacht would quickly rout the Soviets, much the way it had defeated the British and French armies a year earlier. It was also widely believed in both the United Kingdom and the United States that Germany would defeat the Soviet Union in 1941.[134] Indeed, there were good reasons to think that the Red Army would collapse in the face of the German onslaught. Stalin's massive purges of his army in the late 1930s had markedly reduced its fighting power, and almost as if to prove the point, the Red Army performed badly in its war against Finland (1939–40).[135] Plus, the Wehrmacht was a finely tuned fighting force by June 1941. In the end, Hitler and his lieutenants simply miscalculated the outcome of Operation Barbarossa. They made a wrong decision, not an irrational one, and that sometimes happens in international politics.

A final point about Germany's two failed attempts at hegemony. Haffner wrote during the Cold War of the wide belief that it was "a mistake from the very start" for Germany to have attempted to dominate Europe.[136] He emphasized how members of "the younger generation" in what was then West Germany "often stare at their fathers and grandfathers as though they were lunatics ever to have set themselves such a goal." He notes, however, that "it should be remembered that the majority of those fathers and grandfathers, i.e., the generation of the First and that of the Second World War, regarded the goal as reasonable and attainable. They were inspired by it and not infrequently died for it."

Imperial Japan (1937–41)

The indictment against Japan for overexpansion boils down to its decision to start a war with the United States, which had roughly eight times as much potential power as Japan in 1941 (see Table 6.2) and went on to inflict a devastating defeat on the Japanese aggressors.

It is true that Japan had picked fights with the Red Army in 1938 and 1939 and lost both times. But as a result, Japan stopped provoking the Soviet Union and the border between them remained quiet until the last

TABLE 6.2

Relative Share of World Wealth, 1830–1940

	1830	1840	1850	1860	1870	1880	1890	1900	1910	1913	1920	1930	1940
United Kingdom	47%	57%	59%	59%	53%	45%	32%	23%	15%	14%	16%	11%	11%
Germany	4%	4%	3%	9%	13%	16%	16%	21%	20%	21%	14%	14%	17%
France	18%	14%	10%	12%	11%	10%	8%	7%	6%	6%	5%	9%	4%
Russia	13%	8%	6%	3%	2%	2%	3%	6%	5%	6%	1%	6%	13%
Austria-Hungary	6%	6%	6%	4%	4%	3%	4%	4%	4%	4%	—	—	—
Italy	—	—	—	0%	0%	0%	1%	1%	1%	1%	1%	2%	2%
United States	12%	12%	15%	13%	16%	23%	35%	38%	48%	47%	62%	54%	49%
Japan	—	—	—	0%	0%	0%	0%	0%	1%	1%	2%	4%	6%

NOTE: "Wealth" is measured with the same composite indicator used in Table 3.3. Note that the calculations of world wealth used here are based on figures for the relevant great powers. Minor powers are not included, save for the United States in the nineteenth century, when it was not yet a great power.

SOURCES: All data are from J. David Singer and Melvin Small, *National Material Capabilities Data, 1816–1985* (Ann Arbor, MI: Inter-University Consortium for Political and Social Research, February 1993).

days of World War II, when Japan's fate was clearly sealed. It is also true that Japan invaded China in 1937 and became involved in a lengthy war that it was unable to win. However, not only was Japan reluctantly drawn into that conflict, but its leaders were confident that China, which was hardly a formidable military power at the time, would be easily defeated. Although they were wrong, Japan's failure to win a victory in China was hardly a catastrophic failure. Nor was the Sino-Japanese War the catalyst that put the the United States on a collision course with Japan.[137] American policymakers were clearly unhappy about Japanese aggression in China, but the United States remained on the sidelines as the war escalated. In fact, it made little effort to help China until late 1938, and even then it offered the beleagured Chinese only a small package of economic aid.[138]

Two stunning events in Europe—the fall of France in June 1940 and especially Nazi Germany's invasion of the Soviet Union in June 1941—drove the United States to confront Japan, and eventually led to Pearl Harbor. As Paul Schroeder notes, "The United States did not seriously consider stopping the Japanese advance by force of arms, or consider Japan as an actual enemy, until the Far Eastern war had become clearly linked with the far greater (and, to the United States, more important) war in Europe." In particular, it was "opposition to Hitler which began to condition American policy in the Far East more than any other factor."[139]

The Wehrmacht's victory in the west not only knocked France and the Netherlands out of the war, but it also forced a badly weakened United Kingdom to concentrate on defending itself against a German assault from the air and the sea. Since those three European powers controlled most of Southeast Asia, that resource-rich region was now an open target for Japanese expansion. And if Japan conquered Southeast Asia, it could shut down a considerable portion of the outside aid flowing into China, which would increase Japan's prospects of winning its war there.[140] And if Japan controlled China and Southeast Asia as well as Korea and Manchuria, it would dominate most of Asia. The United States was determined to prevent that outcome, and thus in the summer of 1940 it began working hard to deter further Japanese expansion.

Japan was anxious to avoid a fight with the United States, so it moved cautiously in Southeast Asia. By the early summer of 1941, only northern Indochina had come under Japan's control, although Tokyo had been able to get the United Kingdom to shut down the Burma Road between July and October 1940 and the Dutch to provide Japan with additional oil. It seemed by mid-June 1941 that "even if there were little hope of real agreement" between Japan and the United States, "there remained a chance that some kind of temporary and limited settlement might be reached."[141] At the time, it did not seem likely that they would be at war in six months.

Germany's invasion of the Soviet Union on June 22, 1941, however, fundamentally altered relations between Japan and the United States and sent them hurtling down the road to war.[142] Most American policymakers, as noted, believed that the Wehrmacht was likely to defeat the Red Army, thus making Germany the hegemon in Europe. A Nazi victory would also have left Japan as the hegemon in Asia, since the Soviet Union was the only great power with an army in Asia that could check Japan.[143] Thus, if the Soviets lost to the Germans, the United States would have found itself confronting hostile hegemons in Asia as well as Europe. Not surprisingly, the United States was bent on avoiding that nightmare scenario, which meant that the Soviet Union had to survive the German onslaught of 1941 as well as any future German offensives.

Unfortunately for Japan, it was in a position in 1941 to affect the Soviet Union's chances for survival. In particular, American policymakers were deeply worried that Japan would attack the Soviet Union from the east and help the Wehrmacht finish off the Red Army. Not only were Germany and Japan formally allied in the Tripartite Pact, but the United States had abundant intelligence that Japan was considering an attack on the beleaguered Soviet Union, which Japan had fought against just two years earlier.[144] To preclude that possibility, the United States put tremendous economic and diplomatic pressure on Japan in the latter half of 1941. The aim, however, was not simply to deter Japan from striking the Soviet Union, but also to coerce Japan into abandoning China, Indochina, and possibly Manchuria, and more generally, any ambition it might have to dominate Asia.[145] In short, the United States employed massive coercive pressure against Japan to transform it into a second-rate power.

The United States was well-positioned to coerce Japan. On the eve of World War II, Japan imported 80 percent of its fuel products, more than 90 percent of its gasoline, more than 60 percent of its machine tools, and almost 75 percent of its scrap iron from the United States.[146] This dependency left Japan vulnerable to an American embargo that could wreck Japan's economy and threaten its survival. On July 26, 1941, with the situation going badly for the Red Army on the eastern front and Japan having just occupied southern Indochina, the United States and its allies froze Japan's assets, which led to a devastating full-scale embargo against Japan.[147] The United States emphasized to Japan that it could avoid economic strangulation only by abandoning China, Indochina, and maybe Manchuria.

The embargo left Japan with two terrible choices: cave in to American pressure and accept a significant dimunition of its power, or go to war against the United States, even though an American victory was widely agreed to be the likely outcome.[148] Not surprisingly, Japan's leaders tried to cut a deal with the United States in the late summer and fall of 1941. They said that they would be willing to evacuate their troops from Indochina once a "just peace" was reached in China, and they maintained that they would be willing to pull all Japanese troops out of China within twenty-five years after peace broke out between China and Japan.[149] But U.S. policymakers stuck to their guns and refused to make any concessions to the increasingly desperate Japanese.[150] The United States had no intention of allowing Japan to threaten the Soviet Union either in 1941 or later in the war. In effect, the Japanese would be defanged either peacefully or by force, and the choice was theirs.[151]

Japan opted to attack the United States, knowing full well that it would probably lose, but believing that it might be able to hold the United States at bay in a long war and eventually force it to quit the conflict. For example, the Wehrmacht, which was outside the gates of Moscow by November 1941, might decisively defeat the Soviet Union, thus forcing the United States to focus most of its attention and resources on Europe, not Asia.

Furthermore, the U.S. military, a rather inefficient fighting machine in the fall of 1941, might be further weakened by a surprise Japanese attack.[152] Capabilities aside, it was not certain that the United States had the will to fight if attacked. After all, the United States had done little to stop Japanese expansion in the 1930s, and isolationism was still a powerful ideology in America. As late as August 1941, an extension of the one-year term of service for those who were drafted in 1940 passed the House of Representatives by only one vote.[153]

But the Japanese were not fools. They knew that the United States was more likely than not to fight and likely to win the ensuing war. They were willing to take that incredibly risky gamble, however, because caving in to American demands seemed to be an even worse alternative. Sagan puts the point well: "The persistent theme of Japanese irrationality is highly misleading. . . . [T]he Japanese decision for war appears to have been rational. If one examines the decisions made in Tokyo in 1941 more closely, one finds not a thoughtless rush to national suicide, but rather a prolonged, agonizing debate between two repugnant alternatives."[154]

THE NUCLEAR ARMS RACE

My final test of offensive realism is to examine whether its prediction that great powers seek nuclear superiority is correct. The opposing position, which is closely identified with the defensive realists, is that once nuclear-armed rivals find themselves operating in a MAD world—that is, a world in which each side has the capability to destroy the other side after absorbing a first strike—they should willingly accept the status quo and not pursue nuclear advantage. States should therefore not build counterforce weapons or defensive systems that could neutralize the other side's retaliatory capability and undermine MAD. An examination of the superpowers' nuclear policies during the Cold War thus provides an ideal case for assessing these competing realist perspectives.

The historical record makes it clear that offensive realism better accounts for the nuclear policies of the United States and the Soviet Union during the

Cold War. Neither superpower accepted the defensive realists' advice about the virtues of MAD. Instead, both sides developed and deployed large, sophisticated counterforce arsenals, either to gain nuclear advantage or to prevent the other side from doing so. Moreover, both sides sought to develop defenses against the other side's nuclear weapons, as well as elaborate clever strategies for fighting and winning a nuclear war.

U.S. Nuclear Policy

The nuclear arms race between the superpowers did not become serious until about 1950. The United States enjoyed a nuclear monopoly in the early years of the Cold War, and the Soviet Union did not explode its first nuclear device until August 1949. Thus, concepts such as counterforce were irrelevant in the late 1940s, because the Soviets had no nuclear weapons for the United States to target. The main concern of American strategists during this period was how to stop the Red Army from overrunning Western Europe. They believed that the best way to deal with that threat was to launch a nuclear bombing campaign against the Soviet industrial base.[155] In essence, the strategy was "an extension" of the American strategic bombing campaign against Germany in World War II, although "greatly compressed in time, magnified in effect, and reduced in cost."[156]

After the Soviets developed the atomic bomb, the United States sought to develop a splendid first-strike capability—that is, a strike that would preemptively destroy all of the Soviets' nuclear capabilities in one fell swoop. American nuclear policy during the 1950s was called "massive retaliation," although that label was probably a misnomer, since the word "retaliation" implies that the United States planned to wait to strike the Soviet Union until after absorbing a Soviet nuclear strike.[157] In fact, there is considerable evidence that the United States intended to launch its nuclear weapons first in a crisis in order to eliminate the small Soviet nuclear force before it could get off the ground. General Curtis LeMay, the head of the Strategic Air Command (SAC), made this point clear in the mid-1950s, when he declared that the vulnerability of SAC's bombers—a cause for worry at the time—did not concern him much, because his script for a nuclear war called for the United States to strike first and disarm the Soviet Union. "If I see that the Russians are amassing their planes for an attack," he said, "I'm going to kick the shit out of them before they take off the ground."[158] It would thus be more accurate to define U.S. nuclear policy in the 1950s as "massive preemption" rather than massive retaliation. Regardless, the key point is that during the 1950s, the United States was committed to gaining nuclear superiority over the Soviet Union.

Nevertheless, the United States did not achieve a first-strike capability against the Soviet nuclear arsenal during either the 1950s or the early 1960s. Granted, had the United States struck first in a nuclear exchange during that period, it would have inflicted much greater damage on the Soviet Union than vice versa. And American planners certainly did put forth plausible best-case scenarios in which a U.S. first strike eliminated almost all of the Soviet Union's nuclear retaliatory force, thus raising doubts about whether Moscow truly had an assured-destruction capability.[159] The United States, in other words, was close to having a first-strike capability. Still, most American policymakers at the time believed that the United States was likely to suffer unacceptable damage in a nuclear war with the Soviet Union, even if that damage fell short of total destruction of the United States.[160]

By the early 1960s, however, it was readily apparent that the growing size and diversity of the Soviet nuclear arsenal meant that it would soon be impossible, given existing technology, for the United States seriously to contemplate disarming the Soviet Union with a nuclear first strike.[161] Moscow was on the verge of developing an invulnerable and robust second-strike capability, which would put the superpowers squarely in a MAD world. How did American policymakers view this development, and how did they respond to it? They were not only deeply unhappy about it, but for the remainder of the Cold War, they devoted considerable resources to escaping MAD and gaining a nuclear advantage over the Soviet Union.

Consider the sheer number of Soviet targets that the United States was planning to strike in a nuclear war, a number that went far beyond the requirements of MAD. It was generally agreed that to have an assured-destruction capability, the United States, after absorbing a Soviet first strike, had to be able to destroy about 30 percent of the Soviet Union's population and about 70 percent of its industry.[162] That level of destruction could have been achieved by destroying the 200 largest cities in the Soviet Union. This task required about 400 one-megaton weapons, or an equivalent mix of weapons and megatonnage (hereinafter referred to as 400 EMT). However, the actual number of Soviet targets that the United States planned to destroy far exceeded the 200 cities required for assured destruction. For example, SIOP-5, the actual military plan for employing nuclear weapons that took effect on January 1, 1976, listed 25,000 potential targets.[163] SIOP-6, which the Reagan administration approved on October 1, 1983, contained a staggering 50,000 potential targets.

Although the United States never acquired the capability to hit all of those potential targets at once, it deployed a huge arsenal of nuclear weapons, which grew steadily in size from the early 1960s until the Cold War ended in 1990. Moreover, most of those weapons had significant counterforce capability, because American strategic planners were not content merely to incinerate 200 Soviet cities, but were determined to destroy a large portion of the Soviet Union's retaliatory capability as well. For example, 3,127 nuclear bombs and warheads were in the U.S. inventory in December 1960, when SIOP-62 (the first SIOP) was approved.[164] Twenty-three years later, when SIOP-6 was put into effect, the strategic nuclear arsenal had grown to include 10,802 weapons. Although the United States needed a reasonably large retaliatory force for assured-destruction purposes—because it had to assume that some of its nuclear weapons might be lost to a Soviet first strike—there is no question that the size of the American nuclear arsenal during the last twenty-five years of the Cold War went far beyond the 400 EMT required to destroy 200 Soviet cities.

The United States also pushed hard to develop technologies that would give it an advantage at the nuclear level. For example, it went to considerable lengths to improve the lethality of its counterforce weapons. The United States was especially concerned with improving missile accuracy, a concern that its weapons designers allayed with great success. America also pioneered the development of MIRVs (multiple independently targeted re-entry vehicles), which allowed it to increase significantly the number of strategic warheads in its inventory. By the end of the Cold War, the "hard-target kill capability" of U.S. ballistic missiles—that is, U.S. counterforce capability—had reached the point at which the survivability of the Soviets' land-based missile silos was in question. Washington also invested heavily in protecting its command-and-control systems from attack, thus augmenting its capability to wage a controlled nuclear war. In addition, the United States pushed hard, if unsuccessfully, to develop effective ballistic missile defenses. American policymakers sometimes said that the ultimate purpose of missile defense was to move away from a nuclear world that prized offense to a safer, defense-dominant world, but the truth is that they wanted defenses in order to facilitate winning a nuclear war at a reasonable cost.[165]

Finally, the United States came up with an alternative to the strategy of massive retaliation that, it hoped, would allow it to wage and win a nuclear war against the Soviet Union. This alternative strategy was first formulated by the Kennedy administration in 1961 and came to be known as "limited nuclear options."[166] The new policy assumed that neither superpower could eliminate the other side's assured-destruction capability, but that they could still engage in limited nuclear exchanges with their counterforce weapons. The United States would aim to avoid striking Soviet cities so as to limit civilian deaths and would concentrate instead on achieving victory by dominating the Soviet Union in the limited counterforce exchanges that were at the heart of the strategy. It was hoped that the Soviets would fight according to the same rules. This new policy was codified in SIOP-63, which took effect on August 1, 1962. There were four important successor SIOPs over the remainder of the Cold War, and each new SIOP essentially provided smaller, more precise, and more select counterforce options than its predecessor, as well as command-and-control improvements that would facilitate fighting a limited nuclear war.[167] The ultimate aim of these refinements, of course, was to ensure that the United States had an advantage over the Soviet Union in a nuclear war.[168]

In sum, the evidence is overwhelming that the United States did not abandon its efforts to gain nuclear superiority during the last twenty-five years of the Cold War.[169] Nevertheless, it did not gain a meaningful advantage over the Soviets. In fact, it did not come as close to achieving that goal as it had during the 1950s and early 1960s.

Soviet Nuclear Policy

Although we know less about the Soviet side of the story than we do about the American side, it is not difficult to determine whether the Soviets sought nuclear advantage over the United States or were content to live in a MAD world. We not only have details on the size and composition of the Soviet nuclear arsenal during the course of the Cold War, but also have access to a large body of Soviet literature that lays out Moscow's thinking on nuclear strategy.

The Soviet Union, like the United States, built a massive nuclear arsenal with abundant counterforce capability.[170] The Soviets, however, were late bloomers. They did not explode their first nuclear weapon until August 1949, and their arsenal grew slowly in the 1950s. During that decade, the Soviet Union lagged behind the United States in developing and deploying nuclear weapons, as well as the systems to deliver them. By 1960 the Soviet inventory contained only 354 strategic nuclear weapons, compared to 3,127 for the United States.[171] But the Soviet force grew rapidly during the 1960s. By 1970 it numbered 2,216; ten years later it numbered 7,480. Soviet president Mikhail Gorbachev's "new thinking" notwithstanding, the Soviet Union added almost 4,000 bombs and warheads to its nuclear inventory during the 1980s, ending up with 11,320 strategic nuclear weapons in 1989, the year the Berlin Wall came down.

Furthermore, most Soviet strategists apparently believed that their country had to be prepared to fight and win a nuclear war.[172] This is not to say that Soviet leaders were eager to fight such a war or that they were confident that they could gain a meaningful victory. Soviet strategists understood that nuclear war would involve untold destruction.[173] But they were determined to limit damage to the Soviet Union and prevail in any nuclear exchange between the superpowers. There is little evidence to suggest that Soviet leaders bought the defensive realists' arguments about the virtues of MAD and the dangers of counterforce.

American and Soviet strategists did differ, however, on the question of how best to win a nuclear war. It is apparent that Soviet planners never accepted U.S. thinking about limited nuclear options.[174] Instead, they seemed to favor a targeting policy much like the U.S. policy of massive retaliation from the 1950s. Specifically, they maintained that the best way to wage a nuclear war and limit damage to the Soviet Union was to launch a rapid and massive counterforce strike against the entire war-making capacity of the United States and its allies. The Soviets did not emphasize targeting American civilians, as assured destruction demands, although a full-scale nuclear strike against the United States certainly would have killed many millions of Americans.

Thus it seems that both superpowers went to considerable lengths during the Cold War to build huge counterforce nuclear arsenals so that they could gain nuclear advantage over the other. Neither side was content merely to build and maintain an assured-destruction capability.

Misunderstanding the Nuclear Revolution

One may recognize that the superpowers relentlessly sought nuclear superiority but still argue that this behavior was misguided, if not irrational, and that it cannot be explained by balance-of-power logic. Neither side could possibly have gained meaningful nuclear advantage over the other, and, what is more, MAD makes for a highly stable world. Thus, the pursuit of nuclear superiority must have been the result of bureaucratic politics or dysfunctional domestic politics in both the United States and the Soviet Union. This perspective is held by most defensive realists, who recognize that neither superpower accepted its own claims about the merits of MAD and the evils of counterforce.[175]

It is not easy to apply this line of argument to the 1950s and the early 1960s, because the small size of the Soviet arsenal during that period gave the United States a real chance of gaining nuclear superiority. Indeed, some experts believe that the United States did have a "splendid first-strike" capability against the Soviet Union.[176] I disagree with this assessment, but there is little question that during the early Cold War the

United States would have suffered much less damage than its rival in a nuclear exchange. The defensive realists' best case thus covers roughly the last twenty-five years of the Cold War, when both the United States and the Soviet Union had an unambiguous assured-destruction capability. Yet even during this period of strategic parity, each superpower still sought to gain a nuclear advantage over the other.

To begin with, the broad contours of strategic nuclear policy are consistent with the predictions of offensive realism. Specifically, the United States worked hardest at gaining nuclear superiority in the 1950s, when a first-strike capability was arguably within its grasp. Once the Soviet Union approached a secure retaliatory capability, however, the U.S. effort to gain superiority slackened, although it did not disappear. Although American policymakers never embraced the logic of assured destruction, the percentage of U.S. defense spending devoted to strategic nuclear forces declined steadily after 1960.[177] Moreover, both sides agreed not to deploy significant ballistic missile defenses and eventually placed qualitative and quantitative limits on their offensive forces as well. The nuclear arms race continued in a number of different ways, some of which were described above, but neither side made an all-out effort to acquire superiority once MAD was in place.

Moreover, the continuation of the arms race was not misguided, even though nuclear superiority remained an elusive goal. In fact, it made good strategic sense for the United States and the Soviet Union to compete vigorously in the nuclear realm, because military technology tends to develop rapidly and in unforeseen ways. For example, few people in 1914 understood that the submarine would become a deadly and effective weapon during World War I. Few in 1965 foresaw how the brewing revolution in information technology would profoundly affect conventional weapons such as fighter aircraft and tanks. The key point is that nobody could say for sure in 1965 whether some revolutionary new technology might not transform the nuclear balance and give one side a clear advantage.

Furthermore, military competitions are usually characterized by what Robert Pape has called an "asymmetric diffusion of military technology."[178] States do not acquire new technologies simultaneously, which means that the innovator often gains significant, albeit temporary, advantages over the laggard. Throughout the Cold War, for example, the United States maintained a significant advantage in developing technologies to detect the other side's submarines and to hide its own.

Great powers always prefer to be the first to develop new technologies; they have to make sure that their opponents do not beat them to the punch and gain the advantage for themselves. Thus, it made sense for each superpower to make a serious effort to develop counterforce technology and ballistic missile defenses. At a maximum, a successful breakthrough might have brought clear superiority; at a minimum, these efforts prevented the other side from gaining a unilateral advantage. In short, given the strategic benefits that come with nuclear superiority, and the fact that it was hard to know throughout the Cold War whether it was achievable, it was neither illogical nor surprising that both superpowers pursued it.

CONCLUSION

The nuclear arms race between the superpowers and the foreign policy behavior of Japan (1868–1945), Germany (1862–1945), the Soviet Union (1917–91), and Italy (1861–1943) show that great powers look for opportunities to shift the balance of power in their favor and usually seize opportunities when they appear. Moreover, these cases support my claims that states do not lose their appetite for power as they gain more of it, and that especially powerful states are strongly inclined to seek regional hegemony. Japan, Germany, and the Soviet Union, for example, all set more ambitious foreign policy goals and behaved more aggressively as their power increased. In fact, both Japan and Germany fought wars in an attempt to dominate their areas of the world. Although the Soviet Union did not follow suit, that was because it was deterred by American military might, not because it was a satiated great power.

The fallback argument, which allows that the major states have relentlessly pursued power in the past but characterizes this pursuit as self-defeating behavior caused by destructive domestic politics, is not persuasive. Aggression is not always counterproductive. States that initiate wars often win and frequently improve their strategic position in the process. Furthermore, the fact that so many different kinds of great powers have sought to gain advantage over their rivals over such broad spans of history renders implausible the claim that this was all foolish or irrational behavior brought about by domestic pathologies. A close look at the cases that might seem to be prime examples of aberrant strategic behavior—the final twenty-five years of the nuclear arms race, imperial Japan, Wilhelmine Germany, and Nazi Germany—suggests otherwise. Although domestic politics played some role in all of these cases, each state had good reason to try to gain advantage over its rivals *and* good reason to think that it would succeed.

For the most part, the cases discussed in this chapter involve great powers taking active measures to gain advantage over their opponents—exactly what offensive realism predicts. Let us now turn to the American and British cases, which seem at first glance to provide evidence of great powers ignoring opportunities to gain power. As we shall see, however, each of these cases in fact provides further support for the theory.

7

The Offshore Balancers

I have reserved discussion of the American and British cases for a separate chapter because they might appear to provide the strongest evidence against my claim that great powers are dedicated to maximizing their share of world power. Many Americans certainly view their country as a truly exceptional great power that has been motivated largely by noble intentions, not balance-of-power logic. Even important realist thinkers such as Norman Graebner, George Kennan, and Walter Lippmann believe that the United States has frequently ignored the imperatives of power politics and instead acted in accordance with idealist values.[1] This same perspective is evident in the United Kingdom, which is why E. H. Carr wrote *The Twenty Years' Crisis* in the late 1930s. He was warning his fellow citizens about their excessive idealism in foreign policy matters and reminding them that competition for power among states is the essence of international politics.[2]

There are three particular instances where it might seem that the United Kingdom and the United States passed up opportunities to gain power. First, it is usually said that the United States achieved great-power status in about 1898, when it won the Spanish-American War, which gave it control over the fate of Cuba, Guam, the Philippines, and Puerto Rico, and also when it began building a sizable military machine.[3] By

1850, however, the United States already stretched from the Atlantic to the Pacific and, as was shown in Table 6.2, clearly possessed the economic wherewithal to become a great power and compete around the globe with Europe's major powers. Yet it did not build powerful military forces between 1850 and 1898, and it made little effort to conquer territory in the Western Hemisphere, much less outside of it. Fareed Zakaria describes this period as a case of "imperial understretch."[4] The seeming failure of the United States to become a great power and pursue a policy of conquest in the second half of the nineteenth century might seem to contradict offensive realism.

Second, the United States was no ordinary great power by 1900. It had the most powerful economy in the world and it had clearly gained hegemony in the Western Hemisphere (see Table 6.2). Although neither of those conditions changed over the course of the twentieth century, the United States did not attempt to conquer territory in Europe or Northeast Asia or dominate those wealth-producing regions of the world. If anything, the United States has been anxious to avoid sending troops to Europe and Northeast Asia, and when it has been forced to do so, it has usually been anxious to bring them back home as soon as possible. This reluctance to expand into Europe and Asia might appear to contradict my claim that states try to maximize their relative power.

Third, the United Kingdom had substantially more potential power than any other European state during most of the nineteenth century. In fact, between 1840 and 1860, Britain controlled nearly 70 percent of European industrial might, almost five times more than France, its closest competitor (see Table 3.3). Nevertheless, the United Kingdom did not translate its abundant wealth into actual military might and attempt to dominate Europe. In a world where great powers are supposed to have an insatiable appetite for power and ultimately aim for regional hegemony, one might expect the United Kingdom to have acted like Napoleonic France, Wilhelmine Germany, Nazi Germany, and the Soviet Union and pushed hard to become Europe's hegemon. But it did not.

The notion that the United Kingdom and the United States have not been power maximizers over much of the past two centuries is intuitively appealing at first glance. The fact is, however, both states have consistently acted as offensive realism would predict.

American foreign policy throughout the nineteenth century had one overarching goal: achieving hegemony in the Western Hemisphere. That task, which was motivated in good part by realist logic, involved building a powerful United States that could dominate the other independent states of North and South America and also prevent the European great powers from projecting their military might across the Atlantic Ocean. The American drive for hegemony was successful. Indeed, as emphasized earlier, the United States is the only state in modern times to have gained regional hegemony. This impressive achievement, not some purported noble behavior toward the outside world, is the real basis of American exceptionalism in the foreign policy realm.

There was no good strategic reason for the United States to acquire more territory in the Western Hemisphere after 1850, as it had already acquired a huge land mass over which its rule needed to be consolidated. Once that happened, the United States would be overwhelmingly powerful in the Americas. The United States paid little attention to the balance of power in Europe and Northeast Asia during the second half of the nineteenth century, not only because it was focused on gaining regional hegemony, but also because there were no potential peer competitors to worry about in either region. Finally, the United States did not build large and formidable military forces between 1850 and 1898 because there was no significant opposition to the growth of American power in those years.[5] The United Kingdom kept few troops in North America, and the Native Americans possessed little military might. In essence, the United States was able to gain regional hegemony on the cheap.

The United States did not attempt to conquer territory in either Europe or Northeast Asia during the twentieth century because of the difficulty of projecting military forces across the Atlantic and Pacific Oceans against the great powers located in those regions.[6] Every great power would like to dominate the world, but none has ever had or is likely to have the military capability to become a global hegemon. Thus, the ultimate goal of great powers is to achieve regional hegemony and block the rise of peer competitors in distant areas of the globe. In essence, states that gain regional hegemony act as offshore balancers in other regions. Nevertheless, those distant hegemons usually prefer to let the local great powers check an aspiring hegemon, while they watch from the sidelines. But sometimes this buck-passing strategy is not feasible, and the distant hegemon has to step in and balance against the rising power.

American military forces were sent to Europe and Northeast Asia at different times during the twentieth century, and the pattern of commitments follows the logic described above. In particular, whenever a potential peer competitor emerged in either of those regions, the United States sought to check it and preserve America's unique position as the world's only regional hegemon. As emphasized, hegemons are essentially status quo powers; the United States is no exception in this regard. Moreover, American policymakers tried to pass the buck to other great powers to get them to balance against the potential hegemon. But when that approach failed, the United States used its own military forces to eliminate the threat and restore a rough balance of power in the area so that it could bring its troops home. In short, the United States acted as an offshore balancer during the twentieth century to ensure that it remained the sole regional hegemon.

The United Kingdom, too, has never tried to dominate Europe, which is surprising, given that it used its military to forge a vast empire outside of Europe. Furthermore, the United Kingdom, unlike the United States, is a European power. Therefore, one might expect the mid-nineteenth-century United Kingdom to have translated its fabulous wealth into military might to make a run at gaining regional hegemony. The reason it did not do so, however, is basically the same as for the United States: the stopping power of water. Like the United States, the United Kingdom is an insular power that is physically separated from the European continent by a large body of water (the English Channel), which makes it virtually impossible for the United Kingdom to conquer and control all of Europe.

Still, the United Kingdom has consistently acted as an offshore balancer in Europe, as offensive realism would predict. Specifically, it has committed military forces to the continent when a rival great power threatened to dominate Europe and buck-passing was not a viable option. Otherwise, when there has been a rough balance of power in Europe, the British army has tended to stay off the continent. In sum, neither the United Kingdom nor the United States has attempted to conquer territory in Europe in modern times, and both have acted as the balancer of last resort in that region.[7]

This chapter will look more closely at the fit between offensive realism and the past behavior of the United Kingdom and the United States, focusing first on the American bid for regional hegemony in the nineteenth century. The subsequent two sections deal with the commitment of U.S. military forces to Europe and Northeast Asia in the twentieth century, while the section thereafter considers the United Kingdom's role as an offshore balancer in Europe. Some broader implications of the previous analysis are considered in the final section.

THE RISE OF AMERICAN POWER (1800–1900)

It is widely believed that the United States was preoccupied with domestic politics for most of the nineteenth century and that it had little interest in international politics. But this perspective makes sense only if American foreign policy is defined as involvement in areas outside of the Western Hemisphere, especially Europe. For sure, the United States avoided entangling alliances in Europe during this period. Nevertheless, it was deeply concerned with security issues and foreign policy in the Western Hemisphere between 1800 and 1900. Indeed, the United States was bent on establishing regional hegemony, and it was an expansionist power of the first order in the Americas.[8] Henry Cabot Lodge put the point well when he noted that the United States had "a record of conquest, colonization, and territorial expansion unequalled by any people in the nineteenth century."[9] Or the twentieth century, for that matter. When one considers America's aggressive behavior in the Western Hemisphere, and especially the results, the United States seems well-suited to be the poster child for offensive realism.

To illustrate the expansion of U.S. military might, consider the U.S. strategic positions at the beginning and at the end of the nineteenth century. The United States was in a rather precarious strategic situation in 1800 (see Map 7.1). On the plus side, it was the only independent state in the Western Hemisphere, and it possessed all the territory between the Atlantic Ocean and the Mississippi River, save for Florida, which was under Spanish control. On the negative side, however, most of the territory between the Appalachian Mountains and the Mississippi River was sparsely populated by white Americans, and much of it was controlled by hostile Native tribes. Furthermore, Great Britain and Spain had huge empires in North America. Between them, they controlled almost all of the territory west of the Mississippi and most of the territory north and south of the United States. In fact, the population of the Spanish territory that eventually became Mexico was slightly larger than America's population in 1800 (see Table 7.1).

By 1900, however, the United States was the hegemon of the Western Hemisphere. Not only did it control a huge swath of territory running from the Atlantic to the Pacific, but the European empires had collapsed and gone away. In their place were independent states such as Argentina, Brazil, Canada, and Mexico. But none of them had the population size or wealth to challenge the United States, which was the richest state on the planet by the late 1890s (see Table 6.2). Hardly anyone disagreed with Richard Olney, the American secretary of state, when he bluntly told the United Kingdom's Lord Salisbury in his famous July 20, 1895, note, "Today the United States is practically sovereign on this continent, and its fiat is law upon the subjects to which it confines its interposition. . . . Its infinite resources combined with its isolated position render it master of the situation and practically invulnerable as against any or all other powers."[10]

The United States established regional hegemony in the nineteenth century by relentlessly pursuing two closely linked policies: 1) expanding across North America and building the most powerful state in the Western Hemisphere, a policy commonly known as "Manifest Destiny"; and 2) minimizing the influence of the United Kingdom and the other European great powers in the Americas, a policy commonly known as the "Monroe Doctrine."

North America in 1800

MAP 7.1

TABLE 7.1

Population in the Western Hemisphere, 1800–1900

Population in thousands

	1800	1830	1850	1880	1900
United States	5,308	12,866	23,192	50,156	75,995
Canada	362	1,085	2,436	4,325	5,371
Mexico	5,765	6,382	7,853	9,210	13,607
Brazil	2,419	3,961	7,678	9,930	17,438
Argentina	406	634	935	1,737	3,955
Total	14,260	24,928	42,094	75,358	116,366

Percentage of above total

	1800	1830	1850	1880	1900
United States	37%	52%	55%	67%	65%
Canada	3%	4%	6%	6%	5%
Mexico	40%	26%	19%	12%	12%
Brazil	17%	16%	18%	13%	15%
Argentina	3%	3%	2%	2%	3%

NOTE: Because censuses were usually taken at different times in these countries, only the figures for the United States are for the exact dates listed in the table. Also, only the United States was a sovereign state for the entire nineteenth century. The census years and year of independence for the others are as follows: Canada (independent in 1867), 1801, 1831, 1851, 1881, and 1901; Mexico (independent in 1821), 1803, 1831, 1854, 1873, and 1900; Brazil (independent in 1822), 1808, 1823, 1854, 1872, and 1900; Argentina (independent in 1816), 1809, 1829, 1849, 1869, and 1895.

SOURCES: All figures are from B. R. Mitchell, *International Historical Statistics: The Americas, 1750–1988*, 2d ed. (New York: Stockton, 1993), pp. 1, 3–5, 7–8.

Manifest Destiny

The United States started out in 1776 as a weak confederation cobbled together from the thirteen colonies strung along the Atlantic seaboard. The principal goal of America's leaders over the next 125 years was to achieve the country's so-called Manifest Destiny.[11] As noted, the United States had extended its control to the Mississippi River by 1800, although it did not yet control Florida. Over the next fifty years, the United States expanded westward across the continent to the Pacific Ocean. During the second half of the nineteenth century, the United States focused on consolidating its territorial gains and creating a rich and cohesive state.

The expansion of the United States between 1800 and 1850 involved five major steps (see Map 7.2). The huge Louisiana Territory on the western side of the Mississippi River was purchased from France in 1803 for $15 million. Napoleonic France had recently acquired that land from Spain, although it had been under French control from 1682 until 1762. Napoleon needed the proceeds from the sale to finance his wars in Europe. Furthermore, France was in no position to compete with the United Kingdom in North America, because the British had a superior navy that made it difficult for France to project its military might across the Atlantic Ocean. With the acquisition of the vast Louisiana Territory, the United States more than doubled its size. The United States made its next move in 1819 when it took Florida from Spain.[12] American leaders had been devising schemes since the early 1800s to acquire Florida, including a number of invasions by U.S. troops. Spain finally conceded the entire territory after American forces captured Pensacola in 1818.

The last three important acquisitions all occurred in the brief period between 1845 and 1848.[13] Texas won its independence from Mexico in 1836 and shortly thereafter petitioned to join the United States. The petition was rejected, however, mainly because of congressional opposition to admitting Texas as a state in which slavery was legal.[14] But that logjam was eventually broken, and Texas was annexed on December 29, 1845. Six months later, in June 1846, the United States settled a territorial dispute with the United Kingdom over the Oregon Territories, acquiring a

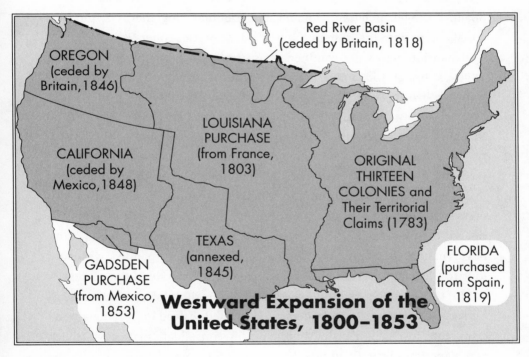

Red River Basin
(ceded by Britain, 1818)

OREGON
(ceded by
Britain, 1846)

LOUISIANA
PURCHASE
(from France,
1803)

ORIGINAL
THIRTEEN
COLONIES and
Their Territorial
Claims (1783)

CALIFORNIA
(ceded by
Mexico, 1848)

TEXAS
(annexed,
1845)

FLORIDA
(purchased
from Spain,
1819)

GADSDEN
PURCHASE
(from Mexico,
1853)

**Westward Expansion of the
United States, 1800–1853**

MAP 7.2

large chunk of territory in the Pacific northwest. In early May 1846, a few weeks before the Oregon agreement, the United States declared war on Mexico and went on to conquer California and most of what is today the American southwest. In the space of two years, the United States had grown by 1.2 million square miles, or about 64 percent. The territorial size of the United States, according to the head of the Census Bureau, was now "nearly ten times as large as that of France and Britain combined; three times as large as the whole of France, Britain, Austria, Prussia, Spain, Portugal, Belgium, Holland, and Denmark together . . . [and] of equal extent with the Roman Empire or that of Alexander."[15]

Expansion across the continent was pretty much complete by the late 1840s, although the United States did acquire a small portion of territory from Mexico in 1853 (the Gadsden Purchase) to smooth out the border between the two countries, and the United States purchased Alaska from Russia in 1867. However, the United States did not acquire all the territory it wanted. In particular, it aimed to conquer Canada when it went to war with the United Kingdom in 1812, and many of its leaders continued to covet Canada throughout the nineteenth century.[16] There was also pressure to expand southward into the Caribbean, where Cuba was considered the prize target.[17] Nevertheless, expansion to the north and south never materialized, and the United States instead expanded westward toward the Pacific Ocean, building a huge territorial state in the process.[18]

The United States had little need for more territory after 1848—at least for security reasons. So its leaders concentrated instead on forging a powerful state inside its existing borders. This consolidation process, which was sometimes brutal and bloody, involved four major steps: fighting the Civil War to eliminate slavery and the threat of dissolution of the union; displacing the Natives who controlled much of the land that the United States had recently acquired; bringing large numbers of immigrants to the United States to help populate its vast expanses of territory; and building the world's largest economy.

During the first six decades of the nineteenth century, there was constant friction between North and South over the slavery issue, especially as it applied to the newly acquired territories west of the Mississippi.

Indeed, the issue was so poisonous that it threatened to tear apart the United States, a result that would have had profound consequences for the balance of power in the Western Hemisphere. Matters finally came to a head in 1861, when the Civil War broke out. The North, which was fighting to hold the United States together, fared badly at first but eventually recovered and won a decisive victory. Slavery was quickly ended in all parts of the United States, and despite the ill will generated by the war, the country emerged a coherent whole that has since remained firmly intact. Had the Confederacy triumphed, the United States would not have become a regional hegemon, since there would have been at least two great powers in North America. This situation would have created opportunities for the European great powers to increase their political presence and influence in the Western Hemisphere.[19]

As late as 1800, Native American tribes controlled huge chunks of territory in North America that the United States would have to conquer if it hoped to fulfill Manifest Destiny.[20] The Natives hardly stood a chance of stopping the United States from taking their land. The Natives had a number of disadvantages, but most important, they were greatly outnumbered by white Americans and their situation only grew worse with time. In 1800, for example, about 178,000 Natives lived within the borders of the United States, which then extended to the Mississippi River.[21] At the same time, the population of the United States was roughly 5.3 million (see Table 7.1). Not surprisingly, the U.S army had little trouble crushing the Natives east of the Mississippi, taking their land, and pushing many of them west of the Mississippi in the first few decades of the nineteenth century.[22]

By 1850, when the present borders of the continental United States were largely in place, there were about 665,000 Native Americans living inside them, of whom roughly 486,000 lived west of the Mississippi. The population of the United States, however, had grown to nearly 23.2 million by 1850. Not surprisingly, then, small and somewhat inept U.S. army units were able to rout the Natives west of the Mississippi and take their land in the second half of the nineteenth century.[23] Victory over the Natives was complete by 1900. They were living on a handful of reservations and their total population had shrunk to about 456,000, of whom 299,000 lived west of the Mississippi. By that time the population of the United States had reached 76 million.

The population of the United States more than tripled during the second half of the nineteenth century, in good part because massive numbers of European immigrants crossed the Atlantic. Indeed, between 1851 and 1900, approximately 16.7 million immigrants came to the United States.[24] By 1900, 34.2 percent of all 76 million Americans were either born outside the United States or had at least one parent born in a foreign land.[25] Many of those immigrants came looking for jobs, which they found in the expanding U.S. economy. At the same time, however, they contributed to the strength of that economy, which grew by leaps and bounds in the latter part of the nineteenth century. Consider, for example, that the United Kingdom was the world's wealthiest country in 1850, with roughly four times the industrial might of the United States. Only fifty years later, however, the United States was the wealthiest country on the globe and had more than 1.6 times the industrial might of the United Kingdom (see Table 6.2).

The United Kingdom and the United States ended their long rivalry in North America during the early years of the twentieth century. In effect, the United Kingdom retreated across the Atlantic Ocean and left the United States to run the Western Hemisphere. A commonplace explanation for this rapprochement is that the United Kingdom had to consolidate its military forces in Europe to check a rising Germany, so it cut a deal with the United States, which was accommodating because it had a vested interest in getting the British out of North America, as well as having them maintain the balance of power in Europe.[26] There is much truth in this line of argument, but there is an even more important reason why the British-American rivalry ended in 1900: the United Kingdom no longer had the power to challenge the United States in the Western Hemisphere.[27]

The two principal indicators of potential military might are population size and industrial might, and the United States was far ahead of the United Kingdom on both indicators by 1900 (see Table 7.2). Furthermore, the United Kingdom had to project power across the Atlantic Ocean into the Western Hemisphere, whereas the United States was physically located there. The U.S.-U.K. security competition was over. Even if there had been no German threat in the early twentieth century, the United Kingdom would almost surely have abandoned the Western Hemisphere to its offspring, which had definitely come of age by then.

The Monroe Doctrine

American policymakers in the nineteenth century were not just concerned with turning the United States into a powerful territorial state, they were also deeply committed to getting the European powers out of the Western Hemisphere and keeping them out.28 Only by doing that could the United States make itself the region's hegemon, highly secure from great-power threats. As the United States moved across North America, it gobbled up territory that previously had belonged to the United Kingdom, France, and Spain, thus weakening their influence in the Western Hemisphere. But it also used the Monroe Doctrine for that same purpose.

The Monroe Doctrine was laid out for the first time in President James Monroe's annual message to Congress on December 2, 1823. He made three main points about American foreign policy.29 First, Monroe stipulated that the United States would not get involved in Europe's wars, in keeping with George Washington's advice in his famous "farewell address" (this policy certainly has not been followed in the twentieth century).30 Second, he put the European powers on notice that they could not acquire new territory in the Western Hemisphere to increase the size of their already considerable empires. "The American Continents," the president said, "are henceforth not to be considered as subjects for future colonization by any European Power." But the policy did not call for dismembering the European empires already established in the Western Hemisphere.31 Third, the United States wanted to make sure that the European powers did not form alliances with the independent states of the Western Hemisphere or control them in any way. Thus, Monroe stated that "with the Governments who have declared their independence and maintained it . . . we could not view any interposition for the purpose of oppressing them, or controlling in any other manner their destiny, by any European power in any other light than as the manifestation of an unfriendly disposition towards the United States."

TABLE 7.2

The United Kingdom and the United States, 1800–1900

Relative share of world wealth

	1800	1830	1850	1880	1900
United Kingdom	na	47%	59%	45%	23%
United States	na	12%	15%	23%	38%

Population (in thousands)

	1800	1830	1850	1880	1900
United Kingdom	15,717	24,028	27,369	34,885	41,459
United States	5,308	12,866	23,192	50,156	75,995

NOTE: na = not available

SOURCES: Figures for world wealth are from Table 6.2. Population figures for the United Kingdom are from B. R. Mitchell, *Abstract to British Historical Statistics* (Cambridge: Cambridge University Press, 1962), pp. 6–8; the figure for 1800 is from the 1801 census, which includes England, Wales, Scotland, and Ireland. All figures for the United States are from Mitchell, *International Historical Statistics: The Americas*, p. 4.

It is understandable that the United States would worry in the early 1800s about further European colonization. The United Kingdom, for example, was a powerful country with a rich history of empire-building around the globe, and the United States was not powerful enough at the time to check the British everywhere in the Western Hemisphere. Indeed, the United States probably did not have sufficient military might to enforce the Monroe Doctrine in the first decades after it was enunciated. Nevertheless, this problem proved illusory, as the European empires shrivelled away over the course of the nineteenth century and no new ones rose in their place.[32] The United States actually had little to do with the collapse of those empires, which were wrecked mainly from within by nationalism.[33] Brazilians, Canadians, and Mexicans, like the American colonists in 1776, did not want Europeans controlling their politics, so they followed the U.S. example and became independent states.

The real danger that the United States faced in the nineteenth century—and continued to face in the twentieth century—was the possibility of an anti-American pact between a European great power and a state in the Western Hemisphere. An alliance like that might ultimately be powerful enough to challenge U.S. hegemony in the Americas, which would adversely affect the country's security. Thus, when Secretary of State Olney sent his famous note to Lord Salisbury in the summer of 1895, he emphasized that "the safety and welfare of the United States are so concerned with the maintenance of the independence of every American state as against any European power as to justify and require the interposition of the United States whenever that independence is endangered."[34]

The United States was able to deal with this threat when it arose during the nineteenth century. For example, France placed an emperor on the throne of Mexico during the American Civil War, but French and Mexican troops together were not a serious threat to the United States, even though it was fighting a bloody internal conflict. When that war ended, the nationalist forces of Benito Juarez and the United States army forced France to withdraw its troops from Mexico. The United States grew more powerful between 1865 and 1900, making it increasingly difficult for any European great power to forge an anti-American alliance with an independent state in the Western Hemisphere. Nevertheless, the problem has not gone away. In fact, the United States had to deal with it three times in the twentieth century: German involvement in Mexico during World War I, German designs on South America during World War II, and the Soviet Union's alliance with Cuba during the Cold War.[35]

The Strategic Imperative

The stunning growth of the United States in the hundred years after 1800 was fueled in good part by realist logic.[36] "The people of the United States have learned," Olney wrote at the end of the nineteenth century, that "the relations of states to each other depend not upon sentiment nor principle, but upon selfish interest."[37] Moreover, American leaders understood that the more powerful their country was, the more secure it would be in the dangerous world of international politics. President Franklin Pierce made the point in his inaugural address on March 4, 1853: "It is not to be disguised that our attitude as a nation and our position on the globe render the acquisition of certain possessions not within our jurisdiction eminently important for our protection."[38]

Of course, Americans had other motives for expanding across the continent. For example, some had a powerful sense of ideological mission.[39] They believed that the United States had created a virtuous republic that was unprecedented in world history and that its citizens had a moral duty to spread its values and political system far and wide. Others were driven by the promise of economic gain, a powerful motor for expansion.[40] These other motives, however, did not contradict the security imperative; in fact, they usually complemented it.[41] This was especially true for the economic motive: because economic might is the foundation of military might, any actions that might increase the relative wealth of the United States would also enhance its prospects for survival. On idealism, there is no question that many Americans fervently believed that expansion was morally justified. But idealist rhetoric also provided a proper mask for the brutal policies that underpinned the tremendous growth of American power in the nineteenth century.[42]

Balance-of-power politics had a rich history in the Western Hemisphere even before the United States declared its independence in 1776.[43] In particular, the British and the French waged an intense security competition in North America during the middle of the eighteenth century, including the deadly Seven Years' War (1756–63). Moreover, the United States ultimately achieved its independence by going to war against Great Britain and making an alliance with France, Britain's arch-rival. James Hutson has it right when he says, "The world the American Revolutionary leaders found themselves in was a brutal, amoral cockpit. . . . [It] was, above all, a world in which power was king."[44] Thus, the elites who managed U.S. national security policy in the decades after the country's independence were steeped in realist thinking.

The politics of the Western Hemisphere in 1800 provided good reasons for those elites to continue thinking in terms of the balance of power. The United States was still operating in a dangerous neighborhood. The British and Spanish empires surrounded it on three sides, making fear of encirclement a common theme among American policymakers, who also worried that Napoleonic France, the most powerful state in Europe, would try to build a new empire in North America. Of course, the French empire never materialized, and indeed, France sold the huge Louisiana Territory to the United States in 1803.

Nevertheless, the Europeans, especially the British, were determined to do what they could to contain the United States and prevent it from further expanding its borders.[45] The United Kingdom actually succeeded at stopping the United States from conquering Canada in the War of 1812. The United Kingdom had few good options for preventing the westward expansion of the United States, but it did form brief alliances with the Native Americans of the Great Lakes region between 1807 and 1815, and later with Texas when it was briefly an independent state.[46] But these efforts never seriously threatened to stop the United States from reaching the Pacific Ocean.

In fact, it appears that any move a European state made to contain the United States had the opposite effect: it strengthened the American imperative to expand. For example, Europeans began speaking openly in the early 1840s about the need to maintain a "balance of power" in North America, a euphemism for containing further American expansion while increasing the relative power of the European empires.[47] The subject was broached before the United States expanded westward beyond the Louisiana Territory. Not surprisingly, it immediately became a major issue in U.S. politics, although there was not much disagreement among

Americans on the issue. President James Polk surely spoke for most Americans when he said that the concept of a balance of power "cannot be permitted to have any application to the North American continent, and especially to the United States. We must ever maintain the principle that the people of this continent alone have the right to decide their own destiny."[48] Shortly after Polk spoke on December 2, 1845, Texas was incorporated into the United States, soon to be followed by the Oregon Territories, California, and the other land taken from Mexico in 1848.

The historian Frederick Merk succinctly summarizes American security policy in the nineteenth century when he writes, "The chief defense problem was the British, whose ambition seemed to be to hem the nation in. On the periphery of the United States, they were the dangerous potential aggressors. The best way to hold them off was to acquire the periphery. This was the meaning of the Monroe Doctrine in the age of Manifest Destiny."[49]

THE UNITED STATES AND EUROPE, 1900–1990

Offensive realism predicts that the United States will send its army across the Atlantic when there is a potential hegemon in Europe that the local great powers cannot contain by themselves. Otherwise, the United States will shy away from accepting a continental commitment. The movement of American forces into and out of Europe between 1900 and 1990 fits this general pattern of offshore balancing. A good way to grasp the broad outlines of American military policy toward Europe is to describe it during the late nineteenth century and in five distinct periods of the twentieth century.

The United States gave hardly any thought to sending an army to Europe between 1850 and 1900, in part because staying out of Europe's wars was deeply ingrained in the American psyche by 1850. Presidents George Washington and James Monroe, among others, had made sure of that.[50] Furthermore, the United States was concerned primarily with establishing hegemony in the Western Hemisphere during the second half of the nineteenth century. But most important, the United States did not contemplate sending troops across the Atlantic because there was no potential hegemon in Europe at that time. Instead, there was a rough balance of power on the continent.[51] France, which made a run at hegemony between 1792 and 1815, was on the decline throughout the nineteenth century, while Germany, which would become a potential hegemon in the early twentieth century, was not powerful enough to overrun Europe before 1900. Even if there had been an aspiring European hegemon, however, the United States surely would have adopted a buck-passing strategy, hoping that the other great powers in Europe could contain the threat.

The first period in the twentieth century covers the time from 1900 to April 1917. It was apparent in the early years of the new century that Germany was not simply the most powerful state in Europe but was increasingly threatening to dominate the region.[52] In fact, Germany precipitated a number of serious diplomatic crises during that period, culminating in the outbreak of World War I on August 1, 1914. Nevertheless, no American troops were sent to Europe to thwart German aggression. The United States pursued a buck-passing strategy instead, relying on the Triple Entente—the United Kingdom, France, and Russia—to contain Germany.[53]

The second period runs from April 1917 until 1923; it covers American participation in World War I, which was the first time in its history that the United States sent troops to fight in Europe. The United States declared war against Germany on April 6, 1917, but was able to send only four divisions to France by the end of that year.[54] However, large numbers of American troops started arriving on the continent in early 1918, and by the time the war ended on November 11, 1918, there were about two million American soldiers stationed in Europe and more on their way. Indeed, General John Pershing, the head of the American Expeditionary Force, expected to have more than four million troops under his command by July 1919. Most of the troops sent to Europe were brought home soon after the war ended, although a small occupation force remained in Germany until January 1923.[55]

The United States entered World War I in good part because it thought that Germany was gaining the upper hand on the Triple Entente and was likely to win the war and become a European hegemon.[56] America's buck-passing strategy, in other words, was unraveling after two and a half years of war. The Russian army, which had been badly mauled in almost every engagement it had with the German army, was on the verge of disintegration by March 12, 1917, when revolution broke out and the tsar was removed from power.[57] The French army was also in precarious shape, and it suffered mutinies in May 1917, shortly after the United States entered the war.[58] The British army was in the best shape of the three allied armies, mainly because it spent the first two years of the war expanding into a mass army and thus had not been bled white like the French and Russian armies. The United Kingdom was nevertheless in desperate straits by April 1917, because Germany had launched an unrestricted submarine campaign against British shipping in February 1917 that was threatening to knock the United Kingdom out of the war by the early fall.[59] Consequently, the United States was forced to enter the war in the spring of 1917 to bolster the Triple Entente and prevent a German victory.[60]

The third period covers the years from 1923 to the summer of 1940. The United States committed no forces to Europe during those years. Indeed, isolationism was the word commonly used to describe American policy during the years between the world wars.[61] The 1920s and early 1930s were relatively peaceful years in Europe, mainly because Germany remained shackled by the strictures of the Versailles Treaty. But Adolf Hitler came to power on January 30, 1933, and soon thereafter Europe was in turmoil again. By the late 1930s, American policymakers recognized that Nazi Germany was a potential hegemon and that Hitler was likely to attempt to conquer Europe. World War II began on September 1, 1939, when Germany attacked Poland and the United Kingdom and France responded by declaring war against Germany. However, the United States made no serious move toward a continental commitment when the war broke out. As in World War I, it initially relied on Europe's other great powers to contain the German threat.[62]

The fourth period covers the five years from the summer of 1940, when Germany decisively defeated France and sent the British army back home via Dunkirk, until the European half of World War II ended in early May 1945. American policymakers had expected the British and French armies to stop a Wehrmacht offensive on the western front and force a protracted war of attrition that would sap Germany's military might.[63] Josef Stalin expected the same outcome, but the Wehrmacht shocked the world by winning a quick and decisive victory in France.[64] With this victory, Germany was well-positioned to threaten the United Kingdom.

More important, however, Hitler could use most of his army to invade the Soviet Union, because he had no western front to worry about. It was widely believed in the United Kingdom and the United States that the Wehrmacht was likely to defeat the Red Army and establish hegemony in Europe.[65] After all, Germany had knocked Russia out of World War I, and in that case Germany was fighting a two-front war and had substantially more divisions fighting against the British and French armies than against the Russian army.[66] This time the Germans would be essentially fighting a one-front war. Also, Stalin's purge of the Red Army between 1937 and 1941 had markedly reduced its fighting power. This weakness was on display in the winter of 1939–40, when the Red Army had trouble defeating the badly outnumbered Finnish army. In short, there was ample reason to think in the summer of 1940 that Germany was on the threshold of dominating continental Europe.

The collapse of France precipitated a dramatic change in American thinking about a continental commitment.[67] Suddenly there was widespread support for providing substantial aid to the United Kingdom, which now stood alone against Germany, and for preparing the American military for a possible war with Germany. By early fall of 1940, public opinion polls showed that for the first time since Hitler came to power, a majority of Americans believed it was more important to ensure that the United Kingdom defeat Germany than to avoid a European war.[68] The U.S. Congress also drastically increased defense spending in the summer of 1940, making it possible to start building an expeditionary force for Europe: on June 30, 1940, the size of the American army was 267,767; one year later, roughly five months before Pearl Harbor, the strength of the army had grown to 1,460,998.[69]

Furthermore, with the passage of the Lend-Lease Act on March 11, 1941, the United States began sending large amounts of war material to the British. It is hard to disagree with Edward Corwin's claim that this step was "a qualified declaration of war" against Germany.[70] During the summer and fall of 1941, the United States became more deeply involved in helping the United Kingdom win its fight with Germany, reaching the point in mid-September where President Franklin Roosevelt instructed the U.S. navy to fire on sight at German submarines in the Atlantic Ocean. The United States did not formally go to war against Germany, however, until December 11, 1941, when Hitler declared war against the United States four days after the Japanese attack at Pearl Harbor. American troops did not set foot on the European continent until September 1943, when they landed in Italy.[71]

The fifth period covers the Cold War, which ran from the summer of 1945 to 1990. The United States planned to bring most of its troops home immediately after World War II ended, leaving just a small occupation force behind to police Germany for a few years, as it had after World War I.[72] By 1950, there were only about 80,000 American troops left in Europe, and they were mainly involved with occupation duty in Germany.[73] But as the Cold War intensified in the late 1940s, the United States formed the North Atlantic Treaty Organization (1949) and eventually made a commitment to remain in Europe and substantially increase its fighting forces on the continent (1950). By 1953, 427,000 American troops were stationed in Europe, which was the high-water mark for the Cold War. The United States also deployed about seven thousand nuclear weapons on European soil during the 1950s and early 1960s. Although there was some variation over time in American troop levels in Europe, the number never dipped below 300,000.

The United States reluctantly kept military forces in Europe after World War II because the Soviet Union controlled the eastern two-thirds of the continent and it had the military might to conquer the rest of Europe.[74] There was no local great power that could contain the Soviet Union: Germany was in ruins and neither France nor the United Kingdom had the military wherewithal to stop the mighty Red Army, which had just crushed the same Wehrmacht that had easily defeated the British and French armies in 1940. Only the United States had sufficient military power to prevent Soviet hegemony after 1945, so American troops remained in Europe throughout the Cold War.

THE UNITED STATES AND NORTHEAST ASIA, 1900–1990

The movement of American troops across the Pacific in the twentieth century follows the same pattern of offshore balancing that we saw at work in Europe. A good way to understand U.S. military policy toward Northeast Asia is to divide the years from 1900 to 1990 into four periods, and describe the practice in each of them.

The first period covers the initial three decades of the twentieth century, during which there was no large-scale commitment of American forces to Northeast Asia.[75] There were, however, small contingents of U.S. military forces in Asia during this period. The United States maintained a small contingent of forces in the Philippine Islands,[76] and it also sent five thousand troops to China in 1900 to help put down the Boxer Rebellion and maintain the infamous "Open Door" policy. As John Hay, the American secretary of state, candidly noted at the time, "the inherent weakness of our position is this: we do not want to rob China ourselves, and our public opinion will not permit us to interfere, with an army, to prevent others from robbing her. Besides, we have no army. The talk of the papers about 'our preeminent moral position giving us the authority to dictate to the world' is mere flap-doodle."[77] A contingent of approximately one thousand U.S. soldiers was deployed to Tientsin, China, from January 1912 to March 1938. Finally, U.S. navy gunboats were on patrol in the region during this period.[78]

The United States did not send a large army to Northeast Asia because there was no potential hegemon in the area. China played an important role in the region's politics, but it was not a great power and it hardly threatened to dominate Northeast Asia. The United Kingdom and France were important actors in Asia in the early twentieth century, but they were interlopers from a distant continent, with all the power-projection problems that role entails. Moreover, they were concerned with containing Germany during most of this period, so most of their attention was focused on Europe at the expense of Northeast Asia. Japan and Russia were candidates for potential hegemon in Northeast Asia, because each was a great power located in the region. But neither fit the bill.

Japan possessed the most formidable army in the region between 1900 and 1930. It soundly defeated the Russian army in the Russo-Japanese War (1904–5).[79] Russia's army went from bad to worse during World War I, finally disintegrating in 1917. The newly created Red Army was essentially a paper tiger throughout the 1920s. Meanwhile, the Japanese army remained an impressive fighting force.[80] But Japan was not a potential hegemon because Russia was the wealthiest state in the region. For example, Russia controlled 6 percent of world industrial might in 1900, while Japan did not even control 1 percent (see Table 6.2). By 1910, Russia's share had shrunk to 5 percent, while Japan's share had grown to 1 percent—still a substantial Russian lead. Italy was actually Japan's closest economic competitor in these years. Japan briefly overtook the Soviet Union in 1920—2 percent vs. 1 percent—but that was only because the Soviet Union was in the midst of a catastrophic civil war. By 1930, Russia controlled 6 percent of world industrial might, while Japan controlled 4 percent. In short, Japan was not powerful enough during the early decades of the twentieth century to drive for supremacy in Northeast Asia.

The second period covers the decade of the 1930s, when Japan went on a rampage on the Asian mainland. Japan conquered Manchuria in 1931, which it turned into the puppet state of Manchukuo. In 1937, Japan went to war against China; its aim was to conquer northern China and key Chinese coastal regions. Japan also initiated a series of border conflicts with the Soviet Union in the late 1930s with the clear intention of making territorial gains at the expense of Moscow. Japan seemed bent on dominating Asia.

The United States did not move troops to Asia in the 1930s because, Japan's grand ambitions notwithstanding, it was not a potential hegemon and China, France, the Soviet Union, and the United Kingdom were capable of containing the Japanese army. The Soviet Union actually gained a significant power advantage over Japan during that decade, mainly because the Soviet Union underwent rapid industrialization after the first Five-Year Plan was put into effect in 1928. The Soviet Union's share of world wealth climbed from 6 percent in 1930 to 13 percent in 1940, while Japan's went from 4 percent to 6 percent over the same period (see Table 6.2). Furthermore, the Red Army developed into an efficient fighting force in the 1930s. Indeed, it played a critical role in containing Japan, inflicting defeats on the Japanese army in 1938 and 1939.[81]

The United Kingdom and China also helped check Japan in the 1930s. The United Kingdom was actually inclined to pull most of its forces out of Asia and strike a deal with Japan in the late 1930s, so that it could concentrate on containing Nazi Germany, which was a more direct and dangerous threat than was Japan.[82] But the United States, playing the role of the buck-passer, told the United Kingdom that any diminution of its force levels in Asia was unacceptable, and that the United Kingdom would have to remain engaged in Asia and balance against Japan. Otherwise, the United States might not help it deal with the growing German threat in Europe. The British stayed in Asia. Although China was not a great power at the time, it managed to pin down the Japanese army in a costly and protracted war that Japan was unable to win.[83] In fact, Japan's experience in China between 1937 and 1945 bears considerable resemblance to the American experience in Vietnam (1965–72) and the Soviet experience in Afghanistan (1979–89).

The third period covers the years between 1940 and 1945, when Japan suddenly became a potential hegemon because of events in Europe. The fall of France in June 1940 and the German invasion of the Soviet Union in June 1941 funadamentally altered the balance of power in Northeast Asia. Germany's quick and decisive victory over France in the late spring of 1940 greatly reduced, if not eliminated, French influence on Japanese behavior in Asia. Indeed, the defeat of France as well as of the Netherlands left their empires in Southeast Asia vulnerable to Japanese attack. With France out of the war, the United Kingdom stood alone against Nazi Germany in the west. But the British army was in shambles after Dunkirk and the Luftwaffe started pounding British cities in mid-July 1940. The United Kingdom also had to contend with fascist Italy in and around the Mediterranean. In short, the British were hanging on for dear life in Europe and therefore could contribute little to containing Japan in Asia.

Nevertheless, the United States made no move to send troops to Asia in 1940, largely because 1) Japan was bogged down in its war with China, and 2) the Soviet Union, which was not involved in the European half of the conflict at that point, was a formidable balancing force against Japan. That situation changed drastically when Germany invaded the Soviet Union on June 22, 1941. Over the next six months, the Wehrmacht inflicted a series of staggering defeats on the Red Army. It appeared likely by the late summer of 1941 that the Soviet Union would collapse as France had the year before. Japan would then be well-positioned to establish hegemony in Northeast Asia, because it would be the only great power left in the region. In effect, the European half of World War II was creating a power vacuum in Asia that Japan was ready to fill.

American policymakers were especially worried that Japan would move northward and attack the Soviet Union from the rear, helping Germany finish off the Soviet Union. Germany would then be the hegemon in Europe, while in Northeast Asia, only China would stand in the way of Japanese hegemony. As offensive realism would predict, the United States began moving military forces to Asia in the fall of 1941 to deal with the Japanese threat.[84] Shortly thereafter, Japan attacked the United States at Pearl Harbor, guaranteeing that massive American military forces would move across the Pacific for the first time ever. Their aim would be to crush Japan before it achieved regional hegemony.

The fourth period covers the Cold War (1945–90). The United States maintained military forces in Asia after World War II for essentially the same reason it accepted a continental commitment in Europe: the Soviet Union, which scored a stunning military victory in Manchuria against Japan's Kwantung Army in the final days of World War II, was a potential hegemon in Northeast Asia as well as in Europe, and there were no local great powers to contain it.[85] Japan was in ruins and China, which was not a great power anyway, was in the midst of a brutal civil war. The United Kingdom and France were in no position to check the Soviet Union in Europe, much less in Asia. So the United States had little choice but to assume the burden of containing the Soviet Union in the Far East.[86] The United States ended up fighting two bloody wars in Asia during the Cold War, while it fired not a shot in Europe.

BRITISH GRAND STRATEGY, 1792–1990

Like the United States, the United Kingdom is separated from the European continent by a substantial body of water, and it, too, has a history of sending troops to the continent. The United Kingdom has also followed an offshore balancing strategy.[87] As Sir Eyre Crowe noted in his famous 1907 memorandum about British security policy, "It has become almost an historical truism to identify England's secular policy with the maintenance of this [European] balance by throwing her weight . . . on the side opposed to the political dictatorship of the strongest single state."[88] Moreover, the United Kingdom has consistently tried to get other great powers to bear the burden of containing potential European hegemons while it remains on the sidelines for as long as possible. Lord Bolingbroke succinctly summarized British thinking about when to commit to the continent in 1743: "We should take few engagements on the continent, and never those of making a land war, unless the conjecture be such, that nothing less than the weight of Britain can prevent the scales from being quite overturned."[89] This commitment to buck-passing explains in good part why other states in Europe have referred to the United Kingdom as "Perfidious Albion" over the past few centuries.

Let us consider British military policy toward the continent from 1792, when the French Revolutionary and Napoleonic Wars started, until the Cold War ended in 1990.[90] Those two centuries can be roughly divided into six periods.

The first period runs from 1792 until 1815 and covers the French Revolutionary and Napoleonic Wars in their entirety. France was by far the most powerful state on the continent during this period, and it was bent on dominating Europe.[91] France was an especially aggressive and formidable great power after Napoleon took over the reigns of power in late 1799. In fact, by the time Napoleon's armies entered Moscow in the fall of 1812, France controlled most of continental Europe. The French drive for hegemony was ultimately thwarted, however, and the British army played an important role in bringing down Napoleon. Great Britain deployed a small army to the continent in 1793, but it was forced to remove those forces in 1795 when the coalition arrayed against France collapsed. Britain placed another army in Holland in August 1799, but it was defeated by and surrendered to the French army within two months. In 1808, the United Kingdom placed an army in Portugal and Spain that eventually helped inflict a decisive defeat on the large French forces in Spain. That same British army helped deliver the final blow against Napoleon at Waterloo (1815).

The second period runs from 1816 to 1904, when the United Kingdom adopted a policy commonly referred to as "splendid isolation."[92] It made no continental commitment during this period, despite the numerous great-power wars raging on the continent. Most important, the United Kingdom did not intervene in either the Austro-Prussian War (1866) or the Franco-Prussian War (1870–71), which led to the creation of a unified Germany. The United Kingdom sent no troops to Europe during those nine decades because there was a rough balance of power on the continent.[93] France, which was a potential hegemon from 1793 until 1815, lost relative power over the course of the nineteenth century, while Germany, which would become the next potential hegemon in the early twentieth century, was not yet powerful enough to dominate Europe. In the absence of a potential hegemon, the United Kingdom had no good strategic reason to move troops to the European mainland.

The third period runs from 1905 to 1930 and was dominated by the United Kingdom's efforts to contain Wilhelmine Germany, which emerged as a potential hegemon in the early twentieth century.[94] It was apparent by 1890 that Germany, with its formidable army, large population, and dynamic industrial base, was rapidly becoming Europe's most powerful state. Indeed, France and Russia formed an alliance in 1894 to contain the growing threat located between them. The United Kingdom would have preferred to let France and Russia deal with Germany. But it was clear by 1905 that they could not do the job alone and would need British help. Not only were the power differentials between Germany and its continental rivals continuing to widen in Germany's favor, but Russia suffered a major military defeat in the Russo-Japanese War (1904–5), which left its army in terrible shape and in no condition to engage the German army. Finally, Germany initiated a crisis with France over Morocco in March 1905, which was designed to isolate France from the United Kingdom and Russia, thus leaving Germany in a position to dominate Europe.

In response to this deteriorating strategic environment, the United Kingdom allied with France and Russia between 1905 and 1907, forming the Triple Entente. In essence, Britain made a continental commitment to deal with the threat of a German hegemon. When World War I broke out on August 1, 1914, the United Kingdom immediately sent an expeditionary force to the continent to help the French army thwart the Schlieffen Plan. As the war progressed, the size of the British expeditionary force grew, until it was the most formidable Allied army by the summer of 1917. It then played the main role in defeating the German army in 1918.[95] Most of the British army exited the continent shortly after the war ended; a small occupation force remained in Germany until 1930.[96]

The fourth period runs from 1930 to the summer of 1939 and covers the years when the United Kingdom pursued a Europe policy commonly referred to as "limited liability." It made no continental commitment in the early 1930s, because Europe was relatively peaceful and there was a rough balance of power in the region. After Hitler came to power in 1933 and began to rearm Germany, the United Kingdom made no move to commit ground forces to fight on the continent. Instead, after much debate, it decided in December 1937 to pass the buck to France to contain Germany. British policymakers eventually realized, however, that France alone did not have the military might to deter Hitler, and that in the event of a war, the United Kingdom would have to send troops to fight Nazi Germany, as it had done against Napoleonic France and Wilhelmine Germany.

The United Kingdom finally accepted a continental commitment on March 31, 1939, which marks the beginning of the fifth period. Specifically, it committed itself to fight with France against Germany if the Wehrmacht attacked Poland. A week later the United Kingdom gave the same guarantee to Greece and Romania. When World War II broke out five months later, British troops were promptly sent to France, as they had been in World War I. Although the British army was pushed off the continent at Dunkirk in June 1940, it returned in September 1943 when it landed with the American army in Italy. British forces also landed at Normandy in June 1944 and eventually fought their way into Germany. This period ended with the surrender of Germany in early May 1945.

The final period runs from 1945 to 1990 and covers the Cold War.[97] With the end of World War II, Britain had planned to move its military forces off the continent after a brief occupation of Germany. However, the emergence of the Soviet threat, the fourth potential hegemon to confront Europe in 150 years, forced the United Kingdom to accept a continental commitment in 1948. British troops, along with American troops, remained on the central front for the duration of the Cold War.

CONCLUSION

In sum, both the United Kingdom and the United States have consistently acted as offshore balancers in Europe. Neither of these insular great powers has ever tried to dominate Europe. It is also clear that American actions in Northeast Asia fit the same pattern. All of this behavior, as well as the U.S. drive for hegemony in the Western Hemisphere during the nineteenth century, corresponds with the predictions of offensive realism.

This chapter raises two issues that bear mentioning. First, insular Japan's conquest of large amounts of territory on the Asian mainland in the first half of the twentieth century might seem to contradict my claim that the stopping power of water made it almost impossible for the United Kingdom in the nineteenth century and the United States in the twentieth century to conquer territory on the European continent. After all, if

Japan was able to project power across the seas separating it from the Asian continent, why is it that the United Kingdom and the United States could not do likewise in Europe?

The answer is that the Asian and European mainlands were different kinds of targets during the periods under discussion. In particular, the European continent has been populated by formidable great powers over the past two centuries, and those states have had both the incentive and the wherewithal to prevent the United Kingdom and the United States from dominating their region. The situation confronting Japan in Asia between 1900 and 1945 looked quite different: Russia was the only great power located on the Asian mainland, but it was usually more concerned with events in Europe than in Asia. Plus, it was a militarily weak great power for much of that period. Russia's immediate neighbors were feeble states like Korea and China, which were inviting targets for Japanese aggression. In short, the Asian continent was open for penetration from abroad, which of course is why the European great powers had empires there. The European continent, on the other hand, was effectively a giant fortress closed to conquest by distant great powers like the United Kingdom and the United States.

Second, I argued earlier that great powers are not seriously committed to maintaining peace but instead aim to maximize their share of world power. On this point, it is worth noting that the United States was not willing at any point between 1900 and 1990 to take on a continental commitment for the purposes of keeping peace in Europe. No American troops were sent across the Atlantic to help prevent World War I or to stop the fighting after war broke out. Nor was the United States willing to accept a continental commitment to deter Nazi Germany or halt the fighting after Poland was attacked in September 1939. In both cases, the United States eventually joined the fight against Germany and helped win the war and create peace in Europe. But the United States did not fight to make peace in either world war. Instead, it fought to prevent a dangerous foe from achieving regional hegemony. Peace was a welcome byproduct of those endeavors. The same basic point holds for the Cold War: American military forces were in Europe to contain the Soviet Union, not to maintain peace. The long peace that ensued was the happy consequence of a successful deterrence policy.

We find a similiar story in Northeast Asia. The United States did not intervene with force to shut down the Russo-Japanese War (1904–5), nor did it send troops to Northeast Asia in the 1930s, when Japan took the offensive on the Asian mainland, conquering Manchuria and large portions of China in a series of brutal military campaigns. The United States began making serious moves to get militarily involved in Asia during the summer of 1941, not because American leaders were determined to bring peace to the region, but because they feared that Japan would join forces with Nazi Germany and decisively defeat the Red Army, making hegemons of Germany in Europe and Japan in Northeast Asia. The United States fought a war in the Far East between 1941 and 1945 to prevent that outcome. As in Europe, American troops were stationed in Northeast Asia during the Cold War to prevent the Soviet Union from dominating the region, not to keep peace.

I have emphasized that when offshore balancers like the United Kingdom and the United States confront a potential hegemon in Europe or Northeast Asia they prefer to buck-pass to other great powers rather than directly confront the threat themselves. Of course, this preference for buck-passing over balancing is common to all great powers, not just offshore balancers. Chapter 8 will consider how states choose between these two strategies.

8

Balancing versus
Buck-Passing

I argued in Chapter 5 that balancing and buck-passing are the main strategies that states employ to defend the balance of power against aggressors, and that threatened states feel a strong impulse to buck-pass. Buck-passing is preferred over balancing because the successful buck-passer does not have to fight the aggressor if deterrence fails. In fact, the buck-passer might even gain power if the aggressor and the buck-catcher get bogged down in a long and costly war. This offensive feature of buck-passing notwithstanding, there is always the possibility that the aggressor might win a quick and decisive victory and shift the balance of power in its favor and against the buck-passer.

This chapter has three aims. First, I explain when threatened states are likely to balance and when they are likely to buck-pass. That choice is mainly a function of the structure of the international system. A threatened great power operating in a bipolar system must balance against its rival because there is no other great power to catch the buck. It is in multipolar systems that threatened states can—and often do—buck-pass. The amount of buck-passing that takes place depends largely on the magnitude of the threat and on geography. Buck-passing tends to be widespread in multipolarity when there is no potential hegemon to contend with, and when the threatened states do not share a common border with the aggressor. But even when there is a dominating threat, endangered rivals will still look for opportunities to pass the buck. In general, the more relative power the potential hegemon controls, the more likely it is that all of the threatened states in the system will forgo buck-passing and form a balancing coalition.

Second, I examine the five most intense cases of security competition in Europe over the past two centuries to test my claims about when threatened states are likely to buck-pass. Specifically, I consider how the great powers responded to the four potential hegemons in modern European history: Revolutionary and Napoleonic France (1789–1815), Wilhelmine Germany (1890–1914), Nazi Germany (1933–41), and the Soviet Union (1945–90).[1] I also look at how the European great powers reacted to Otto von Bismarck's effort to unify Germany with the sword between 1862 and 1870. Bismarckian Prussia, however, was not a potential hegemon. The system was multipolar for all of these cases, save for the bipolar rivalry between the United States and the Soviet Union during the Cold War. Furthermore, all of these security competitions led to great-power wars, except for the conflict between the superpowers.

The evidence from these five cases is largely consistent with my theory on when states buck-pass and when they balance against aggressors. The United States, for example, had no choice but to balance against the Soviet Union during the Cold War, because the system was bipolar. Not surprisingly, the balancing in this case was more timely and more efficient than in any of the multipolar cases. There is significant variation among the four multipolar cases, where passing the buck was an option. Buck-passing is most evident against Bismarck's Prussia, which is not surprising, since Prussia is the one aggressor under study that was not a potential hegemon. Buck-passing is least evident against Wilhelmine Germany, which had a rather impressive balancing coalition arrayed against it about seven years before the start of World War I. There was considerable buck-passing against Revolutionary France and Nazi Germany in the years before they went to war in 1792 and 1939, respectively, and even after both were at war. The variation among these cases can be explained in good part by the relevant distribution of power and by geography, which facilitated buck-passing against Napoleon and Adolf Hitler, but not against Kaiser Wilhelm.

Third, I hope to illustrate my claim that threatened states are inclined to buck-pass rather than balance in the face of aggressors. The discussion in Chapter 7 of how the United Kingdom and the United States have always looked to buck-pass when confronted with a potential hegemon in Europe (or Northeast Asia) provides substantial evidence of that tendency among states. However, I address the issue more directly in this chapter by focusing on five particularly aggressive European states and how their rivals reacted to them.

My explanation for when states buck-pass is laid out in the next section. The five cases are then discussed in chronological order, starting with Revolutionary and Napoleonic France and ending with the Cold War. In the final section, the findings from the different cases are compared and contrasted.

WHEN DO STATES BUCK-PASS?

When an aggressor comes on the scene, at least one other state will eventually take direct responsibility for checking it. Balancing almost always happens, although it is not always successful. This point is consistent with the logic of buck-passing, which is essentially about who does the balancing, not whether it gets done. The buck-passer simply wants someone else to do the heavy lifting, but it certainly wants the threat contained. Buck-passing, on the other hand, does not always occur when an aggressor threatens to upset the balance of power. Passing the buck may be the strategy of choice for threatened great powers, but it is not always a viable option. The task here is to determine when buck-passing makes good strategic sense.

The prospects for buck-passing are largely a function of the particular architecture of the system. What matters most is the distribution of power among the major states, and geography.[2] Power is usually distributed among great powers in three ways.[3] Bipolar systems are dominated by two great powers of roughly equal military might. Unbalanced multipolar systems contain three or more great powers, one of which is a potential hegemon. Balanced multipolar systems have no aspiring hegemon; instead, power is divided rather evenly among the great powers, or at least between the two most powerful states in the system.

No buck-passing takes place among the great powers in bipolarity because there is no third party to catch the buck. A threatened great power has little choice but to balance against its rival great power. It is also not possible to form balancing coalitions with other great powers in a world with just two great powers. Instead, the threatened power has to rely mainly on its own resources, and maybe alliances with smaller states, to contain the aggressor. Because neither buck-passing nor great-power balancing coalitions are feasible in bipolarity, we should expect balancing in this kind of system to be prompt and efficient.

Buck-passing is always possible in multipolarity, because there is always at least one potential buck-catcher in the system. But buck-passing is likely to be rife in balanced multipolar systems, mainly because no aggressor is powerful enough—by definition—to defeat all of the other great powers and dominate the entire system. This means that not every great power is likely to be directly threatened by an aggressor in a counterpoised system, and those that are not in imminent danger of attack will almost certainly opt to pass the buck. States that are directly threatened by the aggressor are likely to try to get another threatened state to handle the problem, so that they can remain unscathed while the buck-catcher defends the balance of power. In short, balancing coalitions are unlikely to form against an aggressor when power is distributed rather evenly among the major states in a multipolar system.

Buck-passing is less likely in an unbalanced multipolar system, because the threatened states have a strong incentive to work together to prevent the potential hegemon from dominating their region. After all, potential hegemons, which are great powers that clearly have more latent power and a more formidable army than any other great power in their region, have the wherewithal to fundamentally alter the balance of power in their favor. Consequently, they are a direct threat to almost every state in the system. Ludwig Dehio, the German historian, maintains that states "seem able to hold together only in one event: when a member of their own circle tries to achieve hegemony," and Barry Posen notes that, "Those states most often identified as history's would-be hegemons have elicited the most intense balancing behavior by their neighbors."[4]

Nevertheless, buck-passing often occurs in unbalanced multipolar systems. Threatened states are reluctant to form balancing coalitions against potential hegemons because the costs of containment are likely to be great; if it is possible to get another state to bear those costs, a threatened state will make every effort to do so. The more powerful the dominant state is relative to its foes, however, the less likely it is that the potential victims will be able to pass the buck among themselves, and the more likely it is that they will be forced to form a balancing coalition against the aggressor. Indeed, at some point, the collective efforts of all the threatened great powers will be needed to contain an especially powerful state. Buck-passing makes little sense in such a circumstance because the buck-catchers are unlikely to be capable of checking the potential hegemon without help.

Whereas the distribution of power tells us how much buck-passing is likely among the great powers, geography helps identify the likely buck-passers and buck-catchers in multipolar systems. The crucial issue regarding geography is whether the threatened state shares a border with the aggressor, or whether a barrier—be it the territory of another state or a large body of water—separates those rivals. Common borders promote balancing; barriers encourage buck-passing.

Common borders facilitate balancing in two ways. First, they provide threatened states with direct and relatively easy access to the territory of the aggressor, which means that the imperiled states are well-positioned to put military pressure on their dangerous opponent. If all the threatened great powers share a border with their common foe, they can readily raise the specter of a multi-front war, which is often the most effective way to deter a powerful aggressor.[5] On the other hand, if a threatened state is separated from its adversary by water or a territorial buffer zone, it will be difficult for the endangered state to use its army to put pressure on the menacing state. A minor power caught in the middle, for example, is often unwilling to invite a threatened great power onto its territory, thus forcing the threatened state to invade the minor power to get at the aggressor. Projecting power across water is also a difficult task, as discussed in Chapter 4.

Second, great powers that share a border with an aggressor are likely to feel particularly vulnerable to attack, and thus they are likely to take matters into their own hands and balance against their dangerous foe. They are not likely to be in a good position to buck-pass, although the temptation to try that strategy will always be present. On the other hand, threatened states separated from an aggressor by a barrier are likely to feel less vulnerable to invasion and therefore more inclined to pass the buck to an endangered state that has a common border with the menacing state. Thus, among threatened states, those that live next door to the aggressor usually get stuck with the buck, while those more distant from the threat usually get to pass the buck. There is some truth to the dictum that geography is destiny.

In sum, buck-passing among the great powers is impossible in bipolarity, and not only possible but commonplace in multipolarity. Indeed, buck-passing is likely to be absent from a multipolar system only when there is an especially powerful potential hegemon and when there are no barriers between the aggressor and the threatened great powers. In the absence of a dominating threat and common borders, substantial buck-passing is likely in multipolarity.

Let us now consider how well this theory explains the historical record, focusing first on how the European great powers reacted to the aggressive behavior of Revolutionary and Napoleonic France some two centuries ago.

REVOLUTIONARY AND NAPOLEONIC FRANCE (1789–1815)

Background

The European great powers were at war almost continuously from 1792 until 1815. Basically, a powerful and highly aggressive France fought against different combinations of the other regional great powers: Austria,

Great Britain, Prussia, and Russia. France, which was bent on becoming Europe's hegemon, reached its expansionist peak in mid-September 1812, when Napoleon's armies entered Moscow. At that point, France controlled almost all of continental Europe from the Atlantic to Moscow and from the Baltic Sea to the Mediterranean. Less than two years later, however, France was a defeated great power and Napoleon was exiled to Elba.

There was no balancing against France between the outbreak of the French Revolution in 1789 and the outbreak of great-power war in 1792. Austria and Prussia actually went to war against Revolutionary France in 1792 to take advantage of it, not to contain it. France quickly built a powerful army, however, and it was a potential hegemon by late 1793. Nevertheless, it was not until 1813—more than twenty years after the fighting began—that all four of France's great-power rivals came together in a balancing coalition and decisively defeated France. In the intervening two decades, there was considerable buck-passing as well as inefficient balancing among France's enemies. In fact, five separate balancing coalitions formed against France between 1793 and 1809, but none contained all of France's rivals and each collapsed after performing poorly on the battlefield. There were also lengthy periods where Britain fought alone against France.

The behavior of France's rivals between 1789 and 1815 can be explained in good part by the distribution of power and by geography. Hardly any balancing took place against France before 1793 because it was not a potential hegemon. Although France became a threat to dominate Europe in late 1793, there was a good deal of buck-passing by Austria, Great Britain, Prussia, and Russia over the next twelve years, mainly because France, although powerful, was not so powerful that all four of its rivals were needed to prevent it from overruning the continent. By 1805, however, the French army had become such a formidable fighting force under Napoleon that only the collective efforts of all the other European great powers could contain it. Yet those powers did not contain it until 1813, in small part because the buck-passing impulse remained at play, but mainly because of inefficient balancing. In particular, Napoleon quickly knocked Austria out of the balance of power in

1805, and then did the same to Prussia in 1806, making it impossible for his foes to form a unified balancing coalition. That situation changed in late 1812 when France suffered a catastrophic defeat in Russia. With France temporarily weakened, Austria, the United Kingdom, Prussia, and Russia were able to join together in 1813 and bring France's run at hegemony to an end.

The Strategic Behavior of the Great Powers

A good way to analyze great-power behavior in Europe between 1789 and 1815 is to start with a brief description of the various targets of French aggression, and then look at the interactions between France and its rivals in four distinct periods: 1789–91, 1792–1804, 1805–12, 1813–15.[6]

France sought to conquer territory all across Europe, although it tended to work its way from west to east over time. Its main targets in western Europe were Belgium, which Austria controlled in 1792; the Dutch Republic; the various German political entities opposite France's eastern border, such as Bavaria, Hanover, and Saxony, which I refer to throughout this chapter as the "Third Germany"[7]; Switzerland; the Italian Peninsula, especially the northern part; Portugal and Spain on the Iberian Peninsula; and Great Britain. France occupied all of those areas at one point or another, save for Britain, which Napoleon planned to invade but never did. In central Europe, France's main targets were Austria, Prussia, and Poland, which was dominated at the time by Austria, Prussia, and Russia. There was one big target in eastern Europe: Russia (see Map 8.1).

The French Revolution, which broke out in the summer of 1789, did not cause France to launch wars to spread its ideology. Nor did it cause Europe's other great powers to wage war against France to crush the revolution and restore the monarchy. In fact, there was peace among the great powers until the spring of 1792, when Austria and Prussia provoked a war with France. But that conflict was motivated mainly by balance-of-power considerations, although it was not a case of two threatened states balancing against a mighty France.[8] On the contrary, Austria and Prussia were ganging up on a weak and vulnerable France to gain power at its expense.

Europe at the Height of Napoleon's Power, 1810

- French Empire
- Satellites
- Subordinate Allies
- Independent Adversaries of France

Atlantic Ocean

NORWAY AND DENMARK

North Sea

Baltic Sea

SWEDEN

RUSSIAN EMPIRE

GREAT BRITAIN

PRUSSIA

GRAND DUCHY OF WARSAW

CONFEDERATION OF THE RHINE (THIRD GERMANY)

EMPIRE OF THE FRENCH

SWITZ.

AUSTRIAN EMPIRE

ILLYRIAN PROVINCES

KINGDOM OF ITALY

Black Sea

PORTUGAL

SPAIN

CORSICA

OTTOMAN EMPIRE

KINGDOM OF SARDINIA

KINGDOM OF NAPLES

KINGDOM OF SICILY

Mediterranean Sea

MAP 8.1

Britain was content to sit on the sidelines and watch this happen, while Russia encouraged Austria and Prussia to fight with France, so that it could make gains in Poland at their expense.

France fared poorly in the opening months of the war, prompting a reorganization and enlargement of the French army in the summer of 1792. It then won a stunning victory against the invading Prussians at Valmy on September 20, 1792. Soon thereafter, France went on the offensive and it remained a relentless and formidable aggressor until Napoleon's final defeat at Waterloo in June 1815.

During the period from 1793 to 1804, France did not attempt to conquer all of Europe. Instead, it sought and achieved hegemony in western Europe. In particular, it gained direct control over Belgium, large parts of Italy, and a portion of the Third Germany. France also dominated the Dutch Republic and Switzerland. But Portugal, Spain, and most important, Britain, were not brought under French control. These gains in western Europe were not made quickly and easily. For example, France won control over Belgium by defeating the Austrians at the Battle of Jemappes on November 6, 1792. But the Austrians won it back at the Battle of Neerwinden on March 16, 1793. France took it back again, however, at the battle of Fleurus on June 26, 1794.

We find a similiar story in Italy. Between March 1796 and April 1797, Napoleon led French armies to victory over the Austrians in northern Italy. France subsequently gained territory and political influence in Italy with the Treaty of Campo Formio (October 18, 1797), which ended the fighting between Austria and France. But they were back at war again on March 13, 1799, and by the fall of that year virtually all French forces had been driven out of Italy. Napoleon returned to Italy in the spring of 1800 and defeated the Austrians in a series of battles, winning back control of much of Italy in the Treaty of Luneville (February 8, 1801), which ended that round of fighting.

France not only had limited territorial ambitions between 1793 and 1804, but also did not make a serious attempt to conquer any of its great-power rivals. France certainly waged successful military campaigns against Austria, Britain, Prussia, and Russia, but it did not seriously threaten to knock any of them out of the balance of power. In effect, France's wars before 1805 were limited in scope, much like the canonical "limited wars" of the preceeding century, which rarely produced decisive victories that led to the conquest of one great power by another.[9]

France's rivals formed two balancing coalitions between 1793 and 1804, but there was still substantial buck-passing among those threatened states. The first coalition was put in place on February 1, 1793, when Britain joined with Austria and Prussia to check French expansion in Belgium and Holland.[10] But Russia did not join the fighting against France, preferring instead to pursue a bloodletting strategy, where Austria and Prussia would wear themselves down fighting against France.[11] Prussia tired of the fighting and quit the coalition on April 5, 1795, which was tantamount to passing the buck to Austria and Britain. In fact, Austria wound up catching the buck, because Britain's small army could not seriously contest the French army on the continent, whereas the Austrian army stood a fighting chance against that powerful aggressor. Austria did not fare well in its subsequent battles with France, however, and it temporarily quit the war in the fall of 1797, leaving Britain to fight alone against France.

A second balancing coalition was in place by December 29, 1798, and its members were Austria, Britain, and Russia, but not Prussia, which preferred to continue buck-passing. The coalition won some battles against France between March and August 1799, but France turned the tables and won impressive victories against the coalition in September and October 1799. Russia quit the coalition on October 22, 1799, leaving Austria and Britain to contain France. Again, the burden fell squarely on Austria, not Britain. After a handful of battlefield defeats by the French army, Austria signed a peace treaty with France on February 9, 1801. The United Kingdom finally quit fighting on March 25, 1802, when it signed the Treaty of Amiens. This was the first time since the spring of 1792 that Europe was free of great-power war. But the peace, which was really just an armed truce, lasted only fourteen months. Fighting broke out again on May 16, 1803, when the United Kingdom declared war against France.

Between 1805 and 1812, Napoleon shattered the limited-war mold that had shaped European conflict for the previous century.[12] Specifically, he sought to conquer all of Europe and make France its hegemon. By the summer of 1809, France held firm control over all of central Europe and it was fighting to conquer Spain and dominate the Iberian Peninsula, the only area on the western part of the continent that France did not dominate.[13] In June 1812, France invaded Russia in hopes of winning control of eastern Europe, too. In pursuit of European hegemony, Napoleon conquered other great powers and knocked them out of the balance of power, something that had not happened in the wars fought between 1792 and 1804. For example, France decisively defeated and conquered Austria in 1805. Prussia met the same fate a year later in 1806. Austria briefly came back from the dead in 1809, but Napoleon's armies decisively defeated it again. In essence, the United Kingdom and Russia were France's only two great-power opponents for much of the period between 1805 and 1812.

Three more balancing coalitions formed against France during this period. There was some buck-passing for sure, but not as much as there had been between 1792 and 1804. The principal problem that Napoleon's rivals faced after 1805 was that they were rather inefficient in putting together a formidable balancing coalition, which allowed Napoleon to defeat them piecemeal and knock some of them out of the balance. In short, diplomacy was slower than the sword.[14]

The third coalition was put in place on August 9, 1805, when Austria joined forces with the United Kingdom and Russia. Prussia initially opted to buck-pass and stay outside the alliance, because it seemed at the time that the combined strength of the three coalition members was sufficient to contain France, which had not fought a major land battle in Europe since late 1800.[15] In fact, Napoleon had been at peace with his three continental foes since early 1801, although he was still highly aggressive on the diplomatic front. "Peace for Napoleon," as Paul Schroeder notes, "was a continuation of war by other means."[16] Moreover, after the United Kingdom and France went back to war in the spring of 1803, Napoleon built a powerful army to cross the English Channel and invade the United Kingdom. La Grande Armée, as it was called, never attacked the United Kingdom, but Napoleon used it to attack the third coalition in the fall of 1805. In the opening round of the fighting, it inflicted a major defeat on the Austrians at Ulm (October 20, 1805).[17] Prussia, recognizing that France was now a serious threat to its survival, took steps to join the coalition. Before that could happen, however, Napoleon defeated the Austrian and Russian armies at Austerlitz on December 2, 1805.[18] After its second major defeat in less than three months, Austria no longer counted as a great power.

Less than a year later, on July 24, 1806, the United Kingdom, Prussia, and Russia formed a fourth coalition. There was no buck-passing this time, for Austria was in no shape to join the coalition. But it mattered little: Napoleon conquered Prussia by winning battles at Jena and Auerstadt on October 14, 1806. Both Austria and Prussia had now been knocked out of the ranks of the great powers. After engaging the Russian army in a bloody stalemate at Eylau (February 8, 1807), Napoleon smashed it on the battlefield at Friedland (June 14, 1807). Soon thereafter, a badly wounded Russia signed the Treaty of Tilsit with Napoleon, which ended the fighting between France and Russia and left France free to wage war against an isolated United Kingdom. Russia was effectively pursuing a buck-passing strategy, pushing France to concentrate on fighting the British, while Russia recovered from its defeats and worked to improve its position in central Europe.

Napoleon's imposing military triumphs after 1805 account in good part for Russia's buck-passing, which was the only significant case of buck-passing in the decade before 1815. Russia passed the buck to the United Kingdom from 1807 until 1812, not only because Austria and Prussia had been conquered by France, and thus were unavailable to join a balancing coalition, but also because the major defeats the Russian army suffered in 1805 and 1807 left it in no position to engage the French army without allies on the continent. Better to let Britain and France batter each other while Russia remained on the sidelines, recovering and waiting for a propitious shift in the balance of power.

Austria had regained enough strength by the spring of 1809 to join with the United Kingdom in a fifth coalition against France. Still smarting from its defeats in 1805 and 1807, Russia opted to remain on the sidelines. Austria fought major battles against Napoleon's armies at Aspern-

Essling (May 21–22, 1809) and Wagram (July 5–6, 1909), but again it was decisively defeated and conquered. With both Austria and Prussia removed from the balance of power, Russia was France's only great power rival on the continent. The Treaty of Tilsit notwithstanding, Napoleon turned on Russia in June 1812, hoping to conquer and eliminate it, too, from the balance of power. The French army, however, suffered a catastrophic defeat in Russia between June and December 1812.[19] At the same time, France's position in Spain was deteriorating rapidly. By early January 1813, Napoleon at last appeared beatable, not invincible.

Not surprisingly, the sixth balancing coalition against France came together in 1813. Prussia, which was given a desperately needed reprieve by Napoleon's debacle in Russia, formed an alliance with Russia on February 26, 1813, and then went to war against France less than a month later, on March 17, 1813. The United Kingdom joined the coalition on June 8, 1813, and Austria followed suit, declaring war against France on August 11, 1813. For the first time since fighting broke out in 1792, all four of France's great-power rivals were allied together in a balancing coalition.[20]

Despite defeat in Russia and the emergence of a powerful enemy coalition, Napoleon was determined to keep fighting. In 1813, war was waged for control of the Third Germany (now called the "Confederation of the Rhine"), which France had dominated for almost a decade. French forces won some impressive victories at Lutzen and Bautzen in May 1813 and even fared well through the summer of 1813, winning a major battle at Dresden on August 26–27, 1813. But France's successes were due in good part to the fact that the sixth coalition was still in the process of coming together. In mid-October 1813, when the coalition was finally in place, Napoleon encountered formidable Austrian, Prussian, and Russian armies at the Battle of Leipzig. France suffered another devastating defeat and lost Germany for good.

By the end of 1813, France's rivals were invading its territory; the fight in 1814 would be for France itself. Napoleon's armies performed surprisingly well in some key battles in February 1814, but despite strains in the balancing coalition, it held together and routed the French army in March, causing Napoleon to abdicate on April 6, 1814.[21] He was eventually exiled to Elba, from which he escaped back to France in early March 1815. The sixth coalition immediately reconstituted itself on March 25, 1815, and defeated Napoleon for the final time at Waterloo on June 18, 1815. France's run at hegemony was over.

The Calculus of Power

It is difficult to establish firmly that France had more latent power than any of its great-power rivals, mainly because there are not much reliable data on population and especially wealth for the period between 1792 and 1815. Still, when you consider what is known about those building blocks of military power, there is reason to think that France had more potential power than any other European state.

Although hardly any comparative data on overall state wealth can be found for the Napoleonic period, scholars generally agree that Great Britain and France were the richest states in the international system. A good indicator of Britain's great wealth is the fact that Britain provided large subsidies to Austria, Prussia, and Russia so that they could build armies that could defeat France, which was certainly not being subsidized by the British or anyone else. The relative wealth of Britain and France is difficult to establish, but there are reasons to think that France was wealthier than Britain, although certainly not by much, for the period in question.[22] For example, France had a much larger population than Britain did in 1800—28 versus 16 million (see Table 8.1)—and given two prosperous economies, the one with the larger population is more likely to possess greater overall wealth. Furthermore, like Nazi Germany, France garnered considerable wealth from its occupation and exploitation of much of Europe. One scholar estimates that "Napoleon's conquests provided the French treasury with 10 to 15 per cent of its annual revenue from 1805 onwards."[23]

Turning to population size, France appears to have had an advantage over its rivals, too. The population figures for 1800 and 1816 in Table 8.1 show that the French outnumbered the British by about 1.5:1 and the Prussians by almost 3:1.[24] But the French did not outnumber either the

Austrians or the Russians. France's population was roughly the same size as Austria's, and it was much smaller than Russia's. Nevertheless, a critical factor at play effectively shifted the population balance in France's favor in both the Austrian and the Russian cases.

TABLE 8.1

Populations of European Great Powers, 1750–1816 (in millions)

	1750	1800	1816
Austria	18	28	29.5
Great Britain	10.5	16	19.5
France	21.5	28	29.5
Prussia	6	9.5	10.3
Russia	20	37	51.3

SOURCES: Figures for 1750 and 1800 are from Paul Kennedy, *The Rise and Fall of the Great Powers: Economic Change and Military Conflict from 1500 to 2000* (New York: Vintage, 1987), p. 99. Figures for 1816 are from J. David Singer and Melvin Small, *National Material Capabilities Database, 1816–1985* (Ann Arbor, MI: Inter-University Consortium for Political and Social Research, February 1993).

Population size, as emphasized in Chapter 3, is an important ingredient of military power because it affects the potential size of a state's army.[25] Large populations allow for large armies. But rival states sometimes have markedly different policies regarding who serves in the military, and in those cases, simple comparisons of population size are not particularly useful. This point is relevant for France and its rivals between 1789 and 1815. Prior to the French Revolution, European armies were rather small in size and they were composed mainly of foreign mercenaries and the dregs of a state's society. In the wake of the revolution, nationalism became a mighty force in France, and it led to the introduction of the novel concept of the "nation in arms."[26] The idea that all persons fit to fight for France should serve the colors was adopted, and thereby the percentage of the population that French leaders could tap for military service increased dramatically. Neither Austria nor Russia, however, was willing to imitate France and adopt the nation-in-arms concept, which meant that compared to France, a significantly smaller percentage of their populations was available for military service. Thus, France was able to raise substantially larger armies than either Austria or Russia, as discussed below.[27]

Let us now consider actual military power. France did not have the most powerful army in Europe from 1789 to 1792, and thus it was not a potential hegemon.[28] In terms of numbers alone, Austria, Prussia, and Russia all had larger armies than did France (see Table 8.2). Only Britain maintained a smaller army than France.[29] Furthermore, the French army did not enjoy a qualitative edge over its rivals. In fact, it was in such disarray in the years right after the revolution that it was not clear that it could even protect France against invasion.[30] This weakness explains why there was no balancing against France before 1793, and why Austria and Prussia ganged up to attack France in 1792.

During the summer of 1792, when the war was going badly for France, it took steps to transform its army into the most powerful fighting force in Europe. By the early fall of 1793, that goal was achieved, and France clearly was a potential hegemon. The French army remained the preeminent army in Europe from 1793 to 1804. Nevertheless, when you consider both relative size and quality, it was not so powerful that all four of its rivals were compelled to ally against it. Instead, its limitations allowed for considerable buck-passing among France's opponents.

The French army, which had numbered 150,000 before war broke out in April 1792, tripled in size to 450,000 by November of that year (see Table 8.2), at which point it was the largest army in Europe. But the army began to shrink in size soon afterward; it was down to 290,000, by February 1793, which made it slightly smaller than the Austrian and Russian armies. However, the famous *levée en masse* was put in place on August 23, 1793, and the size of the army skyrocketed to 700,000 by

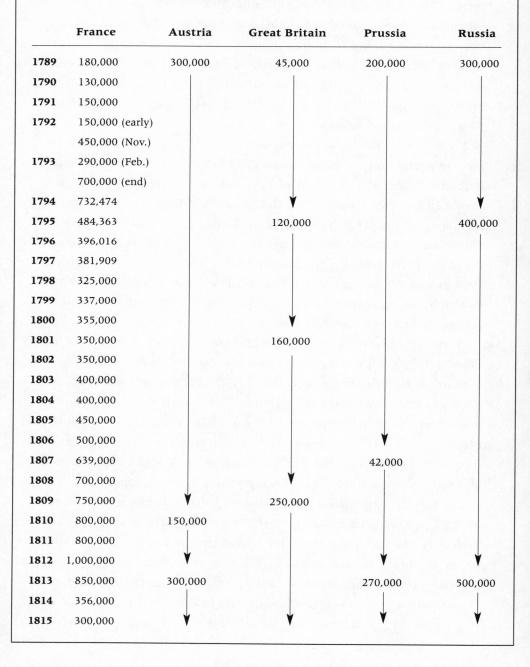

TABLE 8.2

Manpower in European Armies, 1789–1815

	France	Austria	Great Britain	Prussia	Russia
1789	180,000	300,000	45,000	200,000	300,000
1790	130,000				
1791	150,000				
1792	150,000 (early)				
	450,000 (Nov.)				
1793	290,000 (Feb.)				
	700,000 (end)				
1794	732,474				
1795	484,363		120,000		400,000
1796	396,016				
1797	381,909				
1798	325,000				
1799	337,000				
1800	355,000				
1801	350,000		160,000		
1802	350,000				
1803	400,000				
1804	400,000				
1805	450,000				
1806	500,000				
1807	639,000			42,000	
1808	700,000				
1809	750,000		250,000		
1810	800,000	150,000			
1811	800,000				
1812	1,000,000				
1813	850,000	300,000		270,000	500,000
1814	356,000				
1815	300,000				

SOURCES: Figures for the French army are from Jean-Paul Bertaud, *The Army of the French Revolution,* trans. R. R. Palmer (Princeton, NJ: Princeton University Press, 1988), pp. 239 (n. 2), 272; Georges Blond, *La Grande Armée,* trans. Marshall May (London: Arms and Armour Press, 1995), pp. 510–11; David G. Chandler, *The Campaigns of Napoleon* (New York: Macmillan, 1966), p. 333; Owen Connelly, *French Revolution/Napoleonic Era* (New York: Holt, Rinehart, and Winston, 1979), p. 240; Robert A. Doughty and Ira D. Gruber, *Warfare in the Western World,* vol. 1, *Military Operations from 1600 to 1871* (Lexington, MA: D.C. Heath, 1996), p. 213; John R. Elting, *Swords around a Throne: Napoleon's Grande Armée* (New York: Free Press, 1988), pp. 61, 653; Vincent J. Esposito and John Robert Elting, *A Military History and Atlas of the Napoleonic Wars* (New York: Frederick A. Praeger, 1964), p. 35; Alan Forrest, *The Soldiers of the French Revolution* (Durham, NC: Duke University Press, 1990), p. 82; Kennedy, *Rise and Fall,* p. 99; John A. Lynn, *The Bayonets of the Republic* (Urbana: University of Illinois Press, 1984), pp. 48, 53; and Gunther E. Rothenberg, *The Art of Warfare in the Age of Napoleon* (Bloomington: Indiana University Press, 1978), pp. 43, 98. Numbers for 1801–2 and 1810–11 are author's estimates. Figures for the other European armies are given in round numbers based on the following sources: Chandler, *Campaigns of Napoleon,* pp. 42, 666, 750; Connelly, *French Revolution/Napoleonic Era,* p. 268; Clive Emsley, *The Longman Companion to Napoleonic Europe* (London: Longman, 1993), p. 138; David French, *The British Way in Warfare, 1688–2000* (London: Unwin Hyman, 1990), p. 107; Charles J. Esdaile, *The Wars of Napoleon* (New York: Longman, 1995), p. 18; David R. Jones, "The Soviet Defence Burden through the Prism of History," in Carl G. Jacobsen, ed., *The Soviet Defence Enigma: Estimating Costs and Burden* (Oxford: Oxford University Press, 1987), p. 155; Kennedy, *Rise and Fall,* p. 99; Evan Luard, *The Balance of Power: The System of International Relations, 1648–1815* (New York: St. Martin's, 1992), p. 37; Walter M. Pintner, *Russia as a Great Power: Reflections on the Problem of Relative Backwardness, with Special Reference to the Russian Army and Russian Society,* Occasional Paper No. 33 (Washington, DC: Kennan Institute for Advanced Russian Studies, July 18, 1979), p. 29; Rothenberg, *Art of Warfare,* pp. 167, 171–73, 177, 188, 199; and William O. Shanahan, *Prussian Military Reforms, 1786–1813* (New York: AMS, 1966), pp. 33–34, 178, 206, 221.

year's end, making it overwhelmingly larger than any other European army. France could not maintain those large numbers, however, and by 1795, the army had slimmed down to just over 484,000. But it was still the largest army in Europe. Between 1796 and 1804, French army size fluctuated between a low of 325,000 and a high of 400,000, making it always larger than the Austrian army (300,000), but usually not quite as large as the Russian army (400,000).

Numbers, however, tell only part of the story. The French army gained an important qualitative advantage over rival land forces when France became a nation in arms in the summer of 1792.[31] Not only were the ranks then filled with individuals who were motivated to fight and die for France, but merit replaced birthright as the principal criterion for selecting and promoting officers. Furthermore, moving to an army of citizen-soldiers infused with patriotism permitted the introduction of novel tactics, which gave French forces an advantage over their rivals on the battlefield. It also allowed for an army that had greater strategic mobility than either its predecessor or the rival armies of the day.

Although the French army enjoyed a marked qualitative advantage over its opponents (who all remained hostile to the nation-in-arms concept) and was the most powerful army in Europe between 1793 and 1804, it had some serious deficiencies. In particular, the army was neither well-trained nor well-disciplined, and it suffered from high desertion rates. "Messy massive armies," as Geoffrey Best puts it, are what France fought with before 1805.[32]

During the period from 1805 to 1813, the power gap between the French army and its rivals widened significantly. Napoleon was largely responsible for this development. He sharply increased the size of the French army by refining its conscription system and by integrating large numbers of foreign troops into its ranks.[33] Thus, the French army grew from 450,000 in 1805 to 700,000 in 1808, to 1 million in 1812, the year France invaded Russia. Even after that debacle, the French army still numbered 850,000 in 1813. As Table 8.2 makes clear, there was no comparable increase in the size of the other European armies between 1805 and 1813.

Napoleon also substantially raised the quality of the French army. He did not make radical changes in the way the army did business, but instead corrected many of the "imperfections" in the existing system.[34] He improved training and discipline, for example, and he also improved coordination among the infantry, artillery, and cavalry. In short, the French army after 1805 was more professional and more competent than its immediate predecessor had been. Napoleon was also a brilliant military commander, which gave France a further advantage over its foes.[35] France's rivals made minor modifications in their armies in response to Napoleon, but only Prussia adopted the nation-in-arms concept and modernized its army in a fundamental way.[36] Even so, the small Prussian army was no match for the much larger French army in a one-on-one engagement.

France's imposing power advantage over each of its rivals from 1805 until 1813 explains in large part why all four of them came together in 1813 and then remained together until France was defeated and conquered in 1815. One might ask, however, why did that imposing balancing coalition not come together earlier, say in 1806 or 1810? The main reason for the delay, as emphasized earlier in this chapter, was that Napoleon's stunning victories on the battlefield made it impossible for all four rivals to form an alliance. After Napoleon conquered Austria in late 1805, there was no time before 1813 when all four of France's great-power opponents were players in the balance of power. Indeed, for much of the period, both Austria and Prussia were great powers in name only.

Finally, a word about the impact of geography on buck-passing. Austria was the only great power that controlled territory abutting France. Austria and France each shared a border with Italy and the Third Germany, which both of those great powers highly valued as targets. As a result, Austria was too threatened by France to opt out of the fighting by passing the buck. Indeed, it was well-placed to play the unenviable role of buck-catcher. And it did, as it was surely the most put-upon of France's rivals.[37] David Chandler, for example, calculates that among France's rivals on the continent, Austria was at war with it for 13.5 of the relevant 23 years, whereas Prussia and Russia were each at war with France for only 5.5 years.[38]

Britain, which is separated from the continent by a large body of water, was the least vulnerable to invasion of France's foes. Yet Britain was at war with France almost continuously from 1793 onward. Chandler estimates that they were locked in conflict for 21.5 of the relevant 23 years.[39] But Britain buck-passed to its continental allies in the sense that it never raised a powerful army to fight on the continent against France. It preferred instead to send small armies to fight in peripheral places like Spain, while subsidizing its allies to do the brunt of the fighting against the French army.[40] In short, Britain's geographical location allowed it to act as an offshore balancer.

Russia was located on the other end of the continent from France, with Austria and Prussia in between. So a favorable geographic position allowed Russia to buck-pass, too, especially between 1793 and 1804, when France was mainly concerned with winning hegemony in western Europe.[41] In fact, Russia was at war with France for less than one year during that period. Prussia also did a considerable amount of buck-passing, but that behavior cannot be explained by geography, because Prussia was located in the heart of Europe, not far away from France. Prussia's success as a buck-passer was largely due to the fact that neighboring Austria was an ideal buck-catcher.

In sum, the pattern of balancing and buck-passing displayed by France's rivals between 1789 and 1815 can be explained in good part by my theory, which emphasizes the distribution of power and the luck of geography.

Europe was relatively peaceful for almost forty years after the Napoleonic Wars ended in 1815. In fact, no war was fought between any of the great powers until the Crimean War started in 1853. Then the War of Italian Unification, which had Austria and France on opposing sides, broke out in 1859. But neither one of these wars altered the European balance of power in any meaningful way. In contrast, Bismarck initiated a series of wars in the 1860s that transformed Prussia into Germany and fundamentally altered the balance of power in Europe. The next section looks at how the other great powers reacted to this Prussian expansion.

BISMARCKIAN PRUSSIA (1862-70)

Background

Prussia did not become a great power until the mid-eighteenth century, but even then it was probably the weakest European great power until the mid-nineteenth century.[42] The main reason for its weakness was its small population compared to the other great powers. Consider that Prussia's population in 1800 was about 9.5 million, while Austria and France each had roughly 28 million people, and Russia had about 37 million people (see Table 8.1). Prussia's strategic situation changed dramatically between 1864 and 1870, when Bismarck led it to victory in three wars. Prussia actually ceased to exist as a sovereign state after 1870 and instead became the core of a unified Germany that was substantially more powerful than its Prussian predecessor had been.

There was no state called "Germany" when Bismarck was appointed Prussia's minister-president in September 1862. Instead, an assortment of German-speaking political entities were scattered about the center of Europe, loosely tied together in the German Confederation, an ineffectual political organization set up after Napoleon's defeat in 1815. There were two great powers in the confederation: Austria and Prussia. But it also included medium-sized kingdoms such as Bavaria and Saxony, as well as numerous small states and free cities—all of which I refer to as the "Third Germany." It was apparent after the revolutions of 1848 that German nationalism was a potent force that was likely to cause some combination of those German political entities to come together to form a unified German state. The question of the day was whether Austria or Prussia would be the core of that new state—essentially, which great power would absorb the Third Germany? The wars of 1864, 1866, and 1870–71 resolved that issue in Prussia's favor.

Besides Austria and Prussia, there were four other great powers in Europe in the 1860s: the United Kingdom, France, Italy, and Russia (see Map 8.2). But Italy did not have significant influence on the events surrounding German unification, although it did fight with Prussia against Austria in 1866. Italy was a spanking new state that was especially weak relative to the other great powers. Therefore, the key issue is how Austria, the United Kingdom, France, and Russia reacted to Bismarck's efforts to transform Prussia into Germany. As will become apparent, buck-passing was their preferred strategy, and although Austria and France balanced against Prussia at different times, they did so only when they had no alternative.

The Strategic Behavior of the Great Powers

Prussia's first war under Bismarck (1864) was a straightforward case of two great powers, Austria and Prussia, ganging up to attack a minor power, Denmark.[43] Their aim was to take the duchies of Schleswig and Holstein away from Denmark. There was widespread sentiment within the German Confederation that those areas should be part of some

North Sea

DENMARK

Schleswig

Holstein

NETHER-
LANDS

BELGIUM

P   R   U   S   S   I   A

Berlin

Silesia

RUSSIAN

EMPIRE

THE THIRD
GERMANY

FRANCE

Koniggratz

AUSTRIAN

Vienna

EMPIRE

SWITZERLAND

Venetia

ITALY

OTTOMAN

EMPIRE

**Central Europe
in 1866**

MAP 8.2

German political entity, not Denmark, because almost all of Holstein's and about half of Schleswig's population spoke German and thus should be considered German nationals. Austria and Prussia had little difficulty defeating Denmark, but they were unable to agree on who should control Schleswig and Holstein. The United Kingdom, France, and Russia stood aside while Denmark went down to defeat.

Prussia fought Austria in 1866, although Italy, which was a bitter rival of Austria, joined with Prussia in that fight.[44] The war was caused in part by the lingering dispute between Austria and Prussia over what to do with Schleswig and Holstein. But the more important issue at stake was which of these great powers would dominate a united Germany. The Prussian army easily defeated the Austrian army and Prussia gained control of the northern portion of the Third Germany. No other great power intervened to help Austria. Finally, Prussia went to war with France in 1870.[45] Bismarck engineered the war on the assumption that a military victory could be used to complete German unification. France fought mainly for territorial compensation to offset Prussia's gains in 1866. The Prussian army decisively defeated the French army, and Prussia took Alsace and part of Lorraine from France. More important, Prussia gained control of the southern half of the Third Germany, which meant that Bismarck had finally created a united Germany. Europe's other great powers remained on the sidelines while the French army was routed.

It is not surprising that none of the European great powers balanced against Austria and Prussia in 1864, because the stakes were small. Neither Austria nor Prussia was an especially formidable military power, and it was not clear which one of them, if either, would ultimately control Schleswig and Holstein. But the conflicts of 1866 and 1870 are a different matter. Those wars fundamentally altered the European balance of power in Prussia's favor. At first glance, one would have expected the United Kingdom, France, and Russia to have balanced with Austria against Prussia in 1866, and Austria, the United Kingdom, and Russia to have done the same with France in 1870. Instead, they all pursued buck-passing strategies, and Austria was left standing alone against Prussia in 1866, while France found itself in the same position in 1870.

The buck-passing that took place in Europe between 1864 and 1870 was motivated by two different rationales. The United Kingdom and Russia actually welcomed Prussia's victories, because they believed that a unified Germany served their strategic interests.[46] Both felt that France was the most threatening great power in Europe, and that a strong Germany on France's doorstep would help keep it in check. In essence, the United Kingdom and Russia were pursuing a buck-passing strategy, but their aim was not to get another state to balance against Prussia, which they did not consider a threat, but instead to create a powerful Germany that could balance against France, which they did fear. The United Kingdom also thought that a unified Germany would help keep Russia's attention focused on Europe, and away from central Asia, where the British and the Russians were fierce rivals. Furthermore, Russia saw a powerful Germany as a check on Austria, which had recently become Russia's bitter enemy. Still, fear of France was the main driving force behind British and Russian thinking.

Austria and France buck-passed for different reasons. Unlike the United Kingdom and Russia, they feared a unified Germany on their doorstep, because it would pose a direct threat to their survival. Nevertheless, they did not balance together against Prussia; instead they passed the buck to each other, allowing Bismarck to defeat each of them in turn. In fact, there is evidence that France welcomed a bloodletting between Austria and Prussia in 1866, because France believed it would gain relative power in the process.[47] The main reason for this buck-passing was that each thought the other could stop the Prussian army and thwart Bismarck's ambitions without help from another great power. Indeed, it was widely believed in Europe that Austria and France each had the military wherewithal to win a war against Prussia.[48] France not only had Napoleon's legacy on its side, but more concretely, had recently scored victories in the Crimean War (1853–56) and the War of Italian Unification (1859).

There are other reasons why Austria and France failed to form a balancing coalition against Prussia. For example, Bismarck was remarkably skillful at using diplomacy to isolate his targets. Furthermore, Austria and France had fought against each other in 1859, and residual animosity from that conflict hindered relations in the 1860s.[49] Austria also worried in 1870 that if it sided with France, Russia might attack Austria from the east.[50] Finally, the Austrian army was still recuperating in 1870 from the battering it had sustained in 1866, and thus it was not in good shape to take on the Prussian army again. Although these considerations contributed to Austrian and French buck-passing, they would have mattered little if French policymakers had believed Austria needed help against Prussia, and vice versa. In all likelihood, they would have worked togther to stop Bismarck from creating a unified Germany.

The Calculus of Power

This prolific buck-passing during the 1860s can be explained in good part by Prussia's position in the European balance of power. Prussia was certainly not a potential hegemon, and although its army grew increasingly powerful over the course of the decade, it was never so powerful that rival great powers saw fit to form a balancing coalition against it. A potential hegemon, as emphasized throughout this book, must be wealthier than any of its regional rivals and must possess the most powerful army in the area. But the United Kingdom, not Bismarckian Prussia, controlled the largest share of potential power in mid-nineteenth-century Europe. The United Kingdom controlled about 68 percent of European wealth in 1860, whereas France controlled 14 percent and Prussia only 10 percent (see Table 3.3). By 1870, the United Kingdom still controlled roughly 64 percent of European industrial might, while Germany controlled 16 percent and France 13 percent.[51]

Regarding the military balance in the 1860s, there is not much doubt that France and Prussia possessed the most powerful armies. France was surely number one between 1860 and 1866, which is why Britain and Russia looked approvingly on Bismarck's effort to create a unified Germany. Prussia's army was among the weakest European armies at the start of the decade, but it was the most powerful by 1867, and remained in the top position through 1870.[52] Austria had a strong army during the first half of the decade, but its power waned after 1866.[53] Russia maintained a very large but rather inefficient army that had little power-projection capability but was capable of defending Russia against a major attack by another great power.[54] Finally, although the United Kingdom had much more latent power than any of its rivals, it maintained a small and inefficient army that counted for little in the balance of power.[55]

Of course, the United Kingdom's and Russia's relative military weakness hardly mattered for checking Bismarck, because both states wanted Prussia to transform itself into Germany. What mattered most in 1866 and 1870 was how power was distributed among Austria, France, and Prussia.[56] Looking at numbers alone in 1866, the Austrian army was certainly a match for the Prussian army (see Table 8.3).[57] Austria's standing army had an advantage of 1.25:1. After each side's reserves were mobilized, Austria enjoyed a similar advantage. At the crucial battle of Koniggratz on July 3, 1866, an Austrian army of 270,000 faced a Prussian army of 280,000.[58] But the Prussian army was qualitatively better than the Austrian army.[59] Prussian soldiers employed breech-loading rifles, which gave them an important advantage over their Austrian counterparts, who were armed with muzzle-loading rifles. The Prussian army also had a superior staff system, and the Austrian army's multi-ethnic makeup was beginning to impair its fighting power, although the problem was still manageable in 1866. On the other hand, the Austrian army had much better artillery and cavalry than the Prussian army. Considering both quantity and quality, the Prussian army held a distinct though not large power advantage over the Austrian army. This rough balance of power between Austria and Prussia encouraged France to buck-pass in 1866.[60]

France still possessed Europe's most powerful army in 1866, and it could have contained Bismarck by making an alliance with Austria. Unlike Austria and Prussia, France still relied heavily on its standing army, while showing little interest in mobilizable reserves. Nevertheless, France's standing army in 1866 still outnumbered Prussia's fully mobilized army by some 458,000 to 370,000. Furthermore, there was little difference in the quality of the two armies at that point. The balance of power, however, shifted against the French army and in the Prussian army's favor between 1866 and 1870, although that change was not widely recognized at the time.

TABLE 8.3

Manpower in European Armies, 1862–70 (Wars of German Unification)

	1862 Standing army	1864 Standing army	1866 Standing army	1866 Army post-mobilization	1870 Standing army	1870 Army post-mobilization	1870–71 Total Men Mobilized
Austria	255,000	298,000	275,000	460,000	252,000	na	na
United Kingdom	200,000	200,000	176,731	na	174,198	na	na
France	520,000	487,000	458,000	na	367,850	530,870	1,980,000
Prussia	213,000	212,000	214,000	370,000	319,000	1,183,000	1,450,000
Russia	682,000	727,000	742,000	na	738,000	na	na
Italy	185,000	196,100	200,000	na	214,354	na	na

NOTE: na = not available

SOURCES: Numbers for Austria, Prussia, and Russia in 1862 and 1864 are from Singer and Small, *National Material Capabilities Data*. The Russian numbers are actually for 1862 and 1865, as Singer and Small unaccountably put the Russian army at over a million men in 1864. Figures for the United Kingdom are from Michael Stephen Partridge, *Military Planning for the Defense of the United Kingdom, 1814–1870* (Westport, CT: Greenwood, 1989), p. 72. The 1862 figure for Italy is from Singer and Small, *National Material Capabilities*; the 1864 number is from *The Statesman's Year-Book* (London: Macmillan, 1865), p. 312. Standing army figures for Austria, Prussia, and Russia in 1866 are from Singer and Small, *National Material Capabilities Data*; the 1866 figure for the United Kingdom is from Edward M. Spiers, *The Army and Society, 1815–1914* (London: Longman, 1980), p. 38; the 1866 number for France is from Douglas Porch, *Army and Revolution: France, 1815–1848* (London: Routledge and Kegan Paul, 1974), p. 67; the 1866 figure for Italy is from Geoffrey Wawro, *The Austro-Prussian War* (Cambridge: Cambridge University Press, 1996), pp. 52–53. The 1866 numbers for the Austrian and Prussian armies after mobilization are from William McElwee, *The Art of War: Waterloo to Mons* (Bloomington: Indiana University Press, 1974), pp. 53, 62. Standing army figures for Austria, Prussia, and Russia in 1870 are from Singer and Small, *National Material Capabilities Data*; the British number for 1870 is from Spiers, *Army and Society*, p. 36. The 1870 figure for France is from Thomas J. Adriance, *The Last Gaiter Button: A Study of the Mobilization and Concentration of the French Army in the War of 1870* (Westport, CT: Greenwood, 1987), p. 23; the number for Italy in 1870 is from *The Statesman's Year-Book* (London: Macmillan, 1871), p. 312. The figure for the size of the French army after mobilization (as of July 28, 1870) is from Adriance, *Last Gaiter Button*, p. 145; this figure is derived by adding the number of reserves that had arrived in depots by July 28 to the number of men in the standing army. The number for the Prussians (as of August 2, 1870) is from Michael Howard, *The Franco-Prussian War: The German Invasion of France, 1870–1871* (London: Methuen, 1961). p. 60. The figures for the total number of Frenchmen and Prussians mobilized during the 1870–71 war are from Theodore Ropp, *War in the Modern World* (Durham, NC: Duke University Press, 1959). p. 156 (n. 13).

After observing Prussia's success with its mobilized reserves in the war of 1866, France shrunk the size of its standing army and began building a reserve system of its own. Four years later, the French army had a formidable reserve structure on paper. It was inefficient in practice, however, especially compared to the Prussian system, and this difference mattered greatly when France declared war on July 19, 1870.[61] By that point, France's standing army was still more powerful than Prussia's, but whereas Prussia was able to mobilize 1,183,000 soldiers at the start of the war, France could only muster 530,870 soldiers. France eventually managed to mobilize all of its reserves, and over the course of the war, it mobilized more than half a million more men than Prussia. Prussia had a small advantage in army quality by 1870, mainly because it had a superior general staff system and its reserves were better trained than were the French reserves.[62] However, French infantrymen were better armed than their Prussian counterparts, although that advantage was offset by Prussia's breech-loading artillery.

On balance, the Prussian army was markedly more powerful than the French army in 1870, mainly because of the sharp asymmetry between them in short-term mobilization capability. Given this imbalance, Austria should have allied with France against Prussia. But that did not happen, because Austrian and French policymakers miscalculated the balance of power. Both of Prussia's rivals mistakenly believed that the French army could mobilize reserves as rapidly and effectively as the Prussian army.[63] Indeed, France's leaders thought that Prussia would have difficulty mobilizing its reserves, thus providing France with an important military advantage. However, Prussia correctly recognized that France's mobilization would be ragged at best, and that the Prussian army would therefore have a significant advantage on the battlefield.[64] Not surprisingly, Bismarck did not hesitate to go to war against France when the opportunity came in the summer of 1870.

Finally, buck-passing in this case was not heavily influenced by geographical considerations. The United Kingdom was separated from Prussia by the English Channel, but that geographical fact appears to have had little effect on British policy toward Prussia, which was driven mainly by

British fear of France. Austria, France, and Russia all shared a common border with Prussia, so geography cannot help account for their different responses to Bismarck's efforts to create a unified Germany. Prussia's four potential rivals were certainly well-positioned to strike into Prussian territory, had they seen fit to form a balancing coalition. But they did not, mainly because the distribution of power in Europe between 1862 and 1870 encouraged buck-passing.

WILHELMINE GERMANY (1890–1914)

Background

When Bismarck stepped down as chancellor in March 1890, Germany was not yet a potential hegemon, although it had a large and growing population, a dynamic economy, and a formidable army. Those combined assets caused much anxiety among Europe's other great powers in the last decade of the nineteenth century. By the early twentieth century, however, Germany was a full-fledged potential hegemon that was gaining more relative power every year. Not surprisingly, fear of Germany pervaded European politics between 1900 and the outbreak of World War I in August 1914.

Besides Germany, there were five other great powers in Europe during this period: Austria-Hungary, the United Kingdom, France, Italy, and Russia (see Map 6.2).

Austria-Hungary, Italy, and Germany were all members of the Triple Alliance. Austria-Hungary was an especially weak great power with a dim future.[65] In fact, it disintegrated forever at the end of World War I. Nationalism was the principal source of Austria-Hungary's weakness. It was a multinational state, and most of its composite ethnic groups wanted independent states of their own. Austria-Hungary and Germany were closely allied before World War I. Austria-Hungary had serious territorial disputes with Russia in eastern Europe and the Balkans, and needed Germany to help protect it from the tsar's armies. Germany, on the other hand, had a vested interest in keeping Austria-Hungary intact so that it could help block Russian expansion.

Italy was also an especially weak great power. The problem in Italy was not nationalism, which had actually helped unify the country in 1860, but the fact that Italy had little industrial might and an army that was prone to catastrophic defeat.[66] A key British diplomat was not joking when he said in 1909, "We have no desire to seduce Italy from the Triple Alliance, since she would rather be a thorn in the side than any assistance to France and ourselves."[67] Italy was not seriously committed to the Triple Alliance by the early twentieth century, however, because its troubles with France, which are what originally caused the alliance with Germany and Austria-Hungary, had largely gone away, while its relations with Austria-Hungary had deteriorated.[68] In effect, Italy was a neutral state before World War I. Not surprisingly, when the war started, Italy remained neutral and then in May 1915 joined with the Allies to fight against its own erstwhile allies, Austria-Hungary and Germany.

The United Kingdom, France, and Russia were all much more powerful than Austria-Hungary and Italy, and they were determined to stop Germany from establishing hegemony in Europe. Therefore, the key issue is how these three great powers reacted to Wilhelmine Germany's growing might between 1890 and 1914. As will become apparent, there was little buck-passing among the Kaiserreich's rivals. Instead, the United Kingdom, France, and Russia formed a balancing coalition—the Triple Entente—seven years before the start of World War I.

The Strategic Behavior of the Great Powers

France and Russia, the continental powers sitting across Germany's western and eastern borders, negotiated an alliance between 1890 and 1894 that was designed to contain Germany.[69] However, neither partner thought it likely that Germany would attack it at the time or in the immediate future. France and Russia were mainly interested in making sure that Germany did not cause trouble in Europe, so that they could pursue important goals in other regions of the world. Relations between the United Kingdom and Germany experienced a marked chill in the early 1890s, but the United Kingdom showed little inclination to ally with

France and Russia against Germany.[70] In fact, the United Kingdom was frequently at loggerheads with its future allies during the 1890s, and almost went to war with France in 1898 over the Nile fort of Fashoda.[71]

There was no significant change between 1894 and 1904 in how the future members of the Triple Entente reacted to the German threat. France and Russia remained allies, committed to containing the Kaiserreich by threatening it with the specter of a two-front war. Anglo-German relations were badly strained at the turn of the century by Germany's efforts to build a formidable navy with its own version of the British empire (*Weltpolitik*). But the United Kingdom did not join forces with France and Russia to balance against Germany, although fear of Germany caused a marked improvement in Anglo-French relations between 1903 and 1904.[72] They signed the Entente Cordiale on April 8, 1904, which effectively put an end to their bitter rivalry in areas outside of Europe. This agreement was not an alliance against Germany in disguise, although it certainly made that alliance easier to consummate after 1905. In effect, the United Kingdom, acting as a classic offshore balancer, was buck-passing; it was relying on France and Russia to contain German expansion on the European continent. Of course, rejecting a continental commitment meant that the United Kingdom did not have to build a powerful army, which allowed it to concentrate on maintaining the world's most powerful navy.

There was dramatic change in the constellation of forces in Europe between 1905 and 1907, and when the dust had settled, the United Kingdom was allied with France and Russia in the Triple Entente.[73] The United Kingdom was pushed toward accepting a continental commitment by the simple fact that Germany had the earmarkings of a potential hegemon by 1905.[74] But other considerations also affected British calculations. Japan inflicted a devastating defeat on Russia in 1905, effectively knocking it out of the European balance of power and leaving France without its main ally.[75] To make matters worse, while Russia was going down to defeat, Germany initiated a major diplomatic crisis with France over Morocco. The goal was to isolate and humiliate France, which no longer had a reliable Russian ally and was not allied with the United Kingdom at the time.

British policymakers quickly understood that buck-passing was no longer a viable policy, because France alone could not contain Germany.[76] Thus, in late 1905, the United Kingdom began moving toward a continental commitment. Specifically, it began organizing a small expeditionary force to fight alongside the French army on the continent, and it initiated staff talks between the British and French armies to coordinate plans for fighting together against Germany.[77] At the same time, the United Kingdom began working to improve relations with Russia, which were badly strained over their rivalry in Asia. The Anglo-Russian Convention, the third and final leg of the Triple Entente, was consummated on August 31, 1907.[78] The aim was to make sure that the United Kingdom and Russia did not become involved in a serious dispute outside of Europe (especially in central Asia), so that they could work together inside of Europe to contain Germany.

Although the United Kingdom, France, and Russia had formed a balancing coalition against Germany by the summer of 1907, the British impulse to buck-pass never completely disappeared. For example, the United Kingdom never made an explicit commitment to fight with its allies if Germany attacked them.[79] The Triple Entente was not a tightly organized and formal alliance like the North Atlantic Treaty Organization (NATO) would be during the Cold War. Furthermore, when it became apparent in 1911 that the Russian army had recovered from its defeat in the Russo-Japanese War, it was once again possible to imagine France and Russia checking Germany without help from the British army. Consequently, Anglo-Russian relations became testy again and the Triple Entente wobbled a bit.[80] Finally, when war broke out, the United Kingdom tried to get France and Russia to pay the awful price of defeating the mighty German army while it remained on the sidelines, preserving itself for the postwar period.[81] These hesitations notwithstanding, the United Kingdom did not abandon its continental commitment after 1907, and it went to war alongside France and Russia in the early days of August 1914. It also committed a mass army to the western front and did its fair share of fighting against the formidable German army.

In sum, we see relatively efficient balancing against Germany in the two and a half decades before World War I. France and Russia joined forces to check Germany between 1890 and 1905, while the United Kingdom buck-passed. There was little buck-passing after 1905, however, as the United Kingdom joined forces with France and Russia to try to keep the Kaiserreich at bay. This pattern of behavior by Germany's foes can be explained in large part by geography and Germany's evolving position in the European balance of power from 1890 to 1914.

The Calculus of Power

Let us start with the period between 1890 and 1905. Germany was not a potential hegemon until the end of this period, mainly because the United Kingdom controlled more latent power than Germany did until 1903. For example, the United Kingdom controlled 50 percent of European wealth in 1890, while Germany controlled 25 percent (see Table 3.3). France's share was 13 percent, and Russia's was a mere 5 percent. The United Kingdom still held an advantage over Germany in 1900, but it was only 37 percent to 34 percent. Moreover, France's share had shrunk to 11 percent, although Russia's had increased to 10 percent. Germany was rapidly reaching the point where it would have sufficient industrial might to be a potential hegemon. Indeed, it reached that point in 1903, when its share of European wealth reached 36.5 percent, and the United Kingdom's fell to 34.5 percent.[82] There was never much question that by the early twentieth century Germany had substantially more latent power than did either France or Russia.

Regarding actual military power, France and Germany were clearly the two most powerful armies in Europe between 1890 and 1905. As David Herrmann notes, "the French and German armies dominated the stage in the perceptions of military experts," in the pre–World War I era.[83] But the German army was the more formidable of the two fighting forces. The standing armies of France and Germany, as well as their fully mobilized armies, were of roughly equal size during this period (see Tables 6.1 and 8.4). The key difference, however, was in how each army used its reserves. A large portion of Germany's reserves was trained for combat and organized into fighting units that were expected to participate in the opening battles of a major European war. The French, on the other hand, did not believe in training their reserves to fight alongside the standing army. Thus, although there was not much difference in the size of the fully mobilized French and German armies, the German army could generate substantially larger combat forces. If war had broken out in 1905, the Germans would have had roughly 1.5 million soldiers in their fighting armies, whereas the French would have had about 840,000, which translates into a 1.8:1 advantage for Germany.[84] Finally, the German army enjoyed a moderate qualitative edge over its French rival, mainly because of its superior general staff and its advantage in heavy artillery.

Russia possessed Europe's largest army between 1890 and 1905, but it was plagued with serious problems, which relegated it to a distant third place behind the German and French armies.[85] Japan's army took advantage of those deficiencies in the 1904–5 war and inflicted a punishing defeat on the Russian army. The British army was small and ill-prepared for continental warfare before 1905, and thus hardly mattered in the balance of power. As Herrmann notes, "Surveys of the European armies with their strengths and equipment, compiled by general staffs from Paris and Berlin to Vienna and Rome, very often simply left the British out altogether."[86]

Germany was clearly a potential hegemon in the decade before World War I. Regarding latent power, Germany controlled 40 percent of European industrial might by 1913; the United Kingdom controlled 28 percent (see Table 3.3).[87] Also, by that point, Germany had more than a 3:1 advantage in potential power over France and Russia, whose shares of industrial might were 12 percent and 11 percent, respectively. Furthermore, the German army remained the dominant army in Europe after 1905. Indeed, it began a serious expansion program in early 1912. When war broke out in 1914, Germany was able to place 1.71 million soldiers in front-line combat units, while France could muster only 1.07 million (see Table 8.4). Of course, Germany's great advantage in potential power allowed it to mobilize far more men than France over the course of the war: 13.25 million versus 8.6 million. The Russian army was badly crippled by its defeat in the Russo-Japanese War, and began to show signs of recovery only in 1911. However, it was still far inferior to the French

TABLE 8.4

Manpower in European Armies, 1900–1918 (World War I)

	1900		1905		1910		1914		1914–18
	Standing army	War potential	Standing army	War potential	Standing army	War potential	Standing army	War potential	Total mobilized
Austria-Hungary	361,693	1,872,178	386,870	2,580,000	397,132	2,750,000	415,000	1,250,000	8,000,000
United Kingdom	231,851	677,314	287,240	742,568	255,438	742,036	247,432	110,000	6,211,427
France	598,765	2,500,000	580,420	2,500,000	612,424	3,172,000	736,000	1,071,000	8,660,000
Germany	600,516	3,000,000	609,758	3,000,000	622,483	3,260,000	880,000	1,710,000	13,250,000
Russia	1,100,000	4,600,000	1,100,000	4,600,000	1,200,000	4,000,000	1,320,000	1,800,000	13,700,000
Italy	263,684	1,063,635	264,516	1,064,467	238,617	600,000	256,000	875,000	5,615,000

NOTE: "War potential" is as defined in Table 6.1. A country's "fighting army" represents the number of men in the army's fighting units concentrated in the theater of battle and thus immediately available for combat. The distribution of those fighting armies engaged on more than one front in August 1914 is as follows: Austria-Hungary, 1,000,000 in Galicia, 250,000 to invade Serbia; Germany, 1,485,000 to invade France and the Low Countries, 225,000 in East Prussia; Russia, 1,200,000 in Galicia, 600,000 to invade East Prussia.

SOURCES: Figures for standing army and war potential of all states for 1900, 1905, and 1910 are from *The Statesman's Year-Book* (London: Macmillan, various years) except for Austria-Hungary's 1910 war potential, which is the author's estimate. Specific years and page numbers are as follows (years refer to editions of *The Statesman's Year-Book*): Austria-Hungary, 1901, p. 386; 1906, p. 653; 1911, p. 590; United Kingdom, 1901, pp. 57–58; 1906, p. 284; 1911, pp. 52–53; France, 1901, p. 556; 1906, pp. 614–15; 1911, pp. 768–69; Germany, 1901, pp. 629–30; 1906, pp. 936–37; 1911, p. 843; Russia, 1901, p. 991; 1911, p. 1166; Italy, 1902, p. 806; 1906, p. 1088; 1911, p. 963. The figure for the fighting army of France in 1905 is from David G. Herrmann, *The Arming of Europe and the Making of the First World War* (Princeton, NJ: Princeton University Press, 1996), p. 45. The same figure for Germany is the author's estimate based on the discussions in ibid., pp. 44–45, 160, 221; and Jack L. Snyder, *The Ideology of the Offensive: Military Decision Making and the Disasters of 1914* (Ithaca, NY: Cornell University Press, 1984), pp. 41–50, 67, 81, 109–11, 220. Figures for the standing army and mobilized fighting armies of Austria-Hungary in 1914 are from Holger H. Herwig, *The First World War: Germany and Austria-Hungary, 1914–1918* (London: Arnold, 1997), p. 12; and Arthur Banks, *A Military Atlas of the First World War* (London: Leo Cooper, 1989), p. 32. For the United Kingdom, the numbers are from War Office, *Statistics of the Military Effort of the British Empire During the Great War* (London: His Majesty's Stationery Office, 1922), p. 30; and Herwig, *First World War*, p. 98. Figures for the French army are from *Les Armées Françaises dans La Grande Guerre* (Paris: Imprimerie Nationale, 1923), p. 30; and J. E. Edmonds, *History of the Great War: Military Operations, France and Belgium, 1914*, Vol. 1 (London: Macmillan, 1933), p. 18. For Germany, the figures are from Spencer C. Tucker, *The Great War, 1914–1918* (Bloomington: Indiana University Press, 1998), p. 17; and Banks, *Atlas of the First World War*, pp. 30, 32. The figures for the Russian army are from Alfred Knox, *With the Russian Army, 1914–1917* (London: Hutchinson, 1921), p. xviii; and Tucker, *The Great War*, pp. 40, 44. For Italy, the standing army figure is from Herrmann, *Arming of Europe*, p. 234, and the mobilized fighting army figure (which is for May 1915, when Italy entered the war) is from Banks, *Atlas of the First World War*, p. 200. Figures for total number of men mobilized from 1914 to 1918 for Austria-Hungary, the United Kingdom, France, Germany, and Russia are from Roger Chickering, *Imperial Germany and the Great War, 1914–1918* (Cambridge: Cambridge University Press, 1998), p. 195. The figure for Italy is from Judith M. Hughes, *To the Maginot Line: The Politics of French Military Preparation in the 1920s* (Cambridge, MA: Harvard University Press, 1971), p. 12.

and German armies. The post-1905 British army was small, but it was a high-quality fighting force, especially when compared to the Russian army. The British army was probably the third best in Europe during the decade before World War I, while Russia's was fourth best, a reverse of the situation before 1905.

Given that Germany was the most powerful state on the continent from 1890 until 1905 but was not a potential hegemon until 1903, it makes sense that France and Russia balanced together against Germany, while the United Kingdom stayed offshore and pursued a buck-passing strategy. By 1905, however, the Kaiserreich was clearly a potential hegemon, and thus a much more serious threat to the balance of power, especially after the Russian defeat that year. Not surprisingly, the United Kingdom stopped passing the buck and balanced with France and Russia against Germany, a commitment it saw through until Germany was finally defeated in November 1918.

Finally, geography was no hindrance to balancing against the Kaiserreich. France and Russia shared a common border with Germany, which made it easy for them to attack or threaten to attack into German territory. Of course, that proximity also made it easy for Germany to invade France and Russia, which certainly provided them with an incentive to form a balancing coalition against Germany. The United Kingdom was separated from Germany by the English Channel, which made buck-passing a more viable option for the United Kingdom than for either France or Russia. But once the United Kingdom abandoned buck-passing and accepted a continental commitment, it could readily bring pressure to bear against Germany by transporting its army to France, which it did in 1914.

NAZI GERMANY (1933–41)

Background

France was the most powerful state in Europe between the end of World War I (1918) and when Hitler became German chancellor on January 30, 1933. It maintained a formidable army and paid serious attention to defending its eastern border against a German attack (see Table 8.5). Germany presented no threat to France during this period, however, because Weimar Germany was barely capable of defending itself, much less attacking into France. Germany certainly had the requisite population and wealth to build the mightiest army in Europe, but it was hamstrung by the Versailles Treaty (1919), which took the strategically important Rhineland away from Germany and placed it under international control and also prohibited Weimar from building a powerful military machine.

TABLE 8.5

Manpower in European Armies, 1920–30

	1920	1925	1930
United Kingdom	485,000	216,121	208,573
France	660,000	684,039	522,643
Germany	100,000	99,086	99,191
Italy	250,000	326,000	251,470
Soviet Union	3,050,000	260,000	562,000

SOURCES: All figures are from *The Statesman's Year-Book* (various years), except for the Soviet Union in 1920, which is from Singer and Small, *National Material Capabilities Data.* Specific years and page numbers are as follows (years refer to editions of *The Statesman's Year-Book*): United Kingdom, 1920, p. 53; 1925, p. 44; 1931, p. 41; France, 1921, p. 855; 1926, p. 857; 1931, p. 853; Germany, 1921, p. 927; 1926, p. 927; 1931, p. 927; Italy, 1921, p. 1016; 1926, p. 1006; 1931, p. 1023; Soviet Union, 1926, p. 1218; 1931, p. 1238.

The Soviet Union, too, was an especially weak great power in the fifteen years after World War I, which explains in good part why Weimar Germany and the Soviet Union cooperated extensively with each other before 1933.[88] Soviet leaders faced many problems in the 1920s as they tried to rebuild after the destruction wrought by World War I, revolution, civil war, and a lost war against Poland. But the chief problem they faced was their backward economy, which could not support a first-class military establishment. Josef Stalin initiated a major modernization program in 1928 to rectify this problem. It eventually worked, but the fruits of his ruthless industrialization policy were realized only after the Nazis came to power. The United Kingdom maintained a small army in the 1920s that was probably more concerned with fighting in the British Empire than on the European continent. Italy, which had been under Benito Mussolini's rule since 1922, was the weakest great power in Europe.

European leaders realized soon after Hitler took the reins of power that Germany would throw off the shackles of Versailles and attempt to alter the balance of power in its favor. But how quickly Hitler would move, in what directions he would move, and just how aggressive Nazi Germany would be were not clear during his first five years in power. Unlike contemporary students of international relations, Hitler's counterparts across Europe did not have the benefit of hindsight. The picture began to come into focus in 1938, first when he incorporated Austria into the Third Reich, and then when he forced the United Kingdom and France to let him take the Sudetenland from Czechoslovakia. It became crystal clear in 1939. In March 1939, the Wehrmacht conquered all of Czechoslovakia, the first time that Nazi Germany had acquired territory that was not heavily populated with ethnic Germans. Six months later, in September, the Nazis attacked Poland and started World War II. Less than a year later, in May 1940, Hitler invaded France, and a little over a year after that, in June 1941, he sent the Wehrmacht into the Soviet Union.

The same three states that worked to contain Wilhelmine Germany before 1914—the United Kingdom, France, and Russia—were Nazi Germany's principal rivals between 1933 and 1941. Although the cast of characters was essentially unchanged, Hitler's opponents mainly buck-passed among each other in the face of the Third Reich's aggressive behavior, rather than forming a balancing coalition, as their predecessors had.

The Strategic Behavior of the Great Powers

Hitler was not in a good position to act aggressively on the foreign policy front during his early years in office. He first had to consolidate his political position at home and revitalize the German economy. Moreover, the German military he inherited was in no shape to fight a major war anytime soon. Consider that the mobilized German army that went to war in 1914 was composed of 2.15 million soldiers and 102 divisions.[89] The 1933 version of that army had a little over 100,000 soldiers and 7 infantry divisions. Hitler and his generals, however, were determined to rectify that problem by overthrowing the Versailles Treaty and building a formidable military instrument. Still, it took about six years to achieve that goal.

Three major building plans underpinned the growth of the German army.[90] In December 1933, Hitler mandated that the peacetime strength of the army be increased threefold, to 300,000 soldiers and 21 infantry divisions. New reserve units were also to be created, so that the fully mobilized field army would have 63 divisions. In March 1935, a new law stipulated that the peacetime army would grow to 700,000 with 36 infantry divisions. Conscription was introduced at the same time, although it did not go into effect until October 1, 1935, the same month that Hitler decided to build 3 panzer divisons in addition to the 36 infantry divisions. The projected size of the field army, however, remained "practically unchanged at 63 to 73" divisions.[91] Finally, the August 1936 Rearmament Program called for building a peacetime army of 830,000 with roughly 44 divisions by October 1940. The fully mobilized field army was to comprise 4.62 million soldiers and 102 divisions. When World War II started on September 1, 1939, the German army contained 3.74 million soldiers and 103 divisions.

Hitler also pushed to create a powerful navy and air force during the 1930s.[92] The development of the German navy was rather haphazard and unimpressive, but the building of the Luftwaffe was a different story. Germany had no combat-ready air squadrons when Hitler took office in

1933, because the Versailles Treaty outlawed a German air force. By August 1939, however, the Luftwaffe could claim 302 combat-ready squadrons. As Wilhelm Deist notes, "The spectacular development of the Luftwaffe in the six years from 1933 until the outbreak of the war aroused the boundless admiration as well as dark forebodings of contemporaries."[93]

Until Germany had a powerful army, Hitler was not in a good position to redraw the map of Europe by the threat or use of force. Thus, Nazi foreign policy was relatively tame before 1938. Hitler pulled Germany out of the Geneva Disarmament Conference and the League of Nations in October 1933, but he also signed a ten-year non-aggression pact with Poland in January 1934, and a naval treaty with the United Kingdom in June 1935. The Wehrmacht did occupy and remilitarize the Rhineland in March 1936, but that was widely recognized to be German territory, even though the Versailles Treaty mandated that it be permanently demilitarized.[94] There was no overt German aggression in 1938, but Hitler twice used threats that year to acquire new territory. He compelled German-speaking Austria to join the Third Reich in March 1938 (the infamous Anschluss), and then at Munich in September 1938, he used threats and bluster to get the United Kingdom and France to detach the German-speaking Sudetenland from Czechoslovakia and give it to Nazi Germany. By 1939, Hitler finally possessed a potent military instrument, and he turned to overt aggression that same year.

The United Kingdom, France, and the Soviet Union all feared Nazi Germany, and they each paid serious attention to devising a viable containment strategy. However, with the possible exception of the Soviet Union, there was little interest among them in putting together a balancing coalition like the Triple Entente that might deter Hitler by threatening Germany with a two-front war. Instead, each preferred buck-passing. Between 1933 and March 1939, there was no alliance between any of Hitler's great-power rivals. The United Kingdom buck-passed to France, which tried to push Hitler eastward against the smaller states of eastern Europe and possibly the Soviet Union, which in turn tried to pass the buck to the United Kingdom and France. In March 1939, the United Kingdom finally joined forces with France against the Third Reich, but the

Soviet Union did not join with its former allies. After Germany knocked France out of the war in June 1940, the United Kingdom tried to ally with the Soviet Union but failed because the Soviets preferred to continue buck-passing.

Although Hitler's rivals showed little interest in creating an anti-German balancing coalition, both France and the Soviet Union went to considerable lengths in the 1930s to maintain armies that could stand up to the Wehrmacht. They did so to increase the likelihood that buck-passing would work, because the more powerful each was, the less likely that Hitler would attack it. Strong armies were also an insurance policy to protect them in the event that 1) they ended up catching the buck and facing the Nazi war machine alone, or 2) buck-passing worked, but the buck-catcher failed to contain the Wehrmacht.

The United Kingdom's initial strategy for dealing with Hitler was to pass the buck to France, which probably had the most powerful military in Europe during the mid-1930s.[95] British leaders recognized that France would get little assistance from the Soviet Union, which was fine by them, but they hoped that France's alliances with eastern Europe's minor powers (Czechoslovakia, Poland, Romania, and Yugoslavia) would help France contain Hitler. The United Kingdom had powerful incentives to buck-pass in Europe, because it also faced threats from Japan in Asia and Italy in the Mediterranean, and its anemic economy could not provide for a substantial military presence in all three of those regions.

Given this dangerous threat environment, the United Kingdom sharply increased defense spending in 1934, more than tripling its defense budget by 1938.[96] But on December 12, 1937, the United Kingdom decided not to build an army to fight alongside France on the continent. Indeed, the British cabinet decided to starve the army of funds, a move that was certainly consistent with a buck-passing strategy. Spending on the air force was emphasized instead, to deter Hitler from launching the Luftwaffe against the British homeland.

Nevertheless, it became apparent by late 1938 that France needed the United Kingdom's help to contain Nazi Germany. Not only was the Wehrmacht on the verge of becoming a formidable military instrument, but the Anschluss and Munich had delivered the death blow to France's already weak alliance system in eastern Europe. The United Kingdom finally abandoned buck-passing and formed a balancing coalition with France in March 1939, shortly after Hitler conquered Czechoslovakia.[97] At the same time, the United Kingdom began racing to build an army to fight in France in the event of war. The United Kingdom showed a modicum of interest in forging an alliance with the Soviet Union but ultimately found no basis for resurrecting the Triple Entente.[98]

The United Kingdom and France declared war against Germany on September 3, 1939, two days after the Wehrmacht invaded Poland. But they did not fight against the German army until the spring of 1940, when Hitler struck in the west and knocked France out of the war. By the summer of 1940, a badly weakened United Kingdom stood alone against Nazi Germany. British leaders tried to form a balancing coalition with the Soviet Union against Hitler, but they failed, mainly because Stalin continued to pursue a buck-passing strategy. He hoped to see the United Kingdom and Germany engage in a long war, while the Soviet Union stayed out of the fighting.[99] The United Kingdom and the Soviet Union finally came together in an alliance after the Wehrmacht attacked the Soviet Union in June 1941.

France, too, was committed to buck-passing.[100] During the 1920s, well before Hitler came to power, France formed alliances with some of the small states in eastern Europe for the purpose of containing a future German threat. Those alliances remained in place after 1933, which might seem to indicate that France was not buck-passing but was committed to building a balancing coalition against Nazi Germany. In reality, however, those alliances were largely moribund by the mid-1930s, in good part because France had no intention of coming to the aid of its allies, as it demonstrated when it abandoned Czechoslovakia at Munich in 1938.[101] Indeed, France hoped to push Hitler eastward, where it hoped the Wehrmacht would get bogged down in a war in eastern Europe or maybe even the Soviet Union. "France's military policy," as Arnold Wolfers notes, "tends to prove that, notwithstanding her far-flung commitments on the Vistula and the Danube, she was more concerned about receiving than about giving support, more preoccupied with the defense of her own soil than with the protection of small countries."[102]

To encourage Hitler to strike first in the East, French leaders went to some lengths during the 1930s to foster good relations with the Third Reich. That policy remained in place even after Munich.[103] On the other hand, France made no serious effort to form a balancing coalition with the Soviet Union. Geography certainly worked against that alliance (see Map 8.3). The Soviet Union did not share a common border with Germany, which meant that in the event of a Wehrmacht attack against France, the Red Army would have to move through Poland to strike at Germany. Not surprisingly, Poland was categorically opposed to that idea.[104] More generally, a Franco-Soviet alliance would have alienated the minor powers in eastern Europe, since they tended to fear the Soviet Union more than Germany, and it probably would have caused them to ally with Hitler, which would have undermined France's buck-passing strategy.

France was also discouraged from approaching the Soviet Union by concern that a Franco-Soviet alliance would ruin any chance that the United Kingdom might join forces with France against Nazi Germany. Not only were most British leaders hostile to the Soviet Union because they despised and feared communism, but if France had a reliable Soviet ally, it would not need the United Kingdom, which would then be free to continue buck-passing to France.[105] Finally, France did not form an alliance with Stalin because French leaders sought to encourage Hitler to strike first against the Soviet Union rather than France, and in the event that that happened, they had no intention of coming to the aid of Moscow. In short, France was buck-passing to the Soviet Union as well as to the smaller states of eastern Europe.

France's interest in passing the buck to the Soviet Union was reinforced by the widespread belief that Stalin was trying to buck-pass to France, which many French policymakers took as evidence that the Soviets were unreliable alliance partners.[106] Of course, many Soviet policymakers recognized what the French were up to, which just reinforced Stalin's interest in buck-passing, which, in turn, confirmed French suspicions that the Soviets were buck-passing to them.[107] As a consequence of all these fac-

Europe in 1935

MAP 8.3

tors, France showed little interest in allying with the Soviet Union against Hitler during the 1930s.

The United Kingdom's buck-passing notwithstanding, French leaders worked hard throughout the 1930s to get the United Kingdom to commit itself to the defense of France.[108] They prized an Anglo-French alliance because it would increase the likelihood that their buck-passing strategy would work. The combination of British and French military might make a German offensive in the west less likely, and thus increased the probability that the Wehrmacht would strike first in the east. Moreover, if buck-passing failed, fighting with the United Kingdom against the Wehrmacht was clearly preferable to fighting it alone. France also mobilized its own resources to facilitate buck-passing and to protect itself in the event of a buck-passing failure. Little was done to increase French defense spending during Hitler's first two years in office, probably because France had a relatively powerful military when Hitler came to power in 1933. But starting in 1935, the size of the annual defense budget grew constantly and sharply as different French governments sought to maintain a military that could stymie a Wehrmacht offensive. For example, France spent 7.5 billion francs on defense in 1935, 11.2 billion francs in 1937, and 44.1 billion francs in 1939.[109]

Scholars disagree substantially about Soviet policy for dealing with Nazi Germany between 1934 and 1938. Stalin's strategy for the period from 1939 to 1941 is more straightforward and less controversial.

There are three main schools of thought on Soviet policy in the mid-1930s. Some claim that Stalin, not Hitler, was driving events in Europe, and that the Soviet leader pursued a bait-and-bleed strategy. Specifically, it is argued, Stalin intervened in German politics to help Hitler become chancellor because he believed that the Nazis would start a war against the United Kingdom and France, which would work to the Soviets' advantage.[110] Others contend that Stalin was determined to build a balancing coalition with the United Kingdom and France to confront Nazi Germany, but this effort at "collective security" failed because the Western powers refused to cooperate with him.[111] Finally, some argue that Stalin was pursuing a buck-passing strategy,[112] the aim of which was to foster cooperation with Hitler while working to undermine Germany's relations with the United Kingdom and France, so that Hitler would be inclined to attack them first. That approach would not only facilitate passing the buck to the Western great powers but would also create opportunities for Hitler and Stalin to gang up on small states in eastern Europe, such as Poland.

Although Stalin was certainly a clever strategist at times, there is insufficient evidence to support the bait-and-bleed thesis. There is, however, considerable evidence that he pushed both the collective security and buck-passing strategies between 1934 and 1938.[113] This is not surprising, since the political landscape in Europe was undergoing rapid and fundamental change in the wake of Hitler's rise to power, and it was not clear where events were leading. Historian Adam Ulam puts the point well: "Confronted with a terrible danger, the Soviets felt a desperate need to keep all the options open, hoping that one of them would enable the [Soviet Union] to postpone or avoid an actual entanglement in war."[114]

Nevertheless, on balance, the available evidence from the mid-1930s suggests that buck-passing was Stalin's preferred strategy for dealing with Nazi Germany. Buck-passing, of course, is an attractive strategy, which is why the United Kingdom, France, and the Soviet Union were all pursuing it.[115] If it works as designed, the buck-passer avoids the heavy costs of fighting the aggressor and might even gain relative power. Granted, Stalin's buck-passing strategy ultimately failed when France fell in June 1940. But Stalin had no way of knowing that would happen. Indeed, there was good reason at the time to think that the United Kingdom and France would hold their own against the Wehrmacht. Buck-passing in Europe was also attractive because the Soviets faced a serious threat from Japan in the Far East throughout the 1930s.[116]

Furthermore, Stalin surely recognized that there were a host of factors at play in the mid-1930s that made it unlikely he could resurrect the Triple Entente. For example, the French army was not well-suited for offensive operations against Germany, especially after Hitler took back the Rhineland in March 1936. Therefore, Stalin could not depend on France to attack Germany if Hitler struck first against the Soviet Union. Stalin also had abundant evidence that both the United Kingdom and France were committed to buck-passing, which did not bode well for their reliability as allies. This problem was compounded by the deep-seated ideological hostility between Moscow and the Western powers.[117] Finally, as noted, the geography of eastern Europe was a major impediment to the so-called collective security option.

The Soviet Union also mobilized its own resources to protect itself from a German attack and to increase the likelihood that its buck-passing strategy would work. Recall from Chapter 6 that one of the main reasons Stalin began ruthlessly modernizing the Soviet economy in 1928 was to prepare it for a future European war. The Red Army grew substantially in size during the 1930s, almost tripling in size between 1933 and 1938 (see Table 8.6). The quantity and quality of the army's weaponry also improved markedly. For example, Soviet industry produced 952 artillery pieces in 1930, 4,368 in 1933, 4,324 in 1936, and 15,300 in 1940.[118] In 1930, 170 tanks were built; in 1933, 3,509, and in 1936, 4,800. The number dropped to 2,794 tanks in 1940, but that was because the Soviets started producing medium and heavy tanks in 1937, rather than light tanks, which were easier to crank off the assembly line in large numbers. The quality of the fighting forces was good and steadily improving in the mid-1930s. In fact, by 1936, "the Red Army had the most advanced doctrine and the greatest capability for armoured warfare in the world."[119] But Stalin's purges struck the military in the summer of 1937 and seriously damaged its fighting capacity through the early years of World War II.[120]

There is not much debate about Stalin's policy between 1939 and 1941: buck-passing coupled with the search for opportunities to gang up with Hitler on the smaller states of eastern Europe. That policy was formalized in the infamous Molotov-Ribbentrop Pact of August 23, 1939, which not only divided up most of eastern Europe between Germany and the Soviet Union, but also virtually guaranteed that Hitler would go to war with the United Kingdom and France while the Soviet Union sat out the fight. One might have expected Stalin to abandon buck-passing after the collapse of France in the summer of 1940 and instead join forces with the United Kingdom against Hitler. As noted, Stalin continued to pursue a buck-passing strategy, hoping that the United Kingdom and Nazi Germany would become involved in a long and costly war. That approach failed, however, when the Wehrmacht invaded the Soviet Union on June 22, 1941. Only then did the British and the Soviets become allies against the Third Reich.

The Calculus of Power

The distribution of power among the European great powers and geography can account in large part for the buck-passing behavior of Hitler's adversaries during the 1930s. Germany controlled more latent power than did any other European state from 1930 until 1944 (see Tables 3.3 and 3.4). In 1930, Weimar Germany accounted for 33 percent of European wealth, while the United Kingdom, its nearest competitor, controlled 27 percent. France and the Soviet Union possessed 22 and 14 percent, respectively. By 1940, Germany's share of industrial might had grown to 36 percent, but its nearest competitor was now the Soviet Union with 28 percent; the United Kingdom, with 24 percent, had fallen to third place.

For purposes of comparison, Germany had controlled 40 percent of European wealth in 1913, prior to World War I, while the United Kingdom was in second place, with 28 percent. France and Russia accounted for 12 and 11 percent, respectively. Based on latent power alone, it is apparent that Germany was almost as well-positioned to be a potential hegemon in the 1930s as it was earlier in the century. It is also clear that the Soviet Union markedly increased its share of European industrial might during the 1930s, which meant that it had the wherewithal to build a much more formidable army by the end of that decade than it had in either 1914 or 1930.[121]

Despite all of its latent power, Germany was not a potential hegemon until 1939, because it did not have the most powerful army in Europe before then. Hitler inherited a puny army, and it took time to transform it into a well-organized and well-equipped fighting force with the capability to take the offensive against another great power. The critically important August 1936 Rearmament Program, after all, was not expected to be completed until October 1940. Its goals were realized for the most part a year earlier (in the summer of 1939), because rearmament was pushed at a dizzying pace and because of the resources Germany garnered from the acquisition of Austria and Czechoslovakia.[122] But rearming at such a rapid pace caused numerous organizational problems, which left the Wehrmacht in no shape to fight a great-power war before 1939.[123] This general state of unreadiness was the main reason that army leaders were at odds with Hitler during the Munich crisis in 1938. They feared that he would drag Germany into a great-power war that it was ill-prepared to fight.[124]

TABLE 8.6

Manpower in European Armies, 1933–38

	1933	1934	1935	1936	1937	1938
United Kingdom	195,256	195,845	196,137	192,325	190,830	212,300
France	558,067	550,678	642,875	642,785	692,860	698,101
Germany	102,500	240,000	480,000	520,000	550,000	720,000
Italy	285,088	281,855	1,300,000	343,000	370,000	373,000
Soviet Union	534,657	940,000	1,300,000	1,300,000	1,433,000	1,513,000

SOURCES: The numbers for the United Kingdom are from the *League of Nations Armaments Year-Book* (Geneva: League of Nations, June 1940), pp. 58–59. On France, see the annual volumes of the *League of Nations Armaments Year-Book* (dates correspond to volume publication dates): July 1934, p. 259; June 1935, p. 366; August 1936, p. 368; and *The Statesman's Year-Book* (London: Macmillan, various years): 1937, p. 898; 1938, p. 908; 1939, p. 904. The German numbers are from Barton Whaley, *Covert German Rearmament, 1919–1939: Deception and Misperception* (Frederick, MD: University Press of America, 1984), p. 69; Herbert Rosinski, *The German Army* (London: Hogarth, 1939), p. 244; Wilhelm Deist, *The Wehrmacht and German Rearmament* (Toronto: University of Toronto Press, 1981), p. 44; and *The Statesman's Year-Book*, 1938, p. 968. For Italy, see *The Statesman's Year-Book*, 1934, p. 1043; 1935, pp. 1051–52; 1936, p. 1062; 1938, pp. 1066–67; 1939, p. 1066; and Singer and Small, *National Material Capabilities Data*. The Soviet numbers are from the *League of Nations Armaments Year-Book*, 1934, p. 720; June 1940, p. 348; Singer and Small, *National Material Capabilities Data*; and David M. Glantz, *The Military Strategy of the Soviet Union: A History* (London: Frank Cass, 1992), p. 92.

While the Wehrmacht was experiencing growing pains between 1933 and 1939, France and the Soviet Union were expanding their militaries to counter the German buildup. Both the Red Army and the French army were more powerful than the German army through 1937, but their advantage eroded over the next two years, and Germany became the dominant military power in Europe by mid-1939. For this reason, many scholars now believe that Hitler's rivals should have fought the Wehrmacht in 1938 rather than 1939.[125]

The French army, as Table 8.6 makes clear, was substantially larger than its German counterpart as late as 1937. It also enjoyed a qualitative edge, not because the French army was an efficient fighting force (it was not), but because the Wehrmacht's ongoing expansion severely limited its fighting capacity. By 1938, Germany finally had a peacetime army that was larger than France's, but as Table 8.7 makes clear, France could still mobilize a larger wartime army: 100 French versus 71 German divisions. By 1939, Germany had erased that French advantage; they now could mobilize about the same number of divisons for war. Moreover, the German army was qualitatively better than the French army, and it had a superior air force supporting it.[126] Given that Germany possessed significantly more wealth and a much larger population than France, it is hardly surprising that the military power gap between them widened even further by 1940.

The Red Army was also qualitatively and quantitatively superior to the German army between 1933 and 1937. David Glantz is surely correct when he says, "Had the Germans and Soviets fought in the mid-1930s, the Red Army would have had a considerable advantage over its opponent."[127] That advantage slipped away in the late 1930s, however, not just because of the German army's growing strength, but also because of Stalin's purges (see Table 8.8).

Given that Germany was no potential hegemon before 1939, and given that the French army and the Red Army could each have matched the German army through 1938, it makes sense that a balancing coalition like the Triple Entente did not form against Germany before 1939, and that Hitler's rivals instead passed the buck to each other. It also makes sense that the United Kingdom and France formed an alliance against Hitler in March 1939, because the day was fast approaching when the German army would be clearly superior to the French army, which would then need help fending off the Wehrmacht.

TABLE 8.7

Size of French and German Armies after Mobilization, 1938–40 (number of divisions)

	1938	1939	1940
France	100	102	104
Germany	71	103	141

SOURCES: Figures are from Williamson Murray, *The Change in the European Balance of Power, 1938–1939: The Path to Ruin* (Princeton, NJ: Princeton University Press, 1984), p. 242; Richard Overy, *The Penguin Historical Atlas of the Third Reich* (London: Penguin, 1996), p. 67; and Albert Seaton, *The German Army, 1933–1945* (New York: New American Library, 1982), pp. 92–93, 95.

That the Western powers did not join forces with the Soviet Union to recreate the Triple Entente can be explained by the fact that the United Kingdom and France did not have to fear for the Soviet Union's survival in 1939 the way they had feared for Russia's survival before World War I. The Western powers had little choice but to ally with Russia before 1914, because it was barely capable of standing up to a German offensive. The Soviet Union, on the other hand, had much more industrial and military might than its Russian predecessor had, and thus the United Kingdom and France were not compelled to defend it. Stalin, for his part, recognized that the United Kingdom and France together were at least as powerful as Germany, and thus he could buck-pass to them.[128] Finally, the absence of a common border between Germany and the Soviet Union from 1933 until September 1939 greatly hindered efforts to create a united front

TABLE 8.8

Manpower in European Armies, 1939–41

| | 1939 | | | 1940 | | | 1941 | | 1939–45 |
	Standing army	Mobilized army		Fighting army	Total army		Fighting army	Total army	Total men mobilized
United Kingdom	237,736	897,000		402,000	1,888,000		na	2,292,000	5,896,000
France	900,000	4,895,00		2,224,000	5,000,000		na	na	na
Germany	730,000	3,740,000		2,760,000	4,370,000		3,050,000	5,200,000	17,900,000
Italy	581,000	na		na	1,600,000		na	na	9,100,000
Soviet Union	1,520,000	na		na	3,602,000		2,900,000	5,000,000	22,400,000

NOTE: na = not available. "Standing army" is as defined in Table 8.4; "mobilized army" represents the total number of men serving in the army after mobilization was completed in 1939. It is thus not restricted to fighting men. This number is then called "total army" for 1940 and 1941. Comparing the figures given in Table 8.7 with those here, it is apparent that a larger percentage of German soldiers were put in combat divisions rather than support positions; this gave Germany an advantage in fighting power.

SOURCES: The numbers for the United Kingdom are from the *League of Nations Armaments Year-Book* (Geneva: League of Nations, June 1940), p. 59; I.C.B. Dear, ed., *The Oxford Companion to World War II* (Oxford: Oxford University Press, 1995), p. 1148; and John Ellis, *World War II: A Statistical Survey* (New York: Facts on File, 1993), p. 228. The French numbers are from Ellis, *World War II*, p. 227; Pierre Montagnon, *Histoire de l'Armée Française: Des Milices Royales a l'Armée de Métier* (Paris: Editions Pygmalion, 1997), p. 250; Phillip A. Karber et al., *Assessing the Correlation of Forces: France 1940*. Report No. BDM/W-79-560-TR (McLean, VA: BDM Corporation, 1979), table 1; and Dear, ed., *Oxford Companion to World War II*, p. 401. For Germany, see Whaley, *Covert German Rearmament*, p. 69; Dear, ed., *Oxford Companion to World War II*, p. 468; Matthew Cooper, *The German Army, 1933–1945: Its Political and Military Failure* (New York: Stein and Day, 1978), pp. 214, 270; and Ellis, *World War II*, p. 227. The numbers for the Soviet Union are from Glantz, *Military Strategy*, p. 92; Louis Rotundo, "The Creation of Soviet Reserves and the 1941 Campaign," *Military Affairs* 50, No. 1 (January 1985), p. 23; Ellis, *World War II*, p. 228; and Jonathon R. Adelman, *Revolution, Armies, and War: A Political History* (Boulder, CO: Lynne Rienner, 1985), p. 174. For Italy, see Singer and Small, *National Material Capabilities Data*; Dear, ed., *Oxford Companion to World War II*, p. 228; and Ellis, *World War II*, p. 228.

against the Third Reich. Moreover, it made it likely that France (which bordered Nazi Germany), not the Soviet Union, would end up catching the buck.

The British desire to form an alliance with the Soviet Union after June 1940 needs no explanation, as the United Kingdom was already at war with Nazi Germany and naturally wanted all the help it could get. The more interesting question is why the Soviet Union rejected the United Kingdom's overtures and continued buck-passing to it. After all, the German army was far superior to what was left of the British army after Dunkirk, which should have allowed Germany to easily defeat the United Kingdom and then turn its guns against the Soviet Union. The stopping power of water, however, saved the United Kingdom and made buck-passing look like a winning strategy for Stalin. The English Channel made it almost impossible for the Wehrmacht to invade and conquer the United Kingdom, which meant that the British were likely to fight a long war with the Germans in the air, on the seas, and in peripheral areas such as North Africa and the Balkans. Indeed, that is mainly what happened between 1940 and 1945. Allying with the United Kingdom was also unattractive for Stalin because not only would the Soviet Union get dragged into war with the Third Reich, but the Red Army would end up doing most of the fighting against the Wehrmacht, since the United Kingdom was in no position to send a large army to the continent. These considerations notwithstanding, there was an important flaw in Stalin's thinking: he mistakenly assumed that Hitler would not invade the Soviet Union until he decisively defeated the British and solidified his western flank.[129]

Let me conclude with a final word about the contrasting behavior of Germany's rivals in the years before the two world wars. Three key differences account for why the United Kingdom, France, and the Soviet Union tended to buck-pass against the Third Reich but formed a balancing coalition against the Kaiserreich seven years before World War I. First, Nazi Germany was not a formidable military threat until 1939, whereas the kaiser's army was the most powerful fighting force in Europe from at least 1870 until the end of World War I. Indeed, Hitler's

Germany was not a potential hegemon until 1939; Wilhelmine Germany achieved that status in 1903. Second, the Soviet Union controlled considerably more potential as well as actual military power during the 1930s than did pre–World War I Russia. Thus, the United Kingdom and France had less cause to worry about the survival of the Soviet Union than about tsarist Russia. Third, Germany and Russia shared a common border before 1914, but did not before 1939, and separation encouraged buck-passing.

THE COLD WAR (1945–90)

Background

When the Third Reich finally collapsed in April 1945, the Soviet Union was left standing as the most powerful state in Europe. Imperial Japan collapsed four months later (August 1945), leaving the Soviet Union also as the most powerful state in Northeast Asia. No other great power existed in either Europe or Northeast Asia that could stop the mighty Red Army from overrunning those regions and establishing Soviet hegemony. The United States was the only state powerful enough to contain Soviet expansion.

There were reasons, however, to think that the United States might not balance against the Soviet Union. The United States was neither a European nor an Asian power, and it had a long history of avoiding entangling alliances in those areas. In fact, Franklin Roosevelt had told Stalin at Yalta in February 1945 that he expected all American troops to be out of Europe within two years after World War II ended.[130] Furthermore, given that the United States and the Soviet Union were allies in the fight against Nazi Germany from 1941 until 1945, it was difficult for American policymakers to do a sudden 180-degree turn and tell the public that the Soviet Union was now a deadly foe, not a friendly state. There was also a powerful imperative after the war for Stalin and Harry Truman to work together to deal with the defeated Axis powers, especially Germany.

These considerations notwithstanding, the United States acted to check Soviet expansion almost immediately after World War II ended, and it maintained a formidable containment policy until the Soviet threat disappeared some forty-five years later. Marc Trachtenberg puts the point well: "The policy of containment, as it came to be called, was adopted at the beginning of 1946. It was adopted even before the term was coined, certainly well before the rationale for the policy was developed by its chief theoretician, George Kennan."[131] The United States balanced with such alacrity and effectiveness because it was in America's national interest to prevent the Soviet Union from dominating Europe and Northeast Asia, and because there was no other great power that could contain the Soviet army in the bipolar world of the mid-1940s. Simply put, the United States had no buck-passing option, and thus it had to do the heavy lifting itself.[132]

The Strategic Behavior of the Great Powers

Iran and Turkey were important targets of Soviet expansion in the early days of the Cold War.[133] The Soviet Union had occupied northern Iran during World War II but had promised to pull its troops out no later than six months after the war in the Pacific ended. When there was no evidence in early 1946 that the Soviet army was leaving, the United States put pressure on the Soviets to live up to their promise. It worked: Soviet troops were gone from Iran by early May 1946.

Stalin was also interested in expanding into the eastern Mediterranean area. His main target was Turkey. In the summer of 1945, he demanded territory in the eastern part of Turkey and the right to build bases in the Dardanelles, in order to have naval access to the Mediterranean Sea. Furthermore, a powerful communist insurgency raged in Greece between 1944 and 1949, when that country was consumed by civil war. Stalin did not directly support the Greek Communists, but he surely would have benefited if they had won the civil war and ruled Greece.[134] The United States initially relied on the United Kingdom to protect Greece and Turkey from the Soviet Union, but worried throughout 1946 that the British could not do the job. When it became apparent in late February 1947 that the United Kingdom's economy was too weak to provide the necessary economic and military aid to Greece and Turkey, the United States rapidly filled the void.

President Truman went before a joint session of Congress on March 12, 1947, and laid out the famous doctrine that bears his name. He argued in no uncertain terms that it was time for the United States to stand up to the threat of communism, not just in the Mediterranean, but all around the globe. He also requested $400 million in aid for Greece and Turkey. Senator Arthur Vandenberg (R-Mich.) told Truman before-hand that if he wanted that money he would have to "scare hell out of the country."[135] He did, and Congress approved his request. The Greek communists were subsequently defeated and the Soviets got no Turkish territory or bases in the Dardanelles. Greece and Turkey eventually joined NATO in February 1952.

American policymakers also worried throughout 1946 and early 1947 that the Soviet Union would soon dominate Western Europe. Their fear was not that the Soviet army would drive its way to the Atlantic Ocean. Instead, U.S. leaders feared that powerful communist parties with close ties to Moscow might come to power in France and Italy, because their economies were in terrible shape and their populations were deeply dis-satisfied with their destitute status. The United States responded to this problem in early June 1947 with the famous Marshall Plan, which was explicitly designed to fight "hunger, poverty, desperation and chaos" in Western Europe.[136]

At the same time, the United States was also deeply concerned about the future of Germany. Neither the Americans nor, it appears, the Soviets had clear-cut views on the subject when World War II ended.[137] During the early Cold War years the West showed little fear that the Soviets would try to conquer Germany by force. Indeed, there is evidence that Stalin was content to live with a permanently partitioned Germany, pro-vided that the United Kingdom, France, and the United States did not merge their occupation zones and create an independent West German state. But American policymakers came to believe over the course of 1947 that if communism was to be kept out of Western Europe (including the Allied occupation zones in Germany), it was essential to build a prosperous and powerful West Germany that would have close ties with the other states of Western Europe. That outcome was effectively sealed at the London Conference in December 1947; the plan was put into effect over the next two years. The Federal Republic of Germany came into being on September 21, 1949. In short, the United States sought to contain Soviet expansion by building a powerful bulwark in Western Europe, anchored on West Germany.

Not surprisingly, the Soviets viewed the American decision about Germany's future with utter alarm. As Melvyn Leffler notes, "Nothing, of course, agitated the Kremlin more than Anglo-American initiatives in western Germany. The specter of west German self-government horrified the Russians, as did the prospect of German integration into a Western economic bloc."[138] In response, the Soviets facilitated a communist coup in Czechoslovakia in February 1948 and made that country part of their own bulwark against the West. More important, the Soviets started a major crisis in late June 1948 by blockading Berlin, closing the roads and waterways that connected it with the Western occupation zones in Germany.

The United States responded quickly and forcefully to these Soviet actions. In the wake of the coup in Czechoslovakia, the United States began thinking seriously about creating a Western military alliance to deter a future Soviet military threat against Western Europe.[139] Planning began in earnest in May 1948 and eventually led to the creation of NATO on April 4, 1949.[140] Although many in the West thought that Berlin was a strategic liability and should be abandoned, the United States initiated a major airlift of supplies into the beleaguered city.[141] Recognizing that the United States had trumped them, the Soviets lifted the blockade in May 1949.

Stalin also pushed to expand Soviet influence in Northeast Asia during the early Cold War.[142] The Soviets had promised during World War II to pull their troops out of Manchuria by February 1, 1946, but they were still there when that date arrived. The United States protested and the Soviet army was withdrawn by early May 1946. American policymakers were also deeply concerned that Mao Zedong's Communists might defeat Chiang Kai-shek's Nationalists in their long-running civil war and make China an ally of the Soviet Union. Mao and Stalin had complicated relations, but the Soviets were providing modest assistance to the Chinese Communists. The United States, for its part, provided limited aid to the Nationalists. The United States could do little, however, to rescue Chiang's forces from their ultimate defeat in 1949, because they were so corrupt and inefficient. Secretary of State Dean Acheson put the point well in his July 30, 1949, letter transmitting the State Department's famous "White Paper" on China to President Truman: "Nothing that this country did or could have done within the reasonable limits of its capabilities could have changed that result; nothing that was left undone by this country has contributed to it. It was the product of internal Chinese forces which this country tried to influence but could not."[143]

North Korea's invasion of South Korea on June 25, 1950, was widely believed at the time to have been approved and supported by Stalin. The Truman administration reacted immediately to the attack and fought a three-year war against North Korea and China to restore the status quo ante. One consequence of the conflict was that the United States kept a substantial number of troops in South Korea for the remainder of the Cold War. But more important, the Korean War caused the United States to substantially increase defense spending and become even more vigilant in its efforts to contain the Soviet Union. The United States built formidable deterrent structures in Europe, Northeast Asia, and the Persian Gulf that kept the Soviets at bay in those critically important areas from 1950 until 1990. The only places that the Soviets could expand during those four decades were in the Third World, where not only were the gains dubious, but the United States met the Soviets at every turn.[144]

Nevertheless, the American impulse to buck-pass never completely disappeared during the Cold War.[145] For example, to secure Senate approval for the NATO treaty in 1949, Acheson had to emphasize that the United States had no intention of sending large military forces to Europe on a permanent basis. Throughout the 1950s, President Dwight Eisenhower was seriously interested in bringing American forces home and forcing the Western Europeans to defend themselves against the Soviet threat.[146] Indeed, this impulse explains the forceful U.S. support for European integration in the early Cold War. Furthermore, there was strong sentiment in the U.S. Senate in the late 1960s and early 1970s to reduce, if not eliminate, America's continental commitment. Even during the presidency of Ronald Reagan, influential voices called for significant reductions in American troop levels in Europe.[147] But buck-passing was not a serious option for the United States in the bipolar world that existed between 1945 and 1990. From the end of World War II until the end of the Cold War, the United States pursued a tough-minded balancing policy against the Soviet Union that achieved remarkable success.

The Calculus of Power

A brief look at the distribution of power in the wake of World War II shows clearly that no great power or combination of great powers existed in either Europe or Northeast Asia that could prevent the Soviet army from overrunning those regions, and therefore the United States had no choice but to check Soviet expansion. In Northeast Asia, Japan was disarmed and devastated, while China, which had little potential power to start with, was in the midst of a brutal civil war. In Europe, Germany had just been decisively defeated by the Soviet army and was in ruins. It certainly was in no position to build an army in the foreseeable future. Italy's army was wrecked and not likely to recover anytime soon; even when it was intact, it was among the most incompetent fighting forces in modern European history. France had been knocked out of the war in 1940 and then plundered by Germany until the late summer of 1944, when it was finally liberated by the American and British armies. France had a tiny army when the war ended in the spring of 1945, but it was in no position—either economically or politically—to build a mass army as it had before 1940.[148] The United Kingdom built a substantial army in World War II, and it played an important role in defeating the Wehrmacht. But it is apparent on close inspection that the United Kingdom did not have the economic and military wherewithal after 1945 to lead a balancing coalition against the Soviet Union. Only the United States was powerful enough to assume that demanding task.

From the relative size of the American, British, and Soviet military establishments in World War II we can see why the United Kingdom was not in the same league as the Soviet Union and the United States. Between 1939 and 1945, the United Kingdom mobilized about 5.9 million troops, the United States mobilized roughly 14 million, and the Soviet Union mobilized approximately 22.4 million.[149] When World War II ended in 1945, the United Kingdom had about 4.7 million troops under arms, the Americans had roughly 12 million, and the Soviets had about 12.5 million.[150] Regarding army size, the United Kingdom raised 50 divisions over the course of World War II, while the United States raised 90 divisions. The Soviets raised 550 divisions, although they were somewhat smaller than American and British divisions.[151]

Of course, all three military establishments shrunk quite drastically in size after World War II. But the United Kingdom was still no match for the Soviet Union. The Soviets had 2.87 million men under arms in 1948, whereas the United Kingdom had only 847,000. The United States figure for that year was 1.36 million.[152] Furthermore, both the American and the Soviet military establishments grew significantly in size after 1948, while the British military shrunk in size.[153] The United Kingdom's economy was so weak in early 1947, as we saw earlier, that it could not provide aid to Greece and Turkey, prompting the United States to promulgate the Truman Doctrine. The United Kingdom was certainly in no position to defend Western Europe from the Soviet army.

The United Kingdom's problem was not a failure to recognize the Soviet threat, or a lack of will to contain it. On the contrary, British leaders were just as gung-ho as their American counterparts about thwarting Soviet expansion.[154] But the British simply did not have sufficient material resources to compete with the Soviets. In 1950, for example, the Soviet Union had a gross national product (GNP) of $126 billion, and it spent $15.5 billion on defense. The United Kingdom had a GNP of $71 billion and spent $2.3 billion on defense.[155] To make matters worse, the United

Kingdom still possessed a far-flung empire that demanded a large percentage of its precious defense dollars. Not surprisingly, British leaders understood from the beginning of the Cold War that the West would need Uncle Sam to organize and direct the containment of the Soviet Union.

CONCLUSION

Having analyzed each case in detail, let me now step back and summarize the results. Offensive realism predicts that states will be acutely sensitive to the balance of power and will look for opportunities to increase their own power or weaken rivals. In practical terms, this means that states will adopt diplomatic strategies that reflect the opportunities and constraints created by the particular distribution of power. Specifically, the theory predicts that a threatened state is likely to balance promptly and efficiently in bipolarity, because neither buck-passing nor great-power balancing coalitions are feasible when there are only two great powers in the system. The Cold War case appears to support that claim. The Soviet Union emerged from World War II as by far the most powerful state in Europe (and Northeast Asia), and only the United States was capable of containing it.

When confronted with potential European hegemons earlier in the century—Wilhelmine Germany and Nazi Germany—the initial U.S. reaction had been to pass the buck to the other European great powers—the United Kingdom, France, and Russia. But buck-passing was not an option in the Cold War, because there was no great power in Europe that could contain the Soviet Union. So right after World War II ended, the United States moved quickly and forcefully to balance against the Soviet threat, and it stayed the course until the Cold War ended in 1990. Nevertheless, the American impulse to buck-pass was evident throughout the period.

Regarding multipolarity, the theory predicts that buck-passing is most likely in the absence of a potential hegemon but still likely to occur even when there is an especially powerful state in the system. The evidence appears to bear out these claims. Among the four multipolar cases,

Bismarck's Prussia was the only aggressor that was not a potential hegemon. France probably had the most powerful army in Europe between 1862 and 1866, while Prussia was number one from 1867 to 1870. But neither threatened to overrun the continent. As my theory would predict, buck-passing was more widespread here than in any of the cases involving a potential European hegemon. Indeed, no balancing coalition—not even one limited to two states—formed against Prussia while it was winning three wars over an eight-year period. The United Kingdom and Russia actually welcomed Bismarck's efforts to create a unified Germany, which they hoped would serve them in the future as a buck-catcher! The Prussian army directly threatened both Austria and France, making them likely candidates to balance together against Prussia. But they buck-passed instead, allowing Bismarck's army to clobber Austria's in 1866 while France looked on, and then to clobber France's army in 1870 while Austria looked on.

Balancing coalitions did form against the potential hegemons: Napoleonic France, Wilhelmine Germany, and Nazi Germany. Still buck-passing was tried in each case, albeit with significant variations. According to my theory, the balance of power and geography should explain the differences among these cases. Specifically, the more relative power the aspiring hegemon controls, the less likely we are to see buck-passing; common borders are also likely to discourage buck-passing. These arguments appear to account for the different patterns of buck-passing in these three cases of unbalanced multipolarity.

We see the least amount of buck-passing against Wilhelmine Germany. The Triple Entente, which included the United Kingdom, France, and Russia and which was designed to contain Germany, was largely in place by 1907, some seven years before World War I broke out. France and Russia actually formed the first leg of that balancing alliance in the early 1890s, about twenty years before the crisis that sparked World War I. The United Kingdom, although it initially passed the buck to France and Russia, joined the coalition between 1905 and 1907. Power calculations largely account for the formation of the Triple Entente. Germany had an imposing army in the early 1890s, which forced France and Russia to ally.

But Germany was not yet a potential hegemon, and the French and Russian armies together seemed capable of containing the German army. So the United Kingdom was able to remain on the sidelines. But that all changed in the first five years of the twentieth century, when Germany became a potential hegemon (1903) and Russia was dealt a devastating defeat by Japan (1904–5). In response, the United Kingdom stopped buck-passing and the Triple Entente came into being.

Much more buck-passing arose against Nazi Germany than there had been against Wilhelmine Germany. Hitler came to power in January 1933 and almost immediately began building a powerful military. The Third Reich's main rivals—the United Kingdom, France, and the Soviet Union— never formed a balancing coalition against Nazi Germany. In fact, all three pursued buck-passing strategies during the 1930s. Not until March 1939 did the United Kingdom and France come together to oppose Hitler. Nevertheless, the Soviets continued to buck-pass. When the Wehrmacht knocked France out of the war in the spring of 1940, leaving the British to fight alone against the Nazi war machine, Stalin worked to foster a long war between the United Kingdom and Germany while he remained on the sidelines. Operation Barbarossa in the summer of 1941 finally brought the United Kingdom and the Soviet Union together, and the United States joined the Anglo-Soviet coalition in December 1941. That alliance hung together for the next three and a half years to defeat the Third Reich.

All that buck-passing in the 1930s was due in good part to the fact that Germany did not possess a formidable army until 1939, and thus no compelling reason drew Hitler's foes together before then. When Nazi Germany became a potential hegemon in 1939, the United Kingdom and France formed an alliance, mainly because the British recognized that France alone was no match for the Wehrmacht. Yet neither the British nor the French formed an alliance with the Soviet Union, mainly because the Soviet Union was much more powerful than Russia had been before 1914; the Soviets stood a good chance of surviving without help from the United Kingdom and France. After the fall of France, Stalin refused to join forces with the United Kingdom against the Third Reich because he thought that the stopping power of water would make it difficult for

Germany to defeat the United Kingdom quickly and decisively, thus guaranteeing a long war between them that would work to the Soviets' advantage.

Buck-passing was most prevalent in the case of Revolutionary and Napoleonic France, which faced four rival great powers: Austria, Britain, Prussia, and Russia. France actually did not become a potential hegemon until 1793, a year after war broke out. France's rivals passed the buck constantly between 1793 and 1804, mainly because France was not yet so powerful that all of its rivals would have to act in tandem to prevent it from overrunning the continent. By 1805, however, Napoleon had an army in place that threatened to make France Europe's first hegemon. But before all of Napoleon's rivals could form a unified balancing coalition, he knocked Austria and Prussia out of the balance of power and forced Russia to quit fighting and sign a peace treaty. Inefficient balancing, commonplace in multipolarity, allowed Napoleon to win a series of stunning victories between 1805 and 1809 that gave him control of much of Europe. France's rivals got a reprieve in late 1812, when Napoleon suffered a major defeat in Russia. This time they balanced efficiently and decisively defeated France between 1813 and 1815.

Geography also worked to discourage buck-passing against Wilhelmine Germany but to encourage it against Nazi Germany and Napoleonic France. The United Kingdom fought against all three potential hegemons, but it was separated from each of them by the English Channel. Thus, there is no variation in geography across the British cases, so they can be left out of the analysis. The situation on the continent, however, varies markedly among the three cases. Wilhelmine Germany shared a lengthy border with both France and Russia, which made it difficult for either to buck-pass and easy for them to form a balancing coalition, since both were well-positioned to strike directly into Germany. France shared a common border with Nazi Germany, but the Soviet Union was separated from the Third Reich for most of the 1930s by minor powers such as Poland. This buffer zone encouraged buck-passing and made it difficult for France and the Soviet Union to form a balancing coalition to contain Germany. Although the map of Europe changed frequently between 1792 and 1815, Napoleon's rivals often had no common border with France, a situation that facilitated buck-passing and complicated the formation of an effective balancing alliance.

In sum, both geography and the distribution of power play a key role in determining whether threatened great powers form balancing coalitions or buck-pass against dangerous aggressors. The next chapter will switch gears and look at how aggressors behave, focusing on when they are likely to initiate a war with another state. As will become apparent, the distribution of power is also important for explaining the outbreak of great-power war.

9

The Causes of Great Power War

Security competition is endemic to daily life in the international system, but war is not. Only occasionally does security competition give way to war. This chapter will offer a structural theory that accounts for that deadly shift. In effect, I seek to explain the causes of great-power war, defined as any conflict involving at least one great power.

One might surmise that international anarchy is the key structural factor that causes states to fight wars. After all, the best way for states to survive in an anarchic system in which other states have some offensive capability and intentions that might be hostile is to have more rather than less power. This logic, explained in Chapter 2, drives states to strive to maximize their share of world power, which sometimes means going to war against a rival state. There is no question that anarchy is a deep cause of war. G. Lowes Dickinson put this point well in his account of what caused World War I: "Some one state at any moment may be the immediate offender; but the main and permanent offence is common to all states. It is the anarchy which they are all responsible for perpetuating."[1]

Anarchy alone, however, cannot account for why security competition sometimes leads to war but sometimes does not. The problem is that anarchy is a constant—the system is always anarchic—whereas war is not. To account for this important variation in state behavior, it is necessary to consider another structural variable: the distribution of power among the leading states in the system. As discussed in Chapter 8, power in the international system is usually arranged in three different ways: bipolarity, balanced multipolarity, and unbalanced multipolarity. Thus, to explore the effect of the distribution of power on the likelihood of war, we need to know whether the system is bipolar or multipolar, and if it is multipolar, whether or not there is a potential hegemon among the great powers. The core of my argument is that bipolar systems tend to be the most peaceful, and unbalanced multipolar systems are the most prone to deadly conflict. Balanced multipolar sytems fall somewhere in between.

Structural theories such as offensive realism are at best crude predictors of when security competition leads to war. They are not capable of explaining precisely how often war will occur in one kind of system compared to another. Nor are they capable of predicting exactly when wars will occur. For example, according to offensive realism, the emergence of Germany as a potential hegemon in the early 1900s made it likely that there would be a war involving all the European great powers. But the theory cannot explain why war occured in 1914 rather than 1912 or 1916.[2]

These limitations stem from the fact that nonstructural factors sometimes play an important role in determining whether or not a state goes to war. States usually do not fight wars for security reasons alone. As noted in Chapter 2, for instance, although Otto von Bismarck was driven in good part by realist calculations when he took Prussia to war three times between 1864 and 1870, each of his decisions for war was also influenced by nationalism and other domestic political calculations. And yet structural forces do exert a powerful influence on state behavior. It can be no other way if states care deeply about their survival. Thus, focusing exclusively on structure should tell us a lot about the origins of great-power war.

Many theories about the causes of war have been propounded, which is not surprising, since the subject has always been of central importance to students of international politics. Some of those theories treat human nature as the taproot of conflict, while others focus on individual leaders, domestic politics, political ideology, capitalism, economic interdependence, and the structure of the international system.[3] In fact, a handful of prominent theories point to the distribution of power as the key to understanding international conflict. For example, Kenneth Waltz maintains that bipolarity is less prone to war than multipolarity, whereas Karl Deutsch and J. David Singer argue the opposite.[4] Other scholars focus not on the polarity of the system, but on whether there is a preponderant power in the system. Classical realists such as Hans Morgenthau argue that peace is most likely when there is no dominant power, but instead a rough balance of power among the leading states. In contrast, Robert Gilpin and A.F.K. Organski argue that the presence of a preponderant power fosters stability.[5]

Offensive realism, which takes into account polarity as well as the balance of power among the leading states in the system, agrees that bipolarity is more stable than multipolarity but goes beyond that assertion by distinguishing between multipolar systems with or without a potential hegemon. This distinction between balanced and unbalanced multipolar systems, I argue, is important for understanding the history of great-power war. Offensive realism also agrees with the classical realists' claim that peace is more likely if there is no preponderant power in the system, but it goes beyond that perspective by emphasizing that stability also depends on whether the system is bipolar or multipolar.

Showing how offensive realism explains great-power war involves a two-step process. In the next three sections, I spell out my theory and show that the causal logic underpinning it is sound and compelling. In the subsequent two sections, the theory is tested to see how well it explains both the outbreak of great-power war and the periods of relative peace in Europe between 1792 and 1990. Specifically, I look to see how much great-power war there was during the periods when Europe was characterized by bipolarity, by balanced multipolarity, and by unbalanced multipolarity. Finally, my brief conclusion discusses how the presence of nuclear weapons during the Cold War affects the analysis.

STRUCTURE AND WAR

The main causes of war are located in the architecture of the international system. What matters most is the number of great powers and how much power each controls. A system can be either bipolar or multipolar, and power can be distributed more or less evenly among the leading states. The power ratios among all the great powers affect the prospects for stability, but the key ratio is that between the two most formidable states in the system. If there is a lopsided power gap, the number one state is a potential hegemon.[6] A system that contains an aspiring hegemon is said to be unbalanced; a system without such a dominant state is said to be balanced. Power need not be distributed equally among all the major states in a balanced system, although it can be. The basic requirement for balance is that there not be a marked difference in power between the two leading states. If there is, the system is unbalanced.

Combining these two dimensions of power produces four possible kinds of sytems: 1) unbalanced bipolarity, 2) balanced bipolarity, 3) unbalanced multipolarity, and 4) balanced multipolarity. Unbalanced bipolarity is not a useful category, because this kind of system is unlikely to be found in the real world. I know of none in modern times. It is certainly possible that some region might find itself with just two great powers, one of which is markedly more powerful than the other. But that system is likely to disappear quickly, because the stronger state is likely to conquer its weaker rival, who would have no other great power to turn to for help, since by definition there are no other great powers. In fact, the weaker power might even capitulate without a fight, making the more powerful state a regional hegemon. In short, unbalanced bipolar systems are so unstable that they cannot last for any appreciable period of time.

Thus we are likely to find power apportioned among the leading states in three different patterns. Bipolar systems (this is shorthand for balanced bipolarity) are ruled by two great powers that have roughly equal strength—or at least neither state is decidedly more powerful than the other. Unbalanced multipolar sytems are dominated by three or more great powers, one of which is a potential hegemon. Balanced multipolar systems are dominated by three or more great powers, none of which is an aspiring hegemon: there is no significant gap in military strength between the system's leading two states, although some power asymmetries are likely to exist among the great powers.

How do these different distributions of power affect the prospects for war and peace? Bipolar systems are the most stable of the three systems. Great-power wars are infrequent, and when they occur, they are likely to involve one of the great powers fighting against a minor power, not the rival great power. Unbalanced multipolar systems feature the most dangerous distribution of power, mainly because potential hegemons are likely to get into wars with all of the other great powers in the system. These wars invariably turn out to be long and enormously costly. Balanced multipolar sytems occupy a middle ground: great-power war is more likely than in bipolarity, but decidedly less likely than in unbalanced multipolarity. Moreover, the wars between the great powers are likely to be one-on-one or two-on-one engagements, not systemwide conflicts like those that occur when there is a potential hegemon.

Let us now consider why bipolar systems are more stable than multipolar systems, regardless of whether there is a potential hegemon in the mix. Later I will explain why balanced multipolar systems are more stable than unbalanced ones.

BIPOLARITY VS. MULTIPOLARITY

War is more likely in multipolarity than bipolarity for three reasons.[7] First, there are more opportunities for war, because there are more potential conflict dyads in a multipolar system. Second, imbalances of power are more commonplace in a multipolar world, and thus great powers are more likely to have the capability to win a war, making deterrence more difficult and war more likely. Third, the potential for miscalculation is greater in multipolarity: states might think they have the capability to coerce or conquer another state when, in fact, they do not.

Opportunities for War

A multipolar system has more potential conflict situations than does a bipolar order. Consider great-great power dyads. Under bipolarity, there are only two great powers and therefore only one conflict dyad directly involving them. For example, the Soviet Union was the only great power that the United States could have fought during the Cold War. In contrast, a multipolar system with three great powers has three dyads across which war might break out between the great powers: A can fight B, A can fight C, and B can fight C. A system with five great powers has ten great-great power dyads.

Conflict could also erupt across dyads involving major and minor powers. In setting up a hypothetical scenario, it seems reasonable to assume the same number of minor powers in both the bipolar and multipolar systems, since the number of major powers should have no meaningful effect on the number of minor powers. Therefore, because there are more great powers in multipolarity, there are more great-minor power dyads. Consider the following examples: in a bipolar world with 10 minor powers, there are 20 great-minor power dyads; in a multipolar system with 5 great powers and the same 10 minor powers, there are 50 such dyads.

This disparity in the number of great-minor power dyads in the two systems probably should be tilted further in favor of bipolarity, because it is generally less flexible than multipolarity. Bipolar systems are likely to be rigid structures. Two great powers dominate, and the logic of security competition suggests that they will be unambiguous rivals. Most minor powers find it difficult to remain unattached to one of the major powers in bipolarity, because the major powers demand allegiance from the smaller states. This tightness is especially true in core geographical areas, less so in peripheral areas. The pulling of minor powers into the orbit of one or the other great power makes it difficult for either great power to pick a fight with minor powers closely allied with its adversary; as a result, the numbers of potential conflict situations is substantially less. During the Cold War, for example, the United States was not about to use military force against Hungary or Poland, which were allied with the Soviet Union. Thus, there should probably be substantially fewer than 20 great-minor power dyads in our hypothetical bipolar world.

In contrast, multipolar systems are less firmly structured. The exact form multipolarity takes can vary widely, depending on the number of major and minor powers in the system and the geographical arrangement of those states. Nevertheless, both major and minor powers usually have considerable flexibility regarding alliance partners, and minor powers are less likely to be closely tied to a great power than in a bipolar system. This autonomy, however, leaves minor powers vulnerable to attack from the great powers. Thus, the 50 great-minor power dyads in our hypothetical multipolar system is probably a reasonable number.

Wars between minor powers are largely ignored in this study because the aim is to develop a theory of great-power war. Yet minor-power wars sometimes widen and great powers get dragged into the fighting. Although the subject of escalation lies outside the scope of this study, a brief word is in order about how polarity affects the likelihood of great powers' getting pulled into wars between minor powers. Basically, that possibility is greater in multipolarity than in bipolarity, because there are more opportunities for minor powers to fight each other in multipolarity, and thus more opportunities for great-power involvement.

Consider that our hypothetical bipolar and multipolar worlds both contain 10 minor powers, which means that there are 45 potential minor-minor power dyads in each system. That number should be markedly reduced for bipolarity, because the general tightness of bipolar sytems makes it difficult for minor powers to go to war against each other. Specifically, both great powers would seek to prevent fighting between their own minor-power allies, as well as conflicts involving minor powers from the rival camps, for fear of escalation. Minor powers have much more room to maneuver in a multipolar system, and thus they have more freedom to fight each other. Greece and Turkey, for example, fought a war between 1921 and 1924, when Europe was multipolar. But they were in no position to fight with each other during the Cold War, when Europe was bipolar, because the United States would not have tolerated a war between any of its European allies, for fear it would have weakened NATO vis-à-vis the Soviet Union.

Imbalances of Power

Power asymmetries among the great powers are more commonplace in multipolarity than bipolarity, and the strong become hard to deter when power is unbalanced, because they have increased capability to win wars.[8] But even if we assume that the military strength of the great powers is roughly equal, power imbalances that lead to conflict are still more likely in multipolarity than in bipolarity.

Multipolar systems tend toward inequality, whereas bipolar systems tend toward equality, for one principal reason. The more great powers there are in a system, the more likely it is that wealth and population size, the building blocks of military power, will be distributed unevenly among them. To illustrate, let us assume that we live in a world where, regardless of how many great powers populate the system, there is a 50 percent chance that any two great powers will have roughly the same amount of latent power. If there are only two great powers in that world (bipolarity), obviously there is a 50 percent chance that each state will control the same quantity of latent power. But if there are three great powers in that world (multipolarity), there is only a 12.5 percent chance that all of them will have the same amount of latent power. With four great powers (multipolarity), there is less than a 2 percent chance that the ingredients of military might will be distributed evenly among all of them.

One could use a different number for the likelihood that any two states will have equal amounts of latent power—say, 25 percent or 60 percent instead of 50 percent—but the basic story would remain the same. Asymmetries in latent power are more likely to be found among the great powers in multipolarity than in bipolarity, and the more great powers there are in multipolarity, the more remote the chances of symmetry. This is not to say that it is impossible to have a multipolar system in which the great powers possess equal proportions of latent power, but only that it is considerably less likely than in a bipolar system. Of course, the reason for this concern with latent power is that significant variations in wealth and population size among the leading states are likely to lead to disparities in actual military power, simply because some states will be better endowed to pursue an arms race than are others.[9]

But even if we assume that all the major states are equally powerful, imbalances in power still occur more often in multipolarity than in bipolarity. Two great powers in a multipolar system, for example, can join together to attack a third great power, as the United Kingdom and France did against Russia in the Crimean War (1853–56), and Italy and Prussia did against Austria in 1866. This kind of ganging up is impossible in bipolarity, since only two great powers compete. Two great powers can also join forces to conquer a minor power, as Austria and Prussia did against Denmark in 1864, and Germany and the Soviet Union did against Poland in 1939. Ganging up of this sort is logically possible in a bipolar world, but it is highly unlikely because the two great powers are almost certain to be archrivals disinclined to go to war as allies. Furthermore, a major power might use its superior strength to coerce or conquer a minor power. This kind of behavior is more likely in multipolarity than in bipolarity, because there are more potential great-minor power dyads in a multipolar system.

One might argue that balance-of-power dynamics can operate to counter any power imbalances that arise in multipolarity. No state can dominate another if the other states coalesce firmly against it.[10] Indeed, this might be seen as an advantage that multipolarity has over bipolarity, since great-power balancing coalitions are not feasible in a world with only two great powers. But threatened states rarely form effective balancing coalitions in time to contain an aggressor. As Chapter 8 demonstrated, threatened states prefer buck-passing to balancing, but buck-passing directly undermines efforts to build powerful balancing coalitions.

But even when threatened states do balance together in multipolarity, diplomacy is an uncertain process. It can take time to build a defensive coalition, especially if the number of states required to form a balancing alliance is large. An aggressor may conclude that it can gain its objectives before the opposing coalition is fully formed. Finally, geography sometimes prevents balancing states from putting meaningful pressure on aggressors. For example, a major power may not be able to put effective military pressure on a state threatening to cause trouble because they are separated from each other by a large body of water or another state.[11]

The Potential for Miscalculation

A final problem with multipolarity lies in its tendency to foster miscalculation. Multipolarity leads states to underestimate the resolve of rival states and the strength of opposing coalitions. States then mistakenly conclude that they have the military capability to coerce an opponent, or if that fails, to defeat it in battle.

War is more likely when a state underestimates the willingness of an opposing state to stand firm on issues of difference. It then may push the other state too far, expecting the other to concede when in fact it will choose to fight. Such miscalculation is more likely under multipolarity because the shape of the international order tends to remain fluid, due to the tendency of coalitions to shift. As a result, the nature of the agreed international rules of the road—norms of state behavior, and agreed divisions of territorial rights and other privileges—tend to change constantly. No sooner may the rules of a given adversarial relationship be worked out than that relationship becomes a friendship, a new rivalry emerges with a previous friend or neutral, and new rules of the road must be established. Under these circumstances, one state may unwittingly push another too far, because ambiguities as to national rights and obligations leave a wider range of issues on which each state may misjudge the other's resolve. Norms of state behavior can come to be broadly understood and accepted by all states, even in multipolarity, just as basic norms of diplomatic conduct became generally accepted by the European powers during the eighteenth century. Nevertheless, a well-defined division of rights is generally more difficult when the number of states is large and relations among them are in flux, as is the case with multipolarity.

War is also more likely when states underestimate the relative power of an opposing coalition, either because they underestimate the number of states who will oppose them, or because they exaggerate the number of allies who will fight on their own side.[12] Such errors are more likely in a system of many states, since states then must accurately predict the behavior of many other states in order to calculate the balance of power between coalitions. Even assuming that a state knows who is going to fight with and against it, measuring the military strength of multistate coalitions is considerably more difficult than assessing the power of a single rival.

Miscalculation is less likely in a bipolar world. States are less likely to miscalculate others' resolve, because the rules of the road with the main opponent become settled over time, leading both parties to recognize the limits beyond which they cannot push the other. States also cannot miscalculate the membership of the opposing coalition, since each side faces only one main enemy. Simplicity breeds certainty; certainty bolsters peace.

BALANCED VS. UNBALANCED MULTIPOLARITY

Unbalanced multipolar systems are especially war-prone for two reasons. The potential hegemons, which are the defining feature of this kind of system, have an appreciable power advantage over the other great powers, which means that they have good prospects of winning wars against their weaker rivals. One might think that a marked power asymmetry of this sort would decrease the prospects for war. After all, being so powerful should make the potential hegemon feel secure and thus should ameliorate the need to initiate a war to gain more power. Moreover, the lesser powers should recognize that the leading state is essentially a status quo power and relax. But even if they fail to recognize the dominant power's benign intentions, the fact is that they do not have the military capability to challenge it. Therefore, according to this logic, the presence of a potential hegemon in a multipolar system should enhance the prospects for peace.

This is not what happens, however, when potential hegemons come on the scene. Their considerable military might notwithstanding, they are not likely to be satisfied with the balance of power. Instead they will aim to acquire more power and eventually gain regional hegemony, because hegemony is the ultimate form of security; there are no meaningful security threats to the dominant power in a unipolar system. Of course, not only do potential hegemons have a powerful incentive to rule their region, they also have the capability to push for supremacy, which means that they are a dangerous threat to peace.

Potential hegemons also invite war by increasing the level of fear among the great powers.[13] Fear is endemic to states in the international system, and it drives them to compete for power so that they can increase their prospects for survival in a dangerous world. The emergence of a potential hegemon, however, makes the other great powers especially fearful, and they will search hard for ways to correct the imbalance of power and will be inclined to pursue riskier policies toward that end. The reason is simple: when one state is threatening to dominate the rest, the long-term value of remaining at peace declines and threatened states will be more willing to take chances to improve their security.

A potential hegemon does not have to do much to generate fear among the other states in the system. Its formidable capabilities alone are likely to scare neighboring great powers and push at least some of them to create a balancing coalition against their dangerous opponent. Because a state's intentions are difficult to discern, and because they can change quickly, rival great powers will be inclined to assume the worst about the potential hegemon's intentions, further reinforcing the threatened states' incentive to contain it and maybe even weaken it if the opportunity presents itself.

The target of this containment strategy, however, is sure to view any balancing coalition forming against it as encirclement by its rivals. The potential hegemon would be correct to think this way, even though the lesser great powers' purpose is essentially defensive in nature. Nevertheless, the leading state is likely to feel threatened and scared and consequently is likely to take steps to enhance its security, thereby making the neighboring great powers more scared, and forcing them to take additional steps to enhance their security, which then scares the potential hegemon even more, and so on. In short, potential hegemons generate spirals of fear that are hard to control. This problem is compounded by the fact that they possess considerable power and thus are likely to think they can solve their security problems by going to war.

Summary

Thus, bipolarity is the most stable of the different architectures, for four reasons. First, there are relatively fewer opportunities for conflict in bipolarity, and only one possible conflict dyad involving the great powers. When great powers do fight in bipolarity, they are likely to engage minor powers, not the rival great power. Second, power is more likely to be equally distributed among the great powers in bipolarity, an important structural source of stability. Furthermore, there is limited opportunity for the great powers to gang up against other states or take advantage of minor powers. Third, bipolarity discourages miscalculation and thus reduces the likelihood that the great powers will stumble into war. Fourth, although fear is constantly at play in world politics, bipolarity does not magnify those anxieties that haunt states.

Balanced multipolarity is more prone to war than is bipolarity, for three reasons. First, multipolarity presents considerably more opportunities for conflict, especially between the great powers themselves. Wars that simultaneously involve all the great powers, however, are unlikely. Second, power is likely to be distributed unevenly among the leading states, and those states with greater military capability will be prone to start wars, because they will think that they have the capability to win them. There will also be ample opportunity for great powers to gang up on third parties and to coerce or conquer minor powers. Third, miscalculation is likely to be a serious problem in balanced multipolarity, although high levels of fear among the great powers are unlikely, because there are no exceptional power gaps between the leading states in the system.

Unbalanced multipolarity is the most perilous distribution of power. Not only does it have all the problems of balanced multipolarity, it also suffers from the worst kind of inequality: the presence of a potential hegemon. That state both has significant capability to cause trouble and spawns high levels of fear among the great powers. Both of those developments increase the likelihood of war, which is likely to involve all the great powers in the system and be especially costly.

Now that the theory about the causes of war has been presented, let us switch gears and consider how well it explains events in Europe between 1792 and 1990.

GREAT-POWER WAR IN MODERN EUROPE, 1792–1990

To test offensive realism's claims about how different distributions of power affect the likelihood of great-power war, it is necessary to identify the periods between 1792 and 1990 when Europe was either bipolar or multipolar, and when there was a potential hegemon in those multipolar systems. It is then necessary to identify the great-power wars for each of those periods.

System structure, we know, is a function of the number of great powers and how power is apportioned among them. The list of European great powers for the two centuries under discussion includes Austria, Great Britain, Germany, Italy, and Russia.[14] Only Russia, which was known as the Soviet Union between 1917 and 1990, was a great power for the entire period. Austria, which became Austria-Hungary in 1867, was a great power from 1792 until its demise in 1918. Great Britain and Germany were great powers from 1792 until 1945, although Germany was actually Prussia before 1871. Italy is considered a great power from 1861 until its collapse in 1943.

What about Japan and the United States, which are not located in Europe, but were great powers for part of the relevant period? Japan, which was a great power from 1895 until 1945, is left out of the subsequent analysis because it was never a major player in European politics. Japan declared war against Germany at the start of World War I, but other than taking a few German possessions in Asia, it remained on the sidelines. Japan also sent troops into the Soviet Union during the last year of World War I, in conjunction with the United Kingdom, France, and the United States, who were trying to get the Soviet Union back into the war against Germany.[15] Japan, however, was mainly concerned with acquiring territory in Russia's Far East, not with events in Europe, about which it cared little. Regardless, the intervention was a failure.

The United States is a different matter. Although it is located in the Western Hemisphere, it committed military forces to fight in Europe during both world wars, and it has maintained a large military presence in the region since 1945. In those instances in which the United States accepted a continental commitment, it is considered a major actor in the European balance of power. But for reasons discussed in Chapter 7, America was never a potential hegemon in Europe; it acted instead as an offshore balancer. Much of the work on assessing the relative strength of the great powers during the years between 1792 and 1990, especially regarding the crucial question of whether there was a potential hegemon in Europe, was done in Chapter 8. The missing parts of the story are filled in below.

Based on the relevant distribution of power among the major states, European history from the outbreak of the French Revolutionary and Napoleonic Wars in 1792 until the end of the Cold War in 1990 can be roughly divided into seven periods:

1) Napoleonic era I, 1792–93 (1 year), balanced multipolarity;
2) Napoleonic era II, 1793–1815 (22 years), unbalanced multipolarity;
3) Nineteenth century, 1815–1902 (88 years), balanced multipolarity;
4) Kaiserreich era, 1903–18 (16 years), unbalanced multipolarity;
5) Interwar years, 1919–38 (20 years), balanced multipolarity;
6) Nazi era, 1939–45 (6 years), unbalanced multipolarity; and
7) Cold War, 1945–90 (46 years), bipolarity.

The list of wars for each of these seven periods is drawn from Jack Levy's well-regarded database of great-power wars.[16] However, one minor adjustment was made to that database: I treat the Russo-Polish War

(1919–20) and the Russian Civil War (1918–21) as separate conflicts, whereas Levy treats them as part of the same war. Only wars that involved at least one European great power and were fought between European states are included in this analysis. Wars involving a European great power and a non-European state are excluded. Thus the War of 1812 between the United Kingdom and the United States, the Russo-Japanese War (1904–5), and the Soviet war in Afghanistan (1979–89) are omitted.[17] Also excluded are European wars involving only minor powers. Finally, civil wars are not included in the analysis, unless there was substantial outside intervention by at least one European state, as there was in the Russian Civil War. The Spanish Civil War (1936–39) is omitted, although it is a close call.

Great-power wars are broken down into three categories. "Central wars" involve virtually all of the great powers in the system, and the combatants fight with tremendous intensity.[18] "Great power vs. great power wars" involve either one-on-one or two-on-one fights. It should be noted that there is no difference between a central war and a great power vs. great power war in either a bipolar system or a multipolar system with three great powers. No such cases exist, however, in modern Eropean history. Finally, there are "great power vs. minor power wars." During the 199-year period of European history under study, there were a total of 24 great-power wars, including 3 central wars, 6 great power vs. great power wars, and 15 great power vs. minor power wars.

The Napoleonic Era, 1792–1815

Europe was home to five great powers between 1792 and 1815: Austria, Britain/United Kingdom, France, Prussia, and Russia. Although France was clearly the most powerful state during this period, it was not a potential hegemon until the early fall of 1793, because it did not have the most formidable army in Europe before then.[19] Remember that Austria and Prussia went to war against France in 1792 because it was militarily weak and therefore was considered vulnerable to invasion. France retained its exalted status as a potential hegemon until Napoleon was finally defeated in the spring of 1815. Thus, there was balanced multipolarity in Europe from 1792 until 1793, and unbalanced multipolarity from 1793 until 1815.

The period from 1792 to 1815 was dominated by the *French Revolutionary and Napoleonic Wars*. The first year of that conflict is categorized as a great power vs. great power war, because it involved only three great powers: Austria, France, and Prussia. Great Britain and Russia sat on the sidelines throughout 1792 and early 1793. The remaining twenty-two years of that conflict are categorized as a central war. France, which was attempting to become Europe's hegemon, fought against Austria, Britain, Prussia, and Russia—although in different combinations at different times.

There were also three great power vs. minor power wars in the Napoleonic era. The *Russo-Turkish War (1806–12)* was basically an attempt by Russia to take Bessarabia, Moldavia, and Walachia away from Turkey, which was then called the Ottoman Empire. Russian victories in the last year of that war won Bessarabia, but not the other two regions. The *Russo-Swedish War (1808–9)* was caused by French and Russian unhappiness over Sweden's alliance with the United Kingdom. Russia and Denmark went to war against Sweden and were victorious. Sweden had to surrender Finland and the Åland Islands to Russia. The *Neapolitan War (1815)* was fought between Austria and Naples. In the wake of Napoleon's departure from Italy, Austria was determined to reassert its preeminence in the region, while the Neapolitan forces were bent on pushing Austria out of Italy. Austria won the conflict.

The Nineteenth Century, 1815–1902

Six great powers populated the European system for this eighty-eight-year period between the final defeat of Napoleonic France and the rise of Wilhelmine Germany. Austria/Austria-Hungary, the United Kingdom, France, Prussia/Germany, and Russia were great powers for the entire period. Italy joined the club in 1861. There was no potential hegemon in Europe between 1815 and 1902. The United Kingdom was clearly the wealthiest state in Europe during that period (see Table 3.3), but it never translated its abundant wealth into military might. In fact, the United

Kingdom maintained a small and weak army for most of the period in question. The largest armies in Europe between 1815 and 1860 belonged to Austria, France, and Russia, but none of them possessed an army that was powerful enough to overrun Europe (see Tables 9.1 and 9.2).[20] Nor did any of them come close to having enough latent power to qualify as a potential hegemon.

The Prussian army became a formidable fighting force in the 1860s, vying with the Austrian and French armies for the number one ranking in Europe.[21] France occupied that position for the first half of the decade; Prussia held it for the second half. There is little doubt that Germany had the strongest army in Europe between 1870 and 1902, but it was not yet so powerful that it was a threat to the entire continent. Furthermore, Germany did not yet have sufficient wealth to qualify as a potential hegemon. Thus, it seems fair to say that there was balanced multipolarity in Europe during the nineteenth century.

There were four great power vs. great power wars between 1815 and 1902. The *Crimean War (1853–56)* was initially a war between Russia and the Ottoman Empire, with the former trying to make territorial gains at the expense of the latter. But the United Kingdom and France entered the war on the Ottoman Empire's side. Russia was defeated and was forced to make minor territorial concessions. In the *War of Italian Unification (1859)*, France joined forces with Piedmont to drive Austria out of Italy and create a unified Italian state. Austria lost the war and Italy came into being shortly thereafter. In the *Austro-Prussian War (1866)*, Prussia and Italy were arrayed against Austria. Prussia and Austria were essentially fighting to determine which one of them would dominate a unified Germany, while Italy was bent on taking territory from Austria. Austria lost and Prussia made substantial territorial gains at Austria's expense. But German unification was still not completed. The *Franco-Prussian War (1870–71)* was ostensibly fought over Prussian interference in Spain's politics. In fact, Bismarck wanted the war so he could complete German unification, while France wanted territorial compensation to offset Prussia's gains in 1866. The Prussian army won a decisive victory.

TABLE 9.1

Manpower in European Armies, 1820–58

	1820	1830	1840	1850	1858
Austria	258,000	273,000	267,000	434,000	403,000
United Kingdom	114,513	104,066	124,659	136,932	200,000
France	208,000	224,000	275,000	391,190	400,000
Prussia	130,000	130,000	135,000	131,000	153,000
Russia	772,000	826,000	623,000	871,000	870,000

SOURCES: Figures for Austria, Prussia, and Russia are from J. David Singer and Melvin Small, *National Material Capabilities Data, 1816–1985* (Ann Arbor, MI: Inter-University Consortium for Political and Social Research, February 1993). Figures for the United Kingdom are from Edward Spiers, *The Army and Society, 1815–1914* (London: Longman, 1980), p. 36, except for 1858, which is the author's estimate. Figures for France in 1820 and 1830 are from Singer and Small, *National Material Capabilities;* France in 1840 is from William C. Fuller, Jr., *Strategy and Power in Russia, 1600–1914* (New York: Free Press, 1992), p. 239; France in 1850 is from André Corvisier, ed., *Histoire Militaire de la France,* Vol. 2 (Paris: Presses Universitaires de France, 1992), p. 413. France in 1858 (the actual year is 1857) is from Michael Stephen Partridge, *Military Planning for the Defense of the United Kingdom, 1814–1870* (Westport, CT: Greenwood, 1989), p. 76. The year 1858 was chosen instead of 1860 because the War of Italian Unification distorted the numbers for 1860, especially for France.

TABLE 9.2

Manpower in European Armies, 1853–56 (Crimean War)

	1853	1854	1855	1856
Austria	514,000	540,000	427,000	427,000
United Kingdom	149,089	152,780	168,552	168,552
France	332,549	310,267	507,432	526,056
Prussia	139,000	139,000	142,000	142,000
Russia	761,000	1,100,000	1,843,463	1,742,000

SOURCES: Figures for Austria and Prussia are from Singer and Small, *National Material Capabilities Data*. The figures for the United Kingdom are as follows: 1853–54, Hew Strachan, *Wellington's Legacy: The Reform of the British Army, 1830–54* (Manchester: Manchester University Press, 1984), p. 182; 1855–56, Spiers, *Army and Society,* p. 36. Figures for France are from Corvisier, ed., *Histoire Militaire,* p. 413. Figures for Russia, 1853–54 are from Singer and Small, *National Material Capabilities Data,* while those for 1855–56 are from David R. Jones, "The Soviet Defence Burden Through the Prism of History," in Carl G. Jacobsen, ed., *The Soviet Defence Enigma: Estimating Costs and Burden* (Oxford: Oxford University Press, 1987), p. 155.

There were also eight great power vs. minor power wars during the nineteenth century. The *Franco-Spanish War (1823)* stemmed from a revolt in Spain that removed the reigning king from his throne. France intervened to restore peace and the monarchy. *Navarino Bay (1827)* was a brief naval engagement with the United Kingdom, France, and Russia on one side and the Ottoman Empire and Egypt on the other. The great powers were helping the Greeks gain their independence from the Ottoman Empire. In the *Russo-Turkish War (1828–29)*, the Russians went to war against the Ottoman Empire to support Greek independence and to make territorial gains in the Caucasus and other places at the Ottoman Empire's expense. The *First Schleswig-Holstein War (1848–49)* was an unsuccessful effort by Prussia to take the duchies of Schleswig and Holstein away from Denmark and make them a German state.

In the *Austro-Sardinian War (1848)*, the kingdom of Piedmont-Sardinia sought to drive Austria out of Italy and create a unified Italy under its own auspices. This attempt at liberation failed. The *Roman Republic War (1849)* broke out when France sent an army to Rome to restore the pope to power and crush the fledgling republic established there by Giuseppe Mazzini. In the *Second Schleswig-Holstein War (1864)*, Austria and Prussia ganged up to finally take those disputed duchies away from Denmark. Finally, in the *Russo-Turkish War (1877–78)*, Russia and Serbia sided with Bosnia-Herzegovina and Bulgaria in their effort to gain independence from the Ottoman Empire.

The Kaiserreich Era, 1903–18

There was no change in the lineup of great powers after 1903. The same six great powers remained at the center of European politics, save for the fact that the United States became a major player in 1918, when American troops began arriving on the continent in large numbers. Wilhelmine Germany, as emphasized in Chapter 8, was a potential hegemon during this period; it controlled the mightiest army and the greatest amount of wealth in the region. Thus, there was unbalanced multipolarity in Europe from 1903 to 1918.

This period was dominated by *World War I (1914–18)*, a central war involving all of the great powers and many of the minor powers in Europe. There was also one great power vs. great power war during this period. In the *Russian Civil War (1918–21)*, the United Kingdom, France, Japan, and the United States sent troops into the Soviet Union in the midst of its civil war. They ended up fighting some brief but intense battles against the Bolsheviks, who nevertheless survived. Finally, there was one great power vs. minor power conflict during this period: the *Italo-Turkish War (1911–12)*. Italy, which was bent on establishing an empire in the area around the Mediterranean Sea, invaded and conquered Tripolitania and Cyrenaica in North Africa, which were then provinces in the Ottoman Empire (both are part of Libya today).

The Interwar Years, 1919–38

There were five great powers in the European system between the two world wars. Austria-Hungary disappeared at the close of World War I, but the United Kingdom, France, Germany, Italy, and the Soviet Union remained intact. There was no potential hegemon in Europe during these two decades. The United Kingdom was the wealthiest state in Europe during the first few years after the war, but Germany regained the lead by the late 1920s (see Table 3.3). Neither the United Kingdom nor Germany, however, had the most powerful army in the region between 1919 and 1938.[22] Indeed, both states possessed especially weak armies throughout the 1920s and early 1930s. The German army certainly grew more powerful during the late 1930s, but it did not become the strongest army in Europe until 1939. Although it might seem difficult to believe given France's catastrophic defeat in 1940, France possessed the number one army in Europe during the interwar years. But France had nowhere near the wealth and population to be a potential hegemon. Thus, there was balanced multipolarity in Europe during this period.

There were no great power vs. great power wars between 1919 and 1938, but there was one war between a great power and a minor power. In the *Russo-Polish War (1919–20)*, Poland invaded a badly weakened Soviet

Union in the wake of World War I, hoping to detach Belorussia and Ukraine from the Soviet Union and make them part of a Polish-led federation. Although Poland failed to achieve that goal, it did acquire some territory in Belorussia and Ukraine.

The Nazi Era, 1939–45

This period began with the same five great powers that dominated the interwar years. But France was knocked out of the ranks of the great powers in the spring of 1940, and Italy went the same route in 1943. The United Kingdom, Germany, and the Soviet Union remained great powers until 1945. Also, the United States became deeply involved in European politics after it entered World War II in December 1941. As discussed in Chapter 8, Nazi Germany was a potential hegemon from 1939 until it collapsed in defeat in the spring of 1945. Thus, there was unbalanced multipolarity in Europe during this period.

World War II (1939–45), which was a central war, was obviously the dominating event in Europe during this period. There was also one great power vs. minor power war: the *Russo-Finnish War (1939–40)*. In anticipation of a possible Nazi attack on the Soviet Union, Stalin had demanded territorial concessions from Finland in the fall of 1939. The Finns refused and the Red Army invaded Finland in late November 1939. Finland capitulated in March 1940 and the Soviet Union took the territory it wanted.

The Cold War, 1945–90

There was only one great power left in Europe after World War II: the Soviet Union.[23] The United States, however, was determined to prevent the Soviets from dominating the region, so they maintained a massive military presence in Europe throughout the Cold War. This was the first time in its history that the United States stationed large numbers of troops in Europe during peacetime. Europe was therefore bipolar from 1945 to 1990.

There was no war between the two great powers during this period, but there was one great power vs. minor power war. In the *Russo-*

Hungarian War (1956), the Soviet Union successfully intervened to put down an anticommunist revolt in Hungary.

ANALYSIS

Let us now sort this information to see how much great-power war there was in Europe when it was characterized by bipolarity, by balanced multipolarity, and by unbalanced multipolarity. In particular, let us consider the number of wars, the frequency of war, and the deadliness of the wars in each of those kinds of systems. The number of great-power wars in each period is broken down according to the three types of war described earlier: central, great power vs. great power, and great power vs. minor power. Frequency is determined by adding up the years in each period in which a great-power war was being fought. War need only be fought in some part of a year for that year to be counted as a war year. For example, the Crimean War ran from October 1853 until February 1856, and thus 1853, 1854, 1855, and 1856 are counted as war years. Finally, deadliness is measured by counting the number of military deaths in each conflict; civilian deaths are omitted.

Bipolarity seems to be the most peaceful and least deadly kind of architecture (see Table 9.3). Between 1945 and 1990, which was the only period during which Europe was bipolar, there was no war between the great powers. There was, however, one great power vs. minor power war, which lasted less than a month. Thus war took place in Europe during only one of the 46 years in which it was bipolar. Regarding deadliness, there were 10,000 deaths in that conflict.

Unbalanced multipolarity is by far the most war-prone and deadly distribution of power. During the periods when there was a potential hegemon in a multipolar Europe—1793–1815, 1903–18, 1939–45—there were three central wars, one great power vs. great power war, and five great power vs. minor power wars. A war was being fought during 35 of the relevant 44 years, and in 11 of those years two wars were going on at the same time. Finally, there were roughly 27 million military deaths in those

TABLE 9.3

Summary of European Wars by System Structure, 1792–1990

	Number of wars			Frequency of wars			Deadliness of wars
	Central	Great vs. great	Great vs. minor	Total years	War years	% of years with war	Military deaths only
Bipolarity (1945–90)	0	0	1	46	1	2.2%	10,000
Balanced multipolarity (1792–93, 1815–1902, 1919–38)	0	5	9	109	20	18.3%	1.2 million
Unbalanced multipolarity (1793–1815, 1903–18, 1939–45)	3	1	5	44	35	79.5%	27 million

NOTE: I could not find casualty data for the Russo-Turkish (1806–12) and the Russo-Swedish Wars (1808–9), both of which occurred during the Napoleonic Era, so I omitted them from the calculation. Nevertheless, the numbers of combat deaths for those wars are surely small and would hardly affect the huge number of military deaths that occurred when there was unbalanced multipolarity in Europe.

SOURCES: Data on number of wars and total war years are from Jack S. Levy, *War in the Modern Great Power System, 1495–1975* (Lexington: University Press of Kentucky, 1983), pp. 90–91; and J. David Singer and Melvin Small, *Resort to Arms: International and Civil Wars, 1816–1980* (Beverly Hills, CA: Sage, 1982), pp. 82–95. Data on deadliness of wars is from Singer and Small, *Resort to Arms*, pp. 82–95, save for the following exceptions: the Napoleonic Wars, from Charles J. Esdaile, *The Wars of Napoleon* (London: Longman, 1995), p. 300; Navarino Bay, from John Laffin, *Brassey's Battles: 3,500 Years of Conflict, Campaigns and Wars from A–Z* (London: Brassey's Defence Publishers, 1986), p. 299; the Russian Civil War, from Levy, *War*, p. 61; and the Neapolitan War, from Clive Emsley, *Napoleonic Europe* (New York: Longman, 1993).

conflicts (and probably about as many civilian deaths when all the murder and mayhem in World War II is taken into account).

Balanced multipolarity falls somewhere in between the other two kinds of systems. Consider that there were no hegemonic wars, five great power vs. great power wars, and nine great power vs. minor power wars during the times when Europe was multipolar but without a potential hegemon—1792–93, 1815–1902, 1919–38. In terms of frequency, war took place somewhere in Europe during 20 of the relevant 109 years. Thus, war was going on 18.3 percent of the time in balanced multipolarity, compared with 2.2 percent in bipolarity and 79.5 percent in unbalanced multipolarity. Regarding deadliness, there were approximately 1.2 million military deaths in the various wars fought in balanced multipolarity, which is far less than the 27 million in unbalanced multipolarity, but substantially more than the 10,000 in bipolarity.

CONCLUSION

These results appear to offer strong confirmation of offensive realism. Nevertheless, an important caveat is in order. Nuclear weapons, which were first deployed in 1945, were present for the entire time that Europe was bipolar, but they were not present in any of the previous multipolar systems. This creates a problem for my argument, because nuclear weapons are a powerful force for peace, and they surely help account for the absence of great-power war in Europe between 1945 and 1990. It is impossible, however, to determine the relative influence of bipolarity and nuclear weapons in producing this long period of stability.

It would be helpful in dealing with this problem if we could turn to some empirical studies that provide reliable evidence on the effects of bipolarity and multipolarity on the likelihood of war in the absence of nuclear weapons. But there are none. From its beginning until 1945 the European state system was multipolar, leaving this history barren of comparisons that would reveal the differing effects of multipolarity and bipolarity. Earlier history does afford some apparent examples of bipolar systems, including some that were warlike—Athens and Sparta, Rome and Carthage—but this history is inconclusive because it is incomplete.

This problem does not arise, however, when comparing the two kinds of multipolarity, because there were no nuclear weapons before 1945. It is apparent from the analysis that whether a multipolar system contains a potential hegemon like Napoleonic France, Wilhelmine Germany, or Nazi Germany has a profound influence on the prospects for peace. Any time a multipolar system contains a power that has the strongest army as well as the greatest amount of wealth, deadly war among the great powers is more likely.

Little has been said up to this point about international politics after the Cold War. The next and final chapter will consider relations among the great powers in the 1990s, as well as the likelihood of great-power conflict in the century ahead.

10

Great Power Politics in
the Twenty-first Century

A large body of opinion in the West holds that international politics underwent a fundamental transformation with the end of the Cold War. Cooperation, not security competition and conflict, is now the defining feature of relations among the great powers. Not surprisingly, the optimists who hold this view claim that realism no longer has much explanatory power. It is old thinking and is largely irrelevant to the new realities of world politics. Realists have gone the way of the dinosaurs; they just don't realize it. The best that might be said about theories such as offensive realism is that they are helpful for understanding how great powers interacted before 1990, but they are useless now and for the foreseeable future. Therefore, we need new theories to comprehend the world around us.

President Bill Clinton articulated this perspective throughout the 1990s. For example, he declared in 1992 that, "in a world where freedom, not tyranny, is on the march, the cynical calculus of pure power politics simply does not compute. It is ill-suited to a new era." Five years later he sounded the same theme when defending the expansion of the North Atlantic Treaty Organization (NATO) to include some of the formerly communist Warsaw Pact states. Clinton argued that the charge that this expansion policy might isolate Russia was based on the belief "that the great power territorial politics of the 20th century will dominate the 21st century," which he rejected. Instead, he emphasized his belief that "enlightened self-interest, as well as shared values, will compel countries to define their greatness in more constructive ways . . . and will compel us to cooperate in more constructive ways."[1]

The optimists' claim that security competition and war among the great powers has been burned out of the system is wrong. In fact, all of the major states around the globe still care deeply about the balance of power and are destined to compete for power among themselves for the foreseeable future. Consequently, realism will offer the most powerful explanations of international politics over the next century, and this will be true even if the debates among academic and policy elites are dominated by non-realist theories. In short, the real world remains a realist world.

States still fear each other and seek to gain power at each other's expense, because international anarchy—the driving force behind great-power behavior—did not change with the end of the Cold War, and there are few signs that such change is likely any time soon. States remain the principal actors in world politics and there is still no night watchman standing above them. For sure, the collapse of the Soviet Union caused a major shift in the global distribution of power. But it did not give rise to a change in the anarchic structure of the system, and without that kind of profound change, there is no reason to expect the great powers to behave much differently in the new century than they did in previous centuries.

Indeed, considerable evidence from the 1990s indicates that power politics has not disappeared from Europe and Northeast Asia, the regions in which there are two or more great powers, as well as possible great powers such as Germany and Japan. There is no question, however, that the competition for power over the past decade has been low-key. Still, there is potential for intense security competion among the great powers that might lead to a major war. Probably the best evidence of that possibility is the fact that the United States maintains about one hundred thousand troops each in Europe and in Northeast Asia for the explicit purpose of keeping the major states in each region at peace.

These relatively peaceful circumstances are largely the result of benign distributions of power in each region. Europe remains bipolar (Russia and the United States are the major powers), which is the most stable kind of power structure. Northeast Asia is multipolar (China, Russia, and the United States), a configuration more prone to instability; but fortunately there is no potential hegemon in that system. Furthermore, stability is enhanced in both regions by nuclear weapons, the continued presence of U.S. forces, and the relative weakness of China and Russia. These power structures in Europe and Northeast Asia are likely to change over the next two decades, however, leading to intensified security competition and possibly war among the great powers.

The remainder of this chapter is organized as follows. In the next section, I analyze the claims that international politics has changed or is about to change in essential ways, thus undermining realism. Because of space limitations, it is impossible to deal with each argument in detail. Nevertheless, it should be apparent from my analysis that the basic structure of the international system did not change with the end of the Cold War, and that there is little reason to think that change is in the offing. I attempt to show in the following section the considerable evidence from the decade 1991–2000 that security competition among the great powers is not obsolete, either in Europe or in Northeast Asia. In the subsequent four sections, I make the case that we are likely to see greater instability in those important regions over the next twenty years. Finally, in a brief conclusion, I argue that a rising China is the most dangerous potential threat to the United States in the early twenty-first century.

PERSISTENT ANARCHY

The structure of the international system, as emphasized in Chapter 2, is defined by five assumptions about how the world is organized that have some basis in fact: 1) states are the key actors in world politics and they operate in an anarchic system, 2) great powers invariably have some offensive military capability, 3) states can never be certain whether other states have hostile intentions toward them, 4) great powers place a high premium on survival, and 5) states are rational actors who are reasonably effective at designing strategies that maximize their chances of survival.

These features of the international system appear to be intact as we begin the twenty-first century. The world still comprises states that operate in an anarchic setting. Neither the United Nations nor any other international institution has much coercive leverage over the great powers. Furthermore, virtually every state has at least some offensive military capability, and there is little evidence that world disarmament is in sight. On the contrary, the world arms trade is flourishing, and nuclear proliferation, not abolition, is likely to concern tomorrow's policymakers. In addition, great powers have yet to discover a way to divine each other's intentions. For example, nobody can predict with any degree of certainty what Chinese or German foreign policy goals will be in 2020. Moreover, there is no good evidence that survival is a less important goal for states today than it was before 1990. Nor is there much reason to believe that the ability of great powers to think strategically has declined since the Cold War ended.

This description of continuity in great-power politics has been challenged on a variety of fronts by experts who believe that significant changes have recently occurred in the structure of the international system—changes that portend a welcome peace among the great powers. Although there are sharp differences among these optimists about the root causes of this purported transformation, each argument is essentially a direct challenge to one of the realist assumptions described above. The only claim that the optimists do not challenge is the claim that states are rational actors. Instead, they concentrate their fire on the other four realist beliefs about the international system. Let us consider, in turn, their best arguments against each of those core assumptions.

Sovereignty at Bay

Some suggest that international institutions are growing in number and in their ability to push states to cooperate with each other.[2] Specifically, institutions can dampen security competition and promote world peace because they have the capability to get states to reject power-maximizing behavior and to refrain from calculating each important move according to how it affects their position in the balance of power. Institutions, so the argument goes, have an independent effect on state behavior that at least mitigates and possibly might put an end to anarchy.

The rhetoric about the growing strength of international institutions notwithstanding, there is little evidence that they can get great powers to act contrary to the dictates of realism.[3] I know of no study that provides evidence to support that claim. The United Nations is the only worldwide organization with any hope of wielding such power, but it could not even shut down the war in Bosnia between 1992 and 1995, much less push a great power around. Moreover, what little influence the United Nations (UN) holds over states is likely to wane even further in the new century, because its key decision-making body, the Security Council, is sure to grow in size. Creating a larger council, especially one with more permanent members who have a veto over UN policy, would make it virtually impossible to formulate and enforce policies designed to limit the actions of the great powers.

There is no institution with any real power in Asia. Although there are a handful of impressive institutions in Europe, such as NATO and the European Union, there is little evidence that they can compel member states to act against their strategic interests. What is most impressive about international institutions is how little independent effect they seem to have on great-power behavior.

Of course, states sometimes operate through institutions and benefit from doing so. However, the most powerful states in the system create and shape institutions so that they can maintain, if not increase, their own share of world power. Institutions are essentially "arenas for acting out power relationships."[4] When the United States decided it did not want Secretary-General Boutros Boutros-Ghali to head the UN for a second term, it forced him out, despite the fact that all the other members of the Security Council wanted him to stay on the job. The United States is the most powerful state in the world, and it usually gets its way on issues it judges important. If it does not, it ignores the institution and does what it deems to be in its own national interest.

Others argue that the state is being rendered impotent by globalization or by today's unprecedented levels of economic interdependence. In particular, great powers are said to be incapable of dealing with the mighty forces unleashed by global capitalism and are becoming marginal players in world politics.[5] "Where states were once the masters of markets, now it is the markets which, on many crucial issues, are the masters over the governments of states."[6] For some, the key actor in the market is the multinational corporation (MNC), which is seen as threatening to overwhelm the state.[7]

The fact is that the levels of economic transactions among states today, when compared with domestic economic dealings, are probably no greater than they were in the early twentieth century.[8] The international economy has been buffeting states for centuries, and they have proved remarkably resilient in the face of that pressure. Contemporary states are no exception in this regard; they are not being overwhelmed by market forces or MNCs but are making the adjustments necessary to ensure their survival.[9]

Another reason to doubt these claims about the state's impending demise is that there is no plausible alternative on the horizon. If the state disappears, presumably some new political entity would have to take its place, but it seems that nobody has identified that replacement. Even if the state disappeared, however, that would not necessarily mean the end of security competition and war. After all, Thucydides and Machiavelli wrote long before the birth of the state system. Realism merely requires anarchy; it does not matter what kind of political units make up the system. They could be states, city-states, cults, empires, tribes, gangs, feudal principalities, or whatever. Rhetoric aside, we are not moving toward a hierarchic international system, which would effectively mean some kind of world government. In fact, anarchy looks like it will be with us for a long time.

Finally, there is good reason to think that the state has a bright future. Nationalism is probably the most powerful political ideology in the world, and it glorifies the state.[10] Indeed, it is apparent that a large number of nations around the world want their own state, or rather nation-state, and they seem to have little interest in any alternative political arrangement. Consider, for example, how badly the Palestinians want their own state, and before 1948, how desperately the Jews wanted their own state. Now that the Jews have Israel it is unthinkable that they would give it up. If the Palestinians get their own state, they surely will go to great lengths to ensure its survival.

The usual rejoinder to this perspective is to argue that the recent history of the European Union contradicts it. The states of western Europe have largely abandoned nationalism and are well on their way toward achieving political unity, providing powerful evidence that the state system's days are numbered. Although the members of the European Union have certainly achieved substantial economic integration, there is little evidence that this path will lead to the creation of a superstate. In fact, both nationalism and the existing states in western Europe appear to be alive and well. Consider French thinking on the matter, as reflected in the comments of French president Jacques Chirac to the German Bundestag in June 2000: he said that he envisioned a "united Europe of states rather than a United States of Europe."[11] He went on to say, "Neither you nor we envisage the creation of a European superstate that would take the place of our nation states and end their role as actors on the international stage. . . . In the future, our nations will stay the first reference point for our people." But even if Chirac proves wrong and western Europe becomes a superstate, it would still be a state, albeit a powerful one, operating in a system of states.

Nothing is forever, but there is no good reason to think that the sovereign state's time has passed.

The Futility of Offense

Some suggest that great powers no longer have a meaningful offensive military capability against each other, because great-power war has become prohibitively costly. In essence, war is no longer a useful instrument of statecraft. John Mueller maintains that offense had become too costly for rational leaders even before the advent of nuclear weapons.[12]

World War I was decisive proof, he argues, that conventional war among the great powers had degenerated to the point where it was essentially senseless slaughter. The main flaw in this line of argument is that great-power conventional wars do not have to be protracted and bloody affairs. Quick and decisive victories are possible, as Germany demonstrated against France in 1940—which means that great powers can still have a viable offensive capability against one another.

The more persuasive variant of this argument is that nuclear weapons make it almost impossible for great powers to attack each other. After all, it is difficult to imagine winning any kind of meaningful victory in an all-out nuclear war. This argument, too, falls apart on close inspection. There is no question that nuclear weapons significantly reduce the likelihood of great-power war, but as discussed in Chapter 4, war between nuclear-armed great powers is still a serious possibility. Remember that during the Cold War, the United States and its NATO allies were deeply worried about a Soviet conventional attack into Western Europe, and after 1979 about a Soviet invasion of Iran. The fact that both superpowers had massive nuclear arsenals apparently did not persuade either side that the other had no offensive military capability.

Certain Intentions

Democratic peace theory is built on the premises that democracies can be more certain of each other's intentions and that those intentions are generally benign; thus they do not fight among themselves.[13] If all the great powers were democracies, each could be certain that the others had friendly intentions, and thus they would have no need to compete for power or prepare for major war. Since democracy appears to be spreading across the globe, it is reasonable to think that the world will eventually become one giant zone of peace.

As challenges to realism go, democratic peace theory is among the strongest. Still, it has serious problems that ultimately make it unconvincing. The theory's proponents maintain that the available evidence shows that democracies do not fight other democracies. But other scholars who have examined the historical record dispute this claim. Perhaps the most telling evidence against the theory is Christopher Layne's careful analysis of four crises in which rival democracies almost went to war with each other.[14] When one looks at how the decision not to fight was reached in each case, the fact that both sides were democracies appears to have mattered little. There certainly is no evidence that the rival democracies had benign intentions toward each other. In fact, the outcome each time was largely determined by balance-of-power considerations.

Another reason to doubt democratic peace theory is the problem of backsliding. No democracy can be sure that another democracy will not someday become an authoritarian state, in which case the remaining democracy would no longer be safe and secure.[15] Prudence dictates that democracies prepare for that eventuality, which means striving to have as much power as possible just in case a friendly neighbor turns into the neighborhood bully. But even if one rejects these criticisms and embraces democratic peace theory, it is still unlikely that all the great powers in the system will become democratic and stay that way over the long term. It would only take a non-democratic China or Russia to keep power politics in play, and both of those states are likely to be non-democratic for at least part of the twenty-first century.[16]

Social constructivists provide another perspective on how to create a world of states with benign intentions that are readily recognizable by other states.[17] They maintain that the way states behave toward each other is not a function of how the material world is structured—as realists argue—but instead is largely determined by how individuals think and talk about international politics. This perspective is nicely captured by Alexander Wendt's famous claim that "anarchy is what states make of it."[18] Discourse, in short, is the motor that drives international politics. But unfortunately, say social constructivists, realism has been the dominant discourse for at least the past seven centuries, and realism tells states to distrust other states and to take advantage of them whenever possible. What is needed to create a more peaceful world is a replacement discourse that emphasizes trust and cooperation among states, rather than suspicion and hostility.

One reason to doubt this perspective is the simple fact that realism *has* dominated the international relations discourse for the past seven centuries or more. Such remarkable staying power over a lengthy period that has seen profound change in almost every other aspect of daily life strongly suggests that the basic structure of the international system—which has remained anarchic over that entire period—largely determines how states think and act toward each other. But even if we reject my materialist interpretation, what is going to cause the reigning discourse about world politics to change? What is the causal mechanism that will delegitimize realism after seven hundred years and put a better substitute in its place? What determines whether the replacement discourse will be benign or malign? What guarantee is there that realism will not rise from the dead and once again become the hegemonic discourse? The social constructivists provide no answers to these important questions, which makes it hard to believe that a marked change in our discourse about international politics is in the offing.[19]

Social constructivists sometimes argue that the end of the Cold War represents a significant triumph for their perspective and is evidence of a more promising future.[20] In particular, they maintain that in the 1980s a group of influential and dovish Western intellectuals convinced Soviet president Mikhail Gorbachev to eschew realist thinking and instead work to foster peaceful relations with the United States and his neighbors in Europe. The result was Soviet withdrawal from Eastern Europe and the end of the Cold War, a Soviet Union with an enlightened foreign policy, and fundamental change in the norms that underpin great-power politics.

Although Gorbachev surely played the key role in ending the Cold War, there are good reasons to doubt that his actions fundamentally transformed international politics. As discussed in Chapter 6, his decison to liquidate the Soviet empire in Eastern Europe can be explained by realism. By the mid-1980s, it was clear that the Soviet Union was losing the Cold War and that it had little hope of catching up with the United States, which was in the midst of a massive arms buildup. In particular, the Soviet Union was suffering an economic and political crisis at home that made the costs of empire prohibitive and created powerful incentives to cooperate with the West to gain access to its technology.

Many empires collapsed and many states broke apart before 1989, and many of them sought to give dire necessity the appearance of virtue. But the basic nature of international politics remained unchanged. That pattern certainly appears to be holding up in the wake of the collapse of the Soviet Union. Consider that Gorbachev has been out of office and without much influence in Russia since the early 1990s, and there is little evidence that his "new thinking" about international politics carries much weight inside Russia today.[21] In fact, contemporary Russian leaders view the world largely in terms of power politics, as discussed below. Moreover, Western leaders, as well as Russia's neighbors in eastern Europe, continue to fear that a resurgent Russia might be an expansionist state, which explains in part why NATO expanded eastward. In sum, it is not true that the collapse of the Soviet Union was unprecedented, that it violated realist conceptions, or that it is a harbinger of a new, post-realist international system.

Survival in the Global Commons

Realist thinking about survival gets challenged in two ways. Proponents of globalization often argue that states today are concerned more with achieving prosperity than with worrying about their survival.[22] Getting rich is the main goal of post-industrial states, maybe even the all-consuming goal. The basic logic here is that if all the great powers are prospering, none has any incentive to start a war, because conflict in today's interdependent world economy would redound to every state's disadvantage. Why torpedo a system that is making everyone rich? If war makes no sense, survival becomes a much less salient concern than realists would have you believe, and states can concentrate instead on accumulating wealth.

There are problems with this perspective, too.[23] In particular, there is always the possibility that a serious economic crisis in some important region, or in the world at large, will undermine the prosperity that this theory needs to work. For example, it is widely believed that Asia's "economic miracle" worked to dampen security competition in that region before 1997, but that the 1997–98 financial crisis in Asia helped foster a "new geopolitics."[24] It is also worth noting that although the United States led a successful effort to contain that financial crisis, it was a close call, and there is no guarantee that the next crisis will not spread across the globe. But even in the absence of a major economic crisis, one or more states might not prosper; such a state would have little to lose economically, and maybe even something to gain, by starting a war. A key reason that Iraqi dictator Saddam Hussein invaded Kuwait in August 1990 was that Kuwait was exceeding its oil production quotas (set by the Organization of Petroleum Exporting Countries, or OPEC) and driving down Iraq's oil profits, which the Iraqi economy could ill-afford.[25]

There are two other reasons to doubt the claim that economic interdependence makes great-power war unlikely. States usually go to war against a single rival, and they aim to win a quick and decisive victory. Also, they invariably seek to discourage other states from joining with the other side in the fight. But a war against one or even two opponents is unlikely to do much damage to a state's economy, because typically only a tiny percentage of a state's wealth is tied up in economic intercourse with any other state. It is even possible, as discussed in Chapter 5, that conquest will produce significant economic benefits.

Finally, an important historical case contradicts this perspective. As noted above, there was probably about as much economic interdependence in Europe between 1900 and 1914 as there is today. Those were also prosperous years for the European great powers. Yet World War I broke out in 1914. Thus a highly interdependent world economy does not make great-power war more or less likely. Great powers must be forever vigilant and never subordinate survival to any other goal, including prosperity.

Another challenge to the realist perspective on survival emphasizes that the dangers states face today come not from the traditional kind of military threats that realists worry about, but instead from non-traditional threats such as AIDS, environmental degradation, unbounded population growth, and global warming.[26] Problems of this magnitude, so the argument goes, can be solved only by the collective action of all the major states in the system. The selfish behavior associated with realism, on the other hand, will undermine efforts to neutralize these threats. States surely will recognize this fact and cooperate to find workable solutions.

This perspective raises two problems. Although these dangers are a cause for concern, there is little evidence that any of them is serious enough to threaten the survival of a great power. The gravity of these threats may change over time, but for now they are at most second-order problems.[27] Furthermore, if any of these threats becomes deadly serious, it is not clear that the great powers would respond by acting collectively. For example, there may be cases where the relevant states cooperate to deal with a particular environmental problem, but an impressive literature discusses how such problems might also lead to inter-state war.[28]

In sum, claims that the end of the Cold War ushered in sweeping changes in the structure of the international system are ultimately unpersuasive. On the contrary, international anarchy remains firmly intact, which means that there should not have been any significant changes in great-power behavior during the past decade.

GREAT-POWER BEHAVIOR IN THE 1990S

The optimists' contention that international politics has undergone a great transformation applies mainly to relations among the great powers, who are no longer supposed to engage in security competition and fight wars with each other, or with minor powers in their region. Therefore, Europe and Northeast Asia, the areas that feature clusters of great powers, should be zones of peace, or what Karl Deutsch famously calls "pluralistic security communities."[29]

Optimists do not argue, however, that the threat of armed conflict has been eliminated from regions without great powers, such as 1) the South Asian subcontinent, where India and Pakistan are bitter enemies armed with nuclear weapons and caught up in a raging dispute over Kashmir; 2) the Persian Gulf, where Iraq and Iran are bent on acquiring nuclear weapons and show no signs of becoming status quo powers; or 3) Africa, where seven different states are fighting a war in the Democratic Republic

of the Congo that some are calling "Africa's first world war."[30] Nor do optimists claim that great powers no longer fight wars with states in these
troubled regions; thus, the American-led war against Iraq in early 1991 is
not evidence against their position. In short, great powers are not yet out
of the war business altogether, only in Europe and Northeast Asia.

There is no question that security competition among the great powers
in Europe and Northeast Asia has been subdued during the 1990s, and
with the possible exception of the 1996 dispute between China and the
United States over Taiwan, there has been no hint of war between any of
the great powers. Periods of relative peacefulness like this one, however,
are not unprecedented in history. For example, there was little open conflict among the great powers in Europe from 1816 through 1852, or from
1871 through 1913. But this did not mean then, and it does not mean
now, that the great powers stopped thinking and behaving according to
realist logic. Indeed, there is substantial evidence that the major states in
Europe and Northeast Asia still fear each other and continue to worry
about how much relative power they control. Moreover, sitting below the
surface in both regions is significant potential for intense security competition and possibly even war among the leading states.

Security Competition in Northeast Asia

In the large literature on security issues in Northeast Asia after the Cold
War, almost every author recognizes that power politics is alive and well
in the region, and that there are good reasons to worry about armed conflict involving the great powers.[31]

The American experience in the region since 1991 provides considerable evidence to support this pessimistic perspective. The United States
came close to fighting a war against North Korea in June 1994 to prevent
it from acquiring nuclear weapons.[32] War still might break out between
North and South Korea, in which case the United States would automati-
cally become involved, since it has 37,000 troops stationed in South Korea
to help counter a North Korean invasion. If such a war happened,
American and South Korean forces would probably trounce the invading

North Korean army, creating an opportunity for them to strike north of the 38th parallel and unify the two Koreas.[33] This is what happened in 1950, prompting China, which shares a border with North Korea, to feel threatened and go to war against the United States. This could plausibly happen again if there is a second Korean war.

One might argue that the Korean problem is likely to go away soon, because relations are improving between the two Koreas, and there is actually a reasonable chance they will reunify in the decade ahead. Although future relations between North and South Korea are difficult to predict, both sides are still poised to fight a major war along the border separating them, which remains the most heavily armed strip of territory in the world. Moreover, there is hardly any evidence—at least at this point—that North Korea intends to surrender its independence and become part of a unified Korea. But even if reunification happens, there is no reason to think that it will enhance stability in Northeast Asia, because it will surely create pressures to remove American troops from Korea and will also revive competition among China, Japan, and Russia for influence in Korea.

Taiwan is another dangerous place where China and the United States could end up in a shooting war.[34] Taiwan appears determined to maintain its de facto independence from China, and possibly to gain de jure independence, while China seems equally determined to reincorporate Taiwan into China. In fact, China has left little doubt that it would go to war to prevent Taiwanese independence. The United States, however, is committed to help Taiwan defend itself if it is attacked by China, a scenario which could plausibly lead to American troops fighting with Taiwan against China. After all, between July 1995 and March 1996, China fired live missiles into the waters around Taiwan and conducted military exercises off the coast of its Fujian province, just across the strait from Taiwan. China rattled its saber because it thought that Taiwan was taking major steps toward independence. The United States responded by sending two aircraft-carrier battle groups into the waters around Taiwan. Fortunately, the crisis ended peacefully.

The Taiwan problem, however, shows no signs of going away. China is deploying large numbers of missiles (ballistic and cruise) in Fujian province, and it is procuring aircraft and naval ships from Russia that might some day make it risky for the United States to deploy naval forces in the region during a crisis. Furthermore, China issued a document in February 2000 in which it said that it was prepared to go to war before it would allow "the Taiwan issue to be postponed indefinitely."[35] Immediately thereafter, China and the United States exchanged thinly disguised nuclear threats.[36] Taiwan, for its part, is shopping for new weapons to counter China's growing arsenal, while remaining determined to maintain its independence from China. The United States could therefore get pulled into war with China over both Korea and Taiwan.

More needs to be said about China, the principal great-power rival of the United States in Northeast Asia. Many Americans may think that realism is outmoded thinking, but this is not how China's leaders view the world. According to one prominent Sinologist, China "may well be the high church of realpolitik in the post–Cold War world."[37] This is not surprising when you consider China's history over the past 150 years and its present threat environment. It shares borders, a number of which are still disputed, with thirteen different states. China fought over territory with India in 1962, the Soviet Union in 1969, and Vietnam in 1979. All of these borders are still contested. China also claims ownership of Taiwan, the Senkaku/Diaoyutai Islands, and various island groups in the South China Sea, many of which it does not now control.[38]

Furthermore, China tends to view both Japan and the United States as potential enemies. Chinese leaders maintain a deep-seated fear that Japan will become militaristic again, like it was before 1945. They also worry that the United States is bent on preventing China from becoming the dominant great power in Northeast Asia. "Many Chinese foreign- and defense-policy analysts," according to one scholar, "believe that U.S. alliances with Asian countries, particularly with Japan, pose a serious, long-term challenge, if not a threat, to China's national security, national unification, and modernization."[39]

It is worth noting that China's relations with Japan and the United States have gotten worse—not better—since the end of the Cold War.[40] All three states were aligned against the Soviet Union during the 1980s, and they had little cause to fear each other. Even Taiwan was not a major source of friction between China and the United States during the last decade of the Cold War. But times have changed for the worse since 1990, and now China fears Japan and the United States, who, in turn, worry about China. For example, in the immediate aftermath of the Cold War, Japan was confident that growing economic interdependence in Asia would allow it to maintain peaceful relations with China for the indefinite future.[41] By the mid-1990s, however, Japanese views about China had "hardened considerably," and showed evidence of "an anxious realism about China's strategic intentions."[42]

China certainly has not been quick to employ military force over the past decade, although it has demonstrated more than once that it is willing to employ the sword to achieve particular political goals. Besides the missile firings and military maneuvers during the Taiwan crisis, Chinese military forces in early 1995 seized Mischief Reef, one of the disputed Spratly Islands claimed by the Philippines. These incidents notwithstanding, the Chinese military has limited power-projection capability, and therefore it cannot be too aggressive toward other states in the region.[43] For example, China does not have the wherewithal to defeat and conquer Taiwan in a war. To rectify that problem, however, China has embarked on a major military modernization program. Indeed, China decided this year (2001) to increase its defense spending by 17.7 percent, which represents its largest expansion in real terms in the last two decades.[44]

Another indicator of security competition in Northeast Asia is the region's burgeoning arms race in missile technology.[45] North Korea has been developing and testing ballistic missiles throughout the 1990s, and in August 1998 it fired a missile over Japan. In response to the growing North Korean missile threat, South Korea is making moves to increase the range of its own ballistic missiles, while Japan and the United States are moving to build a "theater missile defense" (TMD) system to protect Japan as well as American forces stationed in the region. The United States is also determined to build a "national missile defense" (NMD) system to protect the American homeland from nuclear attacks by small powers such as North Korea. China, however, has made it clear that if Japan and the United States deploy missile defenses of any kind, it will markedly increase its arsenal of ballistic missiles so that it can overwhelm them.

Independent of these developments, China is deploying large numbers of missiles opposite Taiwan, which, not surprisingly, is now trying to acquire defensive systems from the United States. But if the United States aids Taiwan, especially if it helps Taiwan develop its own TMD system, China is sure to increase its arsenal of missiles, which would force the United States to upgrade its TMD system in the region, which would force China to build more missiles, and so on. How all this missile-building will play out over time is difficult to predict, but the key point is that an arms race centered on ballistic missiles is already underway in Asia and shows few signs of abating.

Finally, the fact that the United States maintains one hundred thousand troops in Northeast Asia contradicts the claim that the region is "primed for peace."[46] If that were so, those U.S. forces would be unnecessary and they could be sent home and demobilized, saving the American taxpayer an appreciable sum of money. Instead, they are kept in place to help pacify a potentially volatile region.

Joseph Nye, one of the main architects of post–Cold War American policy in Northeast Asia and a scholar with a well-established reputation as a liberal international-relations theorist (not a realist), made this point in an important 1995 article in *Foreign Affairs*.[47] "It has become fashionable," he notes, "to say that the world after the Cold War has moved beyond the age of power politics to the age of geoeconomics. Such clichés reflect narrow analysis. Politics and economics are connected. International economic systems rest upon international political order." He then makes the "pacifier" argument: "The U.S. presence [in Asia] is a force for stability, reducing the need for arms buildups and deterring the rise of hegemonic forces." Not only do "forward-deployed forces in Asia ensure broad regional stability," they also "contribute to the tremendous political and economic advances made by the nations of the region." In short, "the United States is the critical variable in the East Asia security equation." [48]

Security Competition in Europe

Europe might appear to be a better place than Northeast Asia to make the optimists' case, but on close inspection the evidence shows that security competition and the threat of great-power war remain facts of life in Europe, too. Consider the series of wars that have been fought in the Balkans in the 1990s, and that the United States and its European allies have twice been directly involved in the fighting. American airpower was used against Serb ground forces in Bosnia during the summer of 1995, helping to end the fighting in that embattled country. In the spring of 1999, NATO went to war against Serbia over Kosovo. It was a minor conflict for sure, but the fact remains that in the years since the Cold War ended, the United States has fought a war in Europe, not in Northeast Asia.

The evolution of Russian foreign policy during the 1990s provides further evidence that realism still has a lot to say about inter-state relations in Europe. After the Soviet Union collapsed, it was widely believed that Russia's new leaders would follow in Mikhail Gorbachev's footsteps and eschew the selfish pursuit of power, because they recognized that it made Russia less, not more, secure. Instead, they would work with the United States and its NATO allies to create a peaceful order that reached across all of Europe.

But this is not what has happened. NATO's actions in the Balkans and its expansion eastward have angered and scared the Russians, who now view the world clearly through realist lenses and do not even pay lip service to the idea of working with the West to build what Gorbachev called "a common European home."[49] Russia's hardheaded view of its external environment is reflected in "The National Security Concept of the Russian Federation," a seminal policy document that Russian president Vladimir Putin signed on January 10, 2000. "The formation of international relations," it states, "is accompanied by competition and also by the aspiration of a number of states to strengthen their influence on global politics, including by creating weapons of mass destruction. Military force and violence remain substantial aspects of international relations."[50]

Russia also made it clear in 1993 that it would initiate nuclear war if its territorial integrity was threatened, thus abandoning the Soviet Union's long-standing pledge not to be the first state to use nuclear weapons in a war.[51] Russia's military weakness, however, sharply limits what it can do outside of its borders to challenge the United States over issues such as

NATO expansion and NATO policy in the Balkans. Nevertheless, Russia's actions in the breakaway republic of Chechnya make clear that it is willing to wage a brutal war if it thinks its vital interests are threatened.[52]

More evidence that great-power war remains a serious threat in Europe arises from the fact that the United States maintains one hundred thousand troops in the region, and its leaders often emphasize the importance of keeping NATO intact. If Europe is "primed for peace," as many claim, NATO would surely be disbanded and American forces would be sent home. Instead, they are kept in place. In fact, NATO has moved eastward and incorporated the Czech Republic, Hungary, and Poland into its ranks. Why? Because there is potential for dangerous security competition in Europe, and the United States is determined to keep the forces of trouble at bay. Otherwise why would it be spending tens of billions of dollars annually to maintain a large military presence in Europe?

There is considerable evidence that the pacifier argument is widely accepted among policymakers and scholars on both sides of the Atlantic. For example, President Clinton told the West Point graduating class of 1997, "Some say we no longer need NATO because there is no powerful threat to our security now. I say there is no powerful threat in part because NATO is there."[53] That same year, Secretary of State Madeleine Albright told the U.S. Senate at her confirmation hearing, "We have an interest in European security, because we wish to avoid the instability that drew five million Americans across the Atlantic to fight in two world wars."[54] It appears that many Europeans also believe in the pacifier argument. Between 1990 and 1994, Robert Art conducted more than one hundred interviews with European political-military elites. He found that most believed that "if the Americans removed their security blanket from Europe . . . the Western European states could well return to the destructive power politics that they had just spent the last forty-five years trying to banish from their part of the continent."[55] Presumably that perspective is even more tightly held today, since the early 1990s was the heyday of optimism about the prospects for peace in Europe.

Finally, it is worth noting that Art, Michael Mandelbaum, and Stephen Van Evera, all prominent scholars who believe that Europe is primed for peace, favor keeping American troops there and maintaining a formidable NATO. Might it be that they are ultimately guided by pacifier logic, not their stated belief that great-power war is no longer a danger in Europe?[56]

Structure and Peace in the 1990s

There is no question that the presence of U.S. troops in Europe and Northeast Asia has played an important role in moderating security competition and promoting stability over the past decade. But periods of relative peace in those regions cannot be explained simply by the presence or absence of American forces. After all, there were no U.S. troops in Europe during the nineteenth century, yet there were long periods of relative peace. Moreover, even if the United States had committed military forces to Europe in the late 1930s, there still would have been intense security competition among the great powers, and Nazi Germany might have started a major war anyway.

To understand why the great powers were so tame in the 1990s, it is necessary to consider the overall distribution of power in each area, which means determining how much power is controlled by each major state in the region, as well as by the United States. In essence, we need to know whether the system is bipolar or multipolar, and if it is multipolar, whether it is unbalanced by the presence of a potential hegemon. Bipolar systems, as we saw in Chapter 9, tend to be the most peaceful, whereas unbalanced multipolar systems are the most prone to conflict. Balanced multipolar systems fall somewhere in between.

Europe remains bipolar in the wake of the Cold War, with Russia and the United States as the region's principal rivals. There are three particular aspects of Europe's bipolarity that make it especially stable. First, both Russia and the United States are armed with nuclear weapons, which are a force for peace. Second, the United States behaves as an offshore balancer in Europe, acting primarily as a check on any local great power that tries to dominate the region. It has no hegemonic aspirations beyond the Western Hemisphere, which significantly reduces the threat it presents to the states of Europe.[57] Third, Russia, which is a local great power that might have territorial ambitions, is too weak militarily to cause serious trouble outside of its own borders.[58]

Northeast Asia, on the other hand, is now a balanced multipolar system; China, Russia, and the United States are the relevant great powers, and none has the markings of a potential hegemon. Balanced multipolarity tends to be less stable than bipolarity, but the same three factors that enhanced the prospects for peace in bipolar Europe do likewise in multipolar Northeast Asia. First, China, Russia, and the United States all have nuclear arsenals, which makes them less likely to initiate war with each other. Second, although the United States is clearly the most powerful actor in the region, it is an offshore balancer without territorial aspirations. Third, neither the Chinese nor the Russian military has much power-projection capability, making it difficult for them to behave aggressively toward other states in the area.

There are two possible objections to my description of how power is distributed in Europe and Northeast Asia. Some might argue that the post–Cold War world is unipolar, which is another way of saying that the United States is a global hegemon.[59] If true, there would be hardly any security competition in Europe and Northeast Asia, because there would be no great powers in those areas—by definition—to challenge the mighty United States. This is certainly the state of affairs in the Western Hemisphere, where the United States is the only great power, and it is not involved in security competition with any of its its neighbors. Canada and Mexico, for example, pose no military threat whatsoever to the United States. Nor does Cuba, which is a minor political irritant, not a serious threat to American security.

But the international system is not unipolar.[60] Although the United States is a hegemon in the Western Hemisphere, it is not a global hegemon. Certainly the United States is the preponderant economic and military power in the world, but there are two other great powers in the international system: China and Russia. Neither can match American military might, but both have nuclear arsenals, the capability to contest and probably thwart a U.S. invasion of their homeland, and limited power-projection capability.[61] They are not Canada and Mexico.

Furthermore, hardly any evidence indicates that the United States is about to take a stab at establishing global hegemony. It certainly is determined to remain the hegemon in the Western Hemisphere, but given the difficulty of projecting power across large bodies of water, the United States is not going to use its military for offensive purposes in either Europe or Northeast Asia. Indeed, America's allies worry mainly that U.S. troops will be sent home, not that they will be used for conquest. This lack of a hegemonic impulse outside the confines of the Western Hemisphere explains why no balancing coalition has formed against the United States since the Cold War ended.[62]

Others might argue that America's allies from the Cold War—the United Kingdom, France, Germany, Italy, and Japan—should count as great powers, an accounting that would produce markedly different power distributions in Europe and Northeast Asia. There is little doubt that these states, especially Germany and Japan, have the potential in terms of population and wealth to become great powers (see Tables 10.1 and 10.2). They do not qualify for that ranking, however, because they depend in large part on the United States for their security; they are effectively semi-sovereign states, not great powers. In particular, Germany and Japan have no nuclear weapons of their own and instead rely on the American nuclear deterrent for protection.

In addition, America's allies have little maneuver room in their foreign policy, because of the presence of U.S. troops on their territory. The United States continues to occupy Western Europe and to dominate NATO decision-making, much the way it did during the Cold War, not only making war among its members unlikely, but also making it difficult for any of those states (especially Germany) to cause trouble with Russia.[63] Finally, the United States continues to maintain a formidable military presence in Japan, making it difficult for that potentially powerful state to engage in serious security competition with China.

In sum, a good deal of evidence indicates that power politics has not been stamped out of Europe and Northeast Asia, and that there is potential for serious trouble involving the great powers. Nevertheless, both regions have been largely free of intense security competition and great-power war during the 1990s. The taproot of that stability is the particular distribution of power that has emerged in each area since the Cold War ended and the Soviet Union collapsed. The question we must now ask is whether the structure of power in each of those regions is likely to remain intact over the next two decades.

TABLE 10.1

The Asian Balance of Power, 2000

	Potential power		Actual power	
	GNP	Population	Size of army	Number of nuclear warheads
China	$1.18 trillion	1.24 billion	2,200,000	410
Japan	$4.09 trillion	126 million	151,800	0
Russia	$0.33 trillion	147 million	348,000	10,000

NOTE: Two caveats are in order regarding China's GNP. First, as emphasized in Chapter 3, much more of China's GNP is tied up in agriculture than is the case for either Japan or the United States (18 percent versus 2 percent). As a result, the balance of latent power is a good deal more favorable to Japan than the numbers in this table indicate. Second, the World Bank measure for GNP that I employ is calculated by converting national currency units into dollars at prevailing exchange rates. Another way to measure GNP, however, is to use purchasing power parities; this method gives China a much larger GNP. For a discussion of the two approaches, see *World Development Indicators, 2000* (Washington, DC: World Bank, March 2000), pp. 10–13, 224, 283; *World Bank Atlas 2000*, pp. 14–15; and Murray Weidenbaum and Samuel Hughes, *The Bamboo Network: How Expatriate Entrepreneurs Are Creating a New Economic Superpower in Asia* (New York: Free Press, 1996), pp. 95–100. I use the World Bank's measure, because it does a better job of capturing a state's level of technological development, which is a key ingredient of military power.

SOURCES: GNP and population figures are for 1998 from *World Bank Atlas 2000* (Washington, DC: World Bank, April 2000), pp. 24–25, 42–43. Figures for army size are from International Institute for Strategic Studies [IISS], *The Military Balance, 2000/2001* (Oxford: Oxford University Press, October 2000), pp. 120–21, 194–95, 200. Figures on the nuclear arsenals are from Robert S. Norris and William M. Arkin, "Chinese Nuclear Forces, 2000," *Bulletin of the Atomic Scientists* 56, No. 6 (November–December 2000), pp. 78–79; and Robert S. Norris and William M. Arkin, "Russian Nuclear Forces, 2000," *Bulletin of the Atomic Scientists* 56, No. 4 (July–August 2000), pp. 70-71.

TABLE 10.2

The European Balance of Power, 2000

	Potential power		Actual power	
	GNP	Population	Size of army	Number of nuclear warheads
United Kingdom	$1.26 trillion	59 million	301,150	185
France	$1.47 trillion	59 million	411,800	470
Germany	$2.20 trillion	82 million	516,500	0
Italy	$1.16 trillion	58 million	164,900	0
Russia	$0.33 trillion	147 million	348,000	10,000

SOURCES: GNP and population figures are from the same source as in Table 10.1. Figures for army size are from IISS, *Military Balance, 2000/2001*, pp. 58, 61, 67, 80, 120–21. Figures on the nuclear arsenals are from Robert S. Norris and William M. Arkin, "French and British Nuclear Forces, 2000," *Bulletin of the Atomic Scientists* 56, No. 5 (September–October 2000), pp. 69–71; and Norris and Arkin, "Russian Nuclear Forces, 2000," pp. 70–71.

TROUBLE AHEAD

Predicting what the distribution of power will look like in Europe and Northeast Asia by 2020 involves two closely related tasks: 1) reckoning the power levels of the main actors located in each region, paying special attention to whether there is a potential hegemon among them; and 2) assessing the likelihood that the United States will remain militarily engaged in those regions, which depends largely on whether there is a potential hegemon among the local great powers that can be contained only with American help. It is difficult to predict the balance of power in a region, because it depends in good part on determining how fast each state's economy will grow, as well as its long-term political viability. Unfortunately, we do not have theories that can anticipate economic and political developments with high confidence. For example, it is hard to know how powerful the Chinese and Russian economies will be in 2020, or whether China will survive as a single political entity or break apart like the Soviet Union.

It is still possible, however, to make informed judgments about the architectures that are likely to emerge in Europe and Northeast Asia over the next twenty years. We can start with the conservative assumption that there will be no fundamental change in the *relative* wealth or political fortunes of the principal states in each region. In other words, the existing distribution of potential power remains essentially intact for the next two decades. Alternatively, we can assume significant change in state capabilities, focusing on the most weighty scenarios in each region, such as the complete collapse of Russian power or China's transformation into an economic superpower. The future of the American military presence in each region will depend on whether there is a potential hegemon.

I believe that the existing power structures in Europe and Northeast Asia are not sustainable through 2020. Two alternative futures loom on the horizon, both of which are likely to be less peaceful than the 1990s. If there is no significant change in the relative wealth or the political integrity of the key states located in each region, the United States is likely to bring its troops home, because they will not be needed to contain a potential hegemon. Removing American forces from either region, however, would change the structure of power in ways that would make conflict more likely than it is today. The structural change would be greater in Europe than in Northeast Asia, as would the likelihood of intensified security competition.

But if fundamental economic or political change occurs in either region and a potential hegemon emerges that the local powers cannot contain, U.S. troops are likely to remain in place or come back to the region to balance against that threat. Should that happen, an intense security competition would likely ensue between the potential hegemon and its rivals, including the United States. In short, either the United States will leave Europe or Northeast Asia because it does not have to contain an emerging peer competitor, in which case the region would becomes less stable, or the United States will stay engaged to contain a formidable rival in what is likely to be a dangerous situation. Either way, relations between the great powers are likely to become less peaceful than they were during the 1990s.

Before analyzing future power structures in Europe and Northeast Asia, it is necessary to look more closely at the claim that only the presence of a potential hegemon can keep the United States militarily engaged in those regions. A widely touted alternative perspective claims that American troops will stay put in the absence of a potential hegemon, because peace in those strategically important areas is a vital U.S. interest, and it would be difficult to achieve without the American pacifier. This claim needs to be examined.

THE FUTURE OF THE AMERICAN PACIFIER

The central aim of American foreign policy, as emphasized in Chapter 5, is to be the hegemon in the Western Hemisphere and have no rival hegemon in either Europe or Northeast Asia. The United States does not want a peer competitor. In the wake of the Cold War, U.S. policymakers remain firmly committed to that goal. Consider the following excerpt from an important Pentagon planning document that was leaked to the press in 1992: "Our first objective is to prevent the reemergence of a new rival . . . that poses a threat on the order of that posed formerly by the Soviet Union. . . . Our strategy must now refocus on precluding the emergence of any potential future global competitor."[64]

In pursuit of this goal, the United States has historically behaved as an offshore balancer in Europe and Northeast Asia. As pointed out in Chapter 7, it has committed troops to those areas only when there was a potential hegemon in the neighborhood that the local great powers could not contain by themselves. In effect, the United States has traditionally pursued a buck-passing strategy when faced with a potential peer competitor. Therefore, the future of the U.S. military commitments to Europe and Northeast Asia hinge on whether there is a potential hegemon in either of those regions that can be contained only with American help. If not, the one hundred thousand U.S. troops in each region would likely leave in the near future. As discussed below, no great power is likely to be in a position to overrun either Europe or Northeast Asia anytime soon, with the possible exception of China. Therefore, the United States will probably bring its troops home in the first decade or so of the new century.[65]

America the Peacekeeper

Nevertheless, a different rationale has emerged for maintaing a robust American military presence in those regions. The United States, so the argument goes, has a deep-seated interest in maintaining peace in Europe and Northeast Asia, and bringing its troops home would probably lead to instability, and maybe even great-power war.[66] Peace in these regions is said to be of vital importance to the United States for two reasons. For one thing, American economic prosperity would be undermined by a major war in either area. Given the high levels of economic interdependence among the world's wealthiest powers, a great-power war would not only badly damage the economies of the warring states, it would also seriously hurt the American economy, even if the United States managed to stay out of the fighting.

Moreover, the United States invariably gets dragged into distant great-power wars, which means it is an illusion for Americans to think that they can sit out a big war in either Europe or Northeast Asia. It therefore makes sense for the United States to maintain forces in those regions and preserve the peace, so that large numbers of Americans do not die in a future war. Presumably this perspective leads to an open-ended commitment of U.S. troops across both the Atlantic and the Pacific Oceans.

There is little doubt that peace in Europe and Northeast Asia is a desirable goal for the United States. The key issue, however, is whether peace is important enough to justify putting U.S. troops in harm's way, which is the risk the United States runs if it stations troops in those regions. In fact, peace in these two wealthy regions is not a vital American interest. The rationale for this alternative perspective is unconvincing and it receives little support from the historical record.

Consider the claim that a war in Europe or Northeast Asia would undermine American prosperity. It is based on assertion, not analysis. Indeed, the only study I know of on the subject contradicts that claim. It concludes that "the primary effect of overseas wars on the economies of neutral countries is to redistribute wealth from belligerents to non-combatants, enriching neutrals rather than impovershing them."[67] In essence, the United States would probably become more prosperous in the event of an Asian or a European war, and it would probably also gain relative power over the warring great powers. This is what happened to the United States when it was neutral in World War I: after some initial problems, the American economy flourished, while the economies of the European great powers were badly damaged.[68] There is little reason to think that a major war in Europe or Northeast Asia today would seriously damage the American economy, as it is "roughly as vulnerable to a major great power war in Asia as it was to World War I, but it is only half as vulnerable today to disruptions in Europe as it was early in the 20th Century."[69]

But even if this analysis is wrong and a great-power war in Europe or Northeast Asia would make Americans less prosperous, the United States is still unlikely to fight a major war just to ensure continued economic prosperity. Two prominent cases in recent times support this point. The United States did not use, or even seriously consider using, military force against any of the members of OPEC during the oil crisis of the mid-1970s, even though OPEC's actions at the time undermined American prosperity.[70] Furthermore, in the fall of 1990, the administration of President George H. W. Bush briefly tried to justify the impending Persian Gulf War on the grounds that Iraq's invasion of Kuwait had to be reversed because it threatened American jobs. This argument was heavily criticized and quickly abandoned.[71] If the United States was unwilling to fight a war against weak oil-producing states for the sake of economic prosperity, it is hard to imagine it engaging in a great-power war for the same purpose.

The claim that the United States invariably gets drawn into great-power wars in Europe and Northeast Asia is also not persuasive. Both the United Kingdom and the United States are offshore balancers who get pulled into great-power conflicts only when there is a potential hegemon in the region that the local great powers cannot contain by themselves. For example, both the United Kingdom and the United States were content to sit out the Franco-Prussian War (1870–71) and the Russo-Japanese War (1904–5), because neither was a hegemonic war. Moreover, the United States would not have entered World War I or World War II if the European great powers had been able to contain Germany by themselves. But in early 1917, and again in the summer of 1940, Germany threatened to overrun Europe, forcing the United States to accept a continental commitment.

One might counter that, if the United States stays put in Europe and Northeast Asia, there would be no great-power war and therefore no danger that Americans might have to suffer the horrible costs of war. But there are two related problems with this line of argument. Although an American military presence would probably make war less likely, there is no guarantee that a great-power conflict would not break out. For example, if the U.S. military stays put in Northeast Asia, it could plausibly end up in a war with China over Taiwan. Furthermore, if a great-power war did occur, the United States would surely be involved from the start, which does not make good strategic sense. It would be best for the United States either not to become involved in the fighting or, if it had to join the war, to do so later rather than earlier. That way the United States would pay a much smaller price than would the states that fought from start to finish, and it would be well-positioned at the war's end to win the peace and shape the postwar world to its advantage.

Putting these different rationales aside, what does the historical record tell us about American willingness to play the role of peacemaker or peacekeeper in Europe and Northeast Asia? As we saw in Chapter 7, hardly any evidence before 1990 shows that the United States is willing to commit troops to those regions to maintain peace. American armies were sent there to prevent the rise of peer competitors, not to maintain peace. One might concede this history but argue that the more relevant evidence is what happened during the 1990s, when American troops remained in Europe and Northeast Asia even though no great power threatened to dominate either region.

The 1990s: Anomaly or Precedent?

This is all true, of course, and what has happened so far does appear to contradict the predictions of offensive realism. A closer look at the situation, however, reveals that too little time has passed since the Cold War ended to make a judgment about whether U.S. forces will stay put in Europe and Northeast Asia in the absence of the Soviet Union or an equivalent great-power threat. The Soviet Union broke apart at the end of 1991, only ten years ago, and the last Russian troops were removed from the former East Germany in 1994, a mere seven years ago. Given the suddenness of the Soviet collapse, as well as its profound effect on the balance of power in Europe and Northeast Asia, there was no question that the United States would need time to figure out what the new architectures in each region meant for American interests. To give some historical perspective on this matter, remember that although World War I ended in 1918, U.S. troops were not completely withdrawn from Europe until 1923, and British troops remained on the continent until 1930 (twelve years after the war ended).

Simple inertia is also an important factor in delaying the American withdrawal. The United States has deployed large-scale military forces in Europe since 1943, when it invaded Italy during World War II, and in Northeast Asia since 1945, when it occupied Japan at the end of World War II. Moreover, both NATO and the American alliance structure in Northeast Asia are institutions with deep roots that helped win a spectacular victory in the Cold War. The United States would not walk away from them overnight.[72] Furthermore, maintaining forces in Europe and Northeast Asia since the 1990s has been relatively cheap and painless for the United States. Not only has the American economy flourished during that period, generating large budget surpluses in the process, but China and Russia have been easy to contain, because they are much weaker than the United States.

This matter of a lag time aside, there is considerable evidence that the United States and its allies from the Cold War are "drifting apart."[73] This trend is most apparent in Europe, where NATO's 1999 war against Serbia and its messy aftermath have damaged transatlantic relations and prompted the European Union to begin building a military force of its own that can operate independently of NATO—which means independently of the United States.[74] The United Kingdom, France, Germany, and Italy are slowly but inexorably realizing that they want to provide for their own security and control their own destiny. They are less willing to take orders from the United States than they were during the Cold War. Japan, too, is showing signs of independent behavior.[75] Moreover, the American commitment to defend Europe and Northeast Asia shows signs of weakening. Public opinion polls and congressional sentiment seem to indicate that the United States is at best a "reluctant sheriff" on the world stage, and that over time America's military role in those two strategically important areas is likely to diminish, not increase.[76]

Given that the United States is widely recognized to be a pacifying force in Europe and Northeast Asia, one might wonder why its allies would assert their independence from the United States, a move that is almost certain to cause transatlantic friction, if not a divorce. Some might say that this is evidence that America's former allies are balancing against the mighty United States. But that response is not convincing, because the United States has no appetite for conquest and domination outside of the Western Hemisphere; offshore balancers do not provoke balancing coalitions against themselves. Indeed, their main mission is to balance against dangerous rivals.

No, America's Cold War allies have started to act less like dependents of the United States and more like sovereign states because they fear that the offshore balancer that has protected them for so long might prove to be unreliable in a future crisis. The reliability of the United States was not a serious problem during the Cold War, because the Soviet threat provided a powerful incentive for the United States to protect its allies, who were too weak to defend themselves against an attack by the Warsaw Pact. Without that galvanizing threat, however, America has begun to look like a less dependable ally to states such as Germany and Japan, which are capable of protecting themselves from any threat in their own region.

One source of concern among America's allies in Europe and Northeast Asia is the widespread belief that it will inevitably draw down its forces in those regions; this belief raises doubts about the seriousness of the U.S. commitment, as well as the ability of the United States to act in a crisis to defend its allies.[77] The United States is also sure to pursue policies that will raise doubts about whether it is a wise and reliable ally, if only because U.S. interests are not identical to those of its allies. For example, President Clinton, hoping to improve Sino-American relations, visited China for nine days in 1998 without stopping in Japan. This trip's itinerary was seen by Japanese leaders as evidence that their alliance with the United States was weakening.[78] In Europe, the ongoing Kosovo crisis has raised doubts about American leadership. Moreover, the United States and its European allies have conflicting views about Middle East policy, about employing NATO forces outside of Europe, and especially about developing a national missile defense. Over time, differences of this sort are likely to cause America's allies to provide for their own security, rather than rely on the United States for protection.[79] The international system, as emphasized in Chapter 2, is a self-help world.

In sum, the brief history of the 1990s is not a good indicator of what the future holds for American military involvement in Europe and Northeast Asia. That issue will be resolved in the early years of the twenty-first century, and the determining factor will be whether there is a potential hegemon in either region that the United States must help contain. Only the threat of a peer competitor is likely to provide sufficient incentive for the United States to risk involvement in a distant great-power war. The United States is an offshore balancer, not the world's sheriff.

STRUCTURE AND CONFLICT IN TOMORROW'S EUROPE

Five European states now have sufficient wealth and population to be a great power: the United Kingdom, France, Germany, Italy, and Russia. Furthermore, Germany has the earmarking of a potential hegemon. Among European states, it is clearly the wealthiest, has the largest population save for Russia, and has the most powerful army in the region (see Table 10.2). Nevertheless, Germany is not a great power today, much less a potential hegemon, because it has no nuclear weapons of its own and because it is heavily dependent on the United States for its security. But if American troops were pulled out of Europe and Germany became responsible for its own defense, it would probably acquire its own nuclear arsenal and increase the size of its army, transforming itself into a potential hegemon.

To illustrate Germany's potential military might, consider the population and wealth differentials between Germany and Russia during the twentieth century. Although Russia has always enjoyed a significant population advantage over Germany, its present advantage is smaller than at any other time in the past hundred years. For example, Russia had approximately 2.6 times as many people as Germany in 1913 (175 million vs. 67 million), one year before World War I broke out, and twice as many people in 1940 (170 million vs. 85 million), one year before Nazi Germany invaded the Soviet Union.[80] This population disadvantage notwithstanding, Germany was a potential hegemon in both of those years. In 1987, a representative year of the Cold War, the Soviet Union had roughly 4.7 times as many people as West Germany (285 million vs. 61 million). Russia today, however, has only about 1.8 times as many people as Germany (147 million vs. 82 million).[81]

Despite its smaller population, Germany was a potential hegemon in Europe from 1903 to 1918 and from 1939 to 1945, primarily because it had a marked advantage in wealth over Russia. For example, Germany enjoyed roughly a 3.6:1 advantage in industrial might over Russia in 1913, and an approximately 1.3:1 advantage over the Soviet Union in 1940. Today, Germany has a startling 6.6:1 advantage in wealth over Russia.[82] Thus, Germany now has a significant advantage in latent military power over Russia, much like it had in the early twentieth century, when it was the dominant military power in Europe.

Regarding actual military might, the German army is superior to the Russian army. The size of Germany's standing army is 221,100 soldiers, and it can be quickly augmented by 295,400 reserves, thus creating a highly effective fighting force of more than half a million soldiers.[83] Russia has about 348,000 soldiers in its standing army, and although it has a large pool of reserves, they are poorly trained and Russia would have great difficulty mobilizing any of them quickly and efficiently in a crisis. Thus, those reserves contribute little to Russia's fighting power, and Germany therefore has a somewhat larger army than Russia. In terms of quality, the German army is well-trained and well-led, whereas the Russian army is neither. Only on the nuclear front does Russia dominate, but Germany has the wherewithal to rectify this asymmetry if it decides to acquire its own nuclear deterrent.

Although Germany is likely to become a potential hegemon if it has to provide for its own security, the United States is still likely to pull its forces out of Europe. Despite Germany's significant military potential, the other European powers should be able to keep it from dominating Europe without help from the United States. The United Kingdom, France, Italy, and Russia together have about three times as many people as Germany, and their combined wealth is roughly three times greater than Germany's. Plus, the United Kingdom, France, and Russia have nuclear weapons, which should be a strong deterrent against an expansionist Germany, even if it has its own nuclear weapons.

Yet Europe may not remain peaceful without the American pacifier. Indeed, there is likely to be intense security competition among the great powers, with the ever-present possibility that they might fight among themselves, because upon American withdrawal Europe would go from benign bipolarity to unbalanced multipolarity, the most dangerous kind of power structure. The United Kingdom, France, Italy, and Germany would have to build up their own military forces and provide for their own security. In effect, they would all become great powers, making Europe multipolar. And as we saw above, Germany would probably become a potential hegemon and thus the main source of trouble in the new Europe.

To illustrate the kind of trouble that might lie ahead, consider how particular German measures aimed at enhancing its security might nevertheless lead to instability. As discussed above, Germany would likely move to acquire its own nuclear arsenal if the United States removed its security umbrella from over western Europe. Not only are nuclear weapons an excellent deterrent, a point widely recognized by Germany's governing elites during the Cold War, but Germany would be surrounded by three nuclear-armed states—the United Kingdom, France, and Russia—leaving it vulnerable to nuclear coercion.[84] During the proliferation process, however, Germany's neighbors would probably contemplate using force to prevent it from going nuclear.

Furthermore, without the American military on its territory, Germany would probably increase the size of its army and it certainly would be more inclined to try to dominate central Europe. Why? Germany would fear Russian control of that critically important buffer zone between them, a situation that would directly threaten Germany. Of course, Russia would have the same fear about Germany, which would likely lead to a serious security competition between them for control of central Europe. France would undoubtedly view such behavior by Germany with alarm and take measures to protect itself from Germany. For example, France might increase its defense spending and establish closer relations with Russia. Germany would likely view these actions as hostile and respond with measures of its own.

So, the United States is likely to pull its troops back across the Atlantic Ocean in the years immediately ahead, if there is no significant change in the present distribution of potential power, even though that move is likely to intensify security competition in Europe and render it less peaceful.

Europe's future could turn out differently, however. The two most consequential scenarios involve Russia. In the first, Russia, not Germany, will become Europe's next potential hegemon. For that to happen, Russia, which already has a larger population than Germany, must also become the wealthier of the two states. Although it is difficult to predict the future of the Russian economy, it is hard to imagine Russia becoming wealthier than Germany in the next twenty years. But in the unlikely event that happens and Russia is once again a potential hegemon, the other European powers—the United Kingdom, France, Germany, and Italy—should be able to contain Russia without help from the United States. After all, Germany is now unified and wealthy, and Russia has only about half the population of the former Soviet Union, which makes it almost impossible for Russia to build a military machine as powerful as the Soviet army was in its heyday.[85] Of course, a wealthy Russia would not be a paper tiger, it would simply not be so formidable that American troops would be needed to contain it.

In the other scenario, the Russian economy collapses, possibly causing severe political turmoil, and Russia is effectively removed from the ranks of the great powers. Thus it will be able to do little to help contain Germany. This alternative future is not likely, either, but should it come to pass, U.S. troops would surely remain in Europe to help the United Kingdom, France, Italy, and Russia check German expansion. Both of these scenarios involve a potential hegemon (either Russia or Germany) in a multipolar Europe, a situation that is likely to result in dangerous security competition among the great powers.

STRUCTURE AND CONFLICT IN TOMORROW'S NORTHEAST ASIA

Three Northeast Asian states presently have sufficient population and wealth to be great powers: China, Japan, and Russia. But none is a potential hegemon. Japan is by far the wealthiest state in the region. Its gross national product (GNP) is about 3.5 times as large as China's and more than 12 times as large as Russia's (see Table 10.1). Nevertheless, Japan is not in a position to convert its substantial wealth into a decisive military advantage that could be used to threaten the rest of Northeast Asia.[86] Although Japan has much greater wealth than do either China or Russia, it has a relatively small population, especially compared to China's. In fact, China's population is almost ten times larger than Japan's, and it appears that the gap between them will widen further over the next fifty years.[87] Thus, it would be almost impossible for Japan to build an army that is more powerful than China's army. Japan could certainly build an army that is qualitatively superior to China's, but not so much better that it would offset the 10:1 advantage in numbers that China could maintain because of its huge population.

Japan would also face a serious power-projection problem if it tried to overrun Northeast Asia. It is an insular state that is physically separated from the Asian mainland by a substantial body of water. Thus, unless Japan is able to secure a foothold on the Asian continent—which is unlikely—it would have to invade the Asian mainland from the sea to conquer it. This was not a problem between 1895 and 1945, because China and Korea were so weak that Japan had little difficulty establishing and maintaining a large army on the continent. China and Korea are much more formidable adversaries today, and they would surely use their armies to oppose a Japanese invasion of the Asian mainland. Amphibious operations against territory controlled by China and Korea would be a daunting task. In short, if Japan shakes loose the United States and becomes a great power in the next decade or so, it is more likely to look like the United Kingdom in mid-nineteenth-century Europe than Japan in the first half of the twentieth century.

There is also little chance that Russia will become a potential hegemon in Northeast Asia by 2020. It is hard to imagine Russia building a more powerful economy than Japan's anytime soon. But even if Russia experiences spectacular economic growth, it still has essentially the same population problem vis-à-vis China that Japan faces. Specifically, China has more than eight times as many people as Russia and the gap between them is likely to widen over time.[88] Thus, not even a wealthy Russia is likely to be able to field an army more powerful than China's. Russia's problems are further compounded by the fact it has significant security concerns in Europe and on its southern borders, which limit the military resources it can devote to Northeast Asia.[89]

China is the key to understanding the future distribution of power in Northeast Asia.[90] It is clearly not a potential hegemon today, because it is not nearly as wealthy as Japan. But if China's economy continues expanding over the next two decades at or near the rate it has been growing since the early 1980s, China will likely surpass Japan as the wealthiest state in Asia. Indeed, because of the vast size of China's population, it has the potential to become much wealthier than Japan, and even wealthier than the United States.

To illustrate China's potential, consider the following scenarios. Japan's per capita GNP is now more than 40 times greater than China's.

If China modernizes to the point where it has about the same per capita GNP as South Korea does today, China would have a GNP of $10.66 trillion, substantially larger than Japan's $4.09 trillion economy (see Table 10.3). If China's per capita GNP grew to be just half of Japan's present per capita GNP, China would have a GNP of $20.04 trillion, which would make China almost five times as wealthy as Japan. Finally, if China had about the same per capita GNP as Japan, China would be ten times as wealthy as Japan, because China has almost ten times as many people as Japan.

Another way of illustrating how powerful China might become if its economy continues growing rapidly is to compare it with the United States. The GNP of the United States is $7.9 trillion. If China's per capita GNP equals Korea's, China's overall GNP would be almost $10.66 trillion, which is about 1.35 times the size of America's GNP. If China's per capita GNP is half of Japan's, China's overall GNP would then be roughly 2.5 times bigger than America's. For purposes of comparison, the Soviet Union was roughly one-half as wealthy as the United States during most of the Cold War (see Table 3.5). China, in short, has the potential to be considerably more powerful than even the United States.

TABLE 10.3

China's Economy in Perspective

U.S. GNP (1998)	$ 7.90 trillion
Japan's GNP (1998)	$ 4.09 trillion
China's GNP (1998)	$ 1.18 trillion
China's GNP if it had South Korea's per capita GNP	$ 10.66 trillion
China's GNP if it had half of Japan's per capita GNP	$ 20.04 trillion
China's GNP if it had Japan's per capita GNP	$ 40.08 trillion

SOURCE: All calculations are based on data from *World Bank Atlas 2000*.

It is difficult to predict where the Chinese economy is headed in the twenty-first century and thus whether China will overtake Japan and become a potential hegemon in Northeast Asia.[91] Nonetheless, the principal ingredients of military power in that region are likely to be distributed in one of two ways in the decades ahead.

First, if China's economy stops growing at a rapid pace and Japan remains the wealthiest state in Northeast Asia, neither would become a potential hegemon and the United States would likely bring its troops home. If that happened, Japan would almost surely establish itself as a great power, building its own nuclear deterrent and significantly increasing the size of its conventional forces. But there would still be balanced multipolarity in the region: Japan would replace the United States, and China and Russia would remain the region's other great powers. In short, an American exit would not change the basic structure of power in Northeast Asia, and presumably would not make war more or less likely than it is today.

Nevertheless, substituting Japan for the United States would increase the likelihood of instability in Northeast Asia. Whereas the United States has a robust nuclear deterrent that contributes to peace, Japan has no nuclear weapons of its own and would have to build its own nuclear arsenal. That proliferation process, however, would be fraught with dangers, especially because China, and maybe Russia, would be tempted to use force to prevent a nuclear Japan. In addition, the deep-seated fear of Japan in Asia that is a legacy of its behavior between 1931 and 1945 would surely be fanned if Japan acquired a nuclear deterrent, intensifying security competition in the region. Furthermore, as an offshore balancer, the United States has hardly any interest in conquering territory in Northeast Asia. As noted above, Japan would face profound limits on its ability to project power onto the Asian mainland as long as China remains a great power. Still, Japan has territorial disputes with China over the Senkaku/Diaoyutai Islands, with Korea over the Takeshima/Tokto Islets, and with Russia over the Kurile Islands. Finally, although China is militarily too weak to fight a major war with the mighty United States, China is not likely to be as outgunned by Japan, which simply does not have the population nor the wealth to fully replace America's military power.

The second possible distribution of power would result if China's economy continues growing at a robust pace and it eventually becomes a potential hegemon. The United States would either remain in Northeast Asia or return someday to make sure that China does not become a peer competitor. Japan and Russia together are unlikely to have the wherewithal to contain China, even if India, South Korea, and Vietnam were to join the balancing coalition. Not only would China be much wealthier than any of its Asian rivals in this scenario, but its huge population advantage would allow it to build a far more powerful army than either Japan or Russia could. China would also have the resources to acquire an impressive nuclear arsenal. Northeast Asia would obviously be an unbalanced multipolar system if China threatened to dominate the entire region; as such it would be a far more dangerous place than it is now. China, like all previous potential hegemons, would be strongly inclined to become a real hegemon, and all of its rivals, including the United States, would encircle China to try to keep it from expanding. Engagement policies and the like would not dull China's appetite for power, which would be considerable.

In sum, although the power structures that are now in place in Europe and Northeast Asia are benign, they are not sustainable over the next twenty years. The most likely scenario in Europe is an American exit coupled with the emergence of Germany as the dominant state. In effect, the region will probably move from its present bipolarity to unbalanced multipolarity, which will lead to more intense security competition among the European great powers. In Northeast Asia, the power structure is likely to evolve in one of two ways: 1) If China does not become a potential hegemon, the United States is likely to pull its troops out of the area, causing Japan to become a formidable great power. The system, however, would remain multipolar and balanced. Still, security competition would be somewhat more intense than it is today because of problems associated with Japan's replacing the United States in the regional lineup of great powers. 2) If China emerges as a potential hegemon, Northeast Asia's multipolarity would become unbalanced and the United States would keep forces in the region to contain China.

CONCLUSION

What are the implications of the preceding analysis for future American national security policy? It is clear that the most dangerous scenario the United States might face in the early twenty-first century is one in which China becomes a potential hegemon in Northeast Asia. Of course, China's prospects of becoming a potential hegemon depend largely on whether its economy continues modernizing at a rapid pace. If that happens, and China becomes not only a leading producer of cutting-edge technologies, but the world's wealthiest great power, it would almost certainly use its wealth to build a mighty military machine. Moreover, for sound strategic reasons, it would surely pursue regional hegemony, just as the United States did in the Western Hemisphere during the nineteenth century. So we would expect China to attempt to dominate Japan and Korea, as well as other regional actors, by building military forces that are so powerful that those other states would not dare challenge it. We would also expect China to develop its own version of the Monroe Doctrine, directed at the United States. Just as the United States made it clear to distant great powers that they were not allowed to meddle in the Western Hemisphere, China will make it clear that American interference in Asia is unacceptable.

What makes a future Chinese threat so worrisome is that it might be far more powerful and dangerous than any of the potential hegemons that the United States confronted in the twentieth century. Neither Wilhelmine Germany, nor imperial Japan, nor Nazi Germany, nor the Soviet Union had nearly as much latent power as the United States had during their confrontations (see Tables 3.5 and 6.2). But if China were to become a giant Hong Kong, it would probably have somewhere on the order of four times as much latent power as the United States does, allowing China to gain a decisive military advantage over the United States in Northeast Asia.[92] In that circumstance, it is hard to see how the United States could prevent China from becoming a peer competitor. Moreover, China would likely be a more formidable superpower than the United States in the ensuing global competition between them.

This analysis suggests that the United States has a profound interest in seeing Chinese economic growth slow considerably in the years ahead. For much of the past decade, however, the United States has pursued a strategy intended to have the opposite effect. The United States has been committed to "engaging" China, not "containing" it. Engagement is predicated on the liberal belief that if China could be made both democratic and prosperous, it would become a status quo power and not engage in security competition with the United States. As a result, American policy has sought to integrate China into the world economy and facilitate its rapid economic development, so that it becomes wealthy and, one would hope, content with its present position in the international system.

This U.S. policy on China is misguided. A wealthy China would not be a status quo power but an aggressive state determined to achieve regional hegemony. This is not because a rich China would have wicked motives, but because the best way for any state to maximize its prospects for survival is to be the hegemon in its region of the world. Although it is certainly in China's interest to be the hegemon in Northeast Asia, it is clearly not in America's interest to have that happen.

China is still far away from the point where it has enough latent power to make a run at regional hegemony. So it is not too late for the United States to reverse course and do what it can to slow the rise of China. In fact, the structural imperatives of the international system, which are powerful, will probably force the United States to abandon its policy of constructive engagement in the near future. Indeed, there are signs that the new Bush administration has taken the first steps in this direction.

Of course, states occasionally ignore the anarchic world in which they operate, choosing instead to pursue strategies that contradict balance-of-power logic. The United States is a good candidate for behaving in that way, because American political culture is deeply liberal and correspondingly hostile to realist ideas. It would be a grave mistake, however, for the United States to turn its back on the realist principles that have served it well since its founding.

NOTES

PREFACE

1. C. Wright Mills, *The Sociological Imagination* (New York: Oxford University Press, 1959), p. 221.

CHAPTER ONE

1. The phrase "perpetual peace" was made famous by Immanuel Kant. See his "Perpetual Peace," in Hans Reiss, ed., *Kant's Political Writings*, trans. H. B. Nisbet (Cambridge: Cambridge University Press, 1970), pp. 93–130. Also see John Mueller, *Retreat from Doomsday: The Obsolescence of Major War* (New York: Basic Books, 1989); Michael Mandelbaum, "Is Major War Obsolete?" *Survival* 40, No. 4 (Winter 1998–99), pp. 20–38; and Francis Fukuyama, "The End of History?" *The National Interest*, No. 16 (Summer 1989), pp. 3–18, which was the basis of Francis Fukuyama, *The End of History and the Last Man* (New York: Free Press, 1992).

2. Charles L. Glaser, "Realists as Optimists: Cooperation as Self-Help," *International Security* 19, No. 3 (Winter 1994–95), pp. 50–90.

3. The balance of power is a concept that has a variety of meanings. See Inis L. Claude, Jr., *Power and International Relations* (New York: Random House, 1962), chap. 2; and Ernst B. Haas, "The Balance of Power: Prescription, Concept, or Propaganda?" *World Politics* 5, No. 4 (July 1953), pp. 442–77. I use it to mean the actual distribution of military assets among the great powers in the system.

4. Quoted in Lothar Gall, *Bismarck: The White Revolutionary*, vol. 1, *1851–1871*, trans. J. A. Underwood (London: Unwin Hyman, 1986), p. 59.

5. Nevertheless, the theory has relevance for smaller powers, although for some more than for others. Kenneth Waltz puts the point well when he writes, "A general theory of international politics . . . once written also applies to lesser states that interact insofar as their interactions are insulated from the intervention of the great powers of a system, whether by the relative indifference of the latter or by difficulties of communication and transportation." Waltz, *Theory of International Politics* (Reading, MA: Addison-Wesley, 1979), p. 73.

6. For other definitions of a great power, see Jack S. Levy, *War in the Modern Great Power System, 1495–1975* (Lexington: University Press of Kentucky, 1983), pp. 10–19.

7. There is little disagreement among scholars about which states qualified as the great powers between 1792 and 1990. See Levy, *War,* chap. 2; and J. David Singer and Melvin Small, *The Wages of War, 1816–1965: A Statistical Handbook* (New York: Wiley, 1972), p. 23. I have accepted the conventional wisdom because it appears to be generally consistent with my definition of a great power, and to analyze each potential great power "on a case-by-case basis would be prohibitive in time and resources, and in the end it might make little difference." Levy, *War,* p. 26. Russia (the Soviet Union from 1917 to 1991) is the only state that was a great power for the entire period. The United Kingdom and Germany (Prussia before 1870) were great powers from 1792 to 1945, and France was a great power from 1792 until it was defeated and occupied by Nazi Germany in 1940. Some scholars label the United Kingdom, France, and Germany as great powers after 1945 and classify the much more powerful Soviet Union and United States as superpowers. I do not find these labels useful. Although I sometimes refer to the United States and the Soviet Union as superpowers, they were the great powers in the system during the Cold War, when the United Kingdom, France, and Germany (as well as China and Japan) lacked the military capability to qualify as great powers. Italy is treated as a great power from 1861 until 1943, when it collapsed in World War II. Austria-Hungary (Austria before 1867) was a great power from 1792 until it disintegrated in 1918. Japan is considered a great power from 1895 until 1945, and the United States is usually designated a great power from 1898 until 1990. Regarding the period from 1991 to 2000, China (which is treated as a great power from 1991 onward), Russia, and the United States are considered great powers for reasons discussed in Chapter 10.

8. Quoted in Stephen Van Evera, *Causes of War: Power and the Roots of Conflict* (Ithaca, NY: Cornell University Press, 1999), p. 2.

9. William J. Clinton, "Commencement Address," United States Military Academy, West Point, NY, May 31, 1997. Also see *A National Security Strategy of Engagement and Enlargement* (Washington, DC: The White House, February 1996).

10. Strobe Talbott, "Why NATO Should Grow," *New York Review of Books,* August 10, 1995, pp. 27–28. Also see Strobe Talbott, "Democracy and the National Interest," *Foreign Affairs* 75, No. 6 (November–December 1996), pp. 47–63.

11. Madeleine Albright, "A Presidential Tribute to Gerald Ford," speech at Ford Museum Auditorium, Grand Rapids, MI, April 16, 1997. Also see Madeleine

Albright, "Commencement Address," Harvard University, Cambridge, MA, June 5, 1997; and Richard Holbrooke, "America, A European Power," *Foreign Affairs* 74, No. 2 (March–April 1995), pp. 38–51.

12. On what constitutes a sound theory, see Stephen Van Evera, *Guide to Methods for Students of Political Science* (Ithaca, NY: Cornell University Press, 1997), pp. 17–21.

13. The key work on this subject is Marc Trachtenberg, *A Constructed Peace: The Making of the European Settlement, 1945–1963* (Princeton, NJ: Princeton University Press, 1999).

14. Although NATO employed a defensive strategy vis-à-vis the Warsaw Pact throughout the Cold War, Samuel Huntington argued instead for an offensive strategy in an article that generated considerable controversy within the security community. See Samuel P. Huntington, "Conventional Deterrence and Conventional Retaliation in Europe," *International Security* 8, No. 3 (Winter 1983–84), pp. 32–56.

15. This point is made clear in Michael W. Doyle, *Ways of War and Peace: Realism, Liberalism, and Socialism* (New York: Norton, 1997); and Brian C. Schmidt, *The Political Discourse of Anarchy: A Disciplinary History of International Relations* (Albany: State University of New York Press, 1998).

16. E. H. Carr, *The Twenty Years' Crisis, 1919–1939: An Introduction to the Study of International Relations,* 2d ed. (London: Macmillan, 1962; the first edition was published in 1939); Hans Morgenthau, *Politics among Nations: The Struggle for Power and Peace,* 5th ed. (New York: Knopf, 1973; the first edition was published in 1948); and Waltz, *Theory of International Politics.*

17. Carr, *Twenty Years' Crisis,* chap. 4; Kenneth Waltz, "The Myth of National Interdependence," in Charles P. Kindelberger, ed., *The International Corporation* (Cambridge, MA: MIT Press, 1970), pp. 205–223; and Waltz, *Theory of International Politics,* chap. 7.

18. See Morgenthau, *Politics among Nations,* chaps. 14, 21; and Kenneth N. Waltz, "The Stability of a Bipolar World," *Daedalus* 93, No. 3 (Summer 1964), pp. 881–909.

19. For further evidence of those differences, see *Security Studies* 5, No. 2 (Winter 1995–96, special issue on "Roots of Realism," ed. Benjamin Frankel); and *Security Studies* 5, No. 3 (Spring 1996, special issue on "Realism: Restatements and Renewal," ed. Benjamin Frankel).

20. See F. H. Hinsley, *Power and the Pursuit of Peace: Theory and Practice in the History of Relations between States* (Cambridge: Cambridge University Press, 1967), pt. I; Torbjorn L. Knutsen, *A History of International Relations Theory: An Introduction* (New York: Manchester University Press, 1992), chap. 5; and F. Parkinson, *The Philosophy of International Relations: A Study in the History of Thought* (Beverly Hills, CA: Sage Publications, 1977), chap. 4.

21. See Andrew Moravcsik, "Taking Preferences Seriously: A Liberal Theory of International Politics," *International Organization* 51, No. 4 (Autumn 1997), pp. 513–53.

22. See Michael Howard, *War and the Liberal Conscience* (New Brunswick, NJ: Rutgers University Press, 1978).

23. See *inter alia* Norman Angell, *The Great Illusion: A Study of the Relation of Military Power in Nations to Their Economic and Social Advantage*, 3d rev. and enl. ed. (New York: G. P. Putnam's, 1912); Thomas L. Friedman, *The Lexus and the Olive Tree: Understanding Globalization* (New York: Farrar, Straus and Giroux, 1999); Edward D. Mansfield, *Power, Trade, and War* (Princeton, NJ: Princeton University Press, 1994); Susan M. McMillan, "Interdependence and Conflict," *Mershon International Studies Review* 41, Suppl. 1 (May 1997), pp. 33–58; and Richard Rosecrance, *The Rise of the Trading State: Commerce and Conquest in the Modern World* (New York: Basic Books, 1986).

24. Among the key works on democratic peace theory are Michael E. Brown, Sean M. Lynn-Jones, and Steven E. Miller, eds., *Debating the Democratic Peace* (Cambridge, MA: MIT Press, 1996), pts. I and III; Michael Doyle, "Liberalism and World Politics," *American Political Science Review* 80, No. 4 (December 1986), pp. 1151–69; Fukuyama, "End of History?"; John M. Owen IV, *Liberal Peace, Liberal War: American Politics and International Security* (Ithaca, NY: Cornell University Press, 1997); James L. Ray, *Democracy and International Conflict: An Evaluation of the Democratic Peace Proposition* (Columbia: University of South Carolina Press, 1995); and Bruce Russett, *Grasping the Democratic Peace: Principles for a Post–Cold War World* (Princeton, NJ: Princeton University Press, 1993). Some scholars argue that democracies are more peaceful than non-democracies, regardless of the regime type of their adversary. But the evidence for this proposition is weak; stronger evidence exists for the claim that the pacific effects of democracy are limited to relations between democratic states.

25. See *inter alia* David A. Baldwin, ed., *Neorealism and Neoliberalism: The Contemporary Debate* (New York: Columbia University Press, 1993); Robert O. Keohane, *After Hegemony: Cooperation and Discord in the World Political Economy* (Princeton, NJ: Princeton University Press, 1984); *International Organization* 36, No. 2 (Spring 1982, special issue on "International Regimes," ed. Stephen D. Krasner); Lisa L. Martin and Beth A. Simmons, "Theories and Empirical Studies of International Institutions," *International Organization* 52, No. 4 (Autumn 1998), pp. 729–57; and John G. Ruggie, *Constructing the World Polity: Essays on International Institutionalization* (New York: Routledge, 1998), chaps. 8–10. Regimes and international law are synonymous with institutions, since all are essentially rules that states negotiate among themselves.

26. Carr, *Twenty Years' Crisis*, p. 10.

27. Although realists believe that the international system allows for little variation in the external conduct of great powers, they recognize that there are sometimes profound differences in how governments deal with their own people. For example, although the Soviet Union and the United States behaved similarly toward each other during the Cold War, there is no question that the leaders of each superpower treated their citizens in fundamentally different ways. Thus, one can rather easily distinguish between good and bad states when assessing internal conduct. Such distinctions, however, tell us relatively little about international politics.

28. Morgenthau is something of an exception regarding this second belief. Like other realists, he does not distinguish between good and bad states, and he clearly recognizes that external environment shapes state behavior. However, the desire for power, which he sees as the main driving force behind state behavior, is an internal characteristic of states.

29. Carl von Clausewitz, *On War*, trans. and ed. Michael Howard and Peter Paret (Princeton, NJ: Princeton University Press, 1976), esp. books 1, 8. Also see Richard K. Betts, "Should Strategic Studies Survive?" *World Politics* 50, No. 1 (October 1997), pp. 7–33, esp. p. 8; and Michael I. Handel, *Masters of War: Classical Strategic Thought*, 3d ed. (London: Frank Cass, 2001).

30. Michael J. Smith notes in *Realist Thought from Weber to Kissinger* (Baton Rouge: Louisiana State University Press, 1986) that Carr does not "explain why politics always involves power, an explanation vital to any attempt to channel the exercise of power along lines compatible with an ordered social existence. Is a lust for power basic to human nature—the view of Niebuhr and Morgenthau—. . . [or] is it the result of a security dilemma?" (p. 93).

31. George F. Kennan, *American Diplomacy, 1900–1950* (Chicago: University of Chicago Press, 1951). Smith writes, "Kennan nowhere offers a systematic explanation of his approach to international politics or of his political philosophy in general: he is a diplomat turned historian, not a theologian or a political theorist, and he is concerned neither to propound a doctrine of human nature nor to set forth the recurring truths of international politics in a quasi-doctrinal way." Smith, *Realist Thought*, p. 166.

32. Human nature realism lost much of its appeal in the early 1970s for a variety of reasons. The backlash against the Vietnam War surely contributed to its demise, since any theory that saw the pursuit of military power as inevitable was likely to be unpopular on university campuses by 1970. [Ironically, Morgenthau was an early and vocal critic of the Vietnam War. See Hans J. Morgenthau, *Vietnam and the United States* (Washington, DC: Public Affairs, 1965); and "Bernard Johnson's Interview with Hans J. Morgenthau," in Kenneth Thompson and Robert J. Myers, eds., *Truth and Tragedy: A Tribute to Hans J. Morgenthau* (New Brunswick, NJ: Transaction Books, 1984), pp. 382–84.] Furthermore, the collapse of the Bretton Woods system in 1971, the oil shock of 1973, and the growing power of multinational corporations (MNCs) led many to think that economic issues had become more important than security issues, and that realism, especially Morgenthau's brand, had little to say about questions of international political economy. Some even argued in the early 1970s that MNCs and other transnational forces were threatening the integrity of the state itself. "Sovereignty at bay" was a widely used phrase at the time. Finally, human nature realism was essentially a philosophical theory that was out of sync with the behavioral revolution that was overwhelming the study of international politics in the early 1970s. Morgenthau intensely disliked modern social science theories, but he was badly outnumbered in this war of ideas and his theory lost much of its legitimacy. For Morgenthau's views on social science, see Hans J. Morgenthau, *Scientific Man vs. Power Politics* (Chicago: University of Chicago Press, 1946). For a recent but rare example of human nature realism, see Samuel P. Huntington, "Why International Primacy Matters," *International Security* 17, No. 4 (Spring 1993), pp. 68–71. Also see Bradley A. Thayer, "Bringing in Darwin: Evolutionary Theory, Realism, and International Politics," *International Security* 25, No. 2 (Fall 2000), pp. 124–51.

33. See Morgenthau, *Politics among Nations;* and Morgenthau, *Scientific Man.* Although Morgenthau is the most famous human nature realist, Reinhold Niebuhr was also a major intellectual force in this school of thought. See Niebuhr's *Moral Man and Immoral Society* (New York: Scribner's, 1932). Friedrich Meinecke made the case for human nature realism at considerable length well before Morgenthau began publishing his views on international politics in the mid-1940s. See Meinecke's *Machiavellism: The Doctrine of Raison d'Etat and Its Place in Modern History,* trans. Douglas Scott (Boulder, CO: Westview, 1984), which was originally published in Germany in 1924 but was not published in English until 1957. Morgenthau, who was educated in Germany, was familiar with *Machiavellism,* according to his former student Kenneth W. Thompson. Correspondence with author, August 9, 1999. Also see Christoph Frei, *Hans J. Morgenthau: An Intellectual Biography* (Baton Rouge: Louisiana State University Press, 2001), pp. 207–26.

34. Morgenthau, *Scientific Man,* p. 194. Also see Morgenthau, *Politics among Nations,* p. 208.

35. Morgenthau, *Scientific Man,* p. 192. Despite his claim that "the desire to attain a maximum of power is universal" *(Politics among Nations,* p. 208), Morgenthau distinguishes between status quo and revisionist powers in his writings. *Politics among Nations,* pp. 40–44, 64–73. But there is an obvious problem here: if all states have a "limitless aspiration for power" *(Politics among Nations,* p. 208), how can there be status quo powers in the world? Moreover, although Morgenthau emphasizes that the drive for power is located in human nature, he also recognizes that the structure of the international system creates powerful incentives for states to pursue offense. He writes, for example, "Since . . . all nations live in constant fear lest their rivals deprive them, at the first opportune moment, of their power position, all nations have a vital interest in anticipating such a development and doing unto the others what they do not want the others to do unto them" *(Politics among Nations,* p. 208). However, if all states have a vital interest in taking advantage of each other whenever the opportunity presents itself, how can there be status quo powers in the system? Indeed, this incentive structure would seem to leave no room for satiated powers. Again, Morgenthau provides no explanation for this apparent contradiction. Arnold Wolfers notes this same problem in Morgenthau's work. See Wolfers's *Discord and Collaboration: Essays on International Politics* (Baltimore, MD: Johns Hopkins University Press, 1962), pp. 84–86.

36. Waltz's other key works on realism include *Man, the State, and War: A Theoretical Analysis* (New York: Columbia University Press, 1959); "Theory of International Relations," in Fred I. Greenstein and Nelson W. Polsby, eds., *The Handbook of Political Science,* vol. 8, *International Politics* (Reading, MA: Addison-Wesley, 1975), pp. 1–85; "The Origins of War in Neorealist Theory," in Robert I. Rotberg and Theodore K. Rabb, eds., *The Origin and Prevention of Major Wars* (Cambridge: Cambridge University Press, 1989), pp. 39–52; and "Reflections on *Theory of International Politics:* A Response to My Critics," in Robert Keohane, ed., *Neorealism and Its Critics* (New York: Columbia University Press, 1986), pp. 322–45. Unlike Morgenthau's *Politics among Nations,* Waltz's *Theory of International Politics* clearly qualifies as a work of modern social science (esp. its chap. 1).

37. Structural theories emphasize that the configuration of the international system sharply constrains the behavior of the great powers and forces them to act in similar ways. Thus, we should expect to find common patterns of great-power behavior in anarchic systems. Nevertheless, anarchic systems themselves can be configured differently, depending on the number of great powers and how power is distributed among them. As discussed in subsequent chapters, those structural differences sometimes cause important variations in state behavior.

38. Waltz, *Theory of International Politics,* p. 126. Also see ibid., pp. 118, 127; and Joseph M. Grieco, "Anarchy and the Limits of Cooperation: A Realist Critique of the Newest Liberal Institutionalism," *International Organization* 42, No. 3 (Summer 1988), pp. 485–507, which builds directly on Waltz's claim that states are mainly concerned with preserving their share of world power.

39. Randall L. Schweller, "Neorealism's Status-Quo Bias: What Security Dilemma?" *Security Studies* 5, No. 3 (Spring 1996, special issue), pp. 90–121. Also see Keith L. Shimko, "Realism, Neorealism, and American Liberalism," *Review of Politics* 54, No. 2 (Spring 1992), pp. 281–301.

40. Waltz, *Theory of International Politics,* chaps. 6, 8. The other key work emphasizing that states have a powerful tendency to balance against aggressors is Stephen M. Walt, *The Origins of Alliances* (Ithaca, NY: Cornell University Press, 1987).

41. See Waltz, *Theory of International Politics,* chap. 8; and Waltz, "Origins of War."

42. Waltz, "Origins of War," p. 40.

43. The key works include Robert Jervis, "Cooperation under the Security Dilemma," *World Politics* 30, No. 2 (January 1978), pp. 167–214; Jack L. Snyder, *Myths of Empire: Domestic Politics and International Ambition* (Ithaca, NY: Cornell University Press, 1991), esp. chaps. 1–2; and Van Evera, *Causes of War,* esp. chap. 6. Also see Glaser, "Realists as Optimists"; and Robert Powell, *In the Shadow of Power: States and Strategies in International Politics* (Princeton, NJ: Princeton University Press, 1999), esp. chap. 3. George Quester's *Offense and Defense in the International System* (New York: Wiley, 1977) is an important book on the offense-defense balance, although he is generally not considered a defensive realist. For an overview of the literature on the subject, see Sean M. Lynn-Jones, "Offense-Defense Theory and Its Critics," *Security Studies* 4, No. 4 (Summer 1995), pp. 660–91.

44. Jervis has a more qualified view on this point than either Snyder or Van Evera. See Snyder, *Myths of Empire,* pp. 22–24; Van Evera, *Causes of War,* pp. 118, 191, 255.

45. Grieco, "Anarchy and the Limits of Cooperation," p. 500.

46. Some defensive realists emphasize that great powers seek to maximize security, not relative power. "The ultimate concern of states," Waltz writes, "is not for power but for security." Waltz, "Origins of War," p. 40. There is no question that great powers maximize security, but that claim by itself is vague and provides little insight into actual state behavior. The important question is, How do states maximize security? My answer: By maximizing their share of world power. Defensive realists' answer: By preserving the existing balance of power. Snyder puts the point well in *Myths of Empire* when he writes that both offensive and defensive realists "accept that security is normally the strongest motivation of states in international anarchy, but they have opposite views about the most effective way to achieve it" (pp. 11–12).

47. G. Lowes Dickinson, *The European Anarchy* (New York: Macmillan, 1916). Also see G. Lowes Dickinson, *The International Anarchy, 1904–1914* (New York: Century Company, 1926), esp. chap. 1.

48. Dickinson, *European Anarchy,* pp. 14, 101.

49. Eric Labs, Nicholas Spykman, and Martin Wight also make the case for offensive realism in their writings, although none lays the theory out in any detail.

See Eric J. Labs, "Offensive Realism and Why States Expand Their War Aims," *Security Studies* 6, No. 4, pp.1–49; Nicholas J. Spykman, *America's Strategy in World Politics: The United States and the Balance of Power* (New York: Harcourt, Brace, 1942), introduction and chap. 1; and Martin Wight, *Power Politics,* eds. Hedley Bull and Carsten Holbraad (New York: Holmes and Meier, 1978), chaps. 2, 3, 9, 14, 15. One also catches glimpses of the theory in Herbert Butterfield, *Christianity and History* (New York: Scribner's, 1950), pp. 89–91; Dale C. Copeland, *The Origins of Major War* (Ithaca, NY: Cornell University Press, 2000), passim; Robert Gilpin, *War and Change in World Politics* (Cambridge: Cambridge University Press, 1981), pp. 87–88; John H. Herz, "Idealist Internationalism and the Security Dilemma," *World Politics* 2, No. 2 (January 1950), p. 157; John H. Herz, *Political Realism and Political Idealism* (Chicago: University of Chicago Press, 1951), pp. 14–15, 23–25, 206; A.F.K. Organski, *World Politics,* 2d ed. (New York: Knopf, 1968), pp. 274, 279, 298; Frederick L. Schuman, *International Politics: An Introduction to the Western State System* (New York: McGraw-Hill, 1933), pp. 512–19; and Fareed Zakaria, *From Wealth to Power: The Unusual Origins of America's World Role* (Princeton, NJ: Princeton University Press, 1998), passim. Finally, aspects of Randall Schweller's important work are consistent with offensive realism. See Schweller, "Neorealism's Status-Quo Bias"; Randall L. Schweller, "Bandwagoning for Profit: Bringing the Revisionist State Back In," *International Security* 19, No. 1 (Summer 1994), pp. 72–107; and Randall L. Schweller, *Deadly Imbalances: Tripolarity and Hitler's Strategy of World Conquest* (New York: Columbia University Press, 1998). However, as Gideon Rose makes clear, it is difficult to classify Schweller as an offensive realist. See Gideon Rose, "Neoclassical Realism and Theories of Foreign Policy," *World Politics* 51, No. 1 (October 1998), pp. 144–72.

50. See Inis L. Claude, *Power and International Relations* (New York: Random House, 1962); August Heckscher, ed., *The Politics of Woodrow Wilson: Selections from His Speeches and Writings* (New York: Harper, 1956); and James Brown Scott, ed., *President Wilson's Foreign Policy: Messages, Addresses, Papers* (Oxford: Oxford University Press, 1918).

51. Quoted in Wight, *Power Politics,* p. 29.

52. William J. Clinton, "American Foreign Policy and the Democratic Ideal," campaign speech, Pabst Theater, Milwaukee, WI, October 1, 1992.

53. "In Clinton's Words: 'Building Lines of Partnership and Bridges to the Future,'" *New York Times,* July 10, 1997.

54. See Shimko, "Realism, Neorealism, and American Liberalism."

55. See Seymour Martin Lipset, *American Exceptionalism: A Double-Edged Sword* (New York: Norton, 1996), pp. 51–52, 237. Also see Gabriel A. Almond, *The American People and Foreign Policy* (New York: Praeger, 1968), pp. 50–51.

56. Alexis de Tocqueville, *Democracy in America*, vol. II, trans. Henry Reeve (New York: Schocken Books, 1972), p. 38.

57. Morgenthau, *Scientific Man*, p. 201.

58. See Reinhold Niebuhr, *The Children of Light and the Children of Darkness: A Vindication of Democracy and a Critique of Its Traditional Defense* (New York: Scribner's, 1944), esp. pp. 153–90.

59. Lipset, *American Exceptionalism*, p. 63.

60. See Samuel P. Huntington, *The Soldier and the State: The Theory and Practice of Civil-Military Relations* (Cambridge, MA: Harvard University Press, 1957).

61. For example, it is apparent from archival-based studies of the early Cold War that American policymakers thought largely in terms of power politics, not ideology, when dealing with the Soviet Union. See H. W. Brands, *The Specter of Neutralism: The United States and the Emergence of the Third World, 1947–1960* (New York: Columbia University Press, 1989); Thomas J. Christensen, *Useful Adversaries: Grand Strategy, Domestic Mobilization, and Sino-American Conflict, 1947–1958* (Princeton, NJ: Princeton University Press, 1996); Melvyn P. Leffler, *A Preponderance of Power: National Security, the Truman Administration, and the Cold War* (Stanford, CA: Stanford University Press, 1992); and Trachtenberg, *Constructed Peace*. Also see Keith Wilson, "British Power in the European Balance, 1906–14," in David Dilks, ed., *Retreat from Power: Studies in Britain's Foreign Policy of the Twentieth Century*, vol. 1, *1906–1939* (London: Macmillan, 1981), pp. 21–41, which describes how British policymakers "constantly and consistently employed the concept of the balance of power" (p. 22) in private but employed more idealistic rhetoric in their public utterances.

62. Kennan, *American Diplomacy*, p. 82. For examples of other realists emphasizing this theme, see Walter Lippmann, *U.S. Foreign Policy: Shield of the Republic* (Boston: Little, Brown, 1943); Hans Morgenthau, *In Defense of the National Interest: A Critical Examination of American Foreign Policy* (New York: Knopf, 1951); Norman A. Graebner, *America as a World Power: A Realist Appraisal from Wilson to Reagan* (Wilmington, DE: Scholarly Resources, 1984); and Norman A. Graebner, *Cold War Diplomacy: American Foreign Policy, 1945–1975*, 2d ed. (New York: Van Nostrand, 1977).

63. Carr, *Twenty Years' Crisis*, p. 79. For evidence that this kind of hypocrisy is not limited to Anglo-Saxons, see Markus Fischer, "Feudal Europe, 800–1300: Communal Discourse and Conflictual Practices," *International Organization* 46, No. 2 (Spring 1992), pp. 427–66.

64. The key work on this subject is Ido Oren, "The Subjectivity of the 'Democratic' Peace: Changing U.S. Perceptions of Imperial Germany," *International Security* 20, No. 2 (Fall 1995), pp. 147–84. For additional evidence on the examples discussed in this paragraph and the next, see Konrad H. Jarausch, "Huns, Krauts, or Good Germans? The German Image in America, 1800–1980," in James F. Harris, ed., *German-American Interrelations: Heritage and Challenge* (Tubingen: Tubingen University Press, 1985), pp. 145–59; Frank Trommler, "Inventing the Enemy: German-American Cultural Relations, 1900–1917," in Hans-Jurgen Schroder, ed., *Confrontation and Cooperation: Germany and the United States in the Era of World War I, 1900–1924* (Providence, RI: Berg Publishers, 1993), pp. 99–125; and John L. Gaddis, *The United States and the Origins of the Cold War, 1941–1947* (New York: Columbia University Press, 1972), chap. 2. For discussions of how British policymakers worked to clean up Russia's image during both world wars, see Keith Neilson, *Britain and the Last Tsar: British Policy and Russia, 1894–1917* (Oxford: Clarendon, 1995), pp. 342–43; and P.M.H. Bell, *John Bull and the Bear: British Public Opinion, Foreign Policy and the Soviet Union, 1941–1945* (London: Edward Arnold, 1990).

65. The classic statement on the profound impact of liberal ideas on American thinking is Louis Hartz, *The Liberal Tradition in America: An Interpretation of American Political Thought since the Revolution* (New York: Harcourt, Brace and World, 1955).

CHAPTER TWO

1. Most realist scholars allow in their theories for status quo powers that are not hegemons. At least some states, they argue, are likely to be satisfied with the balance of power and thus have no incentive to change it. See Randall L. Schweller, "Neorealism's Status-Quo Bias: What Security Dilemma?" *Security Studies* 5, No. 3 (Spring 1996, special issue on "Realism: Restatements and Renewal," ed. Benjamin Frankel), pp. 98–101; and Arnold Wolfers, *Discord and Collaboration: Essays on International Politics* (Baltimore, MD: Johns Hopkins University Press, 1962), pp. 84–86, 91–92, 125–26.

2. Milton Friedman, *Essays in Positive Economics* (Chicago: University of Chicago Press, 1953), p. 14. Also see Kenneth N. Waltz, *Theory of International Politics* (Reading, MA: Addison-Wesley, 1979), pp. 5–6, 91, 119.

3. Terry Moe makes a helpful distinction between assumptions that are simply useful simplifications of reality (i.e., realistic in themselves but with unnecessary details omitted), and assumptions that are clearly contrary to reality (i.e., that directly violate well-established truths). See Moe, "On the Scientific Status of Rational Models," *American Journal of Political Science* 23, No. 1 (February 1979), pp. 215–43.

4. The concept of anarchy and its consequences for international politics was first articulated by G. Lowes Dickinson, *The European Anarchy* (New York: Macmillan, 1916). For a more recent and more elaborate discussion of anarchy, see Waltz, *Theory of International Politics*, pp. 88–93. Also see Robert J. Art and Robert Jervis, eds., *International Politics: Anarchy, Force, Imperialism* (Boston: Little, Brown,

1973), pt. 1; and Helen Milner, "The Assumption of Anarchy in International Relations Theory: A Critique," *Review of International Studies* 17, No. 1 (January 1991), pp. 67–85.

5. Although the focus in this study is on the state system, realist logic can be applied to other kinds of anarchic systems. After all, it is the absence of central authority, not any special characteristic of states, that causes them to compete for power. Markus Fischer, for example, applies the theory to Europe in the Middle Ages, before the state system emerged in 1648. See Fischer, "Feudal Europe, 800–1300: Communal Discourse and Conflictual Practices," *International Organization* 46, No. 2 (Spring 1992), pp. 427–66. The theory can also be used to explain the behavior of individuals. The most important work in this regard is Thomas Hobbes, *Leviathan*, ed. C. B. Macpherson (Harmondsworth, UK: Penguin, 1986). Also see Elijah Anderson, "The Code of the Streets," *Atlantic Monthly*, May 1994, pp. 80–94; Barry R. Posen, "The Security Dilemma and Ethnic Conflict," *Survival* 35, No. 1 (Spring 1993), pp. 27–47; and Robert J. Spitzer, *The Politics of Gun Control* (Chatham, NJ: Chatham House, 1995), chap. 6.

6. Inis L. Claude, Jr., *Swords into Plowshares: The Problems and Progress of International Organization*, 4th ed. (New York: Random House, 1971), p. 14.

7. The claim that states might have benign intentions is simply a starting assumption. I argue subsequently that when you combine the theory's five assumptions, states are put in a position in which they are strongly disposed to having hostile intentions toward each other.

8. My theory ultimately argues that great powers behave offensively toward each other because that is the best way for them to guarantee their security in an anarchic world. The assumption here, however, is that there are many reasons besides security for why a state might behave aggressively toward another state. In fact, it is uncertainty about whether those non-security causes of war are at play, or might come into play, that pushes great powers to worry about their survival and thus act offensively. Security concerns alone cannot cause great powers to act aggressively. The possibility that at least one state might be motivated by non-security calculations is a necessary condition for offensive realism, as well as for any other structural theory of international politics that predicts security competition. Schweller puts the point well: "If states are assumed to seek nothing more than their own survival, why would they feel threatened? Why would they engage in balancing behavior? In a hypothetical world that has never experienced crime, the concept of security is meaningless." Schweller, "Neorealism's Status-Quo Bias," p. 91. Herbert Butterfield makes essentially the same point when he writes, "Wars would hardly be likely to occur if all men were Christian saints, competing with one another in nothing, perhaps, save self-renunciation." C. T. McIntire, ed., *Herbert*

Butterfield: Writings on Christianity and History (Oxford: Oxford University Press, 1979), p. 73. Also see Jack Donnelly, *Realism and International Relations* (Cambridge: Cambridge University Press, 2000), chap. 2.

9. Quoted in Jon Jacobson, *When the Soviet Union Entered World Politics* (Berkeley: University of California Press, 1994), p. 271.

10. See Elizabeth Pond, *Beyond the Wall: Germany's Road to Unification* (Washington, DC: Brookings Institution Press, 1993), chap. 12; Margaret Thatcher, *The Downing Street Years* (New York: HarperCollins, 1993), chaps. 25–26; and Philip Zelikow and Condoleezza Rice, *Germany Unified and Europe Transformed: A Study in Statecraft* (Cambridge, MA: Harvard University Press, 1995), chap. 4.

11. Frederick Schuman introduced the concept of self-help in *International Politics: An Introduction to the Western State System* (New York: McGraw-Hill, 1933), pp. 199–202, 514, although Waltz made the concept famous in *Theory of International Politics,* chap. 6. On realism and alliances, see Stephen M. Walt, *The Origins of Alliances* (Ithaca, NY: Cornell University Press, 1987).

12. Quoted in Martin Wight, *Power Politics* (London: Royal Institute of International Affairs, 1946), p. 40.

13. If one state achieves hegemony, the system ceases to be anarchic and becomes hierarchic. Offensive realism, which assumes international anarchy, has little to say about politics under hierarchy. But as discussed later, it is highly unlikely that any state will become a global hegemon, although regional hegemony is feasible. Thus, realism is likely to provide important insights about world politics for the foreseeable future, save for what goes on inside in a region that is dominated by a hegemon.

14. Although great powers always have aggressive intentions, they are not always *aggressors,* mainly because sometimes they do not have the capability to behave aggressively. I use the term "aggressor" throughout this book to denote great powers that have the material wherewithal to act on their aggressive intentions.

15. Kenneth Waltz maintains that great powers should not pursue hegemony but instead should aim to control an "appropriate" amount of world power. See Waltz, "The Origins of War in Neorealist Theory," in Robert I. Rotberg and Theodore K. Rabb, eds., *The Origin and Prevention of Major Wars* (Cambridge: Cambridge University Press, 1989), p. 40.

16. The following hypothetical example illustrates this point. Assume that American policymakers were forced to choose between two different power balances in the Western Hemisphere. The first is the present distribution of power, whereby the United States is a hegemon that no state in the region would dare challenge militarily. In the second scenario, China replaces Canada and Germany takes the place of Mexico. Even though the United States would have a significant military advantage over both China and Germany, it is difficult to imagine any American strategist opting for this scenario over U.S. hegemony in the Western Hemisphere.

17. John H. Herz, "Idealist Internationalism and the Security Dilemma," *World Politics* 2, No. 2 (January 1950), pp. 157–80. Although Dickinson did not use the term "security dilemma," its logic is clearly articulated in *European Anarchy*, pp. 20, 88.

18. Herz, "Idealist Internationalism," p. 157.

19. See Joseph M. Grieco, "Anarchy and the Limits of Cooperation: A Realist Critique of the Newest Liberal Institutionalism," *International Organization* 42, No. 3 (Summer 1988), pp. 485–507; Stephen D. Krasner, "Global Communications and National Power: Life on the Pareto Frontier," *World Politics* 43, No. 3 (April 1991), pp. 336–66; and Robert Powell, "Absolute and Relative Gains in International Relations Theory," *American Political Science Review* 85, No. 4 (December 1991), pp. 1303–20.

20. See Michael Mastanduno, "Do Relative Gains Matter? America's Response to Japanese Industrial Policy," *International Security* 16, No. 1 (Summer 1991), pp. 73–113.

21. Waltz maintains that in Hans Morgenthau's theory, states seek power as an end in itself; thus, they are concerned with absolute power, not relative power. See Waltz, "Origins of War," pp. 40–41; and Waltz, *Theory of International Politics*, pp. 126–27. Although Morgenthau occasionally makes statements that appear to support Waltz's charge, there is abundant evidence in Morgenthau, *Politics among Nations: The Struggle for Power and Peace*, 5th ed. (New York: Knopf, 1973) that states are concerned mainly with the pursuit of relative power.

22. Quoted in Marc Trachtenberg, *A Constructed Peace: The Making of the European Settlement, 1945–1963* (Princeton, NJ: Princeton University Press, 1999), p. 36.

23. In short, the key issue for evaluating offensive realism is not whether a state is constantly trying to conquer other countries or going all out in terms of defense spending, but whether or not great powers routinely pass up promising opportunities to gain power over rivals.

24. See Richard K. Betts, *Surprise Attack: Lessons for Defense Planning* (Washington, DC: Brookings Institution Press, 1982); James D. Fearon, "Rationalist Explanations for War," *International Organization* 49, No. 3 (Summer 1995), pp. 390–401; Robert Jervis, *The Logic of Images in International Relations* (Princeton, NJ: Princeton University Press, 1970); and Stephen Van Evera, *Causes of War: Power and the Roots of Conflict* (Ithaca, NY: Cornell University Press, 1999), pp. 45–51, 83, 137–42.

25. See Joel Achenbach, "The Experts in Retreat: After-the-Fact Explanations for the Gloomy Predictions," *Washington Post,* February 28, 1991; and Jacob Weisberg, "Gulfballs: How the Experts Blew It, Big-Time," *New Republic,* March 25, 1991.

26. Jack Snyder and Stephen Van Evera make this argument in its boldest form. See Jack Snyder, *Myths of Empire: Domestic Politics and International Ambition* (Ithaca, NY: Cornell University Press, 1991), esp. pp. 1, 307–8; and Van Evera, *Causes of War*, esp. pp. 6, 9.

27. Relatedly, some defensive realists interpret the security dilemma to say that the offensive measures a state takes to enhance its own security force rival states to respond in kind, leaving all states no better off than if they had done nothing, and possibly even worse off. See Charles L. Glaser, "The Security Dilemma Revisited," *World Politics* 50, No. 1 (October 1997), pp. 171–201. Given this understanding of the security dilemma, hardly any security competition should ensue among rational states, because it would be fruitless, maybe even counterproductive, to try to gain advantage over rival powers. Indeed, it is difficult to see why states operating in a world where aggressive behavior equals self-defeating behavior would face a "security dilemma." It would seem to make good sense for all states to forsake war and live in peace. Of course, Herz did not describe the security dilemma this way when he introduced it in 1950. As noted, his original rendition of the concept is a synoptic statement of offensive realism.

28. Although threatened states sometimes balance efficiently against aggressors, they often do not, thereby creating opportunities for successful offense. This matter will be discussed at length in Chapters 8 and 9. Snyder appears to be aware of this problem, as he adds the important qualifier "at least in the long run" to his claim that "states typically form balancing alliances to resist aggressors." *Myths of Empire*, p. 11. Aggressors, however, will be tempted to win victory in the short term, hoping they can use their success to shape the long term to their advantage. Regarding the offense-defense balance, it is an amorphous concept that is especially difficult for scholars and policymakers to define and measure. See "Correspondence: Taking Offense at Offense-Defense Theory," *International Security* 23, No. 3 (Winter 1998–99), pp. 179–206; Jack S. Levy, "The Offensive/Defensive Balance of Military Technology: A Theoretical and Historical Analysis," *International Studies Quarterly* 28, No. 2 (June 1984), pp. 219–38; Kier A. Lieber, "Grasping the Technological Peace: The Offense-Defense Balance and International Security," *International Security* 25, No. 1 (Summer 2000), pp. 71–104; Sean M. Lynn-Jones, "Offense-Defense Theory and Its Critics," *Security Studies* 4, No. 4 (Summer 1995), pp. 672–74; John J. Mearsheimer, *Conventional Deterrence* (Ithaca, NY: Cornell University Press, 1983), pp. 24–27; and Jonathan Shimshoni, "Technology, Military Advantage, and World War I: A Case for Military Entrepreneurship," *International Security* 15, No. 3 (Winter 1990–91), pp. 187–215. More important, there is little evidence that defense invariably has a crushing advantage over offense. As discussed in the remainder of this paragraph, states sometimes attack and lose, whereas at other times they attack and win.

29. John Arquilla, *Dubious Battles: Aggression, Defeat, and the International System* (Washington, DC: Crane Russak, 1992), p. 2. Also see Bruce Bueno de Mesquita, *The War Trap* (New Haven, CT: Yale University Press, 1981), pp. 21–22; and Kevin Wang and James Ray, "Beginners and Winners: The Fate of Initiators of Interstate Wars Involving Great Powers since 1495," *International Studies Quarterly* 38, No. 1 (March 1994), pp. 139–54.

30. Although Snyder and Van Evera maintain that conquest rarely pays, both concede in subtle but important ways that aggression sometimes succeeds. Snyder, for example, distinguishes between expansion (successful offense) and overexpansion (unsuccessful offense), which is the behavior that he wants to explain. See, for example, his discussion of Japanese expansion between 1868 and 1945 in *Myths of Empire,* pp. 114–16. Van Evera allows for variation in the offense-defense balance, to include a few periods where conquest is feasible. See *Causes of War,* chap. 6. Of course, allowing for successful aggression contradicts their central claim that offense hardly ever succeeds.

31. See Robert Gilpin, *War and Change in World Politics* (Cambridge: Cambridge University Press, 1981), p. 29; and William C. Wohlforth, *The Elusive Balance: Power and Perceptions during the Cold War* (Ithaca, NY: Cornell University Press, 1993), pp. 12–14.

32. In subsequent chapters, the power-projection problems associated with large bodies of water are taken into account when measuring the distribution of power (see Chapter 4). Those two factors are treated separately here, however, simply to highlight the profound influence that oceans have on the behavior of great powers.

33. For an opposing view, see David M. Edelstein, "Choosing Friends and Enemies: Perceptions of Intentions in International Relations," Ph.D. diss., University of Chicago, August 2000; Andrew Kydd, "Why Security Seekers Do Not Fight Each Other," *Security Studies* 7, No. 1 (Autumn 1997), pp. 114–54; and Walt, *Origins of Alliances.*

34. See note 8 in this chapter.

35. Jacob Viner, "Power versus Plenty as Objectives of Foreign Policy in the Seventeenth and Eighteenth Centuries," *World Politics* 1, No. 1 (October 1948), p. 10.

36. See Mark Bowden, *Black Hawk Down: A Story of Modern War* (London: Penguin, 1999); Alison Des Forges, *"Leave None to Tell the Story": Genocide in Rwanda* (New York: Human Rights Watch, 1999), pp. 623–25; and Gerard Prunier, *The Rwanda Crisis: History of a Genocide* (New York: Columbia University Press, 1995), pp. 274–75.

37. See Scott R. Feil, *Preventing Genocide: How the Early Use of Force Might Have Succeeded in Rwanda* (New York: Carnegie Corporation, 1998); and John Mueller,

"The Banality of 'Ethnic War,' " *International Security* 25, No. 1 (Summer 2000), pp. 58–62. For a less sanguine view of how many lives would have been saved had the United States intervened in Rwanda, see Alan J. Kuperman, "Rwanda in Retrospect," *Foreign Affairs* 79, No. 1 (January–February 2000), pp. 94–118.

38. See David F. Schmitz, *Thank God They're on Our Side: The United States and Right-Wing Dictatorships, 1921–1965* (Chapel Hill: University of North Carolina Press, 1999), chaps. 4–6; Gaddis Smith, *The Last Years of the Monroe Doctrine, 1945–1993* (New York: Hill and Wang, 1994); Tony Smith, *America's Mission: The United States and the Worldwide Struggle for Democracy in the Twentieth Century* (Princeton, NJ: Princeton University Press, 1994); and Stephen Van Evera, "Why Europe Matters, Why the Third World Doesn't: American Grand Strategy after the Cold War," *Journal of Strategic Studies* 13, No. 2 (June 1990), pp. 25–30.

39. Quoted in John M. Carroll and George C. Herring, eds., *Modern American Diplomacy,* rev. ed. (Wilmington, DE: Scholarly Resources, 1996), p. 122.

40. Nikita Khrushchev makes a similar point about Stalin's policy toward Chinese nationalist leader Chiang Kai-shek during World War II: "Despite his conflict with the Chinese Communist Party, Chiang Kai-shek was fighting against Japanese imperialism. Therefore, Stalin—and consequently the Soviet government—considered Chiang a progressive force. Japan was our number one enemy in the East, so it was in the interests of the Soviet Union to support Chiang. Of course, we supported him only insofar as we didn't want to see him defeated by the Japanese—in much the same way that Churchill, who had been our enemy since the first days of the Soviet Union, was sensible enough to support us in the war against Hitler." *Khrushchev Remembers: The Last Testament,* trans. and ed. Strobe Talbott (Boston: Little, Brown, 1974), pp. 237–38.

41. See Walt, *Origins of Alliances,* pp. 5, 266–68.

42. Adam Smith, *An Inquiry into the Nature and Causes of the Wealth of Nations,* ed. Edwin Cannan (Chicago: University of Chicago Press, 1976), Vol. 1, p. 487. All the quotes in this paragraph are from pp. 484–87 of that book.

43. For an overview of the Anglo-Dutch rivalry, see Jack S. Levy, "The Rise and Decline of the Anglo-Dutch Rivalry, 1609–1689," in William R. Thompson, ed., *Great Power Rivalries* (Columbia: University of South Carolina Press, 1999), pp. 172–200; and Paul M. Kennedy, *The Rise and Fall of British Naval Mastery* (London: Allen Lane, 1976), chap. 2. This example has direct bearing on the earlier discussion of relative versus absolute power. Specifically, without the Navigation Act, both England and Holland probably would have made greater absolute gains, because their economies would have benefited from open trade. England, however, probably would not have gained much of a relative advantage over Holland. With the Navigation Act, England gained a significant relative advantage over Holland, but both sides suffered in terms of absolute gains. The bottom line is that relative power considerations drive great-power behavior.

44. William J. Clinton, "Address by the President to the 48th Session of the United Nations General Assembly," United Nations, New York, September 27, 1993. Also see George Bush, "Toward a New World Order: Address by the President to a Joint Session of Congress," September 11, 1990.

45. Bradley Thayer examined whether the victorious powers were able to create and maintain stable security orders in the aftermath of the Napoleonic Wars, World War I, and World War II, or whether they competed among themselves for power, as realism would predict. In particular, he looked at the workings of the Concert of Europe, the League of Nations, and the United Nations, which were purportedly designed to limit, if not eliminate, realist behavior by the great powers. Thayer concludes that the rhetoric of the triumphant powers notwithstanding, they remained firmly committed to gaining power at each other's expense. See Bradley A. Thayer, "Creating Stability in New World Orders," Ph.D. diss., University of Chicago, August 1996. Also see Korina Kagan, "The Myth of the European Concert," *Security Studies* 7, No. 2 (Winter 1997–98), pp. 1–57. She concludes that the Concert of Europe "was a weak and ineffective institution that was largely irrelevant to great power behavior" (p. 3).

46. See Melvyn P. Leffler, *A Preponderance of Power: National Security, the Truman Administration, and the Cold War* (Stanford, CA: Stanford University Press, 1992).

47. For a discussion of American efforts to undermine Soviet control of Eastern Europe, see Peter Grose, *Operation Rollback: America's Secret War behind the Iron Curtain* (Boston: Houghton Mifflin, 2000); Walter L. Hixson, *Parting the Curtain: Propaganda, Culture, and the Cold War, 1945–1961* (New York: St. Martin's, 1997); and Gregory Mitrovich, *Undermining the Kremlin: America's Strategy to Subvert the Soviet Bloc, 1947–1956* (Ithaca, NY: Cornell University Press, 2000).

48. For a synoptic discussion of U.S. policy toward the Soviet Union in the late 1980s that cites most of the key sources on the subject, see Randall L. Schweller and William C. Wohlforth, "Power Test: Evaluating Realism in Response to the End of the Cold War," *Security Studies* 9, No. 3 (Spring 2000), pp. 91–97.

49. The editors of a major book on the Treaty of Versailles write, "The resulting reappraisal, as documented in this book, constitutes a new synthesis of peace conference scholarship. The findings call attention to divergent peace aims within the American and Allied camps and underscore the degree to which the negotiators themselves considered the Versailles Treaty a work in progress." Manfred F. Boemeke, Gerald D. Feldman, and Elisabeth Glaser, eds., *The Treaty of Versailles: A Reassessment after 75 Years* (Cambridge: Cambridge University Press, 1998), p. 1.

50. This paragraph draws heavily on Trachtenberg, *Constructed Peace;* and Marc Trachtenberg, *History and Strategy* (Princeton, NJ: Princeton University Press, 1991), chaps. 4–5. Also see G. John Ikenberry, "Rethinking the Origins of American Hegemony," *Political Science Quarterly* 104, No. 3 (Autumn 1989), pp. 375–400.

51. The failure of American policymakers during the early Cold War to understand where the security competition in Europe was leading is summarized by Trachtenberg, who asks the rhetorical question, "Had anyone predicted that a system of this sort would emerge, and that it would provide the basis for a very durable peace?" His answer: "The predictions that were made pointed as a rule in the opposite direction: that Germany could not be kept down forever; that the Federal Republic would ultimately . . . want nuclear forces of her own; that U.S. troops could not be expected to remain in . . . Europe. . . . Yet all these predictions—every single one—turned out to be wrong." Trachtenberg, *History and Strategy,* pp. 231–32. Also see Trachtenberg, *Constructed Peace,* pp. vii–viii.

52. For more discussion of the pitfalls of collective security, see John J. Mearsheimer, "The False Promise of International Institutions," *International Security* 19, No. 3 (Winter 1994–95), pp. 26–37.

53. See Grieco, "Anarchy and the Limits of Cooperation," pp. 498, 500.

54. For evidence of relative gains considerations thwarting cooperation among states, see Paul W. Schroeder, *The Transformation of European Politics, 1763–1848* (Oxford: Clarendon, 1994), chap. 3.

55. Charles Lipson, "International Cooperation in Economic and Security Affairs," *World Politics* 37, No. 1 (October 1984), p. 14.

56. See Randall L. Schweller, "Bandwagoning for Profit: Bringing the Revisionist State Back In," *International Security* 19, No. 1 (Summer 1994), pp. 72–107. See also the works cited in note 59 in this chapter.

57. See Misha Glenny, *The Fall of Yugoslavia: The Third Balkan War,* 3d rev. ed. (New York: Penguin, 1996), p. 149; Philip Sherwell and Alina Petric, "Tudjman Tapes Reveal Plans to Divide Bosnia and Hide War Crimes," *Sunday Telegraph* (London), June 18, 2000; Laura Silber and Allan Little, *Yugoslavia: Death of a Nation,* rev. ed. (New York: Penguin, 1997), pp. 131–32, 213; and Warren Zimmerman, *Origins of a Catastrophe: Yugoslavia and Its Destroyers—America's Last Ambassador Tells What Happened and Why* (New York: Times Books, 1996), pp. 116–17.

58. See John Maynard Keynes, *The Economic Consequences of the Peace* (New York: Penguin, 1988), chap. 2; and J. M. Roberts, *Europe, 1880–1945* (London: Longman, 1970), pp. 239–41.

59. For information on the Molotov-Ribbentrop Pact of August 1939 and the ensuing cooperation between those states, see Alan Bullock, *Hitler and Stalin: Parallel Lives* (London: HarperCollins, 1991), chaps. 14–15; I.C.B. Dear, ed., *The*

Oxford Companion to World War II (Oxford: Oxford University Press, 1995), pp. 780–82; Anthony Read and David Fisher, *The Deadly Embrace: Hitler, Stalin, and the Nazi-Soviet Pact, 1939–1941* (New York: Norton, 1988); Geoffrey Roberts, *The Unholy Alliance: Stalin's Pact with Hitler* (Bloomington: Indiana University Press, 1989), chaps. 8–10; and Adam B. Ulam, *Expansion and Coexistence: Soviet Foreign Policy, 1917–1973*, 2d ed. (New York: Holt, Rinehart, and Winston, 1974), chap. 6.

60. Waltz maintains that structural theories can explain international outcomes—i.e., whether war is more likely in bipolar or multipolar systems—but that they cannot explain the foreign policy behavior of particular states. A separate theory of foreign policy, he argues, is needed for that task. See *Theory of International Politics*, pp. 71–72, 121–23. Colin Elman challenges Waltz on this point, arguing that there is no logical reason why systemic theories cannot be used as a theory of foreign policy. The key issue, as Elman notes, is whether the particular structural theory helps us understand the foreign policy decisions that states make. I will attempt to show that offensive realism can be used to explain both the foreign policy of individual states and international outcomes. See Colin Elman, "Horses for Courses: Why *Not* Neorealist Theories of Foreign Policy?"; Kenneth N. Waltz, "International Politics Is Not Foreign Policy"; and Colin Elman, "Cause, Effect, and Consistency: A Response to Kenneth Waltz," in *Security Studies* 6, No. 1 (Autumn 1996), pp. 7–61.

CHAPTER THREE

1. Power can be defined in different ways, raising the question of which definition is correct. A scholar's theory, in fact, determines the appropriate definition. Whether my definition makes good sense depends on how well offensive realism explains international politics.

2. For elaboration of these two ways of thinking about power, see Bruce Russett and Harvey Starr, *World Politics: The Menu for Choice* (New York: Freeman, 1989), chap. 6; and William C. Wohlforth, *The Elusive Balance: Power and Perceptions during the Cold War* (Ithaca, NY: Cornell University Press, 1993), pp. 3–5. Furthermore, some scholars (such as Wohlforth) maintain that there is a sharp distinction between how policymakers perceive the balance of power and the actual balance itself, and that what really matters for understanding international politics is the picture of the balance that policymakers have in their heads. I disagree with this line of argument. As will become clear in subsequent chapters, policymakers usually have a good sense of the actual balance of power, although they occasionally miscalculate the power of rival states. Therefore, one need not focus on perceptions of power to explain how states behave.

3. Robert Dahl, "The Concept of Power," *Behavioral Science* 2, No. 3 (July 1957), pp. 202–3. Also see David A. Baldwin, *Paradoxes of Power* (New York: Basil

Blackwell, 1989); and Karl W. Deutsch, *The Analysis of International Relations* (Englewood Cliffs, NJ: Prentice-Hall, 1988), chap. 3.

4. A good example of this literature is A.F.K. Organski and Jacek Kugler, *The War Ledger* (Chicago: University of Chicago Press, 1980), chap. 3. Also see Jacek Kugler and William Domke, "Comparing the Strength of Nations," *Comparative Political Studies* 19, No. 1 (April 1986), pp. 39–70; and Jacek Kugler and Douglas Lemke, eds., *Parity and War: Evaluations and Extensions of the War Ledger* (Ann Arbor: University of Michigan Press, 1998).

5. Geoffrey Blainey, *The Causes of War* (New York: Free Press, 1973), chap. 8. The quote is from p. 119. Also see James D. Fearon, "Rationalist Explanations for War," *International Organization* 49, No. 3 (Summer 1995), pp. 379–414.

6. See Zeev Maoz, "Power, Capabilities, and Paradoxical Conflict Outcomes," *World Politics* 41, No. 2 (January 1989), pp. 239–66. As discussed in the next chapter, military power incorporates the number of fighting forces as well as their quality.

7. John J. Mearsheimer, *Conventional Deterrence* (Ithaca, NY: Cornell University Press, 1983), pp. 33–35, 58–60. Also see Mark Harrison, "The Economics of World War II: An Overview," in Mark Harrison, ed., *The Economics of World War II: Six Great Powers in International Comparison* (Cambridge: Cambridge University Press, 1998), pp. 1–2.

8. See Mearsheimer, *Conventional Deterrence;* T. V. Paul, *Asymmetric Conflicts: War Initiation by Weaker Powers* (Cambridge: Cambridge University Press, 1994); and Dan Reiter, "Military Strategy and the Outbreak of International Conflict," *Journal of Conflict Resolution* 43, No. 3 (June 1999), pp. 366–87.

9. Brian Bond, *France and Belgium, 1939–1940* (London: Davis-Poynter, 1975); Phillip A. Karber et al., *Assessing the Correlation of Forces: France 1940*, Report No. BDM/W-79-560-TR (McLean, VA: BDM Corporation, June 18, 1979); and Barry R. Posen, *The Sources of Military Doctrine: France, Britain, and Germany between the World Wars* (Ithaca, NY: Cornell University Press, 1984), pp. 82–94.

10. On the details of the Schlieffen Plan, see Gerhard Ritter, *The Schlieffen Plan*, trans. Andrew and Eva Wilson (London: Oswald Wolff, 1958). Regarding the claim that Schlieffen's original version probably would have worked, see Gordon Craig, *The Politics of the Prussian Army, 1640–1945* (Oxford: Oxford University Press, 1975), pp. 279–80; Walter Goerlitz, *History of the German General Staff, 1657–1945*, trans. Brian Battershaw (New York: Praeger, 1953), p. 135; and L.C.F. Turner, "The Significance of the Schlieffen Plan," *Australian Journal of Politics and History* 8, No. 1 (April 1967), pp. 52–53, 59–63.

11. During the latter half of the Cold War, there was much interest in doing net assessments of the conventional balance in Europe to determine whether the Warsaw Pact was likely to score a quick and decisive victory against NATO. It was commonplace for analysts of that balance (and others) to focus on the material assets available to each side while paying little attention to the likely strategies that the opposing sides would employ. The underlying assumption was that the balance of power alone would determine the result. However, the outcome of a war between NATO and the Warsaw Pact would surely have depended on strategy as well as numbers. Thus, net assessments of the European balance (and others) should have considered both strategy and the balance of material assets. See John J. Mearsheimer, "Numbers, Strategy, and the European Balance," *International Security* 12, No. 4 (Spring 1988), pp. 174–85.

12. This discussion of Napoleon's campaign in Russia is based largely on David G. Chandler, *The Campaigns of Napoleon* (New York: Macmillan, 1996), pts. 13–14; Christopher Duffy, *Borodino and the War of 1812* (New York: Scribner's, 1973); Vincent J. Esposito and John R. Elting, *A Military History and Atlas of the Napoleonic Wars* (New York: Praeger, 1965); and Georges Lefebvre, *Napoleon: From Tilsit to Waterloo, 1807–1815,* trans. J. E. Anderson (New York: Columbia University Press, 1990), chap. 9.

13. The numbers in this paragraph are from Chandler, *Campaigns of Napoleon,* pp. 750, 754–55, 852–53. Also see the numbers on the size of the French and Russian armies in Table 8.2 of this book.

14. It appears that Russia's strategy was not the result of a conscious policy decision but was forced on it by the unfolding campaign. See Chandler, *Campaigns of Napoleon,* pp. 764–65, 859; and Lefebvre, *Napoleon,* p. 313. Regardless of the reasons behind it, the strategy worked brilliantly.

15. For an excellent statistical graphic of the disintegration of Napoleon's army, see Edward R. Tufte, *The Visual Display of Quantitative Information* (Cheshire, CT: Graphics Press, 1983), pp. 41, 176.

16. See Jonathan Kirshner, "Rationalist Explanations for War?" *Security Studies* 10, No. 1 (Autumn 2000), pp. 153–61. Also see Alan Beyerchen, "Clausewitz, Nonlinearity, and the Unpredictability of War," *International Security* 17, No. 3 (Winter 1992–93), pp. 59–90, which overstates the difficulty of predicting which side will win a war but nevertheless makes some important points on the matter.

17. See Kenneth N. Waltz, *Theory of International Politics* (Reading, MA: Addison-Wesley, 1979), pp. 191–92; and Wohlforth, *Elusive Balance,* p. 4.

18. See Klaus Knorr, *The War Potential of Nations* (Princeton, NJ: Princeton University Press, 1956); and Klaus Knorr, *Military Power and Potential* (Lexington, MA: D. C. Heath, 1970).

19. Among the best works on population and military capability are Kingsley Davis, "The Demographic Foundations of National Power," in Morroe Berger, Theodore Abel, and Charles H. Page, eds., *Freedom and Control in Modern Societies* (New

York: Van Nostrand, 1954), pp. 206–42; Katherine Organski and A.F.K. Organski, *Population and World Power* (New York: Knopf, 1961); and Michael S. Teitelbaum and Jay M. Winter, *The Fear of Population Decline* (Orlando, FL: Academic Press, 1985).

20. The Chinese and Russian figures are from *World Bank Atlas, 2000* (Washington, DC: World Bank, April 2000), pp. 24–25. The U.S. figure is from the Census Bureau.

21. Simon Kuznets, *Modern Economic Growth: Rate, Structure, and Spread* (New Haven, CT: Yale University Press, 1966), chap. 2.

22. On the importance of wealth for military might, see Robert Gilpin, *War and Change in World Politics* (Cambridge: Cambridge University Press, 1981); Paul M. Kennedy, *The Rise and Fall of British Naval Mastery* (London: Allen Lane, 1976); Paul M. Kennedy, *The Rise and Fall of the Great Powers: Economic Change and Military Conflict from 1500 to 2000* (New York: Random House, 1987); A.F.K. Organski, *World Politics*, 2d ed. (New York: Knopf, 1968); and Organski and Kugler, *War Ledger.*

23. On the cost of World War I, see Ernest L. Bogart, *Direct and Indirect Costs of the Great World War* (Oxford: Oxford University Press, 1919), p. 299; Roger Chickering, *Imperial Germany and the Great War, 1914–1918* (Cambridge: Cambridge University Press, 1998) p. 195; Niall Ferguson, *The Pity of War* (New York: Basic Books, 1999), pp. 322–23; and Gerd Hardach, *The First World War, 1914–1918* (Berkeley: University of California Press, 1977), p. 153. The International Institute for Strategic Studies (IISS) estimates that the cost of World War I—measured in 1995 dollars—was about $4.5 trillion, and that World War II cost a staggering $13 trillion. See "The 2000 Chart of Armed Conflict," insert to IISS, *The Military Balance, 2000/2001* (Oxford: Oxford University Press, October 2000).

24. America's GNP in 1940 was $101 billion. These figures are from I.C.B. Dear, ed., *The Oxford Companion to World War II* (Oxford: Oxford University Press, 1995), pp. 1059, 1182. For a more general discussion of the costs of World War II, see Alan S. Milward, *War, Economy, and Society, 1939–1945* (Berkeley: University of California Press, 1979), chap. 3.

25. One might seek to remedy this problem by relying on per capita GNP, since it neutralizes the effect of differences in population size between states. But, as emphasized, it is imperative to account for population size, because it is an important ingredient of latent power. For example, relying only on per capita GNP, one would conclude that Singapore has much more latent power than China does today, because Singapore has a much higher per capita GNP than China. This conclusion obviously makes little sense.

26. See Bernard Brodie, "Technological Change, Strategic Doctrine, and Political Outcomes," in Klaus Knorr, ed., *Historical Dimensions of National Security Problems* (Lawrence: University Press of Kansas, 1976), pp. 263–306; Karl

Lautenschlager, "Technology and the Evolution of Naval Warfare," *International Security* 8, No. 2 (Fall 1983), pp. 3–51; William H. McNeill, *The Pursuit of War: Technology, Armed Force, and Society since AD 1000* (Chicago: University of Chicago Press, 1982), chaps. 6–10; and Merritt Roe Smith, ed., *Military Enterprise and Technological Change: Perspectives on the American Experience* (Cambridge, MA: MIT Press, 1987). Differences in industrial might sometimes have other consequences that affect the balance of latent power. Advanced industrial states usually can build the logistical capacity (roads, trucks, railroads, transport ships, cargo planes) to support large military forces. Industrially backward states invariably cannot create these ingredients of military success. Modern industrial states are also likely to have better-educated populations than do semi-industrialized states, and higher education levels tend to correlate with better military performance. Finally, modern militaries are large and complex organizations that need to be managed, which is why general staffs are indispensable. Highly industrialized states tend to have considerable expertise in managing large organizations, because they are populated with large economic institutions. During World War I, for example, semi-industrialized Russia was plagued with significant logistical problems, poorly educated soldiers, and an inadequate staff system. Highly industrialized Germany, on the other hand, had excellent logistics, well-educated soldiers, and the best staff system among the warring powers.

27. A problem with *The War Ledger* is that Organski and Kugler use GNP to measure power in the late nineteenth and early twentieth centuries. See William B. Moul, "Measuring the 'Balances of Power': A Look at Some Numbers," *Review of International Studies* 15, No. 2 (April 1989), pp. 107–15. They also equate latent power with actual power, which are not always commensurate, as discussed later in this chapter.

28. Although the United Kingdom was an economic colossus during this period, it did not build formidable military forces, for reasons discussed later in this chapter.

29. See William C. Fuller, Jr., *Strategy and Power in Russia, 1600–1914* (New York: Free Press, 1992), chaps. 6–9.

30. The numbers in this paragraph are from *World Bank Atlas, 2000*, pp. 42–43; and World Bank, *Knowledge for Development: World Development Report 1998/1999* (Oxford: Oxford University Press, 1998), p. 212. The 1980 figure is for gross domestic product (GDP), which roughly approximates GNP in these cases.

31. On the importance of energy for measuring wealth, see Oskar Morgenstern, Klaus Knorr, and Klaus P. Heiss, *Long Term Projections of Power: Political, Economic, and Military Forecasting* (Cambridge, MA: Ballinger, 1973), esp. chap. 6. Regarding steel, see Ray S. Cline, *World Power Assessment, 1977: A Calculus of Strategic Drift* (Boulder, CO: Westview, 1977), pp. 68–69.

32. It might seem unusual to switch indicators of latent power, but as Moul notes, "to test a theory in various historical and temporal contexts requires equivalent, not identical, measures." Moul, "Measuring," p. 103.

33. See William T. Hogan, *Global Steel in the 1990s: Growth or Decline?* (Lexington, MA: Lexington Books, 1991); Paul A. Tiffany, "The American Steel Industry in the Postwar Era: Dominance and Decline," in Etsuo Abe and Yoshitaka Suzuki, eds., *Changing Patterns of International Rivalry: Some Lessons from the Steel Industry* (Tokyo: University of Tokyo Press, 1991), pp. 245–65. It is worth noting that when Cline updated *World Power Assessment, 1977* in the early 1990s, steel was no longer considered a key indicator of economic might. See Ray S. Cline, *The Power of Nations in the 1990s: A Strategic Assessment* (Lanham, MD: University Press of America, 1994), pp. 51–68.

34. There is no good comparative data on American and Soviet GNP for every year of the Cold War. The data set I used, which begins in 1960 and covers each remaining year of the Cold War, is from the World Military Expenditures and Arms Transfers Database of the former U.S. Arms Control and Disarmament Agency (ACDA). For the post–Cold War period, I use GNP numbers from the World Bank.

35. There is good reason to think that switching indicators in 1960 does not distort my analysis of the balance of latent power between the superpowers. In 1968 and again in 1976, the Joint Economic Committee of Congress published comparative data on American and Soviet GNP for scattered years of the Cold War. The 1968 publication provides GNP figures for 1950, 1955, 1961, and 1965, and the 1975 study gives GNP figures for 1948, 1950, 1955, 1960, 1965, 1970, and 1975. In each publication, the relative share of GNP that the United States and the Soviet Union control for the relevant years is hardly different from the percentages described in Table 3.5. See U.S. Congress, Joint Economic Committee, *Soviet Economic Performance, 1966–67*, 90th Cong., 2d sess. (Washington, DC: U.S. Government Printing Office, May 1968), p. 16; U.S. Congress, Joint Economic Committee, *Soviet Economy in a New Perspective*, 94th Cong., 2d sess. (Washington, DC: U.S. Government Printing Office, October 14, 1976), p. 246.

36. See J. David Singer and Melvin Small, *National Material Capabilities Data, 1816–1985* (Ann Arbor, MI: Inter-University Consortium for Political and Social Research, February 1993), pp. 108-1, 132-1.

37. These figures are from ibid., p. 132-1.

38. Steven T. Ross, *European Diplomatic History, 1789–1815: France against Europe* (Garden City, NY: Anchor Books, 1969), chap. 11.

39. Roughly 200,000 French troops were fighting in Spain when Napoleon attacked Russia in June 1812. Nevertheless, Napoleon still had 674,000 troops available for the attack on Russia. Chandler, *Campaigns of Napoleon*, pp. 754–55.

About 70 percent of Germany's divisions were on the eastern front in June 1941, including almost all of the Wehrmacht's best units. That ratio remained largely unchanged until late 1943, when Germany began building up its forces in France in anticipation of the Normandy invasion, which came on June 6, 1944. See Jonathan R. Adelman, *Prelude to the Cold War: The Tsarist, Soviet, and U.S. Armies in the Two World Wars* (Boulder, CO: Lynne Rienner, 1988), pp. 130–31; and Jonathan R. Adelman, *Revolution, Armies, and War: A Political History* (Boulder, CO: Lynne Rienner, 1985), pp. 71–72.

40. Adelman, *Prelude*, p. 40; and Adelman, *Revolution*, pp. 69–70. One might argue that this analysis does not account for the fact that the Austro-Hungarian army fought in the east with Germany in World War I but not in World War II. It is clear from what transpired on the battlefield during World War I, however, that the feeble Austro-Hungarian army was probably more of a liability than an asset for the Germans. See Holger H. Herwig, *The First World War: Germany and Austria-Hungary, 1914–1918* (New York: Arnold, 1997). Furthermore, a substantial number of Finnish, Hungarian, Italian, and Romanian forces were fighting with Germany on the eastern front in World War II. See Adelman, *Revolution*, pp. 71–72.

41. Norman Davies, *White Eagle, Red Star: The Polish-Soviet War, 1919–20* (New York: St. Martin's, 1972); Thomas C. Fiddick, *Russia's Retreat from Poland, 1920* (New York: St. Martin's, 1990); Piotr S. Wandycz, *Soviet-Polish Relations, 1917–1921* (Cambridge, MA: Harvard University Press, 1969); and Adam Zamoyski, *The Battle for the Marchlands*, Eastern European Monograph No. 88 (New York: Columbia University Press, 1981).

42. See Francois Crouzet, "Wars, Blockade, and Economic Change in Europe, 1792–1815," *Journal of Economic History* 24, No. 4 (December 1964), pp. 567–90; and Patrick O'Brien and Caglar Keyder, *Economic Growth in Britain and France 1780–1914: Two Paths to the Twentieth Century* (London: Allen and Unwin, 1978), chap. 3. Also see the figures for 1816 in Table 3.3.

43. See Paul Bairoch, "International Industrialization Levels from 1750 to 1980," *Journal of European Economic History* 11, No. 2 (Fall 1982), pp. 281, 292, 294, 296 (some of Bairoch's data is reprinted in Kennedy, *Great Powers*, p. 149); Fuller, *Strategy and Power*, pp. 151–53; Arcadius Kahan, *The Plow, the Hammer, and the Knout: An Economic History of Eighteenth-Century Russia* (Chicago: University of Chicago Press, 1985); and W. W. Rostow, "The Beginnings of Modern Growth in Europe: An Essay in Synthesis," *Journal of Economic History* 33, No. 3 (September 1973), p. 555.

44. See David R. Jones, "The Soviet Defense Burden through the Prism of History," in Carl G. Jacobsen, ed., *The Soviet Defense Enigma: Estimating Costs and Burdens* (Oxford: Oxford University Press, 1987), pp. 154–61; Walter M. Pintner, "Russia as a Great Power, 1709–1856: Reflections on the Problem of Relative

Backwardness, with Special Reference to the Russian Army and Russian Society," Occasional Paper No. 33 (Washington, DC: Kennan Institute for Advanced Russian Studies, July 18, 1978); and Walter M. Pintner, "The Burden of Defense in Imperial Russia, 1725–1914," *Russian Review* 43, No. 3 (July 1984), pp. 231–59.

45. D. N. Collins, "The Franco-Russian Alliance and Russian Railways, 1891–1914," *Historical Journal* 16, No. 4 (December 1973), pp. 777–88.

46. On the weakness of the Russian economy before World War I, see Raymond W. Goldsmith, "The Economic Growth of Tsarist Russia, 1860–1913," *Economic Development and Cultural Change* 9, No. 3 (April 1961), pp. 441–75; Paul R. Gregory, *Russian National Income, 1885–1913* (Cambridge: Cambridge University Press, 1982), chap. 7; Alec Nove, *An Economic History of the USSR, 1917–1991*, 3d ed. (New York: Penguin, 1992), chap. 1; and Clive Trebilcock, *The Industrialization of the Continental Powers, 1780–1914* (New York: Longman, 1981), chaps. 4, 7.

47. All of the quotes and figures in this paragraph are from Adelman, *Revolution*, pp. 88–92. Also see ibid., pp. 85–86; Adelman, *Prelude*, pp. 32–37, 44–45; and Peter Gatrell and Mark Harrison, "The Russian and Soviet Economies in Two World Wars: A Comparative View," *Economic History Review* 46, No. 3 (August 1993), pp. 425–52.

48. For a graphic depiction of the effects of Stalin's economic policies, see the table titled "Soviet Heavy Industry Output, 1928–1945," in Mark Harrison, *Soviet Planning in Peace and War, 1938–1945* (Cambridge: Cambridge University Press, 1985), p. 253. For a more general discussion, see R. W. Davies, Mark Harrison, and S. G. Wheatcroft, eds., *The Economic Transformation of the Soviet Union, 1913–1945* (Cambridge: Cambridge University Press, 1994).

49. These numbers are from Adelman, *Revolution*, p. 92; Adelman uses slightly different numbers in *Prelude*, p. 219. Also see David M. Glantz and Jonathan M. House, *When Titans Clashed: How the Red Army Stopped Hitler* (Lawrence: University Press of Kansas, 1995), p. 306; Harrison, "Economics of World War II," pp. 15–17; and Richard J. Overy, *Why the Allies Won* (New York: Norton, 1996), pp. 331–32.

50. The Soviet Union did not defeat Nazi Germany simply by building more weapons. The fighting skills of the Red Army also improved markedly between 1941 and 1945. During the first two years of the conflict, for example, the Soviets lost between six and seven armored vehicles for every German one. By the fall of 1944, however, the ratio was approximately 1:1. See Overy, *Why the Allies Won*, p. 212. Also see Glantz, *When Titans Clashed*, esp. pp. 286–89; and F. W. von Mellenthin, *Panzer Battles: A Study of the Employment of Armor in the Second World War*, trans. H. Betzler (New York: Ballantine, 1976), pp. 349–67.

51. The Soviet Union's only serious competitor was the United Kingdom, which produced less steel and consumed less energy than the Soviet Union for every year from 1946 to 1950. See Singer and Small, *National Material Capabilities Data, 1816–1985,* pp. 91-1, 188-1. Also see Chapter 8 of this book.

52. Addressing Western diplomats on November 18, 1956, Khrushchev said, "Whether you like it or not, history is on our side. We will bury you." Quoted in William J. Tompson, *Khrushchev: A Political Life* (New York: St. Martin's, 1995), p. 171.

53. Gus Ofer, "Soviet Economic Growth: 1928–1985," *Journal of Economic Literature* 25, No. 4 (December 1987), pp. 1767–833.

54. William E. Odom, "Soviet Force Posture: Dilemmas and Directions," *Problems of Communism* 34, No. 4 (July–August 1985), pp. 1–14; and Notra Trulock III, "Emerging Technologies and Future War: A Soviet View," in Andrew W. Marshall and Charles Wolf, eds., *The Future Security Environment,* report submitted to the Commission on Integrated Long-Term Strategy (Washington, DC: U.S. Department of Defense, October 1988), pp. 97–163. It is commonplace in the post–Cold War world to emphasize the former Soviet Union's inefficiencies, and there were many for sure. Nevertheless, it should not be forgotten that the Soviet Union was good at employing draconian measures to harness underutilized resources, as Stalin showed in the 1930s, and it was good at mobilizing resources under emergency conditions, as happened between 1941 and 1945.

55. This point is made by Stephen M. Walt, *The Origins of Alliances* (Ithaca, NY: Cornell University Press, 1987), pp. 273–81.

56. Students of international political economy sometimes refer to the nineteenth-century United Kingdom as a hegemon. See Stephen D. Krasner, "State Power and the Structure of International Trade," *World Politics* 28, No. 3 (April 1976), pp. 317–47. But this is because they usually focus their attention on economic issues and pay little attention to military power. Students who emphasize the importance of security competition, on the other hand, usually describe Europe in the 1800s as multipolar.

57. See J. M. Hobson, "The Military-Extraction Gap and the Wary Titan: The Fiscal-Sociology of British Defence Policy, 1870–1913," *Journal of European Economic History* 22, No. 3 (Winter 1993), pp. 461–503; Paul M. Kennedy, "The Costs and Benefits of British Imperialism, 1846–1914," *Past and Present,* No. 125 (November 1989), pp. 186–92; Jacek Kugler and Marina Arbetman, "Choosing among Measures of Power: A Review of the Empirical Record," in Richard J. Stoll and Michael D. Ward, eds., *Power in World Politics* (Boulder, CO: Lynne Rienner, 1989), p. 76; and Quincy Wright, *A Study of War,* vol. 1 (Chicago: University of Chicago Press, 1942), pp. 670–71.

58. Some of Germany's leading scholars in the early twentieth century (e.g., Hans Delbruck and Otto Hintze) mistakenly believed that Wilhelmine Germany would lead a balancing coalition against the United Kingdom, because the United

Kingdom was especially wealthy and had a powerful navy. Instead, the United Kingdom, France, and Russia allied against Germany. See Ludwig Dehio, *Germany and World Politics in the Twentieth Century*, trans. Dieter Pevsner (New York: Norton, 1967), pp. 45–47, 51–55. As discussed later in this chapter, Europe's great powers balanced against Germany and not the United Kingdom because Germany had a large army with significant offensive capability, whereas the United Kingdom had a small army with hardly any offensive capability against another great power.

59. Paul Kennedy's *Great Powers* has various tables (pp. 149, 154, 199–203, 243) that illustrate the great wealth as well as the military weakness of the United States during the second half of the nineteenth century. Also see Hobson, "The Military-Extraction Gap," pp. 478–80; and Table 6.2 in this book.

60. R.A.C. Parker, "Economics, Rearmament, and Foreign Policy: The United Kingdom before 1939—A Preliminary Study," *Journal of Contemporary History* 10, No. 4 (October 1975), pp. 637–47; G. C. Peden, *British Rearmament and the Treasury: 1932–1939* (Edinburgh: Scottish Academic Press, 1979); and Robert P. Shay, Jr., *British Rearmament in the Thirties: Politics and Profits* (Princeton, NJ: Princeton University Press, 1977).

61. Robert R. Bowie and Richard H. Immerman, *Waging Peace: How Eisenhower Shaped an Enduring Cold War Strategy* (Oxford: Oxford University Press, 1998), esp. chaps. 4, 6; Aaron L. Friedberg, *In the Shadow of the Garrison State: America's Anti-Statism and Its Cold War Grand Strategy* (Princeton, NJ: Princeton University Press, 2000), pp. 93–98, 127–39; John L. Gaddis, *Strategies of Containment: A Critical Appraisal of Postwar American National Security Policy* (Oxford: Oxford University Press, 1982), chaps. 5–6; and Glenn H. Snyder, "The 'New Look' of 1953," in Warner R. Schilling, Paul Y. Hammond, and Glenn H. Snyder, *Strategy, Politics, and Defense Budgets* (New York: Columbia University Press, 1962), pp. 379–524.

62. The U.S. Central Intelligence Agency usually estimated that the Soviets spent roughly three times as much of their GNP on defense as did the United States, although this number was criticized by some for being too low, and by others for being too high. Nevertheless, almost all the experts agreed that the Soviets spent a larger share of their GNP on defense than did the United States.

63. See Walt, *Origins of Alliances*, pp. 289–91.

64. Japan's GNP in 1979 was $2.076 trillion, while Soviet GNP was $2.445 trillion. Japan closed the gap over the next seven years, so that in 1987, its GNP was $2.772 trillion, while Soviet GNP was $2.75 trillion. All figures are from ACDA's World Military Expenditures and Arms Transfers Database.

65. Peter Liberman, *Does Conquest Pay? The Exploitation of Occupied Industrial Societies* (Princeton, NJ: Princeton University Press, 1996), chap. 3; and Milward, *War, Economy, and Society*, chap. 5.

66. Harrison, *Soviet Planning*, pp. 64, 125. Also see Overy, *Why the Allies Won*, pp. 182–83.

67. Mark Harrison, "Resource Mobilization for World War II: The USA, UK, USSR, and Germany, 1938–1945," *Economic History Review* 2d Ser., Vol. 41, No. 2 (May 1988), p. 185. Also see Dear, ed., *Oxford Companion to World War II*, p. 1218.

68. Overy, *Why the Allies Won*, p. 332.

69. Adelman, *Revolution*, pp. 106–7. These numbers should be considered rough approximations. In fact, Adelman writes in *Prelude* (p. 174) that the Soviets had 488 divisions by January 1945. Furthermore, at least two sources credit the Germans with slightly more than 300 divisions by early 1945. See Dear, ed., *Oxford Companion to World War II*, p. 471; and N. I. Anisimov, *Great Patriotic War of the Soviet Union, 1941–1945: A General Outline* (Moscow: Progress Publishers, 1970), p. 437. Regarding the equipment differences inside the opposing divisions, see R. L. DiNardo, *Mechanized Juggernaut or Military Anachronism? Horses and the German Army of World War II* (Westport, CT: Greenwood, 1991).

70. Harrison, "Economics of World War II," p. 21.

71. One widely cited Soviet study estimates that Lend-Lease accounted for 4 percent of Soviet output during the war. But that figure is probably too low; Adelman estimates that the figure should be 10 percent. See Adelman, *Prelude*, pp. 223–24; Mark Harrison, "The Second World War," in Davies et al., eds., *Economic Transformation*, pp. 250–52; and Boris K. Sokolov, "The Role of Lend-Lease in Soviet Military Efforts, 1941–1945," trans. David M. Glantz, *Journal of Slavic Military Studies* 7, No. 3 (September 1994), pp. 567–86.

72. See Werner Abelshauser, "Germany: Guns, Butter, and Economic Miracles," in Harrison, ed., *Economics of World War II*, pp. 151–70; Alfred C. Mierzejewski, *The Collapse of the German War Economy, 1944–1945: Allied Air Power and the German National Railway* (Chapel Hill: University of North Carolina Press, 1988), chap. 1; Richard J. Overy, *War and Economy in the Third Reich* (Oxford: Clarendon, 1994); and Overy, *Why the Allies Won*, chaps. 6–7.

73. See Wright, *A Study of War*, vol. 1, pp. 670–71, tables 58, 59. As noted, the United Kingdom also spent a smaller percentage of its wealth on defense than did its continental rivals, because it is separated from the continent by a large body of water.

74. Quoted in Hobson, "The Military-Extraction Gap," p. 495. For general discussions of the British army between 1870 and 1914, see Correlli Barnett, *Britain and Her Army, 1509–1970: A Military, Political, and Social Survey* (Harmondsworth, UK: Penguin Books, 1974), chaps. 13–15; David French, *The British Way in Warfare, 1688–2000* (London: Unwin Hyman, 1990), chaps. 5–6; and Edward M. Spiers, *The Late Victorian Army, 1868–1902* (New York: Manchester University Press, 1992). Also see A.J.P. Taylor, *The Struggle for Mastery in Europe, 1848–1918* (Oxford: Clarendon, 1954), introduction.

CHAPTER FOUR

1. Alfred T. Mahan, *The Influence of Sea Power upon History, 1660–1783*, 12th ed. (Boston: Little, Brown, 1918).

2. Giulio Douhet, *The Command of the Air*, trans. Dino Ferrari (New York: Coward-McCann, 1942).

3. This is not to deny that the United States and its allies maintained formidable ground forces in Europe during most of the Cold War, which is why the North Atlantic Treaty Organization (NATO) stood a good chance of thwarting a Soviet conventional attack. See John J. Mearsheimer, "Why the Soviets Can't Win Quickly in Central Europe," *International Security* 7, No. 1 (Summer 1982), pp. 3–39; and Barry R. Posen, "Measuring the European Conventional Balance: Coping with Complexity in Threat Assessment," *International Security* 9, No. 3 (Winter 1984–85), pp. 47–88. Nevertheless, unlike the Soviet army, the U.S. army was never in a position to overrun Europe. In fact, it was probably only the third most powerful standing army on the continent, behind the Soviet and West German armies. On or near the central front of the Cold War were roughly 26 Soviet divisions, 12 West German divisions, and slightly fewer than 6 American divisions. U.S. divisions, however, were bigger and more formidable than their West German and Soviet counterparts. But even allowing for these differences, the American army was still the third most powerful fighting force in Europe. Regarding the relative combat potential of American, West German, and Soviet divisions, see William P. Mako, *U.S. Ground Forces and the Defense of Central Europe* (Washington, DC: Brookings Institution Press, 1983), pp. 105–25.

4. And marines are essentially small armies that go by a different name.

5. Julian S. Corbett, *Some Principles of Maritime Strategy* (1911; rpt., Annapolis, MD: U.S. Naval Institute Press, 1988), p. 16. Corbett also writes that "it scarcely needs saying that it is almost impossible that a war can be decided by naval action alone" (p. 15).

6. See John J. Mearsheimer, *Conventional Deterrence* (Ithaca, NY: Cornell University Press, 1983), esp. chap. 2.

7. On command of the sea, see Corbett, *Principles of Maritime Strategy*, pp. 91–106. For a good primer on naval strategy, see Geoffrey Till et al., *Maritime Strategy and the Nuclear Age* (New York: St. Martin's, 1982).

8. States also aim to command the sea and the air so they can protect their own homeland from attack by the enemy.

9. Not surprisingly, Mahan, who was a staunch advocate of independent naval power, disliked amphibious operations, which required the navy to support the army. See Jon T. Sumida, *Inventing Grand Strategy: The Classic Works of Alfred Thayer Mahan Reconsidered* (Baltimore, MD: Johns Hopkins University Press, 1997), p. 45.

10. This distinction between amphibious assaults and amphibious landings is taken from Jeter A. Isely and Philip A. Crowl, *The U.S. Marines and Amphibious War: Its Theory and Its Practice in the Pacific* (Princeton, NJ: Princeton University Press, 1951), p. 8, although I define the concepts somewhat differently than they do.

11. *Raids* are a fourth kind of amphibious operation. Raids are where a navy briefly places troops on an enemy's coast to destroy particular targets but then takes them back to sea when the mission is completed (or fails). The disastrous Allied landing along the French coast at Dieppe in August 1942 is an example of a raid. See Brian L. Villa, *Unauthorized Action: Mountbatten and the Dieppe Raid* (Oxford: Oxford University Press, 1990). Another example is the British operation at Zeebrugge in April 1918. See Paul G. Halpern, *A Naval History of World War I* (Annapolis, MD: U.S. Naval Institute Press, 1994), pp. 411–16. I largely ignore raids, not because they usually fail, but because they are trivial operations that have little influence on the outcomes of wars.

12. Richard Harding, *Amphibious Warfare in the Eighteenth Century: The British Expedition to the West Indies, 1740–1742* (Woodbridge, UK: Boydell, 1991), p. 81.

13. Quoted in Brian R. Sullivan, "Mahan's Blindness and Brilliance," *Joint Forces Quarterly*, No. 21 (Spring 1999), p. 116.

14. John Lehman, who was secretary of the navy in the administration of President Ronald Reagan, frequently asserted that, in the event of war with the Soviet Union, American aircraft carriers would move close to the Soviet mainland, specifically the Kola Peninsula, and strike important military targets. But hardly an admiral could be found to support that idea. Adm. Stansfield Turner wrote that Lehman "advocates a strategy for the Navy of 'maneuver, initiative, and offense.' Presumably, he is reaffirming his many public statements that our Navy is going to be capable of carrying the war right to the Soviets' home bases and airfields. This sounds stirring and patriotic. The only problem is that I have yet to find one admiral who believes that the U.S. Navy would even attempt it." Letter to the editor, *Foreign Affairs* 61, No. 2 (Winter 1982–83), p. 457. Submarines, however, can now deliver conventionally armed cruise missiles to a rival's homeland with relative impunity. See Owen R. Cote, Jr., *Precision Strike from the Sea: New Missions for a New Navy*, Security Studies Program Conference Report (Cambridge: MIT, July 1998); and Owen R. Cote, Jr., *Mobile Targets from under the Sea: New Submarine Missions in the New Security Environment*, Security Studies Program Conference Report (Cambridge: MIT, April 2000).

15. Quoted in Paul M. Kennedy, *The Rise and Fall of British Naval Mastery* (London: Allen Lane, 1976), p. 253. Also see Sumida, *Inventing Grand Strategy*, pp. 45–47; and Allan Westcott, *Mahan on Naval Warfare: Selections from the Writings of Rear Admiral Alfred T. Mahan* (London: Sampson Low, Marston, 1919), pp. 91–99,

328–41. For Corbett's views on blockade, see *Principles of Maritime Strategy*, pp. 95–102, 183–208. Although Mahan believed that independent sea power, not land power, was the decisive military instrument, it is widely recognized that there are fatal flaws in his analysis. See Philip A. Crowl, "Alfred Thayer Mahan: The Naval Historian," in Peter Paret, ed., *Makers of Modern Strategy: From Machiavelli to the Nuclear Age* (Princeton, NJ: Princeton University Press, 1986), pp. 444–77; Gerald S. Graham, *The Politics of Naval Supremacy: Studies in British Maritime Ascendancy* (Cambridge: Cambridge University Press, 1965); and Kennedy, *British Naval Mastery*, esp. introduction and chap. 7.

16. Two other cases rarely mentioned in the literature on blockade but that might be included in this list are Germany's efforts in World Wars I and II to use its geographic advantage and its navy to stop Russian/Soviet trade with the outside world. I did not include these cases, however, because Germany made only a minor effort to isolate Russia in both conflicts. Nevertheless, the German blockades had little effect on the outcome of either war, and thus they support my argument about the limited utility of independent sea power.

17. Among the best sources on the Continental System are Geoffrey Ellis, *Napoleon's Continental Blockade: The Case of Alsace* (Oxford: Clarendon, 1981); Eli F. Heckscher, *The Continental System: An Economic Interpretation*, trans. C. S. Fearenside (Oxford: Clarendon, 1922); Georges Lefebvre, *Napoleon*, vol. 2, *From Tilsit to Waterloo, 1807–1815*, trans. J. E. Anderson (New York: Columbia University Press, 1990), chap. 4; and Mancur Olson, Jr., *The Economics of the Wartime Shortage: A History of British Food Supplies in the Napoleonic War and in World Wars I and II* (Durham, NC: Duke University Press, 1963), chap. 3.

18. Concerning the United Kingdom's blockade of France between 1792 and 1815, see Francois Crouzet, "Wars, Blockade, and Economic Change in Europe, 1792–1815," *Journal of Economic History* 24, No. 4 (December 1964), pp. 567–90; Kennedy, *British Naval Mastery*, chap. 5; and Herbert W. Richmond, *Statesmen and Seapower* (Oxford: Clarendon, 1946), pp. 170–257. In its various wars with France during the eighteenth century, the United Kingdom tried to bring its rival to its knees by cutting French overseas commerce. See Graham, *Politics of Naval Supremacy*, pp. 19–20. But as Graham notes, "There is no evidence to suggest that the denial of colonial commerce materially altered the French strategic position on the Continent" (p. 19). Also see Michael Howard, *The British Way in Warfare: A Reappraisal*, 1974 Neale Lecture in English History (London: Jonathan Cape, 1975), pp. 15–20.

19. Regarding the French blockade of Prussia, see Michael Howard, *The Franco-Prussian War: The German Invasion of France, 1870–1871* (London: Dorset Press, 1961), pp. 74–76; and Theodore Ropp, *The Development of a Modern Navy: French Naval Policy,*

1871–1904, ed. Stephen S. Roberts (Annapolis, MD: U.S. Naval Institute Press, 1987), pp. 22–25.

20. Some of the best sources on Germany's blockade of Britain in World War I are Olson, *Economics of the Wartime Shortage,* chap. 4; E. B. Potter and Chester W. Nimitz, *Sea Power: A Naval History* (Englewood Cliffs, NJ: Prentice-Hall, 1960), chap. 25; John Terraine, *The U-Boat Wars, 1916–1945* (New York: Putnam, 1989), part 1; and V. E. Tarrant, *The U-Boat Offensive, 1914–1945* (Annapolis, MD: U.S. Naval Institute Press, 1989), pp. 7–76.

21. On the Allied blockade of Germany and Austria in World War I, see A. C. Bell, *A History of the Blockade of Germany, Austria-Hungary, Bulgaria, and Turkey, 1914–1918* (1937; rpt., London: Her Majesty's Stationery Office, 1961); Louis Guichard, *The Naval Blockade, 1914–1918,* trans. Christopher R. Turner (New York: Appleton, 1930); Holger H. Herwig, *The First World War: Germany and Austria-Hungary, 1914–1918* (London: Arnold, 1997), pp. 271–83; and C. Paul Vincent, *The Politics of Hunger: The Allied Blockade of Germany, 1915–1919* (Athens: Ohio University Press, 1985). Also see Avner Offer, *The First World War: An Agrarian Interpretation* (Oxford: Oxford University Press, 1989), pp. 23–78, which provides a detailed description of the effects of the blockade but ascribes too much importance to its impact on the war's outcome.

22. On Germany's blockade of the United Kindom in World War II, see Clay Blair, *Hitler's U-Boat War: The Hunters, 1939–1942* (New York: Random House, 1996); Clay Blair, *Hitler's U-Boat War: The Hunted, 1942–1945* (New York: Random House, 1998); Jurgen Rohwer, "The U-Boat War against the Allied Supply Lines," in H. A. Jacobsen and J. Rohwer, eds., *Decisive Battles of World War II: The German View,* trans. Edward Fitzgerald (New York: Putnam, 1965), pp. 259–312; Tarrant, *U-Boat Offensive,* pp. 81–144; and Terraine, *U-Boat Wars,* pt. 3.

23. For discussions of the Allied blockade of Germany and Italy in World War II, see Kennedy, *British Naval Mastery,* chap. 11; W. N. Medlicott, *The Economic Blockade,* 2 vols. (London: Her Majesty's Stationery Office, 1952, 1959); and Alan S. Milward, *War, Economy, and Society, 1939–1945* (Berkeley: University of California Press, 1979), chap. 9.

24. On the American Civil War, see Bern Anderson, *By Sea and by River: The Naval History of the Civil War* (New York: De Capo, 1989), pp. 26, 34–37, 65–66, 225–34; Richard E. Beringer et al., *Why the South Lost the Civil War* (Athens: University of Georgia Press, 1986), chap. 3; and Potter and Nimitz, *Sea Power,* chaps. 13–17.

25. Among the best sources on the American blockade of Japan are Clay Blair, *Silent Victory: The U.S. Submarine War against Japan* (New York: Lippincott, 1975); U.S. Strategic Bombing Survey (USSBS), *The War against Japanese Transportation,*

1941–1945, Pacific War Report 54 (Washington, DC: U.S. Government Printing Office, 1947); and Theodore Roscoe, *United States Submarine Operations in World War II* (Annapolis, MD: U.S. Naval Institute Press, 1956).

26. My analysis of Japan's decision to surrender relies heavily on Robert A. Pape, *Bombing to Win: Air Power and Coercion in War* (Ithaca, NY: Cornell University Press, 1996), chap. 4, although I assign greater importance than Pape does to the dropping of the two atomic bombs. I also relied in part on Barton J. Bernstein, "Compelling Japan's Surrender without the A-bomb, Soviet Entry, or Invasion: Reconsidering the US Bombing Survey's Early-Surrender Conclusions," *Journal of Strategic Studies* 18, No. 2 (June 1995), pp. 101–48; Richard B. Frank, *Downfall: The End of the Imperial Japanese Empire* (New York: Random House, 1999); and Leon V. Sigal, *Fighting to a Finish: The Politics of War Termination in the United States and Japan, 1945* (Ithaca, NY: Cornell University Press, 1988).

27. See Olson, *Economics of the Wartime Shortage.* Also see L. Margaret Barnett, *British Food Policy during the First World War* (Boston: Allen and Unwin, 1985); Gerd Hardach, *The First World War, 1914–1918* (Berkeley: University of California Press, 1977), chap. 5; and Milward, *War, Economy, and Society,* chap. 8.

28. See Milward, *War, Economy, and Society,* p. 179.

29. The quotations in this and the next paragraph are from pp. 132–33 and 142 of Olson, *Economics of the Wartime Shortage.*

30. Pape, *Bombing to Win,* pp. 21–27.

31. Pape, *Bombing to Win,* p. 25.

32. See Pape, *Bombing to Win,* chap. 4; and USSBS, *The Effects of Strategic Bombing on Japanese Morale,* Pacific War Report 14 (Washington, DC: U.S. Government Printing Office, June 1947).

33. On this basic logic, see Hein E. Goemans, *War and Punishment: The Causes of War Termination and the First World War* (Princeton, NJ: Princeton University Press, 2000).

34. See Wesley F. Craven and James L. Cate, *The Army Air Forces in World War II,* 7 vols. (Washington, DC: Office of Air Force History, 1983), Vol. 2, pp. 681–87, 695–714; Thomas M. Coffey, *Decision over Schweinfurt: The U.S. 8th Air Force Battle for Daylight Bombing* (New York: David McKay, 1977); and John Sweetman, *Schweinfurt: Disaster in the Skies* (New York: Ballantine, 1971).

35. See Trevor N. Dupuy, *Elusive Victory: The Arab-Israeli Wars, 1947–1974* (New York: Harper and Row, 1978), pp. 550–53, 555–56; Insight Team of the London *Sunday Times, The Yom Kippur War* (Garden City, NY: Doubleday, 1974), pp. 184–89; Chaim Herzog, *The War of Atonement, October 1973* (Boston: Little, Brown, 1975), pp. 256–61; Edward Luttwak and Dan Horowitz, *The Israeli Army* (London: Allen Lane, 1975), pp. 347–52, 374; and Eliezer Cohen, *Israel's Best Defense: The First Full Story of* *the Israeli Air Force,* trans. Jonathan Cordis (New York: Orion, 1993), pp. 321–68, 386, 391.

36. The line between interdiction operations that reach far behind an adversary's front lines (deep interdiction) and strategic bombing is sometimes murky. Air forces can also help navies implement a blockade.

37. Carl H. Builder, *The Icarus Syndrome: The Role of Air Power Theory in the Evolution and Fate of the U.S. Air Force* (New Brunswick, NJ: Transaction, 1994), passim; Morton H. Halperin, *Bureaucratic Politics and Foreign Policy* (Washington, DC: Brookings Institution Press, 1974), pp. 28–32, 43–46, 52; and Perry M. Smith, *The Air Force Plans for Peace, 1943–1945* (Baltimore, MD: Johns Hopkins University Press, 1970), chaps. 1–3.

38. There are two main differences between blockade and strategic bombing. First, blockades are indiscriminate in the sense that they aim to cut off *all* of an enemy's imports and exports. Strategic bombers, as noted earlier, can be employed more selectively: they can strike directly at specific industries and ignore others. Second, if the aim is to punish an adversary's civilian population, blockades can do that only indirectly by wrecking the enemy's economy, which would eventually hurt the civilian population. Airpower, on the other hand, can perform that task directly by targeting civilians.

39. See, for example, John A. Warden III, "Employing Air Power in the Twenty-first Century," in Richard H. Schultz, Jr., and Robert L. Pfaltzgraff, Jr., eds., *The Future of Air Power in the Aftermath of the Gulf War* (Maxwell Air Force Base, AL: Air University Press, July 1992), pp. 57–82.

40. For an interesting discussion of how the strategic bombing mission has changed since 1945, see Mark J. Conversino, "The Changed Nature of Strategic Attack," *Parameters* 27, No. 4 (Winter 1997–98), pp. 28–41. Also see Phillip S. Meilinger, "The Problem with Our Airpower Doctrine," *Airpower Journal* 6, No. 1 (Spring 1992), pp. 24–31.

41. On World War I, see H. A. Jones, *The War in the Air,* vol. 3 (Oxford: Clarendon, 1931), chaps. 2–3; H. A. Jones, *The War in the Air,* vol. 5 (Oxford: Clarendon, 1935), chaps. 1–2; and George H. Quester, *Deterrence before Hiroshima: The Airpower Background of Modern Strategy* (New York: John Wiley, 1966), chap. 3. The Allies mounted a minor bombing campaign against Germany late in World War I, but it was of no strategic consequence. See H. A. Jones, *The War in The Air,* vol. 6 (Oxford: Clarendon, 1937), chaps. 1–4; and Quester, *Deterrence before Hiroshima,* chap. 4. On World War II, see Matthew Cooper, *The German Air Force, 1933–1945: An Anatomy of Failure* (London: Jane's, 1981), chaps. 5–6; and John Terraine, *The Right of the Line: The Royal Air Force in the European War, 1939–1945* (London: Hodder and Stoughton, 1985), chaps. 16–25, 77.

42. Richard J. Overy, *Why the Allies Won* (New York: Norton, 1996), p. 124.

43. See Paul Kecskemeti, *Strategic Surrender: The Politics of Victory and Defeat* (Stanford, CA: Stanford University Press, 1958), pp. 72–73; Barrie Pitt, *The Crucible of War: Western Desert 1941* (London: Jonathan Cape, 1980), passim; and Jonathan Steinberg, *All or Nothing: The Axis and the Holocaust, 1941–1943* (New York: Routledge, 1990), pp. 15–25.

44. These figures are from Pape, *Bombing to Win*, pp. 254–55. In addition to Pape (chap. 8), see Craven and Cate, *Army Air Forces*, vol. 3, chaps. 20–22; Max Hastings, *Bomber Command* (New York: Touchstone, 1989); Ronald Schaffer, *Wings of Judgement: American Bombing in World War II* (Oxford: Oxford University Press, 1985), chaps. 4–5; and Charles Webster and Noble Frankland, *The Strategic Air Offensive against Germany, 1939–1945*, vols. 1–4 (London: Her Majesty's Stationery Office, 1961).

45. See Earl R. Beck, *Under the Bombs: The German Home Front, 1942–1945* (Lexington: University Press of Kentucky, 1986).

46. See Craven and Cate, *Army Air Forces*, vol. 2, sec. 4, and vol. 3, secs. 1, 2, 4–6; Haywood S. Hansell, Jr., *The Strategic Air War against Germany and Japan: A Memoir* (Washington, DC: Office of Air Force History, 1986), chaps. 2–3; Alfred C. Mierzejewski, *The Collapse of the German War Economy, 1944–1945: Allied Air Power and the German National Railway* (Chapel Hill: University of North Carolina Press, 1988); and USSBS, *The Effects of Strategic Bombing on the German War Economy*, European War Report 3 (Washington, DC: U.S. Government Printing Office, October 1945).

47. Overy emphasizes that the air war played a key role in defeating Nazi Germany by forcing Hitler to divert precious resources away from the ground war against the Allies and especially the Red Army. See Overy, *Why the Allies Won*, pp. 20, 127–33. The Allies, however, also had to divert enormous resources away from the ground war to the air war. See *General Marshall's Report: The Winning of the War in Europe and the Pacific*, Biennial Report of the Chief of Staff of the United States Army to the Secretary of War, July 1, 1943, to June 30, 1945 (New York: Simon and Schuster, 1945), pp. 101–7. There is no evidence that the Allies diverted fewer resources to fighting the air war than did the Germans. In fact, I believe a convincing case can be made that the Allies diverted greater resources to the air war than did the Germans.

48. Craven and Cate, *Army Air Forces*, vol. 2, chaps. 13–17; Kecskemeti, *Strategic Surrender*, chap. 4; Pape, *Bombing to Win*, pp. 344–45; Philip A. Smith, "Bombing to Surrender: The Contribution of Air Power to the Collapse of Italy, 1943," thesis, School of Advanced Airpower Studies, Air University, Maxwell Air Force Base, AL, March 1997; and Peter Tompkins, *Italy Betrayed* (New York: Simon and Schuster, 1966).

49. The Allied air forces compounded the Italian army's problems with an interdiction campaign against the transportation network that supported its front-line forces.

50. See Craven and Cate, *Army Air Forces,* vol. 5, pp. 507–614; Hansell, *Strategic Air War,* chaps. 4–6; and Schaffer, *Wings of Judgement,* chap. 6.

51. See Martin Caidin, *A Torch to the Enemy: The Fire Raid on Tokyo* (New York: Ballantine, 1960); Craven and Cate, *Army Air Forces,* Vol. 5, chaps. 1–5, 17–23; Schaffer, *Wings of Judgement,* chaps. 6–8; and Kenneth P. Werrell, *Blankets of Fire: U.S. Bombers over Japan during World War II* (Washington, DC: Smithsonian Institution Press, 1996).

52. The U.S. Strategic Bombing Survey reports that the entire air campaign (conventional and nuclear) destroyed about 43 percent of Japan's 66 largest cities, killed roughly 900,000 civilians, and forced the evacuation of more than 8.5 million people from urban areas. USSBS, *Japanese Morale,* pp. 1–2. Two of those 66 cities (Hiroshima and Nagasaki) were destroyed by atomic bombs, not conventional attacks. Moreover, a total of about 115,000 civilians died in the two nuclear attacks. Pape, *Bombing to Win,* p. 105. The firebombing also hurt the Japanese economy somewhat, although the blockade had effectively devastated it by the time the bombers began torching Japan's cities.

53. Angelo Del Boca, *The Ethiopian War, 1935–1941,* trans. P. D. Cummins (Chicago: University of Chicago Press, 1969); J.F.C. Fuller, *The First of the League Wars: Its Lessons and Omens* (London: Eyre and Spottiswoode, 1936); and Thomas M. Coffey, *Lion by the Tail: The Story of the Italian-Ethiopian War* (London: Hamish Hamilton, 1974).

54. Takejiro Shiba, "Air Operations in the China Area, July 1937–August 1945," in Donald S. Detwiler and Charles B. Burdick, eds., *War in Asia and the Pacific, 1937–1949,* Vol. 9 (New York: Garland, 1980), pp. 1–220; and H. J. Timperley, ed., *Japanese Terror in China* (New York: Modern Age, 1938), chaps. 6–7.

55. Mark Clodfelter, *The Limits of Air Power: The American Bombing of North Vietnam* (New York: Free Press, 1989), chaps. 2–4; and Pape, *Bombing to Win,* pp. 176–95.

56. Scott R. McMichael, *Stumbling Bear: Soviet Military Performance in Afghanistan* (London: Brassey's, 1991), chap. 9; Denny R. Nelson, "Soviet Air Power: Tactics and Weapons Used in Afghanistan," *Air University Review,* January–February 1985, pp. 31–44; Marek Sliwinski, "Afghanistan: The Decimation of a People," *Orbis* 33, No. 1 (Winter 1989), pp. 39–56; and Edward B. Westermann, "The Limits of Soviet Airpower: The Bear versus the Mujahideen in Afghanistan, 1979–1989," thesis, School of Advanced Airpower Studies, Air University, Maxwell Air Force Base, AL, June 1997.

57. Eliot A. Cohen et al., *Gulf War Air Power Survey*, 5 vols. (Washington, DC: U.S. Government Printing Office, 1993); and Pape, *Bombing to Win*, chap. 7. The strategic bombing campaign was directed at targets in Iraq such as the city of Baghdad and is distinct from the air attacks directed against Iraqi military targets in Kuwait. The latter campaign inflicted heavy losses on Iraq's army and helped the Allied ground forces win a quick and decisive victory in late February 1991.

58. The U.S. air force's own study of its attacks on Iraqi leadership targets concludes, "The results of these attacks clearly fell short of fulfilling the ambitious hope, entertained by at least some airmen, that bombing the L [leadership] and CCC [command, control, and communications] target categories might put enough pressure on the regime to bring about its overthrow and completely sever communications between the leaders in Baghdad and their military forces." Thomas A. Keaney and Eliot A. Cohen, *Gulf War Air Power Survey Summary Report* (Washington, DC: U.S. Government Printing Office, 1993), p. 70. Also see Pape, *Bombing to Win*, pp. 221–23, 226–40, 250–53.

59. Allen F. Chew, *The White Death: The Epic of the Soviet-Finnish Winter War* (East Lansing: Michigan State University Press, 1971), chap. 5; Eloise Engle and Lauri Paananen, *The Winter War: The Russo-Finnish Conflict, 1939–40* (New York: Scribner's, 1973), chaps. 3, 7, 8; and William R. Trotter, *A Frozen Hell: The Russo-Finnish Winter War of 1939–1940* (Chapel Hill, NC: Algonquin, 1991), chap. 15.

60. The best analysis of this case is Pape, *Bombing to Win*, chap. 5. For detailed descriptions of the bombing campaign, see Conrad C. Crane, *American Airpower Strategy in Korea, 1950–1953* (Lawrence: University Press of Kansas, 2000); and Robert F. Futrell, *The United States Air Force in Korea, 1950–1953*, rev. ed. (Washington, DC: Office of Air Force History, 1983).

61. Clodfelter, *Limits of Air Power*, chaps. 5–6; Pape, *Bombing to Win*, pp. 195–210.

62. John E. Mueller, "The Search for the 'Breaking Point' in Vietnam: The Statistics of a Deadly Quarrel," *International Studies Quarterly* 24, No. 4 (December 1980), pp. 497–519.

63. The best available description of the air campaign over Kosovo is the U.S. air force's official study of the offensive. See *The Air War over Serbia: Aerospace Power in Operation Allied Force*, Initial Report (Washington, DC: U.S. Air Force, 2001). NATO air forces also attacked Yugoslav ground troops in Bosnia during the late summer of 1995, but that was not a strategic bombing campaign. See Robert C. Owen, ed., *Deliberate Force: A Case Study in Effective Air Campaigning* (Maxwell Air Force Base, AL: Air University Press, January 2000).

64. The best available sources include Daniel A. Byman and Matthew C. Waxman, "Kosovo and the Great Air Power Debate," *International Security* 24, No. 4

(Spring 2000), pp. 5–38; Ivo H. Daalder and Michael E. O'Hanlon, *Winning Ugly: NATO's War to Save Kosovo* (Washington, DC: Brookings Institution Press, 2000); Doyle McManus, "Clinton's Massive Ground Invasion That Almost Was; Yugoslavia: After 71 Days of Air War, White House Had in Place a Memo to Send in 175,000 NATO Troops," *Los Angeles Times,* June 9, 2000; and Barry R. Posen, "The War for Kosovo: Serbia's Political-Military Strategy," *International Security* 24, No. 4 (Spring 2000), pp. 39–84.

65. William H. Arkin, "Smart Bombs, Dumb Targeting?" *Bulletin of the Atomic Scientists* 56, No. 3 (May–June 2000), p. 49. The Yugoslav government claims that the number of civilians killed was 2,000. See Posen, "War for Kosovo," p. 81.

66. Pape, *Bombing to Win,* p. 68. For a discussion of why punishment from the air usually fails, see ibid., pp. 21–27; Stephen T. Hosmer, *Psychological Effects of U.S. Air Operations in Four Wars, 1941–1991: Lessons for U.S. Commanders,* RAND Report MR-576-AF (Santa Monica, CA: RAND Corporation, 1996); and Irving L. Janis, *Air War and Emotional Stress: Psychological Studies of Bombing and Civilian Defense* (New York: McGraw-Hill, 1951).

67. There is also some evidence in the public domain that a decapitation strategy was employed against Yugoslavia in 1999. Specifically, it appears from some of the targets that NATO struck (TV stations, Milosevic's house, important government buildings, party headquarters, high-level military headquarters, and the businesses of Milosevic's close friends) that it aimed either to kill him or to precipitate a coup. There is no evidence, however, that this strategy worked.

68. See Pape, *Bombing to Win,* pp. 79–86.

69. See Beck, *Under the Bombs;* Jeffrey Herf, *Divided Memory: The Nazi Past in the Two Germanys* (Cambridge, MA: Harvard University Press, 1997); and Ian Kershaw, *The 'Hitler Myth': Image and Reality in the Third Reich* (Oxford: Oxford University Press, 1987).

70. On this general theme, see Kennedy, *British Naval Mastery,* chap. 7; Robert W. Komer, *Maritime Strategy or Coalition Defense* (Cambridge, MA: Abt Books, 1984); Halford J. Mackinder, "The Geographical Pivot of History," *Geographical Journal* 23, No. 4 (April 1904), pp. 421–37; Halford J. Mackinder, *Democratic Ideals and Reality: A Study in the Politics of Reconstruction* (New York: Henry Holt, 1919); and Martin Wight, *Power Politics,* eds. Hedley Bull and Carsten Holbraad (New York: Holmes and Meier, 1978), chap. 6.

71. Corbett says of the Battle of Trafalgar, "By universal assent Trafalgar is ranked as one of the decisive battles of the world, and yet of all the great victories there is not one which to all appearance was so barren of immediate result. It had brought to a triumphant conclusion one of the most masterly and complex sea campaigns in history, but insofar as it was an integral part of the combined campaign its results are scarcely to be discerned. It gave to England finally the dominion of the seas, but it left Napoleon dictator of the Continent. So incomprehensible was its apparent sterility that to fill the void a legend grew up that it saved England from invasion." Julian S. Corbett, *The Campaign of Trafalgar* (London: Longmans, Green, 1910), p. 408. Also see Edward Ingram, "Illusions of Victory: The Nile, Copenhagen, and Trafalgar Revisited," *Military Affairs* 48, No. 3 (July 1984), pp. 140–43.

72. I estimate that approximately 24 million Soviets died in the fight against Nazi Germany. Of that total, 16 million were civilian and 8 million were military. Of the 8 million military deaths, 3.3 million were prisoners of war who died in captivity. The remaining 4.7 million died either in combat or from combat wounds. Among the best sources on Soviet casualties are Edwin Bacon, "Soviet Military Losses in World War II," *Journal of Slavic Military Studies* 6, No. 4 (December 1993), pp. 613–33; Michael Ellman and S. Maksudov, "Soviet Deaths in the Great Patriotic War: A Note," *Europe-Asia Studies* 46, No. 4 (1994), pp. 671–80; Mark Harrison, *Accounting for War: Soviet Production, Employment, and the Defence Burden, 1941–1945* (Cambridge: Cambridge University Press, 1996), pp. 159–61; and Gerhard Hirschfeld, ed., *The Policies of Genocide: Jews and Soviet Prisoners of War in Nazi Germany* (Boston: Allen and Unwin, 1986), chaps. 1–2. For evidence that the ratio of German casualties between the eastern front and other fronts was probably greater than 3:1, see Jonathan R. Adelman, *Prelude to the Cold War: The Tsarist, Soviet, and U.S. Armies in the Two World Wars* (Boulder, CO: Lynne Rienner, 1988), pp. 128–29, 171–73; and David M. Glantz and Jonathan M. House, *When Titans Clashed: How the Red Army Stopped Hitler* (Lawrence: University Press of Kansas, 1995), p. 284.

73. See Lincoln Li, *The Japanese Army in North China, 1937–1941: Problems of Political and Economic Control* (Oxford: Oxford University Press, 1975).

74. See Potter and Nimitz, *Sea Power,* chap. 19; and the works cited in Chapter 6, note 18 of this book.

75. The Reagan administration's "Maritime Strategy" contained some schemes for using the U.S. navy to influence events on the central front, but those operations were concerned mainly with shifting the strategic nuclear balance against the Soviet Union. Of course the U.S. navy was also concerned with maintaining command of the sea in wartime, so that it could transport troops and supplies across the Atlantic Ocean. See John J. Mearsheimer, "A Strategic Misstep: The Maritime Strategy and Deterrence in Europe," *International Security* 11, No. 2 (Fall 1986), pp. 3–57; and Barry R. Posen, *Inadvertent Escalation: Conventional War and Nuclear Risks* (Ithaca, NY: Cornell University Press, 1991), chaps. 4–5.

76. This point is widely accepted by prominent naval strategists. For example, Adm. Herbert Richmond, one of Britain's leading naval thinkers in the first half of the twentieth century, wrote, "An invasion by sea of a great modern military state may be dismissed as impracticable, even if there were no opposition at sea. The number of men which can be transported would never be sufficient to conduct an invasion in the face of the opposition of the military forces of any great power." Herbert Richmond, *Sea Power in the Modern World* (London: G. Bell, 1934), p. 173.

77. The problem of projecting power across a large body of water is not simply a problem of operating over a long distance. There is a fundamental difference between moving an army over water and moving it over land. A great power separated from an adversary by a large stretch of land can conquer and occupy that land and then move its army and air force right up to the border of its rival, where it can launch a massive ground invasion. (Consider how Napoleonic France conquered the various states that separated it from Russia in the early 1800s and then invaded Russia with a huge army in 1812.) Great powers, however, cannot conquer and occupy water. The sea, as Corbett notes, "is not susceptible to ownership. . . . [Y]ou cannot subsist your armed forces upon it as you can upon enemy's territory." Corbett, *Principles of Maritime Strategy*, p. 93. (Napoleon could not capture the English Channel and station troops on it, which explains in part why he did not invade the United Kingdom). Therefore, navies have to move armies across the sea to strike an adversary. But navies usually cannot project large and powerful armies into enemy territory, and therefore the striking power of seaborne invasion forces is sharply limited.

78. See Piers Mackesy, "Problems of an Amphibious Power: Britain against France, 1793–1815," *Naval War College Review* 30, No. 4 (Spring 1978), pp. 18–21. Also see Richard Harding, "Sailors and Gentlemen of Parade: Some Professional and Technical Problems Concerning the Conduct of Combined Operations in the Eighteenth Century," *Historical Journal* 32, No. 1 (March 1989), pp. 35–55; and Potter and Nimitz, *Sea Power*, p. 67.

79. Raids, on the other hand, were commonplace in great-power wars during the age of sail. For example, Great Britain launched four raids against French port cities in 1778, during the Seven Years' War. See Potter and Nimitz, *Sea Power*, p. 53. Although Britain had a penchant for raids, they were often unsuccessful. Looking at Lisbon (1589), Cadiz (1595 and 1626), Brest (1696), Toulon (1707), Lorient (1746), Rochefort (1757), and Walcheren (1809), Michael Howard sees "an almost unbroken record of expensive and humiliating failures." Howard, *British Way in Warfare*, p. 19. Even the successful raids, however, had little effect on the balance of power.

80. For overviews of how industrialization affected navies, see Bernard Brodie, *Sea Power in the Machine Age*, 2d ed. (Princeton, NJ: Princeton University Press, 1943); Karl Lautenschlager, "Technology and the Evolution of Naval Warfare," *International Security* 8, No. 2 (Fall 1983), pp. 3–51; and Potter and Nimitz, *Sea Power*, chaps. 12, 18.

81. Quoted in Brodie, *Sea Power*, p. 49.

82. On the impact of railroads on war, see Arden Bucholz, *Moltke, Schlieffen, and Prussian War Planning* (New York: Berg, 1991); Edwin A. Pratt, *The Rise of Rail-Power in War and Conquest, 1833–1914* (London: P. S. King, 1915); Dennis E. Showalter, *Railroads and Rifles: Soldiers, Technology, and the Unification of Germany* (Hamden, CT: Archon, 1975); George Edgar Turner, *Victory Rode the Rails: The Strategic Place of the Railroads in the Civil War* (Lincoln: University of Nebraska Press, 1992); and John Westwood, *Railways at War* (San Diego, CA: Howell-North, 1981).

83. See Arthur Hezlet, *Aircraft and Sea Power* (New York: Stein and Day, 1970); and Norman Polmar, *Aircraft Carriers: A Graphic History of Carrier Aviation and Its Influence on World Events* (Garden City, NY: Doubleday, 1969).

84. See USSBS, *Air Campaigns of the Pacific War*, Pacific War Report 71a (Washington, DC: U.S. Government Printing Office, July 1947), sec. 10.

85. I.C.B. Dear, ed., *The Oxford Companion to World War II* (Oxford: Oxford University Press, 1995), pp. 46–50. Also see B. B. Schofield, *The Arctic Convoys* (London: Macdonald and Jane's, 1977); and Richard Woodman, *The Arctic Convoys, 1941–1945* (London: John Murray, 1994).

86. On how submarines affect war, see Arthur Hezlet, *The Submarine and Sea Power* (London: Peter Davies, 1967); and Karl Lautenschlager, "The Submarine in Naval Warfare, 1901–2001," *International Security* 11, No. 3 (Winter 1986–87), pp. 94–140.

87. Halpern, *Naval History of World War I*, p. 48.

88. For a general discussion of naval mines and how they affect the conduct of war, see Gregory K. Hartmann and Scott C. Truver, *Weapons That Wait: Mine Warfare in the U.S. Navy*, 2d ed. (Annapolis, MD: U.S. Naval Institute Press, 1991).

89. Hartmann and Truver, *Weapons That Wait*, p. 15.

90. See U.S. Department of Defense, *Conduct of the Persian Gulf War*, Final Report to Congress (Washington, DC: U.S. Government Printing Office, April 1992), chap. 7; and Michael R. Gordon and Bernard E. Trainor, *The Generals' War: The Inside Story of the Conflict in the Gulf* (Boston, MA: Little, Brown, 1995), pp. 292–94, 343–45, 368–69.

91. Describing British strategy against France during the Napoleonic Wars, Piers Mackesy writes, "No major landing in Western Europe could ever be contemplated unless there was an active war front in the east to hold down the major forces of the French. Mackesy, "Problems of an Amphibious Power," p. 21.

92. Japan's attempt to transport troop reinforcements to the Philippines in late 1944, when the United States dominated the skies over the Pacific, illustrates what happens to one's seaborne forces when one does not have air superiority. American planes decimated the Japanese convoys. See M. Hamlin Cannon, *Leyte: The Return* *to the Philippines* (Washington, DC: U.S. Government Printing Office, 1954), pp. 92–102. Of course, the navy launching the seaborne forces must also have command of the sea. On the importance of sea control for amphibious operations, see P. H. Colomb, *Naval Warfare: Its Ruling Principles and Practice Historically Treated* (London: W. H. Allen, 1891), chaps. 11–18.

93. See Alfred Vagts, *Landing Operations: Strategy, Psychology, Tactics, Politics, from Antiquity to 1945* (Harrisburg, PA: Military Service Publishing Company, 1946), pp. 509–16; and Samuel R. Williamson, Jr., *The Politics of Grand Strategy: Britain and France Prepare for War, 1904–1914* (Cambridge, MA: Harvard University Press, 1969), pp. 43–45.

94. Corbett, *Principles of Maritime Strategy*, p. 98.

95. Quoted in Kennedy, *British Naval Mastery*, p. 201.

96. See Mearsheimer, "A Strategic Misstep," pp. 25–27.

97. Describing American war plans for the period between 1945 and 1950, Steven Ross writes, "Early plans, therefore, called for a rapid retreat from Europe and contained no concept of a second Normandy. Against the might of the Red Army there was little or no prospect of success by direct attack." Steven Ross, *American War Plans, 1945–1950* (New York: Garland, 1988), pp. 152–53.

98. See Piers Mackesy, *Statesmen at War: The Strategy of Overthrow, 1798–1799* (New York: Longman, 1974); and A. B. Rodger, *The War of the Second Coalition, 1798 to 1801: A Strategic Commentary* (Oxford: Clarendon, 1964).

99. See David Gates, *The Spanish Ulcer: A History of the Peninsular War* (New York: Norton, 1986), chaps. 5–7; and Michael Glover, *The Peninsular War, 1807–1814: A Concise Military History* (Hamden, CT: Archon, 1974), chaps. 4–6.

100. The United Kingdom kept a small contingent of troops in Portugal, which had regained its sovereignty in the wake of the British invasion. The British navy transported additional troops to friendly Portugal in April 1809, and those forces, under Lord Wellington's command, played an important role in winning the war on the Iberian Peninsula.

101. See Piers Mackesy, *British Victory in Egypt, 1801: The End of Napoleon's Conquest* (London: Routledge, 1995); Potter and Nimitz, *Sea Power*, chap. 7; and Rodger, *War of the Second Coalition*, chaps. 1–9, esp. chap. 16. Britain and France also conducted a handful of small-scale amphibious operations in the West Indies during the French Revolutionary Wars. See Michael Duffy, *Soldiers, Sugar, and Seapower: The British Expeditions to the West Indies and the War against Revolutionary France* (Oxford: Clarendon, 1987).

102. Among the best works on the Crimean War are Winfried Baumgart, *The Crimean War, 1853–1856* (London: Arnold, 1999); John S. Curtiss, *Russia's Crimean War* (Durham, NC: Duke University Press, 1979); David M. Goldfrank, *The Origins* *of the Crimean War* (New York: Longman, 1994); Andrew D. Lambert, *The Crimean War: British Grand Strategy, 1853–1856* (New York: Manchester University Press, 1990); Norman Rich, *Why the Crimean War? A Cautionary Tale* (Hanover, NH: University Press of New England, 1985); and Albert Seaton, *The Crimean War: A Russian Chronicle* (London: B. T. Batsford, 1977).

103. The numbers in this paragraph are from Potter and Nimitz, *Sea Power,* p. 234; and Hew Strachan, "Soldiers, Strategy and Sebastopol," *Historical Journal* 21, No. 2 (June 1978), p. 321.

104. Quoted in Vagts, *Landing Operations,* p. 411.

105. Among the best works on Gallipoli are C. F. Aspinall-Oglander, *Military Operations: Gallipoli,* 2 vols., Official British History of World War I (London: Heinemann, 1929); Robert R. James, *Gallipoli* (London: B. T. Batsford, 1965); and Michael Hickey, *Gallipoli* (London: John Murray, 1995). Also, the Russians conducted some small-scale amphibious operations against the Turks in the Black Sea region. See Halpern, *Naval History of World War I,* pp. 238–46.

106. Two other well-known amphibious operations in Europe were not directed against the territory of a great power. Germany invaded and conquered Norway (a minor power) in April 1940, and American troops successfully launched seaborne assaults against French-controlled North Africa in November 1942. France, which was decisively defeated by Nazi Germany in the spring of 1940, was not a sovereign state, much less a great power, in 1942. On Norway, see Jack Adams, *The Doomed Expedition: The Norwegian Campaign of 1940* (London: Leo Cooper, 1989); and Maurice Harvey, *Scandinavian Misadventure* (Turnbridge Wells, UK: Spellmount, 1990). On North Africa, see George F. Howe, *Northwest Africa: Seizing the Initiative in the West* (Washington, DC: U.S. Government Printing Office, 1991), pts. 1–3. Furthermore, the Germans and especially the Soviets launched numerous small-scale amphibious operations into territory controlled by the other side on the shores of the Baltic and Black Seas. See W. I. Atschkassow, "Landing Operations of the Soviet Naval Fleet during World War Two," in Merrill L. Bartlett, ed., *Assault from the Sea: Essays on the History of Amphibious Warfare* (Annapolis, MD: U.S. Naval Institute Press, 1983), pp. 299–307; and "Baltic Sea Operations," and "Black Sea Operations," in Dear, ed., *Oxford Companion to World War II,* pp. 106–8, 135–36. One study estimates that the Soviets conducted 113 amphibious invasions between 1941 and 1945. See Atschkassow, "Landing Operations," p. 299. Many failed, but more important, they were all minor operations that took place on the periphery of the main battlefront between the Wehrmacht and the Red Army. Consequently, they had little influence on the war's outcome. Finally, the Soviets launched two minor amphibious operations against Finnish-controlled territory in 1944, one of which failed. See Waldemar Erfurth, *The Last Finnish War* (Washington, DC: University Publications of America, 1979), p. 190.

107. On Sicily, see Albert N. Garland and Howard M. Smyth, *Sicily and the Surrender of Italy* (Washington, DC: U.S. Government Printing Office, 1965), chaps. 1–10. On the Italian mainland, see Martin Blumenson, *Salerno to Cassino* (Washington, DC: U.S. Government Printing Office, 1969), chaps. 1–9.

108. On Anzio, see Blumenson, *Salerno to Cassino*, chaps. 17–18, 20, 22, 24.

109. On Normandy, see Gordon A. Harrison, *Cross-Channel Attack* (Washington, DC: U.S. Government Printing Office, 1951). On southern France, see Jeffrey J. Clarke and Robert R. Smith, *Riviera to the Rhine* (Washington, DC: U.S. Government Printing Office, 1993), chaps. 1–7.

110. Italy was technically still a great power when the Allies invaded Sicily in mid-1943, and Italian as well as German troops were located on that island. But as noted, the Italian army was in tatters and incapable of putting up a serious fight against the Allies. In fact, the Wehrmacht was largely responsible for Italy's defense at the time of the Sicily operation. Italy was out of the war when the Allies invaded the Italian mainland and Anzio.

111. See Paul Kennedy, *Pacific Onslaught: 7th December 1941–7th February 1943* (New York: Ballantine, 1972); and H. P. Willmott, *Empires in the Balance: Japanese and Allied Pacific Strategies to April 1942* (Annapolis, MD: U.S. Naval Institute Press, 1982).

112. Hezlet, *Aircraft and Sea Power*, chap. 8; Isely and Crowl, *U.S. Marines and Amphibious War*, pp. 74, 79; and Hans G. Von Lehmann, "Japanese Landing Operations in World War II," in Bartlett, ed., *Assault from the Sea*, pp. 195–201.

113. "Major U.S. Amphibious Operations—World War II," memorandum, U.S. Army Center of Military History, Washington, DC, December 15, 1960. Each of the fifty-two invasion forces was at least the size of a regimental combat team. Operations involving smaller units are not included. Also, the Australian military conducted three amphibious operations against Japanese forces on Borneo between May and July 1945. These mopping-up campaigns succeeded for essentially the same reasons that the American seaborne invasions gained their objective. See Peter Dennis et al., *The Oxford Companion to Australian Military History* (Oxford: Oxford University Press, 1995), pp. 109–16.

114. USSBS, *Air Campaigns of the Pacific War*, p. 19.

115. Guadalcanal and the Philippines are major exceptions to this rule. See George W. Garand and Truman R. Strobridge, *Western Pacific Operations: History of U.S. Marine Corps Operations in World War II*, vol. 4 (Washington, DC: U.S. Government Printing Office, 1971), pp. 320–21; and Isely and Crowl, *U.S. Marines and Amphibious War*, p. 588.

116. USSBS, *Air Campaigns of the Pacific War*, p. 61.

117. Among the best general surveys of this conflict are Paul S. Dull, *A Battle History of the Imperial Japanese Navy, 1941–1945* (Annapolis, MD: U.S. Naval Institute

Press, 1978); Isely and Crowl, *U.S. Marines and Amphibious War;* Potter and Nimitz, *Sea Power,* chaps. 35–43; and Ronald H. Spector, *Eagle against the Sun: The American War with Japan* (New York: Free Press, 1985).

118. On the disparity in size between the Japanese and American economies, see Table 6.2; Adelman, *Prelude,* pp. 139, 202–3; and Jonathan R. Adelman, *Revolution, Armies, and War: A Political History* (Boulder, CO: Lynne Rienner, 1985), pp. 130–31.

119. By mid-1945, there were about 2 million soldiers in Japan's home army. Dear, ed., *Oxford Companion to World War II,* p. 623. At the same time, there were roughly 900,000 Japanese soldiers in China, 250,000 in Korea, 750,000 in Manchuria, and 600,000 in Southeast Asia. These numbers are from Adelman, *Revolution,* p. 147; Saburo Hayashi and Alvin D. Coox, *Kogun: The Japanese Army in the Pacific War* (Quantico, VA: Marine Corps Association, 1959), p. 173; and Douglas J. MacEachin, *The Final Months of the War with Japan: Signals Intelligence, U.S. Invasion Planning, and the A-Bomb Decision* (Langley, VA: Center for the Study of Intelligence, Central Intelligence Agency, December 1998), attached document no. 4.

120. Although the invading American forces would surely have conquered Japan, they undoubtedly would also have suffered significant casualties in the process. See Frank, *Downfall;* and MacEachin, *Final Months.*

121. Insular powers, however, might be attacked over land by a rival great power if that adversary can deploy troops on the territory of a minor power in the insular state's backyard. As will be discussed in the next chapter, insular great powers worry about this possibility and seek to ensure that it never happens.

122. See Frank J. McLynn, *Invasion: From the Armada to Hitler, 1588–1945* (London: Routledge and Kegan Paul, 1987); and Herbert W. Richmond, *The Invasion of Britain: An Account of Plans, Attempts and Counter-measures from 1586 to 1918* (London: Methuen, 1941).

123. See Felipe Fernández-Armesto, *The Spanish Armada: The Experience of War in 1588* (Oxford: Oxford University Press, 1988); Colin Martin and Geoffrey Parker, *The Spanish Armada* (London: Hamish Hamilton, 1988); Garrett Mattingly, *The Armada* (Boston: Houghton Mifflin, 1959); and David Howarth, *The Voyage of the Armada: The Spanish Story* (New York: Viking, 1981).

124. On Napoleon, see Richard Glover, *Britain at Bay: Defence against Bonaparte, 1803–14* (London: Allen and Unwin, 1973); J. Holland Rose and A. M. Broadley, *Dumouriez and the Defence of England against Napoleon* (New York: John Lane, 1909); and H.F.B. Wheeler and A. M. Broadley, *Napoleon and the Invasion of England: The Story of the Great Terror* (New York: John Lane, 1908). On Hitler, see Frank Davis, "Sea Lion: The German Plan to Invade Britain, 1940," in Bartlett, ed., *Assault from the Sea,* pp. 228–35; Egber Kieser, *Hitler on the Doorstep, Operation 'Sea Lion': The*

German Plan to Invade Britain, 1940, trans. Helmut Bogler (Annapolis, MD: U.S. Naval Institute Press, 1997); and Peter Schenk, *Invasion of England 1940: The Planning of Operation Sealion,* trans. Kathleen Bunten (London: Conway Maritime Press, 1990).

125. Gen. Hans von Seeckt, a prominent German officer, noted in 1916 that "America cannot be attacked by us, and until technology provides us with totally new weapons, England itself neither." Quoted in Vagts, *Landing Operations,* p. 506.

126. The United Kingdom prepared plans for invading the United States until the late 1890s but then gave up on the idea. See Aaron Friedberg, *The Weary Titan: Britain and the Experience of Relative Decline, 1895–1905* (Princeton, NJ: Princeton University Press, 1988), pp. 162–65.

127. As noted, the Allies invaded northwestern France in June 1944 and southern France in August 1944. But France was not a sovereign state at that point; it was part of the Nazi empire.

128. One noteworthy case is left out of this analysis. In the final year of World War I, the United Kingdom, Canada, France, Italy, Japan, and the United States inserted troops into the newly established Soviet Union at Archangel (August 2, 1918), Baku (August 4, 1918), Murmansk (March 6 and June 23, 1918), and Vladivostok (April 5 and August 3, 1918). Those troops eventually fought some battles against the Bolsheviks. This case is not relevant, however, because the Allies' entrance into the Soviet Union was not an invasion in any meaningful sense of that term. The Soviet Union had just been decisively defeated by Germany and was in the midst of a civil war. Consequently, the Bolshevik army did not oppose the coming of Allied forces. In fact, the Allies were welcomed into Baku and Archangel. See John Swettenham, *Allied Intervention in Russia, 1918–1919* (Toronto: Ryerson, 1967); and Richard H. Ullman, *Intervention and the War* (Princeton, NJ: Princeton University Press, 1961).

129. See William Daugherty, Barbara Levi, and Frank von Hippel, "The Consequences of 'Limited' Nuclear Attacks on the United States," *International Security* 10, No. 4 (Spring 1986), pp. 3–45; and Arthur M. Katz, *Life after Nuclear War: The Economic and Social Impacts of Nuclear Attacks on the United States* (Cambridge, MA: Ballinger, 1982).

130. After listening to a Strategic Air Command (SAC) briefing on March 18, 1954, a U.S. navy captain used these words to describe what SAC planned to do to the Soviet Union in the event of war. David Alan Rosenberg, "'A Smoking Radiating Ruin at the End of Two Hours': Documents on American Plans for Nuclear War with the Soviet Union, 1954–1955," *International Security* 6, No. 3 (Winter 1981–82), pp. 11, 25.

131. Herman Kahn coined the phrase "splendid first strike," which is synonymous with a disarming first strike. See Kahn's *On Thermonuclear War: Three Lectures and Several Suggestions,* 2d ed. (New York: Free Press, 1969), pp. 36–37.

132. See Charles L. Glaser, *Analyzing Strategic Nuclear Policy* (Princeton, NJ: Princeton University Press, 1990), chap. 5.

133. See Benjamin Frankel, "The Brooding Shadow: Systemic Incentives and Nuclear Weapons Proliferation," *Security Studies* 2, Nos. 3–4 (Spring–Summer 1993), pp. 37–78; and Bradley A. Thayer, "The Causes of Nuclear Proliferation and the Utility of the Nuclear Nonproliferation Regime," *Security Studies* 4, No. 3 (Spring 1995), pp. 463–519.

134. See Harry R. Borowski, *A Hollow Threat: Strategic Air Power and Containment before Korea* (Westport, CT: Greenwood, 1982); David A. Rosenberg, "The Origins of Overkill: Nuclear Weapons and American Strategy, 1945–1960," *International Security* 7, No. 4 (Spring 1983), pp. 14–18; and Ross, *American War Plans*, passim, esp. pp. 12–15. A yearly inventory of the superpowers' nuclear arsenals for the entire Cold War can be found in Robert S. Norris and William M. Arkin, "Nuclear Notebook: Estimated U.S. and Soviet/Russian Nuclear Stockpile, 1945–94," *Bulletin of the Atomic Scientists* 50, No. 6 (November–December 1994), p. 59. Also see Robert S. Norris and William M. Arkin, "Global Nuclear Stockpiles, 1945–2000," *Bulletin of the Atomic Scientists* 56, No. 2 (March–April 2000), p. 79.

135. During the Cold War, some experts argued that it is possible to achieve nuclear superiority even in a MAD world. Specifically, they claimed that it was possible for the superpowers to fight a limited nuclear war with their counterforce weapons (nuclear weapons designed to destroy other nuclear weapons, rather than cities), while leaving each other's assured destruction capability intact. Each superpower would also try to minimize civilian deaths on the other side. The superpower that emerged from this limited nuclear exchange with an advantage in counterforce weapons would be the winner, having gained significant coercive leverage over the loser. See Colin S. Gray, "Nuclear Strategy: A Case for a Theory of Victory," *International Security* 4, No. 1 (Summer 1979), pp. 54–87; and Paul Nitze, "Deterring Our Deterrent," *Foreign Policy*, No. 25 (Winter 1976–77), pp. 195–210. The case for limited nuclear options, however, is flawed for two reasons. First, it is not likely that such a war would remain limited. The destruction to each side's society would be enormous, making it difficult to distinguish a limited counterforce strike from an all-out attack. Furthermore, we do not know much about escalation dynamics in a nuclear war, especially regarding how command-and-control systems would perform in a nuclear attack. Second, even if it were possible to fight a limited nuclear war and minimize casualties, the side with a counterforce advantage would not win a meaningful victory, as the following example illustrates. Assume that the Soviets won a counterforce exchange between the superpowers; they were left with 500 counterforce warheads, the United States had none. In the process, both sides suffered 500,000 casualties, and their assured destruction capabilities remained intact. The Soviets are purportedly the victors because they have a counterforce advantage of 500:0. In fact, that advantage is meaningless, because there are no targets left in the United States that the Soviets can use their 500 counterforce weapons against, unless they want to strike at America's cities or its assured destruction capability and get annihilated in the process. In short, the result of this limited nuclear war is that both sides suffer equal casualties, both sides have their assured destruction capabilities intact, and the Soviet Union has 500 counterforce weapons that it cannot use in any meaningful military way. That is a hollow victory. Among the best works criticizing limited nuclear options are Glaser, *Analyzing Strategic Nuclear Policy*, chap. 7; and Robert Jervis, "Why Nuclear Superiority Doesn't Matter," *Political Science Quarterly* 94, No. 4 (Winter 1979–80), pp. 617–33.

136. Robert S. McNamara, "The Military Role of Nuclear Weapons: Perceptions and Misperceptions," *Foreign Affairs* 62, No. 1 (Fall 1983), p. 79.

137. The idea that robust stability at the nuclear level allows for instability at the conventional level is often called the "stability-instability paradox." See Glenn H. Snyder, "The Balance of Power and the Balance of Terror," in Paul Seabury, ed., *Balance of Power* (San Francisco: Chandler, 1965), pp. 184–201. Also see Robert Jervis, *The Meaning of the Nuclear Revolution: Statecraft and the Prospect of Armageddon* (Ithaca, NY: Cornell University Press, 1989), pp. 19–22.

138. On accidental nuclear escalation, see Bruce G. Blair, *The Logic of Accidental Nuclear War* (Washington, DC: Brookings Institution Press, 1993); and Scott D. Sagan, *The Limits of Safety: Organizations, Accidents, and Nuclear Weapons* (Princeton, NJ: Princeton University Press, 1993). On inadvertent nuclear escalation, see Posen, *Inadvertent Escalation*. On purposeful nuclear escalation, see Herman Kahn, *On Escalation: Metaphors and Scenarios*, rev. ed. (Baltimore, MD: Penguin, 1968); and Thomas Schelling, *Arms and Influence* (New Haven, CT: Yale University Press, 1966), chaps. 2–3. The best book on the general phenomenon of escalation is Richard Smoke, *War: Controlling Escalation* (Cambridge, MA: Harvard University Press, 1977), although it says little about escalation from the conventional to the nuclear level, or about escalation in a nuclear war.

139. Robert Jervis is probably the most articulate proponent of this perspective. He writes, "The implications of mutual second-strike capability are many and far-reaching. If nuclear weapons have had the influence that the nuclear-revolution theory indicates they should have, then there will be peace between the superpowers, crises will be rare, neither side will be eager to press bargaining advantages to the limit, the status quo will be relatively easy to maintain, and political outcomes will not be closely related to either the nuclear or the conventional balance. Although the evidence is ambiguous, it generally confirms these propositions." Jervis, *Meaning of the Nuclear Revolution*, p. 45. Also see McGeorge Bundy, *Danger and*

Survival: Choices about the Bomb in the First Fifty Years (New York: Random House, 1988).

140. Assume, for example, that Mexico becomes a great power with a survivable nuclear deterrent. Also assume that Mexico becomes interested in conquering a large expanse of territory in the southwestern United States, but otherwise has no interest in conquering American territory. Mexican policymakers might conclude that they could achieve their limited aims without causing the United States to start a nuclear war. In the event, they probably would prove correct. American policymakers, however, would be much more likely to use nuclear weapons if Mexico tried to inflict a decisive defeat on the United States. Shai Feldman makes essentially the same point regarding the decision by Egypt and Syria to attack a nuclear-armed Israel in 1973. Arab policymakers, he argues, thought that Israel would not use its nuclear weapons, because the Arab armies were not bent on conquering Israel but were merely aiming to recapture territory lost to Israel in the 1967 war. Feldman, *Israeli Nuclear Deterrence: A Strategy for the 1980s* (New York: Columbia University Press, 1982), chap. 3. But as Feldman points out, the state that loses a slice of its territory is likely to think that the victor will want to take another slice, and then another slice, and that such "salami tactics" will ultimately lead to its destruction. Ibid., pp. 111–12. The best way to avoid this predicament is to have powerful conventional forces that can deter the initial attack; this once again highlights the importance of the balance of land power.

141. For example, the United States spent roughly five times more money on conventional forces than on nuclear forces during the early 1980s, and about four times as much by the mid-1980s. See Harold Brown, *Department of Defense Annual Report for Fiscal Year 1982* (Washington, DC: U.S. Department of Defense, January 19, 1981), pp. C-4, C-5; and William W. Kaufmann, *A Reasonable Defense* (Washington, DC: Brookings Institution Press, 1986), pp. 21, 27. Over the course of the entire Cold War, roughly 25 percent of American defense spending went to the nuclear forces. See Steven M. Kosiak, *The Lifecycle Costs of Nuclear Forces: A Preliminary Assessment* (Washington, DC: Defense Budget Project, October 1994), p. ii. Another study estimates that about 29 percent of defense spending from 1940 to 1996 went toward nuclear weapons. See Stephen I. Schwartz, ed., *Atomic Audit: The Costs and Consequences of U.S. Nuclear Weapons since 1940* (Washington, DC: Brookings Institution Press, 1998), p. 3. For evidence of the relative importance of U.S. conventional forces in Europe, consider how the fiscal year 1986 U.S. defense budget, which totaled $313.7 billion, was apportioned: roughly $133 billion went to conventional defense of Europe, $54.7 billion went to nuclear forces, $34.6 billion went to conventional defense in the Pacific, $20.9 billion went to conventional defense of the Persian Gulf, and $16.2 billion went to conventional defense of

Panama and the U.S. homeland. These figures are from Kaufmann, *Reasonable Defense*, p. 14. Also see the works cited in Chapter 6, note 177, of this book.

142. See Feldman, *Israeli Nuclear Deterrence*, pp. 106–12, esp. p. 109.

143. See Thomas W. Robinson, "The Sino-Soviet Border Conflict," in Stephen S. Kaplan, ed., *Diplomacy of Power: Soviet Armed Forces as a Political Instrument* (Washington, DC: Brookings Institution Press, 1981), pp. 265–313; Harrison E. Salisbury, *War between Russia and China* (New York: Norton, 1969); and Richard Wich, *Sino-Soviet Crisis Politics: A Study of Political Change and Communication* (Cambridge, MA: Harvard University Press, 1980), chaps. 6, 9.

144. See Sumantra Bose, "Kashmir: Sources of Conflict, Dimensions of Peace," *Survival* 41, No. 3 (Autumn 1999), pp. 149–71; Sumit Ganguly, *The Crisis in Kashmir: Portents of War, Hopes of Peace* (Cambridge: Cambridge University Press, 1999); and Devin T. Hagerty, "Nuclear Deterrence in South Asia: The 1990 Indo-Pakistani Crisis," *International Security* 20, No. 3 (Winter 1995–96), pp. 79–114.

145. As noted in Chapter 3, note 11, full-scale net assessments require more than just measuring the size and quality of the opposing forces. It is also necessary to consider the strategy that both sides would employ and what is likely to happen when the rival forces collide.

146. See Mako, *U.S. Ground Forces*, pp. 108–26; and *Weapons Effectiveness Indices/Weighted Unit Values III (WEI/WUV III)* (Bethesda, MD: U.S. Army Concepts Analysis Agency, November 1979). Also see Phillip A. Karber et al., *Assessing the Correlation of Forces: France 1940*, Report No. BDM/W-79-560-TR (McLean, VA: BDM Corporation, June 18, 1979), which uses this methodology to assess the balance of forces between Germany and the Allies in the spring of 1940.

147. Posen, "Measuring the European Conventional Balance," pp. 51–54, 66–70.

148. For examples of how one might do this kind of analysis, see Joshua Epstein, *Measuring Military Power: The Soviet Air Threat to Europe* (Princeton, NJ: Princeton University Press, 1984); and Posen, *Inadvertent Escalation*, pp. 101–6.

149. The prospects for peace would also be enhanced if each of those states had an ethnically homogeneous population, because then there would be no ethnic civil wars.

CHAPTER FIVE

1. I remind readers that the term "aggressor" is used throughout this book to denote great powers that have both the motive and the wherewithal to use force to gain additional power. As emphasized in Chapter 2, all great powers have aggressive intentions, but not all states have the capability to act aggressively.

2. See Stephen M. Walt, *The Origins of Alliances* (Ithaca, NY: Cornell University Press, 1987); and Kenneth N. Waltz, *Theory of International Politics* (Reading, MA: Addison-Wesley, 1979). Also see Robert Powell, *In the Shadow of Power: States and Strategies in International Politics* (Princeton, NJ: Princeton University Press, 1999), chap. 5, which emphasizes the distinction between bandwagoning and balancing, but unlike Walt and Waltz, argues that threatened states are more likely to bandwagon than balance against their adversaries.

3. For evidence that supports my point, see the debate between Robert Kaufman and Stephen Walt over Allied policy toward Nazi Germany during the 1930s. Their debate is framed explicitly in terms of the dichotomy between balancing and bandwagoning, a contrast that Walt helped make famous. A close reading of the debate, however, makes it clear that, the authors' rhetoric notwithstanding, the real choice facing the Allies was between balancing and buck-passing, not balancing and bandwagoning. See Robert G. Kaufman, "To Balance or to Bandwagon? Alignment Decisions in 1930s Europe," *Security Studies* 1, No. 3 (Spring 1992), pp. 417–47; and Stephen M. Walt, "Alliances, Threats, and U.S. Grand Strategy: A Reply to Kaufman and Labs," *Security Studies* 1, No. 3 (Spring 1992), pp. 448–82.

4. See Steven J. Valone, "'Weakness Offers Temptation': Seward and the Reassertion of the Monroe Doctrine," *Diplomatic History* 19, No. 4 (Fall 1995), pp. 583–99. As discussed in Chapter 7, the United States has worried throughout its history about the threat of distant great powers forming alliances with other states in the Western Hemisphere. Also see Alan Dowty, *The Limits of American Isolation: The United States and the Crimean War* (New York: New York University Press, 1971); and J. Fred Rippy, *America and the Strife of Europe* (Chicago: University of Chicago Press, 1938), esp. chaps. 6–8.

5. These words are not Weber's, but Wolfgang J. Mommsen's synopsis of Weber's views. See Mommsen, *Max Weber and German Politics, 1890–1920*, trans. Michael S. Steinberg (Chicago: University of Chicago Press, 1984), p. 39.

6. Paul M. Kennedy, *The Rise of the Anglo-German Antagonism, 1860–1914* (London: Allen and Unwin, 1980), chaps. 16, 20.

7. See Stephen Van Evera, "Why Europe Matters, Why the Third World Doesn't: American Grand Strategy after the Cold War," *Journal of Strategic Studies* 13, No. 2 (June 1990), pp. 1–51; and Stephen M. Walt, "The Case for Finite Containment: Analyzing U.S. Grand Strategy," *International Security* 14, No. 1 (Summer 1989), pp. 5–49. For an argument that areas with little intrinsic wealth are sometimes strategically important, see Michael C. Desch, *When the Third World Matters: Latin America and United States Grand Strategy* (Baltimore, MD: Johns Hopkins University Press, 1993). Also see Steven R. David, "Why the Third World Matters," *International Security* 14, No. 1 (Summer 1989), pp. 50–85; and Steven R. David,

"Why the Third World Still Matters," *International Security* 17, No. 3 (Winter 1992–93), pp. 127–59.

8. See Barry R. Posen and Stephen Van Evera, "Defense Policy and the Reagan Administration: Departure from Containment," *International Security* 8, No. 1 (Summer 1983), pp. 3–45.

9. Charles L. Glaser, *Analyzing Strategic Nuclear Policy* (Princeton, NJ: Princeton University Press, 1990); Robert Jervis, *The Illogic of American Nuclear Strategy* (Ithaca, NY: Cornell University Press, 1984); Robert Jervis, *The Meaning of the Nuclear Revolution: Statecraft and the Prospects of Armageddon* (Ithaca, NY: Cornell University Press, 1989); and Stephen Van Evera, *Causes of War: Power and the Roots of Conflict* (Ithaca, NY: Cornell University Press, 1999), chap. 8.

10. Norman Angell, *The Great Illusion: A Study of the Relation of Military Power in Nations to Their Economic and Social Advantage,* 3d rev. and enl. ed. (New York: Putnam, 1912). Also see Norman Angell, *The Great Illusion 1933* (New York: Putnam, 1933). For an early critique of Angell, see J. H. Jones, *The Economics of War and Conquest: An Examination of Mr. Norman Angell's Economic Doctrines* (London: P. S. King, 1915).

11. See Robert Gilpin, *War and Change in World Politics* (Cambridge: Cambridge University Press, 1981); and Paul M. Kennedy, *The Rise and Fall of the Great Powers: Economic Change and Military Conflict from 1500 to 2000* (New York: Random House, 1987).

12. For example, see Klaus Knorr, *On the Uses of Military Power in the Nuclear Age* (Princeton, NJ: Princeton University Press, 1966), pp. 21–34; Richard Rosecrance, *The Rise of the Trading State: Commerce and Conquest in the Modern World* (New York: Basic Books, 1986), pp. 34–37; and Van Evera, *Causes of War,* chap. 5.

13. Van Evera makes this argument in *Causes of War,* p. 115.

14. See Ethan B. Kapstein, *The Political Economy of National Security: A Global Perspective* (Columbia: University of South Carolina Press, 1992), pp. 42–52.

15. See the sources cited in Chapter 3, note 57.

16. For example, a number of studies argue that the Soviet Union's system of rigid centralized control of the economy was the main culprit for stifling innovation and growth. See Tatyana Zaslavskaya, "The Novosibirsk Report," *Survey* 28, No. 1 (Spring 1984), pp. 88–108; Abel Aganbegyan, *The Economic Challenge of Perestroika,* trans. Pauline M. Tiffen (Bloomington: Indiana University Press, 1988); Padma Desai, *Perestroika in Perspective: The Design and Dilemmas of Soviet Reform* (Princeton, NJ: Princeton University Press, 1989); and Anders Aslund, *Gorbachev's Struggle for Economic Reform,* rev. ed. (Ithaca, NY: Cornell University Press, 1991). Also see Peter Rutland, *Politics of Economic Stagnation in the Soviet Union: The Role of Local Party Organs in Economic Management* (Cambridge: Cambridge University Press, 1993), which blames the Soviet Union's economic woes on the Communist Party.

17. See Peter Liberman, *Does Conquest Pay? The Exploitation of Occupied Industrial Societies* (Princeton, NJ: Princeton University Press, 1996); and Peter Liberman, "The Spoils of Conquest," *International Security* 18, No. 2 (Fall 1993), pp. 125–53. Also see David Kaiser, *Politics and War: European Conflict from Philip II to Hitler* (Cambridge, MA: Harvard University Press, 1990), pp. 219–22, 246–55; and Alan S. Milward, *War, Economy, and Society, 1939–1945* (Berkeley: University of California Press, 1977), chap. 5.

18. These quotes are from Liberman, *Does Conquest Pay?* p. 28; and Lieberman, "Spoils of Conquest," p. 126. On the Orwellian dimension of information technologies, see Jeffrey Rosen, *The Unwanted Gaze: The Destruction of Privacy in America* (New York: Random House, 2000). In a recent article assessing whether conquest pays, Stephen Brooks concludes that Liberman's claim that repressive conquerors can deal effectively with popular resistance as well as the subversive potential of information technologies is persuasive. Stephen G. Brooks, "The Globalization of Production and the Changing Benefits of Conquest," *Journal of Conflict Resolution* 43, No. 5 (October 1999), pp. 646–70. Brooks argues, however, that conquest is not likely to pay significant dividends, because of "changes in the globalization of production" (p. 653). This argument, which I find unconvincing, is basically the liberal theory that economic interdependence causes peace, updated to take account of globalization. I deal with it briefly in Chapter 10.

19. Liberman, "Spoils of Conquest," p. 139.

20. See Norman M. Naimark, *The Russians in Germany: A History of the Soviet Zone of Occupation, 1945–1949* (Cambridge, MA: Harvard University Press, 1995). Also see Liberman, *Does Conquest Pay?* chap. 7.

21. See Joshua M. Epstein, *Strategy and Force Planning: The Case of the Persian Gulf* (Washington, DC: Brookings Institution Press, 1987); Charles A. Kupchan, *The Persian Gulf and the West: The Dilemmas of Security* (Boston: Allen and Unwin, 1987); and Thomas L. McNaugher, *Arms and Oil: U.S. Military Strategy and the Persian Gulf* (Washington, DC: Brookings Institution Press, 1985).

22. See John W. Wheeler-Bennett, *Brest-Litovsk: The Forgotten Peace, March 1918* (New York: Norton, 1971); and Milward, *War, Economy, and Society,* chap. 8.

23. Clive Emsley, *Napoleonic Europe* (New York: Longman, 1993), p. 146.

24. David G. Chandler, *The Campaigns of Napoleon* (New York: Macmillan, 1966), pp. 754–56.

25. George H. Stein, *The Waffen SS: Hitler's Elite Guard at War, 1939–1945* (Ithaca, NY: Cornell University Press, 1966), p. 137.

26. Edward Homze, "Nazi Germany's Forced Labor Program," in Michael Berenbaum, ed., *A Mosaic of Victims: Non-Jews Persecuted and Murdered by the Nazis* (New York: New York University Press, 1990), pp. 37–38. Also see Ulrich Herbert, *Hitler's Foreign Workers: Enforced Foreign Labor in Germany under the Third Reich,* trans. William Templer (Cambridge: Cambridge University Press, 1997).

27. See Jere C. King, *Foch versus Clemenceau: France and German Dismemberment, 1918–1919* (Cambridge, MA: Harvard University Press, 1960); Walter A. McDougall, *France's Rhineland Diplomacy, 1914–1924: The Last Bid for a Balance of Power in Europe* (Princeton, NJ: Princeton University Press, 1978); and David Stevenson, *French War Aims against Germany, 1914–1919* (Oxford: Oxford University Press, 1982).

28. Max Jakobson, *The Diplomacy of the Winter War: An Account of the Russo-Finnish War* (Cambridge, MA: Harvard University Press, 1961), pts. 1–3; Anthony F. Upton, *Finland, 1939–1940* (London: Davis-Poynter, 1974), chaps. 1–2; and Carl Van Dyke, *The Soviet Invasion of Finland, 1939–1940* (London: Frank Cass, 1997), chap. 1.

29. On Carthage, see Serge Lancel, *Carthage: A History*, trans. Antonia Nevill (Cambridge: Blackwell, 1995), esp. pp. 412–27. On Poland, see Jan T. Gross, *Polish Society under German Occupation: The Generalgouvernement, 1939–1944* (Princeton, NJ: Princeton University Press, 1979); and Richard C. Lukas, *Forgotten Holocaust: The Poles under German Occupation, 1939–1944* (Lexington: University Press of Kentucky, 1986). On the Soviet Union, see Alexander Dallin, *German Rule in Russia, 1941–1945: A Study of Occupation Policies* (London: Macmillan, 1957). Also see David Weigall and Peter Stirk, eds., *The Origins and Development of the European Community* (London: Leicester University Press, 1992), pp. 27–28.

30. Michael Handel writes, "The basic assumption underlying the Israeli political-military doctrine is the understanding that the *central aim of Arab countries is to destroy the state of Israel whenever they feel able to do so,* while doing everything to harass and disturb its peaceful life." Handel, *Israel's Political-Military Doctrine*, Occasional Paper No. 30 (Cambridge, MA: Center for International Affairs, Harvard University, July 1973), p. 64 [emphasis in original]. Also see Yehoshafat Harkabi, *Arab Strategies and Israel's Response* (New York: Free Press, 1977); Yehoshafat Harkabi, *Arab Attitudes to Israel*, trans. Misha Louvish (Jerusalem: Israel Universities Press, 1972); and Asher Arian, *Israeli Public Opinion on National Security, 2000*, Memorandum No. 56 (Tel Aviv: Jaffee Center for Strategic Studies, July 2000), pp. 13–16.

31. Poland was partitioned in 1772, 1793, and 1795 by Austria, Prussia, and Russia, and in 1939 by Germany and the Soviet Union. Furthermore, at the end of World War II, Stalin took the eastern third of Poland and incorporated it into the Soviet Union. One author notes that, "Contrary to conventional wisdom, state death has occurred quite frequently over the last two centuries; 69 of 210 states (about 30%) have died, and most [51 out of those 69] have died violently." Most of the victims were small states that either became an integral part of a great power or part of a great power's empire. Some of the victims eventually came back from the dead and became independent states again. Tanisha M. Fazal, "Born to Lose and Doomed to Survive: State Death and Survival in the International System," paper presented at the Annual Meeting of the American Political Science Association, Washington, DC, August 31–September 3, 2000, pp. 15–16.

32. Wilfried Loth, "Stalin's Plans for Post-War Germany," in Francesca Gori and Silvio Pons, eds., *The Soviet Union and Europe in the Cold War, 1943–53* (New York: St. Martin's, 1996), pp. 23–36; Marc Trachtenberg, *A Constructed Peace: The Making of the European Settlement, 1945–1963* (Princeton, NJ: Princeton University Press, 1999), pp. 57–60, 129–30; and Vladislav Zubok and Constantine Pleshakov, *Inside the Kremlin's Cold War: From Stalin to Khrushchev* (Cambridge, MA: Harvard University Press, 1996), pp. 46–53.

33. See Warren F. Kimball, *Swords or Ploughshares? The Morgenthau Plan for Defeated Nazi Germany, 1943–1946* (Philadelphia: Lippincott, 1976); and Henry Morgenthau, Jr., *Germany Is Our Problem* (New York: Harper, 1945).

34. A brief word on the terms "coercion" and "blackmail." Coercion involves either the use of force or the threat of force to get an adversary to change its behavior. I used the term "coercion" in Chapter 4 to describe the *actual* use of force (naval blockade and strategic bombing) to cause an opponent to quit a war before it was conquered. To avoid possible confusion, I use the term "blackmail" to describe *threats* of force to alter state behavior. Nevertheless, blackmail is generally synonymous with coercion. On coercion see Daniel Ellsberg, "Theory and Practice of Blackmail," RAND Paper P-3883 (Santa Monica, CA: RAND Corporation, 1968); Alexander L. George, William E. Simons, and David K. Hall, *Limits of Coercive Diplomacy: Laos, Cuba, and Vietnam* (Boston: Little, Brown, 1971); Robert A. Pape, *Bombing to Win: Air Power and Coercion in War* (Ithaca, NY: Cornell University Press, 1996); Thomas Schelling, *Arms and Influence* (New Haven, CT: Yale University Press, 1966); and Thomas Schelling, *Strategy of Conflict* (Cambridge, MA: Harvard University Press, 1960).

35. Regarding the pre–World War I crises, see Luigi Albertini, *The Origins of the War of 1914*, vol. I, *European Relations from the Congress of Berlin to the Eve of the Sarajevo Murder*, ed. and trans. Isabella M. Massey (Oxford: Oxford University Press, 1952), chaps. 3–10; Imanuel Geiss, *German Foreign Policy, 1871–1914* (London: Routledge and Kegan Paul, 1979), chaps. 8–17; David G. Herrmann, *The Arming of Europe and the Making of the First World War* (Princeton, NJ: Princeton University Press, 1996); and L.C.F. Turner, *Origins of the First World War* (New York: Norton, 1970).

36. See Christopher Andrew, *Théophile Delcassé and the Making of the Entente Cordiale: A Reappraisal of French Foreign Policy, 1898–1905* (New York: St. Martin's, 1968), chap. 5; Darrell Bates, *The Fashoda Incident: Encounter on the Nile* (Oxford: Oxford University Press, 1984); and Roger G. Brown, *Fashoda Reconsidered: The Impact of Domestic Politics on French Policy in Africa, 1893–1898* (Baltimore, MD: Johns Hopkins University Press, 1969).

37. Herman Kahn, *On Thermonuclear War: Three Lectures and Several Suggestions*, 2d ed. (New York: Free Press, 1960), p. 231; and Henry S. Rowen, "Catalytic Nuclear War," in Graham T. Allison, Albert Carnesale, and Joseph S. Nye, Jr., eds.,

Hawks, Doves, and Owls: An Agenda for Avoiding Nuclear War (New York: Norton, 1985), pp. 148–63.

38. Quoted in T.C.W. Blanning, *The Origins of the French Revolutionary Wars* (London: Longman, 1986), p. 186. There is some evidence that in 1908 Austria-Hungary's foreign minister considered trying to bait Serbia and Bulgaria into a war, so that Austria-Hungary could take advantage of a weakened Serbia in the Balkans. However, the idea was not put into practice. Edmond Taylor, *The Fall of the Dynasties: The Collapse of the Old Order, 1905–1922* (Garden City, NY: Doubleday, 1963), pp. 128–29. Also, some argue that Stalin baited Nazi Germany and the Allies into starting World War II. But as discussed in Chapter 8, there is not sufficient evidence to support that claim.

39. See Charles D. Smith, *Palestine and the Arab-Israeli Conflict*, 2d ed. (New York: St. Martin's, 1992), p. 164; and Michael Bar-Zohar, *Ben-Gurion: A Biography*, trans. Peretz Kidron (New York: Delacorte, 1978), pp. 209–16.

40. Quoted in David McCullough, *Truman* (New York: Touchstone, 1992), p. 262.

41. Wheeler-Bennett, *Brest-Litovsk*, pp. 189–90, 385–91.

42. See Peter Schweizer, *Victory: The Reagan Administration's Secret Strategy That Hastened the Collapse of the Soviet Union* (New York: Atlantic Monthly Press, 1994), pp. xviii, 9, 64–65, 100–101, 116–19, 151–53. Also see Robert P. Hager, Jr., and David A. Lake, "Balancing Empires: Competitive Decolonization in International Politics," *Security Studies* 9, No. 3 (Spring 2000), pp. 108–48.

43. On balancing, see Robert Jervis and Jack Snyder, eds., *Dominoes and Bandwagons: Strategic Beliefs and Great Power Competition in the Eurasian Rimland* (Oxford: Oxford University Press, 1991); Walt, *Origins of Alliances;* and Waltz, *Theory of International Politics.* Some scholars define balancing behavior as a joint effort by the great powers to preserve each other's independence. States have "a conception of a common destiny," writes Edward Vose Gulick in *Europe's Classical Balance of Power* (New York: Norton, 1955), p. 10. Every major power aims to make sure that no rival is eliminated from the system, because that is the best way for each state to guarantee its own survival. "Group-consciousness and group action," so the argument goes, are "the best way of preserving the individual state." Ibid., p. 297. States are not wedded to defending the status quo in this theory; changes in the distribution of power are acceptable, as long as no great power is driven from the system. Indeed, states can be expected to go to war to gain power at the expense of other states. But states fight only limited wars, because they recognize that although it is permissible to alter the balance of power, the independence of all the major powers must be preserved. Thus, states will often demonstrate "restraint, abnegation, and the denial of immediate self-interest." Ibid., p. 33. States will "stop fighting rather than eliminate an essential national actor," because they are motivated by "a theory of the general good." Morton A. Kaplan, *System and Process in International Politics* (New York: John Wiley, 1957), p. 23; and Gulick, *Europe's Classical Balance*, p. 45. The result of all this "attention to group interest" is a fluid but stable equilibrium. Ibid., p. 31. Although this theory focuses on the balance of power and allows for limited wars of aggression, it is not a realist theory, because in it states are concerned mainly with preserving a particular version of world order, not the pursuit of power. For further discussion of this theory, see Inis L. Claude, Jr., *Power and International Relations* (New York: Random House, 1962), chap. 2; Ernst B. Haas, "The Balance of Power: Prescription, Concept, or Propaganda?" *World Politics* 5, No. 4 (July 1953), pp. 442–77; Hans Morgenthau, *Politics among Nations: The Struggle for Power and Peace*, 5th ed. (New York: Knopf, 1973), chap. 11; and Quincy Wright, *A Study of War*, vol. 2 (Chicago: University of Chicago Press, 1942), chap. 20.

44. The examples of balancing and buck-passing mentioned in this section are discussed in detail in Chapter 8.

45. The terms "external" and "internal" balancing were introduced by Waltz in *Theory of International Politics*, pp. 118, 163.

46. Quoted in "Preface" to Keith Neilson and Roy A. Prete, eds., *Coalition Warfare: An Uneasy Accord* (Waterloo, ON: Wilfrid Laurier University Press, 1983), p. vii. Napoleon's views on the matter are reflected in a comment he made to an Austrian diplomat: "How many allies do you have? Five? Ten? Twenty? The more you have, the better it is for me." Quoted in Karl A. Roider, Jr., *Baron Thugut and Austria's Response to the French Revolution* (Princeton, NJ: Princeton University Press, 1987), p. 327. Also see Gordon A. Craig, "Problems of Coalition Warfare: The Military Alliance against Napoleon, 1813–14," in Gordon A. Craig, *War, Politics, and Diplomacy: Selected Essays* (New York: Praeger, 1966), pp. 22–45; and Neilson and Prete, *Coalition Warfare*, passim.

47. On buck-passing, see Mancur Olson, Jr., *The Logic of Collective Action: Public Goods and the Theory of Groups* (Cambridge, MA: Harvard University Press, 1965); Mancur Olson and Richard Zeckhauser, "An Economic Theory of Alliances," *Review of Economics and Statistics* 48, No. 3 (August 1966), pp. 266–79; and Barry R. Posen, *The Sources of Military Doctrine: France, Britain, and Germany between the World Wars* (Ithaca: Cornell University Press, 1984), esp. pp. 63, 74, 232.

48. Thomas J. Christensen and Jack Snyder refer to this as the "chain ganging" problem in "Chain Gangs and Passed Bucks: Predicting Alliance Patterns in Multipolarity," *International Organization* 44, No. 2 (Spring 1990), pp. 137–68.

49. See David French, *British Strategy and War Aims, 1914–1916* (Boston: Allen and Unwin, 1986), pp. 24–25; and David French, "The Meaning of Attrition, 1914–1916," *English Historical Review* 103, No. 407 (April 1988), pp. 385–405.

50. States are also deeply interested in avoiding the terrible costs of war, for reasons unrelated to the balance of power.

51. As noted in Chapter 4 (note 72), roughly 24 million Soviets died in the war against Nazi Germany. The United Kingdom and the United States together suffered about 650,000 deaths in all theaters combined. That figure includes roughly 300,000 U.S. battle deaths, 300,000 British battle deaths, and 50,000 British civilian deaths. See I.C.B. Dear, ed., *The Oxford Companion to World War II* (Oxford: Oxford University Press, 1995), p. 290; and Robert Goralski, *World War II Almanac: 1931–1945* (New York: Putnam, 1981), pp. 425–26, 428.

52. Winston Churchill appears to have been committed to a buck-passing strategy. He did not want the Allies to invade France even in the summer of 1944, and agreed to the D-Day invasion only because of intense American pressure. He preferred to allow the Red Army to crush the Wehrmacht's main forces, while the British and American armies remained on the periphery of Europe, engaging relatively small contingents of German forces. See Mark A. Stoler, *The Politics of the Second Front: American Military Planning and Diplomacy in Coalition Warfare, 1941–1943* (Westport, CT: Greenwood, 1977).

53. See Isaac Deutscher, *Stalin: A Political Biography,* 2d ed. (Oxford: Oxford University Press, 1967), pp. 478–80; and John Erickson, "Stalin, Soviet Strategy and the Grand Alliance," in Ann Lane and Howard Temperley, eds., *The Rise and Fall of the Grand Alliance, 1941–45* (New York: St. Martin's, 1995), pp. 140–41. Recalling his experience as the the Soviet ambassador to the United Kingdom during World War II, Ivan Maisky writes, "From Churchill's point of view, it would be ideal if both Germany and the [Soviet Union] emerged from the war greatly battered, bled white and, for at any rate a whole generation, would be struggling along on crutches, while Britain arrived at the finish line with a minimum of losses and in good form as a European boxer." Ivan Maisky, *Memoirs of a Soviet Ambassador: The War, 1939–1943*, trans. Andrew Rothstein (London: Hutchinson, 1967), p. 271. Similarly, the Italian ambassador to Turkey during World War II remarked, "The Turkish ideal is that the last German soldier should fall upon the last Russian corpse." Selim Deringil, *Turkish Foreign Policy during the Second World War: An "Active" Neutrality* (Cambridge: Cambridge University Press, 1989), pp. 134–35.

54. The key works on bandwagoning include Eric J. Labs, "Do Weak States Bandwagon?" *Security Studies* 1, No. 3 (Spring 1992), pp. 383–416; Randall L. Schweller, "Bandwagoning for Profit: Bringing the Revisionist State Back In," *International Security* 19, No. 1 (Summer 1994), pp. 72–107; Walt, *Origins of Alliances;* and Waltz, *Theory of International Politics.* Schweller's definition of bandwagoning, however, is fundamentally different from the one used by almost all other international relations scholars, including me (Schweller, "Bandwagoning for Profit," pp.

80–83). According to the conventional definition, bandwagoning is a strategy that threatened states employ against their adversaries, and it involves asymmetrical concessions to the aggressor. Bandwagoning in Schweller's lexicon is explicitly not a strategy employed by threatened states but one employed by states looking for opportunities to gain profit through aggression. Specifically, according to Schweller, bandwagoning is where an opportunistic state joins forces with another aggressor to take advantage of a third state, the way the Soviet Union joined forces with Nazi Germany in 1939 to dismember Poland. This kind of behavior, which does not contradict balance-of-power logic, fits squarely under the strategy of war described above.

55. Robert B. Strassler, ed., *The Landmark Thucydides: A Comprehensive Guide to the Peloponnesian War* (New York: Simon and Schuster, 1998), p. 352.

56. After studying balancing and bandwagoning behavior in the Middle East, Walt concludes that "balancing was far more common than bandwagoning, and bandwagoning was almost always confined to especially weak and isolated states." Walt, *Origins of Alliances*, p. 263. Also see ibid., pp. 29–33; and Labs, "Weak States."

57. See Elizabeth Wiskemann, "The Subjugation of South-Eastern Europe, June 1940 to June 1941," in Arnold Toynbee and Veronica M. Toynbee, eds., *Survey of International Affairs, 1939–46: The Initial Triumph of the Axis* (Oxford: Oxford University Press, 1958), pp. 319–36; and Sidney Lowery, "Rumania" and "Bulgaria," in Arnold Toynbee and Veronica M. Toynbee, eds., *Survey of International Affairs, 1939–46: The Realignment of Europe* (Oxford: Oxford University Press, 1955), pp. 285–90, 301–6.

58. This definition of appeasement is found in most dictionaries and is widely employed by historians and political scientists. For example, see Gilpin, *War and Change*, pp. 193–94; and Bradford A. Lee, *Britain and the Sino-Japanese War, 1937–1939: A Study in the Dilemmas of British Decline* (Stanford, CA: Stanford University Press, 1973), pp. vii–viii. Nevertheless, some scholars employ a different definition of appeasement. They describe it as a policy designed to reduce tensions with a dangerous adversary by eliminating the cause of conflict between them. See Stephen R. Rock, *Appeasement in International Politics* (Lexington: University Press of Kentucky, 2000), pp. 10–12. That definition of appeasement certainly allows for conceding power to a rival state but does not mandate it. My definition, on the other hand, requires that the appeaser allow the balance of power to shift against it.

59. See Chapter 7.

60. See Chapter 8.

61. Waltz, *Theory of International Politics*, pp. 127–28. Also see ibid., pp. 74–77; Kenneth Waltz, "A Response to My Critics," in Robert O. Keohane, ed., *Neorealism and Its Critics* (New York: Columbia University Press, 1986), pp. 330–32; and Colin

Elman, "The Logic of Emulation: The Diffusion of Military Practices in the International System," Ph.D. diss., Columbia University, 1999.

62. Waltz, *Theory of International Politics*, pp. 127–28.

63. For example, President George Bush said on November 8, 1990, that "Iraq's aggression is not just a challenge to the security of Kuwait and other Gulf nations, but to the better world that we have all hoped to build in the wake of the Cold War. And therefore, we and our allies cannot and will not shirk our responsibilities. The state of Kuwait must be restored, or no nation will be safe, and the promising future we anticipate will indeed be jeopardized." George Bush, "The Need for an Offensive Military Option," in Micah L. Sifry and Christopher Cerf, eds., *The Gulf War Reader: History, Documents, Opinions* (New York: Times Books, 1991), p. 229. Also see Thomas L. Friedman, "Washington's 'Vital Interests,'" in ibid., pp. 205–6. There is also the possibility that states will bandwagon (in Schweller's sense of the term) with successful aggressors and cause more war.

64. See Matthew Evangelista, *Innovation and the Arms Race: How the United States and the Soviet Union Develop New Military Technologies* (Ithaca, NY: Cornell University Press, 1988); Williamson Murray and Allan R. Millet, eds., *Military Innovation in the Interwar Period* (Cambridge: Cambridge University Press, 1996); Posen, *Sources of Military Doctrine*, pp. 29–33, 54–57, 224–26; and Stephen P. Rosen, *Winning the Next War: Innovation and the Modern Military* (Ithaca, NY: Cornell University Press, 1991).

65. See Richard K. Betts, *Surprise Attack: Lessons for Defense Planning* (Washington, DC: Brookings Institution Press, 1983).

66. See Michael I. Handel, *War, Strategy, and Intelligence* (London: Frank Cass, 1989), chaps. 3–8; and Dan Reiter, *Crucible of Beliefs: Learning, Alliances, and World Wars* (Ithaca, NY: Cornell University Press, 1996).

CHAPTER SIX

1. Only one study deals directly with offensive realism's claim that status quo powers are seldom seen in the international system. Eric Labs examined the war aims of Prussia during the Austro-Prussian War (1866), of Prussia in the Franco-Prussian War (1870–71), of the United Kingdom during World War I (1914–18), and of the United States in the Korean War (1950–53). He sought to determine whether security concerns drove those states to jump at wartime opportunities to gain relative power, as offensive realism would predict, or whether they were content to maintain the status quo. In other words, do war aims tend to remain fixed over the course of a conflict, or are they more likely to expand? He found that all four cases "provide strong support" for offensive realism. "Statesmen expanded their war aims . . . [and] pushed the international system for all its worth," he argued, because they believed that maximizing their relative power was the best way "to secure their interests . . . in a postwar world." Eric J. Labs, "Offensive Realism and Why States Expand Their War Aims," *Security Studies* 6, No. 4 (Summer 1997), pp. 1–49. The quotes are from pp. 21, 46.

2. Although the United States was not a great power until the end of the nineteenth century, its behavior during that entire century is of direct relevance for assessing offensive realism. Also, Japan was not a great power until 1895. However, I consider its behavior between the Meiji Restoration (in 1868) and 1895 because it has direct bearing on events after 1895. For reasons of space, I do not examine the actions of the complete universe of great powers between 1792 and 1990. Specifically, I omit Austria/Austria-Hungary (1792–1918), France (1792–1940), Prussia (1792–1862), and Russia (1792–1917). However, I am confident that a survey of the foreign policy behavior of these states would not contradict—indeed, would support—the main tenets of offensive realism.

3. This phrase is taken from Richard J.B. Bosworth, *Italy, The Least of the Great Powers: Italian Foreign Policy before the First World War* (Cambridge: Cambridge University Press, 1979).

4. The quotation is from Nicholas Spykman, *America's Strategy in World Politics: The United States and the Balance of Power* (New York: Harcourt, Brace, 1942), p. 20.

5. Quoted in Marius B. Jansen, "Japanese Imperialism: Late Meiji Perspectives," in Ramon H. Myers and Mark R. Peattie, eds., *The Japanese Colonial Empire, 1895–1945* (Princeton, NJ: Princeton University Press, 1984), p. 64.

6. W. G. Beasley, *The Modern History of Japan*, 2d ed. (London: Weidenfeld and Nicolson, 1973), chaps. 6–8; and Marius B. Jansen, ed., *The Cambridge History of Japan*, vol. 5, *The Nineteenth Century* (Cambridge: Cambridge University Press, 1989), chaps. 5–11.

7. Akira Iriye, "Japan's Drive to Great-Power Status," in Jansen, ed., *Cambridge History*, vol. 5, pp. 721–82.

8. Among the best surveys of Japanese foreign policy over this period are: W. G. Beasley, *Japanese Imperialism, 1894–1945* (Oxford: Clarendon, 1987); James B. Crowley, "Japan's Military Foreign Policies," in James W. Morley, ed., *Japan's Foreign Policy, 1868–1941: A Research Guide* (New York: Columbia University Press, 1974), pp. 3–117; Peter Duus, ed., *The Cambridge History of Japan*, vol. 6, *The Twentieth Century* (Cambridge: Cambridge University Press, 1988), chaps. 5–7; and Ian Nish, *Japanese Foreign Policy, 1869–1942: Kasumigaseki to Miyakezaka* (London: Routledge and Kegan Paul, 1977).

9. Nobutaka Ike, "War and Modernization," in Robert E. Ward, ed., *Political Development in Modern Japan* (Princeton, NJ: Princeton University Press, 1968), p. 189.

10. Jack Snyder, *Myths of Empire: Domestic Politics and International Ambition* (Ithaca, NY: Cornell University Press, 1991), p. 114. Also see Michael A. Barnhart, *Japan Prepares for Total War: The Search for Economic Security, 1919–1941* (Ithaca, NY: Cornell University Press, 1987), p. 17.

11. Mark R. Peattie, "Introduction," in Myers and Peattie, eds., *Japanese Colonial Empire*, p. 9.

12. E. H. Norman, "Japan's Emergence as a Modern State," in John W. Dower, ed., *Origins of the Modern Japanese State: Selected Writings of E. H. Norman* (New York: Random House, 1975), p. 305. Also see Marius B. Jansen, "Japanese Imperialism: Late Meiji Perspectives," in Myers and Peattie, eds., *Japanese Colonial Empire*, p. 62; and Marius B. Jansen, "Modernization and Foreign Policy in Meiji Japan," in Ward, ed., *Political Development*, pp. 149–88.

13. Quoted in Hiroharu Seki, "The Manchurian Incident, 1931," trans. Marius B. Jansen, in James W. Morley, ed., *Japan Erupts: The London Naval Conference and the Manchurian Incident, 1928–1932* (New York: Columbia University Press, 1984), p. 143.

14. Quoted in Peattie, "Introduction," in Myers and Peattie, eds., *Japanese Colonial Empire*, p. 15.

15. Hilary Conroy, *The Japanese Seizure of Korea, 1868–1910: A Study of Realism and Idealism in International Relations* (Philadelphia: University of Pennsylvania Press, 1960); and M. Frederick Nelson, *Korea and the Old Orders in Eastern Asia* (New York: Russell and Russell, 1945).

16. Beasley, *Japanese Imperialism*, chaps. 4–5.

17. Beasley, *Japanese Imperialism*, chap. 6.

18. Among the best sources on the Russo-Japanese War are Committee of Imperial Defence, *The Official History of the Russo-Japanese War*, 3 vols. (London: His Majesty's Stationery Office, 1910–20); R. M. Connaughton, *The War of the Rising Sun and Tumbling Bear: A Military History of the Russo-Japanese War, 1904–1905* (London: Routledge, 1988); A. N. Kuropatkin, *The Russian Army and the Japanese War*, trans. A. B. Lindsay, 2 vols. (London: John Murray, 1909); Ian Nish, *The Origins of the Russo-Japanese War* (London: Longman, 1985); J. N. Westwood, *Russia against Japan, 1904–1905: A New Look at the Russo-Japanese War* (Albany: State University of New York Press, 1986); and John A. White, *The Diplomacy of the Russo-Japanese War* (Princeton, NJ: Princeton University Press, 1964).

19. Beasley, *Japanese Imperialism*, chap. 7.

20. Beasley, *Japanese Imperialism*, chap. 8.

21. James W. Morley, *The Japanese Thrust into Siberia, 1918* (New York: Columbia University Press, 1957). Also see Chapter 4, note 128, of this book.

22. Emily O. Goldman, *Sunken Treaties: Naval Arms Control between the Wars* (University Park: Pennsylvania State University Press, 1994); and Stephen E. Pelz,

Race to Pearl Harbor: The Failure of the Second London Naval Conference and the Onset of World War II (Cambridge, MA: Harvard University Press, 1974).

23. Crowley, "Japan's Military Foreign Policies," pp. 39–54.

24. Among the best studies of the period are Barnhart, *Japan Prepares for Total War*; Alvin D. Coox, *Nomonhan: Japan against Russia, 1939,* 2 vols. (Stanford, CA: Stanford University Press, 1985); and James B. Crowley, *Japan's Quest for Autonomy: National Security and Foreign Policy, 1930–1938* (Princeton, NJ: Princeton University Press, 1966).

25. Seki, "The Manchurian Incident"; Sadako N. Ogata, *Defiance in Manchuria: The Making of Japanese Foreign Policy, 1931–1932* (Berkeley: University of California Press, 1964); Mark R. Peattie, *Ishiwara Kanji and Japan's Confrontation with the West* (Princeton, NJ: Princeton University Press, 1975), chaps. 4–5; and Toshihiko Shimada, "The Extension of Hostilities, 1931–1932," trans. Akira Iriye, in Morley, ed., *Japan Erupts*, pp. 233–335.

26. Peter Duus, Raymond H. Myers, and Mark R. Peattie, eds., *The Japanese Formal Empire in China, 1895–1937* (Princeton, NJ: Princeton University Press, 1989); and Shimada Toshihiko, "Designs on North China, 1933–1937," trans. James B. Crowley, in James W. Morley, ed., *The China Quagmire: Japan's Expansion on the Asian Continent, 1933–1941* (New York: Columbia University Press, 1983), pp. 3–230.

27. George H. Blakeslee, "The Japanese Monroe Doctrine," *Foreign Affairs* 11, No. 4 (July 1933), pp. 671–81.

28. Ikuhiko Hata, "The Marco Polo Bridge Incident, 1937," trans. David Lu and Katsumi Usui, "The Politics of War, 1937–1941," trans. David Lu, in Morley, ed., *China Quagmire*, pp. 233–86, 289–435.

29. Alvin D. Coox, *The Anatomy of a Small War: The Soviet-Japanese Struggle for Changkufeng-Khasan, 1938* (Westport, CT: Greenwood, 1977); Coox, *Nomonhan*, vols. 1–2; and Hata, "The Japanese-Soviet Confrontation, 1935–1939," trans. Alvin D. Coox, in James W. Morley, ed., *Deterrent Diplomacy: Japan, Germany, and the USSR, 1935–1940* (New York: Columbia University Press, 1976), pp. 113–78.

30. This phase of Japanese expansion is discussed in detail later in this chapter.

31. For a synoptic discussion of Bismarck as a realist and a nationalist, see Bruce Waller, *Bismarck,* 2d ed. (Oxford: Blackwell, 1997), chaps. 2–4. Probably the two best biographies of Bismarck, which deal with these matters in greater detail, are Lothar Gall, *Bismarck: The White Revolutionary,* vol. I, *1851–1871,* trans. J. A. Underwood (Boston: Unwin Hyman, 1986); and Otto Pflanze, *Bismarck and the Development of Germany: The Period of Unification, 1815–1871* (Princeton, NJ: Princeton University Press, 1973).

32. The key works on this subject are Andreas Hillgruber, *Germany and the Two World Wars,* trans. William C. Kirby (Cambridge, MA: Harvard University Press,

1982), chap. 2; and Eberhard Jackel, *Hitler's World View: A Blueprint for Power*, trans. Herbert Arnold (Cambridge, MA: Harvard University Press, 1981), chaps. 2, 5. Also see Dale C. Copeland, *The Origins of Major War* (Ithaca, NY: Cornell University Press, 2000), chap. 5; Gordon A. Craig, *Germany, 1866–1945* (Oxford: Oxford University Press, 1980), pp. 673–77; and Sebastian Haffner, *The Meaning of Hitler*, trans. Ewald Osers (Cambridge, MA: Harvard University Press, 1979), pp. 75–95. Hitler's most comprehensive writings on foreign policy are found not in *Mein Kampf*, but in *Hitler's Secret Book*, trans. Salvator Attanasio (New York: Bramhall House, 1986).

   33. David Calleo, *The German Problem Reconsidered: Germany and the World Order, 1870 to the Present* (Cambridge: Cambridge University Press, 1978), p. 119. Also see Ludwig Dehio, *Germany and World Politics in the Twentieth Century*, trans. Dieter Pevsner (New York: Norton, 1959); Fritz Fischer, *From Kaiserreich to Third Reich: Elements of Continuity in German History, 1871–1945*, trans. Roger Fletcher (London: Allen and Unwin, 1986); Klaus Hildebrand, *The Foreign Policy of the Third Reich*, trans. Anthony Fothergill (Berkeley: University of California Press, 1973), pp. 1–11, 135–47; and Woodruff D. Smith, *The Ideological Origins of Nazi Imperialism* (Oxford: Oxford University Press, 1986).

   34. See Henry A. Turner, *Hitler's Thirty Days to Power, January 1933* (Reading, MA: Addison-Wesley, 1996), pp. 173–74.

   35. Evidence of Germany's ambitious goals is found in the list of war aims drawn up by Chancellor Theobald von Bethmann-Hollweg one month after the outbreak of World War I. See Fritz Fischer, *Germany's Aims in the First World War* (New York: Norton, 1967), pp. 103–6. Also see Stephen Van Evera, *Causes of War: Power and the Roots of Conflict* (Ithaca, NY: Cornell University Press, 1999), pp. 202–3.

   36. See Chapter 8.

   37. Among the best overviews of European politics between 1870 and 1900 are Luigi Albertini, *The Origins of the War of 1914*, vol. I, *European Relations from the Congress of Berlin to the Eve of the Sarajevo Murder*, ed. and trans. Isabella M. Massey (Oxford: Oxford University Press, 1952), chaps. 1–2; Imanuel Geiss, *German Foreign Policy, 1871–1914* (London: Routledge and Kegan Paul, 1979), chaps. 3–9; William L. Langer, *European Alliances and Alignments, 1871–1890* (New York: Alfred A. Knopf, 1939); William L. Langer, *The Diplomacy of Imperialism, 1890–1902*, 2d ed. (New York: Knopf, 1956); Norman Rich, *Friedrich Von Holstein: Politics and Diplomacy in the Era of Bismarck and Wilhelm II*, 2 vols. (Cambridge: Cambridge University Press, 1965), pts. 2–5; Glenn H. Snyder, *Alliance Politics* (Ithaca, NY: Cornell University Press, 1997); and A.J.P. Taylor, *The Struggle for Mastery in Europe, 1848–1918* (Oxford: Clarendon, 1954), chaps. 10–17.

   38. The phrase is W. N. Medlicott's, although he too argues that it is not an accurate description of Bismarck. See W. N. Medlicott, *Bismarck and Modern Germany* (New York: Harper and Row, 1965), p. 180.

39. See George F. Kennan, *The Decline of Bismarck's European Order: Franco-Russian Relations, 1875–1890* (Princeton, NJ: Princeton University Press, 1979), pp. 11–23; and Taylor, *Struggle,* pp. 225–27.

40. Joseph V. Fuller, *Bismarck's Diplomacy at Its Zenith* (Cambridge, MA: Harvard University Press, 1922), chaps. 6–8; William D. Irvine, *The Boulanger Affair Reconsidered: Royalism, Boulangism, and the Origins of the Radical Right in France* (Oxford: Oxford University Press, 1989); and Langer, *European Alliances,* chap. 11.

41. Kennan, *Decline,* p. 338.

42. Richard D. Challener, *The French Theory of the Nation in Arms, 1866–1939* (New York: Russell and Russell, 1965), chaps. 1–2; Allan Mitchell, *Victors and Vanquished: The German Influence on Army and Church in France after 1870* (Chapel Hill: University of North Carolina Press, 1984), chaps. 1–5; Barry R. Posen, "Nationalism, the Mass Army, and Military Power," *International Security* 18, No. 2 (Fall 1993), pp. 109–17; and David Stevenson, *Armaments and the Coming of War: Europe, 1904–1914* (Oxford: Oxford University Press, 1996), pp. 56–58.

43. See Chapter 8.

44. Among the best overviews of European politics between 1900 and 1914 are Albertini, *Origins of the War,* vol. I, chaps. 3–10; Geiss, *German Foreign Policy,* chaps. 8–17; David G. Herrmann, *The Arming of Europe and the Making of the First World War* (Princeton, NJ: Princeton University Press, 1996); Rich, *Holstein,* vol. 2, pts. 5–6; Snyder, *Alliance Politics;* Stevenson, *Armaments and the Coming of War;* and Taylor, *Struggle,* chaps. 17–22.

45. At the start of the crisis in July 1914, Germany wanted a local war in the Balkans involving Austria-Hungary and Serbia. It was willing, however, to accept a continental war that pitted Austria-Hungary and Germany against France and Russia. It did not want a world war, however, which would mean British involvement in the conflict. See Jack S. Levy, "Preferences, Constraints, and Choices in July 1914," *International Security* 15, No. 3 (Winter 1990–91), pp. 154–61. As the crisis evolved, it became increasingly clear that Europe was headed for either a continental or a world war, not a local war. Germany, which had played the key role in fueling the crisis from the start, made little effort to end it as war loomed closer. In fact, Germany saw a major war with France and Russia as an opportunity to 1) break its encirclement by the Triple Entente, 2) crush Russia, which it feared would grow more powerful than Germany in the near future, and 3) establish hegemony in Europe. For evidence that these goals dominated German thinking, see, for example, Copeland, *Origins of Major War,* chaps. 3–4; Fritz Fischer, *War of Illusions: German Policies from 1911 to 1914,* trans. Marian Jackson (New York: Norton, 1975), chaps. 22–23; Imanuel Geiss, ed., *July 1914, The Outbreak of the First World War: Selected Documents* (New York: Norton, 1974); Konrad H. Jarausch, "The Illusion of Limited War: Chancellor Bethmann-Hollweg's Calculated Risk, July 1914," *Central*

European History 2, No. 1 (March 1969), pp. 48–76; Wayne C. Thompson, *In the Eye of the Storm: Kurt Riezler and the Crises of Modern Germany* (Ames: University of Iowa Press, 1980), chaps. 2–3; and the works cited in note 35 of this chapter.

46. The sections of the Versailles Treaty dealing with the size and shape of the German military can be found in U.S. Department of State, *The Treaty of Versailles and After: Annotations of the Text of the Treaty* (Washington, DC: U.S. Government Printing Office, 1947), pp. 301–65.

47. On Germany's fear of Poland, see Michael Geyer, "German Strategy in the Age of Machine Warfare, 1914–1945," in Peter Paret, ed., *Makers of Modern Strategy: From Machiavelli to the Nuclear Age* (Princeton, NJ: Princeton University Press, 1986), pp. 561–63; and Gaines Post, Jr., *The Civil-Military Fabric of Weimar Foreign Policy* (Princeton, NJ: Princeton University Press, 1973), pp. 101–10. The case of Poland in the years immediately after World War I appears to provide additional support for offensive realism. That newly created state briefly enjoyed a marked military advantage over Germany and the Soviet Union, which were both devastated by defeat in World War I. Sensing an opportunity to gain power and enhance its security, Poland set out to break apart the Soviet Union and create a powerful Polish-led federation that included Lithuania, Belorussia, and Ukraine. Poles "dreamed of a reestablishment of the powerful and vast country which once was the Kingdom of Poland." Josef Korbel, *Poland between East and West: Soviet and German Diplomacy toward Poland, 1919–1933* (Princeton, NJ: Princeton University Press, 1963), p. 33. Also see the sources cited in Chapter 3, note 41, of this book.

48. See Edward W. Bennett, *German Rearmament and the West, 1932–1933* (Princeton, NJ: Princeton University Press, 1979); Jon Jacobson, *Locarno Diplomacy: Germany and the West, 1925–1929* (Princeton, NJ: Princeton University Press, 1972); Christopher M. Kimmich, *The Free City: Danzig and German Foreign Policy, 1919–1934* (New Haven, CT: Yale University Press, 1968); Post, *Civil-Military Fabric;* Marshall M. Lee and Wolfgang Michalka, *German Foreign Policy, 1917–1933: Continuity or Break?* (New York: Berg, 1987); and Smith, *Ideological Origins,* chap. 9.

49. Toward this end, on April 16, 1922, Weimar Germany and the Soviet Union signed the secret Rapallo Treaty, "a many-sided, intimate, and long-lasting cooperative arrangement" that allowed Germany to covertly enhance its military capability in violation of the Treaty of Versailles. Jiri Hochman, *The Soviet Union and the Failure of Collective Security, 1934–1938* (Ithaca, NY: Cornell University Press, 1984), p. 17. Also see Hans W. Gatzke, "Russo-German Military Collaboration during the Weimar Republic," *American Historical Review* 63, No. 3 (April 1958), pp. 565–97; Aleksandr M. Nekrich, *Pariahs, Partners, Predators: German-Soviet Relations, 1922–1941* (New York: Columbia University Press, 1997), chaps. 1–2; and Kurt Rosenbaum, *Community of Fate: German-Soviet Diplomatic Relations, 1922–1928* (Syracuse, NY: Syracuse University Press, 1965).

50. Henry L. Bretton, *Stresemann and the Revision of Versailles: A Fight for Reason* (Stanford, CA: Stanford University Press, 1953), p. 25. Also see Manfred J. Enssle, *Stresemann's Territorial Revisionism: Germany, Belgium, and the Eupen-Malmedy Question, 1919–1929* (Wiesbaden, FRG: Franz Steiner, 1980); Hans W. Gatzke, *Stresemann and the Rearmament of Germany* (New York: Norton, 1969); and the works cited in note 48 of this chapter. On the influence of *Machtpolitik* in Weimar, see Post, *Civil-Miliatry Fabric,* pp. 81–82, 164–67, 311–12.

51. Among the best sources on Nazi aggression are Hildebrand, *Foreign Policy of the Third Reich;* Hillgruber, *Germany,* chaps. 5–9; Norman Rich, *Hitler's War Aims: Ideology, the Nazi State, and the Course of German Expansion* (New York: Norton, 1973); Telford Taylor, *Sword and Swastika: Generals and Nazis in the Third Reich* (New York: Simon and Schuster, 1952); Gerhard L. Weinberg, *The Foreign Policy of Hitler's Germany: Diplomatic Revolution in Europe, 1933–36* (Chicago: University of Chicago Press, 1970); and Gerhard L. Weinberg, *The Foreign Policy of Hitler's Germany: Starting World War II, 1937–39* (Chicago: University of Chicago Press, 1980).

52. On the growth of the German military in the 1930s, see Chapter 8.

53. Richard Pipes, *The Formation of the Soviet Union: Communism and Nationalism, 1917–1923* (Cambridge, MA: Harvard University Press, 1957), p. 1. Also see William C. Fuller, Jr., *Strategy and Power in Russia, 1600–1914* (New York: Free Press, 1992); Geoffrey Hosking, *Russia: People and Empire, 1552–1917* (Cambridge, MA: Harvard University Press, 1997), pt. 1; Barbara Jelavich, *A Century of Russian Foreign Policy, 1814–1914* (Philadelphia: J. B. Lippincott, 1964); and John P. LeDonne, *The Russian Empire and the World, 1700–1917: The Geopolitics of Expansion and Containment* (Oxford: Oxford University Press, 1997).

54. Fuller, *Strategy and Power,* p. 132. Also see pp. 34, 125–27, 134–39, 174–75; and Hosking, *Russia,* pp. 3–4, 41.

55. Both quotes are from Stephen M. Walt, *Revolution and War* (Ithaca, NY: Cornell University Press, 1996), p. 129.

56. This phrase is from Jon Jacobson, *When the Soviet Union Entered World Politics* (Berkeley: University of California Press, 1994), p. 3, describing the scholarly consensus on Lenin's foreign policy.

57. Richard K. Debo, *Revolution and Survival: The Foreign Policy of Soviet Russia, 1917–18* (Toronto: University of Toronto Press, 1979), p. 416. Also see Piero Melograni, *Lenin and the Myth of World Revolution: Ideology and Reasons of State, 1917–1920,* trans. Julie Lerro (Atlantic Highlands, NJ: Humanities Press International, 1979), which argues that Lenin did not want a world revolution because it would have brought communist and socialist parties to power in other states that probably would have dominated the European left at the expense of the Bolsheviks.

58. On Stalin as a realist, see P.M.H. Bell, *The Origins of the Second World War in Europe,* 2d ed. (London: Longman, 1997), pp. 136–37; David Holloway, *Stalin and* the Bomb: The Soviet Union and Atomic Energy, 1939–1956 (New Haven, CT: Yale University Press, 1994), pp. 168–69; Henry Kissinger, Diplomacy (New York: Simon and Schuster, 1994), chaps. 13–20; Vojtech Mastny, Russia's Road to the Cold War: Diplomacy, Warfare, and the Politics of Communism, 1941–1945 (New York: Columbia University Press, 1979), p. 223; Adam B. Ulam, Expansion and Coexistence: Soviet Foreign Policy, 1917–1973, 2d ed. (New York: Holt, Rinehart, and Winston, 1974), p. 144; and Vladislav Zubok and Constantine Pleshakov, Inside the Kremlin's Cold War: From Stalin to Khrushchev (Cambridge, MA: Harvard University Press, 1996), pp. 18, 38. Also see Vladimir O. Pechatnov, "The Big Three after World War II: New Documents on Soviet Thinking about Post War Relations with the United States and Britain," Cold War International History Project [CWIHP] Working Paper No. 13 (Washington, DC: Woodrow Wilson International Center for Scholars, July 1995), which makes apparent that at least three of Stalin's main foreign policy advisers saw the world in terms of realpolitik. On Nazi-Soviet cooperation between August 1939 and June 1941, see the works cited in Chapter 2, note 59, of this book.

59. Zubok and Pleshakov, Inside the Kremlin's Cold War, p. 139.

60. Barrington Moore, Jr., Soviet Politics—The Dilemma of Power: The Role of Ideas in Social Change (Cambridge, MA: Harvard University Press, 1950), p. 408. Also see ibid., pp. 350–51, 382–83, 390–92; Francesca Gori and Silvio Pons, eds., The Soviet Union and Europe in the Cold War, 1945–1953 (London: Macmillan, 1996); Walter Lippmann, The Cold War: A Study in U.S. Foreign Policy (New York: Harper and Brothers, 1947); Samuel L. Sharp, "National Interest: Key to Soviet Politics," in Erik P. Hoffmann and Frederic J. Fleron, Jr., eds., The Conduct of Soviet Foreign Policy (Chicago: Aldine-Atherton, 1971), pp. 108–17; Snyder, Myths of Empire, chap. 6; Ulam, Expansion and Coexistence; William C. Wohlforth, The Elusive Balance: Power and Perceptions during the Cold War (Ithaca, NY: Cornell University Press, 1993); and Zubok and Pleshakov, Inside the Kremlin's Cold War.

61. Among the works that emphasize the role of ideology in Soviet foreign policy are Jacobson, When the Soviet Union Entered; Douglas J. Macdonald, "Communist Bloc Expansion in the Early Cold War: Challenging Realism, Refuting Revisionism," International Security 20, No. 3 (Winter 1995–96), pp. 152–88; Teddy J. Uldricks, Diplomacy and Ideology: The Origins of Soviet Foreign Relations, 1917–1930 (London: Sage, 1979); and Walt, Revolution and War, chap. 4.

62. See E. H. Carr, The Bolshevik Revolution, 1917–1923, vol. 3 (New York: Macmillan, 1961), chaps. 21–25; Debo, Revolution and Survival; Richard K. Debo, Survival and Consolidation: The Foreign Policy of Soviet Russia, 1918–1921 (Montreal: McGill–Queen's University Press, 1992); Ulam, Expansion and Coexistence, chap. 3; and Walt, Revolution and War, chap. 4.

63. See John W. Wheeler-Bennett, Brest-Litovsk: The Forgotten Peace, March 1918 (New York: Norton, 1971).

64. See Chapter 4, note 128, of this book.

65. See Debo, *Survival and Consolidation*, chaps. 13–14; James M. McCann, "Beyond the Bug: Soviet Historiography of the Soviet-Polish War of 1920," *Soviet Studies* 36, No. 4 (October 1984), pp. 475–93; and the sources cited in Chapter 3, note 41, of this book. This case supports Eric Labs's claim that states expand their war aims whenever opportunities to conquer territory arise during the fighting. See Labs, "Offensive Realism."

66. As noted earlier, Japan kept its troops in Siberia until 1922 and in northern Sakhalin until 1925.

67. See Carr, *Bolshevik Revolution*, vol. 3, chaps. 26–34; R. Craig Nation, *Black Earth, Red Star: A History of Soviet Security Policy, 1917–1991* (Ithaca, NY: Cornell University Press, 1992), chap. 2; Jacobson, *When the Soviet Union Entered*; Teddy J. Uldricks, "Russia and Europe: Diplomacy, Revolution, and Economic Development in the 1920s," *International History Review* 1, No. 1 (January 1979), pp. 55–83; Ulam, *Expansion and Coexistence*, chap. 4; and Walt, *Revolution and War*, pp. 175–201.

68. See the sources cited in note 49 in this chapter.

69. Quoted in Robert C. Tucker, *Stalin in Power: The Revolution from Above, 1928–1941* (New York: Norton, 1990), p. 9. For a detailed discussion of Stalin's industrialization policy in the decade before World War II, see ibid., chaps. 3–5; and Alec Nove, *An Economic History of the USSR, 1917–1991*, 3d ed. (New York: Penguin, 1992), chaps. 7–9.

70. Jonathan Haslam, *The Soviet Union and the Threat from the East, 1933–1941: Moscow, Tokyo and the Prelude to the Pacific War* (Pittsburgh, PA: University of Pittsburgh Press, 1992).

71. See Chapter 8.

72. See the sources cited in Chapter 5, note 28.

73. Nikita Khrushchev, *Khrushchev Remembers*, trans. and ed. Strobe Talbott (Boston: Little, Brown, 1970), p. 134.

74. Mastny, *Russia's Road to the Cold War*; and Ulam, *Expansion and Coexistence*, chap. 7.

75. Russell D. Buhite, *Decisions at Yalta: An Appraisal of Summit Diplomacy* (Wilmington, DE: Scholarly Resources, 1986), chap. 5; Diane S. Clemens, *Yalta* (Oxford: Oxford University Press, 1970), pp. 58–62, 247–55; Herbert Feis, *Churchill, Roosevelt, Stalin: The War They Waged and the Peace They Sought* (Princeton, NJ: Princeton University Press, 1957), pp. 505–18; and Odd Arne Westad, *Cold War and Revolution: Soviet-American Rivalry and the Origins of the Chinese Civil War, 1944–1946* (New York: Columbia University Press, 1993), chap. 1.

76. Bruce Cumings, *The Origins of the Korean War*, vol. I, *Liberation and the Emergence of Separate Regimes, 1945–1947* (Princeton, NJ: Princeton University Press, 1981); and Kathryn Weathersby, "Soviet Aims in Korea and the Origins of the

Korean War, 1945–1950: New Evidence from Russian Archives," CWIHP Working Paper No. 8 (Washington, DC: Woodrow Wilson International Center for Scholars, November 1993).

77. In 1948, however, American policymakers believed that there were 4 million people serving in the Soviet armed forces, not 2.87 million. See Matthew A. Evangelista, "Stalin's Postwar Army Reappraised," *International Security* 7, No. 3 (Winter 1982–83), pp. 110–38; and the articles by Phillip A. Karber and Jerald A. Combs, John S. Duffield, and Matthew Evangelista in "Assessing the Soviet Threat to Europe: A Roundtable," *Diplomatic History* 22, No. 3 (Summer 1998), pp. 399–449. Despite these inflated U.S. intelligence estimates, Western policymakers in the late 1940s thought it was unlikely that the Red Army would strike into Western Europe. Fear of a Soviet blitzkrieg became a serious concern after North Korea invaded South Korea in June 1950. See Ulam, *Expansion and Coexistence*, pp. 404, 438, 498.

78. Douglas Macdonald writes, "The oral memoirs of both Khrushchev and Molotov, as well as much of the other new evidence, confirm that Stalin's fear of U.S. power was the most important constraint on Soviet expansionism." Macdonald, "Communist Bloc Expansion," p. 161.

79. See Werner Hahn, *Postwar Soviet Politics: The Fall of Zhdanov and the Defeat of Moderation, 1946–1953* (Ithaca, NY: Cornell University Press, 1982); Holloway, *Stalin and the Bomb*, chap. 8; Vojtech Mastny, *The Cold War and Soviet Insecurity: The Stalin Years* (Oxford: Oxford University Press, 1996); Pechatnov, "The Big Three"; Ulam, *Expansion and Coexistence*, chaps. 8–13; and Zubok and Pleshakov, *Inside the Kremlin's Cold War*, chaps. 1–3 and "Postmortem." Also see the quotes from Molotov and Stalin in Marc Trachtenberg, *A Constructed Peace: The Making of the European Settlement, 1945–1963* (Princeton, NJ: Princeton University Press, 1999), pp. 19, 36.

80. Louise L. Fawcett, *Iran and the Cold War: The Azerbaijan Crisis of 1946* (Cambridge: Cambridge University Press, 1992); Bruce Kuniholm, *The Origins of the Cold War in the Near East: Great Power Conflict and Diplomacy in Iran, Turkey, and Greece* (Princeton, NJ: Princeton University Press, 1980), chaps. 3–6; and Natalia I. Yegorova, "The 'Iran Crisis' of 1945–1946: A View from the Russian Archives," CWHIP Working Paper No. 15 (Washington, DC: Woodrow Wilson International Center for Scholars, May 1996).

81. Kuniholm, *The Origins of the Cold War*, chaps. 1, 4–6; Melvyn P. Leffler, "Strategy, Diplomacy, and the Cold War: The United States, Turkey, and NATO, 1945–1952," *Journal of American History* 71, No. 4 (March 1985), pp. 807–25; and Eduard Mark, "The War Scare of 1946 and Its Consequences," *Diplomatic History* 21, No. 3 (Summer 1997), pp. 383–415.

82. The Soviet Union also reached an agreement with the West in 1955 to pull Soviet and NATO forces out of Austria and make it a neutral state in the East-West conflict. But there were good strategic reasons for the Soviets to cut this deal, as Audrey K. Cronin makes clear in *Great Power Politics and the Struggle over Austria, 1945–1955* (Ithaca, NY: Cornell University Press, 1986).

83. Among the best sources on Soviet policy in Asia are Sergei N. Goncharov, John W. Lewis, and Xue Litai, *Uncertain Partners: Stalin, Mao, and the Korean War* (Stanford, CA: Stanford University Press, 1993); Westad, *Cold War and Revolution;* and Michael M. Sheng, *Battling Western Imperialism: Mao, Stalin, and the United States* (Princeton, NJ: Princeton University Press, 1997).

84. Goncharov, Lewis, and Litai, *Uncertain Partners,* chap. 5; Mastny, *The Cold War,* pp. 85–97; Weathersby, "Soviet Aims in Korea"; and Kathryn Weathersby, "To Attack or Not to Attack: Stalin, Kim Il Sung, and the Prelude to War," *CWIHP Bulletin* 5 (Spring 1995), pp. 1–9.

85. See *inter alia* Galia Golan, *The Soviet Union and National Liberation Movements in the Third World* (Boston: Unwin Hyman, 1988); Andrzej Korbonski and Francis Fukuyama, eds., *The Soviet Union and the Third World: The Last Three Decades* (Ithaca, NY: Cornell University Press, 1987); Bruce D. Porter, *The USSR in Third World Conflicts: Soviet Arms and Diplomacy in Local Wars, 1945–1980* (Cambridge: Cambridge University Press, 1984); and Carol R. Saivetz, ed., *The Soviet Union in the Third World* (Boulder, CO: Westview, 1989).

86. See Jeffrey T. Checkel, *Ideas and International Political Change: Soviet/Russian Behavior and the End of the Cold War* (New Haven, CT: Yale University Press, 1997); Matthew Evangelista, *Unarmed Forces: The Transnational Movement to End the Cold War* (Ithaca, NY: Cornell University Press, 1999); Robert G. Herman, "Identity, Norms and National Security: The Soviet Foreign Policy Revolution and the End of the Cold War," in Peter J. Katzenstein, ed., *The Culture of National Security: Norms and Identity in World Politics* (New York: Columbia University Press, 1996), pp. 271–316; and Richard Ned Lebow and Thomas W. Risse-Kappen, eds., *International Relations Theory and the End of the Cold War* (New York: Columbia University Press, 1995).

87. Stephen G. Brooks and William C. Wohlforth, "Power, Globalization, and the End of the Cold War: Reevaluating a Landmark Case for Ideas," *International Security* 25, No. 3 (Winter 2000–2001), pp. 5–53; William C. Wohlforth, "Realism and the End of the Cold War," *International Security* 19, No. 3 (Winter 1994–95), pp. 91–129; and Randall L. Schweller and William C. Wohlforth, "Power Test: Evaluating Realism in Response to the End of the Cold War," *Security Studies* 9, No. 3 (Spring 2000), pp. 60–107. Also see Chapters 3 and 10 of this book; and the comments of former Soviet policymakers in William C. Wohlforth, ed., *Witnesses to the End of the Cold War* (Baltimore, MD: Johns Hopkins University Press, 1996), pt. 1.

88. Ronald G. Suny, *The Revenge of the Past: Nationalism, Revolution, and the Collapse of the Soviet Union* (Stanford, CA: Stanford University Press, 1993).

89. Offensive realism would be falsified if an economically healthy Soviet Union had opted to abandon Eastern Europe because its leaders were convinced that security competition was no longer an important aspect of international politics.

90. Among the best sources on Italian foreign policy are H. James Burgwyn, *Italian Foreign Policy in the Interwar Period, 1918–1940* (Westport, CT: Praeger, 1997); Bosworth, *Italy, the Least of the Great Powers;* Alan Cassels, *Mussolini's Early Diplomacy* (Princeton, NJ: Princeton University Press, 1970); MacGregor Knox, *Mussolini Unleashed, 1939–1941: Politics and Strategy in Fascist Italy's Last War* (Cambridge: Cambridge University Press, 1982); C. J. Lowe and F. Marzari, *Italian Foreign Policy, 1870–1940* (London: Routledge and Kegan Paul, 1987); Christopher Seton-Watson, *Italy from Liberalism to Fascism, 1870–1925* (London: Methuen, 1967); Denis Mack Smith, *Modern Italy: A Political History* (Ann Arbor: University of Michigan Press, 1997); Denis Mack Smith, *Mussolini's Roman Empire* (New York: Viking, 1976); and Brian R. Sullivan, "The Strategy of the Decisive Weight: Italy, 1882–1922," in Williamson Murray, MacGregor Knox, and Alvin Bernstein, eds., *The Making of Strategy: Rulers, States, and War* (Cambridge: Cambridge University Press, 1995), pp. 307–51.

91. Bosworth, *Italy, the Least of the Great Powers,* p. viii. Also see Ottavio Barie, "Italian Imperialism: The First Stage," *Journal of Italian History* 2, No. 3 (Winter 1979), pp. 531–65; and Federico Chabod, *Italian Foreign Policy: The Statecraft of the Founders,* trans. William McCuaig (Princeton, NJ: Princeton University Press, 1996).

92. Maxwell H.H. Macartney and Paul Cremona, *Italy's Foreign and Colonial Policy, 1914–1937* (Oxford: Oxford University Press, 1938), p. 12.

93. Seton-Watson, *Italy,* p. 29.

94. John Gooch, *Army, State, and Society in Italy, 1870–1915* (New York: St. Martin's, 1989); "Italian Military Efficiency: A Debate," *Journal of Strategic Studies* 5, No. 2 (June 1982), pp. 248–77; MacGregor Knox, *Hitler's Italian Allies: Royal Armed Forces, Fascist Regime, and the War of 1940–1943* (Cambridge: Cambridge University Press, 2000); Smith, *Mussolini's Roman Empire,* chap. 13; and Brian R. Sullivan, "The Italian Armed Forces, 1918–40," in Allan R. Millett and Williamson Murray, eds., *Military Effectiveness,* vol. 2, *The Interwar Period* (Boston: Allen and Unwin, 1988), pp. 169–217.

95. Quoted in Gooch, *Army, State, and Society,* p. xi.

96. Sullivan, "Strategy of Decisive Weight."

97. See William A. Renzi, *In the Shadow of the Sword: Italy's Neutrality and Entrance into the Great War, 1914–1915* (New York: Peter Lang, 1987); and Seton-Watson, *Italy,* chap. 11.

98. Smith, *Modern Italy*, p. 89.

99. Seton-Watson, *Italy*, p. 430.

100. A copy of the Treaty of London can be found in René Albrecht-Carrié, *Italy at the Paris Peace Conference* (New York: Columbia University Press, 1938), pp. 334–39. Also relevant is the February 7, 1919, "Italian Memorandum of Claims," presented at the Paris Peace Conference, a copy of which can be found in ibid., pp. 370–87.

101. Taylor, *Struggle*, p. 544.

102. Sullivan, "Strategy of Decisive Weight," p. 343.

103. See Albrecht-Carrié, *Italy at the Paris Peace Conference;* and H. James Burgwyn, *The Legend of the Mutilated Victory: Italy, the Great War, and the Paris Peace Conference, 1915–1919* (Westport, CT: Greenwood, 1993).

104. Smith, *Mussolini's Roman Empire*, p. 60. Also see p. 16.

105. John F. Coverdale, *Italian Intervention in the Spanish Civil War* (Princeton, NJ: Princeton University Press, 1975), pp. 41, 53, 74–78, 127–50, 198–200, 388–89.

106. Knox, *Mussolini Unleashed*, p. 2.

107. See Mario Cervi, *The Hollow Legions: Mussolini's Blunder in Greece, 1940–1941*, trans. Eric Mosbacher (Garden City, NY: Doubleday, 1971); and I.S.O. Playfair, *The Mediterranean and Middle East*, vol. I, *The Early Successes against Italy* (London: Her Majesty's Stationery Office, 1954).

108. Snyder, *Myths of Empire*, p. 21. Also see ibid., pp. 1–3, 61–62; and Van Evera, *Causes of War.*

109. Snyder, *Myths of Empire*, p. 308.

110. Snyder, for example, maintains in *Myths of Empire* that the aggressive behavior of great powers can be explained largely by "logrolling" among selfish interest groups on the home front. Van Evera ascribes their ill-advised behavior to militarism. See Stephen Van Evera, *Causes of War: Misperception and the Roots of Conflict* (Ithaca, NY: Cornell University Press, forthcoming).

111. See Snyder, *Myths of Empire;* Van Evera, *Causes of War;* and Kenneth N. Waltz, *Theory of International Politics* (Reading, MA: Addison-Wesley, 1979). For other evidence of this line of argument, see Charles A. Kupchan, *The Vulnerability of Empire* (Ithaca, NY: Cornell University Press, 1994). For an excellent summary and critique of this perspective, see Fareed Zakaria, "Realism and Domestic Politics: A Review Essay," *International Security* 17, No. 1 (Summer 1992), pp. 177–98. Also see Chapter 2, note 30, of this book.

112. Snyder, *Myths of Empire*, p. 8.

113. As discussed in Chapter 8, the balancing coalition that defeated Napoleon came together in 1813, after the French army that had invaded Russia in 1812 had been routed and destroyed. The balancing coalition that ultimately defeated Hitler came together in December 1941, at roughly the same time that the Red Army was stopping the German blitzkrieg outside of Moscow. At that point, a good number of Wehrmacht commanders thought that the war against the Soviet Union was already lost.

114. J. A. Nichols, *Germany after Bismarck: The Caprivi Era, 1890–1894* (Cambridge, MA: Harvard University Press, 1958); Sidney B. Fay, *The Origins of the World War,* 2d ed. (New York: Macmillan, 1943), pp. 122–24; Geiss, *German Foreign Policy,* chap. 7; and Rich, *Holstein,* vols. 1–2, chaps. 23–35.

115. Charles Kupchan, who accuses Wilhelmine Germany of causing its own encirclement, allows that Germany did not start behaving aggressively until 1897. Kupchan, *Vulnerability of Empire,* p. 360. However, there is a problem with this argument: Germany was encircled by France and Russia well before 1897. Thus, according to Kupchan's own timeline, the formation of the first and most important leg of the Triple Entente cannot be explained by aggressive German behavior. The same problem is found in Snyder, *Myths of Empire,* pp. 68, 72.

116. Medlicott, *Bismarck,* p. 172. Also see ibid., pp. 164–66, 171–73; Fuller, *Bismarck's Diplomacy,* passim; Geiss, *German Foreign Policy,* chaps. 6–7; Kennan, *Decline,* chaps. 18–22; and Taylor, *Struggle,* pp. 317–19.

117. Geiss, *German Foreign Policy,* p. 52. Waller makes the same argument in *Bismarck,* p. 118.

118. This point is the central theme in Paul M. Kennedy, *The Rise of the Anglo-German Antagonism, 1860–1914* (London: Allen and Unwin, 1980), esp. chaps. 16, 20. Also see Calleo, *German Problem Reconsidered;* and Chapter 8 of this book.

119. Hillgruber, *Germany,* p. 13, is excellent on this point. Even if there had been no Moroccan crisis, Russia's defeat by itself would probably have caused the formation of the Triple Entente. However, that crisis alone would not have been enough to prompt the United Kingdom to join forces with France and Russia.

120. Herrmann, *Arming of Europe,* chap. 2.

121. Not only did the United Kingdom fail to give "a clear and timely commitment in support of her allies," but there was also a marked improvement in Anglo-German relations between 1911 and 1914. See Levy, "Preferences," p. 168; Sean M. Lynn-Jones, "Detente and Deterrence: Anglo-German Relations, 1911–1914," *International Security* 11, No. 2 (Fall 1986), pp. 121–50; Scott D. Sagan, "1914 Revisited: Allies, Offense, and Instability," *International Security* 11, No. 2 (Fall 1986), pp. 169–71; and the sources cited in Chapter 8, note 79, of this book. Furthermore, Anglo-Russian relations soured somewhat after 1911, raising doubts about the viability of the Triple Entente. See Keith Neilson, *Britain and the Last Tsar: British Policy and Russia, 1894–1917* (Oxford: Clarendon, 1995), chaps. 10–11.

122. For example, Cyril Falls writes, "The Germans had come within an inch of bringing off a set plan of great length and ending it with the annihilation of their foes." Falls, *The Great War* (New York: Capricorn, 1959), p. 70. Also see Trevor N.

Dupuy, *A Genius for War: The German Army and General Staff, 1807–1945* (Englewood Cliffs, NJ: Prentice-Hall, 1977), pp. 145–47; Herbert Rosinski, *The German Army* (New York: Praeger, 1966), pp. 134–37; and Sagan, "1914," pp. 159–61.

123. Sagan, "1914," pp. 159–60.

124. See Michael C. Desch, *When the Third World Matters: Latin America and United States Grand Strategy* (Baltimore, MD: Johns Hopkins University Press, 1993), pp. 39–44; and Taylor, *Struggle*, pp. xx, 566–67. Also see the discussion in Chapter 7, note 60, of this book.

125. Taylor, *Mastery*, p. 427. Regarding the balance of power in 1905, see Herrmann, *Arming of Europe*, pp. 40–47.

126. There was some sentiment among the German generals in 1905 for launching a preventive war, but apparently Field Marshal Alfred von Schlieffen (the chief of the General Staff) was not among the advocates. Regardless, the kaiser refused to consider the idea. See Geiss, "Origins of the First World War," in Geiss, ed., *July 1914*, pp. 39–40; Martin Kitchen, *A Military History of Germany: From the Eighteenth Century to the Present Day* (Bloomington: Indiana University Press, 1975), pp. 174–75; and Gerhard Ritter, *The Schlieffen Plan: Critique of a Myth*, trans. Andrew and Eva Wilson (London: Oswald Wolff, 1958), pp. 103–28.

127. Hitler emphasized in mid-February 1945, "I had always maintained that we ought at all costs to avoid waging war on two fronts." Francois Genoud, ed., *The Last Testament of Adolf Hitler: The Hitler-Bormann Documents, February–April 1945*, trans. R. H. Stevens (London: Cassell, 1961), p. 63. His views on this subject were hardly unusual in post–World War I Germany. See Post, *Civil-Military Fabric*, p. 151.

128. Hitler told his generals on March 30, 1941, "Now the possibility exists to strike Russia with our rear safe; that chance will not soon come again." Quoted in Joachim C. Fest, *Hitler*, trans. Richard and Clara Winston (New York: Harcourt Brace Jovanovich, 1974), p. 646.

129. Rich, *Hitler's War Aims*, p. xii. Also see Craig, *Germany*, chap. 19, esp. pp. 677–78; Wolfram Wette, "Ideology, Propaganda, and Internal Politics as Preconditions of the War Policy of the Third Reich," in Wilhelm Deist et al., eds., *Germany and the Second World War*, vol. 1, *The Build-up of German Aggression*, trans. P. S. Falla et al. (Oxford: Clarendon, 1990), pp. 83–124.

130. Matthew Cooper and James Lucas, *Panzer: The Armoured Force of the Third Reich* (New York: St. Martin's, 1976), pp. 7–24; Kenneth Macksey, *Guderian: Creator of the Blitzkrieg* (New York: Stein and Day, 1976), chap. 5; Ernest R. May, *Strange Victory: Hitler's Conquest of France* (New York: Hill and Wang, 2000), pt. 3; John J. Mearsheimer, *Conventional Deterrence* (Ithaca, NY: Cornell University Press, 1983), chap. 4; and Barry R. Posen, *Sources of Military Doctrine: France, Britain, and Germany between the World Wars* (Ithaca, NY: Cornell University Press, 1984), chaps. 3, 6.

131. Haffner, *Meaning of Hitler*, p. 49.

132. The phrase is Joachim Fest's, who uses the date 1938 rather than 1940 to make the same point. Fest, *Hitler*, p. 9.

133. Robert Cecil, *Hitler's Decision to Invade Russia* (New York: David McKay, 1975), chap. 8; Matthew Cooper, *The German Army, 1933–1945: Its Political and Military Failure* (New York: Stein and Day, 1978), chaps. 17–18; Geyer, "German Strategy," pp. 587–90; and Barry K. Leach, *German Strategy against Russia, 1939–1941* (Oxford: Clarendon, 1973).

134. Feis, *Churchill, Roosevelt, Stalin*, pp. 9–10; Waldo Heinrichs, *Threshold of War: Franklin D. Roosevelt and American Entry into World War II* (Oxford: Oxford University Press, 1988), pp. 95, 102–3; Warren F. Kimball, *The Juggler: Franklin Roosevelt as Wartime Statesman* (Princeton, NJ: Princeton University Press, 1991), p. 15, 21–41; and William L. Langer and S. Everett Gleason, *The Undeclared War, 1940–1941* (New York: Harper, 1953), chap. 17.

135. See Chapter 8.

136. All quotes in this paragraph are from Haffner, *Meaning of Hitler*, pp. 104–5.

137. This is a key theme in Akira Iriye, *The Origins of the Second World War in Asia and the Pacific* (London: Longman, 1987).

138. Dorothy Borg, *The United States and the Far Eastern Crisis of 1933–1938* (Cambridge, MA: Harvard University Press, 1964); Warren I. Cohen, *America's Response to China: An Interpretative History of Sino-American Relations*, 2d ed. (New York: John Wiley, 1980), chap. 5; Warren I. Cohen, *The Chinese Connection: Roger S. Greene, Thomas W. Lamont, George E. Sokolsky, and American–East Asian Relations* (New York: Columbia University Press, 1978); and Michael Schaller, *The United States and China in the Twentieth Century*, 2d ed. (Oxford: Oxford University Press, 1990), chap. 3.

139. Paul W. Schroeder, *The Axis Alliance and Japanese-American Relations, 1941* (Ithaca, NY: Cornell University Press, 1958), pp. 2, 15. Also see Herbert Feis, *The Road to Pearl Harbor: The Coming of the War between the United States and Japan* (Princeton, NJ: Princeton University Press, 1950), esp. chaps. 5–6. The Japanese military actually thought little about fighting a war against the United States until 1940. See Michael A. Barnhart, "Japanese Intelligence before the Second World War: 'Best Case' Analysis," in Ernest R. May, ed., *Knowing One's Enemies: Intelligence Assessment before the Two World Wars* (Princeton, NJ: Princeton University Press, 1984), pp. 424–55; and Peattie, *Ishiwara Kanji*.

140. About 48 percent of the outside aid flowing into China came across its border with Indochina. Another 31 percent came across China's border with Burma (along the famous "Burma Road"). James W. Morley, ed., *The Final Confrontation: Japan's Negotiations with the United States, 1941*, trans. David A. Titus (New York: Columbia University Press, 1994), pp. xx, 373.

141. Schroeder, *Axis Alliance*, p. 46. Also see Iriye, *Origins of the Second World War*, p. 140.

142. The key work on this point is Heinrichs, *Threshold of War*. Also see Michael A. Barnhart, "Historiography, the Origins of the Second World War in Asia and the Pacific: Synthesis Impossible?" *Diplomatic History* 20, No. 2 (Spring 1996), pp. 241–60; Feis, *Road to Pearl Harbor;* Morley, ed., *Final Confrontation;* and Schroeder, *Axis Alliance*.

143. On the Soviet Union balancing against Japan, see Coox, *Nomonhan*, vols. 1–2; and Hata, "The Japanese-Soviet Confrontation."

144. On the Tripartite Pact, see Chihiro Hosoya, "The Tripartite Pact, 1939–1940," trans. James W. Morley, in Morley, ed., *Deterrent Diplomacy*, pp. 179–257. On American knowledge of Japanese thinking, see Heinrichs, *Threshold of War*, chaps. 5–7.

145. The United States clearly demanded that Japan exit China and Indochina but was ambiguous about Manchuria. Nevertheless, there was good reason for Japan to think that the United States would demand that Manchuria also be abandoned. See Feis, *Road to Pearl Harbor*, p. 276; Morley, ed., *Final Confrontation*, pp. xxviii–xxx, 318, 321–22; and Schroeder, *Axis Alliance*, pp. 35–36.

146. Barnhart, *Japan Prepares for Total War*, pp. 144–46.

147. Iriye, *Origins of the Second World War*, pp. 148–50.

148. Kupchan, *Vulnerability of Empire*, pp. 339–50.

149. Langer and Gleason, *Undeclared War*, pp. 857, 867.

150. For a detailed discussion of this point, see Schroeder, *Axis Alliance*, which should be read in conjunction with Heinrichs, *Threshold of War*, chaps. 4–7. Heinrichs shows how German battlefield successes on the eastern front between June and December 1941 hardened the U.S. negotiating position against Japan.

151. As Heinrichs notes, it is difficult to believe that Roosevelt did not understand that his policies would eventually lead to war between Japan and the United States. Heinrichs, *Threshold of War*, p. 159.

152. Mark S. Watson, *Chief of Staff: Prewar Plans and Operations* (Washington, DC: Department of the Army, 1950), chaps. 4–9; and Stephen D. Westbrook, "The Railey Report and Army Morale, 1941: Anatomy of a Crisis," *Military Review* 60, No. 6 (June 1980), pp. 11–24.

153. Langer and Gleason, *Undeclared War*, pp. 570–74.

154. Scott D. Sagan, "The Origins of the Pacific War," in Robert I. Rotberg and Theodore K. Rabb, eds., *The Origin and Prevention of Major Wars* (Cambridge: Cambridge University Press, 1989), p. 324. This same theme is emphasized in Michael E. Brown, *Deterrence Failures and Deterrence Strategies*, RAND Paper 5842 (Santa Monica, CA: RAND Corporation, March 1977), pp. 3–7; Robert J.C. Butow, *Tojo and the Coming of the War* (Princeton, NJ: Princeton University Press, 1961), chap. 11; Kupchan, *Vulnerability of Empire*, p. 344; Bruce M. Russett, "Pearl Harbor: Deterrence Theory and Decision Theory," *Journal of Peace Research* 4, No. 2 (1967), pp. 89–105; and Schroeder, *Axis Alliance,* pp. 200–201. Also useful is Nobutaka Ike, ed. and trans., *Japan's Decision for War: Records of the 1941 Policy Conferences* (Stanford, CA: Stanford University Press, 1967).

155. Among the best sources on U.S. nuclear strategy from 1945 to 1950 are Harry R. Borowski, *A Hollow Threat: Strategic Air Power and Containment before Korea* (Westport, CT: Greenwood, 1982); David Alan Rosenberg, "The Origins of Overkill: Nuclear Weapons and American Strategy, 1945–1960," *International Security* 7, No. 4 (Spring 1983), pp. 11–22; David Alan Rosenberg, "American Atomic Strategy and the Hydrogen Bomb Decision," *Journal of American History* 66, No. 1 (June 1979), pp. 62–87; Steven T. Ross, *American War Plans, 1945–1950* (New York: Garland, 1988); and Samuel R. Williamson and Steven L. Rearden, *The Origins of U.S. Nuclear Strategy, 1945–1953* (New York: St. Martin's, 1993).

156. Henry S. Rowen, "Formulating Strategic Doctrine," in *Report of the Commission on the Organization of the Government for the Conduct of Foreign Policy,* Appendix K, *Adequacy of Current Organization: Defense and Arms Control* (Washington, DC: U.S. Government Printing Office, June 1975), p. 222.

157. Among the best works on massive retaliation are Rosenberg, "Origins of Overkill," pp. 3–69; Scott D. Sagan, "SIOP-62: The Nuclear War Plan Briefing to President Kennedy," *International Security* 12, No. 1 (Summer 1987), pp. 22–51; and Samuel F. Wells, Jr., "The Origins of Massive Retaliation," *Political Science Quarterly* 96, No. 1 (Summer 1981), pp. 31–52.

158. Quoted in Fred Kaplan, *The Wizards of Armageddon* (New York: Simon and Schuster, 1983), p. 134.

159. See Trachtenberg, *Constructed Peace,* pp. 100–101, 123, 156–58, 179–83, 293–97, 351. Trachtenberg maintains that the United States had nuclear superiority from roughly 1953 to 1963.

160. See Richard K. Betts, *Nuclear Blackmail and Nuclear Balance* (Washington, DC: Brookings Institution Press, 1987), pp. 144–79; and Scott D. Sagan, *Moving Targets: Nuclear Strategy and National Security* (Princeton, NJ: Princeton University Press, 1989), pp. 24–26. Between 1949 and 1955, the United States wrestled with the idea of launching a preventive strike against the Soviets' incipient nuclear capability but always decided that the operation was not feasible. See Tami Davis Biddle, "Handling the Soviet Threat: 'Project Control' and the Debate on American Strategy in the Early Cold War Years," *Journal of Strategic Studies* 12, No. 3 (September 1989), pp. 273–302; Russell D. Buhite and William C. Hamel, "War for Peace: The Question of an American Preventive War against the Soviet Union, 1945–1955," *Diplomatic History* 14, No. 3 (Summer 1990), pp. 367–84; Copeland, *Origins of Major War,* pp. 170–75; and Marc Trachtenberg, "A 'Wasting Asset': American Strategy and the Shifting Nuclear Balance, 1949–1954," *International Security* 13, No. 3 (Winter 1988–89), pp. 5–49.

161. See Kaplan, *Wizards,* chaps. 12–18. Also see Lynn Etheridge Davis, *Limited Nuclear Options: Deterrence and the New American Doctrine,* Adelphi Paper No. 121 (London: International Institute for Strategic Studies, Winter 1975–76); Alfred Goldberg, *A Brief Survey of the Evolution of Ideas about Counterforce,* RM-5431-PR (Santa Monica, CA: RAND Corporation, October 1967, rev. March 1981); Klaus Knorr and Thornton Read, eds., *Limited Strategic War* (New York: Praeger, 1962); and Marc Trachtenberg, *History and Strategy* (Princeton, NJ: Princeton University Press, 1991), chap. 1.

162. On the criteria for assured destruction, see Alain C. Enthoven and K. Wayne Smith, *How Much Is Enough? Shaping the Defense Program, 1961–1969* (New York: Harper and Row, 1971), pp. 174–75, 207–10; Milton Leitenberg, "Presidential Directive (PD) 59: United States Nuclear Weapons Targeting Policy," *Journal of Peace Research* 18, No. 4 (1981), pp. 312–14; and Stephen Van Evera, "Analysis or Propaganda? Measuring American Strategic Nuclear Capability, 1969–1988," in Lynn Eden and Steven E. Miller, eds., *Nuclear Arguments: Understanding the Strategic Nuclear Arms and Arms Control Debates* (Ithaca, NY: Cornell University Press, 1989), pp. 209–21.

163. SIOP stands for Single Integrated Operational Plan. The numbers for potential targets in this paragraph are from Desmond Ball, "The Development of the SIOP, 1960–1983," in Desmond Ball and Jeffrey Richelson, eds., *Strategic Nuclear Targeting* (Ithaca, NY: Cornell University Press, 1986), p. 80.

164. Figures for the size of the U.S. nuclear arsenal are from Robert S. Norris and William M. Arkin, "Nuclear Notebook: Estimated U.S. and Soviet/Russian Nuclear Stockpiles, 1945–94," *Bulletin of the Atomic Scientists* 50, No. 6 (November–December 1994), p. 59.

165. Frances FitzGerald, *Way Out There in the Blue: Reagan, Star Wars, and the End of the Cold War* (New York: Simon and Schuster, 2000); and David Goldfischer, *The Best Defense: Policy Alternatives for U.S. Nuclear Security from the 1950s to the 1990s* (Ithaca, NY: Cornell University Press, 1993).

166. Among the best sources on American nuclear policy between 1961 and 1990 are Desmond Ball, *Politics and Force Levels: The Strategic Missile Program of the Kennedy Administration* (Berkeley: University of California Press, 1980); Ball, "Development of the SIOP"; Desmond Ball, "U.S. Strategic Forces: How Would They Be Used?" *International Security* 7, No. 3 (Winter 1982–83), pp. 31–60; Desmond Ball and Robert Toth, "Revising the SIOP: Taking War-Fighting to Dangerous Extremes," *International Security* 14, No. 4 (Spring 1990), pp. 65–92; Aaron L. Friedberg, "A History of U.S. Strategic 'Doctrine'—1945 to 1980," *Journal of Strategic Studies* 3, No. 3 (December 1980), pp. 37–71; Leitenberg, "Presidential Directive (PD) 59"; Eric Mlyn, *The State, Society, and Limited Nuclear War* (Albany: State University of New York Press, 1995); Jeffrey Richelson, "PD-59, NSDD-13 and the Reagan Strategic

Modernization Program," *Journal of Strategic Studies* 6, No. 2 (June 1983), pp. 125–46; Rowen, "Formulating Strategic Doctrine," pp. 219–34; Sagan, *Moving Targets;* and Walter Slocombe, "The Countervailing Strategy," *International Security* 5, No. 4 (Spring 1981), pp. 18–27. For a discussion of why limited nuclear options was not a viable strategy, see Chapter 4, note 135, of this book.

167. They included the Ford administration's SIOP-5 (which took effect January 1, 1976); the Carter administration's SIOP-5F (October 1, 1981); the Reagan administration's SIOP-6 (October 1, 1983); and the George H.W. Bush administration's SIOP-6F (October 1, 1989). For a summary chart describing the differences among these SIOPs, see Ball and Toth, "Revising the SIOP," p. 67.

168. Desmond Ball, a leading expert on the history of American nuclear planning, succinctly summarizes American nuclear policy between 1961 and 1990: "Since the early 1960s, the overriding objective of U.S. strategic nuclear policy has been the development of a strategic posture designed to enable the United States to control any nuclear exchange in order to limit damage at the lowest possible levels while ensuring that the outcomes are favorable to the United States." Desmond Ball, "Soviet Strategic Planning and the Control of Nuclear War," in Roman Kolkowicz and Ellen P. Mickiewicz, eds., *The Soviet Calculus of Nuclear War* (Lexington, MA: D. C. Heath, 1986), p. 49. For evidence that the Soviets thought that the United States was deploying counterforce weapons to gain military advantage, see Henry A. Trofimenko, "Illusion of a Panacea," *International Security* 5, No. 4 (Spring 1981), pp. 28–48. All the emphasis on limited nuclear options notwithstanding, "the doctrine of the overwhelming massive strike still had a strong hold" in some quarters of the U.S. national security establishment. Rowen, "Formulating Strategic Doctrine," p. 233. Given that the Soviet Union rejected the notion of fighting limited nuclear wars and instead favored massive nuclear strikes against the United States (see the next section of this chapter), this residual interest in massive retaliation is not surprising.

169. During the late 1960s and throughout much of the 1970s, it was fashionable on both the right and the left to argue that the United States had abandoned counterforce targeting and adopted a straightforward MAD strategy in its place. Senator Malcolm Wallop (R-Wyo.), for example, wrote in 1979 that "over the past fifteen years, at least four American Presidents, and their leading defense advisers, have built weapons and cast strategic plans well nigh exclusively for the purpose of inflicting damage upon the enemy's society." Malcolm Wallop, "Opportunities and Imperatives of Ballistic Missile Defense," *Strategic Review* 7, No. 4 (Fall 1979), p. 13. It is now well established among students of the nuclear arms race that this claim is a groundless myth perpetrated by experts and policymakers who surely knew better. The seminal piece exposing this myth is Desmond Ball, *Déjà Vu: The Return* *to Counterforce in the Nixon Administration* (Santa Monica: California Seminar on Arms Control and Foreign Policy, December 1974). Also see Leitenberg, "Presidential Directive (PD) 59"; Mlyn, *The State;* and Rowen, "Formulating Strategic Doctrine."

170. Henry Rowen writes, "Over the years the number of weapons in both the U.S. and Soviet forces has increased enormously, as has the number of targets assigned to these weapons, but the number of urban-industrial targets . . . has increased little." Rowen, "Formulating Strategic Doctrine," p. 220. As discussed later in this section, Soviet strategists did not emphasize the concept of assured destruction, and therefore they did not spell out criteria for achieving that mission. However, based on U.S. criteria, the Soviets faced roughly the same task confronting the United States. Specifically, they had to destroy the 200 largest American cities, which contain about 33 percent of the U.S. population and 75 percent of the industrial base. That task probably could have been accomplished with 400 EMT, if not half that number. See Ashton B. Carter, "BMD Applications: Performance and Limitations," in Ashton B. Carter and David N. Schwartz, eds., *Ballistic Missile Defense* (Washington, DC: Brookings Institution Press, 1984), pp. 103, 163, 168–69.

171. All numbers in this paragraph are from Norris and Arkin, "Nuclear Notebook," p. 59. For a detailed description of the growth and evolution of the Soviet nuclear arsenal, see Robert P. Berman and John C. Baker, *Soviet Strategic Forces: Requirements and Responses* (Washington, DC: Brookings Institution Press, 1982).

172. Robert L. Arnett, "Soviet Attitudes towards Nuclear War: Do They Really Think They Can Win?" *Journal of Strategic Studies* 2, No. 2 (September 1979), pp. 172–91; Ball, "Soviet Strategic Planning"; David Holloway, *The Soviet Union and the Arms Race* (New Haven, CT: Yale University Press, 1983), chap. 3; Benjamin Lambeth, "Contemporary Soviet Military Policy," in Kolkowicz and Mickiewicz, eds., *Soviet Calculus of Nuclear War*, pp. 25–48; William T. Lee, "Soviet Nuclear Targeting Strategy," in Ball and Richelson, eds., *Nuclear Targeting*, pp. 84–108; and Richard Pipes, "Why the Soviet Union Thinks It Could Fight and Win a Nuclear War," *Commentary* 64, No. 1 (July 1977), pp. 21–34.

173. See Benjamin S. Lambeth, "Uncertainties for the Soviet War Planner," *International Security* 7, No. 3 (Winter 1982–83), pp. 139–66.

174. Benjamin S. Lambeth, *Selective Nuclear Options in American and Soviet Strategic Policy*, R-2034-DDRE (Santa Monica, CA: RAND Corporation, December 1976); and Jack L. Snyder, *The Soviet Strategic Culture: Implications for Limited Nuclear Options*, R-2154-AF (Santa Monica, CA: RAND Corporation, September 1977).

175. Robert Jervis, for example, has written a book titled *The Illogic of American Nuclear Strategy* (Ithaca, NY: Cornell University Press, 1984).

176. See note 159 in this chapter.

177. One author estimates that the ratio of conventional to nuclear spending in the U.S. defense budget was roughly 1.45:1 in 1961, 4:1 in 1971, and 6.7:1 in 1981. See William W. Kaufmann, *A Reasonable Defense* (Washington, DC: Brookings Institution Press, 1986), p. 21. Also see Ball, *Politics and Force Levels*, chap. 6; and Chapter 4, note 141, of this book.

178. Robert A. Pape, "Technological Sources of War and Peace," manuscript, April 2001.

CHAPTER SEVEN

1. See the works cited in Chapter 1, note 62.

2. E. H. Carr, *The Twenty Years' Crisis, 1919–1939: An Introduction to the Study of International Relations*, 2d ed. (London: Macmillan, 1962; first edition published in 1939).

3. James L. Abrahamson, *America Arms for a New Century: The Making of a Great Military Power* (New York: Free Press, 1981); and Allan R. Millett and Peter Maslowski, *For the Common Defense: A Military History of the United States of America* (New York: Free Press, 1984), chaps. 8–10.

4. Zakaria writes, "The period 1865–1908, particularly before 1890, presents us with many instances in which the country's central decision-makers noticed and considered clear opportunities to expand American influence abroad and rejected them. . . . The United States would thus seem to represent an exception to the historical record and a challenge to the great power rule." Fareed Zakaria, *From Wealth to Power: The Unusual Origins of America's World Role* (Princeton, NJ: Princeton University Press, 1998), p. 5. "Imperial Understretch" is the title of chap. 3 in Zakaria's book.

5. There is one exception to this rule: both sides built massive armies during the American Civil War (1861–65).

6. The United States probably could have conquered substantial territory in Northeast Asia between 1900 and 1945, because unlike Europe, the region was open to outside penetration. (See the comparison of the Asian and European mainlands as targets for aggression in the conclusion of this chapter.) Nevertheless, it is unlikely that the United States could have conquered Japan and Russia, the two great powers located in Northeast Asia, and dominated that region the way it does the Western Hemisphere.

7. Nicholas Spykman makes this point elegantly: "The position of the United States with regard to Europe as a whole is, therefore, identical to the position of Great Britain in regard to the European Continent. The scale is different, the units are larger, and the distances are greater, but the pattern is the same. . . . It is not surprising, then, that we have pursued a similar policy and have apparently become involved in the same vicious cycles of isolation, alliance and war. We, like the British, would prefer to achieve our aim with the least possible amount of sacrifice." Nicholas J. Spykman, *America's Strategy in World Politics: The United States and the Balance of Power* (New York: Harcourt, Brace, 1942), p. 124. Also see ibid., pp. 103–7.

8. Joseph Chamberlain described the United States in 1895 as "being untroubled by any foreign policy." Henry Cabot Lodge agreed that this statement was essentially true "outside of the Americas," but he maintained that "we had a very definite" foreign policy within the Western Hemisphere: the United States had to be "supreme." William C. Widenor, *Henry Cabot Lodge and the Search for an American Foreign Policy* (Berkeley: University of California Press, 1980), p. 106.

9. Quoted in Anders Stephanson, *Manifest Destiny: American Expansionism and the Empire of Right* (New York: Hill and Wang, 1995), p. 104.

10. July 20, 1895, letter from Richard Olney to Thomas F. Bayard, in *Foreign Relations of the United States, 1895*, pt. 1 (Washington, DC: U.S. Government Printing Office, 1896), p. 558. Hereinafter referred to as Olney Note.

11. The phrase "Manifest Destiny" was actually not coined until 1845. Nevertheless, as early as "the middle of the eighteenth century, the idea that the English settlements in America were destined to embrace most of the continent was well-engrained in American and European thinking." Reginald Horsman, *The Diplomacy of the New Republic* (Arlington Heights, IL: Harlan Davidson, 1985), p. 5. Also see Marc Egnal, *A Mighty Empire: The Origins of the American Revolution* (Ithaca, NY: Cornell University Press, 1988).

12. D. W. Meinig, *The Shaping of America: A Geographical Perspective on 500 Years of History*, vol. 2 (New Haven CT: Yale University Press, 1993), pp. 24–32.

13. David M. Pletcher, *The Diplomacy of Annexation: Texas, Oregon, and the Mexican War* (Columbia: University of Missouri Press, 1973).

14. On how race affected expansion, see Reginald Horsman, *Race and Manifest Destiny: The Origins of American Racial Anglo-Saxonism* (Cambridge, MA: Harvard University Press, 1981); and Michael L. Krenn, ed., *Race and U.S. Foreign Policy: From the Colonial Period to the Present: A Collection of Essays*, vols. 1–2 (Levittown, PA: Garland, 1998).

15. Quoted in Meinig, *Shaping of America*, vol. 2, p. 159.

16. Reginald C. Stuart, *United States Expansionism and British North America, 1775–1871* (Chapel Hill: University of North Carolina Press, 1988).

17. Lester D. Langley, *Struggle for the American Mediterranean: United States–European Rivalry in the Gulf-Caribbean, 1776–1904* (Athens: University of Georgia Press, 1976); and Robert E. May, *The Southern Dream of a Caribbean Empire, 1854–1861* (Baton Rouge: Louisiana State University Press, 1973). Some Americans were also determined to acquire Mexico. See John D.P. Fuller, *The Movement for the Acquisition of All Mexico, 1846–1848* (Baltimore, MD: Johns Hopkins University Press, 1936).

18. One might argue that America's failure to conquer Canada and Mexico and make them part of the United States is a strike against offensive realism. Although neither state ever had the wherewithal to challenge the United States by itself, there was always the risk that a distant hegemon might form an anti-American alliance with Canada or Mexico, or maybe both of them. The United States, so the argument goes, could have precluded this possibility by expanding northward and southward as well as westward. The strategic benefits of controlling virtually all of North America notwithstanding, the United States did not attempt to conquer and assimilate Canada and Mexico after 1812 because it would have been an enormously difficult and costly task. For sure, the United States would have had little trouble conquering its neighbors after 1850. But because of the power of nationalism, subduing the people in those countries and turning them into Americans would have been a difficult if not impossible task. It made much more sense for the United States to remain on friendly terms with Canada and Mexico and help thwart the rise of a distant hegemon who might ally with them. Indeed, that approach worked well. If it had failed, however, the United States might then have considered occupying Canada or Mexico.

19. Fear of disunion was a major concern of American policymakers from the founding until the Civil War. For example, John Quincy Adams wrote in 1796, "There is no one article of my political creed more clearly demonstrated to my mind than this, that we shall proceed with giant strides to honor and consideration, and national greatness, if the union is preserved; but that if it is once broken, we shall soon divide into a parcel of petty tribes at perpetual war with one another, swayed by rival European powers, whose policy will agree perfectly in the system of keeping us at variance with one another." Quoted in Samuel Flagg Bemis, *John Quincy Adams and the Foundations of American Foreign Policy* (New York: Knopf, 1965), p. 181. Also see W. L. Morton, "British North America and a Continent in Dissolution, 1861–71," *History* 47, No. 160 (June 1962), pp. 139–56.

20. Martin Gilbert, *Atlas of American History*, rev. ed. (New York: Dorset, 1985), pp. 37–38, 62; and Alex Wexler, *Atlas of Westward Expansion* (New York: Facts on File, 1995), pp. 43, 122, and esp. 216.

21. Roughly 739,000 Native Americans lived west of the Mississippi River in 1800, bringing the total within the present borders of the continental United States to roughly 916,000. All Native American population figures in this section are compiled from Douglas H. Ubelaker, "North American Indian Population Size: Changing Perspectives," in John W. Verano and Douglas H. Ubelaker, eds., *Disease and Demography in the Americas* (Washington, DC: Smithsonian Institution Press, 1992),

p. 173, table 3. There is no consensus on how many Natives were in the Western Hemisphere at the time of initial European contact in 1492. There is substantial agreement, however, on the numbers of Natives in North America from 1800 to 1900.

22. Meinig, *Shaping of America*, Vol. 2, pp. 78–103, 179–88; Wexler, *Atlas*, pp. 42–48, 85–96; and T. Harry Williams, *The History of American Wars: From 1745 to 1918* (Baton Rouge: Louisiana State University Press, 1981), pp. 139–43.

23. During the 1870s, for example, the U.S. army deployed about nine thousand troops west of the Mississippi to deal with the Natives. Williams, *History of American Wars*, p. 310. Also see Robert M. Utley, *Frontier Regulars: The United States Army and the Indian, 1866–1891* (New York: Macmillan, 1973); and Robert Wooster, *The Military and United States Indian Policy, 1865–1903* (New Haven, CT: Yale University Press, 1988).

24. W. S. Woytinsky and E. S. Woytinsky, *World Population and Production: Trends and Outlook* (New York: Twentieth Century Fund, 1953), p. 83, table 40.

25. Ibid., p. 84, table 41.

26. See, for example, R. G. Neale, *Great Britain and United States Expansion: 1898–1900* (East Lansing: Michigan State University Press, 1966); and Stephen R. Rock, *Why Peace Breaks Out: Great Power Rapprochement in Historical Perspective* (Chapel Hill: University of North Carolina Press, 1989), chap. 2.

27. Some scholars make this point. See Kenneth Bourne, *Britain and the Balance of Power in North America, 1815–1908* (Berkeley: University of California Press, 1967), chap. 9; Bradford Perkins, *The Great Rapprochement: England and the United States, 1895–1914* (New York: Atheneum, 1968), pp. 8–9; and Samuel F. Wells, Jr., "British Strategic Withdrawal from the Western Hemisphere, 1904–1906," *Canadian Historical Review* 49, No. 4 (December 1968), pp. 335–56. Bourne argues that the United Kingdom recognized after the American Civil War (1861–65) that "it could never again hope to challenge the will of the United States on the continent of North America." Kenneth Bourne, *The Foreign Policy of Victorian England, 1830–1902* (Oxford: Oxford University Press, 1970), p. 96. Indeed, one reason Britain did not intervene on the Confederacy's side during the Civil War is that its leaders believed that the North would prevail even if the South received British assistance. See Bourne, *Britain and the Balance*, chaps. 7–8; Brian Jenkins, *Britain and the War for the Union*, 2 vols. (Montreal: McGill–Queen's University Press, 1974, 1980), passim; and Morton, "British North America."

28. See Samuel F. Bemis, *The Latin American Policy of the United States: An Historical Interpretation* (New York: Harcourt, Brace, 1943); Michael C. Desch, *When the Third World Matters: Latin America and United States Grand Strategy* (Baltimore, MD: Johns Hopkins University Press, 1993); David G. Haglund, *Latin America and the*

Transformation of U.S. Strategic Thought, 1936–1940 (Albuquerque: University of New Mexico Press, 1984); Spykman, *America's Strategy;* and Arthur P. Whitaker, *The Western Hemisphere Idea: Its Rise and Decline* (Ithaca, NY: Cornell University Press, 1954).

29. Among the best studies of the Monroe Doctrine are Bemis, *John Quincy Adams,* esp. chaps. 28–29; Ernest R. May, *The Making of the Monroe Doctrine* (Cambridge, MA: Harvard University Press, 1975); and Dexter Perkins, *A History of the Monroe Doctrine* (Boston: Little, Brown, 1963). For a copy of Monroe's address laying out the doctrine, from which the quotes in this paragraph are taken, see pp. 391–93 of the Perkins book.

30. See Felix Gilbert, *To the Farewell Address: Ideas of Early American Foreign Policy* (Princeton, NJ: Princeton University Press, 1961).

31. The United States had already made clear on January 15, 1811, that no European state could transfer any part of its empire to another European state.

32. Richard Olney effectively made this point in 1895: "That America is in no part open to colonization, though the proposition was not universally admitted at the time of its first enunciation [1823], has long been universally conceded." Olney Note, p. 554.

33. Benedict Anderson, *Imagined Communities: Reflections on the Origin and Spread of Nationalism* (London: Verso, 1983), chap. 4; and John Lynch, *The Spanish American Revolutions, 1808–1826,* 2d ed. (New York: Norton, 1986).

34. Olney Note, p. 557.

35. Desch, *Third World Matters,* chaps. 2–5.

36. Norman A. Graebner, ed., *Ideas and Diplomacy: Readings in the Intellectual Tradition of American Foreign Policy* (Oxford: Oxford University Press, 1964), pp. 154–212; Lawrence S. Kaplan, *Thomas Jefferson: Westward the Course of Empire* (Wilmington, DE: SR Books, 1999); Robert W. Tucker and David C. Hendrickson, *Empire of Liberty: The Statecraft of Thomas Jefferson* (Oxford: Oxford University Press, 1990), esp. pp. 234–36; and Richard W. Van Alstyne, *The Rising American Empire* (Oxford: Basil Blackwell, 1960).

37. Olney Note, pp. 558–59.

38. *Inaugural Addresses of the Presidents of the United States* (Washington, DC: U.S. Government Printing Office, 1974), p. 105. This was a common theme among American policymakers before 1850. For example, Thomas Jefferson defended the Louisiana Purchase as well as the expropriation of Native American lands on the grounds that if the United States did not control the territory, a rival state might. See Meinig, *Shaping of America,* vol. 2, p. 14; and Wilcomb E. Washburn, *Red Man's Land/White Man's Law: A Study of the Past and Present Status of the American Indian* (New York: Charles Scribner's, 1971), p. 56.

39. This perspective is reflected in many of the selections in Norman A. Graebner, ed., *Manifest Destiny* (Indianapolis, IN: Bobbs-Merrill, 1968). Also see Thomas R. Hietala, *Manifest Design: Anxious Aggrandizement in Late Jacksonian America* (Ithaca, NY: Cornell University Press, 1985); and Stephanson, *Manifest Destiny.*

40. Charles A. Beard and Mary R. Beard, *The Rise of American Civilization,* 2 vols. (New York: Macmillan, 1931); Norman A. Graebner, *Empire on the Pacific: A Study in Continental Expansion* (New York: Ronald Press, 1955); and William A. Williams, *The Roots of the Modern American Empire: A Study of the Growth and Shaping of Social Consciousness in a Marketplace Society* (New York: Random House, 1969).

41. Hietala, *Manifest Design;* and Albert K. Weinberg, *Manifest Destiny: A Study of Nationalist Expansionism in American History* (1935; rpt. Chicago: Quadrangle Books, 1963).

42. Michael H. Hunt, *Ideology and U.S. Foreign Policy* (New Haven, CT: Yale University Press, 1987), chap. 2; and Daniel G. Lang, *Foreign Policy in the Early Republic: The Law of Nations and the Balance of Power* (Baton Rouge: Louisiana State University Press, 1985).

43. Max Savelle, *The Origins of American Diplomacy: The International History of Angloamerica, 1492–1763* (New York: Macmillan, 1967). Also see Walter L. Dorn, *Competition for Empire, 1740–1763* (New York: Harper, 1940).

44. James H. Hutson, "Intellectual Foundations of Early American Diplomacy," *Diplomatic History* 1, No. 1 (Winter 1977), p. 9. Also see Theodore Draper, *A Struggle for Power: The American Revolution* (New York: Times Books, 1996); Jonathan R. Dull, *A Diplomatic History of the American Revolution* (New Haven, CT: Yale University Press, 1985); Horsman, *Diplomacy;* James H. Hutson, *John Adams and the Diplomacy of the American Revolution* (Lexington: University Press of Kentucky, 1980); and Bradford Perkins, *The Cambridge History of American Foreign Relations,* vol. 2, *The Creation of a Republican Empire, 1776–1865* (Cambridge: Cambridge University Press, 1995), chaps. 1–5.

45. H. C. Allen, *Great Britain and the United States: A History of Anglo-American Relations, 1783–1952* (London: Odhams, 1954), chaps. 9–14; Kinley J. Brauer, "The United States and British Imperial Expansion, 1815–60," *Diplomatic History* 12, No. 1 (Winter 1988), pp. 19–37; and Pletcher, *Diplomacy of Annexation.*

46. Ephraim D. Adams, *British Interests and Activities in Texas, 1838–1846* (Baltimore, MD: Johns Hopkins University Press, 1910); Sam W. Haynes, "Anglophobia and the Annexation of Texas: The Quest for National Security," in Sam W. Haynes and Christopher Morris, eds., *Manifest Destiny and Empire: American Antebellum Expansionism* (College Station: Texas A&M University Press, 1997), pp. 115–45; Reginald Horsman, "British Indian Policy in the Northwest, 1807–1812," *Mississippi Valley Historical Review* 45, No. 1 (June 1958), pp. 51–66; and J. Leitch

Wright, Jr., *Britain and the American Frontier, 1783–1815* (Athens: University of Georgia Press, 1975).

47. This subject is discussed at length in Frederick Merk, *The Monroe Doctrine and American Expansionism, 1843–1849* (New York: Knopf, 1966). Also see Pletcher, *Diplomacy of Annexation.*

48. Quoted in Merk, *Monroe Doctrine*, p. 6. Also see Sam W. Haynes, *James K. Polk and the Expansionist Impulse* (New York: Longman, 1997).

49. Merk, *Monroe Doctrine*, p. 289.

50. There is evidence that the founders' resistance to a continental commitment was influenced by eighteenth-century British debates on the subject. See Gilbert, *To the Farewell Address*, chap. 2.

51. See Chapter 6.

52. See Chapter 8.

53. William C. Askew and J. Fred Rippy, "The United States and Europe's Strife, 1908–1913," *Journal of Politics* 4, No. 1 (February 1942), pp. 68–79; and Raymond A. Esthus, "Isolationism and World Power," *Diplomatic History* 2, No. 2 (Spring 1978), pp. 117–29.

54. On the movement of American troops to Europe, see Leonard P. Ayres, *The War with Germany: A Statistical Summary* (Washington, DC: U.S. Government Printing Office, 1919); and David Trask, *The AEF and Coalition Warmaking, 1917–1918* (Lawrence: University Press of Kansas, 1993).

55. Henry T. Allen, *The Rhineland Occupation* (Indianapolis, IN: Bobbs-Merrill, 1927); and Keith L. Nelson, *Victors Divided: America and the Allies in Germany, 1918–1923* (Berkeley: University of California Press, 1975).

56. See Edward H. Buehrig, *Woodrow Wilson and the Balance of Power* (Bloomington: Indiana University Press, 1955); Patrick Devlin, *Too Proud to Fight: Woodrow Wilson's Neutrality* (Oxford: Oxford University Press, 1975), pp. 671–88; George F. Kennan, *American Diplomacy, 1900–1950* (Chicago: University of Chicago Press, 1951), chap. 4; Robert Lansing, *War Memoirs of Robert Lansing, Secretary of State* (Indianapolis, IN: Bobbs-Merrill, 1935), pp. 18–26, 203–37; Walter Lippmann, *U.S. Foreign Policy: Shield of the Republic* (Boston: Little, Brown, 1943), pp. 33–39; and Daniel M. Smith, *The Great Departure: The United States and World War I, 1914–1920* (New York: John Wiley, 1965). This is not to deny that other factors contributed to the American decision to enter World War I. For example, see Ernest May, *The World War and American Isolation, 1914–1917* (Chicago: Quadrangle, 1966), esp. chap. 19.

57. See Nicholas N. Golovine, *The Russian Army in the World War* (New Haven, CT: Yale University Press, 1931), chap. 11; Sir Alfred Knox, *With the Russian Army, 1914–1917: Being Chiefly Extracts from the Diary of a Military Attaché*, vol. 2 (London: Hutchinson, 1921), chaps. 16–19; W. Bruce Lincoln, *Passage through Armageddon:*

The Russians in War and Revolution, 1914–1918 (New York: Simon and Schuster, 1986), pts. 3–4; and Allan K. Wildman, *The End of the Russian Imperial Army: The Old Army and the Soldiers' Revolt* (March–April 1917), vol. 1 (Princeton, NJ: Princeton University Press, 1980).

58. See Philippe Pétain, "Crisis of Morale in the French Nation at War, 16th April–23 October, 1917," trans. Rivers Scott, in Edward Spears, ed., *Two Men Who Saved France: Pétain and DeGaulle* (London: Eyre and Spottiswoode, 1966), pp. 67–128; Leonard V. Smith, *Between Mutiny and Obedience: The Case of the French Fifth Infantry Division during World War I* (Princeton, NJ: Princeton University Press, 1994), chaps. 7–8; and Richard M. Watt, *Dare Call It Treason* (New York: Simon and Schuster, 1963), chaps. 10–12.

59. See Paul G. Halpern, *A Naval History of World War I* (Annapolis, MD: U.S. Naval Institute Press, 1994), chap. 11; Holger H. Herwig and David F. Trask, "The Failure of Imperial Germany's Undersea Offensive against World Shipping, February 1917–October 1918," *The Historian* 32, No. 4 (August 1971), pp. 611–36; and Arthur J. Marder, *From the Dreadnought to Scapa Flow: The Royal Navy in the Fisher Era, 1904–1919*, vol. 4, *1917: Year of Crisis* (Oxford: Oxford University Press, 1969), chaps. 4–6.

60. Had the United States not entered the war, Germany might have defeated the British and French armies in the spring of 1918. See the sources cited in Chapter 6, note 124, of this book. This is not to say that the United States played the key role in defeating Germany in 1918. In fact, the British army spearheaded the Allied victory in the final year of the war. See the sources cited in note 95 of this chapter. The arrival of the U.S. army on the western front, however, markedly shifted the balance of forces against the German army at a critical juncture in the war. It is also possible that the United Kingdom might have succumbed to the German submarine campaign if the United States had not entered the war on the Allies' side. Another dimension to the American decision to join the war against Germany also bears mentioning. As emphasized in Chapter 5, the principal reason that the United States sought to prevent a European hegemon is fear that such a power would be free to intervene in the Western Hemisphere. In early 1917, Germany proposed that Mexico (and possibly Japan) form an alliance against the United States. In a secret telegram that fell into American hands, the German foreign minister called for Germany and Mexico to make war together against the United States for the purpose of helping Mexico reconquer Arizona, New Mexico, and Texas. Germany's main aim, of course, was to get the United States bogged down in a war on its own territory, so that it could not fight against Germany in Europe. This episode played a key role in bringing the United States into the war against Germany. See Desch, *Third World Matters*, chap. 2; and Barbara W. Tuchman, *The Zimmerman Telegram* (New York: Macmillan, 1966).

61. Among the best works on isolationism are Selig Adler, *The Isolationist Impulse: Its Twentieth-Century Reaction* (London: Abelard-Schuman, 1957); Wayne S. Cole, *Roosevelt and the Isolationists, 1932–1945* (Lincoln: University of Nebraska Press, 1983); and Manfred Jonas, *Isolationism in America, 1935–1941* (Ithaca, NY: Cornell University Press, 1966).

62. See Robert A. Divine, *The Reluctant Belligerent: American Entry into World War II* (New York: John Wiley, 1965); William L. Langer and S. Everett Gleason, *The Challenge to Isolation, 1937–1940* (New York: Harper and Brothers, 1952); Frederick W. Marks III, *Wind over Sand: The Diplomacy of Franklin Roosevelt* (Athens: University of Georgia Press, 1988); Arnold A. Offner, *American Appeasement: United States Foreign Policy and Germany, 1933–1938* (New York: Norton, 1976); and Arnold Offner, "Appeasement Revisited: The United States, Great Britain, and Germany, 1933–1940," *Journal of American History* 64, No. 2 (September 1977), pp. 373–93.

63. Kenneth S. Davis, *FDR: Into the Storm 1937–1940, A History* (New York: Random House, 1993), pp. 543–44; Eric Larrabee, *Commander in Chief: Franklin Delano Roosevelt, His Lieutenants, and Their War* (New York: Harper and Row, 1987), pp. 46–47; David Reynolds, "1940: Fulcrum of the Twentieth Century?" *International Affairs* 66, No. 2 (April 1990), pp. 325–26, 329, 334, 337; and Gerhard L. Weinberg, *A World at Arms: A Global History of World War II* (Cambridge: Cambridge University Press, 1994), pp. 84–85, 121.

64. Alan Bullock, *Hitler and Stalin: Parallel Lives* (New York: Vintage, 1993), p. 670; Robert Conquest, *Stalin: Breaker of Nations* (New York: Viking Penguin, 1991), p. 229; Reynolds, "1940," p. 337; R. C. Raack, *Stalin's Drive to the West, 1938–1945: The Origins of the Cold War* (Stanford, CA: Stanford University Press, 1995), pp. 25–26, 52, 187 (note 23), 195 (note 34); and Adam B. Ulam, *Stalin: The Man and His Era* (New York: Viking, 1973), p. 524.

65. See the sources cited in Chapter 6, note 134.

66. See Chapter 3.

67. Cole, *Roosevelt and the Isolationists,* chap. 26; Langer and Gleason, *Challenge to Isolation,* chaps. 14–15; Warren F. Kimball, *The Most Unsordid Act: Lend-Lease, 1939–1941* (Baltimore, MD: Johns Hopkins University Press, 1969), chap. 2; David L. Porter, *The Seventy-sixth Congress and World War II* (Columbia: University of Missouri Press, 1979), chaps. 6–7; and Marvin R. Zahniser, "Rethinking the Significance of Disaster: The United States and the Fall of France in 1940," *International History Review* 14, No. 2 (May 1992), pp. 252–76.

68. Cole, *Roosevelt and the Isolationists,* pp. 11, 364–65.

69. Mark S. Watson, *Chief of Staff: Prewar Plans and Preparations* (Washington, DC: Department of the Army, 1950), pp. 16, 202.

70. Quoted in Kimball, *Unsordid Act,* p. 233.

71. William L. Langer and S. Everett Gleason, *The Undeclared War, 1940–1941*

(New York: Harper and Brothers, 1953), chaps. 8–9, 14, 17–18, 21–23; and Richard M. Leighton and Robert W. Coakley, *Global Logistics and Strategy, 1940–1943* (Washington, DC: Department of the Army, 1955), pt. I. Even if Hitler had not declared war on the United States, Washington would have declared war on Germany soon after Pearl Harbor, just as it had declared war on Germany in World War I. The Roosevelt administration was clearly trying to get the United States into a fight with Germany by the fall of 1941. Its main concern was finding a pretext to enter the war. Fortunately, Hitler provided a neat solution to that problem.

72. Walter W. Rostow, *The Division of Europe after World War II, 1946* (Austin: University of Texas Press, 1981), pp. 5–6, 54–55, 92; Mark S. Sheetz, "Exit Strategies: American Grand Designs for Postwar European Security," *Security Studies* 8, No. 4 (Summer 1999), pp. 1–43; Michael S. Sherry, *Preparing for the Next War* (New Haven, CT: Yale University Press, 1977), pp. 97–98; Jean E. Smith, ed., *The Papers of General Lucius D. Clay: Germany, 1945–1949*, vol. 1 (Bloomington: Indiana University Press, 1974), pp. 242–43; and Phil Williams, *The Senate and US Troops in Europe* (New York: St. Martin's, 1985), chap. 2.

73. The numbers in this paragraph are from Daniel J. Nelson, *A History of U.S. Military Forces in Germany* (Boulder, CO: Westview, 1987), pp. 45, 81, 103; and Phil Williams, *US Troops in Europe*, Chatham House Paper No. 25 (Boston: Routledge and Kegan Paul, 1984), p. 19. Also see William P. Mako, *U.S. Ground Forces and the Defense of Central Europe* (Washington, DC: Brookings Institution Press, 1983), p. 8.

74. See Chapter 8.

75. See Brian M. Linn, *Guardians of Empire: The U.S. Army and the Pacific, 1902–1940* (Chapel Hill: University of North Carolina Press, 1997); and Edward S. Miller, *War Plan Orange: The U.S. Strategy to Defeat Japan, 1897–1945* (Annapolis, MD: U.S. Naval Institute Press, 1991). For a useful survey of American policy in the Far East between 1900 and 1930, see A. Whitney Griswold, *The Far Eastern Policy of the United States* (New York: Harcourt, Brace, 1938), chaps. 1–8.

76. The figures for each year can be found in Linn, *Guardians of Empire*, pp. 253–54.

77. Quoted in Walter LaFeber, *The Cambridge History of American Foreign Relations*, vol. 2, *The American Search for Opportunity, 1865–1913* (Cambridge: Cambridge University Press, 1995), p. 175.

78. See Kemp Tolley, *Yangtze Patrol: The U.S. Navy in China* (Annapolis, MD: U.S. Naval Institute Press, 1971); and Dennis L. Noble, *The Eagle and the Dragon: The United States Military in China, 1901–1937* (Westport, CT: Greenwood, 1990).

79. On the Russo-Japanese War, see the sources cited in Chapter 6, note 18.

80. On the Japanese army in the 1920s, see Meiron and Susie Harries, *Soldiers of the Sun: The Rise and Fall of the Imperial Japanese Army* (New York: Random House, 1991), pt. 3. On the Soviet army in the 1920s, see John Erickson, *The Soviet High*

Command: A Military-Political History, 1918–1941 (New York: St. Martin's, 1962), chaps. 5–10; and Dimitri F. White, *The Growth of the Red Army* (Princeton, NJ: Princeton University Press, 1944), chaps. 6–9.

81. Stalin's purges did weaken Soviet units stationed in the Far East, although the purges there lacked "the ferocity and intensity exhibited elsewhere in the Red Army." See Erickson, *Soviet High Command*, p. 467. For a general discussion of the purges, see ibid., chaps. 14–16; and Robert Conquest, *The Great Terror: A Reassessment* (Oxford: Oxford University Press, 1990), pp. 427–31. Despite its manifest military capabilities, the Soviet Union was not a potential hegemon in Asia. The bulk of Soviet military resources was by necessity deployed in Europe and could only be shifted to the Far East if the Soviets first gained hegemony in Europe, which was not a serious possibility in the late 1930s.

82. See Paul Haggie, *Britannia at Bay: The Defence of the British Empire against Japan, 1931–1941* (Oxford: Clarendon, 1981), pp. 161–63; and Peter Lowe, *Great Britain and the Origins of the Pacific War: A Study of British Policy in East Asia, 1937–1941* (Oxford: Clarendon, 1977), chap. 4.

83. Among the best works describing Japan's problems winning its war in China are Frank Dorn, *The Sino-Japanese War, 1937–1941: From Marco Polo Bridge to Pearl Harbor* (New York: Macmillan, 1974); Edward L. Dreyer, *China at War, 1901–1949* (London: Longman, 1995), chaps. 6–7; and Lincoln Li, *The Japanese Army in North China, 1937–1941: Problems of Political and Economic Control* (Oxford: Oxford University Press, 1975).

84. See Wesley F. Craven and James L. Cate, *The Army Air Forces in World War II*, vol. I, *Plans and Early Operations, January 1939–August 1942* (Washington, DC: Office of Air Force History, 1983), pp. 175–93; and Louis Morton, *The Fall of the Philippines* (Washington, DC: Department of the Army, 1953), chaps. 2–3.

85. On the defeat of the Kwantung Army, see David M. Glantz, *August Storm: The Soviet 1945 Strategic Offensive in Manchuria*, Leavenworth Paper No. 7 (Fort Leavenworth, KS: Army Command and General Staff College, February 1983); and David M. Glantz, *August Storm: Soviet Tactical and Operational Combat in Manchuria, 1945*, Leavenworth Paper No. 8 (Fort Leavenworth, KS: Army Command and General Staff College, June 1983).

86. See Marc S. Gallicchio, *The Cold War Begins in Asia: American East Asian Policy and the Fall of the Japanese Empire* (New York: Columbia University Press, 1988).

87. There is a difference between British and American motives for maintaining a balance of power on the European continent. The United States, as emphasized, worries little about a direct military threat from a European hegemon, but instead is concerned about the possibility of a European (or Asian) great power forming an alliance with a state in the Western Hemisphere. The United Kingdom does not have to worry about that problem, because it is the only state on the island it occupies. Instead, it worries that a European hegemon would pose a direct military threat to its survival, either by sending an invasion force across the English Channel or by defeating the British navy and severing British trade with the outside world, thus wrecking its economy.

88. Eyre Crowe, "Memorandum on the Present State of British Relations with France and Germany," January 1, 1907, in G. P. Gooch and Harold Temperley, eds., *British Documents on the Origins of the War, 1898–1914*, vol. 3 (London: His Majesty's Stationery Office, 1928), p. 403. For other statements to this effect, see the November 27, 1911, and August 3, 1914, speeches of Sir Edward Grey (the secretary of state for foreign affairs) before the House of Commons, which can be found in Edward Grey, *Speeches on Foreign Affairs, 1904–1914* (London: Allen and Unwin, 1931), pp. 145–71, 297–315; and Paul M. Kennedy, *The Realities Behind Diplomacy: Background Influences on British External Policy, 1865–1980* (Boston: Allen and Unwin, 1981), p. 139.

89. Quoted in Richard Pares, "American versus Continental Warfare, 1739–1763," *English Historical Review* 51, No. 203 (July 1936), p. 430. Twenty years earlier, in 1723, Prime Minister Robert Walpole had said, "My politics are to keep free from all engagements as long as we possibly can." Quoted in Gilbert, *To the Farewell Address*, p. 22.

90. For an excellent analysis of British strategy toward the continent over the past three centuries, see Steven T. Ross, "Blue Water Strategy Revisited," *Naval War College Review* 30, No. 4 (Spring 1978), pp. 58–66. Also see Michael Howard, *The Continental Commitment: The Dilemma of British Defence Policy in the Era of Two World Wars* (London: Pelican, 1974); Paul M. Kennedy, *The Rise and Fall of British Naval Mastery* (London: Allen Lane, 1976); Pares, "American versus Continental Warfare," pp. 429–65; and R. W. Seton-Watson, *Britain in Europe, 1789–1914: A Survey of Foreign Policy* (New York: Macmillan, 1937), pp. 35–37. B. H. Liddell Hart argued in the late 1930s that "the British way in warfare" was to avoid continental commitments and rely instead on its navy to influence the outcome of European wars. See B. H. Liddell Hart, *The British Way in Warfare* (London: Faber, 1932); and B. H. Liddell Hart, *When Britain Goes to War* (London: Faber, 1935). This line of argument has been largely discredited by Brian Bond, *Liddell Hart: A Study of His Military Thought* (London: Cassell, 1977), chap. 3; and Michael Howard, *The British Way in Warfare: A Reappraisal*, 1974 Neale Lecture in English History (London: Cape, 1975).

91. See Chapter 8.

92. Christopher Howard, *Splendid Isolation* (New York: St. Martin's, 1967), pp. xi–xv.

93. The one exception is during the Crimean War (1853–56), in which the United Kingdom and France invaded Russia's Crimean Peninsula. However, the

United Kingdom was not motivated by fear of Russian expansion into central Europe; it went to war because of fear that Russian expansion at Turkey's expense in the Black Sea region would threaten British lines of communication with India. Andrew D. Lambert, *The Crimean War: British Grand Strategy, 1853–56* (New York: Manchester University Press, 1990).

94. See Chapter 8.

95. For a short summary of the British contribution, see Brian Bond, *British Military Policy between the Two World Wars* (Oxford: Oxford University Press, 1980), pp. 1–6. For more detail, see James E. Edmonds, ed., *Military Operations: France and Belgium, 1918,* 5 vols., Official British History of World War I (London: Macmillan, 1935–47); Hubert Essame, *The Battle for Europe, 1918* (New York: Scribner's, 1972); and John Terraine, *To Win a War: 1918, the Year of Victory* (New York: Doubleday, 1981). Also see John J. Mearsheimer, *Liddell Hart and the Weight of History* (Ithaca, NY: Cornell University Press, 1988), chap. 3.

96. David G. Williamson, *The British in Germany, 1918–1930: The Reluctant Occupiers* (New York: Berg, 1991).

97. As noted in Chapter 1, the United Kingdom was not a great power after 1945, yet it still acted as an offshore balancer in Europe.

CHAPTER EIGHT

1. These dates represent the time frame I examine in each case, which includes some years before either Napoleonic France, Wilhelmine Germany, or Nazi Germany (but not the Soviet Union) became a potential hegemon. As will become clear, Napoleonic France was a potential hegemon from 1793 to 1815, Wilhelmine Germany from 1903 to 1918, and Nazi Germany from 1939 to 1945. The Soviet Union was a potential hegemon from 1945 until 1990, which is the entire time frame for that case. Also, I will sometimes refer to Revolutionary and Napoleonic France (1789–1815) as simply Napoleonic France, although Napoleon did not take control of France until November 10, 1799. Finally, the Cold War case will include a discussion of the superpower rivalry in Northeast Asia as well as in Europe.

2. Barry Posen emphasizes these same factors, as well as military technology, in *The Sources of Military Doctrine: France, Britain, and Germany between the World Wars* (Ithaca, NY: Cornell University Press, 1984), pp. 63–67. For a different perspective, which emphasizes perceptions of the offense-defense balance, see Thomas J. Christensen and Jack Snyder, "Chain Gangs and Passed Bucks: Predicting Alliance Patterns in Multipolarity," *International Organization* 44, No. 2 (Spring 1990), pp. 137–68.

3. This framework is discussed in more detail in Chapter 9.

4. Ludwig Dehio, *Germany and World Politics in the Twentieth Century,* trans. Dieter Pevsner (New York: Norton, 1967), p. 29; and Posen, *Sources,* p. 63.

5. See Scott Sagan, "1914 Revisited: Allies, Offense, and Instability," *International Security* 11, No. 2 (Fall 1986), pp. 151–76; and Stephen Van Evera, *Causes of War: Power and the Roots of Conflict* (Ithaca, NY: Cornell University Press, 1999), pp. 152–54.

6. There is a huge literature on great-power politics between 1789 and 1815. Among the key works that inform the following discussion are Geoffrey Best, *War and Society in Revolutionary Europe, 1770–1870* (Montreal: McGill–Queen's University Press, 1998), chaps. 5–13; T.C.W. Blanning, *The Origins of the French Revolutionary Wars* (New York: Longman, 1986); David G. Chandler, *The Campaigns of Napoleon* (New York: Macmillan, 1966); Vincent J. Esposito and John R. Elting, *A Military History and Atlas of the Napoleonic Wars* (New York: Praeger, 1965); David Gates, *The Napoleonic Wars, 1803–1815* (London: Arnold, 1997); Georges Lefebvre, *Napoleon,* vol. I, *From 18 Brumaire to Tilsit, 1799–1807,* and vol. 2, *From Tilsit to Waterloo, 1807–1815,* trans. H. F. Stockhold and J. E. Anderson, respectively (New York: Columbia University Press, 1990); Steven T. Ross, *European Diplomatic History, 1789–1815: France against Europe* (Garden City, NY: Anchor, 1969); Paul W. Schroeder, *The Transformation of European Politics, 1763–1848* (Oxford: Oxford University Press, 1994), chaps. 1–11; and Stephen M. Walt, *Revolution and War* (Ithaca, NY: Cornell University Press, 1996), chap. 3.

7. The phrase is from William Carr, *The Origins of the Wars of German Unification* (London: Longman, 1991), p. 90.

8. That the French Revolutionary Wars were caused and fueled by calculations about relative power, not ideology, is a main theme in Blanning, *French Revolutionary Wars;* Ross, *Diplomatic History;* and Schroeder, *Transformation.* Walt agrees that power politics drove these wars, but he maintains that ideological considerations influenced how the relevant actors assessed the balance of power. Walt, *Revolution and War,* chap. 3.

9. On eighteenth century warfare, see Best, *War and Society,* chaps. 1–4; Hans Delbruck, *History of the Art of War: Within the Framework of Political History,* vol. 4, *The Modern Era,* trans. Walter J. Renfroe, Jr. (Westport, CT: Greenwood, 1985), pp. 223–383; Michael Howard, *War in European History* (Oxford: Oxford University Press, 1976), chap. 4; and R. R. Palmer, "Frederick the Great, Guibert, Bulow: From Dynastic to National War," in Peter Paret, ed., *Makers of Modern Strategy: From Machiavelli to the Nuclear Age* (Princeton, NJ: Princeton University Press, 1986), pp. 91–119.

10. Historians usually date the first coalition to February 7, 1792, when Austria and Prussia came together to invade France. That alliance, however, was obviously not a balancing coalition.

11. As one Russian diplomat put it, "The present war, despite the laxity with which Prussia wages it, continues to exhaust it, and depending on how long it lasts its means will be considerably diminished. You will say that this will be as much the case with Austria, but imagine how we will remain fresh and intact, and how we will set a weight in the balance which will carry everything before it." Quoted in Schroeder, *Transformation*, p. 145.

12. The best description of the profound impact that Napoleon had on warfare is Carl Von Clausewitz, *On War*, eds. and trans. Michael Howard and Peter Paret (Princeton, NJ: Princeton University Press, 1976), pp. 585–610. Also see Jean Colin, *The Transformations of War*, trans. L.H.R. Pope-Hennessy (London: Hugh Rees, 1912).

13. On the conflict in Spain, see David Gates, *The Spanish Ulcer: A History of the Peninsular War* (New York: Norton, 1986); and Michael Glover, *The Peninsular War, 1807–1814: A Concise Military History* (Hamden, CT: Archon, 1974).

14. Hans Delbruck writes, "When Napoleon was involved with several enemies, he was able to overcome all of them, one after the other. In 1805 he had defeated the Austrians at Ulm before the Russians arrived; then he defeated the Russians with the remnants of the Austrians at Austerlitz before the Prussians intervened. In 1806 he again defeated the Prussians before the Russians were on hand (at Jena), and in 1807 he defeated the Russians before the Austrians had pulled themselves together again." Delbruck, *History*, Vol. 4, p. 422.

15. Peter Paret, "Napoleon and the Revolution in War," in Paret, *Makers*, p. 123.

16. Schroeder, *Transformation*, p. 289.

17. As noted in Chapter 4, the United Kingdom won a decisive naval victory over France one day later at Trafalgar (October 21, 1805). But as should be clear from the discussion below, the British success at sea had little effect on Napoleon's armies, which continued winning major victories against rival great powers through at least 1809.

18. Commenting on Napoleon's situation after Ulm, but before Austerlitz, Harold Deutsch writes, "To strike down the allies while Prussia was still hesitating constituted his one great chance of victory." Harold C. Deutsch, *The Genesis of Napoleonic Imperialism* (Cambridge, MA: Harvard University Press, 1938), p. 402. For a description of Prussia's behavior in the wake of Ulm, see ibid., chaps. 21–24.

19. On the Russian campaign, see Chapter 3.

20. A further indicator of the seriousness of purpose of France's rivals after 1812 is that almost 40 percent of the United Kingdom's subsidies to the continent between 1792 and 1815 were doled out in the last three years of the conflict. Michael Duffy, "British Diplomacy and the French Wars, 1789–1815," in H. T. Dickinson, ed., *Britain and the French Revolution, 1789–1815* (New York: St. Martin's,

1989), p. 142. The seminal book on the subject is John M. Sherwig, *Guineas and Gunpowder: British Foreign Aid in the Wars with France, 1793–1815* (Cambridge, MA: Harvard University Press, 1969).

21. Those strains, which were caused in part by the ever-present but muted impulse to buck-pass among coalition members, were successfully dealt with in the Treaty of Chaumont (March 1, 1814). See Charles K. Webster, *The Foreign Policy of Castlereagh, 1812–1815: Britain and the Reconstruction of Europe* (London: G. Bell, 1931), pp. 211–32.

22. See the works cited in Chapter 3, note 42.

23. Brian Bond, *The Pursuit of Victory: From Napoleon to Saddam Hussein* (Oxford: Oxford University Press, 1998), p. 37. Among the best works on France's plundering of conquered states are Owen Connelly, *Napoleon's Satellite Kingdoms: Managing Conquered Peoples* (Malabar, FL: Krieger, 1990); David Kaiser, *Politics and War: European Conflict from Philip II to Hitler* (Cambridge, MA: Harvard University Press, 1990), pp. 212–23, 246–52; and Stuart Woolf, *Napoleon's Integration of Europe* (London: Routledge, 1991), esp. chap. 4.

24. Ireland, which was hostile to British rule, accounted for about 5 million of Britain's total population figure of 16 million in 1800. André Armengaud, "Population in Europe, 1700–1914," in Carlo M. Cipolla, ed., *The Fontana Economic History of Europe*, vol. 3, *The Industrial Revolution* (London: Collins, 1973), p. 29. Leaving out Ireland's population, France's population advantage over Britain would increase from 1.5:1 to 2.5:1 (28 versus 11 million).

25. Population size also can influence a state's overall wealth, as just discussed.

26. On the differences in the size and social structure of eighteenth-century armies versus the post-1789 French army, see Best, *War and Society*, chaps. 2–7; Howard, *War in European History*, chaps. 4–5; and Hew Strachan, *European Armies and the Conduct of War* (Boston: Allen and Unwin, 1983), chaps. 2–3.

27. France's conquest of foreign territory also helped tilt the population balance against Austria and Russia. Paul Kennedy, for example, maintains that "Napoleon's conquests of bordering lands increased the number of 'Frenchmen' from 25 million in 1789 to 44 million in 1810." Paul M. Kennedy, *The Rise and Fall of the Great Powers: Economic Change and Military Conflict from 1500 to 2000* (New York: Random House, 1987), p. 131.

28. It is worth noting that the pre-revolutionary French army was not a formidable fighting force. See Steven Ross, *From Flintlock to Rifle: Infantry Tactics, 1740–1866* (Cranbury, NJ: Associated University Presses, 1979), chap. 1; Gunther E. Rothenberg, *The Art of Warfare in the Age of Napoleon* (Bloomington: Indiana University Press, 1978), chap. 1; and Spenser Wilkinson, *The French Army before Napoleon* (Oxford: Clarendon, 1915).

29. Not only did Britain have a small army, but only a small part of it could be committed to fight on the continent, because sizable forces were needed to police the empire and to protect Britain itself from invasion. See Piers Mackesy, "Strategic Problems of the British War Effort," in Dickinson, ed., *Britain and the French Revolution*, pp. 156–57. Consider that out of an army of 250,000, British forces in Spain numbered 47,000 at their peak—i.e., less than 20 percent of the army. Ibid., p. 163.

30. See Jean-Paul Bertaud, *The Army of the French Revolution: From Citizen-Soldiers to Instrument of Power*, trans. R. R. Palmer (Princeton, NJ: Princeton University Press, 1988), chaps. 1–2; and Samuel F. Scott, *The Response of the Royal Army to the French Revolution: The Role and Development of the Line Army, 1787–93* (Oxford: Clarendon, 1978), chaps. 1–4.

31. Bertaud, *Army of the French Revolution*, chaps. 3–14; John A. Lynn, *The Bayonets of the Republic: Motivation and Tactics in the Army of Revolutionary France, 1791–94* (Urbana: University of Illinois Press, 1984); Ross, *Flintlock*, chap. 2; and Rothenberg, *Art of Warfare*, chap. 4.

32. Best, *War and Society*, p. 88.

33. On conscription, see Isser Woloch, "Napoleonic Conscription: State Power and Civil Society," *Past and Present*, No. 111 (May 1986), pp. 101–29. On Napoleon's use of foreign troops, see Best, *War and Society*, pp. 114–17; John R. Elting, *Swords around a Throne: Napoleon's Grande Armée* (New York: Free Press, 1988), chaps. 18–19; Rothenberg, *Art of Warfare*, pp. 158–62; and Woolf, *Napoleon's Integration*, pp. 156–74.

34. Clausewitz, *On War*, p. 592. On the qualitative improvements Napoleon made in the French army, see Chandler, *Campaigns*, pts. 3, 6; Colin, *Transformations*, esp. pp. 117–35, 228–95; Christopher Duffy, *Austerlitz, 1805* (London: Seeley Service, 1977), chap. 2; Elting, *Swords;* Ross, *Flintlock*, chap. 3; and Rothenberg, *Art of Warfare*, chap. 5. Also useful is Robert S. Quimby, *The Background of Napoleonic Warfare: The Theory of Military Tactics in Eighteenth-Century France* (New York: Columbia University Press, 1957). The quality of Napoleon's armies diminished somewhat after 1807, and certainly after the Russian campaign of 1812.

35. Almost all students of the period between 1792 and 1815, to include most military historians, emphasize Napoleon's genius as a military commander. Consider, for example, this description from Clausewitz's *On War* (p. 170): "One has to have seen the steadfastness of one of the forces trained and led by Bonaparte in the course of his conquests—seen them under fierce and unrelenting fire—to get some sense of what can be accomplished by troops steeled by long experience of danger, in whom a proud record of victories has instilled the noble principle of placing the highest demands on themselves. As an idea alone it is unbelievable." For a rare critical assessment of Napoleon's military leadership, see Owen Connelly, *Blundering to Glory: Napoleon's Military Campaigns* (Wilmington, DE: Scholarly Resources, 1987).

36. See Best, *War and Society*, chaps. 10, 11, 13; Gates, *Napoleonic Wars*, chap. 5; Ross, *Flintlock*, chap. 4; and Rothenberg, *Art of Warfare*, chap. 6. The key work on Prussia's response is Peter Paret, *Yorck and the Era of Prussian Reform, 1807–1815* (Princeton, NJ: Princeton University Press, 1966). Because three of Napoleon's four great-power rivals refused to imitate the French model and increase their armies' fighting power, they had a strong incentive to form a balancing coalition against France.

37. That Austria usually got left holding the buck is a central theme in Schroeder, *Transformation*.

38. David G. Chandler, *On the Napoleonic Wars: Collected Essays* (London: Greenhill, 1994), p. 43. Also, Austria was knocked out of the balance of power for seven years, Prussia for six years, and Russia for none.

39. Chandler, *Napoleonic Wars*, p. 43.

40. On British strategy, see Duffy, "British Diplomacy"; Mackesy, "Strategic Problems"; Rory Muir, *Britain and the Defeat of Napoleon, 1807–1815* (New Haven, CT: Yale University Press, 1996); Sherwig, *Guineas and Gunpowder;* and Webster, *Foreign Policy.* Not surprisingly, Britain's allies deeply resented its strategy for defeating France. See Duffy, "British Diplomacy," pp. 137–38; and A. D. Harvey, "European Attitudes to Britain during the French Revolutionary and Napoleonic Era," *History* 63, No. 209 (October 1978), pp. 356–65.

41. Russia was at war with France for less than one year between 1793 and 1804.

42. Sebastian Haffner, *The Rise and Fall of Prussia*, trans. Ewald Osers (London: Weidenfeld and Nicolson, 1980), chaps. 1–5.

43. On the 1864 war, see Carr, *Wars of German Unification*, chap. 2; and Otto Pflanze, *Bismarck and the Development of Germany: The Period of Unification, 1815–1871* (Princeton, NJ: Princeton University Press, 1963), chap. 11.

44. On the Austro-Prussian War, see Carr, *Wars of German Unification*, chap. 3; Lothar Gall, *Bismarck: The White Revolutionary*, vol. 1, *1815–1871*, trans. J. A. Underwood (London: Unwin Hyman, 1986), chap. 8; Pflanze, *Bismarck*, chaps. 13–14; Richard Smoke, *War: Controlling Escalation* (Cambridge, MA: Harvard University Press, 1977), chap. 5; and Geoffrey Wawro, *The Austro-Prussian War: Austria's War with Prussia and Italy in 1866* (Cambridge: Cambridge University Press, 1996).

45. On the Franco-Prussian War, see Carr, *Wars of German Unification*, chap. 4; Michael Howard, *The Franco-Prussian War: The German Invasion of France, 1870–1871* (New York: Dorset, 1990); Pflanze, *Bismarck*, chaps. 18–20; and Smoke, *War*, chap. 6.

46. W. E. Mosse, *The European Powers and the German Question, 1848–1871: With Special Reference to England and Russia* (New York: Octagon, 1969). Also see Richard Millman, *British Foreign Policy and the Coming of the Franco-Prussian War* (Oxford: Clarendon, 1965).

47. Haffner, *Rise and Fall of Prussia,* p. 124; and Smoke, *War,* p. 92.

48. Carr, *Wars of German Unification,* pp. 129, 203; William C. Fuller, Jr., *Strategy and Power in Russia, 1600–1914* (New York: Free Press, 1992), pp. 272–73; Haffner, *Rise and Fall of Prussia,* pp. 124–26; and Smoke, *War,* pp. 89, 92–93, 101, 117, 128–33.

49. Mosse, *European Powers,* p. 372.

50. Pflanze, *Bismarck,* pp. 419–32, 460–62; and Smoke, *War,* pp. 127, 134–35.

51. For further comparisons see Tables 3.1 and 3.2.

52. Michael Howard writes that in 1860, Prussia was "the least of the continent's major military powers." Howard, *Franco-Prussian War,* p. 1. For a good survey of the state of the French and Prussian armies between 1860 and 1870, see ibid., chap. 1. Also see Thomas J. Adriance, *The Last Gaiter Button: A Study of the Mobilization and Concentration of the French Army in the War of 1870* (Westport, CT: Greenwood, 1987), chaps. 1–3; Richard Holmes, *The Road to Sedan: The French Army, 1866–70* (London: Royal Historical Society, 1984); Trevor N. Dupuy, *A Genius for War: The German Army and General Staff, 1807–1945* (Englewood Cliffs, NJ: Prentice-Hall, 1977), chaps. 7–8; and Barry R. Posen, "Nationalism, the Mass Army, and Military Power," *International Security* 18, No. 2 (Fall 1993), pp. 100–106.

53. Istvan Deak, *Beyond Nationalism: A Social and Political History of the Habsburg Officer Corps, 1848–1918* (Oxford: Oxford University Press, 1992), chap. 2; and Gunther E. Rothenberg, *The Army of Francis Joseph* (West Lafayette, IN: Purdue University Press, 1976), chap. 6.

54. Fuller, *Strategy and Power,* pp. 273–89; and Bruce W. Menning, *Bayonets before Bullets: The Imperial Russian Army, 1861–1914* (Bloomington: Indiana University Press, 1992), chap. 1.

55. Correlli Barnett, *Britain and Her Army, 1509–1970: A Military, Political and Social Survey* (Harmondsworth, UK: Penguin, 1974), chap. 12; David French, *The British Way in Warfare, 1688–2000* (London: Unwin Hyman, 1990), chap. 5; and Edward M. Spiers, *The Army and Society, 1815–1914* (London: Longman, 1980), chaps. 2, 4.

56. A.J.P. Taylor captures this point when he writes, "Both Russia and Great Britain had virtually eliminated themselves from the European balance; this gave the years between 1864 and 1866 a character unique in recent history. The struggle for mastery in Europe was fought out on a stage limited to western Europe." Taylor, *The Struggle for Mastery in Europe, 1848–1918* (Oxford: Clarendon, 1954), p. 156.

57. Unless noted otherwise, all subsequent numbers in this section are from Table 8.3.

58. Carr, *Wars of German Unification,* p. 137. Also, Austria deployed three of its ten corps against Italy during the 1866 war. Gordon A. Craig, *The Battle of Koniggratz* (London: Weidenfeld and Nicolson, 1965), p. 21.

59. Carr, *Wars of German Unification,* pp. 137–38; Craig, *Koniggratz,* pp. 15–39; Deak, *Beyond Nationalism,* pp. 51–52; Howard, *Franco-Prussian War,* p. 5; and James J. Sheehan, *German History, 1770–1866* (Oxford: Clarendon, 1993), pp. 901–5.

60. It also explains why Prussia's military leaders maintained that war against Austria was not feasible unless Prussia had an ally (Italy) that could pin down part of the Austrian army. Gall, *Bismarck,* pp. 283–84; and Smoke, *War,* p. 85.

61. See Howard, *Franco-Prussian War,* chaps. 1–5.

62. Carr, *Wars of German Unification,* pp. 203–4; Smoke, *War,* pp. 128–29; and the other works cited in note 59 of this chapter.

63. Smoke, *War,* pp. 129–32.

64. Howard, *Franco-Prussian War,* pp. 43–44.

65. See Deak, *Beyond Nationalism,* chap. 2; David G. Herrmann, *The Arming of Europe and the Making of the First World War* (Princeton, NJ: Princeton University Press, 1996), pp. 33–34, 97–100, 123–24, 201–2; C. A. Macartney, *The Habsburg Empire, 1790–1918* (London: Weidenfeld and Nicolson, 1968); Rothenberg, *Army of Francis Joseph,* chaps. 9–11; and A.J.P. Taylor, *The Habsburg Monarchy, 1809–1918: A History of the Austrian Empire and Austria-Hungary* (London: Hamish Hamilton, 1948).

66. See Tables 3.3, and 6.1; John Gooch, *Army, State, and Society in Italy, 1870–1915* (New York: St. Martin's, 1989); Herrmann, *Arming of Europe,* pp. 34–35, 101–5, 206–7; and "Italian Military Efficiency: A Debate," *Journal of Strategic Studies* 5, No. 2 (June 1982), pp. 248–77.

67. Quoted in Richard Bosworth, *Italy and the Approach of the First World War* (New York: St. Martin's, 1983), p. 62.

68. Bosworth, *Italy and the Approach;* Richard Bosworth, *Italy, the Least of the Great Powers: Italian Foreign Policy before the First World War* (Cambridge: Cambridge University Press, 1979); Herrmann, *Arming of Europe,* pp. 105–11; and Christopher Seton-Watson, *Italy from Liberalism to Fascism, 1870–1925* (London: Methuen, 1967), chaps. 9–11.

69. See Fuller, *Strategy and Power,* pp. 350–62, 377–93; George F. Kennan, *The Fateful Alliance: France, Russia, and the Coming of the First World War* (New York: Pantheon, 1984); William L. Langer, *The Franco-Russian Alliance, 1890–1894* (New York: Octagon, 1977); William L. Langer, *The Diplomacy of Imperialism, 1890–1902,* 2d ed. (New York: Knopf, 1956), chaps. 1–2; and Taylor, *Mastery,* chap. 15.

70. For a comprehensive survey of Anglo-German relations between 1890 and 1914, see Paul M. Kennedy, *The Rise of the Anglo-German Antagonism, 1860–1914* (London: Allen and Unwin, 1980), pts. 3–5.

71. See Prosser Gifford and William R. Louis, eds., *France and Britain in Africa: Imperial Rivalry and Colonial Rule* (New Haven, CT: Yale University Press, 1971); J.A.S. Grenville, *Lord Salisbury and Foreign Policy: The Close of the Nineteenth Century* (London: Athlone, 1964); Langer, *Diplomacy of Imperialism;* Keith Neilson, *Britain and the Last Tsar: British Policy and Russia, 1894–1917* (Oxford: Clarendon, 1995), pt. 2; and the sources cited in Chapter 5, note 36, of this book.

72. Christopher Andrew, *Théophile Delcassé and the Making of the Entente Cordiale: A Reappraisal of French Foreign Policy, 1898–1905* (New York: St. Martin's, 1968), chaps. 9–10; George Monger, *The End of Isolation: British Foreign Policy, 1900–1907* (London: Thomas Nelson and Sons, 1963), chaps. 6–7; Stephen R. Rock, *Why Peace Breaks Out: Great Power Rapprochement in Historical Perspective* (Chapel Hill: University of North Carolina Press, 1989), chap. 4; and Taylor, *Mastery,* chap. 18.

73. See Monger, *End of Isolation,* chaps. 8–12; and Taylor, *Mastery,* chap. 19.

74. Kennedy, *Anglo-German Antagonism,* chaps. 16, 20.

75. On this significant event, see Herrmann, *Arming of Europe;* David Stevenson, *Armaments and the Coming of War: Europe, 1904–1914* (Oxford: Oxford University Press, 1996), chap. 2; and Taylor, *Mastery,* chap. 19.

76. Herrmann, *Arming of Europe,* chap. 2.

77. See John Gooch, *The Plans of War: The General Staff and British Military Strategy c. 1900–1916* (New York: John Wiley, 1974), chap. 9; Nicholas d'Ombrain, *War Machinery and High Policy: Defence Administration in Peacetime Britain, 1902–1914* (Oxford: Oxford University Press, 1973), chap. 2; and Samuel R. Williamson, Jr., *The Politics of Grand Strategy: Britain and France Prepare for War, 1904–1914* (Cambridge, MA: Harvard University Press, 1969).

78. Monger, *End of Isolation,* chap. 11; Neilson, *Britain and the Last Tsar,* chap. 9; Zara Steiner, *Britain and the Origins of the First World War* (London: Macmillan, 1977), chaps. 4, 6; and Williamson, *Politics of Grand Strategy,* chap. 1.

79. See John W. Coogan and Peter F. Coogan, "The British Cabinet and the Anglo-French Staff Talks, 1905–1914: Who Knew What and When Did He Know It?" *Journal of British Studies* 24, No. 1 (January 1985), pp. 110–31; Keith M. Wilson, "To the Western Front: British War Plans and the 'Military Entente' with France before the First World War," *British Journal of International Studies* 3, No. 2 (July 1977), pp. 151–68; and Keith M. Wilson, "British Power in the European Balance, 1906–1914," in David Dilks, ed., *Retreat from Power: Studies in Britain's Foreign Policy of the Twentieth Century,* vol. 1, *1906–1939* (London: Macmillan, 1981), pp. 21–41.

80. See Neilson, *Britain and the Last Tsar,* chaps. 10–11.

81. See the sources cited in Chapter 5, note 49.

82. This calculation is based on the same indicator and data base used to compile Table 3.3. For a good discussion of the evolution of the balance of economic might between Britain and Germany in the decades before World War I, see Charles P. Kindelberger, *Economic Response: Comparative Studies in Trade, Finance, and Growth* (Cambridge, MA: Harvard University Press, 1978), chap. 7. Also see Tables 3.1 and 3.2.

83. Herrmann, *Arming of Europe,* p. 112. On the French army see ibid., pp. 44–47, 80–85, 202–4; and Douglas Porch, *The March to the Marne: The French Army, 1871–1914* (Cambridge: Cambridge University Press, 1981). On the German army, see Herrmann, *Arming of Europe,* pp. 44–47, 85–92, 200–201.

84. Germany actually might have had better than a 1.8:1 advantage in a 1905 war, since some German officers believed that the Kaiserreich could mobilize a field army of 1.95 million soldiers. The French military, however, concluded that Germany could mobilize a fighting force of only 1.33 million soldiers. Herrmann, *Arming of Europe,* p. 45. I estimate the German number at roughly 1.5 million based on the discussion in ibid., pp. 44–45, 160, 221; and Jack L. Snyder, *The Ideology of the Offensive: Military Decision Making and the Disasters of 1914* (Ithaca, NY: Cornell University Press, 1984), pp. 41–50, 67, 81, 109–11, 220.

85. Fuller, *Strategy and Power,* chaps. 8–9; Herrmann, *Arming of Europe,* pp. 40–41, 61–63, 92–95, 112–46, 204–6; Pertti Luntinen, *French Information on the Russian War Plans, 1880–1914* (Helsinki: SHS, 1984), passim; Menning, *Bayonets before Bullets,* chaps. 5–7; and William C. Wohlforth, "The Perception of Power: Russia in the Pre-1914 Balance," *World Politics* 39, No. 3 (April 1987), pp. 353–81.

86. Herrmann, *Arming of Europe,* p. 97. On the British army, see Barnett, *Britain and Her Army,* chaps. 14–15; Herrmann, *Arming of Europe,* pp. 42–43, 95–97, 206; and Edward M. Spiers, *The Late Victorian Army, 1868–1902* (New York: Manchester University Press, 1992).

87. Also see Tables 3.1 and 3.2.

88. See, for example, the discussion and sources in Chapter 6, note 49.

89. Wilhelm Deist, *The Wehrmacht and German Rearmament* (Toronto: University of Toronto Press, 1981), p. 45.

90. The numbers in this paragraph are from Deist, *The Wehrmacht,* chaps. 2–3; and Wilhelm Deist, "The Rearmament of the Wehrmacht," in Militärgeschichtliches Forschungsamt, ed., *Germany and the Second World War,* vol. 1, *The Build-up of German Aggression,* trans. P. S. Falla, Dean S. McMurry, and Ewald Osers (Oxford: Clarendon, 1990), pp. 405–56. Also see Matthew Cooper, *The German Army, 1933–1945: Its Political and Military Failure* (New York: Stein and Day, 1978), chaps. 1–12; and

Albert Seaton, *The German Army, 1933–1945* (New York: New American Library, 1982), chaps. 3–4.

91. Deist, *The Wehrmacht*, p. 38.

92. On the German air force and navy, see Deist, *The Wehrmacht*, chaps. 4–6; Deist, "The Rearmament of the Wehrmacht," pp. 456–504; and Williamson Murray, *The Change in the European Balance of Power, 1938–1939: The Path to Ruin* (Princeton, NJ: Princeton University Press, 1984), pp. 38–47.

93. Deist, "The Rearmament of the Wehrmacht," p. 480.

94. See Arnold Wolfers, *Britain and France between Two Wars: Conflicting Strategies of Peace from Versailles to World War II* (New York: Norton, 1966), pp. 337–51.

95. Martin S. Alexander, *The Republic in Danger: General Maurice Gamelin and the Politics of French Defence, 1933–1940* (Cambridge: Cambridge University Press, 1992), chap. 9; Brian Bond, *British Military Policy between the Two World Wars* (Oxford: Oxford University Press, 1980), chaps. 8–9; Norman H. Gibbs, *Grand Strategy*, vol. 1, *Rearmament Policy* (London: Her Majesty's Stationery Office, 1976), chaps. 12, 16; and Posen, *Sources*, chap. 5.

96. Robert P. Shay, Jr., *British Rearmament in the Thirties: Politics and Profits* (Princeton, NJ: Princeton University Press, 1977), p. 297.

97. Bond, *British Military Policy*, chaps. 10–11; and Gibbs, *Grand Strategy*, chaps. 13, 17, 18.

98. Gibbs, *Grand Strategy*, chap. 29.

99. On Stalin as a buck-passer between June 1940 and June 1941, see Steven M. Miner, *Between Churchill and Stalin: The Soviet Union, Great Britain, and the Origins of the Grand Alliance* (Chapel Hill: University of North Carolina Press, 1988), chaps. 1–4. For evidence that Stalin thought Britain could hold out against Nazi Germany in a protracted war, see ibid., pp. 62–63, 69, 71–72, 90–91, 95, 118–19, 123; and Gabriel Gorodetsky, *Grand Delusion: Stalin and the German Invasion of Russia* (New Haven, CT: Yale University Press, 1999), pp. 58–59, 65, 135. Stalin also reasoned that even if the United Kingdom were ultimately defeated in a war, Germany would be badly weakened in the process. See Earl F. Ziemke, "Soviet Net Assessment in the 1930s," in Williamson Murray and Allan R. Millett, eds., *Calculations: Net Assessment and the Coming of World War II* (New York: Free Press, 1992), p. 205. Stalin was inclined to buck-pass to Britain, in part, because he believed that the British were trying to pass the buck to him. See Gorodetsky, *Grand Delusion*, pp. 4–6, 36, 39, 43, 89–90.

100. Nicole Jordan, *The Popular Front and Central Europe: The Dilemmas of French Impotence, 1918–1940* (Cambridge: Cambridge University Press, 1992), esp. chaps. 1–2; Posen, *Sources*, chap. 4; and Wolfers, *Britain and France*, chaps. 1–10.

101. On French behavior at Munich, see Anthony Adamthwaite, *France and the Coming of the Second World War, 1936–1939* (London: Cass, 1977), chaps. 11–13; and Yvon Lacaze, *France and Munich: A Study of Decision Making in International Affairs*

(New York: Columbia University Press, 1995). On the sorry state of France's alliances in eastern Europe by the mid-1930s, see Alexander, *Republic in Danger*, chap. 8; Jordan, *Popular Front*, chaps. 1–2; Anthony T. Komjathy, *The Crises of France's East Central European Diplomacy, 1933–1938* (New York: Columbia University Press, 1976); and Piotr S. Wandycz, *The Twilight of French Eastern Alliances, 1926–1936: French-Czechoslovakia-Polish Relations from Locarno to the Remilitarization of the Rhineland* (Princeton, NJ: Princeton University Press, 1988). It is worth noting that there was considerable buck-passing among the smaller states in eastern Europe as well as among Hitler's great-power rivals. See Robert G. Kaufman, "To Balance or to Bandwagon? Alignment Decisions in 1930s Europe," *Security Studies* 1, No. 3 (Spring 1992), pp. 417–47.

102. Wolfers, *Britain and France*, p. 75. Further evidence of France's heavy emphasis on buck-passing is the fact that it held essentially the same view toward its neighbor Belgium that it held towards its allies in the east. Specifically, if the Wehrmacht attacked in the west, French leaders were determined to fight the war in Belgium, not in France. See Alexander, *Republic in Danger*, chap. 7.

103. Adamthwaite describes the situation: "The Rhineland, *Anschluss*, [and] Munich had interrupted but not changed the long-range objective of French statesmen—the search for agreement with Germany. Relief at a hair-breadth escape from war in September 1938 brought a determination to work all the harder for a Franco-German settlement." Adamthwaite, *France and the Coming*, p. 280, and chap. 16 more generally.

104. Jiri Hochman writes, "In 1935 as well as in later years, however, the principal factor limiting the possibility of military coordination was the absence of a common border between the Soviet Union and Germany." Hochman, *The Soviet Union and the Failure of Collective Security, 1934–1938* (Ithaca, NY: Cornell University Press, 1984), p. 54. For more details on this matter, see ibid., chaps. 2–3; Patrice Buffotot, "The French High Command and the Franco-Soviet Alliance, 1933–1939," trans. John Gooch, *Journal of Strategic Studies* 5, No. 4 (December 1982), pp. 548, 554–56; and Barry R. Posen, "Competing Images of the Soviet Union," *World Politics* 39, No. 4 (July 1987), pp. 586–90.

105. Anthony Adamthwaite, "French Military Intelligence and the Coming of War, 1935–1939," in Christopher Andrew and Jeremy Noakes, eds., *Intelligence and International Relations, 1900–1945* (Exeter: Exeter University Publications, 1987), pp. 197–98; and Buffotot, "French High Command," pp. 548–49.

106. On French suspicions that the Soviets were buck-passing, see Alexander, *Republic in Danger*, pp. 299–300; Buffotot, "French High Command," pp. 550–51; Jordan, *Popular Front*, pp. 70–71, 260, 307; and Robert J. Young, *In Command of France: French Foreign Policy and Military Planning, 1933–1940* (Cambridge, MA: Harvard University Press, 1978), pp. 145–50.

107. On Soviet suspicions that France was buck-passing, see Jordan, *Popular Front*, pp. 259–60; and Alexander M. Nekrich, *Pariahs, Partners, Predators: German-Soviet Relations, 1922–1941*, trans. Gregory L. Freeze (New York: Columbia University Press, 1997), pp. 77, 106–7, 114, 269n. 10.

108. Adamthwaite, *France and the Coming*, chap. 13; Alexander, *Republic in Danger*, chap. 9; Nicholas Rostow, *Anglo-French Relations, 1934–36* (New York: St. Martin's, 1984); and Young, *Command*, passim, esp. chaps. 5, 8.

109. Robert Frankenstein, *Le prix du reármement français (1935–1939)* (Paris: Publications de la Sorbonne, 1982), p. 307. Also see Adamthwaite, *France and the Coming*, chap. 10; and Alexander, *Republic in Danger*, chaps. 4–5.

110. See Robert C. Tucker, *Stalin in Power: The Revolution from Above, 1928–1941* (New York: Norton, 1990), pp. 223–37, 338–65, 409–15, 513–25, 592–619. Also see R. C. Raack, *Stalin's Drive to the West, 1938–1945: The Origins of the Cold War* (Stanford, CA: Stanford University Press, 1995), introduction, chaps. 1–2; and Viktor Suvorov [pseudonym for Viktor Rezun], *Icebreaker: Who Started the Second World War?* trans. Thomas B. Beattie (London: Hamish Hamilton, 1990).

111. See Jonathan Haslam, *The Soviet Union and the Search for Collective Security, 1933–1939* (New York: St. Martin's, 1984); Geoffrey K. Roberts, *The Soviet Union and the Origins of the Second World War: Russo-German Relations and the Road to War* (New York: St. Martin's, 1995); and Teddy J. Uldricks, "Soviet Security Policy in the 1930s," in Gabriel Gorodetsky, ed., *Soviet Foreign Policy, 1917–1991: A Retrospective* (London: Frank Cass, 1994), pp. 65–74.

112. Hochman, *Soviet Union and the Failure;* Miner, *Between Churchill and Stalin;* Nekrich, *Pariahs;* and Adam B. Ulam, *Expansion and Coexistence: Soviet Foreign Policy, 1917–73*, 2d ed. (New York: Holt, Rinehart, and Winston, 1974), chap. 5.

113. Those who advocate that Stalin pushed collective security provide substantial evidence in their writings that he also pursued buck-passing. For examples, see Jonathan Haslam, "Soviet-German Relations and the Origins of the Second World War: The Jury Is Still Out," *Journal of Modern History* 69, No. 4 (December 1997), pp. 785–97; Roberts, *The Soviet Union;* and Uldricks, "Soviet Security Policy."

114. Ulam, *Expansion and Coexistence*, p. 238.

115. Most of the literature dealing with Stalin's German policy operates from the assumption that buck-passing is a misguided strategy. Hochman, for example, portrays Stalin as an immoral opportunist pursuing a strategy that was guaranteed to fail. See Hochman, *Soviet Union and the Failure*. Haslam, on the other hand, believes that Stalin sought the correct strategy (collective security), but was forced to accept a bankrupt alternative (buck-passing) because the Western allies themselves were foolishly passing the buck. See Haslam, *Soviet Union and the Search*.

116. Jonathan Haslam, *The Soviet Union and the Threat from the East, 1933–1941: Moscow, Tokyo and the Prelude to the Pacific War* (Pittsburgh, PA: University of Pittsburgh Press, 1992).

117. Michael J. Carley, *1939: The Alliance That Never Was and the Coming of World War II* (Chicago: Ivan R. Dee, 1999). Stalin's calculation also reflected the core Marxist tenet that the capitalist states were doomed to fight each other.

118. Mark Harrison, *Soviet Planning in Peace and War, 1938–1945* (Cambridge: Cambridge University Press, 1985), p. 8. Harrison provides similarly impressive numbers for rifles and aircraft. Also see Jonathan R. Adelman, *Prelude to Cold War: The Tsarist, Soviet, and U.S. Armies in the Two World Wars* (Boulder, CO: Lynne Rienner, 1988), chap. 5.

119. Strachan, *European Armies,* p. 159. Also see Colin Elman, "The Logic of Emulation: The Diffusion of Military Practices in the International System," Ph.D. diss., Columbia University, 1999, chap. 4; and Sally W. Stoecker, *Forging Stalin's Army: Marshal Tukhachevsky and the Politics of Military Innovation* (Boulder, CO: Westview, 1998).

120. David M. Glantz, *Stumbling Colossus: The Red Army on the Eve of World War II* (Lawrence: University Press of Kansas, 1998).

121. See Jonathan R. Adelman, *Revolution, Armies, and War: A Political History* (Boulder, CO: Lynne Rienner, 1985), chaps. 4–7.

122. Regarding the resources Germany garnered from the Anschluss and Munich, see Murray, *Change in the European Balance,* pp. 151–53; Deist, "The Rearmament of the Wehrmacht," pp. 450–51; and Seaton, *The German Army,* pp. 94–95.

123. Williamson Murray concludes that, in 1938, German "rearmament had not yet progressed to the point where her armed forces had much prospect of winning anything more than a conflict with one of the smaller European nations." Murray, *Change in the European Balance,* p. 127. For more general discussion, see ibid., chaps. 1, 7; and Cooper, *German Army,* chap. 12.

124. Manfred Messerschmidt, "Foreign Policy and Preparation for War," in *Build-up of German Aggression,* pp. 658–72; and Murray, *Change in the European Balance,* pp. 174–84.

125. See Adamthwaite, *France and the Coming,* chap. 10; Murray, *Change in the European Balance;* and Telford Taylor, *Munich: The Price of Peace* (Garden City, NY: Doubleday, 1979), chap. 33.

126. For a good discussion of the qualitative edge that the German army held over the French army once the former had rearmed, see Williamson Murray, "Armored Warfare: The British, French and German Experiences," in Williamson Murray and Allan R. Millet, eds., *Military Innovation in the Interwar Period*

(Cambridge: Cambridge University Press, 1996), pp. 6–49. Regarding the German advantage in the air, see Richard R. Muller, "Close Air Support: The German, British, and American Experiences, 1918–1941," in ibid., pp. 155–63; Alexander, *Republic in Danger,* chap. 6; and Posen, *Sources,* pp. 133–35.

127. David M. Glantz and Jonathan M. House, *When Titans Clashed: How the Red Army Stopped Hitler* (Lawrence: University Press of Kansas, 1995), p. 10. For a size comparison of the two armies, see Table 8.6. On the low quality of the German army during the mid-1930s, see the discussion earlier in this chapter. On the generally high quality of the Red Army between 1933 and 1937, see Glantz, *When Titans Clashed,* pp. 6–10; Ziemke, "Soviet Net Assessment," pp. 175–215; and the sources listed in note 119 of this chapter.

128. On the balance between Germany and the western Allies, see the sources cited in Chapter 3, note 9.

129. Gorodetsky, *Grand Delusion,* p. 135.

130. Ulam, *Expansion and Coexistence,* pp. 369–70, 410.

131. Marc Trachtenberg, *A Constructed Peace: The Making of the European Settlement, 1945–1963* (Princeton, NJ: Princeton University Press, 1999), p. 41. Melvyn Leffler makes the same point in *A Preponderance of Power: National Security, the Truman Administration, and the Cold War* (Stanford, CA: Stanford University Press, 1992), pp. 60–61. Other important works that emphasize this theme include Dale C. Copeland, *The Origins of Major War* (Ithaca, NY: Cornell University Press, 2000), chap. 6; Marc S. Gallicchio, *The Cold War Begins in Asia: American East Asian Policy and the Fall of the Japanese Empire* (New York: Columbia University Press, 1988); John L. Gaddis, *The United States and the Origins of the Cold War, 1941–1947* (New York: Columbia University Press, 1972), esp. chaps. 7–10; Bruce Kuniholm, *The Origins of the Cold War in the Near East: Great Power Conflict and Diplomacy in Iran, Turkey, and Greece* (Princeton, NJ: Princeton University Press, 1980); Geir Lundestad, *America, Scandinavia, and the Cold War, 1945–1949* (New York: Columbia University Press, 1980); Chester J. Pach, Jr., *Arming the Free World: The Origins of the United States Military Assistance Program, 1945–1950* (Chapel Hill: University of North Carolina Press, 1991); Michael Schaller, *The American Occupation of Japan: The Origins of the Cold War in Asia* (Oxford: Oxford University Press, 1985); and Odd Arne Westad, *Cold War and Revolution: Soviet-American Rivalry and the Origins of the Chinese Civil War, 1944–1946* (New York: Columbia University Press, 1993). Not surprisingly, the Soviets fully grasped soon after World War II ended that the United States was determined to pursue an aggressive containment policy against them. See Vladislav Zubok and Constantine Pleshakov, *Inside the Kremlin's Cold War: From Stalin to Khrushchev* (Cambridge, MA: Harvard University Press, 1996).

132. The fact that the United States implemented a hard-nosed balancing policy against the Soviet Union so soon after World War II ended helps "Cold War revisionists" make their case that the United States, not the Soviet Union, was responsible for starting the Cold War. For an excellent example of this phenomenon, see Carolyn W. Eisenberg, *Drawing the Line: The American Decision to Divide Germany, 1944–1949* (Cambridge: Cambridge University Press, 1996). For an offensive realist, neither side can be blamed for starting the Cold War; it was the international system itself that caused the intense security competition between the superpowers.

133. See Charles A. Kupchan, *The Persian Gulf: The Dilemmas of Security* (Boston: Allen and Unwin, 1987), chaps. 1–2; Mark J. Gasiorowski, *U.S. Foreign Policy and the Shah: Building a Client State in Iran* (Ithaca, NY: Cornell University Press, 1991); and the sources cited in Chapter 6, notes 80–81, of this book.

134. See Peter J. Stavrakis, *Moscow and Greek Communism, 1944–1949* (Ithaca, NY: Cornell University Press, 1989); Lawrence S. Wittner, *American Intervention in Greece, 1943–1949* (New York: Columbia University Press, 1982); and Artiom A. Ulunian, "The Soviet Union and the 'Greek Question,' 1946–53: Problems and Appraisals," in Francesca Gori and Silvio Pons, eds., *The Soviet Union and Europe in the Cold War, 1945–53* (London: Macmillan, 1996), pp. 144–60.

135. Quoted in Norman A. Graebner, *Cold War Diplomacy: American Foreign Policy, 1945–1960* (New York: Van Nostrand, 1962), p. 40.

136. Graebner, *Cold War Diplomacy*, p. 154. On the tight linkage between economic and strategic calculations in U.S. thinking during the late 1940s, see Melvyn P. Leffler, "The United States and the Strategic Dimensions of the Marshall Plan," *Diplomatic History* 12, No. 3 (Summer 1988), pp. 277–306; and Robert A. Pollard, *Economic Security and the Origins of the Cold War, 1945–1950* (New York: Columbia University Press, 1985). Also see Michael J. Hogan, *The Marshall Plan: America, Britain, and the Reconstruction of Western Europe, 1947–1952* (Cambridge: Cambridge University Press, 1987); and Alan S. Milward, *The Reconstruction of Western Europe, 1945–1951* (Berkeley: University of California Press, 1984).

137. Among the best sources on American thinking about how to deal with Germany are Eisenberg, *Drawing the Line;* Gaddis, *Origins of the Cold War,* chap. 4; Bruce Kuklick, *American Policy and the Division of Germany: The Clash with Russia over Reparations* (Ithaca, NY: Cornell University Press, 1972); and Trachtenberg, *Constructed Peace.* On Soviet thinking about Germany, see Caroline Kennedy-Pipe, *Stalin's Cold War: Soviet Strategies in Europe, 1943 to 1956* (New York: Manchester University Press, 1995); Wilfried Loth, "Stalin's Plans for Post-War Germany," in Gori and Pons, eds., *The Soviet Union and Europe,* pp. 23–36; Norman M. Naimark, *The Russians in Germany: A History of the Soviet Zone of Occupation, 1945–1949* (Cambridge, MA: Harvard University Press, 1995); and Zubok and Pleshakov, *Inside the Kremlin's Cold War,* pp. 46–53.

138. Leffler, *Preponderance of Power,* p. 204. Trachtenberg argues convincingly in *Constructed Peace* that the main cause of friction between the superpowers from

1945 until 1963 was their conflict over Germany. The decisions to create and then arm West Germany, possibly with nuclear weapons, infuriated Soviet leaders and led them to precipitate crises over Berlin in the hope that they could reverse U.S. policy. There is much support for this line of argument in Zubok and Pleshakov, *Inside the Kremlin's Cold War.*

139. American policymakers considered Czechoslovakia to be within the Soviet sphere of influence in Eastern Europe, and they were reconciled to Soviet control of that region. See Geir Lundestad, *The American Non-Policy Towards Eastern Europe, 1943–1947: Universalism in an Area Not of Essential Interest to the United States* (Oslo: Universitetsforlaget, 1978). Thus, the United States was not prepared to directly confront the Soviets over the communist coup in Czechoslovakia. Nevertheless, that event set off alarm bells in the West. See Trachtenberg, *A Constructed Peace,* pp. 79–80.

140. On the creation of NATO, see John Baylis, *The Diplomacy of Pragmatism: Britain and the Formation of NATO, 1942–1949* (Kent, OH: Kent State University Press, 1993); Timothy P. Ireland, *Creating the Entangling Alliance: The Origins of the North Atlantic Treaty Organization* (Westport, CT: Greenwood, 1981); Lawrence S. Kaplan, *The United States and NATO: The Formative Years* (Lexington: University of Kentucky Press, 1984); Joseph Smith, ed., *The Origins of NATO* (Exeter: University of Exeter Press, 1990).

141. Avi Shlaim, *The United States and the Berlin Blockade, 1948–1949: A Study in Crisis Decision-Making* (Berkeley: University of California Press, 1983).

142. See Chapter 6.

143. *The China White Paper,* August 1949 (Stanford, CA: Stanford University Press, 1967), p. xvi. Also see Tang Tsou, *America's Failure in China, 1941–1950,* 2 vols. (Chicago: University of Chicago Press, 1975). Some scholars argue that the United States still could have formed an alliance with communist China against the Soviet Union but failed to do so because of rigid and irrational anti-communism. Thus, the United States is guilty of inefficient balancing against the Soviet threat. For an excellent discussion of this issue that casts serious doubts on the feasibility of a U.S.-China balancing coalition in the late 1940s and early 1950s, see the five articles in "Symposium: Rethinking the Lost Chance in China," *Diplomatic History* 21, No. 1 (Winter 1997), pp. 71–115. Nevertheless, the United States searched for opportunities after 1949 to split apart the Chinese-Soviet alliance. Gordon Chang, *Friends and Enemies: The United States, China, and the Soviet Union, 1948–1972* (Stanford, CA: Stanford University Press, 1990).

144. See H. W. Brands, *The Specter of Neutralism: The United States and the Emergence of the Third World, 1947–1960* (New York: Columbia University Press, 1989); Robert E. Harkavy, *Great Power Competition for Overseas Bases: The Geopolitics of*

Access Diplomacy (New York: Pergamon, 1982), chaps. 4–5; Douglas J. Macdonald, *Adventures in Chaos: American Intervention for Reform in the Third World* (Cambridge, MA: Harvard University Press, 1992); Peter W. Rodman, *More Precious Than Peace: The Cold War and the Struggle for the Third World* (New York: Scribner's 1994); and Marshall D. Shulman, ed., *East-West Tensions in the Third World* (New York: Norton, 1986).

145. For a brief overview, see Phil Williams, *US Troops in Europe*, Chatham House Paper No. 25 (Boston: Routledge and Kegan Paul, 1984), chap. 2. Also see Phil Williams, *The Senate and US Troops in Europe* (New York: St. Martin's, 1985).

146. As Marc Trachtenberg notes, "During the crucial formative period [of NATO] in the early 1950s, everyone wanted a permanent American presence in Europe—everyone, that is, except the Americans themselves. It is hard to understand why the intensity and persistence of America's desire to pull out as soon as she reasonably could has never been recognized, either in the public discussion or in the scholarly literature, because it comes through with unmistakable clarity in the *Foreign Relations* documents." Marc Trachtenberg, *History and Strategy* (Princeton, NJ: Princeton University Press, 1991), p. 167. Also see the works cited in Chapter 7, note 72, of this book. The buck-passing impulse was alive in the United Kingdom as well during the 1950s. See Saki Dockrill, "Retreat from the Continent? Britain's Motives for Troop Reductions in West Germany, 1955–1958," *Journal of Strategic Studies* 20, No. 3 (September 1997), pp. 45–70.

147. See the sources cited in Stephen Van Evera, "Why Europe Matters, Why the Third World Doesn't: American Grand Strategy after the Cold War," *Journal of Strategic Studies* 13, No. 2 (June 1990), pp. 34–35, note 1.

148. See William I. Hitchcock, *France Restored: Cold War Diplomacy and the Quest for Leadership in Europe, 1944–1954* (Chapel Hill: University of North Carolina Press, 1998), chaps. 2–3; Irwin M. Wall, *The United States and the Making of Postwar France, 1945–1954* (Cambridge: Cambridge University Press, 1991), chap. 2.

149. The numbers for Britain and the Soviet Union are from Table 8.8. The number for the United States is from Adelman, *Revolution,* p. 174.

150. The American and British numbers are from I.C.B. Dear, ed., *The Oxford Companion to World War II* (Oxford: Oxford University Press, 1995), pp. 1148, 1192, 1198. The Soviet number is from Phillip A. Karber and Jerald A. Combs, "The United States, NATO, and the Soviet Threat to Western Europe: Military Estimates and Policy Options, 1945–1963," *Diplomatic History* 22, No. 3 (Summer 1998), p. 403.

151. The numbers on divisions are from Adelman, *Prelude,* p. 212.

152. The Soviet number is from Karber and Combs, "The United States, NATO, and the Soviet Threat" pp. 411–12. The American and British numbers are from J. David Singer and Melvin Small, *National Material Capabilities Data,*

1816–1985 (Ann Arbor, MI: Inter-University Consortium for Political and Social Research, February 1993).

153. For the relevant data on the years after 1948, see Singer and Small, *National Material Capabilities Data.*

154. See Elisabeth Barker, *The British between the Superpowers, 1945–1950* (Toronto: University of Toronto Press, 1983); Alan Bullock, *Ernest Bevin: Foreign Secretary, 1945–1951* (New York: Norton, 1983); David Reynolds, "Great Britain," in David Reynolds, ed., *The Origins of the Cold War in Europe: International Perspectives* (New Haven, CT: Yale University Press, 1994), pp. 77–95; and Victor Rothwell, *Britain and the Cold War, 1941–1947* (London: Jonathan Cape, 1982).

155. Kennedy, *Great Powers*, p. 369. Also see William C. Wohlforth, *The Elusive Balance: Power and Perceptions during the Cold War* (Ithaca, NY: Cornell University Press, 1993), p. 60. For data on the relative industrial might of the United States and the Soviet Union during the early Cold War, see Table 3.5. For excellent surveys of the United Kingdom's problem, see Correlli Barnett, *The Audit of War: The Illusion and Reality of Britain as a Great Power* (London: Macmillan, 1986); and Correlli Barnett, *The Lost Victory: British Dreams, British Realities, 1945–1950* (London: Macmillan, 1995). Also see Randall L. Schweller, *Deadly Imbalances: Tripolarity and Hitler's Strategy of World Conquest* (New York: Columbia University Press, 1998), which uses a variety of measures to argue that the world was tripolar before World War II and that the United Kingdom was not one of the three great powers, which were Germany, the Soviet Union, and the United States.

CHAPTER NINE

1. G. Lowes Dickinson, *The European Anarchy* (New York: Macmillan, 1916), p. 14.

2. To the best of my knowledge, no existing theory has the capability to predict exactly when war will occur.

3. For an excellent survey of the causes of war literature, see Jack S. Levy, "The Causes of War and the Conditions of Peace," *Annual Review of Political Science* 1 (1998), pp. 139–65. Also see Dale C. Copeland, *The Origins of Major War* (Ithaca, NY: Cornell University Press, 2000), chap. 1; Stephen Van Evera, *Causes of War: Power and the Roots of Conflict* (Ithaca, NY: Cornell University Press, 1999), chap. 1; and Kenneth N. Waltz, *Man, the State and War: A Theoretical Analysis* (New York: Columbia University Press, 1959).

4. Karl W. Deutsch and J. David Singer, "Multipolar Power Systems and International Stability," *World Politics* 16, No. 3 (April 1964), pp. 390–406; Kenneth N. Waltz, "The Stability of a Bipolar World," *Daedalus* 93, No. 3 (Summer 1964), pp. 881–909; and Kenneth N. Waltz, *Theory of International Politics* (Reading, MA:

Addison-Wesley, 1979), chap. 8. Also see Robert Jervis, *System Effects: Complexity in Political and Social Life* (Princeton, NJ: Princeton University Press, 1997), chap. 3.

5. Robert Gilpin, *War and Change in World Poliics* (Cambridge: Cambridge University Press, 1981); Hans Morgenthau, *Politics among Nations: The Struggle for Power and Peace*, 5th ed. (New York: Knopf, 1973); and A.F.K. Organski, *World Politics*, 2d ed. (New York: Knopf, 1968), chap. 14.

6. For a more complete definition of a potential hegemon, see Chapter 2.

7. Among the key works on bipolarity and multipolarity are the sources cited in note 4 of this chapter; Thomas J. Christensen and Jack Snyder, "Chain Gangs and Passed Bucks: Predicting Alliance Patterns in Multipolarity," *International Organization* 44, No. 2 (Spring 1990), pp. 137–68; and Richard N. Rosecrance, "Bipolarity, Multipolarity, and the Future," *Journal of Conflict Resolution* 10, No. 3 (September 1966), pp. 314–27.

8. Although a balance of power is more likely to produce deterrence than is an imbalance of power, balanced power does not guarantee that deterrence will work. As discussed in Chapter 3, states sometimes design innovative military strategies that allow them to win wars, even though they have no advantage in the size and quality of their fighting forces. Furthermore, the broader political forces that move states toward war sometimes force leaders to pursue highly risky military strategies, impelling states to challenge opponents of equal or even superior strength. See John J. Mearsheimer, *Conventional Deterrence* (Ithaca, NY: Cornell University Press, 1983), esp. chap. 2.

9. A second argument is sometimes made to support the claim that power disparities are more common in multipolarity than in bipolarity. States in multipolarity facing a more powerful adversary are likely to pursue buck-passing, which usually means that they are content to live with an imbalance of power, because they believe that another state will deal with the threat. But even when states balance in multipolarity, they are often tempted to seek security through alliances rather than by building up their own strength. External balancing of this sort is attractive because it is cheaper than the alternative. Nevertheless, it leaves the original power imbalance largely intact and hence leaves in place the dangers that such a power gap creates. The number two state in a bipolar system, on the other hand, can hope to balance against the leader only by mobilizing its own resources, since it has no great-power alliance partners or buck-catchers. Internal balancing of this sort is likely to produce a rough balance of power between the opposing great powers. In fact, I made this argument in John J. Mearsheimer, "Back to the Future: Instability in Europe after the Cold War," *International Security* 15, No. 1 (Summer 1990), pp. 13–19. But there are two problems with this line of argument. As Dale Copeland notes, it contradicts my claim that states maximize their share of world power. If states are power maximizers, they are not going to tolerate imbalances of power that they have the capability to rectify. See Dale C. Copeland, "The Myth of Bipolar Stability: Toward a New Dynamic Realist Theory of Major War," *Security Studies* 5, No. 3 (Spring 1996), pp. 38–47. Furthermore, while there is no question that buck-passing is a popular option among threatened states in multipolarity (see Chapter 8), buck-passing is most likely to succeed if the threatened state also builds formidable military forces and erases any power gap that might exist between it and the aggressor (see Chapter 5).

10. There is one exception to this general point: if there were only three great powers in a multipolar system, two of them could gang up on the third, and there would be no allies available for the victim state.

11. Balancing coalitions are most likely to form when there is a potential hegemon that can be contained only by the joint efforts of all the threatened great powers. But as discussed in the next section, war is highly likely when there is a potential hegemon in a multipolar system.

12. This point is the central theme of Waltz, "Stability of a Bipolar World." Also see Geoffrey Blainey, *The Causes of War* (New York: Free Press, 1973), chap. 3.

13. The claim that multipolarity is more stable than bipolarity is often based on the belief that as the number of states in a system increases, the amount of attention that states can focus on each other diminishes, because other states demand attention as well. See, for example, Deutsch and Singer, "Multipolar Power Systems," pp. 396–400. This claim, however, assumes rough equality in the size and strength of the relevant actors. But in multipolar systems with a potential hegemon, the other great powers are surely going to pay an inordinate amount of attention to that especially powerful state, largely vitiating the claim that multipolarity means "limited attention capability."

14. To review my criteria for selecting great powers, see Chapter 1, note 7.

15. See Chapter 6.

16. Jack S. Levy, *War in the Modern Great Power System, 1495–1975* (Lexington: University Press of Kentucky, 1983), chap. 3.

17. The other great-power wars that are excluded because they involve a non-European state include the Anglo-Persian War (1856–57), the Franco-Mexican War (1862–67), the Sino-French War (1883–85), the Sino-Soviet War (1929), the Italo-Ethiopian War (1935–36), the Soviet-Japanese War (1939), and the Sinai War (1956).

18. Levy uses the term "general war" instead of "central war," whereas Copeland refers to these conflicts as "major wars." See Copeland, *Origins*, pp. 27–28; and Levy, *War*, pp. 3, 52, 75. Others refer to them as "hegemonic wars," because they usually involve a state that is attempting to dominate the entire system.

19. See Chapter 8.

20. Although the Russian army was more than twice as large as the Austrian and French armies, it had significant qualitative deficiencies, which became more

acute over time and account in good part for Russia's defeat by the United Kingdom and France in the Crimean War (1853–56). See John S. Curtiss, *The Russian Army under Nicholas I, 1825–1855* (Durham, NC: Duke University Press, 1965); and William C. Fuller, Jr., *Strategy and Power in Russia, 1600–1914* (New York: Free Press, 1992), chaps. 6–7. On the Austrian army, see Istvan Deak, *Beyond Nationalism: A Social and Political History of the Habsburg Officer Corps, 1848–1918* (Oxford: Oxford University Press, 1992), pp. 29–41; and Gunther E. Rothenberg, *The Army of Francis Joseph* (West Lafayette, IN: Purdue University Press, 1976), chaps. 1–4. On the French army, see Paddy Griffith, *Military Thought in the French Army, 1815–1851* (Manchester, UK: Manchester University Press, 1989); and Douglas Porch, *Army and Revolution, 1815–1848* (London: Routledge and Kegan Paul, 1974).

21. See Chapter 8.

22. See Chapter 8.

23. See Chapter 8.

CHAPTER TEN

1. William J. Clinton, "American Foreign Policy and the Democratic Ideal," campaign speech, Pabst Theater, Milwaukee, WI, October 1, 1992; "In Clinton's Words: 'Building Lines of Partnership and Bridges to the Future,' " *New York Times*, July 10, 1997. Rhetoric aside, Clinton's foreign policy was largely consistent with the predictions of realism. See Stephen M. Walt, "Two Cheers for Clinton's Foreign Policy," *Foreign Affairs* 79, No. 2 (March–April 2000), pp. 63–79.

2. See the sources cited in Chapter 1, note 25.

3. See Joseph Grieco, "Anarchy and the Limits of Cooperation: A Realist Critique of the Newest Liberal Institutionalism," *International Organization* 42, No. 3 (Summer 1988), pp. 485–507; Stephen D. Krasner, "Global Communications and National Power: Life on the Pareto Frontier," *World Politics* 43, No. 3 (April 1991), pp. 336–66; John J. Mearsheimer, "The False Promise of International Institutions," *International Security* 19, No. 3 (Winter 1994–95), pp. 5–49; John J. Mearsheimer, "A Realist Reply," *International Security* 20, No. 1 (Summer 1995), pp. 82–93; and Baldev Raj Nayer, "Regimes, Power, and International Aviation," *International Organization* 49, No. 1 (Winter 1995), pp. 139–70. It is worth noting that in a recent survey of the international institutions literature by two prominent institutionalists, little evidence is provided that institutions have caused states to alter their behavior in fundamental ways. See Lisa L. Martin and Beth A. Simmons, "Theories and Empirical Studies of International Institutions," *International Organization* 52, No. 4 (Autumn 1998), pp. 729–57.

4. Tony Evans and Peter Wilson, "Regime Theory and the English School of International Relations: A Comparison," *Millennium: Journal of International Studies*

21, No. 3 (Winter 1992), p. 330. Also see Lloyd Gruber, *Ruling the World: Power Politics and the Rise of Supranational Institutions* (Princeton, NJ: Princeton University Press, 2000).

5. Prominent examples of this perspective include Philip G. Cerny, "Globalization and the Changing Logic of Collective Action," *International Organization* 49, No. 4 (Autumn 1995), pp. 595–625; William Greider, *One World, Ready or Not: The Manic Logic of Global Capitalism* (New York: Simon and Schuster, 1997); Kenichi Ohmae, *The End of the Nation State: The Rise of Regional Economies* (New York: Free Press, 1996); Saskia Sassen, *Losing Control? Sovereignty in an Age of Globalization* (New York: Columbia University Press, 1995); and Walter B. Wriston, *The Twilight of Sovereignty: How the Information Revolution is Transforming Our World* (New York: Scribner's, 1992).

6. Susan Strange, *The Retreat of the State: The Diffusion of Power in the World Economy* (Cambridge: Cambridge University Press, 1996), p. 4.

7. See Richard J. Barnet and John Cavanagh, *Global Dreams: Imperial Corporations and the New World Order* (New York: Simon and Schuster, 1994); and David C. Korten, *When Corporations Rule the World* (West Hartford, CT: Kumarian Press, 1995). Similar claims about the dominating influence of multinational corporations were heard in the 1970s. See Raymond Vernon, *Sovereignty at Bay: The Multinational Spread of U.S. Enterprises* (New York: Basic Books, 1971). For the case against Vernon, see Robert Gilpin, *U.S. Power and the Multinational Corporation: The Political Economy of Foreign Direct Investment* (New York: Basic Books, 1975).

8. See Paul Hirst and Grahame Thompson, *Globalization in Question: The International Economy and the Possibilities of Governance,* 2d ed. (Cambridge: Polity Press, 1999); Janice E. Thomson and Stephen D. Krasner, "Global Transactions and the Consolidation of Sovereignty," in Ernst-Otto Czempiel and James N. Rosenau, eds., *Global Changes and Theoretical Challenges: Approaches to World Politics for the 1990s* (Lexington, MA: Lexington Books, 1989), pp. 195–219; and Robert Wade, "Globalization and Its Limits: Reports of the Death of the National Economy Are Greatly Exaggerated," in Suzanne Berger and Ronald Dore, eds., *National Diversity and Global Capitalism* (Ithaca, NY: Cornell University Press, 1996), pp. 60–88.

9. See Paul N. Doremus et al., *The Myth of the Global Corporation* (Princeton, NJ: Princeton University Press, 1998); Geoffrey Garrett, "Global Markets and National Politics: Collision Course or Virtuous Circle?" *International Organization* 52, No. 4 (Autumn 1998), pp. 787–824; Eric Helleiner, *States and the Reemergence of Global Finance: From Bretton Woods to the 1990s* (Ithaca, NY: Cornell University Press, 1994); Ethan B. Kapstein, *Governing the Global Economy: International Finance and the State* (Cambridge, MA: Harvard University Press, 1994); Stephen D. Krasner, *Sovereignty: Organized Hypocrisy* (Princeton, NJ: Princeton University Press, 1999); Steven K. Vogel, *Freer Markets, More Rules: Regulatory Reform in Advanced Industrial Countries*

(Ithaca, NY: Cornell University Press, 1996); Linda Weiss, *The Myth of the Powerless State* (Ithaca, NY: Cornell University Press, 1998); and "The Future of the State," *Economist*, Special Supplement, September 20, 1997.

10. These points are clearly reflected in almost all the seminal works on nationalism. See, for example, Benedict Anderson, *Imagined Communities: Reflections on the Origins and Spread of Nationalism*, rev. ed. (London: Verso, 1991); Walker Connor, *Ethnonationalism* (Princeton, NJ: Princeton University Press, 1993); Ernest Gellner, *Nations and Nationalism* (Ithaca, NY: Cornell University Press, 1983); and Anthony D. Smith, *The Ethnic Origins of Nations* (New York: Blackwell, 1989).

11. All quotes in this paragraph are from Suzanne Daley, "French Leader, in Berlin, Urges a Fast Track to Unity in Europe," *New York Times*, June 28, 2000. Also see Suzanne Daley, "French Premier Opposes German Plan for Europe," *New York Times*, May 29, 2001; and William A. Hay, "Quiet Quake in Europe: The French and the Germans Divide," Foreign Policy Research Institute's *Watch on the West* 1, No. 9 (October 2000).

12. John Mueller, *Retreat from Doomsday: The Obsolescence of Major War* (New York: Basic Books, 1989). Also see Michael Mandelbaum, "Is Major War Obsolete?" *Survival* 40, No. 4 (Winter 1998–99), pp. 20–38.

13. See the works cited in Chapter 1, note 24.

14. Christopher Layne, "Kant or Cant: The Myth of the Democratic Peace," *International Security* 19, No. 2 (Fall 1994), pp. 5–49. Other key works challenging democratic peace theory include Michael E. Brown, Sean M. Lynn-Jones, and Steven E. Miller, eds., *Debating the Democratic Peace* (Cambridge, MA: MIT Press, 1996), pts. 2–3; Miriam Fendius Elman, ed., *Paths to Peace: Is Democracy the Answer?* (Cambridge, MA: MIT Press, 1997); Miriam Fendius Elman, "The Never-Ending Story: Democracy and Peace," *International Studies Review* 1, No. 3 (Fall 1999), pp. 87–103; and Joanne Gowa, *Ballots and Bullets: The Elusive Democratic Peace* (Princeton, NJ: Princeton University Press, 1999).

15. For evidence of backsliding, see Samuel P. Huntington, *The Third Wave: Democratization in the Late Twentieth Century* (Norman: University of Oklahoma Press, 1991), chaps. 5–6; and Juan J. Linz and Alfred Stepan, eds., *The Breakdown of Democratic Regimes: Crisis, Breakdown, and Reequilibration* (Baltimore, MD: Johns Hopkins University Press, 1978).

16. Markus Fischer, in "The Liberal Peace: Ethical, Historical, and Philosophical Aspects," BCSIA Discussion Paper 2000–07 (Cambridge, MA: John F. Kennedy School of Government, Harvard University, April 2000), discusses the difficulty of creating and sustaining liberal democracy around the world.

17. The key work in this genre is Alexander Wendt, *Social Theory of International Politics* (Cambridge: Cambridge University Press, 1999). For other important social constructivist tracts, see the sources cited in Mearsheimer, "False Promise," p. 37 (n.

128). Also see Peter J. Katzenstein, ed., *The Culture of National Security: Norms and Identity in World Politics* (New York: Columbia University Press, 1996); John G. Ruggie, *Constructing the World Polity: Essays on International Institutionalization* (New York: Routledge, 1998); and John G. Ruggie, "What Makes the World Hang Together? Neo-Utilitarianism and the Social Constructivist Challenge," *International Organization* 52, No. 4 (Autumn 1998), pp. 855–85.

18. Alexander Wendt, "Anarchy Is What States Make of It: The Social Construction of Power Politics," *International Organization* 46, No. 2 (Spring 1992), pp. 391–425.

19. For further elaboration of my critique of social constructivism, see Mearsheimer, "False Promise," pp. 37–47; and Mearsheimer, "Realist Reply," pp. 90–92.

20. See the works cited in Chapter 6, note 86.

21. For Gorbachev's views, see Mikhail Gorbachev, *Perestroika: New Thinking for Our Country and the World* (New York: Harper and Row, 1987).

22. See the sources listed in Chapter 1, note 23.

23. See *inter alia* Katherine Barbieri, "Economic Interdependence: A Path to Peace or a Source of Interstate Conflict?" *Journal of Peace Research* 33, No. 1 (February 1996), pp. 29–49; Barry Buzan, "Economic Structure and International Security: The Limits of the Liberal Case," *International Organization* 38, No. 4 (Autumn 1984), pp. 597–624; Dale C. Copeland, "Economic Interdependence and War: A Theory of Trade Expectations," *International Security* 20, No. 4 (Spring 1996), pp. 5–41; Norrin M. Ripsman and Jean-Marc F. Blanchard, "Commercial Liberalism under Fire: Evidence from 1914 and 1936," *Security Studies* 6, No. 2 (Winter 1996–97), pp. 4–50; David M. Rowe, "World Economic Expansion and National Security in Pre–World War I Europe," *International Organization* 53, No. 2 (Spring 1999), pp. 195–231; and Kenneth N. Waltz, "The Myth of National Interdependence," in Charles P. Kindelberger, ed., *The International Corporation* (Cambridge, MA: MIT Press, 1970), pp. 205–23.

24. Paul Dibb, David D. Hale, and Peter Prince, "Asia's Insecurity," *Survival* 41, No. 3 (Autumn 1999), pp. 5–20. Also see Robert A. Manning and James J. Przystup, "Asia's Transition Diplomacy: Hedging against Futureshock," *Survival* 41, No. 3 (Autumn 1999), pp. 43–67. For a discussion of the fragility of the contemporary world economy, see Robert Gilpin, *Global Capitalism: The World Economy in the 21st Century* (Princeton, NJ: Princeton University Press, 2000).

25. See "The Glaspie Transcript: Saddam Meets the U.S. Ambassador," in Micah L. Sifry and Christopher Cerf, eds., *The Gulf War Reader: History, Documents, Opinions* (New York: Times Books, 1991), pp. 122–33.

26. For examples of this perspective, see Hilary French, *Vanishing Borders: Protecting the Planet in the Age of Globalization* (New York: Norton, 2000); Carl Kaysen,

Robert A. Pastor, and Laura W. Reed, eds., *Collective Responses to Regional Problems: The Case of Latin America and the Caribbean* (Cambridge, MA: American Academy of Arts and Sciences, 1994); Ronnie D. Lipschutz and Ken Conca, eds., *The State and Social Power in Global Environmental Politics* (New York: Columbia University Press, 1993); Ronnie D. Lipschutz, "Reconstructing World Politics: The Emergence of Global Civil Society," *Millennium: Journal of International Studies* 21, No. 3 (Winter 1992), pp. 389–420; Jessica Tuchman Matthews, ed., *Preserving the Global Environment: The Challenge of Shared Leadership* (New York: Norton, 1991); Paul Wapner, *Environmental Activism and World Civic Politics* (Albany: State University of New York Press, 1996); and World Commission on Environment and Development, *Our Common Future* (Oxford: Oxford University Press, 1987).

27. See Julian L. Simon, ed., *The State of Humanity* (Cambridge, MA: Blackwell, 1995); and Julian L. Simon, *The Ultimate Resource 2* (Princeton, NJ: Princeton University Press, 1996).

28. See Nazli Choucri and Robert C. North, *Nations in Conflict: National Growth and International Violence* (San Francisco: W. H. Freeman, 1975); William H. Durham, *Scarcity and Survival in Central America: Ecological Origins of the Soccer War* (Stanford, CA: Stanford University Press, 1979); Peter H. Gleick, "Water and Conflict: Fresh Water Resources and International Security," *International Security* 18, No. 1 (Summer 1993), pp. 79–112; Thomas F. Homer-Dixon, *Environment, Scarcity, and Violence* (Princeton, NJ: Princeton University Press, 1999); and Arthur H. Westing, ed., *Global Resources and International Conflict: Environmental Factors in Strategic Policy and Action* (Oxford: Oxford University Press, 1986).

29. Karl W. Deutsch et al., *Political Community and the North Atlantic Area: International Organization in the Light of Historical Experience* (Princeton, NJ: Princeton University Press, 1957), pp. 5–9.

30. Ian Fisher and Norimitsu Onishi, "Many Armies Ravage Rich Land in the 'First World War' of Africa," *New York Times,* February 6, 2000.

31. See, for example, the many articles on Asian security published over the past decade in *Foreign Affairs, International Security,* and *Survival.* Some of the best pieces from *International Security* are published in Michael E. Brown, Sean M. Lynn-Jones, and Steven E. Miller, eds., *East Asian Security* (Cambridge, MA: MIT Press, 1996).

32. See Leon V. Sigal, *Disarming Strangers: Nuclear Diplomacy with North Korea* (Princeton, NJ: Princeton University Press, 1998); and Don Oberdorfer, *The Two Koreas: A Contemporary History* (New York: Basic Books, 1997), chaps. 11–13.

33. For the best net assessments of the military balance on the Korean Peninsula, see Nick Beldecos and Eric Heginbotham, "The Conventional Military Balance in Korea," *Breakthroughs* 4, No. 1 (Spring 1995), pp. 1–8; and Michael O'Hanlon, "Stopping a North Korean Invasion: Why Defending South Korea Is

Easier Than the Pentagon Thinks," *International Security* 22, No. 4 (Spring 1998), pp. 135–70.

34. On the Taiwan problem, see Bernice Lee, *The Security Implications of the New Taiwan,* Adelphi Paper No. 331 (London: International Institute for Strategic Studies, October 1999); James R. Lilley and Chuck Downs, eds., *Crisis in the Taiwan Strait* (Washington, DC: National Defense University Press, 1997); Denny Roy, "Tension in the Taiwan Strait," *Survival* 42, No. 1 (Spring 2000), pp. 76–96; Andrew Scobell, "Show of Force: The PLA and the 1995-1996 Taiwan Strait Crisis," discussion paper (Stanford, CA: Asia/Pacific Research Center, Stanford University, January 1999); and Suisheng Zhao, ed., *Across the Taiwan Strait: Mainland China, Taiwan, and the 1995–1996 Crisis* (New York: Routledge, 1999).

35. Taiwan Affairs Office and the Information Office of the State Council, People's Republic of China, "The One-China Principle and the Taiwan Issue," February 21, 2000.

36. In response to China's white paper, the U.S. undersecretary of defense warned China that it would face "incalculable consequences" if it attacked Taiwan. Steven Mufson and Helen Dewar, "Pentagon Issues Warning to China: U.S. Officials Criticize Beijing White Paper Backing Use of Force against Taiwan," *Washington Post,* February 23, 2000. Shortly thereafter, China's official military newspaper emphasized that China "is a country that has certain abilities of launching strategic counterattack and the capacity of launching a long-distance strike." Bill Gertz, "China Threatens U.S. with Missile Strike," *Washington Times,* February 29, 2000. China made a similar threat in January 1996. See Patrick E. Tyler, "China Threatens Taiwan, It Makes Sure U.S. Listens," *New York Times,* January 24, 1996.

37. Thomas J. Christensen, "Chinese Realpolitik," *Foreign Affairs* 75, No. 5 (September–October 1996), p. 37. Also see Alastair Iain Johnston, *Cultural Realism: Strategic Culture and Grand Strategy in Chinese History* (Princeton, NJ: Princeton University Press, 1995); and Andrew J. Nathan and Robert S. Ross, *The Great Wall and the Empty Fortress: China's Search for Security* (New York: Norton, 1997).

38. Mark J. Valencia, *China and the South China Sea Disputes,* Adelphi Paper No. 298 (London: International Institute for Strategic Studies, October 1995).

39. Yu Bin, "Containment by Stealth: Chinese Views of and Policies toward America's Alliances with Japan and Korea after the Cold War," discussion paper (Stanford, CA: Asia/Pacific Research Center, Stanford University, September 1999), p. 5. Also see Richard Bernstein and Ross H. Munro, "China I: The Coming Conflict with America," *Foreign Affairs* 76, No. 2 (March–April 1997), pp. 18–32; Thomas J. Christensen, "China, the U.S.-Japan Alliance, and the Security Dilemma in East Asia," *International Security* 23, No. 4 (Spring 1999), pp. 49–80; Christensen, "Chinese Realpolitik," pp. 37–52; Michael Pillsbury, *China Debates the Future Security*

Environment (Washington, DC: National Defense University Press, 2000); David Shambaugh, "China's Military Views the World: Ambivalent Security," *International Security* 24, No. 3 (Winter 1999–2000), pp. 52–79; Allen S. Whiting, *China Eyes Japan* (Berkeley: University of California Press, 1989); and Jianwei Wang and Xinbo Wu, "Against Us or with Us? The Chinese Perspective of America's Alliances with Japan and Korea," discussion paper (Stanford, CA: Asia/Pacific Research Center, Stanford University, May 1998).

40. Bin, "Containment by Stealth," p. 7; and David Shambaugh, "Sino-American Strategic Relations: From Partners to Competitors," *Survival* 42, No. 1 (Spring 2000), pp. 97–115.

41. See Yoichi Funabashi, "Japan and the New World Order," *Foreign Affairs* 70, No. 5 (Winter 1991–92), pp. 58–74.

42. Michael J. Green, "The Forgotten Player," *National Interest*, No. 60 (Summer 2000), pp. 44–45. Also see Benjamin L. Self, "Japan's Changing China Policy," *Survival* 38, No. 2 (Summer 1996), pp. 35–58; and Gerald Segal, "The Coming Confrontation between China and Japan?" *World Policy Journal* 10, No. 2 (Summer 1993), pp. 27–32.

43. On Chinese military weakness, see Bates Gill and Michael O'Hanlon, "China's Hollow Military," *National Interest*, No. 56 (Summer 1999), pp. 55–62; Robert S. Ross, "China II: Beijing as a Conservative Power," *Foreign Affairs* 76, No. 2 (March–April 1997), pp. 33–44; and Gerald Segal, "Does China Matter?" *Foreign Affairs* 78, No. 5 (September–October 1999), pp. 24–36. For a contrasting view, see James Lilley and Carl Ford, "China's Military: A Second Opinion," *National Interest*, No. 57 (Fall 1999), pp. 71–77. Thomas Christensen argues that China will have the capability to challenge American interests in Asia even if it remains a relatively weak military power. See Christensen, "Posing Problems without Catching Up: China's Rise and Challenges for U.S. Security Policy," *International Security* 25, No. 4 (Spring 2001), pp. 5–40.

44. See John Pomfret, "China Plans Major Boost in Defense Spending for Military," *Washington Post*, March 6, 2001. Also see James C. Mulvenon and Richard H. Yang, eds., *The People's Liberation Army in the Information Age* (Santa Monica, CA: RAND Corporation, 1999); Mark A. Stokes, *China's Strategic Modernization: Implications for the United States* (Carlisle Barracks, PA: Strategic Studies Institute, U.S. Army War College, 1999); and Michael Swaine, "Chinese Military Modernization and Asian Security," discussion paper (Stanford, CA: Asia/Pacific Research Center, Stanford University, August 1998).

45. Paul Bracken, *Fire in the East: The Rise of Asian Military Power and the Second Nuclear Age* (New York: HarperCollins, 1999). For more general discussions of the arms buildup in the region see Kent E. Calder, *Asia's Deadly Triangle: How Arms,*

Energy and Growth Threaten to Destabilize the Asia-Pacific (London: Nicholas Brealey, 1997); and Tim Huxley and Susan Willett, *Arming East Asia,* Adelphi Paper No. 329 (London: International Institute of Strategic Studies, July 1999).

46. The phrase "primed for peace" was coined by Stephen Van Evera to describe post–Cold War Europe. See Stephen Van Evera, "Primed for Peace: Europe after the Cold War," *International Security* 15, No. 3 (Winter 1990–91), pp. 7–57.

47. Joseph S. Nye, Jr., "East Asian Security: The Case for Deep Engagement," *Foreign Affairs* 74, No. 4 (July–August 1995), pp. 90–102. The quotes in this paragraph are from pp. 90–91, 102. Also see Department of Defense, *United States Security Strategy for the East Asia–Pacific Region* (Washington, DC: U.S. Department of Defense, February 1995); and Department of Defense, *The United States Security Strategy for the East Asia–Pacific Region: 1998* (Washington, DC: U.S. Department of Defense, November 1998). This perspective enjoys wide support on both sides of the Pacific. See, for example, United States Commission on National Security/21st Century, *New World Coming: American Security in the 21st Century,* Phase I Report (Washington, DC: U.S. Commission on National Security, September 15, 1999), p. 82. One notable exception is Chalmers Johnson and E. B. Keehn, "East Asian Security: The Pentagon's Ossified Strategy," *Foreign Affairs* 74, No. 4 (July–August 1995), pp. 103–14.

48. The argument that the United States can serve as a "pacifier" in regions such as Europe and Northeast Asia was first laid out in Josef Joffe, "Europe's American Pacifier," *Foreign Policy,* No. 54 (Spring 1984), pp. 64–82.

49. Gorbachev, *Perestroika,* pp. 194–95.

50. The document was originally published in *Nezavisimoye Voennoye Obozreniye* on January 14, 2000. For key translated excerpts, from which this quote is taken, see "Russia's National Security Concept," *Arms Control Today* 30, No. 1 (January–February 2000), pp. 15–20. For a discussion of the evolution of Russian thinking about security during the 1990s, see Celeste A. Wallander, "Wary of the West: Russian Security Policy at the Millennium," *Arms Control Today* 30, No. 2 (March 2000), pp. 7–12. It should be emphasized, however, that rhetoric aside, Russia has been acting like a traditional great power since the early 1990s. See the sources cited in Mearsheimer, "False Promise," p. 46 (n. 175, 176).

51. See Serge Schmemann, "Russia Drops Pledge of No First Use of Atom Arms," *New York Times,* November 4, 1993. NATO, which has always rejected a no-first-use policy regarding nuclear weapons, remains firmly wedded to that policy. For example, the "NATO Alliance Strategic Concept," which was approved by the North Atlantic Council on April 24, 1999, states that "the Alliance's conventional forces alone cannot ensure credible deterrence. Nuclear weapons make a unique contribution in rendering the risks of aggression against the Alliance incalculable and unacceptable. Thus they remain essential to preserve peace. . . . They demonstrate that aggression of any kind is not a rational option."

52. Russian public opinion polls from November 1999 show that 85 percent of the population believe that Russia must once again become a "great empire." Only 7 percent disagree. Michael Wines, "Russia Pines for a New Savior: Victory," *New York Times,* November 21, 1999, Sec. 4.

53. William J. Clinton, "Commencement Address," United States Military Academy, West Point, NY, May 31, 1997.

54. Madeleine Albright, prepared statement before the U.S. Senate Foreign Relations Committee, Washington, DC, January 8, 1997.

55. Robert J. Art, "Why Western Europe Needs the United States and NATO," *Political Science Quarterly* 111, No. 1 (Spring 1996), pp. 5–6. The views of Christoph Bertram, a former director of the International Institute for Strategic Studies in London and one of Germany's foremost strategic thinkers, are also instructive on this point. He wrote in 1995 that "to disband NATO now would throw Europe into deep insecurity. . . . It would be a strategic disaster." He goes on to say that "if the United States turned its back on Europe, NATO would collapse and the European Union would be strained to the point of disintegration. Germany would stand out as the dominant power in the West of the continent, and Russia as the disturbing power in the East. The United States would lose much of its international authority as well as the means to help prevent European instability from igniting international conflict once again." Bertram, *Europe in the Balance: Securing the Peace Won in the Cold War* (Washington, DC: Carnegie Endowment for International Peace, 1995), pp. 17–18, 85. Also see pp. 10–11.

56. Regarding their views on the obsolescence of great-power war in Europe, see Robert J. Art, "A Defensible Defense: America's Grand Strategy after the Cold War," *International Security* 15, No. 4 (Spring 1991), pp. 45–46; Mandelbaum, "Is Major War Obsolete?"; and Van Evera, "Primed for Peace." For evidence that they are influenced by the pacifier argument, see Art, "Why Western Europe," esp. pp. 4–9, 35–39; Michael Mandelbaum, *The Dawn of Peace in Europe* (New York: Twentieth Century Fund, 1996), esp. chaps. 1, 9; Van Evera, "Primed for Peace," pp. 16, 54–55; and Stephen Van Evera, "Why Europe Matters, Why the Third World Doesn't: American Grand Strategy after the Cold War," *Journal of Strategic Studies* 13, No. 2 (June 1990), pp. 9–11.

57. President Clinton put this point well when he noted that although there are good reasons to be critical of American foreign policy in the twentieth century, "no one suggests that we ever sought territorial advantage." President William J. Clinton, "Remarks to the American Society of Newspaper Editors Regarding the Situation in Kosovo," San Francisco, CA, April 15, 1999.

58. On the diminished state of the Russian military, see Alexei G. Arbatov, "Military Reform in Russia: Dilemmas, Obstacles, and Prospects," *International Security* 22, No. 4 (Spring 1998), pp. 83–134; Robert W. Duggleby, "The Disintegration of the Russian Armed Forces," *Journal of Slavic Studies* 11, No. 2 (June 1998), pp. 1–24; and Sergey Rogov, *Military Reform and the Defense Budget of the Russian Federation* (Alexandria, VA: Center for Naval Analyses, August 1997).

59. Charles Krauthammer, "The Unipolar Moment," *Foreign Affairs* 70, No. 1 (Winter 1990–91), pp. 23–33; Michael Mastanduno, "Preserving the Unipolar Moment: Realist Theories and U.S. Grand Strategies after the Cold War," *International Security* 21, No. 4 (Spring 1997), pp. 49–88; and William C. Wohlforth, "The Stability of a Unipolar World," *International Security* 24, No. 1 (Summer 1999), pp. 5–41.

60. For an interesting discussion of this point, see Samuel P. Huntington, "The Lonely Superpower," *Foreign Affairs* 78, No. 2 (March–April 1999), pp. 35–49. Also see Christopher Layne, "The Unipolar Illusion: Why New Great Powers Will Rise," *International Security* 17, No. 4 (Spring 1993), pp. 5–51; and Kenneth N. Waltz, "The Emerging Structure of International Politics," *International Security* 18, No. 2 (Fall 1993), pp. 44–79. Wohlforth, who makes the most compelling case for unipolarity, defines it as "a structure in which one state's capabilities are too great to be counterbalanced." Wohlforth, "Stability," p. 9. Although I agree with that definition, I take issue with his assessment that China and Russia do not have the wherewithal to stand up to the United States.

61. On what defines a great power, see Chapter 1.

62. China and Russia have been on friendly terms in recent years, and both have made clear their displeasure with different aspects of American foreign policy. But they have not formed a serious balancing coalition against the United States, and few believe that they will do so in the future. See Jennifer Anderson, *The Limits of Sino-Russian Strategic Partnership*, Adelphi Paper No. 315 (London: International Institute for Strategic Studies, December 1997); Mark Burles, *Chinese Policy toward Russia and the Central Asian Republics* (Santa Monica, CA: RAND Corporation, 1999); and "Can a Bear Love a Dragon?" *Economist*, April 26, 1997, pp. 19–21. Also, there is a potential source of serious trouble between China and Russia: large-scale illegal immigration from China into Russia for the past decade, which could lead to ethnic conflict or territorial disputes. See David Hale, "Is Asia's High Growth Era Over?" *National Interest*, No. 47 (Spring 1997), p. 56; and Simon Winchester, "On the Edge of Empires: Black Dragon River," *National Geographic*, February 2000, pp. 7–33.

63. Many argue that it is difficult to imagine security competition, much less war, between France and Germany. The current happy situation, however, did not come about because those longtime rivals, who fought wars against each other in

1870–71, 1914–18, and 1940, suddenly learned to like and trust each other in 1945. The presence of a large American army in Western Europe since World War II has made it almost impossible for France and Germany to fight with each other and thus has eliminated the main cause of fear between them. In essence, hierarchy replaces anarchy in areas directly controlled by U.S. forces. Josef Joffe puts the point well: "Only the permanent intrusion of the United States into the affairs of the Continent changed the terms of state interaction to the point where West Europeans no longer had to conduct their business in the brooding shadow of violence. By promising to protect Western Europe against others and against itself, the United States swept aside the rules of the self-help game that had governed and regularly brought grief to Europe in centuries past." Joffe, "Europe's American Pacifier," p. 72.

64. "Excerpts from Pentagon's Plan: 'Prevent the Re-Emergence of a New Rival,'" *New York Times,* March 8, 1992. Also see Patrick E. Tyler, "U.S. Strategy Plan Calls for Insuring No Rivals Develop," *New York Times,* March 8, 1992.

65. See Eugene Gholz, Daryl G. Press, and Harvey M. Sapolsky, "Come Home, America: The Strategy of Restraint in the Face of Temptation," *International Security* 21, No. 4 (Spring 1997), pp. 5–48; and Christopher Layne, "From Preponderance to Offshore Balancing: America's Future Grand Strategy," *International Security* 22, No.1 (Summer 1997), pp. 86–124.

66. The Clinton administration certainly bought this view. Secretary of State Madeleine Albright, for example, told the U.S. Senate that "European stability depends in large measure on continued American engagement and leadership. And as history attests, European stability is also vital to our national interests. As a result we will remain engaged." Madeleine Albright, prepared statement before the U.S. Senate Foreign Relations Committee, January 8, 1997. This perspective also enjoys broad support among academics. For example, see Art, "Why Western Europe"; Bertram, *Europe in the Balance;* Mandelbaum, *Dawn of Peace;* Van Evera, "Why Europe Matters"; and Barry R. Posen and Andrew L. Ross, "Competing Visions for U.S. Grand Strategy," *International Security* 21, No. 3 (Winter 1996–97), pp. 5–53, esp. note 14. Also see Mark S. Sheetz, "Exit Strategies: American Grand Designs for Postwar European Security," *Security Studies* 8, No. 4 (Summer 1999), pp. 1–3, which describes the broad appeal of this perspective.

67. Eugene Gholz and Daryl G. Press, "Economic Externalities of Foreign Wars," manuscript accepted for publication in *Security Studies.*

68. David M. Kennedy, *Over Here: The First World War and American Society* (Oxford: Oxford University Press, 1980), chap. 6. Japan's economy also benefited significantly from sitting out the fighting in World War I.

69. Gholz and Press, "Economic Externalities." This analysis assumes that a great-power war in Europe or Northeast Asia would be protracted and involve virtually all of the regional powers—i.e., a central war like World War I. However, a future great-power war, like many of those in the past, might be short or might involve only two major states. A more limited conflict of this sort would surely have less effect (positive or negative) on the U.S. economy than would a central war.

70. See U.S. Congress, House Committee on International Relations, *Oil Fields as Military Objectives: A Feasibility Study*, 94th Cong., 1st sess. (Washington, DC: U.S. Government Printing Office, August 21, 1975), esp. Annex A.

71. See James A. Baker III, *The Politics of Diplomacy: Revolution, War and Peace, 1989–1992* (New York: Putnam, 1995), pp. 335–39; and George Bush and Brent Scowcroft, *A World Transformed* (New York: Knopf, 1998), pp. 399–400.

72. See Lawrence S. Kaplan, *The Long Entanglement: NATO's First Fifty Years* (Westport, CT: Praeger, 1999); and Robert B. McCalla, "Why NATO Survives," *International Organization* 50, No. 3 (Summer 1996), pp. 456–61, 470–72.

73. See Peter W. Rodman, *Drifting Apart? Trends in U.S.-European Relations* (Washington, DC: Nixon Center, 1999); and Stephen M. Walt, "The Ties That Fray: Why Europe and America Are Drifting Apart," *National Interest*, No. 54 (Winter 1998–99), pp. 3–11. Also see Robert D. Blackwill and Michael Sturmer, eds., *Allies Divided: Transatlantic Policies for the Greater Middle East* (Cambridge, MA: MIT Press, 1997); Roger Cohen, "Storm Clouds over U.S.-Europe Relations," *New York Times*, March 26, 2001; Roger Cohen, "To European Eyes, It's America the Ugly," *New York Times*, May 7, 2001; John Deutch, Arnold Kanter, and Brent Scowcroft, "Saving NATO's Foundation," *Foreign Affairs* 78, No. 6 (November–December 1999), pp. 54–67; Philip H. Gordon, "Recasting the Atlantic Alliance," *Survival* 38, No. 1 (Spring 1996), pp. 32–57; Camille Grand, "Missile Defense: The View from the Other Side of the Atlantic," *Arms Control Today* 30, No. 7 (September 2000), pp. 12–18; and Lawrence F. Kaplan, "Surrender," *New Republic*, November 20, 2000, pp. 12–13.

74. The negative consequences for NATO of the Kosovo war are captured in the following comment from *Der Spiegel:* "After ten weeks of war in Yugoslavia, one thing has become clear across Europe: the hegemony of the U.S. and NATO is limited as a model for the future." Quoted in Jeffrey Gedmin, "Continental Drift: A Europe United in Spirit against the United States," *New Republic*, June 28, 1999, p. 23. Also see the comments of Adm. Leighton W. Smith, Jr., a former commander of NATO forces in southern Europe, in George C. Wilson, "Kosovo May Be NATO's Last Hurrah," *National Journal* 32, No. 16 (April 15, 2000), pp. 1218–19. Friction between the United States and its European allies over the Balkans also flared during the 2000 presidential campaign. See Michael R. Gordon, "Bush Would Stop U.S. Peacekeeping in Balkan Fights," *New York Times*, October 21, 2000; and Steven Erlanger, "Europeans Say Bush's Pledge to Pull Out of Balkans Could Split NATO," *New York Times*, October 25, 2000.

75. For example, Japan, which has the second largest defense budget in the world, is developing its own spy satellites, against American wishes. Moreover, each house of Japan's Diet has established a commission to review its pacifist constitution, a move widely seen as a victory for Japan's nationalists. An important defense official, Shingo Nishimura, was forced to resign in October 1999, because he suggested that Japan develop its own nuclear deterrent. See "Japan's Naval Power: Responding to New Challenges," International Institute for Strategic Studies' *Strategic Comments* 6, No. 8 (October 2000); "Japan Reviews Pacifism," *London Times*, January 21, 2000; Clay Chandler, "Japanese Official Forced to Quit after Endorsing Nuclear Arms," *Washington Post*, October 21, 1999; Howard French, "Japan Signals Peaceful Intentions, but Reaffirms Armament Plans," *New York Times*, April 28, 2001; and "Satellite Program Endorsed as a Response to N. Korean Rocket," *Chicago Tribune*, November 7, 1998. Also see Christensen, "China, the U.S.-Japan Alliance," pp. 74–80; and Milton Ezrati, *Kawari: How Japan's Economic and Cultural Transformation Will Alter the Balance of Power among Nations* (Reading, MA: Perseus, 1999), chaps. 7–8.

76. The phrase "reluctant sheriff" is from Richard N. Haas, *The Reluctant Sheriff: The United States after the Cold War* (New York: Council on Foreign Relations Press, 1997). An important source of evidence of America's waning commitment to Europe and Northeast Asia is John E. Rielly, ed., *American Public Opinion and U.S. Foreign Policy 1999* (Chicago: Chicago Council on Foreign Relations, 1999). The study finds, for example, that only 44 percent of the public and 58 percent of U.S. leaders think that "defending our allies' security" is a "very important" goal. Furthermore, if Russia invaded Poland, a NATO member, a mere 28 percent of the American public favors using U.S. ground troops to defend Poland. Ibid., pp. 16, 26. Also see James M. Lindsay, "The New Apathy: How an Uninterested Public Is Reshaping Foreign Policy," *Foreign Affairs* 79, No. 5 (September–October 2000), pp. 2–8.

77. See Steve Glain, "Fearing China's Plans and a U.S. Departure, Asians Rebuild Forces," *Wall Street Journal*, November 13, 1997; and Manning and Przystup, "Asia's Transition Diplomacy," pp. 48–49.

78. See Ted Galen Carpenter, "Roiling Asia: U.S. Coziness with China Upsets the Neighbors," *Foreign Affairs* 77, No. 6 (November–December 1998), pp. 2–6. The United States raised suspicions about its reliability earlier in 1996 when it said that its security guarantee to Japan did not apply to any crisis arising over the Senkaku/Diaoyutai Islands, which both China and Japan claim. See Yoichi Funabashi, *Alliance Adrift* (New York: Council on Foreign Relations Press, 1999), pp. 401–15.

79. It is apparent from this discussion that even if I am wrong and the United States assumes the role of peacekeeper in Europe and Northeast Asia, there is still likely to be fundamental change in the power structures in those regions. In particular, America's allies, especially Germany and Japan, are not likely to remain wards of the United States, but instead are likely to establish themselves as great powers.

80. These population numbers are from J. David Singer and Melvin Small, *National Material Capabilities Data, 1816–1915* (Ann Arbor, MI: Inter-University Consortium for Political and Social Research, February 1993). Jonathan Adelman writes that the Russians had a 2.7:1 advantage in 1914 (180 million vs. 67.5 million) and a 2.4:1 advantage in 1941 (187 million vs. 78 million). See Jonathan R. Adelman, *Revolution, Armies, and War: A Political History* (Boulder, CO: Lynne Rienner, 1985), pp. 105, 229.

81. These population figures are from Table 10.2; and *The Military Balance 1988–1989* (London: International Institute for Strategic Studies, 1988), p. 33.

82. These figures are drawn from Tables 3.3 and 10.2.

83. For a detailed breakdown of the size and structure of the German and Russian armies, see International Institute for Strategic Studies, *The Military Balance, 2000–2001* (Oxford: Oxford University Press, 2000), pp. 61–62, 120–21. There is evidence that the Russian army will shrink further in the near future, possibly going as low as 220,000. See Simon Saradzhyan, "Lopsided Army Cuts Show Kremlin Fears," *Moscow Times*, September 29, 2000. Germany is also considering cutbacks, although its reductions would be smaller than Russia's. See Cecilie Rohwedder, "Germany to Modernize Military, Trim Defense Spending by 2.5 Percent," *Wall Street Journal*, June 15, 2000.

84. On German thinking about nuclear weapons during the Cold War, see Marc Trachtenberg, *A Constructed Peace: The Making of the European Settlement, 1945–1963* (Princeton, NJ: Princeton University Press, 1999), pp. 203, 230–40, 398.

85. As noted, the Soviet Union had about 285 million people in 1987, whereas Russia's present population is about 147 million.

86. There was considerable speculation in the early 1990s that Japan would grow powerful and replace the Soviet Union as America's main rival in Northeast Asia. See George Friedman and Meredith LeBard, *The Coming War with Japan* (New York: St. Martin's, 1991); and Samuel P. Huntington, "Why International Primacy Matters," *International Security* 17, No. 4 (Spring 1993), pp. 68–83. On why Japan is unlikely to become a highly aggressive state, see Robert S. Ross, "The Geography of the Peace: East Asia in the Twenty-first Century," *International Security* 23, No. 4 (Spring 1999), pp. 81–118.

87. As noted in Table 10.1, Japan has 126 million people, and China has 1.24 billion. The United Nations forecasts that Japan's population will shrink to roughly 100 million by 2050, while China's population will increase to about 1.5 billion by that date. "Emerging Market Indicators," *Economist*, February 1, 1997, p. 108.

88. As noted in Table 10.1, Russia has 147 million people, China has 1.24 billion. The United Nations forecasts that Russia's population will shrink to roughly 120 million by 2050, while China's population will increase to about 1.5 billion by that date. "Emerging Market Indicators," *Economist*, February 1, 1997, p. 108.

89. See Steven E. Miller, "Russian National Interests," in Robert D. Blackwill and Sergei Karaganov, eds., *Damage Limitation or Crisis? Russia and the Outside World*, CSIA Studies in International Security (Washington, DC: Brassey's, 1994), pp. 77–106; and Sergey Rogov, *Security Concerns of the New Russia*, vol. 1, *The Challenges of Defending Russia*, Occasional Paper (Alexandria, VA: Center for Naval Analyses, July 1995).

90. See Zalmay Khalilzad et al., *The United States and a Rising China: Strategic and Military Implications* (Santa Monica, CA: RAND Corporation, 1999); and Michael D. Swaine and Ashley J. Tellis, *Interpreting China's Grand Strategy: Past, Present, and Future* (Santa Monica, CA: RAND Corporation, 2000).

91. For a generally optimistic assessment of the future of China's economy, see World Bank, *China 2020: Development Challenges in the New Century* (Washington, DC: World Bank, 1997). For more pessimistic assessments, see the articles in "The FPRI Conference on China's Economy," *Orbis* 43, No. 2 (Spring 1999), pp. 173–294; and Nicholas R. Lardy, *China's Unfinished Economic Revolution* (Washington, DC: Brookings Institution Press, 1998). Also see Richard K. Betts and Thomas J. Christensen, "China: Getting the Questions Right," *National Interest*, No. 62 (Winter 2000–2001), pp. 17–29.

92. Hong Kong's per capita gross national product (GNP) in 1998 dollars is equal to about 80 percent of U.S. per capita GNP ($23,660 vs. $29,240). See *World Bank Atlas 2000* (Washington, DC: World Bank, April 2000), pp. 42–43. But China has roughly five times as many people as the United States and is projected to maintain that advantage over the first half of the new century. Also see Table 10.3 for some alternative scenarios involving a wealthy China.

INDEX

Page numbers from 403 to 533 refer to endnotes.